Kṛtibodha Series
No. 1

General Editor
Sudha Gopalakrishnan

Kr̥tibodha Series

The Kṛtibodha ("Knowledge on Texts") Series is the project of the National Mission for Manuscripts to promote academic interest and scholarship in the area of manuscript studies. Previously unpublished and rare texts will be published as critical editions, with detailed introduction, analyses and commentaries under this series.

VĀDHŪLA GṚHYĀGAMAVṚTTIRAHASYAM

of

Nārāyaṇa Miśra

नारायणमिश्रविरचितं

वाधूलगृह्यागमवृत्तिरहस्यम्

विशदभूमिकया विविधाभिरनुक्रमणीभिश्च समलङ्कृतं
पाठविमर्शादियुतं समालोचनात्मकं संस्करणम्

सम्पादकः
व्रजबिहारी चौबे

राष्ट्रीय पाण्डुलिपि मिशन
नई दिल्ली

एवं

डी० के० प्रिण्टवर्ल्ड (प्रा०) लि०
नई दिल्ली

VĀDHŪLA GṚHYĀGAMAVṚTTIRAHASYAM

of

Nārāyaṇa Miśra

Critically edited with detailed Introduction and Indices

by

Braj Bihari Chaubey

NATIONAL MISSION FOR MANUSCRIPTS
New Delhi

and

D.K. PRINTWORLD (P) LTD.
New Delhi

Cataloguing in Publication Data — DK
[Courtesy: D.K. Agencies (P) Ltd. <docinfo@dkagencies.com>]

Miśra, Nārāyaṇa.
Vādhūlagṛhyāgamavṛttirahasyam : viśadabhūmikayā vividhābhiranukramaṇībhiśca samalaṅkṛtaṁ pāṭhavimarśadiyutaṁ samālocanātmakaṁ saṁskaraṇam / Nārāyaṇamiśraviracitaṁ : sampādaka, Vrajabihāri Caube.
xvii, 36, 472 p. 23 cm. — (Kṛtibodha series ; 1)
In Sanskrit; includes pref. and introd. in English.
Added t.p. title: Vādhūla gṛhyāgamavṛttirahasyam of Nārāyaṇa Miśra.
On Hindu rituals; critical edition.
ISBN 8190402919

1. Hinduism — Rituals. I. Chaubey, B.B. (Braj Bihari), 1940- II. Title. III. Title: Vādhūla gṛhyāgamavṛttirahasyam of Nārāyaṇa Miśra. IV. Series: Kṛtibodha series ; 1.

DDC 294.538 22

ISBN 81-904029-1-9
First published in India in 2006

Published by:
National Mission for Manuscripts
Indira Gandhi National Centre for the Arts Building
No. 5, Dr. Rajendra Prasad Road
New Delhi - 110 001
Phone: (011) 2338 3894; *Fax:* 2307 3340
E-mail: director.namami@nic.in

and co-published by:
D.K. Printworld (P) Ltd.
Regd. Office: 'Sri Kunj', F-52, Bali Nagar
Ramesh Nagar Metro Station, New Delhi-110 015
Phones: (011) 2545 3975; 2546 6019; *Fax*: (011) 2546 5926
E-mail: dkprintworld@vsnl.net
Website: www.dkprintworld.com

Printed by: D.K. Printworld (P) Ltd., New Delhi.

FOREWORD

THE National Mission for Manuscripts was launched in February 2003, by the Government of India under the Ministry of Tourism and Culture with the mandate of identifying, protecting and making accessible the manuscript heritage of India, believed to be the largest repository of hand-written manuscripts in the world. Found on materials such as birch, palm-leaf, handmade paper and cloth, in different languages and scripts, and spread throughout the country in different public and private repositories, these manuscripts are the precious reserve of Indian knowledge systems. They represent different areas of intellectual activity such as streams of science, philosophy, arts and culture.

While the National Mission for Manuscripts strives to promote and propagate interest in the "traditional" knowledge contained in manuscripts, it also aims to re-contextualize the approach to this knowledge so that it remains alive and vital to the present and future generations. In an effort to engage with Indian knowledge systems, the Mission seeks to publish rare and unpublished manuscripts through bringing out critical editions of important texts, supplemented with informative introduction, detailed analyses and commentaries. Titled Kṛtibodha, this series of publications is intended to generate academic and public interest in Indian systems of learning.

The first of the Series is being launched with the present publication, the *Vādūlagṛhyāgamavṛttirahasya* of Nārāyaṇa Miśra. It is a versified commentary on the *Vādūlagṛhyāsūtravṛtti*, which itself is a short commentary on the *Vādūlagṛhyasūtra*. The text is critical not only for the wealth of information it contains on religious and domestic **rites and rituals** especially related to Gṛhya and Smārtakarma, but its reference to other important texts such as Kaṭha-

Āraṇyaka, Vādhūlāgama and Vṛta Saṁgraha which have so far not seen the light of day.

The text has been critically edited, with detailed introduction and indices by Professor Braj Bihari Chaubey, a Sanskritist and a well-known scholar on Vedic Studies.

In continuation of the Series, the Mission intends to follow this critical edition with other important texts on India's knowledge systems.

Sudha Gopalakrishnan

PREFACE

In 1975, I undertook a project of bringing out the critical editions of the texts belonging to the Vādhūla recension which were not known even by name at that time, and those which were known through catalogues were under wrong nomenclatures. Under this project the *Vādhūla Śrautasūtra* was published in 1993, Vādhūla-smṛti with Hindi translation in 2000, the *Vādhūla Anvākhyāna* in 2001, the *Vādhūla Yajñaprāyaścittam* in 2001. They were all published from the Katyayan Vaidik Sahitya Prakashan, Hoshiarpur (Punjab) with detailed introductions and various Indices. The present edition is based on the three MSS deposited in — (i) the Government Oriental Manuscript Library, Madras, under MS No. 1239; (ii) the Oriental Research Institute and Manuscript Library, Trivandrum, under MS No. T 1072; and (iii) the Oriental Institute, Maharaja Sayajirao University of Baroda under MS No. 3436. With the efforts of Dr Siniruddh Das of Madras University, I got a xerox copy of the MS from GOML, Madras in 1995. Since at that time I was busy with other projects, I could not start working immediately after procuring the MS. In 1998, when I joined as a Visiting Professor for one year (1.5.98 – 30.4.99) at Maharshi Dayanand Saraswati University, Ajmer on the request of Prof. P.L. Chaturvedi, the then Vice-Chancellor, sufficient time was at my disposal to devote on this project. I started copying the MS which I had procured from Madras. I was able to accomplish the basecopy of the entire text within a year. In connection with delivering lectures at a workshop on Palaeography and Manuscriptology organized by Indira Gandhi National Centre for the Arts (IGNCA), New Delhi in collaboration with the Oriental Research Institute and Manuscript Library, University of Kerala, Trivandrum, I visited the Institute and stayed there for a week (March 22-27, 1999). There, with the help of Dr P.L. Shaji, I got the xerox copy of the MS No. 71072, deposited at the Institute. While starting the collation work from the two MSS, I was confronted with a problem which I had already faced in preparing critical edition of the *Vādhūlasmṛti*. The problem was related to the fixing of the two hemistiches of the verses. In most of the cases the first hemistich formed the second hemistich of the preceding verse and the second hemistich the first of the following one. In the versified texts generally the first hemistich is shown by putting one *daṇḍa* and the second hemistich by putting two *daṇḍa*s at the end. But in the MSS there were violations of this rule. And once this violation occurred, there was the likelihood of continuous violations. For example see verses I.15. 53, 58, 62, 71, 91, etc. Such violations occur due to existence of *Dvipadā* verses between the two verses. In the MSS *Dvipadā* verses are not shown separately. This affects the continuous numbering of the text. In such cases, I have separated such *Dvipadā* verses by assigning क syllable to the previous verse number taking into consideration the semantic relation of the following *Dvipadā* verse with the preceding verse. For example, 14क, 52क, 57क, 61क, 71क, 90क, etc.

None of the MSS give the title of the topics dealt within the text. With a view to making easy the understanding of the text, I have given within brackets the subject-headings which have been dealt within a group of verses. As the text is a versified commentary on *Vādhūlagṛhyasūtravṛtti,* which in itself is a commentary (*vṛtti*) on *Vādhūlagṛhyasūtra,* this text will render great help in preparing the critical editions of *Vādhūlagṛhyasūtra and Vādhūlagṛhyasūtravṛtti.* This text refers to the existence of a *Prayogaklṛpti* as its source in the very introductory verses (1.4) and the *Kāṭhaka Āraṇyaka* comprising four *prapāṭhaka*s (4.319). I am sure, with the publication of this important text, many new facts related to *gṛhya* rituals and sacraments would come to light. For example, no text available so far on *gṛhya* rituals, dealing with sacraments, gives in detail the complete procedure of the *Samāvartana*, a ritual performed at the completion of the studentship, as this text does.

Now, I feel great pleasure in presenting this critical edition of the *Vādhūlagṛhyāgamavṛttirahasya* for the first time in the hands of scholars for which they were anxiously waiting.

On this auspicious occasion, I take the opportunity to express my deep sense of gratitude to the Institutions, scholars and well-wishers who helped me in many ways in preparing and bringing out the critical edition of the *Vādhūlagṛhyāgamavṛtti-rahasya*. First of all I am thankful to the Directors/Librarians and other authorities of — (i) The Government Oriental Manuscript Library, Madras; (ii) The Oriental Research Institute and MSS Library, University of Kerala, Trivandrum; and (iii) The Oriental Research Institute, Maharaja Sayajirao University of Baroda, who very kindly supplied me the xerox copies of the *Vadhūla-gṛhyāgamavṛttirahasya* and gave some necessary information about the text. I am thankful to my friends Dr T.N. Dharmadhikari, former Director, Vaidika Saṃśodhana Maṇḍala, Pune, and Dr H.G. Ranade, former Professor in the Dictionary Department at Deccan College, Pune with whom I frequently discussed about many doubtful readings.

I am thankful to Prof. Ghanshyam Uniyal of Vishveshvaranand Vishwa Bandhu Institute of Sanskrit and Indological Studies, Panjab University, Hoshiarpur (now retired), who very carefully went through the proofs and helped in correcting a number of grammatical mistakes. I place on record my appreciation of my daughters-in-law Dr Aruna Shukla, M.A. (Sanskrit, Hindi; and Vedacharya) and Smt. Sandhya, M.A.

(Veda) for helping me in preparation of several Indices to the text.

The complete text of the *Vādhūlagṛhyāgamavṛtti-rahasya* critically edited with detailed Introduction and three Indices: I - उद्धृत-मन्त्रानुक्रमणी (Mantra Index), II - श्लोकानुक्रमणी (Verse-Index), III - प्रमुखपदानुक्रमणी (Important Word-Index) was ready for, publication in 2004. In the meantime, it came to my notice that the National Mission for Manuscripts, New Delhi, under Ministry of Culture, Govt. of India, had made a plan to publish critical editions of ancient texts. I thought it would be in the fitness of things, if this important text was brought out as the first publication under the Kṛtibodha Series. Accordingly, I submitted the complete copy of the text to Dr Sudha Gopalakrishnan, the Mission Director, for consideration of its publication under the Kṛtibodha Series. I am happy to say that the committee constituted for the purpose approved this text to be published under the said series. I am very grateful to Dr Sudha Gopalakrishnan, all the members of the committee and also the concerned Ministry for according necessary sanction for its publication.

Śrāvanī Pūrnimā vs 2063
September 5, 2006

Prof. B.B. Chaubey
Former Director
VVBIS & IS, (Panjab University)
Hoshiarpur (Punjab)
Resi: Chaturveda Niketan
Jodhamal Road, Hoshiarpur

CONTENTS
विषयानुक्रमणिका

षष्ठोऽध्याय:

INTRODUCTION

1. Critical Apparatus used for the Present Edition

The *Vādhūlagṛhyāgamavṛttirahasya* (*VadhGṛVR*) is an important text dealing with the Gṛhya rites accompanied with Smārta *prayogas* as prevalent in the Vādhūla tradition. The present critical edition of the text is based on the following MSS —

M. A paper MS of the *VādhGṛVR,* deposited in the Government Oriental Manuscript Library, Madras under No. 1239; Devanāgarī script; pages 343; 20 lines on a page. It was transcribed in 1920-21 from a MS acquired through K.C. Venkata Subramaniam Sastri of Iriñjālakkuḍa, Cochin, Kerala and the same is deposited in the Government Oriental Manuscript Library, Madras under No. R3439, Total No. of folios 172. The folio Nos. of the original MS is also given on the left-side margin of the pages of the transcribed copy. The MS is at places broken and full of errors. At the top of the first page the MS reads.

श्री:

'अथ वाधूलवृत्तिरहस्यम् प्रारभ्यते'

'अविघ्नमस्तु'

The title of the text is not given on the head of the folio. However, at the end of each chapter the title of the text along with its author's name is given in the colophons:

इति सङ्गमग्रामवासिमिश्रविरचिते नारायणीये वाधूलगृह्यागमवृत्तिरहस्ये प्रथमोऽध्याय: (p. 56)

इति. . . वाधूलकगृह्यागमसंग्रहे द्वितीयोऽध्याय: (p. 91)

इति. . . वाधूलके गृह्यागमसंग्रहे तृतीयोऽध्याय: (p. 132)

इति. . . वाधूलके गृह्यागमवृत्तिरहस्ये चतुर्थोऽध्याय: (p. 178)

इति. . . वाधूलके गृह्यागमवृत्तिरहस्ये पञ्चमोऽध्याय: (p. 226)

इति. . . वाधूलगृह्यागमवृत्तिरहस्ये षष्ठोऽध्याय: (p. 288)

इति. . . वाधूलगृह्यागमवृत्तिरहस्ये [सप्तमोऽध्याय:] (p. 322)

In the eighth chapter MS is broken after verse 200, and the loss of remaining text is indicated with remark :

'इतः परं ग्रन्थपाताः' (p. 343)

The MS also mentions the No. of chapters in the beginning of each chapter before giving the text, e.g.

अथ द्वितीयोऽध्यायः, अथ तृतीयोऽध्यायः, etc.

T. A MS of the *VādhGṛVR*, deposited in the Oriental Research Institute and Manuscript Library, Trivandrum under No. T 1072. This MS was transcribed in Devanāgarī script from a MS which was in possession of Neḍumpilli Mana, Iriñjālakkuḍa, Cochin, Kerala; pages 347; 20 lines on a page. On the outer cover of the MS following informations have been given :

कर्त्ता नारायणः (सङ्गमग्रामनिवासिमिश्र)

स्वामी Neḍumpilli Manakkol (Written in Malayalam)

ग्रन्थाङ्कः 3

लेखकः आर् अनन्ताचार्यः

पुटसंख्या 347

I have compared this whole with Anantacharya

(Sd) ना. अनन्तकृष्ण शर्मा 23.2.1115 ME (= 1940)

I have compared this text with Anantakrishna Sharma

(Sd) R. Anantacharya Sastri 23.2.1115 ME (=1940)

The MS begins with ॐ on the top of the first page. From page No. 2 onwards the title of the text is given on the top of every left page as वाधूलगृह्यागमवृत्तिरहस्ये and the No. of the chapter on the top of every right page as प्रथमोऽध्यायः, द्वितीयोऽध्यायः, etc. In the colophons at the end of each chapter, the MS gives the name of the author and the title of the text invariably as 'इति सङ्गमग्रामनिवासिविरचिते नारायणीयमिश्र वाधूलकगृह्यागमवृत्तिरहस्ये प्रथमोऽध्यायः' etc.

B. A MS of the *VādhGṛVR,* mentioned in the catalogue of Oriental Institute, M. S. University of Baroda, with the title *Vādhūlavṛttirahasyam*, deposited in the same Institute under No. R3436; paper MS; size 10-5/8 x 9-3/8, lines 20 on the page, Devanāgarī script, condition- good; It is a copy of Madras MS (M).

2. Nomenclature of the Text

The title of the text as recorded in the catalogues is *Vādhūlavṛttirahasya*. All the MSS, mentioned above, give the same title on their face. But, while working on this text I found that the nomenclature of the text, as given in the colophons at the end of *adhyāyas*, differs a little bit . In the colophons of the first, sixth and seventh chapters of Madras MS (M) the text is designated as *Vādhūlagṛhyāgamavṛttirahasya*, while in the second, fourth and fifth chapters as *Vādhūlakagṛhyāgamavṛttirahasya*. Again, in the colophon of the third chapter the title of the text is given as *Vādhūlakagṛhyāgamasaṁgraha*. In the Trivandrum MS (T.1092) the title of the text is given as *Vādhūlakagṛhyāgamavṛttirahasya* on the outer cover and the *Vādhūlagṛhyāgamavṛttirahasya* on the top of every left page. However, on most of the left pages *Vādhūlakagṛhyāgamavṛttirahasya* is also given. This title is invariably given in the colophons of the each *adhyāya* (the eighth being incomplete, the colophon is missing).

Now we have four titles of the same text, viz. *Vādhūlagṛhyāgamavṛttirahasya*, *Vādhūlakagṛhyāgamavṛttirahasya*, *Vādhūlagṛhyāgamasaṁgraha*, and *Vādhūlavṛttirahasya*. As regards the difference between Vādhūla and Vādhūlaka there are two possibilities: first, the two names may be for the one and the same person, the difference being only verbal; and the second, the two different names may refer to two different personalities. In the former case there is no proof to establish the identity of the two, whereas in the latter case ample evidences are available to prove the two names of different personalities. Vādhūla has been mentioned among the *Gotrapravartaka ācāryas*. He was the promulgator of a Vedic Śākhā among the Kṛṣṇa Yajurvedins, and on his name Vādhūla Śākhā became popular. He was the original *Pravacanakāra* of the *Vādhūla-Anvākhyānam*,[1] *Vādhūla-Śrautasūtram*,[2] *Vādhūla-mantra Saṁhitā* (not discovered so far) as is evident from mention of his name in the *Vādhūla-*

---

1. Edited by B.B. Chaubey, Katyayan Vaidik Sahitya Prakashan, Hoshiarpur (2001).
2. Edited by B.B. Chaubey, Katyayan Vaidik Sahitya Prakashan, Hoshiarpur (1993).

Anvākhyānam.[1] Probably Vādhūlaka may have been a disciple of Vādhūla and as such he himself might have compiled those texts which were originally promulgated by the latter. Both Vādhūla and Vādhūlaka have been mentioned by name in the later Sūtra texts.[2] The authorship of the *VādhGS* may be ascribed to Vādhūlaka and as such the nomenclature of the text as *Vādhūlaka Gṛhyāgamavṛttirahasya* may be the correct one. Pāṇini's reference to *Vādhūleya* in *Kārttakaujapādigaṇa* (*Pā* VI.2.37) may be referring to Vādhūlaka. Paying of homage to Vādhūlaka in the benedictory verse just after paying homage to Ramāpati (Viṣṇu) in the first verse, too, may give weightage to the nomenclature of the text as *Vādhūlakagṛhyāgamavṛttirahasya*. However, keeping in view the tradition of giving names to the texts belonging to any Śākhā, it would be in the fitness of things to designate the Gṛhyasūtra text, too, like *VādhŚS* as *Vādhūlagṛhyasūtra* on the name of Vādhūla, the promulgator of the Vādhūla Śākhā, even though it might have been compiled or authored by one of his disciples, or followers of that Śākhā.

Now regarding Vṛtti. The word *vṛtti* meaning short commentary on Sūtras, refers to the existence of a text called *Vādhūlagṛhyasūtravṛtti*. There is no doubt about the compiler or author of the *Vādhūlagṛhyasūtra* as Vādhūlaka, but who was the author of *Vṛtti* on it ? A salutation, however, has been offered to the author of the *Vṛtti* (*Vṛttikṛt*) in the second verse of the text (1.2), on which the present text, viz. *VādhGṛVR* seems to have been based. It may be pointed out that the term *rahasya* in the *Vādhūlagṛhyāgamavṛttirahasya* refers to a genre of composition, intended to give exhaustive exposition of the topics dealt with in the *Vādhūlagṛhyasūtravṛtti*. That is to say, it is a detailed exposition on the topics which have been referred to very briefly in the *Vādhūlagṛhyasūtravṛtti*. I would like to mention here that the *Vādhūlagṛhyāgamavṛttirahasya* is not the only text of this

---

1. एतद सौबभ्रुवो वाधूलाय प्रोच्योवाच, प्र न्वै वयं यास्कायाग्न्याधेयमवोचामेति। *VādhAnvā*, I.7.8.
2. अथाभिदग्धानि सदो हविर्धानानि समस्तदेवयजनमावृतैव क्रियेरन्नावृता वा वसतीवरीः प्रथमं गृह्णीयादिति वाधूलकस्य मतम्। – *BaudhŚS* XXIX. 1: 368. 1-3.
   आपस्तम्बः प्रशिष्योऽभूत यस्य वाधूलकस्य तु।
   अग्निवेश्यगुरुः सोऽयमृषिरस्मानिहावतु। *Prayogaklṛpti*, Intro. verse, 1.

type. For example, we may make mention of the *Āpastamba-Śulba-rahasyaprakāśanabhāṣya*[1] of Gopāla, son of Gārgya Śrī Narasiṁhasomasut and the disciple of Śri Raṅgarājamiśra of Vādhūla *gotra*, on the *Āpastambaśulbasūtra*.

As I have mentioned above, the title of the text, as recorded in the catalogues, *Vādhūlavṛttirahasya*, seems to be an abridged form of *Vādhūlagṛhyāgamavṛtti-rahasya,* or *Vādhūlakagṛhyāgamavṛtti-rahasya*. It was entered in the catalogues on the basis of the fact that this name was given in the beginning of the MS (M) itself: 'अथ वाधूलवृत्तिरहस्यः प्रारभ्यते' (p.1). P.V. Kane in his *History of Dharmaśāstra* (p. 1599) has recorded this text in the list of works on *Dharmaśāstras* as *Vādhūlavṛttirahasya*, or *Vādhūlagṛhyāgamavṛtti-rahasya* in bracket.

3. Nature of the Text

From the foregoing discussion on the nomenclature of the text, it is obvious that the *VādhGṛVR* is a versified commentary on the *VādhGSV*, which itself is a brief commentary on the *VādhGS*. But neither the *VādhGS* nor the *VādhGSV* has come to light so far. However, the existence of the text of *VādhGS* is found in the composite Madras MS (M) with the title *Vādhūlakalpavyākhyā* under No. R4375. The contents of the first 28 pages of this MS belong to the Gṛhyasūtra-text of the Vādhūlas. The contents of the first 55 pages (up to line 11) of the Hoshiarpur MS H (which is a copy of M) under No. 1126A, belong to the Gṛhyasūtra text. Another Hoshiarpur MS (H_1) (independent from M) under No. 5657 up to first 28 pages (line 6) belongs to the *VādhGS*.

Besides these MSS, Prof. Ikari has procured the following MSS from Kerala:

K_1 : No. 95, Kiṭaṅṅaśśeri Mana, Iriñjālakkuḍa, 131 leaves (including fragments) composite MS of *GS, ŚS, Anvākhyāna*.

K_2 : No. 101, Kiṭaṅṅaśśeri Mana, Iriñjālakkuḍa, 148 leaves, composite MS of *GS, ŚS*. According to Prof. Ikari this MSS covers almost complete description of *GS*.

N_3 : No. 145, Neḍumpilli Mana, Iriñjālakkuḍa, 52 leaves, composite MS of *Gṛhyasūtra* and *Gṛhyaprayoga*

1. Edited by Damodar Jha, Hoshiarpur, 1988.

(Skt. & Malayālam), title — *Pākayajña.*

About the nature of the text of the Gṛhyasūtra portion of the Madras MS, Caland had expressed his view that it was a commentary of the Gṛhyasūtra, owing to the title in the colophon *Vādhūlagṛhyakalpavyākhyā*. But Prof. Witzel for the first time pointed out that the *Gṛhya* material given at the beginning of the Madras MS (M) was nothing but that of the Gṛhyasūtra. His assertion was based upon the comparison of the text fragments with the parallel passages of the *ĀgnGS.*[1] When I started working on the critical edition of the *VādhŚS*, I, too, found that the contents of the entire composite copy of Madras MS (M), not only its Gṛhyasūtra but the Śrautasūtra and the Anvākhyāna portions, too, were the original texts. Prof. Ikari is of the view that the fragmental condition of the original MS of Madras did not allow anyone to reconstruct the full text of original. Now he is in possession of several old MSS from Iriñjālakkuḍa and on basis of those MSS, he has planned to edit the entire *VādhGS* text. He has given a list of the following provisional contents[2] of the *VādhGS* on the basis of various Malayalam MSS to which he has access :

1. Upanayana
   Samāvartana
   Vivāha
   Aṣṭakā
   Aupāsanāgni
2. Pitṛmedha Brāhmaṇa 1
   Pitṛmedha Brāhmaṇa 2
   Śrāddha
   Antyeṣṭi [with a Śānti *mantra* at the beginning and end]
   Dahanavidhi
   Asthisañcayana

---

1. Michael Witzel, 'Eine fünfte Mitteilung über das Vādhūlasūtra,' *Studien Zur Indologie und Iranistic*, Reinbeck, Germany, 1975, pp. 84-88.
2. Yasuke Ikari, A Survey of the New Manuscripts of the Vādhūla School, *Zinbun*, 1998, No. 33, p. 14.

Mṛtabali

Ekoddiṣṭa

Sapiṇḍīkaraṇa

A text of *Vādhūlagṛhyasūtravṛtti*, though not mentioned in any of the catalogues, is found in the composite MS with the title *Vādhūlakalpavyākhyā,* or *Vādhūla-kalpāgamasaṁgraha,* or *Vādhūlakalpasūtravyākhyā,* deposited at following MSS-collections —

1. Government Oriental Manuscript Library Madras under No. R. 2978, Devanāgarī script, composite MS containing (i) the *Kalpāgamasaṁgraha* of Āryadāsa, (pages 1-377), (ii) *Prayogaklṛpti* of Śivaśroṇa, (pp. 377-498) and (iii) *Vādhūlagṛhyakalpavṛtti* with some miscellaneous *prayoga*s (pp. 498-522). At the close of the MS 'इति वाधूलकल्पसूत्रव्याख्या समाप्ता। समाप्तश्चायं ग्रन्थः' is given. This MS was copied from the MS which was in possession of Neḍumpilli Mana, Iriñjālakkuḍa, and compared with that of Kiṭaṅnaśśeri Mana.
2. Adyar MSS Library, Madras under No. TR 636.1-3 (acc No. 63371-73) in three volumes, Devanāgarī script, composite MS containing (i) *Kalpāgamasaṁgraha* of Āryadāsa (vols. I-II, 1-772), (ii) *Prayogaklṛpti* of Śivaśroṇa (vol. III, pp. 772-994) and (iii) *Gṛhyasūtravṛtti* with some miscellaneous passages (994-1071). This MS is a copy of Madras MS (M) No. R 2978 as it is clear from the colophon : 'मद्रपुरस्थराजकीयपुस्तकमालायां मूलमातृकायाः विलिखितमिदं पुस्तकं.' This copy was prepared by Narayana Sharma and completed on 18.11.1923. It may be pointed out that though it is a copy of Madras MS, it fills most of the lacunae found in the latter.
3. Oriental Research Institute (M.S. University) Baroda, 102 pages serially paginated. It covers the commentary of *VādhŚS* by Āryadāsa from beginning to the fifth Prapāṭhaka, Anuvāka 2, as it is mentioned on p. 201 : 'इति पञ्चमप्रपाठके द्वितीयः'. However, the text of the commentary as given at the end does not belong to

Prapāṭhaka 5, Anuvāka 2. It rather belongs to the commentary of *VādhŚS* XI.22.12, i.e. Prapāṭhaka 11, Anuvāka 8, which deals with the Aśvamedha. This MS is a copy of Madras MS No. R. 2978, prepared in 1922. It is incomplete.

4. Oriental Research Institute (M.S. University) Baroda, under acc. No. 13080 in two parts (a) and (b); Devanagari script, folios 1-211 (a), and 212-313 (b); composite MS containing the *Kalpāgamasaṁgraha* of Āryadāsa, from Prapāṭhaka 5, Anuvāka 3 to description of Ṛṣabhasava and *Vādhūla Prayogaklṛpti* of Śivaśroṇa. After that the second part of the *Vādhūlaprayogaklṛpti* of Śivaśroṇa starts and runs up to the end. It does not have the text of the *Gṛhyakalpasūtravṛtti*.

5. Oriental Research Institute and MSS Library (University of Kerala), Trivandrum under Nos. T 1083 (Sr. No. 16276) and T 1147 (Sr. No. 16277); composite MS containing the *Kalpāgamasaṁgraha* of Āryadāsa, *Prayogaklṛpti* of Śivaśroṇa and *Vādhūla-gṛhyaprayoga*.

From the above descriptions of the MSS at different MSS-collections, it is obvious that among the available MSS, the Kerala MS is the oldest one and the others are copies thereof. From the contents of these MSS it comes to our knowledge that there existed a text with the title *Vādhūlagṛhyakalpasūtravṛtti*. In my opinion this *Gṛhyasūtra-vṛtti* must be a *vṛtti*, i.e. commentary on the *Vādhūlagṛhyasūtra* dealing with the following topics :

1. Baliharaṇam (M, p. 499)
2. Jātakarma (M, p. 499)
3. Nāmakaraṇam (M, p. 499)
4. Niṣkramaṇam (M, p. 500)
5. Annaprāśanam (M, p. 500)
6. Caulakarma (M, p. 500)
7. Ābhyudayika (Nāndīśrāddha) (M, pp. 500-01)
8. Darśapūrṇamāseṣṭi (M, p. 501)
9. Ṛtusaṁveśanam (M, p. 502)
10. Puṁsavanam (M, p. 502)
11. Sīmantonnayanam (M, p. 503)
12. Ādityopasthānam (M, p. 504)
13. Parva-snānam (M, p. 504)
14. Kāṇḍavratāni (M, p. 504)
15. Kārīrivratam (M, p. 505)
16. Kārāvratam (M, p. 505)

17. Godānam (M, pp. 506-07)
18. Upākarma (M, pp. 507-09)
19. Snānam (M, pp. 510-11)
20. Vivāha-prayoga (M, p. 512)
21. Sthālīpākaprayoga
22. Dahanavidhi
23. Anupetonmatta-vidhi
24. Mṛtabaliharaṇam
25. Ekoddiṣṭavidhi
26. Arghyadānam
27. Snātakasnānavidhi

Again after a description of some Śrauta rituals, viz. Rājayajña, Pravargya, Vājapeya, Sakṛtpravargyākhyakratu, Ekāha, Agnihoma-Yajñakārikā and Śulbasūtra, the rituals related to Vivāha, Aṣṭakākārya, Upanayana of Prayoga-type have been described. Since the text is not critically edited so far, it is not possible to ascertain the correct nature of the text. These rituals described above may be regarded as provisional contents of the *Vādhūlagṛhyasūtra* and that of the *vṛtti* thereon.

To have an idea regarding the correlation among the three texts, viz. *VādhGS, VādhGSV* and *VādhGṛVR*, some relevant specimens of the texts are given below:

1. *VādhGS* — ***अष्टमे मासि बलिहरणमिति।***

Vṛtti — अष्टमे मासि बलिहरणमिति। मास शब्दो व्याख्यात:।

VādhGS — ***वैष्णवं सूक्तं प्रवोचमिति।***

Vṛtti — वैष्णवं सूक्तं प्रवोचमिति। 'विष्णोर्नु कं', 'तदस्य प्रियम्' इत्येवं पठितं षट्ष्वृक्षु सूक्तस्य समाप्ति:, प्रत्यृचं होम:।

VādhGS — ***अग्रेणाग्निं हरेदेतेनैवेति।***

Vṛtti — अग्रेणाग्निं हरेदेतेनैवेति। एतस्यै देवताया इति वचनं मन्त्रलिङ्गेनैव सिद्धेरनर्थकं देवता प्रतिपादनं तस्मादेव तच्छब्द: प्रतिपादितम्। सान्निध्यमत्र विधीयते देवताया:। न च तदापादयितुं शक्यम् अतीन्द्रियत्वात्। तस्मात् सन्निधानबुद्ध्या भक्त्या देवतार्चनं कृत्वा तत्समीपे बलिहरणं कर्तव्यमिति केचिन्मन्यन्ते। एतेनैव सूक्तेनैवेत्यादि सम्बन्ध:। बलिहरणमस्य निवेदनं प्रत्यृचम्।

The above texts of the *VādhGS* and the *VādhGSV* describe the *gṛhya* ritual of *Baliharaṇam*, which is mentioned as *Viṣṇubali* in the *VādhGṛVR*. This *Viṣṇubali* is performed in the eighth month of the *Garbhādhāna*. The whole ritual has been explained in *VādhGṛVR*, 2.143-160.

2. *VādhGS* — ***अथ नाम्नाऽस्मान्निदधाति***

Vṛtti — यथा एषां ब्राह्मणानां गुह्यं भवति तथा कुर्यादिति। एषामित्यत्र पुल्लिंगस्य विवक्षितत्वान् मातरि प्रकाशनमनु जायते। यथा न केचित्पठन्ति। तन्मातापितरौ विद्यातामोपनयनादिति च। नान्येषु प्रकाशनप्रसङ्गः। कथं गुह्यपूर्वमित्येतावतैव ब्राह्मणेष्वप्यप्रकाशनस्य सिद्धत्वान्नियमार्थमेतद्वचनं भवति। एषामेव सन्निहितानामेव गुह्यं स्यादिति। सन्निहितेषु पुंसामेव गुह्यं स्यादिति वा । तत्र पूर्वस्मिन्नियमे गुह्यपूर्वमित्यनर्थकं भवति, उत्तरे तु न कश्चिद् दोषः। तस्माद् गुह्यपूर्वमित्यन्येषां गुह्यत्वं यथैषां गुह्यत्वं स्यादिति। एतेन मातरि प्रकाशनं विधीयत इति।

VadhGS — ***अमुस्मै स्वस्तीति ब्राह्मणान् स्वस्ति वाचयेत्।***

Vṛtti — स्वस्तिवाचनः शब्दः समाधीयतामित्येवमादौ प्रसिद्धः तेन युष्मान् ब्राह्मणान् संपूज्य 'मनः समाधीयताम्' इत्यादि वाचयित्वा 'स्वस्ति भवन्तो ब्रुवन्तु' इत्यस्मात्पूर्वं चतुर्थ्यन्तं नाम ब्रूयात्। नाम्नो लक्षणं मङ्गल्यं ब्राह्मणस्येत्यादि द्रष्टव्यम्। तदेव स्वस्तिवाचकं सर्वेष्वाभ्युदयिकेषु कर्मसु पूर्वं कर्तव्यात् समाचारात्। अत्र द्विर्होमात्पूर्वं नामकरणे च।

The above texts of *VādhGS* and *VādhGSV* describe the *gṛhya* ritual of *nāmakaraṇa*. The *VādhGṛVR* explains the whole ritual in 2.197-214.

In both the above-cited cases the nature of the three texts is very clear. There remains no doubt that *VādhGṛVR* is a versified commentary of the *VādhGSV,* which itself is a commentary on *VādhGS*. Since the *VādhGS* and *VādhGSV* are not edited and published so far, it is very difficult to ascertain up to what extent there is agreement in their treatment of the topics related to *gṛhya* rituals. Moreover, the texts of both the works, as found in the available MSS, are very mutilated, full of lacunae and the order of the treatment of *gṛhya* rituals is also not correct, possibly due to displacement and loss of the original folios from which the existing MSS have been copied. This *VādhGṛVR* will certainly help us to a great extent in preparing critical editions of the two texts.

That the *VādhGṛVR* is based on the two texts, viz. the *VādhGS* and the *VādhGSV,* is also evident from the fact that the author of the *VādhGṛVR* quotes the views of the Gṛhyasūtrakāra and the Vṛttikāra. In the very opening verses the author has paid his homage to Vādhūlaka, and the *vṛttikṛt*. Most probably, Vādhūlaka may be the compiler of the *Vādhūlagṛhyakalpa*, but who is Vṛttikāra, in this regard there may be some speculations. From the use of the word *vṛttikṛdbhiḥ* (4.240), it seems that there may have been many *vṛttikāra*s, but the occurrence of the words *vṛttikāreṇa* (2.52), *vṛttikṛtoditam* (2.186), *vṛttikṛnmatam* (2.57; 63) in singular, also lead us to believe some definite personality whose work the author is referring to. This speculation seems to reach a conclusion when at two places the *VādhGṛVR* mentions the name of Kauṇḍinya as the author of the *vṛtti*.[1] He has been referred to as *vṛttikāra*. Āryadāsa in his commentary on the *VādhŚS*, called *Kalpāgamasaṁgraha*, refers to Kauṇḍinya as one of the four branches of Vādhūlas. Therefore, it is possible that he had written *vṛtti* on the *VādhGS*.[2]

4. Contents of the *VādhGṛVR*

The *VādhGṛVR* deals with all the topics dealt with in the *VādhGS* and *VādhGSV* in independent ways. It gives a description of the *gṛhya* rituals and gives their *prayoga*s, too, in free verses. It consists of eight chapters. The first chapter deals with basic common acts which are essential to be performed in any religious rite, related to *gṛhya* and *smārtakarma*. The purpose of the author is to correlate the *gṛhya* rites with the *smārtakarma*. What is the proper time for *smārtakarma*; which *mantra*s are to be pronounced in low voice (*upāṁśu*); how one should put on *yajñopavīta* while performing rituals related to *devakarma*,

1. षोडश स्युस्तथा मन्त्रा वैशम्पायनकादयः।
आत्रेयः पदकारान्तः कौण्डिन्यो वृत्तिकारवान्ङ्क — 4.361
उखं चैव तथात्रेयं पदकारमनन्तरम्।
कौण्डिन्यं वृत्तिकारं महान्तं सौबभ्रुवं ततः — 4.383

2. चतुर्णां वाधूलानामिति। के ते चत्वारो वाधूलाः। कौण्डिन्याग्निवेश्यगार(ल)वशाङ्खानां कल्पाः। तथाहि-शुल्ब उक्तम्-वाधूलाः सवाधूलाश्चत्वारो विहिताः।
Quoted by Ravi Varma in the *ĀgnGS*, Trivandrum Sanskrit Series CXLIV, Sr. No. 11, 1940, Intro. p. iii

pitṛkarma or *manuṣyakarma*; how one should sip and sprinkle sacred waters in the beginning of any religious rite; how one should set-up *aupāsanāgni* for the performance of *homa*s; how the oblations should be prepared and placed on *vedi*; how the enclosures (*paridhi*) are made around the fire; how the *homa*s of cooked food are to be performed; how and where one should offer *homa*s like *jaya, rāṣṭrabhṛt, pārvaṇa,* etc.; and how the expiatory rites are to be performed in the loss of sacrificial fire — all these form the contents of the first chapter.

The second, third and fourth chapters are directly related to the *gṛhya* rituals. The *ṛtusaṁveśanaṁ (garbhādhāna), puṁsavana, sīmantonnayana, viṣṇubali, jātakarma, nāmakaraṇa, janmanakṣatreṣṭi-prayoga, carvākhya-āyuṣyakarma, niṣkramaṇa, annaprāśana, caulakarma, ābhyudayika śrāddha* and *vidyārambha* in this very order, form the contents of the second chapter. It is pertinent to note that a very important question has been discussed regarding whether a female child is entitled to *saṁskāras* like *nāmakaraṇa, niṣkramaṇa,* etc. or not. The author of the text very clearly mentions that according to Vādhūla, all *saṁskāras*, where *homakarma* does not take place, are to be equally performed for both male and female child. But where *homakarma* is involved, *homakarma* will be performed, but without uttering *mantra*s in the case of female child. However, the rite of *puṇyāhavācana,* i.e. "wishing a person happy or auspicious day" is equally prescribed for the female also (2.217). In *caulakarma*, clarified butter is said to be anointed on her head.

The third chapter deals with the *upanayana* in detail. It may be mentioned that here *upanayana* is described as a part (*aṅga*) of study (*adhyayana*). Who is entitled to *upanayana*; what is the proper time for *upanayana* and what is its significance — all this has been discussed in detail. The ritual procedure of performing *upanayana* as a *smārtakarma* has also been described here. A *Brahmacārin,* whose initiatory rite has been performed by the *ācārya*, is supposed to obey the rules of discipline as prescribed by the *ācārya*, or *guru*. How should a *brahmacārin* pay his daily homage to his *guru* (3.231-36) and how should a *guru* bestow his blessings on his pupil, have been explained here. What should he eat and what he should not, this has been prescribed here. The procedures and methods of imparting *Sāvitrī-Gayātrī mantra*, and putting on *sūtra*, *daṇḍa*, *mekhalā*, etc. have been given here.

The fourth chapter, after prescribing the rules of *yama-niyama*, deals with *vrata*s like *kāṇḍa-vrata*, *śukriya-vrata*, *godānakarma*, *kārā-vrata*, *karīri-vrata*, *upākarma*, etc. as preliminary rites for the study of the Vedas (*vedādhyayana*). Stress is given on the study of one's own *Śākha-saṁhitā*. The study of Vedāṅgas as a part of *svādhyāya* like Vedas has also been prescribed. In this connection references to the study of *pitṛ-vidhi*, *pravargya-vidhi*, *kāṭhakānām-vidhi*, *kārīri-vidhi*, *aruṇāmnāya-vidhi*, *śatarudra-vidhi* have been made (4.330). *Mantra*s occurring in the Kalpasūtras in regard to the sacrifices should also be studied by the students of the Vedas (4.331-32). A detailed list of *anadhyāya*s, i.e. periods of time when study is prohibited, has also been given (2.297-317). The *utsarga-vidhi*, i.e. leaving of the study period at the end of studentship has been laid down here (2.333-366). It is pertinent to note that a detailed list of seers and *ācārya*s who are to be satiated by offering waters by the students at the end of the period of studentship, has been given. This ritual is called *tarpaṇa*. A common ritual for daily *tarpaṇa* for the use of all is also given (4.399-401).

The fifth chapter deals with a detailed discussion on the *samāvartana*, the last ceremony to be performed at the end of the period of studentship. After having performed this ceremony students return to their houses. After dealing with the *samāvartana saṁskāra*, the text gives a detailed account of the *vivāha* rites and the duties of the couple to be observed in the *gṛhastha āśrama*. In this connection the text deals with *pañca-mahāyajñas*, *aupāsanahoma*, *gṛhya-vaiśvadevakarma*, *balivaiśvadevakarma*, etc.

The sixth chapter deals with the topics which are not directly related to the *gṛhya* rites. These topics come under the purview of the Smṛtis. The rules of keeping physical purity and cleanliness, such as *viṭśauca*, *mūtraśauca*, *ācamana*, *dantadhāvana*, *snāna*, *vastradhāraṇa*, *ūrdhvapuṇḍradhāraṇa*, etc. have been codified. This portion does not seem to be original. It is rather a collection of *smṛtivacana*s, sometimes in full and sometimes in modified form, related to the topics mentioned above. Here, a list of routine work to be done in the different periods of the day from morning to going to bed is given. In this connection while dealing with *sandhyopāsanā* and *sūryopāsanā*, the secret and significance of worshipping Gāyatrī is given. The recitation of Gāyatrī *mantra* with the accompaniment of *oṁ*, called *praṇava* and the mystical utterances of the seven worlds, viz. *bhūḥ*, *bhuvaḥ*, *svaḥ*, *mahaḥ*, *janaḥ*, *tapaḥ* and *satyam*, called *vyāhṛti*s, have been prescribed. The presiding deity of Gāyatrī *mantra* is threefold, viz. Gāyatrī, Sāvitrī and Sarasvatī. Gāyatrī should be worshipped in the morning, Sāvitrī in the mid-day and Sarasvatī in the evening, by the same *mantra*. The *ādhyātmika* relation of *praṇava* (*oṁ*) and the seven *vyāhṛti*s has been established. The prevalence of worship of one's own *iṣṭadevatā* in waters, fire, heart, sun, *sthaṇḍila* (a piece of squired ground prepared for offering *homa*) and the idols (*pratimā*) has been referred to. But the worship of Viṣṇu or Śiva with Vedic *mantra*s has been regarded as the best one, as there is no worship superior to it (6.456-464). The worship of both Viṣṇu and Śiva with Puruṣa-sūkta has been prescribed for a household in both the schools, viz. Vādhūla and Baudhāyana. Here the unity of Viṣṇu and Śiva has been firmly established. At the close of the chapter the daily routine of a housewife has been prescribed.

The seventh chapter exclusively deals with the *śrāddhakarma*: types, times, and significance of their performances. Who and how many persons are to be served with meal, what materials are to be used, and what is the procedure of performing *śrāddha*, have been discussed in detail.

The eighth chapter deals with the *rajodharma*, i.e. code of conduct of a woman during her menses period, and thereafter. The means of purification and expiations in the violation of rules have also been described. This chapter, like the sixth, is based on Smṛti rules in the matter of treatment of the topics concerned.

5. Authorities Mentioned in the Text

The author of the *VadhGṛVR* refers to many authorities in connection with dealing with the topics therein. We may classify these authorities under the following groups —

(i) Authorities mentioned by using the words *-kāra, -kṛt* with some genre of literature.

(ii) Authorities mentioned by specific names of the class of literature.

(iii) Authorities quoted by referring to specific texts.

(iv) *ṛṣi*s and *ācārya*s mentioned by name.

(i) Authorities mentioned by using the words *-kāra, -kṛt* with some genre of literature — In this class the following authorities have been mentioned:

Kalpakāra, Kalpakṛt — The author of the *kalpa* text has been referred to by the appellation *kalpakāra* twice (3.116; 5.5), and *kalpakṛt* 11 times (1.66; 2.34; 48, 162; 3.87; 89; 346; 359[2], 5.5; 226). In all these cases, both the appellations seem to have been referring to Vādhūla, the author/promulgator of the Kalpasūtra. The views of the *kalpakāra/kalpakṛt* have been quoted as an authority in the matters of *gṛhya* and *smārtakarma*.

Gṛhyakāra, Gṛhyakṛt — The author of the *gṛhya* text has been referred to by the appellation *gṛhyakāra* (5.117) and *gṛhyakṛt* (4.163). Here both appellations seem to have been referring to Vādhūla, the author/promulgator of the *VādhGS*.

Padakāra — The text refers to the author of the *pada*-text by using the appellation *padakāra* and ascribes the *padapāṭha* to Ātreya (4.383). The *padapāṭha* of the *Taittirīya Saṁhitā* is ascribed to Ātreya.

Vṛittikāra, Vṛttikṛt — The author of a *vṛtti* text has been referred to by the appellation *vṛttikāra* twice (2.52; 4.361) and *vṛttikṛt* four times (1.2; 2.57; 63; 186) and the authorship of the said *vṛtti* has been ascribed to Kauṇḍinya (4.361). However, the use of the word *vṛttikṛdbhiḥ* (4.240) in plural also suggests the existence of many authors of the *vṛtti* texts. From this it appears that there existed many texts under the title *vṛtti* and, as such, there may have been many *vṛttikāra*s. The author of the *VādhGṛVR* must have before him many *vṛtti*-texts as it is also evident from the fact that in the very beginning he has paid homage to the authors of the *vṛtti*-texts, whom he regarded as *guru*s (1.2).

Sūtrakāra, Sūtrakṛt — The author of the *sūtra*-text has been referred to by the appellation *sūtrakāra* (4.384) and *sūtrakṛt* (4.362). However, these appellations are not confined to a particular *sūtrakāra*. These have also been used for Vādhūla, Kaṇva, Baudhāyana, and Āpastamba, individually (4.362).

Smṛtibhāṣyakṛt — The text refers to a commentator of a Smṛti text by the appellation *smṛtibhāṣyakṛt* (6.76). But who is intended here by this appellation is not clear. In the name of a Smṛti-text of the Vādhūlas, the *Vādhūla-Smṛti*[1] is available to us. But its commentary is not known to us so far. Here the *smṛtibhāṣyakāra* is quoted in connection with prescribing various occasions (*nimitta*s) where sipping of sacred waters (*ācamana*) has been prescribed.

(ii) Authorities mentioned by specific names of the class of literature

Āraṇyaka — The Āraṇyaka, a particular type of literature, forming a part of Veda, is referred to in connection with prescribing its study in the day-time, not in night (2.295; 322) Āraṇyaka is also mentioned by the name *rahasya* (4.43). It is said that *rahasya* should not be studied in the *kṛṣṇa-pakṣa.*

Itihāsa-Purāṇa — The text refers to the *Itihāsa* and Purāṇa to be satiated in the *tarpaṇakarma* (4.381). Under the class *Itihāsa-Purāṇa*, which texts are intended is not specified in the text. In the *ācamana vidhi,* it is stated that one should cleanse the lips for the satisfaction of *Itihāsa-Purāṇa* (1.197). One should hear regularly the *Itihāsa* and Purāṇas in the sixth and seventh part of the day (6.598).

Kalpa — The text refers to the *kalpa*, a part of Vedāṅga, consisting of Śrauta, Gṛhya, Dharma and Śulba texts as authority in the matters of *smārtakarma* (1.77; 81; 100; 120; 242; 268; 288; 299; 380; 540; 2.32; 33; 38; 40; 44; 195; 4.25; 327; 329; 300; 331; 5.12; 97; 7.41; 44)

Gṛhya — The text refers to the *gṛhya* texts as authorities in the matters of *gṛhya* and *smārtakarma* (1.23; 101; 102; 118; 120; 223; 380; 434; 2.139; 2.195; 4;142; 143; 5.279)

Jyotiḥśāstra — The text refers to the *jyotiḥśāstra* in connection with prescribing time for performance of the rituals (1.123; 2.124; 321; 5.318).

Dharmaśāstra — The text refers to the authority of

1. Edited by B.B. Chaubey, Katyayan Vaidik Sahitya Prakashan, Hoshiarpur (2002).

Dharmaśāstra. Any *smārtakarma* is authentic when it is performed according to the rules of Dharmaśāstra (5.30; 391).

Bhiṣak-Śāstra — The text refers to the authority of the Bhiṣak-Śāstra in the matters of giving meals to a woman in her pregnancy period (2.116). It is also said that the accomplishment of the efficiency in a physician comes by performing the *Śrāddhakarma* (7.67).

Mīmāṁsā — The text refers to Mīmāṁsā and gives its meaning *vikalpanā*, i.e. difference of perception (5.39) and also refers to *Mīmāṁsānyāya* (3.83). The *Mimāṁsā*-style of discussion and its terminologies have been used very frequently in the treatment of the *saṁskāra*s.

Lokaśāstra — The text refers to the authority of the Lokaśāstras, to be followed in the matter of observing *lokācāra* for prevention of miscarriage of the pregnancy (2.115). A thing which is deemed as baseful in *loka*, that should be prohibited in one's life (3.271; 6.4). The *lokācāra* has been accepted as an authority in the matter of performance of the rituals (2.313).

Lokāyatika — The text refers to *lokāyatika*s, i.e. persons experienced in the ways of the world, or materialistic ones, They have been regarded as *nāstika*s, i.e. atheists (6.434), as they do not believe in Vedic rituals.

Veda — The text refers to the Veda as supreme authority in all matters. Therefore, it must be studied by a *dvija* (4.110). It may be pointed out here that Veda is a common designation of all the Saṁhitās with their Brāhmaṇas, Āraṇyakas and the Upaniṣads of all the recensions. However, for study and performance of the rituals one's own *Śākhā Saṁhitā* with its Brāhmaṇa, Āraṇyaka and Upaniṣad, is accepted. (4.111-15).

Vedāṅga — The text refers to the Vedāṅgas as the subject of study like Veda (3.244). But its study has been ordained in the *kṛṣṇa pakṣa* of the month (4.43). The number of Vedāṅgas is said to be six (5.23).

Śaucakalpa — The text refers to the existence of many works dealing with *śauca*, according to different *āśrama*s (6.33).

Smṛti — The text very frequently refers to the authority of Smṛti-texts in the matter of religious performances and code of conduct related to *smārtakarma*. (For reference to Smṛtis, see Index pp. 467-68.)

(iii) Authorities quoted by referring to the specific Texts

Atharvaveda — The text refers to the *Atharvaveda* occupying the fourth position among the Vedas, in connection with the *tarpaṇakarma* (4.380). It has also been referred to by the appellation *Atharvāṅgiras* (4.381).

Ṛgveda — The text refers to the *Ṛgveda* in connection with the *tarpaṇakarma* (4.380). Among the four Vedas it occupies the first position.

Kāṭhaka — The text refers to the *Kāṭhaka Saṁhitā* and ordains its study in the day-time, not in the night (4.322).

Kāṭhaka Āraṇyaka — The text refers to the *Kāṭhaka-Āraṇyaka*, consisting of *hotṛkāṇḍa, pravargyakāṇḍa, upaniṣad-vidhi* and *aruṇāmnāya-vidhi*. It is stated that this Āraṇyaka is not to be studied by an *avratī*, i.e. one who has not undergone *vrata* (4.319).

Narāyaṇa-Upaniṣad — The text refers to the *Nārāyaṇa-Upaniṣad*, as being prescribed for study under *Kāṇḍavrata* (4.237).

Prayogakḷpti — The text refers to the *Prayogakḷpti*,[1] a text dealing with the *śrauta-prayoga*s (1.4). This text is ascribed to Śivaśroṇa. The text is available in the composite MSS of Kerala, Madras, Trivandrum and Baroda, as above (pp. 7-8).

Mānava — The text refers to the *Manu-Smṛti* by the title *Mānava* on the name of Manu (2.68; 13; 162; 260; 7.44).

Yujurveda — The text refers to the *Yajurveda* in connection with the *tarpaṇa* of the four Vedas (4.380). Among the four Vedas it occupies the second position.

Vādhūlāgama — A text called *Vādhūlāgama* has been mentioned here (5.359). It is stated that according to the *Vādhūlāgama* the *arthakrama*, i.e. the order of

1. The text has been edited by the present Editor.

performance is better than the *pāṭhakrama,* i.e. order as given in the text. Therefore, on the authority of the *Vādhūlāgama* the *brahmayajña* should be performed first in the order of sequence of the *pañca-mahāyajña*s. This text is not available or known to us so far. We know about *Vādhūla-kalpāgama*, a commentary on *VādhŚS* by Āryadāsa. Whether the *Vādhūlāgama* and the *Vādhūlakalpāgama* are two separate texts, or one and the same text, is yet to be ascertained. What is relation between *Vādhūlāgama* and *Vādhūlagṛhyāgama* is also yet to be decided.

Vratasaṁgraha — The text refers to the *Vratasaṁgraha*, a collection of *vrata*s (4.70).

Śeṣa-Yajñapārśva — The text seems to refer to two works, viz. *(Pari-)Śeṣa* and *Yajñapārśva* together (1.35). The *Yajñapārśva* has been published.[1] But by *Śeṣa* which work is intended, is not clear. Most probably *Śeṣa* refers to the nature of the *Yajñapārśva* as a *Pariśiṣṭa*.

Sāmaveda — The text refers to the *Sāmaveda* as third in order of sequence of the Vedas to be satiated in *tarpaṇa karma* (4.380).

(iv) Ṛṣis and Ācāryas mentioned by name

Agastya — The text mentions Agastya, a seer of the *ṚV*, who is satiated with water on an *ākhara*, also called *sthaṇḍila*, prepared for the purpose to the south of the *ākhara* of Viśvāmitra and Aṣṭaka (4.348, 357, 372).

Agni — The text refers to Agni as a *ṛṣi* of the Āgneyakāṇḍa of the *TaittS* (4.46).

Aghamarṣaṇa — A reference has been made to the recitation of the *Sūkta* (*ṚV* X.190) of *ṛṣi* Aghamarṣaṇa on whose name the *Sūkta* is also called *Aghamarṣaṇa* (6.170; 170 क ; 378).

Aṅgirasas — The text refers to the satiation of Aṅgirasas on an *ākhara*, made for the purpose in the *utsarga-karma* (4.357; 371). At one place it is stated that among the followers of the Āṅgirasa *gotra* marriage takes place even in their own *gotra* (5.181).

1. The text with English Translation edited by C.G. Kashikar, B.O.R.I., Pune, 1998.

Atri — The text refers to the satiation of Atri a seer of the *ṚV* (*Maṇḍala* 5) on the *ākhara* made for the purpose in the *utsargakarma* (4.372).

Apratiratha — A reference has been made to a *Sūkta* of Apratirath (7.313), a *ṛṣi* of the *ṚV* (X.103).

Arundhatī — A reference has been made to the *tarpaṇa* of Arundhatī along with Vasiṣṭha in the *utsargakarma* (4.372). Arundhatī as a star is also referred to (5.277).

Aṣṭaka — A seer of the *ṚV* quoted along with Viśvāmitra, in connection with *tarpaṇa* of the seers (4.348-58).

Āgniveśya — Āgniveśya has been referred to as a *sūtrakāra* to be satiated in *tarpaṇa* (4.384). His opinion has also been quoted in connection with making the student put on new clothes in the *upanayana* (3.313). Here the opinion of Āgniveśya is said to be in accordance with an Āgama (probably *Vādhūlāgama*, a text referred to above). The author of the *VādhGṛVR* accepts the *mantra* 'यज्ञस्योपवीतेन' as authoritative in connection with putting on the *yajñopavīta* (3.320) with this *mantra* (see *ĀgnGS* II.4.9). The view of Āgniveśya has been quoted as an authority regarding the time of *upanayana* of a brāhmaṇa in Vasanta (3.113; cf *ĀgnGS* 1.1)

Āpastamba — Āpastamba has been quoted at 4 places in the text (3.118; 4.362; 384; 5.463). According to Āpastamba, the father and mother give birth to the body of the child, but the *guru* by *upanayana* gives a better birth to it (3.118). He has been referred to as a *sūtrakāra* (4.362). He is one of the *ācārya*s, mentioned in connection with the *tarpaṇa* in *utsargakarma* (4.384). Āpastamba is said to have prescribed the sprinkling of milk, butter, honey at the arrival of an *āhitāgni* (5.463).

Kaṇva — The text refers to Kaṇva along with Baudhāyana in connection with *tarpaṇa* in the *utsargakarma* (4.362; 384).

Kāśyapa — Kāśyapa is mentioned among the seven *ṛṣi*s to whom *tarpaṇa* is offered in the *utsargakarma* (4.372). He has also been quoted as expressing his view regarding seven types of *paunarbhavā kanyā*s, i.e. widow-virgins giving birth to a child after being remarried (5.248क)

Kṛṣṇadvaipāyana — A group of five *ācārya*s headed by Kṛṣṇadvaipāyana Vyāsa has been referred to as those who put on the *yajñopavita* around their neck (4.360). It is stated that for these *ācārya*s *ākhara* is prepared with northward slope (4.349), and *tarpaṇa* is made to them (4.373). At one place by Vyāsa the author of the *Mahābhārata* seems to be intended (6.238).

Kauṇḍinya — Kauṇḍinya has been mentioned eight times. He is quoted in connection with putting on *mekhalā* in the waist and clothes. According to him, a *brahmacārin* should first put on *mekhalā,* and thereafter the clothes (3.321). He is said to be the author of a *vṛtti*, most probably the *VādhGSV* (4.361). He is satiated by *tarpaṇa* in the *utsargakarma* (4.383). His view has been quoted in connection with *punarādhāna* of the Aupāsanāgni. A *smārta prayoga*, based on Kauṇḍinya's *vṛtti*, has been given in the text (1.495 ff.). The *mantra* applied for putting on *palāśadaṇḍa* is said to be in accordance with the view of Kauṇḍinya (3.323). He has been quoted as having an opinion that in the *vivāha* rite the *sviṣṭakṛt*-offering should consist of *ājya* with parched rice-grain (*lājā*) in accompaniment of the *mantra* 'यदस्य कर्मणो', etc. (5.275).

Gautama — Gautama is referred to in connection with *tarpaṇa* in *utsargakarma* (4.372). Since this Gautama is mentioned among the seven *ṛṣi*s, he should be taken as the seer of Vedic *sūkta*s (*ṚV*. I. 74-93; 9.31; 9.67.7-9; 10.137.3). Another Gautama, the author of the *Gautama-Smṛti* has been quoted in connection with prescribing a code of conduct for a student regarding what he should do and what he should not (3.282). This view of Gautama is found in the *Gautama-Smṛti* (2.4). At one place a quotation 'विद्यान्ते गुरुरर्थेन निमन्त्र्य' has been given in the name of Gautama (5.17). Here, he is quoted as prescribing a *brahmacārin* to get married after *samāvartana* with the permission of his *ācārya*, or live in forest continuing his study (5.17).

Jamadagni — The text refers to Jamadagni, one of the

Vedic seers to whom *tarpaṇa* is offered in the *utsargakarma* (4.371). At another place he is mentioned as Vedic *ṛṣi* from whom a particular *gotra* called Jāmadagnya started on his name (5.180). He is a *gotrapravartaka ṛṣi*. He is also equated with one of the seven *vyāhṛti*s (6.369).

Jātūkarṇa — The text refers to Jātūkarṇa to whom *tarpaṇa* is offered in the *utsargakarma* (4.373). He is one of the promulgators of a Vedic Śākhā-Saṁhitā, belonging to *Śukla Yajurveda*.

Tarukṣa — The text refers to Tarukṣa, a Vedic personality (*ṚV* 8.46.32), to whom *tarpaṇa* is offered (4.373).

Tittiri — The text refers to *ācārya* Tittiri, the promulgator of the Taittirīya school (4.162), to whom *tarpaṇa* is offered in the *utsargakarma* (4.382).

Dhanañjaya — The text refers to Dhanañjaya, most probably a Vedic personality, to whom *tarpaṇa* is offered in the *utsargakarma* (4.376).

Nārāyaṇa — The text refers to Nārāyaṇa, the *ṛṣi* of Puruṣa Sūkta (6.407; 504).

Parāśara — The text refers to Parāśara to whom *tarpaṇa* is offered (4.377). He was one of the promulgators of a Śākhā under the Bāṣkala school. He is also regarded as one of the 15 Śākhā-promulgators of the *Śukla Yajurveda* under Yājñavalkya.

Prajāpati — The text refers to Prajāpati as *ṛṣi* of the Prājāpatya Kāṇḍa (4.45; 59). Another Prajāpati, the author of a Smṛti text is also mentioned (8.92; 182).

Bṛhadukṣa/Bṛhaduktha — The text refers to Bṛhadukṣa to whom *tarpaṇa* is offered in *utsargakarma* (4.373). He is most probably the *ṛṣi* of *ṚV* X.54-56).

Bodhāyana — The text refers to Bodhāyana 12 times. He is mentioned in connection with expressing his views about the *pākayajña* and *darvihoma*, the former, according to him, should be performed with *āghārāhuti* in the beginning, while the latter is performed without *āghārāhuti* (1.94-95). He is again quoted in connection with discussing the types of putting on the *yajñopavīta*. According to Bodhāyana, there are four types of putting on the *yajñopavīta*, viz. *upavīta, adhovīta, nivīta* and *prācīnāvīta* (1.158-1;59). The *lakṣaṇa*s, too, have been given by him. According to Bodhāyana, sipping of sacred water (*ācamana*) should always be accompanied with *mantra*s (1.203). He is again quoted as prescribing *darvihoma* and thereafter going to the newly wedded wife after performing the *caturthī-karma* (2.42). He is again quoted as prescribing the recitation of *mantra*s at the time of going to the wife after her first menses and thereafter as well (2.58). He is quoted as prescribing recitation of *mantra*s in giving knot in the ritual of *mekhalādhāraṇa* (3.322). According to Bodhāyana, *prāyaścitti* offerings are to be made before performing the acts related to sacrifice (4.191). He is also quoted in connection with *śukriyavrata* (4.204; 237). He is offered *tarpaṇa* in *utsargakarma* (4.384). The text gives in detail the rules and procedures of *ātithyavidhi* as laid down by Bodhāyana (5.463 क ff.). Bodhāyana is also mentioned in connection with having his own opinion regarding taking bath (6.416) and worshipping of a deity (6.483).

Bharadvāja — The text refers to Bharadvāja, the seer of the sixth *maṇḍala* of the *ṚV,* in connection with *tarpaṇa* of the *ṛṣi*s (4.372). He is mentioned as a *ṛṣi* after whose name Bhāradvāja *gotra* started and further divided into many branches (5.180). He has been equated with one of the seven *vyāhṛti*s (6.364).

Bhṛgu — The text refers to Bhṛgu to whom *tarpaṇa* is offered in the *utsargakarma* (4.371). He has been referred to as *ṛṣi* from whom Bhṛgu *gotra* started and further divided into many branches (5.180). It is also said that among the followers of Bhṛgu marriage takes place in their own *gotra* (5.181)

Manu — The text refers to Manu by name six times in connection with offering salutation to him (1.2), making *yajñopavīta* with cotton (1.181), putting fire-sticks (*samit*) in fire with *mantra* 'एषा ते अग्ने', etc. (3.168), prescribing duties of *a brahmacārin* (3.278), *aupāsana-homa* (5.407) and *pākṣika śrāddha* (7.3), respectively.

Yakṣa — The text refers to Yakṣa in connection with offering *tarpaṇa* in *utsargakarma* (4.375).

Yama — The text refers to Bhagavān Yama, an author of a Smṛti-text, in connection with giving *bhikṣā* (5.451).

Vasiṣṭha — The text refers to Vasiṣṭha in connection with *tarpaṇa* in the *utsargakarma* (4.375; 378). At one place he has been equated with one of the seven *vyāhṛti*s (6.364).

Vātsyāyana — The text refers to Vātsyāyana, the author of *Kāmasūtra*, in connection with putting on *maṇibandha* in the right hand (5.84).

Vādhūla — The text refers to Vādhūla among the *ācārya*s to whom *tarpaṇa* is offered in *utsargakarma* (4.384). He is also referred to with a patronymic name Saubabhruva, i.e. the son of Subabhru (4.383). But the mention of words *mahāntam saubabhruvam* (4.383) and *mahāntaṁ yakṣaṁ Vādhūlam* (4.3834) together creates doubt whether Saubabhruva and Vādhūla are one and the same person, or two separate personalities. Again the expression *mahāntam yakṣam* creates doubt whether *yakṣa* and *mahāntam* are two adjectives used for Vādhūla, or *yakṣam* is a proper name with whom the adjective *mahāntam* is connected. This problem is solved by the statement of the *Vādhūla Anvākhyāna,* where it is clearly mentioned that Saubabhruva proclaimed the knowledge of *agnyādheya* to Vādhūla.[1] This Saubabhruva and Vādhūla are not one and the same person, but the former is the teacher and the latter his *śiṣya*. Prof. Caland, too, regards Saubabhruva and Vādhūla as two separate personalities. The problem regarding *yakṣa* whether it is a proper name, or an adjective of Vādhūla also seems to be solved by accepting *yakṣam* as a variant reading of Yaska of the *VādhAnvā*. In the *Baudhāyana-Pravarasūtra* Yaska has been mentioned as a *gotra* under which Vādhūla comes.[2] Referring to the *gotra*s who belong to Nārāśaṁśa group in their *āprī* hymns both Vādhūla and Yaska along with some others have been mentioned.[3] From

---

1. एतद सौबभ्रुवो वाधूलाय प्रोच्योवाच, प्र न्वै वयं यास्कायाग्न्याधेयमवोचामेति। *VādhAnvā*, 1.7.8.
2. यस्का मौनो मूको वाधूलो वर्षपुष्यो. . . इत्येते यस्काः। — *BaudhPrS*. 6.421.5.
3. नाराशंसान्व्याख्यास्यामः। आत्रेयवाध्र्यश्ववाधूलवसिष्ठकण्वशुनकसंकृतियस्का इत्येते नाराशंसाः प्रकीर्तिताः। — *BaudhPrS* 54:456.11-12.

these references it becomes clear that Vādhūla and Yaska are two persons. Difference between Yaska and Yakṣa seems to be due to textual variation. Thus, the *VādhGṛVR,* maintains the personalities of Yakṣa and Vādhūla as different. The adjective *mahāntam* should be attached with Yakṣa.

Vāmadeva — The text refers to Vāmadeva, the *ṛṣi* of the fourth *maṇḍala* of the *ṚV*, in connection with the *tarpaṇa* of *ṛṣi*s in *utsargakarma* (4.375).

Viśvāmitra — The text refers to Viśvāmitra, the *ṛṣi* of the 3rd *maṇḍala* of *ṚV*, in connection with the *tarpaṇa* of *ṛṣi*s in *utsargakarma*. (4.352; 371)

Viśvedevā — The text refers to Viśvedevā as the seer of the *Vaiśvadevakāṇḍa* of the *TaitS* (4.46).

Viṣṇu — Referred to in connection with *tarpaṇa* in *utsargakarma* (4.383). It may be mentioned that this Viṣṇu seems to be an author of Dharmasūtra-text, as he is mentioned here along with Tittiri and Vaiśampāyana, not with deities like Śiva, Brahmā, etc.

Vaiśampāyana — Referred to in connection with *tarpaṇa* in *utsargakarma* (4.361; 382). Vaiśampāyana is the promulgator of the *Yajurveda Saṁhitā.*

Śaṅkara — The text refers to Ācārya Śaṅkara in connection with the interpretation of Gāyatrī *mantra* (6.307). The Gāyatrī *mantra* along with *praṇava* and *śiras* has been explained by the author of the text, according to Ācārya Śaṅkara.

Śātātapa — The text refers to Śātātapa, an author of a Smṛti text, in connection with a discussion regarding the right of virgin to get married with another person if her first husband is not found as having a noble family and good character (6.243). According to Śātātapa, the father has the right to bring his daughter back from the husband who does not belong to a noble family and does not have a good character, and give her to another person of a noble family and a good character.

Śālīki — The text refers to Śālīki in connection with whether *mantra* should be recited at the time of coition.

According to Śālīki, coition with one's wife after menstruation should be accompanied with *mantra* (2.59).

Sindhudvīpa — The text refers to Sindhudvīpa, the *ṛṣi* of *Āpohiṣṭhīya Sūkta* (*ṚV* X.9) (6.169).

Soma — The text refers to Soma, a seer of the *Somyakāṇḍa* of the *TaitS* (4.46).

Saubabhruva — The text refers to Saubabhruva, to whom *tarpaṇa* is offered in the *utsargakarma* (4.383). (Also see under Vādhūla.)

6. About the Author of the Text

From the colophons given at the end of each chapter (except 8th, being broken at the end) it is clear that the author of the text is Nārāyaṇa Miśra, a resident of Saṅgamagrāma. From the expression 'नारायणीये वाधूलगृह्यागमवृत्तिरहस्ये' one can easily understand that the author is Nārāyaṇa on whose name the text is mentioned as *Nārāyaṇīya*. But who is Nārāyaṇa and when did he flourish is very difficult to know, as among the commentators of Vedic texts several authors by the name Nārāyaṇa are known to us.

1. One Nārāyaṇa is said to be the commentator of the *ṚV*. Veṅkaṭa Mādhava in his commentary, called *Ṛgārthadīpikā,* in the beginning of the 4th chapter of the 8th *aṣṭaka* mentions that Skandasvāmin, Nārāyaṇa and Udgītha together wrote a commentary on the *ṚV*. This Nārāyaṇa flourished in about sixth century CE, as the date of Skandasvāmin, the teacher of Harisvāmin, has been fixed as sixth century CE. This Nārāyaṇa cannot be the author of the *VādhGṛVR*, as he did not belong to Vallabhi. The colophons clearly mention Nārāyaṇa, the author of the text, a resident of Saṅgamagrāma, not of Vallabhi.

2. Another Nārāyaṇa was the author of the *Āśvalāyana Śrautasūtravṛtti*. He was son of Narasiṁha and belonged to Gārgya *gotra*. This Nārāyaṇa cannot be the author of the *VādhGṛVR*, as the latter belonged to *Vādhūla gotra* not to Gārgya *gotra*.

3. Another Nārāyaṇa was the author of *Āśvalāyana Gṛhyavivaraṇa*. At the end of his *Vivaraṇa* he writes:

आश्वलायनगृह्यस्य भाष्यं भगवता कृतम्।
देवस्वामिसमाख्येन विस्तीर्णं तत्प्रसादतः ॥
दिवाकरद्विजवर्यसूनुना नैध्रुवेण वै।
नारायणेन विप्रेण कृतेयं वृत्तिरीदृशी ॥

This Nārāyaṇa flourished before vs 1323. This Nārayaṇa too, cannot be the author of *VādhGṛVR,* as the author of *VādhGṛVR* belonged to Vādhūla school.

4. Keśavasvāmin, the author of the *Baudhāyana-prayogasāra,* has mentioned the name of a Nārāyaṇa as the author of the *prayogagrantha*s. He writes :

नारायणादिभिः प्रयोगकारैरेकैकं पक्षमाश्रित्य दर्शपूर्णमासादीनां प्रयोग उक्तः। आचार्यपादैः द्वैधे पक्षान्तराण्युक्तानि। भवस्वामिमतानुसारिणा मया तु उभयमङ्गीकृत्यप्रयोगसारः लिख्यते।

This Nārāyaṇa, whom Keśava quotes, is the author of *Baudhāyanasūtra-prayoga*. From the above statement of Keśava mentioning the name of Nārāyaṇa as the author of the *Baudhāyana Prayogasāra*, he possibly refers to Nārāyaṇa the author of *VādhGṛVR*. *Trikāṇḍa-maṇḍana*, a work of eleventh century vs makes mention of Keśava (*Trikāṇḍ*, 1.10.1) and the latter mentions the authors of the prayogagranthas. This Nārāyaṇa whom Keśava has mentioned as the author of *prayogagrantha*s, may be taken as also the author of *VādhGṛVR,* besides the *Baudhāyanasūtra-prayoga*. But to reach this conclusion more evidences are required. At this stage, on the basis of the *VadhGṛVR* we can only say that —

1. Nārāyaṇa Miśra is the author of *VādhGṛVR*.
2. He was the resident of Saṅgamagrāma.
3. He was the follower of Vādhūla school of the *Kṛṣṇa Yajurveda*. It is evident from the fact that the use of the words अस्मदीयाः (1.77; 6.466), अस्मदादीयेन (7.162), अस्माभिः (1.104) clearly refers to his association with the Vādhūlas. In chapter 6, two types of procedures of worshipping a deity have been described. The first *vidhi* is said to be prevalent among the followers of the Vādhūla recension. The other *vidhi* is said to be prevalent among the followers of Baudhāyana school.

The first *vidhi* which is followed by the followers of Vādhūla-school is mentioned as अस्मदीयाः (6.466). This word 'अस्मदीयाः' proves that Nārāyaṇa Miśra was the follower of Vādhūla. In chapter 1, a *vidhi* of *Gṛhyakarmaprayoga* is given (1.27-80). Nārāyaṇa, here emphatically says that this *vidhi* is always followed by us (1.77).

7. Some salient features of the *VādhGṛVR*

The *VadhGṛVR* is a unique work having a triple character: versified combined commentary of both *VādhGS* and *VādhGSV*, an Āgama text dealing with the *smārta* rituals, and a *prayoga* of both the *gṛhya* and *smārta* rituals. In dealing with the topics concerned, it has some salient features which may be mentioned as under:

1. The *VādhGṛVR*, while dealing with the *saṁskāra*s adopts their order as *garbhādhāna, puṁsavana, sīmantonnayana, viṣṇubali, jātakarma, nāmakaraṇa, niṣkramaṇa, annaprāśana, caulakarma, vidyārambha, upanayana, godāna, vedādhyayana, samāvartana* and *vivāha*. These *saṁskāra*s are performed in three ways — *laukika, vaidika* and *smārta*. The text describes all the procedures of performing the above-mentioned *saṁskāra*s. In the treatment of the *saṁskāra*s the text refers to some deviation from the order as given in the *Gṛhyasūtra* (2.195-196). Most of the *Gṛhyasūtra*s describe the *vivāha* ritual in the beginning, because without marriage a child cannot be born. *vivāha* is a *saṁskāra* of a woman. The *VādhGṛVR* deals with *vivāha* at the end, becausee it is not concerned with the treatment of *saṁskāra*s only, but also with the duties of the couple in their whole span of life.

2. The *VādhGṛVR,* dealing with the *vedādhyayana,* prescribes some *vrata*s like *kāṇḍavrata, śukriyavrata, kārāvrata, kārīrivrata*, etc. to be observed by a student. In connection with the observance of *kāṇḍavrata,* it gives the order of the *kāṇḍa*s of the Saṁhitā-text, which a student should follow in the course of his study. The name and order of the *kāṇḍa*s of the Saṁhitā-text is given as Prājāpatya-kāṇḍa, Saumyakāṇḍa, Āgneyakāṇḍa and

Vaiśvadeva-kāṇḍa (2.46). It is said that the *mantras*, employed in Darśapūrṇamāsa along with its Brāhmaṇa-portion, constitute the Prājāpatyakāṇḍa. The *mantras*, employed in the Soma sacrifices along with Brāhmaṇa-portion, constitute the Saumyakāṇḍa; the *mantras* related to *agnyādhāna* along with its Brāhmaṇa-portion constitute the Āgneyakāṇḍa. All the remaining *mantras* together with their Brāhmaṇa-portion constitute the Vaiśvadevakāṇḍa (4.46-48). Now the question is whether this Saṁhitā, consisting of four *kāṇḍas*, belongs to the Vādhūla school or to the Taittirīya school, or to both the schools. It is possible that the author of the text may have been referring to the *Vādhūla-Saṁhitā* which is not yet discovered. Notwithstanding the mention of the *mantras* of the *TaittS*, beginning with 'इषे त्वा', the reference to an *anuvāka* containing the phrase 'सौबभ्रुवो ह वाधूलाय' (*VādhAnvā* 1.7.8) confirms its relation with the Saṁhitā text of the Vādhūlas (4.162.67). Besides the names of the *kāṇḍas*, the text refers to the *anuvākas*, such as Pavamānānuvāka (6.405). The mention of the *anuvākas* for the section of the Saṁhitā text has been made at many places (2.222; 223; 4.100; 164; 167; 224; 239; 242; 5.347; 352). The text also refers to differences of opinions regarding the order of studying the Vedic texts. For example, *Śukriya-mantras* have been prescribed by Bodhāyana to be studied under Saumayakāṇḍa, whereas, according to Vādhūla, they are to be studied under Aupaniṣadkāṇḍa. These *vratas* should be observed according to the order of the text (4.241).

3. In the *Gṛhyasūtras* Vedic *mantras* are prescribed to be uttered in accompaniment of the rituals to be performed. There is no scope for *smārta-mantras* in the *gṛhya* rituals. But in the *VādhGṛVR* both types of *mantras* have been prescribed,[1] which make its character as being related to the *gṛhyasūtras* as well as to the *smārta*-texts. It may be pointed out that the use of *smārta mantras* in

1. See Index-I :*Uddhṛtamantrānukramaṇī.*

performance of the *gṛhya* rituals may have started to make the rituals simple and practicable for the common man, too. These two types of *mantra*s were prevalent side by side at the time of the present text.

4. The *VādhGṛVR* gives a detailed description and *prayoga* of *tarpaṇakarma* as a part of *utsargavidhi* to be performed by a student at the close of his studentship. Such a long description we do not have elsewhere in any of the texts on the subject available to us. The deities, viz. Brahmā, Prajāpati, Bṛhaspati, Agni, Vāyu, Sūrya, Candramā, Indra, Yama, Varuṇa, Soma, Vaiśravaṇa, Vasus, Rudras, Ādityas, Viśvedevā, Sādhyas, Ṛbhus, Bhṛgus and Maruts have been satiated in the first group (4.368-371). In the second group the *ṛṣi*s of the Vedas, viz. Atharvans, Aṅgirases, Viśvāmitra, Jamadagni, Bharadvāja, Gautama, Atri, Kāśyapa, Vasiṣṭha, Arundhatī and Agastya have been satiated (4.371-372). The third group consists of the *ācārya*s who are the promulgators of the *Śākhā-saṁhitā*s. Under this category come Kṛṣṇa-Dvaipāyana Vyāsa, Jātūkarṇa, Bṛhaduktha, Tarukṣa, Tṛṇabindu, Somaśuṣmin, Somaśravas, Vājaśusmin, Vājaśravas, Vājaratna, Vāmadeva, Varuthin, Sanadvāja, Haryajin, Damaya, Udamaya, Hūṇañjaya, Tṛṇañjaya, Kṛtañjaya, Dhanañjaya, Babhru, Tryāruṇa, Trivṛṣa, Tridhāta, Śiśna, Parāśara, and Vasiṣṭha (4.373-377). In the fourth group deities like Indra, Mṛtyu, Kartṛ, Dhātṛ, Tvaṣṭṛ, Vidhātṛ, Savitṛ, Suśravas, Stutaśravas and Vasantaśravas have been mentioned to be satiated (4.378-379). In the fifth group Sāvitrī, Chandas, *Ṛgveda, Yajurveda. Sāmaveda, Atharvaveda, Itihāsa-Purāṇa*, Atharvāṅgiras have been offered *tarparṇa* (4.380-381). In the sixth group the remaining deities like *Sarvabhūta*s, *sarvagaṇa*s, and other *utsargadevatā*s have been mentioned to be satiated (4.381-382). The seventh group seems to consist of the names of the *ācārya*s, promulgators and their followers all belonging, most probably, to the *Kṛṣṇa Yajurveda*. This group includes the names of Vaiśampāyana, Viṣṇu, Tittirī, Ukha, Ātreya, Kauṇḍinya, Saubabhruva, Yakṣa, Vādhūla, Kāṇva, Bodhāyana, Āpastamba, Āgniveśya and other

ācāryas (4.382-385). The forefathers to be satiated by *tarpaṇa* include father, grandfather, great-grandfather; mother, grandmother, great-grandmother; father of the mother, grandfather of the mother, great-grandfather of the mother; father of the grandmother, grandfather of the grandmother, and great-grandfather of the grandmother; father of the great-grandmother, grandfather of the great-grandmother; great-grandfather of the great-grandmother (4.385-389). With which *mantra* the *tarpaṇakarma* is to be performed, the *VādhGṛVR* prescribes that the word 'तर्पयामि' should be accompanied with the name of the person to whom *tarpaṇa* is to be made, in accusative case, for example 'ब्रह्माणं तर्पयामि'. The author has enumerated all the names in accusative — case to whom offering is to be made to make it easy for the slow-witty persons. (367-68)

5. While dealing with the topics, specially prescribing some injunctions, the author uses the Mīmāṁsā-style of discussion. In this connection he uses Mīmāṁsā terminologies like *dṛṣṭādṛsta* (3.21), *apūrva* (1.94; 518), *apūrvavidhi* (1.117), *vidhi, arthavāda* (1.111; 2.73), *utpattividhi* (3.12क; 84) *svādhyāya-codanā* (3.33), *adhīticodanā* (3.42; 68), *vidvadviṣayatā* (3.35), *avidvadviṣayatā* (3.35), *parisaṅkhyāphalatva* (1.19) *prayoktṛtā* (3.4), etc. How *upanayana* is a part of *vedādhyayana* and who is entitled to it has been discussed in detail following the Mīmāṁsā-style (3.1-122).

6. In the case of plurality of views on the particular injunction, when the author establishes his view he uses the phrase इति स्थितम् (3.42; 5.105), इति स्थितिः (1.117; 134; 389; 3.249; 4.38 क).

7. In course of explaining some words, occurring in *VādhGS* or *VādhGSV*, the author takes notice of grammatical peculiarities of the word. Why a particular verb has been used in *ātmanepada* and why in *parasmaipada* that has also been discussed at places (3.13; 20; 22). He sometimes quotes the relevant *sūtras* of Pāṇini, e.g. 'स्वरितञित्' (3.23; *Pāṇ*. 1.3.72), पत्युर्न यज्ञसंयोगे (5.195; *Pāṇ*. 4.1.133). 'षष्ठ्यसौ युष्मदस्मदोः' (6.325; *cf Pāṇ*. 8.1.20), etc. The application of

grammatical rules has been extended to the observance of rituals. For example, 'आदेशवद् विसर्गः' (3.390) prescribes the treatment of *visarga(ḥ)* according to the prescription. In *VādhGṛVR* this has been quoted in support of the fact that since the ritual of *vedādhyayana* is started by the *ācārya*, hence, he must perform the closing ceremony, too. The text at places gives grammatical derivations and etymologies of the words. For example, explaining the Gāyatrī *mantra* the text derives the word 'धीमहि' from √ध्यै चिन्तायाम् (6.320); नः is the substitute for the pronominal stem अस्मद् in the plural of accusative, dative and genitive cases for अस्मान्, अस्मभ्यम् and अस्माकम् (6.325). Giving etymology of the word *ācārya* he follows Yāska when he says *ācārya* is he who inculcates good conduct and fourfold values of life in his pupil (3.49; cf. *Nir.* I.2).

8. The *VādhGṛVR* deals with rituals as found described in the Gṛhyasūtras and Smṛti-texts, as well as prevalent in the contemporary tradition (1.4).

9. The text, at places, uses proper names for the *sūkta*s and *mantra*s on the basis of the names of the *ṛsi*s, *chanda*s *devatā* or some words occurring in the *mantra*s, e.g. *Aghamarṣaṇa-sūkta* (6.170; 378), *Viṣṇu-sūkta* (2.148-150)), *Svasti-sūkta* (6.460; 503), *Rākṣoghna* (7.184; 312), *Raudrī* (6.529), *Śatarudrīya* (2.293), etc.

10. The text refers to the rivers, viz. Godāvarī, Bhīmarathī, Kṛṣṇavarṇā, Sarasvatī, Tuṅgabhadrā, Suprayogā, Sahyā, Kāverikā, Dugdhodā, Revā, Vāriśitā, Kalasvanā and many great rivers originating from Sahya mountain (6.151; 152). Among the rivers of the north, mention has been made of Gaṅgā (2.139; 6.82) and Yamunā (6.82). Gaṅgā has been mentioned by the name Jāhnavī also (6.78; 150; 212).

    It may be pointed out that the mention of a Sarasvatī among the rivers of south may indicate the existence of a Sarasvatī in south which is different from the well-known Sarasvatī of the Vedic Period. Among all the rivers Gaṅgā, Sarasvatī, Yamunā and Narmadā have been regarded as most pious ones. The water of the Gaṅgā purifies a person immediately after taking bath therein;

the waters of Sarasvatī after three days; the waters of Yamunā after five days (6.141). Again it is said that the water of Gaṅgā purifies immediately after taking bath but the Narmadā purifies one even by seeing her (6.142). Here the importance of Narmadā has been established.

8. Relation between *VādhGṛVR* and Smṛti-texts

The *VādhGṛVR* is very much influenced by the Smṛti-texts, among which special mention may made of *Manu-Smṛti, Yājñavalkya-Smṛti, Vādhūla-Smṛti, Āśvalāyana-Smṛti, Vasiṣṭha-Smṛti, Samvarta-Smṛti, Śaṅkha-Smṛti, Auśanasa-Smṛti, Baudāyana-Smṛti, Pārāśara-Smṛti, Bṛhatpārāśara-Smṛti, Bṛhaspati-Smṛti, Kātyāyana-Smṛti, Āpastamba-Smṛti, Atri-Smṛti, Śātātapa-Smṛti* and *Nārada-Smṛti.* The stanzas from the Smṛti texts have been quoted sometimes in full and sometimes in modified form at places even without mentioning their names. A chapterwise verse number with corresponding stanza-number of the Smṛti texts is given below for ready reference —

VādhGṛVR	*Smṛti text*		*VādhGṛVR*	*Smṛti text*	
2.3	Manu	3.46	3.198	Manu	4.51
2.16	,,	3.47	3.199	,,	4.48
2.17	,,	3.48	3.201	,,	4.52
2.37	Vasiṣṭha	1.17.62	3.202	,,	4.152
2.68	Manu	9.7	3.203	,,	4.46
2.74	,,	2.28	3.204	,,	4.47
2.199	Āśva	6.1	3.232	,,	2.122
	Yājña	1.12	3.233	,,	2.124
3.102	Manu	2.40	3.237	,,	2.125
3.103	,,	2.41	3.243	,,	2.142
3.104	,,	2.42	3.244	,,	2.141
3.121	,,	2.173	3.245	Nārada	4.10
3.121क	,,	2.171	3.246	Manu	2.145
3.122	,,	2.172	3.251	,,	2.133
3.124	,,	2.42	3.252	,,	2.120
3.125	,,	2.45	3.253	,,	2.121
3.157	,,	2.108	3.254	,,	2.123
3.196	Vādh	8	3.255	,,	2.126

VādhGṛVR	*Smṛti text*		*VādhGṛVR*	*Smṛti text*	
3.261	,,	2.183	4.139	Auśa	3.81
3.264	Yājña	1.32	4.264	Baudh	1.2.5
3.265	Manu	2.184	4.272	,,	2.165
3.266	,,	2.51	4.298	,,	4.118
3.267	,,	2.52	4.314	,,	4.115
3.268	,,	2.53	5.13	Yājña	1.49
3.269	,,	2.54	5.16	Manu	3.4
3.271	,,	2.57	5.17	Gautam	2.11
3.275	,,	2.182	5.36	Manu	4.36
3.276	Vādh	7	5.102	,,	3.3
3.284	Manu	4.37	5.103	,,	3.3
3.293	,,	2.50	5.164	,,	3.4
3.294	,,	2.51	5.174	,,	3.10
3.316	,,	2.169	5.184	,,	3.6
3.338	,,	2.48	5.185	,,	3.7
3.341	Saṁvarta	92	5.186	,,	3.8
4.17	Manu	2.196	5.189	,,	3.9
4.24	,,	2.199	5.190	,,	3.9
4.25	,,	2.200	5.241	,,	9.72
4.26	,,	2.202	5.250	,,	9.71
4.27	,,	2.203	5.256	,,	3.28
4.28	,,	2.204	5.257	,,	3.21
4.29	,,	2.218	5.258	,,	3.30
4.30	Śaṅkh	5.10	5.259	,,	3.38
4.118	Manu	2.74	5.263	,,	9.90
4.120	,,	2.116	5.265	,,	3.31
4.131	,,	2.112	5.266	,,	3.32
4.132	,,	2.109	5.267	,,	3.33
4.134	,,	8.199	5.268	,,	3.34
4.135	,,	2.97	5.363	,,	3.68
4.136	,,	2.166	5.364	,,	3.69
4.138	,,	2.168	5.365	,,	3.71
4.263	,,	3.1	5.441	,,	3.92

VādhGṛVR	*Smṛti text*	
5.451	Yājña	1.108
5.454	Manu	3.108
5.470	,,	3.107
5.473	,,	3.111
5.474	,,	3.112
5.475	Baudh	3.3.17
5.476	Manu	3.103
5.478	,,	3.101
6.4	,,	4.176
6.18	,,	4.51
6.20	,,	4.48
6.23	,,	4.47
6.54	,,	5.138
6.96	Vādh	30
6.108	,,	35
6.124	,,	37
6.130	,,	69
6.134-36	Pārāśara	12.9-11
6.138	Manu Vādh	4.203; 64
6.159	Vādh	26
6.190	,,	56
6.193	Vādh Pārāśara	59; 12.12
6.194	Vādh Pārāśara	60 12.13
6.195	BṛhadYājña	7.44
6.196	BṛhatPārā.	7.350
6.199	Vādh.	110
6.200	,,	112
6.201	,,	113

VādhGṛVR	*Smṛti text*	
6.215	,,	116
6.243	,,	117
6.244	,,	118
6.245	,,	119
6.342	,,	125
6.347	,,	124
6.348	,,	120
6.349	,,	121
6.350	,,	122
6.362	,,	137
6.390	Āśva	1.74
6.392	Manu	4.3
6.393	,,	10.115
6.394	,, Vādh.	4.4; 167
6.395	,,	4.5
6.396	,,	4.6
6.397	,,	4.7
6.425	,,	5.85
6.433	,,	12.55
6.441	,,	4.129
6.445	Vādh.	43
6.457	Bṛ Pārāśara	4.119
6.516	Gītā	9.26
6.581	Pārāśara	11.8
7.45	Manu	3.122
7.92	,,	1.135
7.97	,,	3.125
7.142	,,	3.125
7.143	,,	3.126
7.205	MānavDS	3.25.9
7.208	Likhit	60

VādhGṛVR	*Smṛti text*		*VādhGṛVR*	*Smṛti text*	
8.2	Manu	9.7	8.166	,,	4.57
8.3	,,	9.2	8.167	,,	4.59
8.4	,,	9.10	8.168	,,	4.38
8.8	,,	5.147	8.169(b)	Yājña	1.161
8.9	,,	5.148	8.170	,,	1.163
8.10 29	Nārada	4.13.28-	8.171	,,	1.164
			8.172	Manu Yājña	4.214, 1.165
8.11	,,	4.13.29			
8.16	Manu	5.154	8.173	,,	1.167
8.18	,,	9.80	8.174	,,	1.168
8.20	,,	11.5	8.175	,,	1.170
8.32	Bṛhaspati	11.22	8.176	,,	1.171
8.60	Manu	9.13	8.177	,,	176
8.65	,,	9.75	8.178	Manu	5.24
8.66	Yājña	1.84	8.179	,,	5.10
8.67	,,	1.86	8.180	,,	5.125
8.68	Kātyāyana	19.12	8.182	,,	4.248
8.86	Āpastamba	7.3	8.183	,,	4.212
8.111	Atri	5.60	8.186	,,	4.87
8.119	Śātātapa	3.5	8.187	,,	4.84-86
8.144	Manu	4.35	8.189	Yājña	1.153
8.145	,,	4.39	8.190	,,	154-155
8.149	,,	4.34	8.190क	,,	156
8.150	,,	4.43	8.191	Yājña (Prāya.)	2.35
8.152	,,	4.55	8.192	,,	2.36
8.153	Yājña	1.135	8.193	,,	2.37
8.159	Manu	4.70	8.194	,,	2.38
8.161	,,	4.73	8.195	,,	2.39
8.162	,,	4.60	8.196	Manu	10.94
8.163	,,	4.61	8.197	,,	10.91
8.164	,,	4.57	8.198	,,	10.92
8.165	,,	4.55	8.200	,,	10.97

॥ श्रीः॥

नारायणमिश्रविरचितं

वाधूलगृह्यागमवृत्तिरहस्यम्

अथ प्रथमोऽध्यायः[1]

[गृह्यकर्मोपक्रमः]

नीलोत्पलदलश्यामं नीरजायतलोचनम् ।
क्वणत्किङ्किणिनृत्यन्तं नमस्यामो रमापतिम् ॥१॥
वाधूलकं महाप्राज्ञं वृत्तिकृत्प्रमुखान्गुरून् ।
मन्वादीन्सूत्रकारांश्च विघ्नेशस्कन्दभास्करान् ॥२॥
गिरं[2] देवीं श्रियं शम्भुं प्रणम्याथ मयाऽधुना ।
वाधूलकल्पितस्मार्तप्रयोगोऽयं निबध्यते ॥ ३ ॥
प्रयोगक्लृप्तौ[3] पूर्वस्यां प्रयोगा बहुधोदिताः ।
समाचारानुसारेण प्रयोग इह कीर्त्यते ॥ ४ ॥
गृहकल्पसमाचारस्मृतिशास्त्रानुसारतः ।
पुरुषस्येह यत्कृत्यं तच्च लेशेन वर्ण्यते ॥ ५ ॥
चत्वारिंशद्धि संस्कारा अष्टावात्मगुणाश्च ये ।
तैः समेतो द्विजो विद्वान् ब्रह्म प्राप्नोति शाश्वतम् ॥ ६ ॥
ऋणत्रयसमायोगान्नियोगात्करणं मतम् ।
ब्रह्मचर्यस्य यज्ञानां प्रजोत्पादनकर्मणाम् ॥ ७ ॥
निषेकादिश्मशानान्तः संस्कारः स्मृतिचोदितः ।
द्विजातेरपि तु स्त्रीणां नित्य एषोऽवगम्यते ॥ ८ ॥
स्वभावामेध्यशुक्तादि[4]देहाशुद्धिनिरासतः ।
श्रौतस्मार्ताधिकारार्थं गर्भाधानादयः स्मृताः ॥ ९ ॥
न चाधिकारः संसिध्येच्छ्रुतिस्मृत्युक्तकर्मसु ।
पतितोत्पादितस्यापि संस्कारैर्विधिवत्कृतैः ॥ १० ॥
[5]इष्टोत्पादनशेषत्वं संस्काराणां प्रसज्यते ।

१.MT. Not mentioned. २.T गिरां. ३.M प्रयोग...प्तेन. ४.M शुक्त्यादि, T शुक्ला.
५.MT दुष्टो°.

नैमित्तिकत्वे नित्यत्वं बाध्येत [१]स्मार्तसम्मतम् ॥ ११ ॥
आचार्याधिकृतेर्यद्वदुपनेयस्य संस्कृतिः ।
पित्राद्यधिकृतेस्तद्वत्[२] संस्कृतेर्गर्भशेषता[२] ॥ १२ ॥
[३]पैतृकर्णविमुक्त्यर्थं प्रजामुत्पादयेदिति ।
विहितत्वात्प्रजोत्पादे[४] पित्रोरेवाधिकारिता[५] ॥ १३ ॥
उत्पादने[६] प्रयत्नोऽतः कार्यस्तस्मादृतावृतौ[७] ।
एवं तयोर्न दोषः स्यात् प्रत्यवायोऽन्यथा भवेत् ॥ १४ ॥
ऋतुकालाभिगामी[८] स्यात् स्त्रियः सेव्या इति स्मृतेः॥ १४क ॥
ऋतुस्नातां[९] तु यो भार्यां[१०] सन्निधौ नोपगच्छति[११] ।
तस्या रजसि तं मासं पितरस्तस्य शेरते ॥ १५ ॥
भर्तुः प्रतिनिवेशने[१२] या भार्या स्कन्दयेदृतुम् ।
तां ग्राममध्ये[१३] विख्याप्य भ्रूणघ्नीं[१४] निष्क्रमेद्[१५] गृहात्॥ १६ ॥
ऋतावागमने चापि प्रायश्चित्तं समीरितम्[१६] ।
दारव्यतिक्रमे [१७]चर्तुव्यतिक्रम इदं त्विति ॥ १७ ॥
[१८]ऋतावुपेयात्सर्वत्र वा निषिद्धं विवर्जयन् ।
इच्छया गमनं[१९] [२०]प्राप्ते नियमोऽत्रोपपद्यते ॥ १८ ॥
परिसंख्याफलत्वे तु सूत्रद्वयमनर्थकम् ।
इच्छया गमनं तत्र सामर्थ्यादेव सिध्यति ॥ १९ ॥
अतो नियोगतः[२१] कार्यं गर्भाधानादिकर्म[२२] यत् ।
लोकाद्यवाप्तये चापि पुत्रस्योत्पादनं[२३] स्मृतम् ॥ २० ॥
पुत्रेण लोकाञ्जयति पौत्रेणानन्त्यमश्नुते ।
अथ पुत्रस्य पौत्रेण ब्रध्नस्याप्नोति विष्टपम् ॥ २१ ॥

---

१. M °तन्मर्तृ°, T स्मार्त्तृ°. २-२.M तद्वस्त्र्यंस्कृते°, T °कृतेगर्भ°. ३.M पैतृकण्ठ°. ४.M °प्रजोत्वादे. ५.M °धित्रोकारितः. ६.M कृत्वादने. ७.T °तद्यानृतावृतौ, M ताद्यामृ. ८.MT °भिनामी. ९.T °स्नानान्तु. १०.M भार्याः. ११.M नोव°. १२.T °निवेशेन. १३.M ग्रामध्ये. १४.M भ्रूणघ्नं. १५.M निर्घ्नमेत्. १६.M °रितः. १७.M भर्तु°. १८.MT °पेयान्. १९.MT न मनः. २०.T प्राप्तेर्नि°. २१.M °गतं. २२.M °दिकार्ययोः. २३.M °त्वादनं.

पुत्रपौत्रप्रतिष्ठस्य बह्वपत्यस्य जीवतः[१] ।
अच्छिन्नवेदयज्ञस्य हस्तप्राप्तं[२] त्रिविष्टपम् ॥ २२ ॥
गृह्योदितानामन्येषां नित्यनैमित्तिकात्मनाम् ।
आकाङ्क्षितानां धर्माणां कथं स्यादिह पूरणम् ॥ २३ ॥
आकाङ्क्षापूर्तिरत्र स्यादाचार्यवचनैर्यदि ।
परार्थैरपि वा लिङ्गैः स्यान्निराकाङ्क्षता ततः ॥ २४ ॥
तदभावे शेषयज्ञपार्श्वाभ्यां[३] निगमादिभिः ।
पूर्वपूर्वबलीयस्त्वं तेषामपि च संमतम्[४] ॥ २५ ॥
निराकाङ्क्षा अपि स्नानशौचादिविधयस्तथा ।
कार्या एव [५]पुमर्थत्वात्तेषां शास्त्रविधानतः ॥ २६ ॥

[गृह्यकर्मप्रयोग-साधारणविधिः]

साधारणविधिं तावत्प्रयोगे गृह्यकर्मणाम् ।
प्रवक्ष्यामः समासेन शेषकल्पादिसंश्रयाः[६] ॥ २७ ॥
आज्यानुलिप्ताः समिधः स्वाहाकारसमन्विताः ।
प्रादेशमात्रीराधाय सर्वत्र जुहुयात्तथा ॥ २८ ॥
गणा एकसमित्काः[७] स्युरेकनामान एव ते ।
एकसंख्यान्विताश्चापि गणा एव प्रकीर्तिताः ॥ २९ ॥
चतुर्गृहीतसम्बन्धे [८]गणेष्वपि पृथक्पृथक् ।
आधाय समिधो होमं कुर्याज्जान्वाच्य दक्षिणम् ॥ ३० ॥
[९]दर्वीहोमेषु जुहुयात्सव्यं जान्वाच्य पैतृके ॥३०क॥
हुत्वा परिमितं[१०] चेध्ममन्नहोमाञ्जुहोति यत् ।
अधर्मकेषु चैतत् स्याद् [११]धर्मवत्स्वेकविंशतिः ॥ ३१ ॥
ओषध्यः सक्तवः पुष्पाः काष्ठमूलफलं तृणम् ।
[१२]एतद्धस्तेन होतव्यं नान्यत् किञ्चिदचोदनात् ॥ ३२ ॥

१.M जिह्मतः. २.M °प्राप्तस्त्रि°. ३.M °पाश्वर्वाद्यान्नि°. ४.M संमतः. ५.M पुमार्थ°. ६.T संश्रयाम्. ७.M °समित्ता. ८.M संबन्धेर्गणेष्वधि. ९.M दर्वि°. १०.M °मितश्चेधृमन्न°. ११.M धर्ममुपत्स्वेक°. १२.M एधतस्तेन.

नानन्तर्हित[१]यज्ञाङ्गं सादयेदिति चोदनात् ।
तृणेषु सर्वहोमादिसाधनानां च सादनम् ॥ ३३ ॥
दर्व्यास्त्वतो[२]ऽग्रतः पात्रं दीर्घं स्याच्चतुरङ्गुलम् ।
पृथुस्तु द्व्यङ्गुलं कार्यं दण्डो विंशतिरङ्गुलः ॥ ३४ ॥
यजमानस्य वाऽध्वर्योरङ्गुष्ठोपरि पर्वणा ।
तिर्यङ्मानं तु कर्तव्यमङ्गुलाख्यं च तद् भवेत् ॥ ३५ ॥
दशाङ्गुलं तु प्रादेशो वितस्तिर्द्वादशाङ्गुलम् ।
द्विवितस्तिररत्निः स्यात् किष्कुर्वा सममेव[३] वा ॥ ३६ ॥
[४]किष्कुर्व्युष्टियुतो हस्त इति चाप्यपरे विदुः ।
दैविकेषु बिलं त्वज्ञः[५] पैतृकेषु तु मज्जतः ॥ ३७ ॥
मूलान् पिण्डद[६]दानीयमग्राद्धोमार्थ[७]मिष्यते ।
औदुम्बराणि पात्राणि पैतृकेष्विति चोदितम्[८] ॥ ३८ ॥
नित्योपस्तरणाद्यर्था दर्वी[९] पर्णमयीष्यते ।
आयामः पंचभागः स्यात् त्रिभागो दण्ड इष्यते ॥ ३९ ॥
द्विभागं पात्रमित्याहुरेतदायामलक्षणम् ।
विस्तारा द्विगुणं पात्रं ग्रीवाविस्तारमर्धतः ॥ ४० ॥
ग्रीवार्धं तु बिलं कुर्यादेतत् पात्रस्य लक्षणम् ।
[१०]अरत्निमात्र्योर्हस्त्योष्ठ्यः प्रसेचनसमन्विताः ॥ ४१ ॥
काकपुच्छा[११] हंसमुख्यः स्रुचो[१२] वा स्युरितीरितम्[१३] ।
औषधार्थे[१४] व्रीहियवौ[१५] श्यामाकाश्च प्रियङ्गवः ॥ ४२ ॥
नीवारा वा[१६] वेणुयवाः कन्दमूलफलानि च ।
तरसः[१७] सक्तवस्तोय[१८]मित्येतं ग्राह्यमीरितम् ॥ ४३ ॥
कोद्रवो [१९]द्वारवरकमावर्ज्यमित्युदीरितम्[२०] ।

१.MT °हीतं. २.MT °स्त्वत्तो. ३. MT शम°. ४.M द्विष्कु°. ५.M तूक्तः. ६.M पिण्डं°. ७.MT द्धोमर्थ°. ८.T चादि°. ९.M दर्वि. १०.M अह्नोरत्नि°. ११.M °पच्छाङ्गः. १२.M स्राचो. १३.M कुरीरितः. १४.M ओषधार्थे. १५.M °यवो. १६.M om. १७.T तर.... १८.M सोऽय°. १९.T broken between द्वार and वरकमाव [Mच] र्ज्ज° [T र्ज]. २०.MT °मितीरितम्.

दर्भाः[१] कुशाश्च दर्भल्लाः[२] क्षीरदर्भांश्च मुञ्जकाः ॥ ४४ ॥
आश्ववालेक्षवश्चेति विहितानि तृणानि च ।
शूकञ्च[३] शरशीर्यञ्च बल्बजं[४] मृतवन्नडम्[५] ॥ ४५ ॥
[६]चुरुल्लका ध्रुवकाद्याः[६] शुष्ठश्चेति विवर्जयेत् ॥४५क॥
शास्त्रेष्वप्रतिषिद्धानि तृणान्यविहितान्यपि ।
ग्राह्याणीति विधेश्चेह निषेधादवगम्यते ॥ ४६ ॥
पलाशः[७] खदिरो बिल्वः प्लक्षो लोहितकस्तथा ।
[८]विकङ्कतौदुम्बरकंकथौ[९]दुम्बरकस्तथा[१०] ॥ ४७ ॥
न्यग्रोधका[११] अमी...................... ।
इध्माः[१२] कार्याः कद्वदन्तान्नादध्यादित्यपीरितम्[१३] ॥ ४८ ॥
धातकाद्याः[१४] कद्वदन्तास्तथाप्यर्को[१४] न दुष्यति ।
अक्षादिवर्जं वृक्षाणामिध्मत्वमपि चोदितम् ॥ ४९ ॥
विशेषवचनाभावे कार्याः परिधयोऽपि ते ।
त्रिप्रादेशाः परिधयो द्विप्रादेशा अपीध्मता ॥ ५० ॥
अङ्गुष्ठपरिणाहाः स्युरङ्गुल्याः संमिता अपि ।
प्रादेशसंमिता अन्या होमेष्वेवंविधाः[१५] श्रुताः ॥ ५१ ॥
द्राघीयान्दक्षिणः कार्यः परिधिः सर्वकर्मसु ।
स्थविष्ठो मध्यमः कार्य उक्ततोऽणुतरः शिशुः ॥ ५२ ॥
परिधीनां निधानान्ते सर्वत्रोर्ध्वसमिद्धुतिः ॥५२क॥
पाटितान्[१६] कृमिदष्टांश्च [१७]निस्त्वक्कानग्निदूषितान् ।
आर्द्रानिनिष्टान्[१८] क्षुद्रांश्च वर्जयेच्छिष्टगर्हितान् ॥ ५३ ॥
गव्यमाज्यं दधि क्षीरमाजं माहिषमेव वा[१९] ।
तिलजर्तिलयोस्तैलं[२०] सर्षपस्य फलस्य वा ॥ ५४ ॥

१.MT दर्भा. २.MT दर्भल्वाः. ३.M शूकश्च. ४.T बद्बजं. ५.T मुत°. ६–६.M चरुल्लकाद्या°. ७.MT पलाशं. ८.T विकं...तौ°. ९.M कंतौ. १० M कश्चथ, T कश्वथ. ११.M न्यग्राधका. १२.M इमाः. १३.M °रितः. १४–१४.T °द्यास्तद्वद°. १५.MT °विधा. १६.MT पाटिता १७.M निष्त्वर्कानन्निदू°, T °त्वक्कानग्नि. १८.M °ष्ठान्. १९.T Corrected as च. २०.M तिल. ..त्तिल.

पयो वा[१] पिष्टसंसृष्टं जलं वा सति सर्पिषी ।
दक्षिणानां च काले स्युर्मूलं[२] भक्षः फलानि वा ॥ ५५ ॥
प्रभुः प्रथमकल्पस्य योऽनुकल्पेन वर्तते ।
न चादृष्टं फलं तस्य दुर्मतेरिह विद्यते ॥ ५६ ॥
आज्यस्थाली प्रोक्षणी च संमिते [३]कुडवेन ते ।
द्वाभ्यां प्रणीता त्वष्टाभिश्चरुस्थालीमितोदिता ॥ ५७ ॥
प्रादेशसंमितं [४]यज्ञवृक्षोत्थं मेक्षणं मतम् ॥५७क॥
नक्षत्रं ब्राह्मणा देवा विप्रास्तेषां च वाक् शुभा[५]।
इति ब्राह्मणमाहात्म्यात्सर्वकर्मसु यत्नतः ॥ ५८ ॥
आदितः श्रोत्रियान्विप्रान्[६] प्राप्याभ्यर्च्य प्रसाद्य तान् ।
अनुज्ञाप्य ततः कुर्याद्यत्तत् कर्म चिकीर्षितम् ॥ ५९ ॥
शुक्लः[७] शुक्लाम्बरः स्नात उपवीती शिखी[८] शुचिः ।
बद्धकक्ष्यो बद्धपादः समाचान्तोऽस्पृशन्परान्[९] ॥ ६० ॥
आत्मानं वाऽशुचिद्रव्यशूद्रादीन्नावलोकयन् ।
श्रद्दधानो जितक्रोध आत्मवानास्तिकः[१०] शुभः ॥ ६१ ॥
उदङ्मुखः[११] प्राङ्मुखो वा स्वासीनः[१२] सपवित्रकः[१३] ॥६१क॥
प्रदक्षिणं दैवकर्म कुर्यात्प्रागपवर्गवत् ।
प्राचीनावीतवत्पित्र्यं प्रसव्यं दक्षिणामुखम् ॥ ६२ ॥
याम्यापवर्गकं कुर्यात् पात्राणां सादनं च यत् ।
दैवेषूत्तरतः कार्यं याम्यायां पैतृके दिशि ॥ ६३ ॥
लौकिकं वैदिकं स्मार्तं कर्णवेधादिकं[१४] च यत् ।
तत्र सर्वत्र[१५] पुण्याहवाचनं कार्यमादितः ॥ ६४ ॥
यस्मिन्नहनि कर्म स्यात्तस्मिन् पुण्याहवाचनम् ।
पुण्याहं वाचयित्वा तदहः कर्मेति चोदनात् ॥ ६५ ॥

१.M om. २.M °मूलमभक्षः. ३.MT कुडुबेन°. ४.M °प्रक्षोत्थं, T बक्षोत्थं. ५.M शुभाः. ६.MT द्विप्रा°. ७.MT शुक्ल. ८.M धिखी. ९.M वरान्. १०.M °स्तितः. ११.M उद्मुखः. १२.M स्वाघीनः. १३.M °कृत्. १४.M कण्ठवेदा°. १५.M adds सर्वं after सर्वत्र.

हरिरादौ समभ्यर्च्यो भक्त्या[1] सर्वार्थदो ह्यसौ ।
कल्पकृद्धि हरेर्नामकीर्तनं प्राह मन्त्रतः ॥ ६६ ॥
आदित्यस्य सदा पूजां तिलकं[2] स्वादिनं तथा ।
महागणपतेश्चैवं कुर्वन् सिद्धिमवाप्नुयात् ॥ ६७ ॥
मङ्गलाचारयुक्तानां नित्यं च प्रयतात्मनाम् ।
जपतां जुह्वतां चैव विनिपातो न विद्यते ॥ ६८ ॥
विनायकादीन्[3] संपूज्य सपत्नीको द्विजोत्तमान् ।
मृष्टान्नदानसन्तुष्टान् वेदशास्त्रविदः शुचीन् ॥ ६९ ॥
प्राङ्मुखानासनेष्वन्येषूपविष्टानुदङ्मुखः ।
तृणपाणिर्जलाद्यैस्तु गन्धपुष्पाक्षतैः शुभैः ॥ ७० ॥
होमादिभिर्दक्षिणाभिः शक्त्या संपूजयेत्ततः ॥ ७०क ॥
सूपलिप्ते स्थितं कुम्भं पूरयित्वाऽच्छवारिणा ।
गन्धपुष्पाक्षतफलसंयुतं सपिधानकम् ॥ ७१ ॥
आदायोभयतो दर्भं धारयंस्तमुदङ्मुखः ।
स्थितस्तृणेषु तिष्ठत्सु प्राङ्मुखेष्वग्रजन्मसु ॥ ७२ ॥
युग्मेषु वाचयेत् स्वामिन्यस्य दक्षिणपार्श्वतः ।
अन्वारभ्य स्थिते पत्न्यां स्थितायां स्वामिसन्निधौ ॥ ७३ ॥
स्वामी चेत्कर्म कुर्वीत [4]वाचयेत्स्वयमेव तु ।
ऋत्विग्वाचयिता[5] कर्म यदि तत्कर्तृकं भवेत् ॥ ७४ ॥
प्रयुज्य प्रणवं पूर्वं वाचयेन् 'मन' आदिना ।
तथैव ते प्रतिब्रूयुर्देवतायां तथोच्चरेत् ॥ ७५ ॥
यद्देवत्यं भवेत्कर्म गृह्णीयान्नाम तस्य यत्[6] ।
प्रधानदेवतास्तत्र [7]वक्तव्यास्ता यथोचितम्[8] ॥ ७६ ॥
प्रजापतेर्वा नामैव गृह्णीयात् सर्वकर्मसु ।

१.M भक्ता°. २.MT तिलक°. ३.M °कादि. ४.T broken between कुर्वीत and येत्.
५.M °वाचत्रिता. ६.M याम्. ७.M वर्तव्या°. ८.M यधोऽपितम्.

अस्मदीया[१] इमं कल्पमनुतिष्ठन्ति[२] सर्वदा ॥ ७७ ॥
तृणपाणय एवाथ[३] कुम्भाद्भिः प्रतिमन्त्रकम् ।
सदारं स्वामिनं मन्त्रैर्मार्जयेयुर्यथोदितैः[४] ॥ ७८ ॥
'हिरण्यवर्णा' इत्यादिरपांस्तोत्रमुदीरितम्[५] ।
[६]'पवमानः सुवर्चादिः'[७] पावमान[८] इहोदितः ॥ ७९ ॥
'आ. भूर्भुवः सुव'रिति मार्जयेयुस्तथान्ततः ।
गृह्यार्थकथनद्वारा[९] प्रयोगोऽथ प्रदर्श्यते ॥ ८० ॥

[गृह्य-स्मार्त-पाकयज्ञादिकर्मप्रयोगः]

पाकयज्ञान् स्मार्तधर्मान्दर्वि[१०]होमादिशब्दितान्[११] ।
कल्पोक्तान् वक्ष्यमाणांश्च [१२]स्मार्तवह्निसमाश्रयान् ॥ ८१ ॥
विस्तरेणाभिधास्यामो यतः संक्षिप्य दर्शिताः ।
पाकयज्ञदर्विहोमभूतिकर्मादयस्ततः ॥ ८२ ॥
वक्तुमारभ्यते तेषामितिकर्तव्यतामिह ।
व्याख्यास्याम इतीहोक्तमन्यथा न समञ्जसम् ॥ ८३ ॥
तर्ह्यत्रैव[१३] समाम्नातं कल्पितानां[१४] भवेन्नहि ।
विशेषविहिता धर्माः सम्भवन्तीह केचन ॥ ८४ ॥
ऐष्टिका उपहोमाद्याः स्युः[१५] स्मार्तेष्वपि कर्मसु ।
एकत्रैव समाम्नाने लाघवं च भवेदिति ॥ ८५ ॥
वक्ष्यमाणैस्तथा सूत्रैरयमर्थोऽवगम्यते ।
सर्वेषां पाकयज्ञत्वे भेदोक्तिः कथमुच्यते ॥ ८६ ॥
दर्विहोमं चतुर्थेऽह्नि जुहुयादिति वक्ष्यति ।
पाकयज्ञदर्विहोमा[१६] भेद एव प्रतीयते[१७] ॥ ८७ ॥
[१८]स्थालीपाकबलात् पाकयज्ञाख्या स्मार्तकर्मणाम् ।

१.M °दीयां. २.M °मन्वतिष्ठन्ति. ३.M एव स्थः. ४.M °मार्जयेद्यथो°. ५.T °त्रमितीरि°. ६.M adds तं before पवमानः. ७.T °वर्च्चाभिः. ८.M पव°. ९.M °क...न°. १०.T दर्वी. ११.M °ताम्. १२.M स्मार्तव हिसमा°, T °वर्त्मसमा°. १३.T त्रैवासमा°. १४.M कल्पिकानां १५.M oms. १६.T होमाः. १७.M प्रवदन्ति ते. १८.M स्थालीपाकान्वलात्°.

एतेषां [१]दर्विहोमाख्या [२]दर्विहोमविधानतः ॥ ८८ ॥
इत्यादिनामव्युत्पत्ते[३]रभेदोऽप्युपपद्यते ॥ ८८क ॥
दध्याज्यहोमनियमे सिद्धे साधारणे विधौ ।
[४]दर्विहोमसमाम्नानं कस्मात्तदभिधीयते ॥ ८९ ॥
पाकयज्ञा भूतिकर्म [४]दर्विहोमाहुतीरणात् ।
प्राप्तभेदनिवृत्त्यै[५] तदभेदप्रतिपत्तये ॥ ९० ॥
यतो ह्यत्रोदिता धर्मा नियताः सर्वकर्मसु ॥ ९०क ॥
यावद्वचनमित्युक्तं शुक्रियादिषु कर्मसु ।
समानमेव सर्वेषामेतावदिति भाषितम् ॥ ९१ ॥
विरुध्यतेऽन्यथा तस्मात्तयोर्भेदो न युज्यते ।
इतिकर्तव्यता क्लृप्तौ[६] विवाहादौ समीरिता ॥ ९२ ॥
प्रदर्शनार्थमन्येषां परिसंख्यार्थमेव वा ।
अतो न दोषः पक्षेऽस्मिन् कश्चिदप्युपलभ्यते ॥ ९३ ॥
अथवा दर्विहोमोऽयमपूर्वोऽत्र विधीयते ।
आघारवदपूर्वार्थौ विधी[७] बोधायनोदितौ ॥ ९४ ॥
आघारवान्पाकयज्ञो[८] दर्विहोमस्त्वपूर्वकः ।
क्लृप्तौ च पाकयज्ञस्य दर्विहोमस्य भेदतः ॥ ९५ ॥
वचनादर्थनानात्वं तयोरध्यवसीयते ।
गृह्येऽपि पाकयज्ञाख्यकर्मव्याख्यानमादितः ॥ ९६ ॥
प्रतिज्ञायाभिधायैतत् स्वरूपमविशेषतः ।
औपासनाग्निसाध्यत्वं गृहिणो वक्तुमस्य तु ॥ ९७ ॥
तदुद्भवं[९] कर्म चात्र विधाय तदनन्तरम् ।
काल्पिकानामपूर्वाणां वक्तुमौपासनान्वयम् ॥ ९८ ॥
उक्तधर्मान्वये नित्ये चतुर्थदिवसाहुतेः ।

१.T दर्वी°. २.MT दाहोम°. ३.M व्युत्वत्तै°. ४-४.T दर्वी°. ५.M निवृत्याथ, T निवृत्या. ६.MT क्लृप्तो. ७.M विधि. ८.M °यज्ञ T °यज्ञः. ९.M तदुभयं.

दर्विहोमं चतुर्थेऽह्नि जुहुयादिति चोदितम् ॥ ९९ ॥
अन्यथा दर्विहोमाभिधानं ह्यत्र निरर्थकम् ।
[1]कल्पपाठोऽपि च[1] स्मार्तकर्मणामुपपद्यते ॥ १०० ॥
पुनः [2]श्रुतिर्विवाहादौ धर्माणामनियुज्यते ।
गृह्योक्तानामपूर्वत्वं काल्पिकानां च युज्यते ॥ १०१ ॥
गृह्योक्तधर्मसंबंधः[3] काल्पिकानां पुरोदितः ।
अतो विकल्पः सर्वेषु तयोः स्मार्तेषु कर्मसु ॥ १०२ ॥
नन्वस्माकं दर्विहोमविधानं नोपलभ्यते ।
सामर्थ्यादागमाच्चेह तद्विधानं प्रकल्पितम्[4] ॥ १०३ ॥
सामर्थ्यमागमश्चेति मानमस्माभिरिष्यते ।
होमापूर्वस्य साध्यत्वं जुहुयादिति गम्यते[5] ॥ १०४ ॥
अतश्च संस्कृतो [6]वह्निरवेक्ष्य श्रौतवह्निवद्[7] ।
तदाधारस्थलस्यापि संस्कारस्तत इष्यते ॥ १०५ ॥
दर्विहोमसमाख्यानाद् दर्व्या होमोऽवगम्यते ।
अविशेषश्रुतौ [8]दर्व्यमाज्यं योग्यं च तत्ततः ॥ १०६ ॥
दर्व्याऽऽज्यवह्निसंस्कारः सामर्थ्यादेव सिध्यति ।
स्नानादिकर्तृसंस्कारः सामान्ये दैवचोदितः ॥ १०७ ॥
एवं सामर्थ्यतः[9] प्राप्ताविति कर्तव्यताऽन्यतः ।
समानविधितो ग्राह्या पाकयज्ञात् पुरोदितात् ॥ १०८ ॥
इत्यागमस्ततः पूर्वमुपख्यानादुदीरितः[10] ।
[11]ब्रह्म प्रणीतारहितं कार्यमापरिधानतः ॥ १०९ ॥
अलङ्कृतिर्गन्धपुष्पैराचारादेव सिध्यति ।
मन्त्रवत्परिषेकोऽपि काल्पिकः कार्य आगमात् ॥ ११० ॥
आधाय समिधं हुत्वा चक्षुषी चार्थवादतः ।

१-१.M कुपाठो°, T क-पाठोऽपि च. २.M श्रुतिवि°. ३.M °धर्म सकाल्पि° सकाल्पि°. ४.T प्रकल्प्यताम्. ५.M नम्यते. ६.T वह्नी°. ७.M °वह्निवम्, °वह्निवा. ८.M °माज्ययोग्यं, T °द्रव्यमाज्यं. ९.T सामान्यतः. १०.M व्यानादुदी°, T व्यानाद्युदीरितम्. ११.T ब्रह्मं.

हुत्वा यथोदितैर्मन्त्रैर्मन्त्रवत्परिषेचनम् ॥ १११ ॥
कुर्यादापूर्विकमिदं विधानमिह कल्पितम् ।
यथासामर्थ्यमन्येषु कर्मस्वेवं प्रकल्प्यताम् ॥ ११२ ॥
चरुवत्सु चरुं चापि श्रपयेत् पाकयज्ञवत् ।
विशेषविहितो धर्मः काल्पिको येषु विद्यते ॥ ११३ ॥
तावानसावनुष्ठेयो [1][यावान्तत्र] यथोदितः[2] ।
अमितं [3]चेध्ममाधाय स्वाहाकारेण चक्षुषी ॥ ११४ ॥
हुत्वा चरौ स्रुचा हुत्वा दर्व्या [4]तस्य विधौ[4] सति ।
हव्यवाहं स्विष्टकृतं ततः[5] .... ॥ ११५ ॥
आम्नाते तेन मन्त्रेण मन्त्रवत्परिषेचनम् ।
कृत्वा होमविधिं कृत्स्नं यथोदितमथाचरेत् ॥ ११६ ॥
अपूर्वविधिरेवैकः पैतृकेषु प्रवर्तते ।
प्रवृत्तिरुभयोर्दैवकर्मस्वेवेति च स्थितिः ॥ ११७ ॥

[स्मार्तकर्मकालनियमः]

गृह्योक्तधर्मसंबंधः सर्वेषां सर्वथा भवेत् ।
उक्तमर्थं दृढीकुर्वन्नाह कालमनन्तरम् ॥ ११८ ॥
[6]यद्व्याख्यार्थोऽयमारम्भस्तेषां कालाः[7] पुरोदिताः[8] ।
यत्किञ्चित्पुण्यमित्यादौ किमर्थमिदमुच्यते ॥ ११९ ॥
कल्पोदितत्वात्[9] कालानां गृह्योक्तानां तु कर्मणाम् ।
मा भूत् कालान्तरमिति[10] सूत्रमर्थवदेव तत् ॥ १२० ॥
पाकयज्ञादिकं चापि क्लृप्तावारभ्य चोदितम् ।
उदीक्ष्य तानि नक्षत्रं कुर्वीतेत्यविशेषतः ॥ १२१ ॥
अयनस्य मुहूर्तस्य करणस्य तिथेरपि ।
प्रदर्शनार्थं नक्षत्रग्रहणं काल्पिकं मतम् ॥ १२२ ॥

१.MT broken. २.T °दितम्. ३.T चेत्समाधाय. ४-४.T तस्याविष्यौ. ५.MT broken after ततः. ६.M यदर्थो°. ७.M कालां. ८.M °दिताम्. ९.M °दितत्वां. १०.M °न्तरमिदं.

ज्योतिःशास्त्रोदिते गृह्यश्रुतिस्मृत्यादिचोदिते ।
काले कर्म सदा कार्यमकाले निष्फलं हि[1] तत् ॥ १२३ ॥
तत्कालवचनं पूर्वमत एवेह युज्यते ॥१२३क॥
येषु कालविशेषो[2] वा नोक्तः[2] कर्मसु तेषु तु[3] ।
सामान्येनोदिताः[4] काला ग्राह्या इति विधीयते ॥ १२४ ॥
व्यवस्थयोदिताः काला दैविके पैतृके गणे ।
पूर्वाह्णः पूर्वपक्षोऽहर्दैविकेषूत्तरायणम् ॥ १२५ ॥
अपराह्णः कृष्णपक्षो रजनी दक्षिणायनम् ।
पैतृकेषु वसन्ताद्यं तत्रोदगयनं भवेत् ॥ १२६ ॥
तन्नेष्टं [5]मकराद्यं तन्मिथुनान्तमिहेष्यते ।
[6]कुलीराद्यवशिष्टं यद्दक्षिणायनमुच्यते ॥ १२७ ॥
आम्नायेऽपि च पुण्यर्क्षं ज्ञात्वा कुर्यादिति श्रुतम् ।
शास्त्रान्तरानुसारेण पुण्यर्क्षं तत्र गम्यते ॥ १२८ ॥
कन्यादानादिकर्माणि विहितान्यत्र[7] केषुचित् ।
निषिध्यन्ते[8] चतुष्टेऽह्नि विशेषेण पुनः श्रुतौ ॥ १२९ ॥
कृत्तिकादिविशाखान्तेष्वृक्षेषु विहितं च यत् ।
व्यस्ताश्चैते समस्ताश्च ग्राह्याः कर्मानुसारतः ॥ १३० ॥
अनित्यत्वादृतोः स्त्रीणां गर्भाधानादिकर्मसु ।
ग्राह्याः काला यथायोगं वेदार्थादिव्रतेष्वपि[9] ॥ १३१ ॥
दक्षिणायन एतद्धि वेदाध्ययनमिष्यते ।
अतस्तेषूदगयनं[10] न प्राप्तमिति गम्यते ॥ १३२ ॥
उत्तरायण एव स्याद्[11] गोदानं शुक्रियं व्रतम् ।
संभवे पूर्वपक्षस्य न कार्यं कृष्णपक्षके ॥ १३३ ॥

१.M दितम्. २-२.M °शोऽपनोक्तं. ३.M oms. ४.M °दितात्. ५.M कर्मकरा°. ६.M कुन्तळी°, T कुळीरा°. ७.M विहिन्य°. ८.MT °षिध्यते [T त्ये]. ९.M वेदार्थत्वाव्रतेष्वपि, T वेदार्थत्वादितेष्वपि. १०.M °गनं. ११.M स्यात्.

पूर्वाह्णसंभवे नापराह्णे दैविकमिष्यते ॥ १३३क ॥
यस्य यत्र निषेधो वा विधिर्वा नोपलभ्यते ।
तत्र काला[1] इमे ग्राह्या यथायोगमिति स्थितिः ॥ १३४ ॥

[कर्माङ्गभूतमन्त्राणामुपांशुत्वविधानम्]

उक्त्वा साधारणं कालं स्मार्तानां सर्वकर्मणाम् ।
कर्माङ्गभूतमन्त्राणामुपांशुत्वमथोच्यते ॥ १३५ ॥
उपांशु यजुषेत्यस्य स्मार्तान्वयविधित्सया ।
तेषामुपांशुतन्त्रं[2] स्यादशब्दं[3] करणान्वितम्[4] ॥ १३६ ॥
अमानसं भवेन्मन्त्रवचनं गृह्यकर्मसु ।
उच्चैष्ट्वमेव प्रैषाणां परबोधार्थिनामिह ॥ १३७ ॥
स्रुक्संमार्गादिधर्माणां दृष्टानां श्रौतकर्मसु ।
प्रोक्षण्याज्यादिसंस्कारधर्माः श्रुत्युदिता इह ॥ १३८ ॥
आकाङ्क्षता मन्त्रवर्जं कार्या इत्यधुनोच्यते ।
अत एव स्रुगिध्मादिमनाकृत्याद्यवेक्षितम् ॥ १३९ ॥
श्रुतिकल्पादिनिर्दिष्टं ग्राह्यमित्यवगम्यते ॥ १३९क ॥
उपलक्ष्येत यज्ञेषु यज्ञमित्यादिशासनात् ।
यज्ञाङ्गेषु च यज्ञाङ्गं सृजेदित्यविशेषतः ॥ १४० ॥
आकाङ्क्षापूरणं युक्तं परार्थैरपि दर्शनैः ।
समानतन्त्रवचनैः परतन्त्रेरितैरपि ॥ १४१ ॥
अतिदिश्य श्रौतधर्मान् स्मार्तकर्मस्वपेक्षितान् ।
व्याख्यास्यमानधर्माणां संप्राप्तौ शुक्रियादिषु ॥ १४२ ॥
यावद्वचनमित्येषु तन्निवृत्त्यर्थमुच्यते ।
निषिध्यन्ते न सामान्यधर्मा आचमनादयः ॥ १४३ ॥
होमसामान्यधर्माश्च शास्त्रन्यायानुसारिणः[5] ।

१.M काल. २.MT तन्त्र. ३.M om between स्य and शब्दं; thus in T. ४.T करणं न्वितम्. ५.T °सारतः.

औपासनाहुतिः सायं प्रातर्होमोऽभिधीयते ॥ १४४ ॥
व्याख्यास्यमानधर्मेषु सीमन्तादिष्वनन्तरम् ।
गृह्यकर्मसु शम्यानां[1] परिधित्वं विधीयते ॥ १४५ ॥
श्रौतकर्माङ्गशम्यावच्छम्याकारत्वमिष्यते ।
शम्याकारानतः[2] कुर्यात् परिधीन् पूर्वचोदितान् ॥ १४६ ॥
यद्व्याख्यार्थोऽयमारम्भो येषां कालाः[3] पुरोदिताः ।
येषामुपांशुतन्त्रं स्याद्येषु श्रौतक्रियेष्यते ॥ १४७ ॥
यद्विशेषेषु विहिता विशेषः शुक्रियादिषु ।
तान् पाकयज्ञानारब्धुकामः[4] पूर्वोक्तलक्षणः ॥ १४८ ॥
यज्ञोपवीतं कुर्वीत श्रुतिस्मृत्युक्तवर्त्मना ।
आरम्भार्थः प्रयोगः स्यादुपव्यानादिरेव सः ॥ १४९ ॥
आरम्भवचनं पूर्वं कर्तृवैचित्र्यसिद्धये ।
स्वयंकर्तृत्वमेवेह केषुचिद् गम्यते स्फुटम् ॥ १५० ॥
विवाहादिषु मन्त्राणां प्रत्यगाशीःष्विलिङ्गतः ।
द्वितीयजन्मपर्यन्तं संस्कारा अन्यकर्तृकाः ॥ १५१ ॥
प्रतिषेधादसामर्थ्याल्लिङ्गतश्च तथाऽपरे ।
उपाकर्मादयः शिष्येष्वन्वारब्धेष्वितीरणात्[5] ॥ १५२ ॥
अग्न्याधेयं पाकयज्ञानग्निष्टोमादिकान् मखान् ।
यः[6] करोति वृतो[7] यस्य स तस्यर्त्विगिहोच्यते[8] ॥ १५३ ॥
इत्यस्मात् पाकयज्ञेषु कर्तृत्वमिति गम्यते ।
करिष्यन् स्वयमार्त्विज्यमित्याद्यपि च कल्पितम् ॥ १५४ ॥
अतो विकल्प एवेह पाकयज्ञेषु गम्यते ।
पैतृकेषु ततेत्यादिलिङ्गादाचारतोऽपि च ॥ १५५ ॥
स्वयंकर्तृकमेव स्याद्विकल्पोऽन्यत्र संमतः ।

१.M शल्यानां. २.M शम्याकरा°. ३.M कालां. ४.M °यज्ञानामारब्धु°. ५.M °रब्धेष्वती°.
७.MT यं. ७.M पृतो, T व्रतो. ८.M °र्त्विनिहो.

[यज्ञोपवीतधारणनियमाः]

यज्ञोपवीतं कृत्वेति वचनं सर्वकर्मसु ॥ १५६ ॥
दैविकेषूपवीतित्वनियमार्थमिहेष्यते ।
अधोवीतित्वमेवास्य प्राप्तं लौकिककर्मसु ॥ १५७ ॥
अतो यज्ञोपवीत्येव कुर्याद् दैवमितीर्यते ।
चत्वारः सूत्रविन्यासा उक्ता बौधायनीयके[1] ॥ १५८ ॥
उपवीतमधोवीतं निवीतं पैतृकं च यत् ।
प्राचीनावीतमित्येषां लक्षणं चापि दर्शितम्[2] ॥ १५९ ॥
सव्यांसमूलहृदयग्रीवापृष्ठाश्रयं स्थितम् ।
दक्षिणस्य करस्याधो नाभ्यावस्थ्युपवीतकम्[3] ॥ १६० ॥
अधोवीतमधोनाभेर्देहस्य पतितोद्धृतम् ।
[4]उपरिष्टादथांसाभ्यां ग्रीवां हृदयमेव च ॥ १६१ ॥
परिगृह्य हृदोऽधस्तादूर्ध्वं नाभेः स्थितं तु यत् ।
निवीतमृषितृप्तौ[5] तत्कराङ्गुष्ठद्वयान्वितम् ॥ १६२ ॥
दक्षिणस्य करस्योर्ध्वं ग्रीवां हृदयपृष्ठकम् ।
सव्यपाणेरधश्चैव परिगृह्य स्थितं तु यत् ॥ १६३ ॥
प्राचीनावीतमित्युक्तं व्यवस्थाऽत्रापि दर्शिता ।
देवानामुपवीतं स्यान्मनुष्याणां निवीतकम् ॥ १६४ ॥
मानुषाणि च कार्याणि द्विविधानि[6] मतानि तु ।
ऋषीणां तर्पणं पुत्रसंस्कारा ऋतुसंगतिः ॥ १६५ ॥
[7]मूत्राद्युत्सर्जनं प्रेतवहनादीनि यानि च ।
मनुष्यकार्यमित्येतदामुष्मिकमितीरितम् ॥ १६६ ॥
[8]आञ्जनाभ्यञ्जनोन्मर्दा लेपनादीनि यानि तु ।
ऐहिकान्येष्वधोवीतमेतेष्वेवोपपद्यते ॥ १६७ ॥

१.T बोधा°. २.M दर्शतम्. ३.M नाभ्यावस्युप°, T नाम्यावस्युप°. ४.M उपादिष्टा°, उपरिष्ठा°. ५.M °तृप्तेन. ६.M द्विधानि. ७.M पुत्राद्यु°. ८.T अञ्ज°.

विहितत्वान्नियोगेन[१] विनियोगस्य कुत्रचित् ।
प्राप्त आमुष्मिके चान्यविधानादिह तद् भवेत् ॥ १६८ ॥
लौकिके कर्मणि प्राप्तमधोवीतमितीह[२] तु[३] ।
उपवीतित्वनियमः सूत्रेणानेन वक्ष्यते[४] ॥ १६९ ॥
सदोपवीतिना भाव्यं सदा बद्धशिखेन च ।
इत्यादिवचनान्नित्यमुपवीतित्वमिष्यते ॥१७० ॥
यज्ञोपवीतमित्यत्र यज्ञाङ्गं तत्प्रतीयते ।
अतो नियोगतश्चान्यत् कर्माङ्गत्वेन चोद्यते ॥ १७१ ॥
इति चेन्नैतदेवं स्याद्देवकार्यार्थमेव हि ।
सदोपवीतिना भाव्यमित्यादिवचनं यतः ॥ १७२ ॥
विशिखोऽप्युपवीतश्च यत्करोति न तत्कृतम् ।
इत्यादिवाक्यशेषेण कर्माङ्गत्वं प्रतीयते ॥ १७३ ॥
निवीतादेर्विधानस्य वैयर्थ्यं चान्यथा भवेत् ।
यज्ञशेषत्वमस्येति समाख्याप्यत्र[५] युज्यते ॥ १७४ ॥
नित्ययज्ञोपवीतीति नित्यं सूत्रस्य धारणम् ।
उपवीतस्य [६]कार्पासनिर्मितत्वं यतः स्मृतम् ॥ १७५ ॥
मन्त्रपूतं स्थितं कार्ये यस्य यज्ञोपवीतिकम्[७] ।
नोत्तारयेत्ततः प्राज्ञो यदीच्छेच्छ्रेय आत्मनः ॥ १७६ ॥
यदि सर्वत्र कर्माङ्गमुपवीतस्य धारणम् ।
ब्रह्मचारिण एकं तु स्नानप्रभृति तु[८] द्वयम् ॥ १७७ ॥
एकमेव यतीनां स्यादिति शास्त्रस्य निश्चयः ।
इत्यादिवचनात्तत्र नियमो युज्यते कथम् ॥ १७८ ॥
अतो यज्ञोपवीतत्वनियमार्थमिदं कृतम् ।
अजिनं वास इत्यादि यज्ञार्थं यच्छ्रुतौ श्रुतम् ॥ १७९ ॥

१.M °नियोगस्य. २.M प्राप्त मेधावीत°. ३.M ते. ४.M वत्स्यते. ५.M समख्या°. ६.M कार्पासं. ७.M °वीतितम्. ८.M om.

यज्ञोपवीतं कृत्वेति तदर्थं वा वचो भवेत् ।
वाससश्च तथाभावे सूत्रं शास्त्रान्तरे स्मृतम् ॥ १८० ॥
तच्चोपवीतं कार्पाससूत्रनिर्मितमिष्यते[1] ।
कार्पासमुपवीतं स्याद्विप्रस्येति मनूक्तितः ॥ १८१ ॥
कौशं सौत्रं त्रिस्त्रिवृत् स्यादित्यादि स्मरणाच्च तत् ।
त्रिवारं त्रिगुणी कार्यमेकग्रन्थिसमन्वितम् ॥ १८२ ॥
स्मृत्यन्तरसमाम्नानान्नवसूत्रकृतं च तत् ।
पृष्ठदेशे[2] च नाभ्यां[2] च धृतं यद्विन्दते कटिम् ॥ १८३ ॥
तद्धार्यमुपवीतं स्यान्नातिलम्बं न चोच्छ्रितम् ।
स्तनादूर्ध्वमधो नाभेर्न कर्तव्यं कथञ्चन ॥ १८४ ॥
दक्षिणं बाहुमित्यादि श्रुतौ यल्लक्षणं श्रुतम् ।
उत्थिते[3] दक्षिणे पाणावित्यादिवचनं च यत् ॥ १८५ ॥
न्यासस्वरूपज्ञप्त्यर्थमुक्तमेतदितीरितम् ।
कार्पासाभाव एव स्यात् कुशरज्ज्वादिनिर्मितम्[4] ॥ १८६ ॥
सूत्रं सरोमकं चेत्स्यात्ततः[5] कृत्वा विलोमकम्[6] ।
सावित्र्या दशकृत्वोऽद्भिर्मन्त्रिताभिस्तदुक्षयेत्[7] ॥ १८७ ॥
विच्छिन्नं[8] वाप्यधो यातं भुक्त्वा निर्मितमुत्सृजेत् ।
मुहूर्तमप्यप्रयतं स्यान्न शक्ताविति स्मृतेः ॥ १८८ ॥

[आचमननियमाः]

आचम्येत्यत्र वचनं कर्माङ्गत्वविवक्षया ।
समाख्यानाच्च तत्कार्यं विहिताङ्गसमन्वितम् ॥ १८९ ॥
यत्स्मृतौ विहितं सद्भिर्यदत्राब्ग्रहणं कृतम् ।
तद्गुणग्रहणार्थं तदक्षारा[9] अश्नता अतः ॥ १९० ॥
दुष्टगन्धादिरहिताः फेनबुद्बुदवर्जिताः ।

१.M °तदिष्यते. २-२.M °देशेऽपराभ्यां. ३.T उद्धृते. ४.MT °रज्चादि°. ५.M चैतस्या°. ६.M विलोमतः. ७.M °क्षये. ८.M अवि°. ९.M °क्षरा.

आप आचमने ग्राह्यास्तत्प्रकारोऽधुनोच्यते ॥ १९१ ॥
उदङ्मुखः प्राङ्मुखो वा प्रागुदङ्मुख एव वा ।
शुचौ देशे समासीनो मृद्भिरद्भिः समाहितः ॥ १९२ ॥
प्रक्षाल्य पादौ पाणी च मणिबन्धात्तथा मुखम् ।
प्रक्षाल्य जानुमध्यस्थौ करौ कृत्वाऽथ दक्षिणम् ॥ १९३ ॥
गोकर्णाकृतिवत्कृत्वा माषसंमज्जनोचिताः ।
अप उद्धृत्य तीर्थेन ब्राह्मेण हृदयङ्गमाः ॥ १९४ ॥
वीक्षितास्त्रिः पिबेत् पूर्वमृग्यजुःसामतृप्तये ।
अङ्गुष्ठदेशिनी[1]सन्धिः पित्र्यं तीर्थमिति स्मृतम् ॥ १९५ ॥
दैवमङ्गुलिमूलं स्यात्तासामग्रं तथार्षकम् ।
अङ्गुष्ठमूलं ब्राह्मं स्यादनेनैव सलोमकौ ॥ १९६ ॥
ओष्ठावथर्वतृप्त्यर्थमितिहासादितृप्तये ।
परिमृज्याद्[2] द्विरङ्गुष्ठानामिकाभ्यां च चक्षुषी ॥ १९७ ॥
चन्द्रभास्करतृप्त्यर्थं क्रमात् स्पृष्ट्वा जलान्वितः।
अङ्गुष्ठेन प्रदेशिन्या नासिके प्राणतृप्तये ॥ १९८ ॥
अपां[3] तृप्तये स्पृष्ट्वा कर्णौ[4] दिक्तृप्तये पृथक् ।
कनिष्ठया च साङ्गुष्ठया स्पृशेदात्मतृप्तये ॥ १९९ ॥
तलेन हृदयं स्पृष्ट्वा श्रियं ध्यात्वाऽथ मूर्धनि ।
साङ्गुष्ठा अङ्गुलीः सर्वा युक्ता न्यस्येदिदं सकृत् ॥ २०० ॥
कृत्वात आद्यैरब्लिङ्गमन्त्रैः पीत्वा क्रमादपः ।
त्रिः [5]प्रमृज्याद् व्याहृतिभिस्तूष्णीं खानि च संस्पृशेत्॥ २०१ ॥
शिष्टाचारस्थितेरेवं कुर्याद्धोमादिकर्मसु ।
मन्त्राचमनमेतद्वाऽत्राचम्येति विधीयते ॥ २०२ ॥
एतद्धि मन्त्रवत्कार्यमिति बोधायनोदितम् ।

१.T °भेदिनी. २.M °मृज्य द्विर°. ३.T a gap after अपा. ४.M कण्ठेन. ५.MT प्रमृज्य द्वयाहृ°.

[स्थण्डिलकर्म]

अथ प्रविश्य भवनं मार्जनालेपनोचितम् ॥ २०३ ॥
तस्य पूर्वोत्तरे भागे प्रागाद्यवनते शुचौ ।
केशकीटादिरहिते गोमयान्वितवारिणा ॥ २०४ ॥
गोचर्ममात्रमालिप्य तस्य [१]पश्चाच्छुभासने ।
जान्वाच्य दक्षिणं मौनी प्राङ्मुखः सन् पवित्रवान् ॥ २०५ ॥
आसीनः[२] स्थण्डिलं मध्ये [३]प्रागाद्यास्वष्टदिक्षु च ॥२०५क॥
अरत्निमात्रान्तरालं याज्ञीयशकलेन तु ।
उद्धृत्य शकलं प्रोक्ष्य [४]नैर्ऋत्यां दिशि सन्त्यजेत् ॥ २०६ ॥
खनने प्रासने च्छेदे भेदने स्पर्शनेऽपि च ।
नाभेरधः खसंस्पर्शे [५]पितृरौद्रादिकर्मणि ॥ २०७ ॥
कृते चाप उपस्पृश्य कार्यमन्यदितीरितम् ।
संप्रोक्ष्य स्थण्डिलं वह्निं याज्ञिकेन्धनवर्धितम्[६] ॥ २०८ ॥
धूमालातविनिर्मुक्तं[७] विप्रं गावं[८] यथाहृतम्[८] ।
मध्य आलिप्तदेशस्य प्रक्षिपेद्यदनग्निकम्[९] ॥ २०९ ॥
[१०]औपासनाग्निसद्भावे तदाविष्करणं तु यत् ।
[११]तदेवोपसमाधायेत्यनेनात्राभिधीयते ॥ २१० ॥

[औपासनाग्निः]

[१२]अपरौपासनाख्योऽग्निर्भार्यासंस्कारकृत्त्रयः[१३] ।
कर्म स्मार्तं विवाहाग्नौ[१४] कुर्वीतेति यतः स्मृतम् ॥ २११ ॥
नन्वग्निहोत्रवच्छ्रौते स्मार्तं वैवाहिकेऽनले ।
नियम्यते ततोऽनग्नेः कथं स्मार्तक्रियोच्यते ॥ २१२ ॥

१.M वच्छाशुभा°. २.M आसीन. ३.M प्रागाद्यास्स्वष्ट°. ४.MT मेनमृत्या. ५.T प्रतृरौद्रालि°. ६.T याज्ञिशेन्धनवद्धितम्. ७.T °विनिमुक्तं. ८-८.MT गावसथाहृ°. ९.M °क्षिपेद्यद्यनग्नि°. १०.T आपास°. ११.M °धायान्येना°. १२.M अपानोपास°, T अपारौपास°. १३.M °ससा°, T °र्भर्यासंस्कारतुत्तयः. १४.T विपानेन.

यत्तु वैवाहिके वह्नौ स्मार्तकर्म नियम्यते ।
तदेतत्तद्व्रतो युक्तं गृहिणः स्वार्थकर्मसु ॥ २ १ ३ ॥
जातस्य नामकरणं निष्क्रमादेरसंभवात् ।
[1]पित्रोरौपासनेनैव कर्म जातस्य चोचितम्[2] ॥ २ १ ४ ॥
पुत्रोत्पत्तिर्हि विहितं[3] पुत्रमुत्पादयेदिति ।
उत्पन्नसंस्कृतं नामकरणाद्यास्तथा[4] स्मृतिः ॥ २ १ ५ ॥
ज्येष्ठेन[5] जातमात्रेण पुत्री भवति मानवः ।
ऋणं च सन्नयत्यस्मिन्नमृतत्वं च गच्छति ॥ २ १ ६ ॥
पिता पुत्रस्य जातस्य पश्येच्चेज्जीवतो मुखम् ।
परार्थकर्मकरणं पराह्णे[6] न हि युज्यते ॥ २ १ ७ ॥
अनुशिष्टस्य पुत्रस्य लोकहेतुतया श्रुतेः ।
पितृभ्यामेव कर्तव्यं जातकर्मादि यत्स्मृतम् ॥ २ १ ८ ॥
ऋत्विग्भिः कारयित्वापि न दोष इह विद्यते ॥ २१८क ॥
प्राग्विवाहादतो[7] वह्नौ लौकिके संस्कृतिर्भवेत् ।
ब्रह्मौदने [8]समस्ताग्निविनियोगसमीरणात् ॥ २१९ ॥
आहिताग्नेरष्टकादेर्नित्यत्वाल्लौकिकेऽनले[9] ।
[10]तत्क्रियार्थात्तन्निषेधः सामर्थ्यात्तद्व्रतो भवेत् ॥ २२० ॥
सत्यौपासन एवातो नियमः स्मृतिदर्शितः ।
अग्न्यन्तरे यथाश्रौतं तस्यान्यत्र कृतं वृथा ॥ २२१ ॥
औपासने यदा कुर्यात्तदायतनसंस्कृतिः ।
न कार्याकार्यशून्यत्वात् पूर्वमेतद्धि संस्कृतम् ॥ २२२ ॥
काष्ठैरप्रतिषिद्धैस्तं[11] शोभयेज्ज्वलयेत्तरम्[12] ॥ २२२क ॥
अप्रोक्षितानि काष्ठानि क्लिन्नानि विहितान्यपि ।
आम्रनिम्बकरञ्जादिवेणुकान् ताँश्च वर्जयेत् ॥ २२३ ॥

१.M पित्रौरौपा°. २.T a gap between जातस्य and चितम्. ३.T a gap between वि and पुत्र [T प्रजा] मुत्या°. ४.M °करणाद्यथा°, T °करणाद्या तथा. ५.M जेष्ठेन. ६.T परानो. ७.M °वादतो. ८.M °स्तानि. ९.M °देस्त्वित्यवा लौकिके तत्. १०.M oms तत्. ११.M °षिद्धस्तं. १२.M °तरः.

[परिस्तरणविधिः]

एवमग्निं शोभयित्वा[१] सकृत्परिसमूहनम् ।
तथा पर्युक्षणं कृत्वा परिस्तरणमारभेत् ॥ २२४ ॥
साग्रैर्दर्भादिभिः पूर्वमुक्तैरग्न्याद्यदूषितैः[२] ।
उदगग्रैः पूर्वपक्षं प्रथमं स्तृणुयादथ[३] ॥ २२५ ॥
[४]प्रागग्रैर्दक्षिणं [५]पक्षमुत्तराग्रैस्तदापदम् ।
प्राक्कूलैरुत्तरं पूर्वपश्चिमोपरि दक्षिणम् ॥ २२६ ॥
पूर्वापरस्तरणयोरध उत्तरसंस्तृतिः[६] ।
उत्तरोत्तरवर्षिष्ठदर्भानादाय[७] संस्तरेत्[८] ॥ २२७ ॥
परिषिच्य सकृद् वह्नेर्देशे दक्षिणतो बहून् ।
संस्तीर्य दर्भान्प्रागग्रानग्नेरुत्तरतोऽपि च ॥ २२८ ॥

[पात्रासादनम्]

आस्तीर्य तेषु पात्राणि न्युब्ज्य[९] द्वन्द्वानि सादयेत् ।
प्रोक्षणीपात्रदर्व्यौ च जुहूं [१०]सादयेन्मेक्षणम् ॥ २२९ ॥
प्रणीताऽऽज्यार्थपात्रे द्वे [११]चरोरिध्मतृणानि च ॥ २२९क ॥
तन्त्रोऽपरो[१२] चरुस्थालीमपिधानीं जुहूं विना ।
सादयेदत्र सर्वा ते मेक्षणं सतृणं क्षिपेत् ॥ २३० ॥
चरोश्चेति[१३] च शब्देन पात्रस्य च समुच्चयात् ।
पाकार्थस्यात्र पात्रस्य विधानार्थस्य संग्रहः ॥ २३१ ॥
द्वादशद्वयसंख्यातः परिधित्रयमेव[१४] वा[१४] ।
जुहू[१५] प्रग्रहितः साद्य इध्मो मुष्टिसमन्वितः ॥ २३२ ॥
एकविंशतिमित्येवमाधाने वक्ष्यतेऽत्र हि ।
ऊर्ध्वेव[१६] समिधौ नित्ये [१७]अनूयाजार्थयान्विते ॥ २३३ ॥

१.T शोधयि°. २.M °मूषिकैः. ३.M तृणयादथ, T तृणुयादथ. ४.M प्रागग्रद°. ५.M पक्षं अन्तराग्रै°. ६.M संस्मृतिः. ७.M वर्षिष्ठंदर्भा°. ८.M संस्करेत्. ९.T न्युब्ज. १०.MT सादय. ११.T चरोश्च...तृणानि. १२.M तन्त्रौ चरौ. १३.M चरोश्चेदति. १४-१४.T broken after मे. १५.M broken before प्रग्र°. १६.M ऊर्ध्वेऽप. १७.T आनु°.

सप्तविंशतिसंख्यात [१]इध्मोऽतः साद्यमत्र तु[१] ।
पवित्रकर्मणादीनि सादिताद् दर्भमुष्टितः[२] ॥ २३४ ॥

[ब्रह्मकर्म]

[३]ऋत्विग्लक्षणसंपन्नो ब्रह्मा बद्धशिखः शुचिः ।
आचम्य मन्त्रतो द्वारा पूर्वयाऽन्तः[४] प्रविश्य तु ॥ २३५ ॥
[५]अग्नेर्दक्षिणतस्तीर्णतृणानामेकमाहरेत् ।
अङ्गुष्ठानामिकाभ्यां [६]तन्नैर्ऋत्यां दिशि संत्यजेत् ॥ २३६ ॥
सपवित्र उपस्पृश्य तृणेषूपविशेत्ततः ।
कृताकृतसमीक्षार्थं कृत्वोपस्थ उदङ्मुखः ॥ २३७ ॥
अशीर्णाग्रौ समौ दर्भौ तरुणौ गर्भवर्जितौ ।
आदायाग्रे गृहीत्वैतौ[७] प्रसलैः परिवेष्य[८] च ॥ २३८ ॥
दक्षिणेन करेणाधो गमयित्वा प्रदक्षिणम् ।
[९]आवेष्ट्योपयुतोद्गृह्य तृणलोष्ठेन्धनादिकम् ॥ २३९ ॥
अन्तर्धाय पवित्रे ते छित्वा प्रादेशसंमिते ।
उपस्पृश्य निधायोर्व्यां प्रोक्ष्यादाय पवित्रके ॥ २४० ॥
प्रोक्षणीपात्रमुत्तानं कृत्वा त्रीन् प्रोक्ष्य वारिणा ।
पात्रे पवित्रे प्रागग्रे निधायापो निनीय च ॥ २४१ ॥
अनुमृज्य त्रिरुत्पूय तथोदिङ्गनमाचरेत् ।
कल्पोदितमिदं[१०] सर्वं संस्कृत्येत्यमुनोदितम् ॥ २४२ ॥
एतदेव दृढीकर्तुं प्रोक्षिताभिरितीतरम् ।
निष्टप्येत्यादिवचनमपि[११]श्रौतानुवादकम् ॥ २४३ ॥

[अनुमार्जनादिविधिः]

अथानुमार्जनादीनां स्वरूपमभिधीयते ।
करेण[१२] सव्येनादाय पवित्रेऽन्येन तद्द्वयम् ॥ २४४ ॥

१-१.M इध्मातस्याद्यमतत्र तु. २.M °मुष्टिकः. ३.M ऋत्विग्दक्षिण°. ४.M °यान्यः. ५.M त्रीणितृणा°. ६.M तनैत्र्ऋ°. ७.M ग्रही°. ८.M °पेष्य. ९.T आवेष्ट्योवयुथो°. १०.T °मिमं. ११.M वचनं वि. १२.M करण.

प्राक्संस्थमुन्मृजेदेतदनुमार्जनमुच्यते ।
साङ्गुष्ठानामिकाभ्यां यदुत्तानाभ्यां पवित्रके ॥ २४५ ॥
आदाय ताभ्यां प्राक्संस्थमपामुन्मार्जनं तु यत् ।
तदुत्पवनमित्युक्तं सपात्रं तज्जलं करे ॥ २४६ ॥
सव्ये न्यस्त्वा[१] महानाम्न्यामासज्य च पवित्रके ।
दक्षिणेन जलादूर्ध्वं क्षिप्त्वा[२] पात्रे पुनः क्षिपेत् ॥ २४७ ॥
उदिङ्गनमिदं ज्ञेयं त्रयमेतत्सनिष्टपम्[३] ।
अपोऽवनं[४] प्रोक्षणं च संमार्गः परिलेखने ॥ २४८ ॥
समारोपणमग्नेश्च तस्य प्रत्यवरोहणम् ।
परिवेशनं[५] बर्हिषां त्रिः कार्यं दैविके सकृत् ॥ २४९ ॥
पैतृके सर्वमेतत्स्यादिति शेषेषु चोदितम् ।
द्रव्यापनयनं[६] चात्र स्वात्माभिमुखमीरितम् ॥ २५० ॥
संप्रोक्षणप्रणीतार्थां वाऽऽज्यादानयनं ततः ।
स्थितात् पात्रस्य पुरतः स्वात्माभिमुखमाचरेत् ॥ २५१ ॥
कृत्वोदिङ्गनमन्याभिस्त्रिरद्भिः[७] प्रोक्ष्य तज्जलम् ।
[८]उत्तानीकृत्य पात्राणि विस्रस्येध्मं स्पृशेदपः ॥ २५२ ॥

[स्थालीपाकविधिः]

अथ त्रिः प्रोक्ष्य पात्राणि तेन संस्कृतवारिणा ।
चमसे भाजने कांस्ये मृन्मये वा पवित्रके ॥ २५३ ॥
निधायोपबिलं पात्रं पूरयित्वा यथोदितम् ।
मुखसंमितमेवैता नीत्वाग्नेरुत्तरत्र तु ॥ २५४ ॥
ईषत्प्राग्गतदर्भेषु[९] सादयित्वा कुशादिभिः ।
प्रतिच्छाद्य समुद्धृत्य[१०] पवित्रे सचरौ विधौ ॥ २५५ ॥
स्थालीं प्रक्षाल्य वह्नौ तामधिश्रित्य पवित्रवत्[११] ।
पयो जलं वा संसिच्य तस्मिन्नुष्णीकृते सति ॥ २५६ ॥

१.M नस्त्वा. २.M हृत्वा, T च्छित्वा. ३.M °निष्टकम्. ४.M योऽवनं, T योवनं. ५.MT °देशनं. ६.M द्रव्यानयन°. ७.M °रद्भिस्त्रीं. ८.M उत्तानि°. ९.M °गतर्भेषु. १०.M °द्धृत. ११.M पवित्रवित्.

त्रिः फलीकृत्य धवलान् त्रिः प्रक्षालिततण्डुलान् ।
प्रक्षिपेद् दैविके पित्र्ये[1] तद्द्वयं सकृदिष्यते ॥ २५७ ॥
द्विर्मानुषे[2] मेक्षणेन सम्यगालोड्य तञ्चरुम् ।
तं[3] द्विधा[4] श्रपयेद् दैव उपर्यर्धं तु पैतृके ॥ २५८ ॥
अर्धपात्रोऽपि दग्धः स सुशृतः स्याद्यथा चरुः ।
तथा तच्छ्रपणं कार्यं [5]विदाहोत्सेचनादिषु ॥ २५९ ॥
श्रौतं[6] नैमित्तिकं कार्यं दर्विहोमेष्वपीष्यते ।
श्रप्यमाणे तु हविषि कार्यं दर्व्यादिमार्जनम् ॥ २६० ॥
नन्वप्रणयनादूर्ध्वं दर्वीसंमार्जनं श्रुतम् ।
तन्मध्ये श्रपणं कस्मात् चरोरत्राभिधीयते ॥ २६१ ॥
स्थालीपाकस्य कार्यत्वात् स्रुचा तद्धोमदर्शनात् ।
अलौकिकाग्निपक्वस्य[7] होमयोग्यत्वदर्शनात् ॥ २६२ ॥
औपासने चाष्टकादौ[8] श्रपणप्रतिपादनात्[9] ।
अस्मिन्नग्नौ चरुः श्रप्य इति तस्मात्प्रतीयते[10] ॥ २६३ ॥
यज्ञाङ्गाद्यज्ञसृष्ट्युक्ते[11] श्रौते[12] प्रणयनाद्वाऽपः[13] ।
स्रुवसंमार्जनात् पूर्वं[14] हविरुत्पत्तिदर्शनात् ॥ २६४ ॥
अयमेवात्र कालः स्यात् परसूत्रतयोच्यते[15] ।
[16]दर्व्यादिमार्जनं त्वत्र वेदकार्यासमन्वयात् ॥ २६५ ॥
सर्वार्थान् मुष्टितो दर्भैराहृतैः[17] कार्यमिष्यते ।
आदाय दर्वीं[18] निष्टप्य त्रिरग्रैस्तद्बिलं तथा ॥ २६६ ॥
संमृज्याधः[19] सकृन्मूलं मूलेन त्रिर्यथाश्रुति ।
संमृज्य सकृदेवोर्ध्वं निष्टप्य[20] निदधाति ताम् ॥ २६७ ॥
प्रयच्छतीति कल्पोक्तेस्तत्प्रदानं विकल्पते ।

१.M नित्ये. २.MT द्विष्मा°. ३.T om. ४.T विधा. ५.T विदाहो सेच°. ६.M श्रौतान्नै°. ७.T °कानिपक्व°. ८.M चाष्ट चाष्टकादौ. ९.M श्रवण°. १०.MT ता तत्प्रती°. ११.M °द्यज्ञ संसृष्युक्ते. १२.M om. १३.M °द्वापोरम्, T नात् (पापो). १४.M °र्जनां पूर्वां. १५.T तथोन्यते. १६.T दर्व्यादि°. १७.M °हृतेः. १८.T दर्वीं. १९.M °मृज्याथ. २०.T निष्ठप्य.

निधानमेव वाऽत्र स्यान्निराकाङ्क्षतया यदि ॥ २६८ ॥
चरुं स्रुचं च पालाशीमधिकाराद्यथोदितम् ।
पृथङ् निष्टप्य संमृज्य निदध्यादपरौ विधौ ॥ २६९ ॥
अपक्वे पक्वमित्यादि विधिना हूयते यदा ।
निधाय दर्विं[1] संमृज्य तदर्थत्वेन मेक्षणम् ॥ २७० ॥
तथा निष्टप्य[2] संमृज्याद्धोमाभावान्न[3] चान्यथा ।
अद्भिः[4] संस्पृश्य संमार्गतृणान्यग्नौ[5] प्रहृत्य च ॥ २७१ ॥
पवित्रद्वयमुद्धृत्य चरोराज्यार्थभाजने ।
[6]न्यस्त्वा प्रागग्रमाज्यं च विगृह्य चतुरानयेत् ॥ २७२ ॥
आज्यं चतुर्विगृह्णीयान्निर्वपन्निशि शेषतः ।
निरुह्योत्तरतोऽङ्गारानुपस्पृश्याज्यमेष्वथ[7] ॥ २७३ ॥
अधिश्रित्य ततोऽङ्गारमयोदर्व्या[8] समाददत् ।
पर्यग्नि कृत्वा [9]प्रसलाग्रैश्चर्वाज्यादि यद्धविः ॥ २७४ ॥
अङ्गारमविसृज्याज्यमुदगुद्वास्य तानपि ।
सु प्रत्यूह्य ततोऽङ्गारानुपस्पृश्याज्यमाहृतम् ॥ २७५ ॥

[हविरासादनम्]

सादयित्वा परेणाग्निं तृणेष्वेतन्निमील्य[10] तम् ।
अवेक्ष्य पुनराहारं त्रिरुत्पूय पवित्रके ॥ २७६ ॥
विस्रस्यावोक्ष्य[11] वह्नौ संप्रक्षिप्याज्याभिघारितम् ।
चरुमुत्तरतो वह्नेः [12]प्रतिष्ठाप्याभिघार्य च[12] ॥ २७७ ॥
[13]तृणेषु दक्षिणेनाज्यं सादयेत्सुप्रतिष्ठितम् ।
[14]उपस्पृश्य समुक्ष्याथ .... ।
प्रहृत्याग्नौ तथाज्येनाभिघार्य चरुमुत्तरे ॥ २७८ ॥

१.T दर्वी. २.M निष्टव्य. ३.M °ज्याधोमाभाव चाह्न. ४.M अजिस्. ५.M °न्यन्नो. ६.M अन्य°. ७.M °ष्यथ. ८.M °मयोर्दर्व्या. ९.T °सलै ग्रीश्च°. १०.M °ष्वतिनि°. ११.M विस्रस्य वोक्ष्य, T °स्याऽपोक्ष्य. १२-१२.M °भिधारयेत्. १३.M adds स च before तृणेषु. १४. M gives the text as ‘उपस्पृश्य समुक्ष्याथ प्रहृत्याग्नौ तथा ज्येनाभिघार्य चरुमुत्तरे; T gives the text as उपस्पृश्य समुक्ष्य त...........। प्रहृत्याग्नौ तथाज्येनाभिधार्य चरुमुत्तरे।।

अग्नेर्भागं समुद्वास्य[१] पुनरप्यभिघार्य च ।
आज्यस्य दक्षिणे भागे तृणेष्वेव[२] तु सादयेत् ॥ २७९ ॥
स्थालीपाकान् स्रुचा होमैः स्थालीपाको यदीत्यपि ।
उच्यतेऽथापि तस्यात्र पाको नैवोपदिश्यते ॥ २८० ॥
लौकिकस्यैव हविष [३]आदानं तेन गम्यते[३] ।
अस्मिन् पक्षे[४]ऽपरेणाग्निं लोकाग्नौ सुशृतं चरुम्[५] ॥ २८१ ॥
[६]तृणेन सह[६] संसाद्य संप्रोक्ष्य प्रोक्षणीजलैः ।
अस्मिन्नग्नावधिश्रित्य कृत्वा पर्यग्नि साज्यकम् ॥ २८२ ॥
अभिघार्य समुद्वास्य पुनरप्यभिघार्य च ।
पूर्ववत् सादयेच्चान्यत् साद्यमत्रैव सादयेत् ॥ २८३ ॥
आज्यधर्मा नियम्यन्ते श्रौतास्तद्वचनादिह ।
स्वस्वधर्मगणैः सार्धमनुष्ठेया अमी ततः ॥ २८४ ॥
अध्वर्यवेक्षणं श्रौतमवेक्ष्येति नियम्यते ।
अवेक्ष्योत्पूय परिधीन् परिदध्यादितीह हि ॥ २८५ ॥
समानकर्तृकं सर्वमेतदित्यवगम्यते ।
समानकर्तृकं यच्च नित्यं तद्धि नियम्यते ॥ २८६ ॥
स्वयंकृतेः[७] पाक्षिकत्वादनित्यं[८] स्वामिदर्शनम् ।
[९]स्वामिद्वयेक्षणं तस्मान्न स्यात् स्मार्तेषु कर्मसु ॥ २८७ ॥
स्वयंकरणपक्षेऽपि सकृत् स्यादाज्यवीक्षणम्[१०] ।
पुनराहारमित्यत्र कल्पानुक्तं नियम्यते ॥ २८८ ॥
[११]अबुत्पवनवत् कृत्वानुद्धृत्य प्राक् पवित्रके ।
पश्चादेवोद्धरेन्नीत्वा पुनराहारमेव तत् ॥ २८९ ॥

[परिधिपरिधानविधिः]

हविरासाद्य परिधीन् परिदध्यात्तदुच्यते ॥ २८९क ॥

१.M °र्भासमु°, T °र्भा..समु°. २.M तृणेष्वपि. ३-३.M आदावन्तेन गम्येते. ४.T पक्षे परेणा°. ५.M चरु. ६-६.M तृणेनु ह. ७.M कृते. ८.M °कत्वमनित्यं. ९.M adds स्व before स्वामि°. १०.T मीक्षणं. ११.M अम्बूत्पवनवत् कृत्वा, T अबुत्पवनं कृत्वा.

उदगग्रं प्रतिष्ठाप्य मध्यमं लक्षणान्वितम् ।
तस्योपरि निधायान्यं प्रागग्रं[1] दक्षिणार्धकम् ॥ २९० ॥
मध्यमस्य तथाधस्तात् स्पृष्टं प्रागग्रमुत्तरम् ।
निधाय प्राक् स्थितं सूर्यं परिधित्वेन संस्मरेत् ॥ २९१ ॥
दक्षिणार्धं च परिधिमग्रेणानियन्त्रितम् ।
व्यवायाभावतो नेह युक्तं तत्समुदीरितम् ॥ २९२ ॥
सामो हवींषि वाऽऽज्यानि द्रव्याणि स्वामिनौ तथा ।
ऋत्विजः[2] कर्मसंयत्ता [3]एते वाह्या[3] यथाक्रमम् ॥ २९३ ॥
परिध्यादय उच्यन्ते संभारा द्रव्यशब्दतः ।
इष्टौ व्यवायसिद्धिः स्यादपराह्णानुसारतः[4] ॥ २९४ ॥
परिध्येन[5] प्रभृत्येव स्वाम्यन्वारंभ इष्यते ।
ऊर्ध्वाग्रे समिधौ कृत्वा युगपद्दक्षिणोत्तरे ॥ २९५ ॥
वह्नेर्दक्षिणपार्श्वस्थामाधायान्यामथोत्तराम् ।
तस्यैवोत्तरपार्श्वस्थामाधाय परिषिच्य च ॥ २९६ ॥

[इध्मपरिषेचनविधिः]

अग्नौ स्थण्डिलदेशस्य प्रागाद्यासु[6] दशासु[7] च ।
गन्धपुष्पैरलंकृत्य परिषिच्य विनायकम् ॥ २९७ ॥
यज्ञेशभास्करादीनभ्यर्च्य कुसुमादिभिः ।
स्वलंकृतो[8] गन्धमाल्यैः परिषिञ्चेच्च मन्त्रवत्[9] ॥ २९८ ॥
मन्त्रादिग्रहणादत्र[10] कल्पोक्तपरिषेचनम् ।
सूचितं तत्प्रकारेण तस्मात् स्यात्परिषेचनम् ॥ २९९ ॥
होमादावन्त इत्युक्तं सिद्धे पाठात् क्रमेऽत्र यत्[11] ।
यद्धोममात्रशेषत्वज्ञापनाय[12] तयेरितः[12] ॥ ३०० ॥
नैमित्तिके शुक्रियादौ[13] समस्तापूर्विकेष्वपि ।

१.M प्रागर्धं. २.M द्विजः, T ऋत्विजः. ३-३.T हितेऽऽवाह्या. ४.T °परानु°. ५.M परिधौ. ६.M प्राद्यासु. ७.M दिशासु. ८.M अलंकृतो. ९.T °षिञ्चेच्च मन्त्र°. १०.M °ग्रहणं तत्र. ११.M तु. १२-१२.M °ज्ञावानयतोरतः, T तयोरतः. १३.M शुक्रियादा.

अविधानेऽपि[१] तत्प्राप्तिः प्राक्संस्थं परिषेचनम् ॥ ३०१ ॥
कृत्वा दक्षिणतः [२]पश्चादुदक्संस्थमथोत्तरम् ।
प्राक्संस्थं प्रसलैः [३]कुर्यात् समन्तात्परिषेचनम्[३] ॥ ३०२ ॥
अभिघार्येध्ममाज्येन तस्मात् समिधमाहृताम् ।
प्रणीतासु निधायेध्मबन्धनं चापनीय तम् ॥ ३०३ ॥
एकविंशतिसंख्यातममितं[४] वा ततः परम् ।
[५]आमध्यान्मन्त्रवत् स्वामी सम्यगुद्दिश्य देवताम् ॥ ३०४ ॥
मन्त्राभिधेयां सर्वत्र त्यजेद् द्रव्यं स्वयंकृतौ ।
विधाय होमं तत् कुर्यादथेतीध्मादनन्तरम्[६] ॥ ३०५ ॥

[पक्वहोमविधिः]

आज्यहोमविधानार्थमुच्यते तच्च कर्मणः[७] ।
अन्यस्य ज्ञापकं ज्ञेयं स्रुचा पक्वाहुतौ[८] ततः ॥ ३०६ ॥
स्रुच्युपस्तीर्य हविषः पश्चात्प्रागवदाय च ।
अविक्तमभिघार्याज्यं प्रसज्य जुहुयात्ततः ॥ ३०७ ॥
अधस्तादुपरिष्टाच्च[९] तस्याज्यमपि हूयते ।
दर्विहोमसमाख्यानाद् दर्व्या कृत्स्नाहुतौ वचः[१०] ॥ ३०८ ॥
दर्व्येत्यपक्वद्रव्याज्येत्यर्थतां[११] वक्तुमर्थवत् ।
अत एव स्रुचा[१२] स्थालीपाकहोमो नियम्यते ॥ ३०९ ॥
ननु दर्व्यैव होमः स्यात् समाख्या बाध्यतेऽन्यथा ।
दर्व्या होतव्यमित्येवं गुणो नेह विधीयते ॥ ३१० ॥
समाख्या दर्विहोमोऽत्र न सा स्याद् गुणचोदना[१३] ।
[१४]एतमर्थमभिप्रेत्यानुपदेशार्थमीरितम्[१५] ॥ ३११ ॥

१.M अपिधाने°. २.M पार्श्वादु°. ३-३.M कुर्यां समन्त परि°. ४.M °तं मिमीतं. ५.M आध्यान्म°. ६.M इध्मानन्तरम्. ७.M कर्मणाम्. ८.MT चर्वापक्वाहुतौ. ९.T a lacuna between °परिष्टा (T ष्ठा) and ज्यमपि. १०.M वच, T broken. ११.M द्रव्ये°; T gives a sign of gap of one syllable between °ज्या and र्थतां which is not shown in M. १२.M adds an additional स्थाली between स्रुचा and स्थालीपाक°. १३.T चोदिना. १४.M एनम°. १५.M °देशमितीरितम्.

नायं गुणोपदेशः स्यात् समाख्या कर्मणामियम् ।
चरुहोमः[1] स्रुचा तस्मादिहापि न विरुध्यते ॥ ३१२ ॥
इत्यर्थान्तरं[2] वा [3]स्याद्विशेषेणाभिधीयते ।
पक्वहोमस्य च तत्र यत्र दर्व्या विधीयते ॥ ३१३ ॥
अष्टकादौ स्रुचा तस्मात् तद्धोमो न प्रदर्श्यते ।
उपदेशादृते पक्वं स्रुचैव जुहुयादिति ॥ ३१४ ॥
स्थालीपाके द्वितीयोक्त्या कृत्स्नहोमो विवक्षितः ।
[4]स्विष्टकृद्धवनाच्छेषप्राशनाच्च नृजन्मनि ॥ ३१५ ॥
स्रुचा प्रधानहोमार्थ[5]प्रसङ्गादेतदीरितम्[6] ।
आज्यहोमगुणायैव सूत्रमारभ्यतेऽपरम् ॥ ३१६ ॥
जुहोति सन्धेरारभ्य वह्नेरित्यत्र योजना ।
जुहोतीति पदं चाथशब्दात् प्रागनुषज्यते ॥ ३१७ ॥
दर्व्या संस्पृश्य परिधी सन्धिमुत्तरमक्ष्णया[7] ।
अग्नेर्वायौ समारभ्य स्वकोणावधिसन्ततम् ॥ ३१८ ॥
उक्त्वा[8] दक्षिणतोऽप्येवं सन्धेरारभ्य पूर्ववत् ।
[9]निर्ऋत्यादीशपर्यन्तं जुहुयान्मनसा श्रुतेः ॥ ३१९ ॥
'प्रजापतय' इत्युक्त्वा स्वाहेत्युच्चैः समुच्चरन् ।
जुहुयाद्यत्र मनसा होमो न्यायोऽयमिष्यते ॥ ३२० ॥
तत उत्तरपूर्वस्मिन् वह्नेः प्राग् दक्षिणेऽपि च ।
भागेऽग्नये[10] च सोमायेत्येते सर्वत्र चक्षुषी ॥ ३२१ ॥
दर्विहोमेऽपि जुहुयादथेत्येवमिहार्थवत् ।
मध्येऽग्नेर्विहिताः सर्वा [11]अग्न्याद्याहुतयो गणे ॥ ३२२ ॥
पाकयज्ञेऽपि तत्प्राप्ति[12]र्मध्य इत्यादिनोदिता ।
जुहोतीत्यनुवादेन तद्विधानार्थमर्थवत् ॥ ३२३ ॥

१.M होम. २.M इत्यर्थोऽन्तरं. ३.M स्यावि°. ४.M स्विष्टकृद्वचनाच्छेष°. ५.M होमार्थ. ६.M °देदितीरितम्. ७.M °मक्षया. ८.M भुक्त्वा. ९.MT निर्ऋत्या° (T ऋ). १०.M भागौ ये. ११.M अग्निद्या°. १२.M प्रप्तिं.

प्राक्संस्था आहुतीर्मध्ये रीतिशो[1] जुहुयात्ततः[2] ।
एवं व्याहृतिहोमान्त उक्तः साधारणो विधिः ॥ ३२४ ॥
सर्वेषां पाकयज्ञानामेतदग्निमुखं मतम् ।
एवमग्निमुखं कर्म कृत्वा साधारणं ततः ॥ ३२५ ॥
स्वस्वविध्यनुसारेण कार्यमित्यधुनोच्यते ।
असाधारणकर्माणि प्रक्षेप्तव्यानि यानि तु ॥ ३२६ ॥
तेषां स्थानमिदं ज्ञेयं द्विविधान्येव तानि तु ।
होमाहोमस्वरूपाणि होमस्तेषां नियम्यते ॥ ३२७ ॥
यावद्धोमान्तमित्यत्रावापस्य[3] द्विविधस्य[4] तु ।
होमरूपमिहावापं[5] कृत्वा हुत्वा जयादिकान् ॥ ३२८ ॥
अहोमरूपं कुर्वीत प्रणीतामार्जनात्परम् ।
प्रधानहोमान् पठितान् वारुणीभिः समैर्हविः[6] ॥ ३२९ ॥
[7]आमात्यादिषु तत्रासां निवृत्त्यर्थमिहोच्यते ।
[8]आवारुणीभ्य इत्येतदन्यथा वृत्तिरत्र हि ॥ ३३० ॥
या तिरश्च्यादिवत् तस्मान्नियमः स्यादिहार्थवान् ।
प्रधानहोमवचनो होमशब्दो विवक्षितः ॥ ३३१ ॥
उपहोमोऽत्र विहितो वारुणीभ्यः पुरा यतः ।
जयादयो विधीयन्ते स्मार्ताग्नौ जुहुयादिति ॥ ३३२ ॥
वैदिकेष्वेव तत्प्राप्तिः श्रौतत्वात् स्यान्नियोगतः[9] ।
येन सत्कर्मणेत्येतद्वाक्यं [10]साधारणं यतः[10] ॥ ३३३ ॥

[उपस्तरणादीनां स्वरूपम्]

अथोपस्तरणादीनां स्वरूपमभिधीयते ।
अवत्ते वाऽनवत्ते वा हविष्युपरि सेचनम् ॥ ३३४ ॥

१.M ईदृशो. २.T जुहुयाद्यतः. ३.T व्याकस्य. ४.M द्विविधास्यते. ५.M °ह वापं; T °मिह...कृत्वा. ४.M सममै°. ७.M हविरामा°. ८.MT प्रावारुणीभ. ९.MT श्रौतत्वास्या°. १०-१०.M साधारणया च.

अभिघारणमित्युक्तमवदानात्पुरा तु यत् ।
अवदाननिधानार्थपात्र आज्यावसेचनम् ॥ ३३५ ॥
स्रुच्यन्यत्रापि[1] वा तत् स्यादुपस्तरणशब्दितम् ।
बदरीपत्रमात्रं स्यादवदानं चरोरपि ॥ ३३६ ॥
अङ्गुष्ठपर्वमात्रं वा ज्यायः स्यात् स्विष्टकृत्ततः ।
अवशिष्टे तु होतव्ये पुनराज्यावसेचनम् ॥ ३३७ ॥
अवत्तदेशे तद्[2] ज्ञेयं प्रत्यञ्जनपदोदितम् ।
अवदानं च पश्चात्प्राग्घविषः[3] स्विष्टकर्मणि ॥ ३३८ ॥
सकृदुत्तरपूर्वार्द्धा[4]न्मेक्षणेनावदाय तत् ।
अभिघार्य द्विरन्यासामाहुतीनां [5]बहिर्दिशि ॥ ३३९ ॥
ऐशान्यां हव्यवाहस्य स्विष्टाद्याभ्यां जुहोत्यथ ।
प्रहृत्य मेक्षणं स्रुक्थसंस्रावेणाभिघार्य च ॥ ३४० ॥
हुत्वोपरिष्टाच्चरुमप्युदङ्[6] नीत्वेध्मबन्धनम् ।
विस्रस्याधाय समिधं प्रहृत्य प्रोक्षणान्वितम् ॥ ३४१ ॥

[जयादिहोमविधानम्]

जयादीञ्जुहुयात्पूर्वमावापात्त्व[7]विकल्पितान् ।
'चित्ताये'त्यादिभिर्मन्त्रैर्हुत्वा तु द्वादशाहुतीः ॥ ३४२ ॥
त्रयोदशेन मन्त्रेण प्रजाद्येन[8] हुताशनम् ।
उपतिष्ठेत् प्राञ्जलिः सन्ननु मन्त्र उपस्थितौ ॥ ३४३ ॥
विधीयते प्राञ्जलित्वमेतद्विध्यवशेषते ।
अभ्यातानाख्यमन्त्राणामनुषङ्ग इहेष्यते ॥ ३४४ ॥
'स माऽवत्वि'ति निर्दिश्या'स्मिन्ब्रह्म'त्यादिना ततः ।
रुद्रादिमन्त्रहोमान्ते वारुणस्पाश[9] इष्यते ॥ ३४५ ॥

[राष्ट्रभृद्-होमविधिः]

हुत्वा शिष्टैरुपस्थाय पित्र्येण पितृगत्ततः[10] ।

१.M वि. २.M तं. ३.M °प्राक्च्छीर्ष. ४.M पूर्वाद् वा. ५.M बहूदिशि. ६.T °नित्वेध्म°. ७.M °वापत्वा°. ८.M प्रज्याद्येन. ९.M broken between वा and णस्पाश; T broken between वा and इष्यते. १०.M पितृवत्ततः.

जुहुयाद्राष्ट्रभृद्भिस्तद्विशेष इह कथ्यते ॥ ३४६ ॥
'अग्निर्गन्धर्व' इत्युक्त्वा 'स इदं ब्रह्म' तत्परम्[१] ।
'क्षत्रं पात्वि'ति निर्दिश्य तस्मै स्वाहेत्यथापरम्[२] ॥ ३४७ ॥
'तस्यौषधय' [३]इत्याद्य ऊर्जौ[४] नामेत्युदीरिते ।
'ता इदं क्षत्र'पर्यन्तमुक्त्वा 'ताभ्यां पान्त्वि'त्युदीर्य च ॥ ३४८ ॥
'ताभ्यः स्वाहे'ति मन्त्रैस्तैर्हुत्वैता द्वादशाहुतीः[५] ।
'भुवनस्ये'त्युपस्थाय 'स नो रास्वा'न्वितेन[६] तु ॥ ३४९ ॥
'परमेष्ठ्या'दिभिर्मन्त्रैर्हुत्वाऽष्टाभिरुपस्थितिम्[७] ।
अन्त्येन वसनाद्येन कुर्यादेवं जयादिकान् ॥ ३५० ॥
हु'त्वेममि'त्यादिभिर्मन्त्रैर्जुहुयादिति वर्तते ।
'प्रजापते न त्वदि'ति हुत्वा सौविष्टकृत्यतः ॥ ३५१ ॥
सर्वस्माद्धविषः [८]कार्या यदन्त्येति विशेषणम् ।
[९]मध्येऽन्यत्स्विष्टकृत्प्राप्तिः सूचकत्वात्तदर्थवत् ॥ ३५२ ॥
चरुश्चेत् स्या'द्धव्यवाहं' 'स्विष्टमग्न' इति द्वयम् ।
स्यात् स्विष्टकृत इत्येवं योजनीयं चरोस्ततः ॥ ३५३ ॥
प्रधानहोमे निर्वृत्ते [१०]कार्या स्विष्टकृदाहुतिः ।
अचरुद्रव्यशेषस्य लाजादेः प्रतिपत्तये ॥ ३५४ ॥
आज्येन सह सर्वस्मादिति निर्दिष्टमर्थवत् ।
एवं साधारणं होमं विधाय तदनन्तरम् ॥ ३५५ ॥

[राष्ट्रभृद्वारुण्योर्मध्य उपहोमविधिः]

[११]राष्ट्रभृद्वारुणीमध्य उपहोमो विधीयते ।
[१२]आभ्यन्तर्याद्वारुणीभ्यः पुरस्तादुपहोमकान्[१३] ॥ ३५६ ॥
ऐष्टिका विहिताः प्राप्ताः स्युरज्यान्यादयो[१४] यदि ।
हुत्वोपहोमान् जुहुयाद्वास्तोष्पत्याहुती[१५] गृहे ॥ ३५७ ॥

१.M तच्चरुम्. २.T °थापरः. ३.M तस्यै नृषधय. ४.T ऊर्जो. ५.M °हुतिः. ६.MT °राज्यान्वि°. ७.M °तम्. ८.MT कार्य. ९.T °ऽन्य स्वि°. १०.M कार्यस्, T कार्यः. ११.M राष्ट्राभिर्द्वा°,T राष्ट्रभिद्वा. १२.M आद्यं कुर्याद्वारु°. १३.M परादुहोम°, T पुरादु..होम°. १४.M स्यु राजन्यादयो, T स्युरज्यान्यदयो. १५.T °हुतीर्गृहे.

होमश्चेत् क्रियतेऽरण्ये न[1] स्यातामाहुती[1] इमे ।
[2]अज्ञातदोषशान्त्यर्थं प्राजापत्याहुतेः पुरा ॥ ३५८ ॥
प्रायश्चित्ताहुतीः कुर्यात् पुरुषाणां प्रमादतः ।
मिन्दाहुती[3] व्याहृतयस्तन्तुमत्यो मनस्वती ॥ ३५९ ॥
अनाज्ञातत्रिकं दुर्गासिन्तत्याभिः[4] समृद्धयः ।
'भूरग्नये' चेत्याद्याः स्युरिह[5] व्याहृतयो 'मनः' ॥ ३६० ॥
इत्यारभ्य दधात्वन्ते 'बृहस्पतिरि'तीरिते ।
[6]'तनुतामिममि'त्युक्त्वाहो 'विश्वे'त्यादिका तु या॥ ३६१ ॥
आद्या तन्तुमती 'तन्तु' 'त्वमग्न' इति तत्परे ।
[7]मनस्वतीमज्योतिर्या इष्टाप[8] उषसोऽन्विता ॥ ३६२ ॥
[9]अनाज्ञातत्रिक'मनाज्ञातं' 'पुरुषसंमितम्'[10] ।
'यत्पाकत्रे'ति दुर्गा स्याज्जातवेदस ऋङ्मता[11] ॥ ३६३ ॥
सन्ततिस्तु 'मनो[12] ज्योतिरिमं नो यज्ञ'मित्ययम् ।
[13]विशेषस्तन्तुमत्येयमाख्यातान्यविशेषतः ॥ ३६४ ॥
'आभिर्गीर्भिर्यदि'त्याद्या त्विष्टेभ्यः[14] स्युः[15] समृद्धयः ।
प्रजापत्यां च मनसा हुत्वा स्विष्टकृदन्विताम्[16] ॥ ३६५ ॥
संमृज्य[17] परिधीन् [18]दर्व्या परिषिच्य च मन्त्रवत् ।
प्रहृत्य परिधीन्दर्व्या संस्रावेणाभिघार्य तान् ॥ ३६६ ॥
गां ब्रह्मणे[19] दक्षिणां च दत्त्वा वह्निं प्रदक्षिणम् ।
आहृत्य च प्रणीतास्तत् [20]पश्चान्यस्त्वाभिपूर्य [21]ताम्॥ ३६७ ॥
दर्भपाणिर्मार्जयित्वा दिशः[22] पूर्वादिकास्ततः[23] ।
तास्वात्माभिमुखं भूमौ निनीयात्मानमम्बुभिः ॥ ३६८ ॥

१-१.M न्याहुती. २.M अज्ञादोष, T अज्ञानदोष. ३.M मन्दाहुतीर्व्या°. ४.M °त्यादिस्. ५.M स्युदिह. ६.M तनुतामिमित्यु°. ७.M मनस्वतिम°. ८.T इष्टा. ९.M °तकमना°. १०.T सदाज्ञा पुरुषस्थितम्. ११.M given in the next line after the sign of broken text. १२.M °तिधूः. १३.M विशेषन्तु मत्ये. १४.M स्विष्टेभ्यः. १५.M न्युस्. १६.M °दन्विता. १७.M समज्य. १८.M परिधिर्दव्या, T परिर्धीर्द°. १९.MT ब्राह्मणे. २०.M पश्चान्य°. २१.M °पूर्वताम्. २२.M दिशं. २३.T °कांस्ततः.

मार्जयेत् स्वयमात्मानं स्वामिनौ नान्यकर्तृके ।
विधाय स्विष्टकृद्धोमपर्यन्तं होममादितः ॥ ३६९ ॥
नियम्य [1]लोपहोमानामिह स्थानान्तरं ततः[1] ।
वास्तोष्पत्यौ विशेषेण विधाय तदनन्तरम् ॥ ३७० ॥
[2]अपराप्यूर्ध्वमित्यादि न तन्त्रे विधिरुच्यते ।
मन्त्रवत्परिषिच्योर्ध्वं [3]समन्तात्परिषेचनम् ॥ ३७१ ॥
कार्या द्विवचनं श्रुत्या प्रसिद्धं परिषेचनम् ।
इत्येकवचनं यस्मान्मन्त्रवत्परिषेचने ॥ ३७२ ॥
दृश्यते परिषेकेभ्य ऊर्ध्वमित्यन्यथोदितम्[4] ।
[5]स्रुचा पक्वाहुतिर्यस्मिन् होमेन विधिचोदिता ॥ ३७३ ॥
अनेन विधिना तत्र पक्वहोमो विधीयते ।
चरुं लोकाग्निसुश्रृतं[6] संसाद्य प्रोक्ष्य पूर्ववत् ॥ ३७४ ॥
आसाद्य परिषेकान्तं होमं कृत्वाऽभिघार्य च ।
संसिच्याज्येन जुहुयान्मेक्षणेन प्रदक्षिणम् ॥ ३७५ ॥
मध्ये यथोदितैर्मन्त्रैर्हुत्वा स्विष्टकृदन्तिमम्[7] ।
मेक्षणं च प्रहृत्याग्नौ [8]समन्तात्परिषिच्य च ॥ ३७६ ॥
चरुमुद्वास्य परिधीन् संप्रहृत्याभिघार्य च ।
प्रणीतामार्जनं कृत्वा [9]वह्न्युद्वसितभस्मना ॥ ३७७ ॥
कृत्वानुलेपनं वह्निमर्चयेत् कुसुमादिभिः ।
एवं साधारणं धर्मं सर्वेषां स्मार्तकर्मणाम् ॥ ३७८ ॥

[विवाहाग्निसाध्यत्वकर्मविधानम्]

कृत्वा[10] तेषां [11]विवाहाग्निसाध्यत्वनियमाय तु ।
कृते विवाहे यत्कार्यं यस्मिन्नित्यादिनोच्यते[12] ॥ ३७९ ॥
क्लृप्तौ विवाहमुक्त्वेह[13] तच्छेषप्रतिपादनात् ।

१-१.M वोच होमाहमिहस्थानन्तरन्तरम्. २.M अपरापूर्वमित्यादि. ३.M समन्तपरि°. ४.M °न्यथापितम्. ५.T स्रुचाऽपक्वा°. ६.T सुश्रुत°. ७.M स्विष्टन्त्विदम्. ८.M समन्तं. ९.M वह्नयुत्थसित°. १०.T उक्त्वा. ११.M विवाहानि. १२.M न्नीत्वादि° T यस्मिन्नि...दिनो°. १३.M मक्त्वेव°.

गृह्योक्तैरन्वितं [१]कल्पविहितानां च गम्यते ॥ ३८० ॥

यस्मिन्नग्नौ [२]व्यवायाख्यसंस्कारं कुरुते तु तम् ।
स्मार्तधर्माश्रयं कुर्याद्यदि ताभ्यां व्रतान्वितम् ॥ ३८१ ॥

वार्योऽसावनलोऽन्यस्मिन् काल उत्पादनं यदि ।
व्रतवद्धारणं तत्र नास्तीत्यर्थादिहोच्यते ॥ ३८२ ॥

मृते पितरि दत्ते च पिण्ड एकादशेऽहनि ।
विभज्य दायमुत्पाद्य[३] वह्निकर्माचरेदिति[४] ॥ ३८३ ॥

इदमर्थमभिप्रेत्य यदीत्यत्रोपवर्णितम् ।
भार्यादिरग्निर्दायादिर्वेति हि स्मर्यते स्मृतौ ॥ ३८४ ॥

न चात्रौपासनस्याग्नेः[५] पाक्षिकत्वं[६] विवक्षितम् ।
सर्वस्मृतिषु नित्यत्वमुच्यते स्मार्तकर्मणाम् ॥ ३८५ ॥

स्मार्तं[७] कर्म विवाहाग्नौ कुर्वीतेति नियम्यते ।
तमग्निमिति[८] चाप्येवं युज्यतेऽत्र विशेषणम् ॥ ३८६ ॥

कालान्तरे तदाधानसूचनार्थं यदीत्यतः ।
सूतकाग्नेरुपादानं नाचार्येणेष्यते च[९] तत् ॥ ३८७ ॥

विवाहे लौकिकस्यैव वह्नेराधानमुच्यते ।
कृते विवाहे सामर्थ्ये सति कर्मारिभेत्ततः ॥ ३८८ ॥

निर्धनत्वे तदारंभे दायकाल इति स्थितिः ।
उद्वाहकर्मणा वह्निः स्मार्त उत्पद्यते न च ॥ ३८९ ॥

व्रतवद्धारणेनेह तदुत्पत्तिर्विधीयते ।
व्रतवद्धारणं [१०]यद्वाऽत्राहिताग्नेर्विधीयते ॥ ३९० ॥

इहापि तद्वदेवास्य धारणं युज्यते यतः ।
व्रतवद्धारणं वह्नेर्होमश्चेह त्र्यहं ननु ॥ ३९१ ॥

तदूर्ध्वं हि चतुर्थेऽह्नि दर्विहोमो विधास्यते ।

१.M कल्पं. २.M व्यवाख्य. ३.M °भज्यादय°. ४.T कर्माचरेदिति. ५.M °त्रौवासरस्याग्नेः, T °ग्ने. ६.M पाक्षिकेवं. ७.M स्मार्तः. ८.M °ग्निमिचाप्येवं. ९.M य. १०.M यत्राहिता°, T यद्वादाहिता°.

विवाहशेषता वाऽस्य[१] दर्विहोमस्य गम्यते ॥ ३९२ ॥
'यास्यै तनू पतिघ्नी'ति स्त्रीफलत्वनिदर्शनात् ।
तस्मिन्नित्यादिना नित्यं कर्म तत्र विधीयते ॥ ३९३ ॥
यावज्जीवित एवायं होमः श्रौताग्निहोत्रवत् ।
कृते विवाह आरभ्य कार्यत्वात्तदनन्तरम् ॥ ३९४ ॥
व्रतवद्धारणं वह्नेर्होमश्चेह विधीयते ।
अत एव पुनर्दर्विहोमोऽप्यत्र विधास्यते ॥ ३९५ ॥
काल्पिकं गमनं प्राप्तं[२] विवाहानन्तरं यतः ।
[३]चर्मोपवेशनान्तं तं विधीय तदनन्तरम् ॥ ३९६ ॥
संवेशनं[४] तदैवोक्तं तदङ्गत्वादमुष्य च ।
इहोक्तस्य तदा प्राप्तौ व्रतवद्धारणे[५] सति ॥ ३९७ ॥
त्रिरात्रेऽपगते[६] तत्र कार्यत्वात्तत्र चोदितम्[७] ।
प्रतिसंख्याय होमादिर्विच्छेदे शास्त्रचोदितः ॥ ३९८ ॥
विरुध्यतेऽन्यथा तस्मान्नित्यत्वं तस्य युज्यते ।
लब्ध्वा कन्यां गृहान्प्राप्य सार्धमुद्वाहवह्निना ॥ ३९९ ॥
शुचौ देशे समुद्धत्य संप्रोक्ष्याधाय पावकम् ।
[८]द्वारेऽग्निमभिमृश्योपविश्य चर्मणि रोहिते ॥ ४०० ॥
कुर्याद् होमं विवाहाग्नौ तस्य सायमुपक्रमः ।
रात्रौ कृते विवाहेऽपि प्रातर्होमं विधाय तु ॥ ४०१ ॥
उपक्रमेत्सायमेव रवावस्तंगते सति ।
सन्निधौ वर्तते सायं [९]व्रतशब्दोऽत्र सन्ध्ययोः ॥ ४०२ ॥
[१०]यावद्वचनमित्युक्तमुक्तधर्मनिवृत्तये ।
आपूर्विको विधिस्तस्माद्यावदर्थं प्रवर्तते ॥ ४०३ ॥
वाचयित्वा स्वस्त्ययनमुपवीती शिखी शुचिः[११] ।
आशम्य शोभयित्वाग्निं परिस्तीर्य यथाविधि ॥ ४०४ ॥

१.M चास्य. २.M om. ३.T प वेशना°. ४.M °वेशनान्त°. ५.M °द्धारणं. ६.M °ऽवगते. ७.T चोदितः. ८.T पारेयीमभि°. ९.MT व्रतश्. १०.M या वचन°, T या-द्वचन°. ११.M शुचिम्.

विशुद्धे भाजने सर्पिषोऽवस्तीर्य[1] विशोधितात्[2] ।
[3]अवदानसमान्व्रीहीन् विरोच्य पृथगाहितान् ॥ ४०५ ॥
अभिघार्यानधिश्रित्य पर्यग्न्यौषधिभिस्तथा ।
कृत्वा सुगन्धिकुसुमैरलंकृत्य हुताशनम् ॥ ४०६ ॥
मन्त्रवत्परिषिच्याग्नावाज्याक्तां समिधं शुभाम् ।
स्वाहेत्याधाय तस्यां च द्व्यङ्गुले देवतीर्थवत् ॥ ४०७ ॥
हस्तेन जुहुयाद् व्रीहीनग्नये पार्श्वतस्ततः ।
ज्यायसो जुहुयाद् भूय उत्तरत्र प्रजापतेः ॥ ४०८ ॥
प्रज्वाल्य चेन्धनैरग्निं मन्त्रवत्परिषिच्य च ।
भस्मानुलेपनं कृत्वा कुर्यादग्नेरलंकृतिम् ॥ ४०९ ॥

[व्रताचरणविधानम्]

देवव्रतान्यपि [4]चरेन्नानृतं स वदेत् त्र्यहम् ।
मांसाशनं स्त्रीगमनं [5]वासपल्पूलनं तथा ॥ ४१० ॥
आञ्जनाभ्यञ्जने कोशीधान्यं खट्वासनादिकम्[6] ।
शूद्रोच्छिष्टं तथा श्राद्धं मृन्मयेन जलाशनम् ॥ ४११ ॥
अन्यच्च न हितं[7] कर्म वर्जयेद् भोजनं हविः[8] ।
कृत्वा विवाहमागत्य धारयित्वानलं त्र्यहम् ॥ ४१२ ॥
दर्विहोमञ्चतुर्थेऽह्नि जुहुयादुक्तधर्मवत् ।
रात्रौ[9] चतुर्थ्यां गमनं शास्त्रान्तर उदीरितम् ॥ ४१३ ॥
उपसंवेशनाङ्गत्वमत एवास्य गम्यते ।
संवत्सरं[10] मैथुनं न चरेदित्यादिनापि च ॥ ४१४ ॥
[11]काल्पिकोपगमादूर्ध्वं ब्रह्मचर्यं नियम्यते ।
अतः संवत्सरं नेति यस्मादत्राभिधास्यते ॥ ४१५ ॥

१.M सर्विषोपस्ती°. २.M विशाधितात्. ३.M अपारा°. ४.MT वरे°. ५.M वासवत्पूलनं, T वास.. न्मूलनं. ६.M खद्यास°. ७.M भीतं. ८.M हणिम्. ९.M रत्रौ, T रात्र्यौ. १०.M सत्सर. ११.T कल्पितोऽपग°.

होमश्च तत्र भवति यत्रोपगमनं ततः ।
अहः शब्दोऽत्र दिवसवाचकः[१] पूर्ववत्ततः ॥ ४१६ ॥
रात्रौ स्वस्त्ययनं कृत्वा होमं कृत्वाऽथ संविशेत् ।
उपसंवेशनादूर्ध्वं कुर्यात्पार्वणमित्यतः ॥ ४१७ ॥

[पार्वणहोमकर्म]

दर्विहोमं विधायेह पार्वणं च विधीयते ।
उपसंवेशनाङ्गत्वं दर्विहोमस्य दर्शितम् ॥ ४१८ ॥
[२]तदनन्तरमेवेह समवायो निषिध्यते[३] ।
दर्विहोमो विधातव्यः[४] प्राङ्निषेधात्ततोऽन्यथा ॥ ४१९ ॥
तथैवेह समाचारः शिष्टानामुपलभ्यते ।
पर्वशब्दः[५] पक्षसन्धौ तत्र होमो विधीयते ॥ ४२० ॥
श्रुतिः सन्धौ यजेतेति [६]दुर्ज्ञेयत्वादमुष्य च ।
अभितो ये तिथी तेन लक्ष्यतेऽत्र तथा श्रुतिः ॥ ४२१ ॥
यजेत सन्धिमभित इत्याद्या श्रूयते यतः ।
पर्वणो यश्चतुर्थांश[७] आद्याप्रतिपदस्त्रयः[८] ॥ ४२२ ॥
यागकालः स विज्ञेयः प्रातरुक्तो मनीषिभिः ।
प्रतिपद्येव होमोऽयं समत्वे पर्वणो भवेत् ॥ ४२३ ॥
पौर्णमासीं यजेत्पूर्व[९]ममावास्यां तथोत्तरम् ।
इति सन्धिर्भवेद्यस्मिन् पर्वणो [१०]होमस्तत्र च ॥ ४२४ ॥
प्रतिपद्याग[११] एव स्यात् पौर्णमासचरुस्तथा ।
आमावास्यमेवात्र[१२] स्यात्तुरीयांशो न चेद् भवेत् ॥ ४२५ ॥
न यष्टव्यं चतुर्थांऽशे यागैः प्रतिपदः क्वचित् ।
अनयाऽत्र दिशाकालो ज्ञातव्यः पार्वणस्य तु ॥ ४२६ ॥
[१३]संदिश्यतेऽत्र तद्धर्मः पूर्णमासवदित्यतः[१४] ।

१.M पावकं. २.M तदन्तर°. ३.M भिषीध्यते. ४.M °धातव्या. ५.M °शब्द. ६.M दुर्ज्येय°. ७.M चतुर्थेशा. ८.M °पदस्त्रयम्. ९.T °पूर्वाम°. १०.M हानि, होत्र तत्र. ११.MT प्रतिपद्भाग. १२.M °पात्रं, T अमावास्य वात्र. १३.M अतिदिश्यते°. १४.M °वतीत्यतः.

पौर्णमासेन सादृश्यं धर्माणां हविषामपि ॥ ४२७ ॥
देवतानां च संप्राप्तं स्थालीपाकोपदेशनात् ।
सादृश्यं देवतानां तद्धोमस्येह विधीयते ॥ ४२८ ॥
[१]तत्तुल्यदेवताहोमाः कार्या इति विधिस्ततः ।
बह्व्योऽत्र देवता होमबहुत्वं चावसीयते ॥ ४२९ ॥
अग्निः सोमः पौर्णमास्यामग्नीषोमौ च देवताः ।
अग्निर्विष्णुस्तथेन्द्राग्नी इतरत्र प्रकीर्तिताः ॥ ४३० ॥
[२]तद्देवत्या अनूच्यार्चो[३] याज्यादिर्जुहुयाच्चरोः ।
'हव्यवाहं' 'स्विष्टमि'ति[४] चरुस्विष्टकृदीरणम् ॥ ४३१ ॥
एक एव चरुः[५] श्रप्यः स्थालीपाकमितीरणात्[६] ।
'हव्यवाहं' 'स्विष्टमि'ति चोपदेशाच्चरोरिह ॥ ४३२ ॥
'पिप्रीह्यग्ने[७]' 'यदस्येति[८]' न स्यातां स्विष्टकृत्यृचौ ।
आमावास्यं विहायापि पौर्णमासमुपक्रमेत् ॥ ४३३ ॥
श्रौतवद् गृह्यवचनं च्छन्दोगैः परिपठ्यते ।
अग्न्यायतनसंस्कारोद्धृते[९]ऽग्नौ न प्रवर्तते ॥ ४३४ ॥
परिलेपनमेवेह कार्यमसकृदम्भसा[१०] ।
वाचयित्वा स्वस्त्ययनं विहृत्य ज्वलितेऽनले ॥ ४३५ ॥
सं परिस्तीर्य संसाद्य सूपविष्टे[११] च वेधसि ।
संप्रोक्ष्य संस्कृताम्भोभिः प्रणीतां[१२] सं प्रणीय च ॥ ४३६ ॥
चरुमग्नौ समुत्पाद्य दर्विस्रुङ्मार्जनादिकम् ।
कृत्वा चरुं समुद्वास्य परिधीन् परिधाय च ॥ ४३७ ॥
मन्त्रवत्परिषिच्येध्ममाधाय च यथोदितम् ।
हुत्वा व्याहृतिपर्यन्तं चरोः स्रुच्यवदाय च ॥ ४३८ ॥
'अग्निर्मूर्द्धे'त्यनुद्रुत्य[१३] 'भुव' इत्यादिनाऽग्नये ।
'त्वं नः सोमे'ति सोमाय 'या ते धामा'द्यया तथा ॥ ४३९ ॥

१.M तत्तुर्य. २.T स्युर्देव°. ३.M अनूव्यार्चो, T °व्यार्च्यो. ४.T स्विष्ठ°. ५.M चरु. ६.M °रणाम्. ७.T विव्रीह्यग्ने. ८.M यदद्येषि. ९.M °रोधृत°. १०.M कार्यं सशकृद°. ११.M °विष्टेव. १२.M प्रणीता, T प्रणीतां. १३.M अग्निमूर्धेत्य°, T अग्निर्मूर्धेत्यनुश्रुत्य.

हुत्वाग्नीषोमयो'रग्नीषोमा स' 'युवमि'त्यपि ।
चरुं[1] स्विष्टकृतं हुत्वा प्रहृत्यापि च मेक्षणम् ॥ ४४० ॥
संस्रावं च स्रुचा हुत्वा जयाद्युक्तं समाचरेत् ।
'इदं विष्णु''स्तदस्ये'ति द्वितीया दर्श इष्यते ॥ ४४१ ॥
'इन्द्राग्नी रोचना'द्येनं तथादित्यादिना परा ।
प्रकृतिः पाकयज्ञानां[2] स्थालीपाकोऽयमीरितः[3] ॥ ४४२ ॥

[इष्टिविधानम्]

नित्या नैमित्तिकाः काम्या इष्टिकल्पादिचोदिताः ।
स्थालीपाकविधानेन [4]कार्यास्तद्विधिरुच्यते ॥ ४४३ ॥
[5]नित्यमाग्रयणे तच्च व्रीहिभिर्वा यवैरिति ।
एकेष्टिविधं[6] तस्या कृतौ दोषाद्युदीरणम्[7] ॥ ४४४ ॥
शरदि व्रीहिभिस्तत् स्याद्वसन्ते स्याद्यवैर्यदि ।
इष्टिकल्पोदिता धर्मा इहापि स्युरितीरितम् ॥ ४४५ ॥
आमावास्येन[8] हविषा हुत्वा स्वस्त्ययनान्वितम् ।
होमे प्रणीताप्रणयपर्यन्ते पूर्ववत्कृते ॥ ४४६ ॥
[9]दर्विस्रुगाज्यसंस्कारे कृतेऽप्यग्नावलंकृते ।
गृहीत्वा च सकृज्जुह्वां[10] समन्तात्[11]परिषिच्य तु ॥ ४४७ ॥
'आकूत्यै त्वे'ति मन्त्राभ्यां समिदाधानपूर्वकम् ।
हुत्वैकामाहुतिं तद्वद् गृहीत्वा जुहुयात्पराम् ॥ ४४८ ॥
'अग्नेस्त्वा तेजसा'ज्येन[12] श्रपयित्वा चरुं ततः ।
पर्यग्नि कृत्वौषधीभिर्नवतण्डुलसाधितम् ॥ ४४९ ॥
आसाद्य परिधानादि व्याहृत्यन्तं यथोदितम् ।
कृत्वेन्द्राग्नीनथ[13] वृत्रं[14] 'विश्वे देवा ऋतावृधः' ॥ ४५० ॥
'विश्वे देवाश्च श्रृणुत' 'द्यावा नः' 'प्रादि पूर्वजे' ।

१.MT चरुस्विष्ट°. २.M °पामस्थाली°. ३.M °पाकस्समीरितम्. ४.MT कार्यान्तविधि°. ५.M नियमा°, T °यणे. ६.T वितन्तस्या°. ७.M दोषराद्युदी°, T दोषाद्युदी°. ८.M आमावास्यौ. ९.T दर्वी०. १०.T जुह्वया. ११.M समन्तं. १२.M °साद्येन. १३.M °त्रथ. १४.M दृत्रं, T ..त्रं.

आहुतीर्जुहुयात्तिस्रश्चरोः स्विष्टकृदादिकम् ॥ ४५१ ॥
हुत्वोपहोमाञ्जुहुयादज्यानीभिः[१] स्वके स्थले ।
द्यावापृथिव्याहुतेः प्रागादिदिक्षु तथोपरि ॥ ४५२ ॥
होमशेषं समाप्याथ पुरुषाराधनादिकम् ।
वैश्वदेवं विधायास्यां[२] नवान्नहविषा स्वयम् ॥ ४५३ ॥
उपविश्यापरेणाग्निं 'भद्रान्नः श्रेय' इत्यृचा ।
प्राश्नीयात् पत्न्यपि तथा वैश्वदेवावशेषितम् ॥ ४५४ ॥
पुराणमिश्रसंसिद्धनवान्नं चेन्निरग्निकम् ।
ब्राह्मणान् भोजयित्वा वा तच्छिष्टं भद्रमन्त्रवत् ॥ ४५५ ॥
नवाग्रयणयागात्प्राङ् नवान्नेन यजेद् गृही ।
नाश्नीयादुभयत्रापि कुर्याद्वैश्वानरं हविः ॥ ४५६ ॥
विधिराग्रयणप्रोक्तस्तस्य स्यात्प्राशनं विना ।
'पृष्टो [३]दिवी'त्यनूच्यात्र [४]'व्रता ते अग्न'[४] इत्यृचा ॥ ४५७ ॥
हुत्वा पक्वान्नकं[५] स्विष्टकृदाद्यं[६] होममाचरेत् ।
'उदु त्यं' 'चित्रमि'त्याभ्यां जुहुयादुपहोमकौ ॥ ४५८ ॥
पुत्रजन्मधनावाप्तितन्नाशादावपीष्यते[७] ।
इष्टिकल्पोदितैर्धर्मैः संभवद्भिरितीरितम् ॥ ४५९ ॥
दर्शकालातिपत्तौ च कृत्वैतत्पथिकृन्मुखम् ।
अतिपन्नं च कुर्वीत पौर्णमासादिपातने ॥ ४६० ॥
अनेन याऽनुवाक्ये'हा[८] देवानामि'ति चापरा ।
वैश्वानरसमानोऽसावनड्वान्[९]दक्षिणाऽस्य तु ॥ ४६१ ॥
पीतत्वेनैतयोः प्राप्तिः कालपात इतीतरे ।
चरुर्वातपतस्तद्वद् व्रतलोपो[१०] विधीयते ॥ ४६२ ॥

१.T °यादाज्यानेभि. २.M °स्मान्नवान्न हविषस्स्व°. ३.M दिविभ्यनू°. ४-४.M व्राताते अग्र, T प्रताते. ५.MT पक्वान्सकं. ६.M स्विस्टकाद्यं. ७.M °दापवीष्यते. ८.M °वाक्येह देवा°. ९.M °ध्वान्. १०.M °पतस्तद्व्रत, T °व्रतलोपे.

'त्वमग्ने व्रतपा'[१] 'यद्वो वयमि'[२]त्यादिना चरोः ।
होतव्य उपहोमोऽपि 'त्वं नः' 'स त्वं न' इत्यपि ॥ ४६३ ॥
'त्वं नस्तन्तुः' स्वयं कृत्वा नितितान्तु मते चरौ ।
याज्यानुवाक्ये शेषस्तु विधिर्वातपतो भवेत् ॥ ४६४ ॥
ब्रह्म प्रणीतारहितं परिधानात्पुरोदितम् ।
कृत्वा वह्निमलंकृत्य मन्त्रवत्परिषिच्य च ॥ ४६५ ॥
आधायेध्ममसंख्यातं [३]स्वाहेतीष्ट्वा च[३] चक्षुषी ।
पक्वाद्धुत्वा[४] यथाम्नातमपक्वे [५] स्विष्टकृत्यपि ॥ ४६६ ॥
[६]हुत्वोपहोमान्विहितान्हुत्वा स्विष्टकृतं ततः ।
मिन्दाहुती[७] व्याहृतीश्च [८]परिषिञ्चेच्च मन्त्रवत् ॥ ४६७ ॥
आपूर्विको विधिरयं दर्विहोमेषु पाक्षिकः ।
आवापहोमात्प्राग्वैते समृध्यौ जुहुयादिह ॥ ४६८ ॥
[९]इष्टिकल्प समाम्नाताः [१०]संभवद्धर्मसंयुताः ।
अनेन विधिना कार्या स्मार्तवह्नौ यथोदिताः ॥ ४६९ ॥

[औपासनाग्नेरुपास्तिविधिः]

औपासनाग्निसाध्यत्वं सर्वेषां गृह्यकर्मणाम् ।
[११]नियम्याग्निमतस्तस्य तदुपास्तिर्विधीयते ॥ ४७० ॥
यस्मिन्नग्नौ विवाहः[१२] स्यात्तदनन्तरमेव तत् ।
यावज्जीवमुपासीत शुश्रूषादिभिरन्वहम् ॥ ४७१ ॥
अतो ब्रह्मौदने[१३] कृत्स्नविनियोगो न युज्यते ।
अग्निहोत्रिण एवैष राजसूयेऽवगम्यते ॥ ४७२ ॥
महिषी गृहयागाग्निरौपासन[१४] उदीरितः[१५] ।
स्मार्तं कर्म विवाहाग्नौ[१६] सामान्येन नियम्यते ॥ ४७३ ॥
अष्टकादि च यन्नित्यं लौकिकेऽग्नौ निषिध्यते ।

१.T प्रतपा. २.M यद्वोपयाममि°, T पयमि°. ३-३.M स्वाहाति पाच. ४.M पक्वादु द्वा. ५.M °म्नातं पक्के. ६.M °पहोऽन्विहि°. ७.T °हुतीर्व्याहृ°. ८.M मपरि°. ९.T इष्टिकर्म°. १०.M संभवन्धर्म°. ११.M °म्यानि°. १२.M विवाह. १३.T ब्रह्मोदने. १४.M °यागानि°. १५.M °रितम्. १६.T विवाहोऽग्नौ.

न पैतृयज्ञिको होमो लौकिकेऽग्नौ विधीयते ॥ ४७४ ॥
व्रीहिहोमादि यन्नित्य अग्निहोत्रादिकः[1] स्मृतः ।
श्रौत्राग्निहोत्रिणः सर्वं कृतार्थत्वान्निवर्तते ॥ ४७५ ॥
दर्शादियागवादश्च चरुणैव समञ्जसः[2] ।
उपयुक्तो न सर्वं चेदिति वाक्यानुसारतः ॥ ४७६ ॥
ब्रह्मौदने समस्तस्य विनियोगो हि[3] गम्यते ।
इति लौकिक एवाग्नौ शिष्टाः कुर्वन्ति केचन ॥ ४७७ ॥
अजस्रवचनाच्चास्य नित्यधारणमिष्यते ।
न समारोपणं तस्मादनापदि समाचरेत् ॥ ४७८ ॥
देशान्तरे च गमनमुपासनविधानतः ।
अनापदि न कुर्वीत धनार्थं गमनं[4] स्मृतम् ॥ ४७९ ॥
धनैर्हि संभवेत् कर्म गृहस्थस्य महद्यतः ।
अतस्तीर्थादिसेवार्थं गमनं नास्य विद्यते ॥ ४८० ॥

[अग्निप्रणाशे प्रायश्चित्तं पुनराधानं च]

यदि नश्येत्प्रमादेन प्रायश्चित्तमनन्तरम् ।
कार्यमित्यधुना तत्र प्रायश्चित्तं विधीयते ॥ ४८१ ॥
अग्निसंस्कारकृद्धोमः परसूत्रात्प्रतीयते ।
प्रायश्चित्तमकृत्वैव[5] न स्यात्कर्मान्तरं ततः ॥ ४८२ ॥
गृहीत्वाऽथेति होमस्य तदानन्तर्यमुच्यते ।
अतः पूर्वोदिता धर्मा न भवन्तीति गम्यते ॥ ४८३ ॥
आपूर्विकविधिस्तस्मादस्मिन्होमे प्रवर्तते ।
उद्धताद् भस्म सन्त्यज्य गोमयेनावलिप्य च ॥ ४८४ ॥
'अहं त्वदा'दि मन्त्रेण यथा यत्नवता[6] पुनः।
श्रौत्रियागारसंभूतमग्निं[7] तस्मिन्विनिक्षिपेत् ॥ ४८५ ॥
[8]ज्वलयित्वाऽथ परितः समूहादि चतुष्टयम् ।

१.M °होत्रादिविस्मृतम्. २.M °जसम्. ३.M वि. ४.M न मनं. ५.M °कृत्वेन. ६.M यथवता.
७.MT °भूत अग्निं. ८.M ज्वाल°.

कृत्वा दर्वीं [१]ससमिधमाज्यस्थालीं तृणानि च ॥ ४८६ ॥
प्रोक्षणीपात्रमेतानि संसाद्य प्रोक्षणीजलैः ।
संप्रोक्ष्य दर्वीं संमृज्य चाज्यमुत्पाद्य मन्त्रतः ॥ ४८७ ॥
परिषिच्यापि समिधमाधाया'या'दिमन्त्रवत् ।
हुत्वा मिन्दाहुती हुत्वा व्याहृतिभिश्च मन्त्रवत् ॥ ४८८ ॥
परिषिञ्चेत्सर्वहोमेषु साधारणविधिर्भवेत्[२] ।
विनाशानन्तरं भस्म समारोप्य समन्त्रकम् ॥ ४८९ ॥
तद्[३] भस्म वहता[४] मन्त्रमुक्त्वा संप्रोक्ष्य तत्पुनः ।
सन्त्यज्य गोमयेनाथ परिलिप्य समाहृतम्[५] ॥ ४९० ॥
अग्निं व्याहृतिभिर्न्युप्य[६] स तत्र[७] समिधं क्षिपेत् ।
'आजुह्वो'द्'बुध्य' मन्त्राभ्यां स्वाहाकारसमन्वितम्॥ ४९१ ॥
आज्यं पूर्ववदुत्पाद्य[८] मन्त्रवत्परिषिच्य च ।
'अयाश्चाग्नेः' पञ्चहोत्रा दशात्मकमनस्वती ॥ ४९२ ॥
मिन्दाहुती[९] व्याहृतीश्च जुहोत्येकोनविंशतिः[१०] ।
आद्वादशाहादुद्वास्य[११] प्रायश्चित्तमिहेरितम् ॥ ४९३ ॥
परतः पुनराधानमग्निविच्छेद इष्यते ।
आरोहे[१२] विकले तद्वदवरोहे[१३] तथाम्भसा ॥ ४९४ ॥
अग्निनाशे तदेव स्यादमेध्यादेश्च संगमे ।
कौण्डिन्योक्तो विधिश्चेह पुनराधान उच्यते ॥ ४९५ ॥
[१४]पाणिग्रहादिरग्निस्तमित्यादिः [१५]पठ्यतेऽत्र यः[१५] ।
तदर्थवर्णनेनाथ प्रयोगः कल्प्यतेऽधुना ॥ ४९६ ॥
पाणिग्रहान्निरग्निः[१६] स्यात् स्मार्तकर्मप्रसिद्धये ।
योऽग्निरेवं समुत्पन्नस्तमौपासनमित्यतः ॥ ४९७ ॥

१.M समिध°. २.T विधिश्च (रेत) M wrongly gives the verse आ जुह्वोद्बुध्य=परिषिच्य च (see verse no. 491 b and 492 a) between 489 a and 489 b. ३.M om. ४.M भस्मापहता. ५.M °हतम्. ६.MT °भिस्सुप्य. ७.T तत्रा. ८.M पूर्वमुत्पा°. ९.M °हुति. १०.M °शति. ११.M °दुद्वाश्च. १२.M आमोहे. १३.M °दपरोहे. १४.M वासगृहादि°. १५-१५.T प्रकृते त्रयः. १६.M °ग्रहादिरग्नि.

आचक्षते च विद्वांस उपासनविधानतः ।
तस्मिन्नौपासने कार्यं[1] गृहकर्म यथोदितम् ॥ ४९८ ॥
[2]विवाहेऽग्निं समुत्पाद्य यः करोति यथाविधि ।
व्रीहिहोमेन चास्य स्यादग्निहोत्रित्वमेव वा[3] ॥ ४९९ ॥
पौर्णमासादियजनं चरुणैव कृतं भवेत् ।
श्रौतकर्मेह यच्चान्यन्नित्यनैमित्तिकादिकम् ॥ ५०० ॥
चरुणाऽऽज्यादिना वात्र क्रियते तत्कृतं ततः ।
इति चाचक्षते तस्मादग्निर्धार्यो निरन्तरम् ॥ ५०१ ॥
कर्माणि च यथाकालं प्रकुर्वीत समाहितः ।
द्वादशाहानि होमस्य विच्छेदेऽग्निर्विनश्यति[4] ॥ ५०२ ॥
अतः स पुनराधेयो वक्ष्यमाणेन वर्त्मना ।
यद्वा तन्तुमतीं कृत्वा प्रायश्चित्तं यथाविधि ॥ ५०३ ॥
प्रतिसंख्याय होमाँश्च जुहुयादेष युज्यते ।
अग्निहोत्राद्यकरणे षण्मासादौ विधीयते ॥ ५०४ ॥
प्रायश्चित्तं तथा पक्षहोमः शास्त्रान्तरोदितम् ।
होमविच्छेद एवाग्नेर्विच्छेदश्च यदा सह ॥ ५०५ ॥
तदोक्तं पुनराधानं होम एवान्यथा भवेत् ।
द्वाद्वशाहादिवाक्यस्य व्याख्यानान्तरमेव वा ॥ ५०६ ॥
उद्वाते[5]ऽग्नौ द्वादशाहात्पुरो नोत्पादयेद्यदि[6] ।
आधानं तत्र कुर्वीत होमाँश्च जुहुयात्ततः ॥ ५०७ ॥
होमाधिकारविच्छित्तिरग्न्यभावादिति[7] भ्रमात् ।
समतिक्रान्तहोमादेर्निवृत्तेरपि संभवात् ॥ ५०८ ॥
प्रतिसंख्याय होमान्वा जुहुयादित्यपीरितम् ।
अतिपन्नं च दर्शादिकार्यं चित्तान्वितं ततः ॥ ५०९ ॥

१.M कार्या. २.M विवाहाग्नि°. ३.T च. ४.M °च्छेदेनि°. ५.M उद्वाहे°. ६.M नो पाद भयेद्यदि, T नोपादयेद्यदि. ७.M °रग्निभावा°.

विच्छेददोषशान्त्यर्थं[1] प्रदद्याद् ब्राह्मणाय गाम्[2] ।
चिरकालसमुच्छेदे कृच्छ्रादेश्च समुच्चय:[3] ॥ ५१० ॥
पुण्याहवाचनं कृत्वा सपत्नीक: सपद्मज:[4] ।
उपविश्य परिश्रित्य समुद्धत्य समुक्ष्य च ॥ ५११ ॥
स्थण्डिले सिकता न्युप्य[5] प्लक्षशाखाभिरेव वा ।
उदुम्बरभवद्भिर्वा समाच्छाद्य हुताशनम् ॥ ५१२ ॥
यज्ञवृक्षसमुद्भूतं[6] विप्रागारोद्भवं तु वा ।
घटेऽवधाय ज्वलितमन्ततस्तत्र निक्षिपेत् ॥ ५१३ ॥
ज्वलयित्वा[7] परिस्तीर्य सादनाद्यपि पूर्ववत् ।
कृत्वाग्निमुखपर्यन्तं यथोक्तं जुहुयात्तत: ॥ ५१४ ॥
प्राजापत्याश्च[8] मनसा दशहोतारमेव च[9] ।
हुत्वा जयादिकं सर्वं पश्चाद्धोमं समापयेत् ॥ ५१५ ॥
वारुण्यादे: प्रधानार्थहोमो नास्तीति भाषितम् ।
अपक्वे पक्वहोमश्च विहितोऽत्रापि विद्यते ॥ ५१६ ॥
ऋद्धिवाचनपर्यन्तं तत: पुण्याहवाचनम् ।
कृत्वा संप्रोक्ष्य तूष्णीं त्रि: स्थालीपाकमथाचरेत् ॥ ५१७ ॥
आघारवानपूर्वो वा तत्रापूर्वो[10] निबध्यते ।
ज्वलयित्वा परिस्तीर्य प्रणीतारहितं तु यत् ॥ ५१८ ॥
हविरासादनान्तं तत्सर्वं कृत्वा यथाविधि ।
गन्धपुष्पैरलंकृत्य मन्त्रवत्परिषिच्य च ॥ ५१९ ॥
असंख्यातसमिद्धोमं कृत्वा हुत्वा च चक्षुषी ।
'अग्निर्मूर्धे'त्यनुद्रुत्य[11] 'भुव' इत्यादिना तत: ॥ ५२० ॥
अवदाय [12]चरोर्हुत्वा पूर्वोक्तविधिना तथा ।
[13]'हव्यवाहा'दिमन्त्राभ्यां हुत्वा स्विष्टकृतं चरुम्॥ ५२१ ॥

१.M विच्छेदादश्मशा°. २.M नाम्. ३.M °च्चयम्. ४.M °पद्मजम्. ५.T °न्यस्य. ६.M °वृक्षस्समु°. ७.M °यित्वोपरि°. ८.M व्रातापद्याद्व, T प्रातापव्याश्च° but corrected as प्राजापत्याश्च. ९.M वा. १०.M तत्राप्तव्ये. ११.T °श्रत्य. १२.M परो हु°. १३.M हव्यव्यवाहा°.

हुत्वास्य जुहुयान्मिन्दाहुती व्याहृतिपश्चिमम्[१] ।
मन्त्रवत्परिषिच्याथ दत्त्वा गां ब्रह्मणे[२] ततः ॥ ५२२ ॥
ऋत्विजे दक्षिणां दद्याद्यदि[३] कर्ताऽपरो[४] भवेत् ।
ब्रह्मोपवेशनं चात्र [५]पृथङ्नेच्छन्ति[५] पण्डिताः ॥ ५२३ ॥
अन्यत्रापूर्विके पक्षे ब्रह्मणो[६] नोपवेशनम् ।
सभार्यो यदि गच्छेत[७] गृहाद् देशान्तरं ततः ॥ ५२४ ॥
अग्निं प्रज्वाल्य समिधि पालाश्यं मन्त्रमुच्चरन्[८] ।
त्रिः समारोप्य तेनैव सह गच्छेत्समाहितः ॥ ५२५ ॥
यदि पत्नी गृहे साद्याद्धोमाद्यन्येन कारयेत् ।
इष्टं देशं समागम्य[९] शुचौ देशे यथाविधि ॥ ५२६ ॥
उद्धत्य स्थण्डिलं प्रोक्ष्य विप्रागारादिसंभवम् ।
आधाय वह्निं प्रज्वाल्य समिधं तत्र निक्षिपेत् ॥ ५२७ ॥
'आजुह्वोद्बुध्य'मन्त्राभ्यां स्वाहाकारान्तमुच्चरन्[१०] ।
अमेध्यादेरुपस्पर्शे पावमानं[११] समाचरेत् ॥ ५२८ ॥
अग्निं प्रज्वाल्य समिधि समारोप्य यथाविधि ।
भस्माग्निमुद्धता त्यक्त्वा शकृता[१२] परिलिप्य च ॥ ५२९ ॥
अग्निमाधाय समिधमादध्यात्तां समन्त्रकम् ।
प्रज्वाल्यग्निं परिस्तीर्य व्याहृत्यन्तं यथाविधि ॥ ५३० ॥
उक्तमग्निमुखं कृत्वा पश्चाच्च[१३] जुहुयात्ततः ।
'अग्न आयूँषि' मन्त्राभ्यां पवमानाग्नये[१४] तथा ॥ ५३१ ॥
'अग्ने पावक'मन्त्राभ्या'मग्नये पावकाय' च ।
'अग्निः शुचि'रु'दग्ने'ति द्वाभ्यां च[१५] शुचयेऽग्नये ॥ ५३२ ॥
हुत्वा स्विष्टकृतं हुत्वा पश्चाद्धोमं समापयेत् ।
आपूर्विकविधानेन कुर्याद्वासमुदीरितम् ॥ ५३३ ॥

१.T व्याहृ°. २.T ब्राह्मणे. ३.M दद्यादभि. ४.M कर्ता broken. ५-५.M पृथक् गच्दन्ति. ६.M ब्राह्मणो. ७.M नच्छेत. ८.M °च्चरेत्. ९.M समानम्य. १०.M स्वाहाकारं तमुच्चरेत्. ११.M वाचमानं. १२.T शकृदा. १३.M पक्वाच्च. १४.M °मानग्नये. १५.M द्वश.

[१]पूर्णाहुतिरशक्तौ स्यात् [२]स्रुवाहुतिरथापि वा ।
सर्वेष्वग्न्युपघातेषु 'पुनस्त्वे'ति समिन्धनम् ॥ ५३४ ॥
विहितं देशकालादिसमीक्ष्यैतत्समाचरेत् ॥ ५३४क ॥
विहायाग्निं सभार्यश्चेत् सीमामुल्लंघ्य[३] गच्छति ।
होमकालव्यपेतस्य[४] पुनराधानमिष्यते ॥ ५३५ ॥
प्रोषिते तु यदा पत्नी यदि ग्रामान्तरं व्रजेत् ।
होमकाले यदि प्राप्ता न सा दोषेण युज्यते ॥ ५३६ ॥
तथैव तत्र वसति होमकालव्यतिक्रमे ।
[५]लौकिकोऽग्निर्विधीयेत काले श्रुतिदर्शनात् ॥ ५३७ ॥
यावत्यो ग्राममर्यादा नद्यो वा तद्व्यतिक्रमे[५] ।
तावेवान्वारभेयातामन्यथा लौकिको भवेत् ॥ ५३८ ॥
कृत्वा विवाहं सहितः पत्न्या देवव्रतानि च ।
चरित्वाथ चतुर्थेऽह्नि होमं कृत्वा यथाविधि ॥ ५३९ ॥
'अभि त्वे'त्यादिना कल्पविहितं गमनं च यत् ।
कृत्वोर्ध्वं ब्रह्मचारी स्यात् संवत्सरमतः परम् ॥ ५४० ॥
ऋतुकाले यथाम्नातं गमनं च समाचरेत् ।
यावद्वा पुष्पसद्भाव ऋतुकालः पुरैव तु ॥ ५४१ ॥
संवत्सरादृतौ तन्वीं स्त्रियं गच्छद्यथाविधि ॥ ५४१क॥

इति सङ्गमग्रामवासिमिश्रविरचिते नारायणीये
वाधूलगृह्यागमवृत्तिरहस्ये
प्रथमोध्यायः

१.M पूजा°. २.M स्रुता°. ३.M °मुल्लच्य. ४.M होमव्यालल्यवेतस्य. ५-५.M om; T काके.

अथ द्वितीयोऽध्यायः

[ऋतुसंवेशनम्]

ऋतौ संवेशनं यत्तु गमनं पुत्रसिद्धये ।
ऋतुसंवेशनं तत्स्यादृतुरत्राभिधीयते ॥ १ ॥
रजोदर्शनमारभ्य कालः षोडश रात्रयः ।
ऋतुसंज्ञो भवेत्तत्र नारीणां गर्भसिद्धितः ॥ २ ॥
ऋतुः स्वाभाविकः स्त्रीणां रात्रयः षोडश स्मृताः ।
चतुर्भिरितरैः सार्धमहोभिः सद्विगर्हितैः ॥ ३ ॥
त्रिरात्रादूर्ध्वमेवर्तुमेतमिच्छन्ति केचन ।
सहवासस्पर्शनादेर्निषेधाद् गत्यसंभवात् ॥ ४ ॥
त्रिरात्राभ्यन्तरे चापि प्रायश्चित्तविधानतः ।
यावद्वा पुष्पमित्युक्तेः परतो गमने[1]ऽसति ॥ ५ ॥
त्रियहे पर्युपेते[2] तामित्यादिवचनान्न तत् ।
युज्यते मानवे चापि चतुर्भिः[3] सद्विगर्हितैः ॥ ६ ॥
इत्यस्माद् गर्हितत्वेन चतूरात्रं निषिध्यते ।
त्रिरात्रादूर्ध्वमेवैष इति वक्तुं न शक्यते ॥ ७ ॥
रजःसंबन्धमेवास्या गमनप्रतिषेधतः ।
रजस्युपरते साध्वी स्नानेन स्त्री रजस्वला ॥ ८ ॥
स्त्रियः पवित्रमतुलं नैता[4] दुष्यन्ति[5] कर्हिचित् ।
मासि मासि रजो ह्यासां दुष्कृतान्यपकर्षति ॥ ९ ॥
रजस्तत्राशुचिकरं तच्च पुंसि न विद्यते ।
सहासनादिसकलं प्रतिषिध्य श्रुतावपि ॥ १० ॥
अन्नमेव निषिद्धं तदभ्यञ्जनमितीरितम् ।
अभ्यञ्जनं च गमनं वाक्यशेषानुसारतः ॥ ११ ॥

१.T °मने सति. २.T पर्यपेते. ३.M चतुर्थः. ४.M नैत. ५.दूष्यन्तु.

मलवद्वाससं यां चेत्यत्रापि मलवच्छ्रुतेः ।
गर्हितं स्याच्चतूरात्रं पुष्पसंभावतः परम् ॥ १२ ॥
रजोनिवृत्तिसिध्यर्थं शुद्धवासश्च मन्त्रवत्[1] ॥ १२क ॥
मानवे रात्रिवचनान्निषिद्धं गमनं दिवा ।
न[2] दिवा[2] मैथुनं कुर्यादित्यादि श्राद्ध उच्यते ॥ १३ ॥
रजस्वला चतुर्थेऽह्नि स्नानाच्छुद्धिमवाप्नुयात् ।
चतुर्थीप्रभृतीत्यादेश्चतुर्थ्यां गमनं स्मृतम् ॥ १४ ॥
रजोनिवृत्तावेव स्यात्तथात्रापि प्रतीयते ।
नैतच्छलं[3] [4]गर्हितत्वाद्वर्जयेदित्यपि स्मृतेः ॥ १५ ॥
तासामाद्याश्चतस्रस्तु निन्दितैकादशी च या ।
त्रयोदशी च शेषास्तु प्रशस्ता दश रात्रयः ॥ १६ ॥
युग्मासु पुत्रा जायन्ते स्त्रियोऽयुग्मासु रात्रिषु ।
तस्माद्युग्मासु[5] पुत्रार्थी [6]संविशेदार्तवे स्त्रियम् ॥ १७ ॥
रात्रौ चतुर्थ्यां पुत्रः स्यादल्पायुर्धनवर्जितः ।
पञ्चम्यां पुत्रिणा नारी षष्ठ्यां पुत्रस्तु मध्यमः ॥ १८ ॥
सप्तम्यामप्रजा योषिदष्टम्यामीश्वरः सुतः ।
नवम्यां सुभगा दारा दशम्यां च वरः पुमान् ॥ १९ ॥
एकादश्यामधर्मा स्त्री द्वादश्यां पुरुषोत्तमः ।
त्रयोदश्यां सुता[7] तस्य तस्य वर्णसंकरकारिणी ॥ २० ॥
धर्मध्वजः कृतज्ञः स्यादात्मवेदी दृढव्रतः ।
प्रजायते चतुर्दश्यां गुणौघैर्जगतां[8] पतिः[8] ॥ २१ ॥
राजपत्नी महाभागा राजवंशगताऽथवा ।
जायते पञ्चदश्यां तु बहुपुत्रा पतिव्रता ॥ २२ ॥

१.M मन्त्रतुजाः. २-२.M यदि वा. ३.M च्छठंत्तं. ४.M गर्हित्वाद्व°. ५.MT om. ६.MT om सं; M wrongly adds स्त्रियं for सं. ७.M सुसुता. ८-८. M जगतः पतिम्.

विद्यालक्षणसंपूर्णः सत्यवादी जितेन्द्रियः ।
आश्रयः सर्वभूतानां षोडश्यां जायते पुमान् ॥ २३ ॥
स्त्रियाः शुक्रेऽधिके स्त्री स्यात्पुमान्पुंसोऽधिके भवेत् ।
तस्माच्छुक्रविवृद्ध्यर्थं वृष्यं स्निग्धं च भक्षयेत् ॥ २४ ॥
लघ्वाहारां स्त्रियं कुर्यादेवं संजनयेत्सुतम् ।
पित्र्यं पौष्णं नैर्ऋतं वापि[१] पक्षं[१] ...... ॥ २५ ॥
त्यक्त्वा[२] नारीं सुप्रसन्नां प्रसन्नां[३] पृष्ठदक्षिणाम् ।
पुत्रकामोऽभिगच्छेत् सल्लक्षण्यं पुत्रमाप्नोति ॥ २६ ॥
[४]अष्टमीयुगलं पर्वद्वयं जन्मत्रयं तथा ।
चतुर्दशी [५]पुनस्तद्वद्दृतावपि निषिध्यते ॥ २७ ॥
यथोक्तेऽस्मिन् शुभे काले रात्रौ पुण्याहवाचनम् ।
कृत्वाग्निमुखपर्यन्तं होमं कृत्वा यथाविधि ॥ २८ ॥
[६]'नेजमेषे'ति मन्त्राभ्यां हुत्वा चैवाहुतिद्वयम् ।
जयादिसकलं होम[७]मन्नपक्वसमन्वितम् ॥ २९ ॥
कृत्वा स्थालीगतं शिष्टमाज्यांशं[८] प्राशयेत्स्वयम्[९] ।
मन्त्रं पठंस्ततो भुक्त्वा तत्समीपे स्वयं ततः ॥ ३० ॥
गत्वा च'मूहं' मन्त्रेण समाहूय सुसंस्तृते ।
शयने शयितां भार्यामुत्तानां संविशेत्ततः ॥ ३१ ॥
'आ ते योन्या'दि मन्त्रेण कल्पोक्तविधिना ततः ।
[१०]प्राणः प्राप्तौ मुखेनास्याः स्वमुखं सन्निधाय च ॥ ३२ ॥
[११]त्रिरभिप्राणनं कुर्यान्मन्त्रैः कल्पसमीरितैः ।
'संयुध्यन्तमसौ' स्थाने तस्या[१२] नामकमुच्चरन्[१३] ॥ ३३ ॥

१-१.MT broken after वापि पक्षं (T वा विचर्क्ष). २.MT त्यक्त्वा for गत्वा. ३.T broken after प्रसन्नां. ४.MT add (T in bracket) पुत्रम् before अष्टमी (M मि). ५.M युगस्तद्वदृता च वि नि°. ६.M नौज°. ७.M होमन्त्र्य, T °मन्स. ८.M °माज्यतां. ९.M प्राशय°. १०.M प्राणः, T प्रा... ११.M त्रिरद्भिः. १२.M तस्यां. १३.M नाम तमुच्चरेत्.

ऋतुसंवेशनाङ्गत्वं[1] मन्त्राणां कल्पकृन्मतम्[2] ।
तत्र ह्यृतुमतीमेनां संविशेदित्युदीरितम् ॥ ३४ ॥
मन्त्रसामर्थ्यमप्यत्र युज्यते ह्यृतुसंगतौ[3] ।
गर्भप्रसवशङ्कादौ तत्स्थैर्याद्यर्थवर्णनात् ॥ ३५ ॥
ऋतुमत्या विवाहस्य निन्दितत्वं स्मृतावपि ।
प्रदानं प्रागृतोः कार्यं प्राग्वासो बोधतोऽपि च ॥ ३६ ॥
प्रयच्छेन्नग्निकां कन्यामृतुकालभयात्पिता ।
ऋतुमत्यां हि तिष्ठन्त्यां दोषः पितरमृच्छति ॥ ३७ ॥
अपि चेह विवाहस्य कल्पोक्तस्यानुवादतः ।
तदूर्ध्वं यद् गृहस्थस्य कार्यं तदुपदिश्यते ॥ ३८ ॥
[अथ][4] विवाहशेषत्वमत्रोक्तस्यावगम्यते ॥ ३८क ॥
पुष्पसद्भावतश्चोर्ध्वं राग[5]प्राप्ते च संगमे ।
काल्पिकं गमनं तत्र कुर्यादिति नियम्यते ॥ ३९ ॥
तत्रानुक्तविधिं कालविशिष्टं समुदीर्य च ।
कल्पोक्तेन प्रकारेण संवेशनमनूद्यते ॥ ४० ॥
कुर्यात्संवेशनं चेति तस्मादेवं[6] समञ्जसम् ।
चतुर्थ्यां पक्वहोमं[7] स्यादुपसंवेशनं तथा ॥ ४१ ॥
इति बोधायनेनोक्तमाचार्येणापि वर्णितम् ।
दर्विहोमश्चतुर्थेऽह्नि गमनं चात्र सूचितम् ॥ ४२ ॥
ततः संवत्सरं नेति ततः शब्दप्रयोगतः ।
प्रागृतोर्गमने प्राप्ते निषेधोऽप्युपपद्यते ॥ ४३ ॥
ऋतावेव यतः कल्पे गमनं समुदीरितम् ।
उपस्थस्पर्शनस्यापि गत्यर्थत्वं समञ्जसम् ॥ ४४ ॥
क्षतयोनित्वसिध्यर्थमुपस्थस्पृष्टिरीरिता ।

१.MT त्व°. २.M मतः. ३.M संगतः. ४.MT broken. M, however, does not show the sign of broken text. ५.M चोर्ध्वं..न. ६.M °देवमसम°. ७.M °होम.

सति दृष्टेन चादृष्टमिह कल्पयितुं क्षमम् ॥ ४५ ॥
सर्वत्र गम्यमानञ्चाप्यानन्तर्यमथेति यत् ।
अविरोधेन तत्त्याज्यमन्यथा तन्निरर्थकम् ॥ ४६ ॥
संवत्सरं द्वादशाहमहोरात्रमितीरितम्[१] ।
मैथुनप्रतिषेधे च समावर्तनकर्मणि ॥ ४७ ॥
विवाहानन्तरं चातो गमनं कल्पकृन्मतम् ।
'आ ते योन्या'दिमन्त्राणामिहानुक्तेः[२] प्रयोजने ॥ ४८ ॥
विवाहे वचनस्यापि चिन्त्यमानेऽवगम्यते ।
विवाहाङ्गं च गमनं मन्त्रेणैव भवेदिति ॥ ४९ ॥
ऋतुमत्याश्च गमनं विवाहे समुदीरितम् ।
सर्वेष्वृतुषु मन्त्रेण संवेशनविधित्सया ॥ ५० ॥
एनां [३]संविशेदित्येवमनुक्त्वा प्रति संविशेत् ।
इति प्रतीति वीप्सा च मन्त्रावृत्तौ समञ्जसम् ॥ ५१ ॥
एतद् व्याख्यानसमये वृत्तिकारेण वर्णितम् ।
सर्वेष्वृतुषु मन्त्रेण प्रथमं गमनं त्विति ॥ ५२ ॥
तथा संवेशनं चैवेत्यवधारणमन्त्रवत् ।
ऋत्वन्तरेषु होमस्य[४] निवृत्त्यर्थं तदिष्यते ॥ ५३ ॥
विवाहवत्स्त्रियश्चासौ संस्कारत्वोपपत्तितः ।
[५]सर्वगर्भोपकारित्वं न्यायतो[६] युज्यते यतः ॥ ५४ ॥
आधास्यमानस्य गर्भस्य संस्कारोऽयं न युज्यते ।
विद्यमानस्य संस्कारः सर्वत्र ह्युपपद्यते ॥ ५५ ॥
आनर्थक्यं कदापि स्यात् गर्भानुत्पत्तितोऽपि च ।
स तु कारणमेवातो न्यायप्राप्यानुवादतः[७] ॥ ५६ ॥
[८]द्योतयत्येवकारोऽत्र तदेव वृत्तिकृन्मतम् ।

१.T °महोरात्रे इती°. २.T °हाद्युक्तेः. ३.M संविशदि° T समविशः. ४.M होमेषु.
५.M °गर्भोपभावित्व. ६.M ह्यायते. ७.M °प्राप्तानु°. ८.M दद्यातयत्ये°.

वचनानां च सर्वेषामपि विधौ[१] भवेत्तथा ॥ ५७ ॥
बोधायनेन विहितं [२]मन्त्रवद् गमनं सदा ।
यच्चादौ गमनं तद्वदृतौ यद् गमनं भवेत् ॥ ५८ ॥
तदेतन्मन्त्रतः कुर्यादिति शालीकिसंमतिः[३] ।
अतो यथोक्त एवार्थ इत्येतदिह निश्चितम् ॥ ५९ ॥
भगाभिमर्शनं त्वत्र[४] प्रकृतार्थत्वान्निवर्तते ।
एवमुक्ते शुभे काले सर्वेष्वृतुषु मन्त्रतः ॥ ६० ॥
प्रथमं हृष्ट एवैनां हृष्टां गच्छेदतन्द्रितः ।
अनेकभार्यो गच्छेत्[५] [..................] ॥ ६१ ॥
[......][६] मृतूनां चेद् ग्रहणं[७] क्रमशो व्रजेत् ।
[..][८] पूर्वं पुत्रिण्यो यदि काश्चन ॥ ६२ ॥
न[९] चैतस्यां[१०] समुत्पाद्यः[११] पुत्रः[१२] तेन वृत्तिकृन्मतम्[१२] ।
स्त्रिया तयाधिकारो हि न्यायतो गृहिणः समम् ॥ ६३ ॥
बह्वपत्यतासिध्यर्थं जातपुत्रोऽप्यृतौ व्रजेत् ।
'भवासि[१३] माता[१४] पुत्राणां जातानां जनयासि च' ॥ ६४ ॥
'दशास्यां पुत्रानाधेहि पतिमेकादशं कृधि' ।
'सा प्रसूर्धेनुकें'त्येवमादि मन्त्रानुसारतः ॥ ६५ ॥
अशून्योपस्थता[१५] लिङ्गमन्यत्राप्यवगम्यते[१६] ॥ ६५क ॥
एष्टव्या[१७] बहवः पुत्रा यद्येकोऽपि गयां व्रजेत् ।
गौरीं वा वरयेत्कन्यां नीलं[१८] वा वृषमुत्सृजेत् ॥ ६६ ॥
अनृतावपि गच्छेत स्त्रीकामात्तद्वरः[१९] श्रुतेः[१९] ।
स्वदारनिरतत्वेन रक्षणं च भवेत्स्त्रियाः ॥ ६७ ॥

१.M °मपिधो, T °षाम..विधौ. २.M मन्त्रवत्. ३.M संमितिः. ४.T चात्र. ५.MT broken after गच्छेत. ६.MT broken before मृतूनां. ७. ग्रहण. ८.MT broken before पूर्वं. ९.M om. १०.MT चैतस्यात्. ११.M °पाद्य, T °पाद्यं. १२-१२.M पुत्रन्तेनकृन्मतं. T पुत्रं तेन.... १३.M मासि, T भासि. १४.T मातासि. १५.M °पस्थका°. १६.M °द्यव°. १७.M adds बहव्या between एष्टव्या and बहवः. १८.MT नीलव्या°. १९-१९.M °कामात्तद्वदाश्रिते.

स्वां प्रसूतिं चरित्रं च कुलमात्मानमेव च ।
स्वं च धर्मं प्रयत्नेन [१]जायां रक्षन् हि[१] रक्षति ॥ ६८ ॥
ऋतुकालाभिगामी स्यात् स्वदारनिरतः सदा ।
या[२] स्यादनतिचारेण रतिः सा धर्मसंश्रिता ॥ ६९ ॥
रतिपुत्रफला नारीत्येवमादि स्मृतावपि ।
नातिप्रसङ्गः कर्तव्यः[३] कामात्मत्वनिषेधतः ॥ ७० ॥

[गृहीतगर्भायाः कर्तव्यम्]

विधानतो नियोगेन गमनं समुदीरितम् ।
गर्भाधानाख्यसंस्कारः प्रथमो मनुजस्य सः ॥ ७१ ॥
आधीयमानगर्भस्य मन्त्रसाध्यस्य संस्कृतिः ।
उपपन्ना तथा वेदे मन्त्रसामर्थ्यलिङ्गतः ॥ ७२ ॥
'एतस्य यजुषो वीर्येणे'त्यादेरर्थवादतः ।
स्मृतिष्वपि च संस्कारेष्वस्य[४] प्राथम्यमुच्यते ॥ ७३ ॥
वैदिकैः[५] कर्मभिः पुण्यैर्निषेकादिर्द्विजन्मनः ।
कार्यः शरीरसंस्कारः पावनः[६] प्रेत्य चेह च ॥ ७४ ॥
गर्भे गृहीते नार्या यत्[७] कर्तव्यं वर्ज्यमेव यत् ।
पुराणादिषु निर्दिष्टं तच्च लेशेन[८] वर्ण्यते[९] ॥ ७५ ॥
सद्योगृहीतगर्भायाः[१०] श्रमो[११] ग्लानिः[१२] प्रवासया[१३] ।
सक्थ्योः संसादनं योनिस्फुरणादि भवेत्ततः ॥ ७६ ॥
नावस्करेषूपविशेन्मुसलोलूखलादिषु ।
जलं च नावगाहेत शून्यागारं[१४] च वर्जयेत् ॥ ७७ ॥
वल्मीकं नाधितिष्ठेत न चोद्विग्नमना भवेत् ।
न नखैर्विलिखेद् भूमिं नाङ्गारेण[१५] न भस्मना ॥ ७८ ॥
[१६]न शयालुः सदा तिष्ठेद् व्यायामं च विवर्जयेत् ।

१-१.M जयं रक्ष हि. २.M दास्यादीनति°. ३.M कर्तव्या. ४.T संस्कारैर्यस्य. ५.MT वैदिके. ६.M प्रापनं, T पावनं. ७.M नार्या यं, T नार्या यः. ८.T पेशेन. ९.T वत्स्यते. १०.MT °या. ११.M सद्यो. १२.M °निं. १३.M विवा°. १४.M शून्या नारं. १५.M ना गारेण. १६.M om.

न तुषाङ्गारभस्मास्थिकपालेषु समाविशेत् ॥ ७९ ॥
वर्जयेत्कलहं लोके गात्रभङ्गं तथैव च ।
न मुक्तकेशी तिष्ठेत्तु नाशुचिः स्यात्कदाचन ॥ ८० ॥
न [१]शयीतोत्तरशिरा न चैवाधःशिराः क्वचित् ।
न वस्त्रहीना नोद्विग्ना न चार्द्रचरणा[२] सती ॥ ८१ ॥
नामङ्गल्यं वदेद्वाक्यं न [३]दन्तास्याधिका भवेत् ।
कुर्याच्छ्वशुरयोर्नित्यं[४] पूजां[५] मङ्गल्यतत्परा ॥ ८२ ॥
तिष्ठेत् प्रसन्नवदना भर्तुः प्रियहिते रताः ।
सन्ध्यायां नैव भोक्तव्यं वृक्षमूलं च वर्जयेत् ॥ ८३ ॥
सर्वौषधिभिर्वोष्णेन[६] वारिणा स्नानमाचरेत् ।
कृतरक्षा सुभूषा च [७]वास्तुपूजनतत्परा ॥ ८४ ॥
दानशीला तृतीयायां पार्वत्यानक्तमाचरेत् ।
इतिवृत्ता भवेन्नारी विशेषेण तु गर्भिणी ॥ ८५ ॥
यस्तु तस्या भवेत्पुत्रः [८]शीलायुर्वृद्धिसंयुतः ।
अन्यथा गर्भपतनमवाप्नोति न संशयः ॥ ८६ ॥
व्यवसायं चाति[९]तृप्तिं [१०]रात्रिजागरणं यतः[११] ।
[१२]यानारोहं दिवास्वप्नं[१२] कुक्कुटासनमेव च ॥ ८७ ॥
वेगस्य धारणं चैव[१३] शोणितस्यापि[१४]मोक्षणम् ।
वर्जयेद् गर्भिणी नित्यं गर्भापायनिवृत्तये ॥ ८८ ॥
गृहनिर्माणमुदधिस्नानं[१५] चौलं[१६] सुतस्य च ।
न कुर्याद् दूरयात्रां च गर्भिणी गृहिणी यदि ॥ ८९ ॥
क्षौरं श्मशानगमनं [१७]नखकृन्तनमेव च ।

१.M शमितो°. २.M °चरणादिभिः. ३.M चन्तास्य°, T one syllable broken before न्तास्य°. ४.M कुर्याच्चिशुरयो नि°. ५.M पूजा. ६.M °स्तोष्णेन, T °षधीभिस्तोष्णेन. ७.M वास्त°. ८. M शिला°. ९.M चापि. १०.T रात्रिं. ११.T broken. १२-१२.M नारौ हरि वा स्वप्नं, T यारौहरिवास्वप्नं. १३.M broken. १४.M °तस्याविमो°. १५.M °दधिस्स्ना°. १६.M चो.... १७.M नवकृ°.

अन्तर्वत्न्यां पतिः कुर्वन्नप्रजो[१] भवति ध्रुवम् ॥ ९० ॥
वहनं दहनं चैव शवानुगमनं तथा ।
अन्तर्वत्न्यां च जायायां न कुर्वीत विचक्षणः ॥ ९१ ॥
मातामह्यां पितामह्यां मातुले पूर्वजे मृते ।
गुरुश्वश्रुरपत्नीषु गर्भवानपि वाहयेत्[२] ॥ ९२ ॥
ज्येष्ठस्य [३]चानपत्यस्य मातुलस्यासुतस्य च ।
अपुत्रस्य पितृव्यस्य श्वसुरस्याप्यसन्ततेः ॥ ९३ ॥
भ्रुवक्षिकोष्ठलोमानि वर्जयित्वा शिखामपि ।
केशान्निवापये[४]त्पित्रोर्मरणे गर्भवानपि ॥ ९४ ॥

[पुंसवनम्]

व्याध्यरुच्या[५]दिभिर्लिङ्गैर्गर्भोत्पत्तिः सुनिश्चिता[६] ।
तदा द्वितीयं संस्कारं कुर्यात्पुंसवनं तदा ॥ ९५ ॥
तृतीये मास एवैतद् व्यक्तता प्रायशो भवेत् ।
अतस्तृतीयमासे तत् कार्यमित्येतदीरितम् ॥ ९६ ॥
स्पन्दनाच्च पुरा कैश्चित् पुंजन्म[७] समुदीरितम् ॥ ९६ क ॥
पुष्यनक्षत्र एवैतदनापदि समाचरेत् ।
आपदि श्रवणे वापि[८] शास्त्रान्तरविधानतः ॥ ९७ ॥
पुन्नक्षत्रेष्वपि तथा कर्मैतज्ज्योतिरीरितम् ।
संस्कारोऽप्यवधानेन गर्भस्यैष समीरितः ॥ ९८ ॥
विद्यमानस्य गर्भस्य [९]पुंस्त्वापादकताऽस्य हि ।
कृत्वा यवेन पुल्लिङ्गं [१०]प्राशयेदिति वक्ष्यति ॥ ९९ ॥
[११]अत आवृत्तिरेवास्य[११] सर्वगर्भेषु युज्यते ।
'पुंसां बहूनां स्यामें'ति स्त्रीफलत्वाद्बहुश्रुतेः ॥ १०० ॥

१.M °व्रजो. २.M वाचयेत्. ३.M चोन°. ४.MT °न्निवाप°. ५.T व्याध्यरु..दिभि..ङ्गै :. ६.M °ताः. ७.M पूजेन्मनमु°. ८.M चापि. ९.M स्त्वावार°, T °स्त्वापद°. १०.M प्राश्रये°. ११-११.M अतन्त्रवृत्ति°.

सकृच्च[१] संस्कृता नारी सर्वगर्भेषु संस्कृता ।
इत्यादिवचनाच्चास्य सकृत्कारणमेव चेत् ॥ १०१ ॥
नैतदाचार्य एवात्र व्यक्ते गर्भ इति ब्रुवन् ।
गर्भसंबद्धमेवेदं[२] कर्म ज्ञापयति स्वयम् ॥ १०२ ॥
अन्यथाऽव्यक्तगर्भाया इत्यवक्षत्तथाख्यया ।
गर्भसंबद्धमेवैतं स्त्रीफलत्वं च युज्यते ॥ १०३ ॥
अधिकारो[३] यतः पित्रोः प्रजोत्पत्तिविधानतः ।
भवानींगतभाव[४]त्वमित्यादौ च बहुश्रुतेः[५] ॥ १०४ ॥
तथा प्रथमगर्भाया इति सीमन्त उच्यते ।
अतः सर्वेषु गर्भेषु कर्मैतत्स्यादिति स्थितम् ॥ १०५ ॥
पुण्याहवाचनं कृत्वा चरुमुत्पाद्य[६] पूर्ववत् ।
व्यावृत्यन्तं[७] कर्म कृत्वा चरोः स्रुच्यवदाय च ॥ १०६ ॥
'प्रजापते' च[८] तनुवो हुत्वा स्विष्टकृदादिकम् ।
पश्चाद्धोमं समाप्यास्याः पाणौ[९] दक्षिण एव च ॥ १०७ ॥
माषद्वयं मुष्कबुध्या निधायाथ तदन्तरा ।
यवः पुल्लिङ्गबुध्यैव निधाय[१०] दधिसंयुतम् ॥ १०८ ॥
'सहस्रशीर्षे'त्येतयर्चा[११] तां[१२] प्राशयेत्ततः ।
[१३]आचान्तायामाज्यशेषं संयुतं [१४]हुतशेषतः ॥ १०९ ॥
[१५]चरोस्तत्प्राशयेन्मन्त्रैश्चतुर्भिः स पृथक्पृथक् ।
पाणिप्रक्षालनं चास्याः[१६] प्राशने पृथगिष्यते ॥ ११० ॥
शिष्टं चरुं ततोऽश्नीयात् सैव पत्नीति गम्यते ।
एकया जुहुयाद्दर्वीहोमं कुर्यादिति श्रुतेः ॥ १११ ॥
एकया दर्विहोमेषु होमोऽस्तीत्यवगम्यते ।
अतः पुरोनुवाक्यार्थं मन्त्रावृत्तिः पुरेरिता[१७] ॥ ११२ ॥

१.M समुच्च. २.T °मेवैदं. ३.M अप्रकाशो. ४.M broken between भाव and इत्या° and T between भवानीं and मित्य°. ५.T °श्रुतम्. ६.M चरुमुक्त्वाद्य. ७.M व्यावृत्यं तत्. ८.M व. ९.M वरणौ. १०.M °सिससं°, T नधायद्धीसं°. ११.M °त्येतत् यच्च, T °यर्च्चा. १२.T ताः. १३.M आवान्तायामाज्यशेषा. १४.T इत°. १५.M चरोस्ताः प्रा°. १६.MT चास्यां. १७. M परैरिता, T परे°.

नेह ग्राह्या यथापाठं होम एवात इष्यते ।
[1]गर्भप्रस्रवशङ्कायां यत्कर्तव्यं तदुच्यते ॥ ११३ ॥
शुष्कगोमयपिण्डान्स्त्रीनग्नावादीप्य भस्म यत्[2] ।
कांसादौ तन्निधायाद्भिरभ्यानीय[3] च पाययेत् ॥ ११४ ॥
'अस्थाद् द्यौ'रिति[4] मन्त्रेण गर्भस्थैर्यप्रसिद्धये ।
अन्यच्च लोकशास्त्रेषु गर्भस्थैर्यादिसिद्धये ॥ ११५ ॥
यत्प्रसिद्धं समुद्दिष्टं तच्च[5] कुर्यात्तथैव च ॥ ११५क ॥
भोजनादौ विशेषेण रुचिर्यस्मिन्भवेत्स्त्रियाः ।
भिषक्शास्त्रानुसारेण तच्च दातव्यमेव हि ॥ ११६ ॥

[सीमन्तोन्नयनम्]

गर्भोत्पत्तिं समारभ्य चतुर्थे मास एव तु ।
सीमन्तोन्नयनं कुर्याद् गर्भिण्याः[6] संस्कृतिं ततः॥ ११७ ॥
न च गर्भस्य संस्कारो व्यवधानादयं भवेत् ॥ ११८ ॥
स्त्रिया [7]विशिष्टावयवः सीमन्ताख्यः[8] प्रसिद्धितः ।
तस्योर्ध्वनयनं चापि प्राधान्येन[9] विधीयते ॥ ११९ ॥
यतः प्रथमगर्भायाः स्त्रिया एव विधीयते ।
'कल्याण्यविधवे'त्यादिमन्त्रलिङ्गोपपत्तितः ॥ १२० ॥
स्त्रीसंस्कारनिमित्तत्वं गर्भोत्पत्तेश्च युज्यते ।
सीमन्तिनीति ह्याख्या च स्त्रिया एव[10] समञ्जसम् ॥ १२१ ॥
गर्भसंस्कारकत्वं च सीमन्तोन्नयनस्य तु ।
स्त्रीद्वारेणैव स्मृत्युक्तं विवाहादिवदेव तत् ॥ १२२ ॥
सकृत्संस्कृतसंस्काराः सीमन्तेन द्विजस्त्रियः ।
यं यं गर्भं प्रसूयन्ते स सर्वः संस्कृतो भवेत् ॥ १२३ ॥
मासश्चतुष्प्रकारः स ज्योतिःशास्त्रे समीरितः ।

१.T °प्रसव°. २.T तत्. ३.T °धायाभि°. ४.M अस्थाभ्योरिति. ५.M adds तां after तच्च. ६.MT गर्भिण्यां. ७.T स्त्रियोपि शि°. ८. MT °ख्य. ९.T प्राधेन्येन. १०.T एवं.

सौर्यः सार्धदिनस्त्रिंशत्त्रिंशदेव तु सावनः ॥ १२४ ॥
नक्षत्रमासो विज्ञेयः कृत्स्नो नक्षत्रपर्ययः ।
अहर्द्विषष्टिभागोनः[1] सौर्यादुद्धृत्य पार्वणः ॥ १२५ ॥
पुंनक्षत्र इदं कार्यं पूर्वपक्ष इति स्मृतिः ।
सवेनापि समुद्दिष्टमेतच्च स्पन्दिते शिशौ ॥ १२६ ॥
प्राग्वैतत्प्रसवात्कार्यमिति शास्त्रान्तरेष्वपि ।
कालान्तरेषु निर्दिष्टमापद्येव[2] समाचरेत्[3] ॥ १२७ ॥
सीमन्तोन्नयने[4] चौले विवाहे स्नानकर्मणि ।
उपनीतौ च कुर्वीत श्राद्धं गोदानकर्मणि ॥ १२८ ॥
कृत्वा नान्दीमुखं श्राद्धं कृत्वा पुण्याहवाचनम् ।
शम्याकारांश्च परिधीन् समुत्पाद्याथ[5] पूर्ववत् ॥ १२९ ॥
कृत्वाग्निमुखपर्यन्तं[6] चरोः स्रुच्यवदाय च ।
'धाता प्रजाया' हुत्वाऽन्या आज्येन जुहुयात्ततः ॥ १३० ॥
'सिनीवाली'ति वैका स्याद् 'यासुपाणि'रितीतराः ।
आहुतीर्द्वादशाज्येन हुत्वा स्विष्टकृदादिकम् ॥ १३१ ॥
अन्त्य[7]पक्वविहीनं च पूर्ववद्धोममाचरेत् ॥ १३१क ॥
शल्यपृष्ठसमुद्भूता सूच्यग्रा शललीर्यते[8] ।
सा च त्रिषु प्रदेशेषु श्वैत्या[9] त्रैणीति कीर्त्यते ॥ १३२ ॥
यवैर्विरचिता माला यवस्रगिह कथ्यते ॥ १३२क ॥
अपरेण ततोऽग्निं प्राङ्मुखीं पत्नीं निवेश्य तु[10] ।
उदुम्बरभवां शाखां दर्भांस्त्रीञ्छललीं[11] स्रजा ॥ १३३ ॥
संबध्य मूलदेशेन तेषां तस्य ललाटतः ।
उपर्यारभ्य मन्त्राभ्यामाशिरो मध्यतः सकृत् ॥ १३४ ॥
अन्ते विभज्य केशाँस्तान्शाखादींस्तत्र निक्षिपेत् ।
प्रतिच्छाद्य ततः [12]केशैर्यवैस्तान्शिरसि स्पृशेत् ॥ १३५ ॥

१.M °षष्टिर्भागोनः. २.M द्येवं. ३.M स्वमा°. ४.M नयन. ५.M समुत्वद्या°. ६.M पर्यन्तमा. ७.T युञ्ज्य. ८.M °वीर्यते, T °वीर्यभे. ९.T श्वैका. १०.M त. ११.MT त्रिञ्जललीं. १२.M कोशैर्जपै°, T केशैर्जपै.

'इत्याहु'रिति[१] मन्त्रस्यावयवोऽत्र[२] निगद्यते ।
[३]'विवृत्तचक्रास्तीरेण' [४]नदीत्यादि तवा'न्तिकम्[५] ॥ १३६ ॥
हुत्वाऽपनीय[६] शाखादीन् विस्रस्यैनां स्रजं ततः ।
गर्भिण्या दक्षिणे हस्ते तया[७] बध्नाति[८] मन्त्रतः ॥ १३७ ॥
[९]यस्या नद्याः[९] समीपेऽस्य होमस्य करणं भवेत् ।
तस्या नद्या नाम मन्त्रे त्वसौ स्थाने विनिर्दिशेत् ॥ १३८ ॥
संबुध्यन्तं यथा 'गङ्गे तवे'त्यादि प्रयुज्यते ।
अक्षरार्थः समासेन गृह्यस्येहाधुनोच्यते[१०] ॥ १३९ ॥
चतुर्थे मासि कर्तव्यं सीमन्तोन्नयनं स्त्रियाः ।
[११]आवापाहुतयस्तस्य सीमन्तोन्नयनस्य ताः ॥ १४० ॥
वक्ष्यन्त इति शेषात्र धानाद्या ऋत एव याः ।
ताभिरेताः[१२] सुसंपाद्याः[१३] पूर्वोक्ताहुतयो यथा ॥ १४१ ॥
चरोर्द्वे आहुती हुत्वा प्रथमे आज्यतोऽपराः ।
हुत्वाहुतीस्ततः कृत्वा पश्चाद्धोमं यथाविधि ॥ १४२ ॥
त्रेणिमित्यादि सकलं यथाविधि समापयेत् ।

[विष्णुबलिः]

गर्भाष्टमे बलिं विष्णोर्मासे कुर्यादनन्तरम् ॥ १४३ ॥
शुक्लपक्षे शुभे काले रोहिण्यां श्रवणेऽथवा ।
द्वादश्यां वाथ सप्तम्यामेतत्कर्म विधीयते ॥ १४४ ॥
पुण्याहवाचनं कृत्वा प्रणीताप्रणयान्तिकम् ।
कर्म कृत्वा गृहे वह्नेर्दर्भान् संस्तीर्य तेष्वथ[१४] ॥ १४५ ॥
वैष्णवीं प्रतिमां प्रत्यङ्मुखीं लक्षणलक्षिताम्[१५] ।
निवेश्य पीठमिष्ट्वा तु समावाह्य[१६] जगत्पतिम् ॥ १४६ ॥

१.T °हुतिरिति. २.M स्यापय गोत्र. ३.MT विविक्तगर्भास्तौ°. ४.MT नन्दी°. ५.T भवा°. ६.M हुत्वोप°. ७.T मया. ८.M मथ्नाति, T मथ्नाभि. ९-९.MT यद्यानस्याः°. १०.M °धुरोच्य°. ११.MT आवावाहु°. १२.M °रेतां. १३.MT सुसंवाद्यां (T द्या). १४.M तेऽन्त्यथ. १५.M लक्षणपक्षि°. १६.M समा...न्य.

अष्टाक्षरेण मन्त्रेण[१] दर्वी[२]संमार्जनादिकम् ।
परिधीनां[३] निधानान्तं कर्म कृत्वा ततो हरिम् ॥ १४७ ॥
[४]अर्चयेद्विष्णुसूक्तेन यथान्यैश्च जलादिभिः[५] ।
ततः पुष्पाञ्जलिं कृत्वा सूक्तेनाष्टाक्षरेण च ॥ १४८ ॥
[६]केशवादिभिरन्यैश्च नामभिर्नमसान्वितैः ।
मन्त्रवत्परिषिच्याग्निमुखं कृत्वा यथाविधि ॥ १४९ ॥
'विष्णोर्नुकं' 'तदस्येति' 'प्र तद्विष्णुस्तवा'पि[७] च ।
'विचक्रमे' च 'त्रिर्देव'[८] इत्येतद्विष्णुसूक्तकम् ॥ १५० ॥
'त्रेधोरुगाय' इत्यन्तः प्रथमस्य मनो[९] भवेत् ।
आज्यस्यैतेन सूक्तेन दर्व्या हुत्वा यथोदितम् ॥ १५१ ॥
अन्त्यपक्वान्वितं सर्वं पश्चाद्धोमं समाप्य च ।
देवस्यापरतो दर्भेष्वेतेन हविषा बलिम्[१०] ॥ १५२ ॥
निवेद्य रूपं[११] सूक्तेन स्वाहान्तेन पृथक् पृथक् ।
[१२]दत्त्वाष्टाक्षरमन्त्रेण भूयो दत्त्वा यथाविधि ॥ १५३ ॥
पूजां समापयेन्नित्यमेतत्कर्म विधानतः ।
अस्य गर्भार्थता शास्त्रे कर्मभिः[१३] समुदीरिता ॥ १५४ ॥
प्रतिगर्भं भवेत्तस्मादेनदित्यवधार्यते ।
अष्टमे मासि गर्भस्य रक्षा कार्या विशेषतः ॥ १५५ ॥
अस्मिन्मासे विनाशोऽस्य शास्त्रान्तरसमीरितः[१४] ।
पुनर्गर्भं पुनर्धात्रीमोजस्तस्य प्रधावति ॥ १५६ ॥
अष्टमे मास्यतो गर्भो जातः प्राणैर्वियुज्यते ।
अतः कल्याणकर्माणि गर्भरक्षार्थमाचरेत् ॥ १५७ ॥
चिरं[१५] यदि विजायेत तत्रोपायोऽधुनोच्यते ।
शीघ्रप्रसवसिध्यर्थमद्भिः संपूर्य चाञ्जलिम् ॥ १५८ ॥

१.M मनुगा, T मनुना. २.M दर्वि°. ३.M परिधीगान्नि°. ४.M अव्यये°, T व्य corrected as र्च. ५.M यथान्यौञ्जला°, T यथान्येनज्जलि°. ६.M केशान्तादि°. ७.M चेमापि. ८. MT चतुर्देव. ९.T मनोर्भ°. १०.T बलिः. ११.T रूपस्सू°. १२.M दत्वाष्टारम°. १३.M कर्म, T text after कर्म broken. १४.M °रिता. १५.T गिरं.

'दशमासाञ्छशयान' इति मन्त्रं समीर्य च ।
निनीय[1] तस्याः शिरसि क्षिप्रमेव विजायते ॥ १५९ ॥
न [2]जरायुर्बहिर्गच्छेत्तत्राप्येवं[2] समाचरेत् ।
'न मांसेष्वि'ति मन्त्रोऽत्र [3]प्रथमे वाभ्युपैति तत्[3] ॥ १६० ॥

[जातकर्म]

यदि जातः पुमान् गर्भो जातकर्म तदाचरेत् ।
स्त्रीजन्मनि न कुर्वीत पुमांसं जनयेद्यदि ॥ १६१ ॥
इति कल्पकृता कर्म स्त्रिया एतन्निषिध्यते ।
मानवे पुंस इत्यस्य पुमर्थत्वं प्रतीयते ॥ १६२ ॥
अवधार्य सुतं जातं पिता स्नानं समाचरेत् ।
[4]एतन्नैमित्तिकं स्नानं रात्रावपि विधीयते ॥ १६३ ॥
रात्रिस्नाने तु संप्राप्ते स्नायादनलसन्निधौ ।
स्नात्वा सचेल[5] आगत्य विघ्नेशाराधनादिकम् ॥ १६४ ॥
कृत्वाथाभ्युदयश्राद्धं रात्रावपि समाचरेत् ।
द्रव्यालाभे द्विजालाभे प्रवासे पुत्रजन्मनि ॥ १६५ ॥
होमश्राद्धं प्रकुर्वीत यस्य भार्या रजस्वला ।
दैववत्सकलं कुर्याद्युग्मांश्च[6] द्विजसत्तमान् ॥ १६६ ॥
द्वे दैवे[7] पितृकार्ये तु द्वौ चत्वारः समास्तथा ।
सकुल्या अपि गृह्णीयुरस्मिन् श्राद्धे तथा स्मृतेः ॥ १६७ ॥
जाते कुमारे तदहः कामं कुर्यात्प्रतिग्रहम् ।
[8]हिरण्यधान्यगोवासस्तिलान्नगुडसर्पिषान् ॥ १६८ ॥
अत्र सर्वं प्रतिग्राह्यं कृतान्नं तु विवर्जयेत् ।
भक्षयित्वा [9]तु तन्मोहात्[9] द्विजश्चान्द्रायणं चरेत् ॥ १६९ ॥
सर्वेषां च सकुल्यानां[10] द्विपदश्च चतुष्पदः ।

१.M puts निनीय between समीर्य and च. २-२.M °युर्विच्छेत्तत्राह्येवं. ३-३.M प्रमेवाम्यवैतित्, T प्रथमेपाम्युपैति तत्. ४.T एकं. ५.M सचे°लं आ°. ६.M द्युमाश्च. ७.M दैवेऽपि. ८.M दानं. ९-९.M कृतन्मो°. १०.M सकल्या°.

हिरण्यं धान्यमित्येतद्दद्यादित्यपि च स्मृतिः ॥ १७० ॥
[१]एतच्छ्राद्धादिसकलं नाभिच्छेदनतः पुरा ।
कर्तव्यं तदहर्वेति विकल्पेन समीरितम् ॥ १७१ ॥
आशौचे तु समुत्पन्ने पुत्रजन्म यदा भवेत् ।
[२]कर्तुस्तात्कालिकी शुद्धिः पितुरित्यपि च स्मृतिः ॥ १७२ ॥
सूतीगृहं[३] प्रविश्याथ हस्ताभ्यां जातमुद्धरेत् ।
उपविश्य तमुत्सङ्ग आधाय तदुपस्थितिम् ॥ १७३ ॥
'अङ्गा"दश्मे'ति[४] मन्त्राभ्यां 'यं दिवि[५] स्वि'त्यनेन च ।
कृत्वा 'ब्रह्मे'ति संप्रोक्ष्य[६] मुखमस्य ततः परम् ॥ १७४ ॥
तूष्णीमङ्गानि चान्वीक्ष्य विप्रेभ्यो दानमाचरेत् ।
स्वर्णपिष्टसमायुक्तं मध्वेनं[७] प्राशयेत्ततः ॥ १७५ ॥
पञ्चभिः पञ्चभिर्दर्भैर्विषूच्यग्रैः[८] सकृत् सकृत्[८] ।
[९]यत्राग्रदर्भमेतेषां[९] तैरग्रैः [१०]प्राशयेन्मधु ॥ १७६ ॥
'मधुषो वाच'मित्यादि मध्वादायाथ 'भूर्ऋचाम्'[११] ।
[१२][इत्याधाय रसं यया त्वमधि] मेधया'[१३] ॥ १७७ ॥
अमुमित्यत्र नक्षत्रनाम निर्दिश्य कृत्तिकम् ।
'आ विशे'ति द्वितीयान्तं यथानक्षत्रमादिशेत् ॥ १७८ ॥
रौहिणं रैवतं ज्यैष्ठं[१४] माघं[१५] चैत्रं [१५]च श्रावणम् ।
प्रोष्ठपादं मार्गशीर्षं तथैवाश्वयुजं[१६] मतम् ॥ १७९ ॥
[१७]तद्वस्य शातभिषजं[१७] तथापभरणं[१८] भवेत् ।
आर्द्रकं[१९] मूलकं तद्वदनूराधं च फल्गुनम्[२०] ॥ १८० ॥

१.MT °च्छास्त्रादि°. २.M °स्तां कालि°. ३.M व्रतीगृ°. ४.M अङ्गाजश्मेति, T अङ्गाज्जश्मेति. ५.M यं... स्वित्य°, T यंदि स्वित्य°; Text not clear. ६.T संप्रोक्ष्य. ७.M मुध्वैनं. ८-८.M पृथक् पृथक्. ९-९.M यत्राग्रत्रमे°, T यत्राग्र..मे°. १०.T प्राशयन्म°. ११.M भूरुचा, T भू. चा. १२.MT broken; cf. Vâdhús 15.19.1. १३.T समेधया. १४.M ज्येष्ठं. १५-१५.M broken between माघं [M मखं] and च; T broken between ज्यैष्ठं and च. १६.M °वश्व°. १७-१७.M तद्वस्याश्चातभिषजं, T तद्वस्याश्चभिषजं. १८.MT तथावभर°. १९.T शूद्रकं. २०.M फाल्गुनम्.

आषाढं च तथा स्वातिं विशाखं च पुनर्वसुम् ।
अनूराधं[१] च हस्तं च पुष्यमाश्लेषमेव च ॥ १८१ ॥
श्रविष्ठामिति मन्त्रेषु प्रयुक्तिरिह कल्प्यताम् ॥१८१क ॥
रोरेममृज्येचिषु[२] वृद्धिरादौ [३]ष्ठात्पे च वान्त्यश्रवशाश्वयुक्षु[३] ।
शेषेषु नाम्वोः[४] कपरः[५] स्वरोन्त्यः स्वाप्वोरदीर्घः[६] सविसर्ग इष्टः ॥ १८२ ॥
चतुर्ष्वपि च[७] मन्त्रेषु 'यया त्वम'नुषज्यते ।
चतुर्भिः प्राशयित्वैनं [८]कुमारं तु[८] प्रदाय च ॥ १८३ ॥
'प्रक्षालयस्व' संप्रेष्य तस्मिन्प्रक्षालिते शिशौ ।
स्तनौ दर्भेण[९] संस्पृश्य जनन्याः प्राशयेच्छिशुम् ॥ १८४ ॥
'अहं कुमार' मन्त्रेण चा'वेहि [१०]निऋते'त्यपि ।
शयितस्य कुमारस्य पूर्वभागे निहन्त्यथ ॥ १८५ ॥
औदुम्बरीं फलवतीं स्थूणां मन्त्रेण तां पुनः ।
स्नात्वैवैतन्निहननमिति वृत्तिकृतोदितम् ॥ १८६ ॥
कृतकार्योऽथ सन्ध्यायां जंभभैषज्यमाचरेत् ।
गृहाङ्गणे[११] प्राङ्मुखस्य तिष्ठन्नेकं कपालकम् ॥ १८७ ॥
प्राच्यां दिशि बहिरन्यदेवं[१२] दक्षिणतस्तथा ।
पश्चिमायामुत्तरायामूर्ध्वायां दिशि तद्धतिम् ॥ १८८ ॥
तत्तदाशामुखः कृत्वा समाचम्य विधानतः ।
आधायाग्निं शोभयित्वा समूह्य परिषिच्य च ॥ १८९ ॥
फलीकृतीर्नवे पात्र उपस्तीर्णाभिघारिताः ।
निक्षिप्य कृत्वा पर्यग्नि गन्धाद्यैरग्न्यलंकृतिम् ॥ १९० ॥
मन्त्रवत्परिषेकं च कृत्वैकां समिधं ततः ।
आधायाश्वत्थपात्रेण मन्त्रैः स्वाहासमन्वितैः ॥ १९१ ॥

१.T आनूराधं; M आराधं. २.M °मृज्येष्वपि. ३-३.M ष्मालवेव वाज्यश्रवशाश्च युक्षु, T षाल्लोपवाज्यश्रवशाश्वयुक्षु. ४.M नाभ्यः, T नाभ्योः. ५.M कवरः. ६.MT स्वाच्चोरदीर्घः. ७. M om. ८-८.M कुमाराय. ९.M दर्भौ. १०.M निरुते°. ११.MT गृहाङ्क्णे. १२.T बहिर्न-देवं.

पञ्चभिर्जुहुयादेता मन्त्रवत्परिषेचनम् ।
कुर्यादेवं दशाहं च सायं प्रातः समाचरेत् ॥ १९२ ॥
अहन्येकादशे चापि प्रातः कर्मैतदिष्यते ।
[1]जंभभैषज्यमित्यादेर्जातरक्षार्थमीरणात् ॥ १९३ ॥
कर्मासङ्करसिध्यर्थादेवातः शब्दवादतः ।
स्थूणादिहननं युक्तं ततः प्राशनतः परम् ॥ १९४ ॥
गृह्योक्तक्रममुल्लंघ्य[2] जातकर्म समीरितम् ।
क्रमप्राप्तस्य[3] कल्पे च[4] वचनस्य प्रयोजनम् ॥ १९५ ॥
पुत्रार्थता विवाहादेरित्येतदवगम्यते ।
तदनन्तरमेवातो यत्कर्तव्यं तदुच्यते ॥ १९६ ॥

[नामकरणम्]

सूतीगृहात्समुत्थाप्य कुमारं यत्र नामनी[5] ।
निदध्यात्कर्म [6]तज्ज्ञेयमुत्थानवदशब्दितम्[7] ॥ १९७ ॥
जननाद्दशरात्रे समतीते[8] तदिहेष्यते ।
व्युष्टे तु[9] दशरात्रे [10]तन्नाम कुर्यादिति स्मृतेः ॥ १९८ ॥
अहन्येकादशे नाम द्वादशाहनि[11] वा शुभे ।
काले स्मृत्यादिविहिते तत्र पुण्याहवाचनम् ॥ १९९ ॥
कृत्वाग्निमुखपर्यन्तं होमं कृत्वा यथाविधि ।
'प्रजापते न त्वदि'ति 'रयीणां पतिं'मित्यपि ॥ २०० ॥
'प्रजापते त्वं निधिपा''स्तवेमे' च 'प्रजापतिम्' ।
'यो राय' इति मन्त्रैस्तैः प्राजापत्यैरमानसैः ॥ २०१ ॥
हुत्वाज्यं होमशेषं[12] चाप्यन्त्यपक्वसमन्वितम् ।
कृत्वा कुर्वीत पुण्याहवाचनं[13] स्वस्तिवाचनात् ॥ २०२ ॥
पूर्वं तद्विहितं कृत्वा चोदकुंभेऽन्यधारिते ।

१.MT दंभ°. २.M °कर्म उल्लंघ्य. ३.T क्रमः प्रागस्य. ४.M om. ५.M नामनि. ६.MT तद् ज्ञेयं. ७.M °शब्दितः. ८.M °त्रेऽनुमिमीते. ९.M oms. १०.M तु नाम. ११.MT द्वादशान्यत्र. १२.M नामशेषं. १३.M °वचनं.

पुत्रमादाय तस्याथ दक्षिणे श्रवणे[1] पिता[1] ॥ २०३ ॥
एकाक्षरं द्व्यक्षरं वा चतुरक्षरमेव वा ।
नाम कृत्वा गुह्यमेव मात्रे विज्ञाप्य तत्पुनः ॥ २०४ ॥
अन्यन्नाम चतुर्थ्यन्तं तथा शर्मपदान्वितम् ।
'आ॰ कृष्णशर्मणे स्वस्ति भवन्तोऽपि[2] ब्रुवन्तु' च ॥ २०५ ॥
इत्याद्युक्त्वा प्रदायैनं कुंभमादाय पूर्ववत् ।
ऋद्धिं च वाचयित्वैनानुपविश्याथ सज्जलैः ॥ २०६ ॥
तूष्णीं त्रिः प्रोक्ष्य चादाय सुतं तद्दक्षिणश्रुतौ ।
संबुध्यन्तं नाम वदेत् स्वस्तिवाचन ईरितम् ॥ २०७ ॥
'पिता माता च दधतुर्नामे'ति श्रुतिलिङ्गतः ।
देवताकुलनक्षत्र[3]संबद्धं नाम तत्पिता ॥ २०८ ॥
करोतीति स्मृतेश्चापि [4]पितैवैतत्समाचरेत् ।
असंभवेऽन्यकर्तृत्वं[5] न दोषाय तथा स्मृतेः ॥ २०९ ॥
अन्यो वा कुलवृद्धस्तन्नाम कुर्यादितीरितम् ।
गुह्यपूर्वं तदित्युक्त्वा यथैषां गुह्यमित्यपि ॥ २१० ॥
उक्तं सन्निहितैर्विप्रैर्नाम न ज्ञायते यथा ।
गुह्यपूर्वं ततः कुर्यान्मात्रा सह पिता ततः ॥ २११ ॥
[6]न वैषामेव[6] गुह्यत्वं ब्राह्मणानां विवक्षितम् ।
एवं हि वचनं[7] चेदं गुह्यपूर्वं निरर्थकम् ॥ २१२ ॥
माता पिता च विद्यातां[8] तदोपनयनादिति ।
स्मृतिरप्येतमेवार्थं दृढयत्यत्र संशये ॥ २१३ ॥
घोषाक्षराद्यनाम स्यादन्तःस्थामध्यसंयुतम्[9] ।
विसर्जनीयान्तगतमिति शास्त्रान्तरोदितम् ॥ २१४ ॥

[जन्मनक्षत्रेष्टिप्रयोगः]

दर्विहोमविधानेन नक्षत्रेष्टिर्विधीयते ।

१-१.M °णेऽपि ताः. २.T भवन्तो हि. ३.M नक्षत्रं. ४.MT पित्रैवैत°. ५.M °भवेन्नकर्तृतां. ६-६.MT नवेषा°. ७.MT वलनं. ८.M विद्यातन्. ९.MT °स्था मध्य°.

कुमारजन्मनक्षत्रे[१] तत्प्रयोगोऽधुनोच्यते ॥ २१५ ॥
पुण्याहं वाचयित्वाग्निमुखं कृत्वा यथाविधि ।
'अग्निर्मूर्धा' 'भुव' इति मन्त्राभ्यां पक्वमादितः ॥ २१६ ॥
[२]हुत्वा जन्मर्क्ष[२]मन्त्राभ्या'मनुनोऽद्या'ऽ'न्विद'त्तथा[३] ।
हुत्वा स्विष्टकृतं कृत्वा स्वस्थान उपहोमकाः ॥ २१७ ॥
यथर्क्षमीरितैर्मन्त्रैः कृत्वा 'चन्द्रमसे'ऽपि च ।
'प्रतीदृश्या'दिभिर्मन्त्रैर्मासान्ते मासिके ततः ॥ २१८ ॥
ऋत्वन्तैर्वत्सरादर्वाग्वत्सरान्तैश्च वत्सरैः[४] ।
हुत्वा 'वास्तोष्पतीयादि' होमशेषं समापयेत् ॥ २१९ ॥
पौर्णमास्या अभिजितोऽमावस्यायास्तथा पृथक्[५] ।
ऋक्षत्वाभावतस्तासां ग्रहणं नेह विद्यते ॥ २२० ॥
नक्षत्रदेवताहोमावित्यनक्षत्रजस्य तु ।
प्राचीनावीतिना कार्यश्चरोरन्यत्तु दैववत् ॥ २२१ ॥
संवत्सरे व्यतीते तु जन्मनक्षत्र एव च ।
'नवो नवो'ऽनुवाकोक्तैः[६] [७]प्रथमान्तैर्यथाक्रमम् ॥ २२२ ॥
मन्त्रैः पूर्ववदिष्टेऽग्नौ होममानुमतादिकम् ।
कृत्वोपहोमान्कुर्वीत 'चन्द्रमावा'नुवाकगैः ॥ २२३ ॥
ततो 'वास्तोष्पतीया'दि होमशेषं समापयेत् ।
नक्षत्रहोमं नामेदमायुष्यं कर्म वर्णितम् ॥ २२४ ॥

[आयुष्यचर्वाख्यकर्म]

कर्माथायुष्यचर्वाख्यं प्रसङ्गादधुनोच्यते ।
दुर्निमित्तेषु दृष्टेषु सर्वेषु मृतिहेतुषु ॥ २२५ ॥
तद्दोषशान्तये कार्यमिदं कर्म तथोदितम् ।
दुर्दर्शनं विनाप्येतदायुष्याद्यर्थमादरात् ॥ २२६ ॥

१.T कुमारज...क्षत्रे. २-२.M कृत्वा जनुषम°. ३.M °न्विद्रत्तथा. ४.M वत्सरे. ५.M wrongly puts पृथक् in the beginning of the 3rd pada. ६.MT नवोनवारवाकोक्तैः. ७.M प्रथदन्तै°.

जन्मर्क्षे च विशेषेण कर्मायुष्यं समाचरेत् ॥ २२६क ॥
दर्पणादावुपाधौ स्वौ चाक्षुषौ पुरुषौ यदि ।
न दृश्येतेऽ[१]चिरादेव म्रियते स न संशयः ॥ २२७ ॥
दृष्टयोः शिरसी यस्य न दृश्येते म्रियेत सः ।
उदङ्मुखं शशं चन्द्रे प्राङ्मुखं यदि पश्यति ॥ २२८ ॥
इत्यन्तं प्रेत इत्येतं विद्यादित्यनुषज्यते ।
व्यवधानेऽपि चैतस्य सामर्थ्यमत्रगम्यते ॥ २२९ ॥
दिवासीत्सङ्गतः पृथ्वी[२] विरहे ते[३] परस्परम् ।
व्यवहृत्य विनिश्चित्य पृथिवी हृदयं स्वकम् ॥ २३० ॥
दिविस्थे चन्द्रमस्येतददधा[४]त्कृष्णमत्र यम् ।
[५]प्लाक्षनिर्झरमूलात् समारभ्योत्तरतो भुवि ॥ २३१ ॥
प्रादेशमात्रे हृदये पूषाख्या[६] द्यौस्तथा भवेत्[७] ॥ २३१क ॥
वेदे [८]वास्ते [८]स्वहृदये तयोर्यस्तस्य नेहतुः ।
भवत्यकाले मरणमग्नेर्हेत्यादि पूर्ववत् ॥ २३२ ॥
आयुर्वृद्धिसमर्थेऽस्मिन् वेदनेऽभिहिते पुनः ।
[९]पुंसर्गस्याभिधानेन मृतिहेत्वभिधानतः ॥ २३३ ॥
आयुर्वृद्धिफलं कर्म साङ्गमत्राभिधीयते ।
प्राणघोषश्रुतिस्तत्र महदुक्थस्य शंसनम् ॥ २३४ ॥
तमोवृतं यदा वस्तु[१०] वर्षास्ववगतास्वपि ।
इत्यादि सर्वमत्रोक्तं[११] समालोच्यावधार्यताम् ॥ २३५ ॥
साग्निरौपासने कुर्यात्कर्मैतल्लौकिके परम्[१२] ।
आज्यमित्यादि संप्रेष्य परिधानात्पुरोदितम् ॥ २३६ ॥
कृत्वा तिरःपवित्रं ताः कमण्डलुभवा अपः ।
पीत्वा पुरुषमन्त्रेण समाप्याचमनं ततः ॥ २३७ ॥

१.M दृश्येत चि°, T दृश्यते चि°. २.T पृथ्वि. ३.M विरहेत्वे, T विरहेतो. ४.M °तददधस्तात्कृ°. ५.M प्लाक्षंनिञ्छर°. ६.M पूषाख्यां, T चूषाख्यां. ७.T दध्यात्. ८-८.M वास्तोष्प ह°. ९.M पुंसर्गास्या°. १०.M मस्तु. ११.M सर्वमन्त्रोक्तं. १२.T परः.

व्याहृत्यन्तं कर्म कृत्वा जुहोत्याज्येन रीतिशः ।
पक्वाद्धुत्वा[1] स्विष्टकृतं हुत्वा होमं समाप्य च ॥ २३८ ॥
उपस्तीर्णे च कंसादौ यावदर्थं समुद्धृतम् ।
अभिघार्य चरुं तत्र कर्तं श्लक्ष्णं विधाय च ॥ २३९ ॥
च्छायादर्शनयोग्येऽस्मिन् बह्वाज्यमुपसिच्य तु ।
'यन्मे मनः परे'त्यादिनाज्ये स्वात्मानमीक्षते ॥ २४० ॥
'अश्मेवे'त्यादिभिर्मन्त्रैस्तस्मात्संप्राश्य सप्तभिः ।
आचम्य दद्यात्तच्छिष्टं ब्राह्मणाय प्रियाय तु ॥ २४१ ॥
यद्याज्यस्थं स्वमात्मानं न पश्येत्तं चरुं तदा ।
प्राश्नीयात्कृत्स्नमेतस्मिन् [2]पक्ष्येऽन्यस्मै न दीयते ॥ २४२ ॥
स्थालीगतं च यच्छिष्टं प्रियेभ्यस्तत्प्रदीयते ।
तृणपाणिरथात्माख्यं हृदयं [3]संस्पृशञ्जपेत् ॥ २४३ ॥
अनुषङ्गश्च कर्तव्यो मन्त्रेष्वत्र प्रदर्श्यते ॥ २४३क ॥
श्रितः प्राणः श्रितं[4] चक्षुः श्रितं[5] श्रोत्रं श्रितं[6] मनः ।
श्रितं[7] रेतश्च हृदये[8] श्रिता लोमान्यतत्वरम् ॥ २४४ ॥
श्रितं[9] शरीरं हृदये श्रितो मूर्धा श्रितं[10] बलम् ।
श्रितो मन्युः श्रित आत्मा हृदये हृदयमपि ॥ २४५ ॥
अथोत्थाय[11] रविं भूय उपस्थायोपविश्य च ।
उपस्पृश्याथ हस्ताभ्यां तप्ताभ्यां भस्मना सह ॥ २४६ ॥
शरीरव्यापकं कुर्यात् त्रिवारं[12] दर्भसंयुतम् ॥ २४६क ॥

[निष्क्रमणम्]

जन्मारभ्य चतुर्थेऽथ मासे निष्क्रमणं गृहात् ।
पूर्ववत्सकलं कृत्वा वाचःस्थाने यथोदितः ॥ २४७ ॥
स्वस्तिसूक्तेन हुत्वाज्यं होमशेषं समाप्य च ।
रात्रिर्बन्धुः[13] सवित्रादि[14] मात्रादिभिर्ज्ञातिभिः सह ॥ २४८ ॥

१.M पक्वाहुत्वा. २.T वक्ष्ये. ३.M सस्पृश°. ४.M श्रितश्च°. ५.M श्रिता. ६.T श्रितो. ७.M श्रिता. ८.M °दयं, T °दयः. ९.MT श्रिता. १०.M श्रितो. ११.M अथ...त्थाय. १२.M श्रीवारं. १३.T रातिसन्धुः. १४.T सवित्रादिमाता°.

अलङ्कृतकुमारस्य[1] कटिसूत्राद्यलंकृतिः ।
कृत्वा स्वस्त्ययनं विप्रैर्जपद्भिर्मङ्गलान्वितम्[2] ॥ २४९ ॥
शिशुं प्रवास्य स्वगृहात्पुण्यवृक्षप्रदक्षिणम् ।
समाचारानुसारेण कृत्वा स्वगृहमानयेत् ॥ २५० ॥

[अन्नप्राशनम्]

षष्ठे मासि शुभे काले वत्सरे वा यथास्मृति ।
आशिषो वाचयित्वाऽग्निमुखं हुत्वा[3] यथोदितम् ॥ २५१ ॥
'अहमस्म्या'दिभिर्मन्त्रैरष्टाभिः [4]प्रत्यृचं घृतम्[4] ।
हुत्वा जयादिकं होमं कृत्वा स्वस्त्ययनं ततः ॥ २५२ ॥
ऋध्यन्तं वाचयित्वाऽन्नं तूष्णीं संप्रोक्ष्य तज्जलैः ।
शुचौ देशे पिता[5] मध्ये मङ्गलादिसमन्विते ॥ २५३ ॥
उपविश्य शिशुं स्नातमलंकृत्योपवेश्य च ॥ २५३क ॥
आहृतं काञ्चने भाण्डे समाचारानुसारतः[6] ।
अन्नं दध्ना घृतेनापि मधुना विषमेण तु ॥ २५४ ॥
संयुज्य मन्त्रैः षड्भिस्तं प्रत्यृचं प्राशयेद्यथा ।
[7]'या जाता' इत्यनुद्रुत्य[7] 'भूर्भुवः सुव'रित्यपि ॥ २५५ ॥
मन्त्रान्ते प्राशयित्वैनं प्रक्षाल्य स्वकरं ततः ।
'शतमि'त्यादिभिर्मन्त्रैरेवं संप्राशयेत्पृथक् ॥ २५६ ॥

[चौलकर्म]

जन्मारभ्य तृतीयेऽब्दे प्रथमे वत्सरेऽपि वा ।
चौलकर्म कुमारस्य कार्यस्तदधुनोच्यते ॥ २५७ ॥
संवत्सरगतैकत्वत्रित्वे अत्र विवक्षिते ।
प्रथमस्य द्वितीयस्य तृतीयत्वं न विद्यते ॥ २५८ ॥
अतस्त्रिष्विति कालस्य तृतीयाब्दत्वसिद्धये ।

१.MT °कृतः कुमारस्य [M °शन्यः]. २.T °लानितम्. ३.T हुत्वा. ४-४.M प्रत्यृचान्वितम्.
५.M तानाध्ये, T विता नाध्ये ६.M समचारा°. ७-७.M यद्भाताइत्य. T याद् भ्राता इत्यनुश्रुत्य.

चूडाकर्म द्विजातीनां सर्वेषामेव धर्मतः[१] ॥ २५९ ॥
प्रथमेऽब्दे तृतीये वेत्येवं मानव ईरितम्[२] ।
किं च संस्कारकर्मत्वादस्यावृत्तिर्न युज्यते ॥ २६० ॥
तच्चान्नप्राशनादूर्ध्वं तदूर्ध्वपठनाद्भवेत् ।
द्वितीये वर्षे कर्तव्यं पञ्चमे वेत्यपि स्मृतिः ॥ २६१ ॥
उद्गते रवौ शुक्लपक्षे पुण्यदिने शुभे ।
पुष्यादौ चौलकर्मेति शास्त्रान्तर उदीरितम् ॥ २६२ ॥

[आभ्युदयिकश्राद्धम्]

पूर्वेद्युस्तद्दिने वापि श्राद्धमभ्युदयात्मकम् ।
कार्यं दैववदेवैतत्तथा च स्मृतिशासनम् ॥ २६३ ॥
पितॄणां [३]रूपमास्थाय देवा अन्नमदन्ति हि[४] ।
अतो यज्ञोपवीतित्वं ब्राह्मणानां च युग्मता ॥ २६४ ॥
विकृतिः पार्वणस्यैतच्छ्राद्धमित्यपि च स्मृतम् ।
आमात्यं संपरिस्तीर्येत्येवमादेरिहोक्तितः ॥ २६५ ॥
अपूर्वता च सर्वत्र[५] कर्मणोऽत्रावगम्यते ।
[६]न चोत्सर्गवदि[७]त्युक्तेर्यावदुक्तमिहेष्यते[७] ॥ २६६ ॥
उत्सर्गवद् वाऽलंकुर्यादित्युक्ते व्रतकर्मणि ।
तद्धर्मस्यातिदिष्टत्वादग्नेरुत्तरभागतः ॥ २६७ ॥
इति देशस्य वचनमाखराणां निवृत्तये ।
प्रागग्रता च दर्भाणां दिगन्तत्वनिवृत्तये ॥ २६८ ॥
एतैरेताभ्य इत्युक्तिस्तद्वैव[८]निवृत्तये ।
ओदनादिनिवृत्त्यर्थं व्रीह्यादिवचनं मतम् ॥ २६९ ॥
तस्मादुत्सर्गवत्सर्वं कल्पनादियथोदितम् ।
संस्तीर्येत्यनुवादोऽत्र [९]कल्पनस्यांगता यतः ॥ २७० ॥

१.T सम्मतः. २.M ईरितः. ३.T तृच°. ४.M नि. ५.M सर्वस्य. ६.M oms. ७-७.M oms. ८.T °स्त...वत°. ९.M कल्पान°.

अत उत्सर्गवत्स्त्रीत्वाद् दुर्गांशेषु बलिं हरेत् ।
द्वौ देवौ ब्राह्मणौ भोज्यौ पित्रर्थे द्वौ समा अपि[१] ॥ २७१ ॥
अभिवाद्य द्विजान्[२] पूर्वं नान्दीमुखवदान्पुरम्[३] ।
श्राद्धे विश्वेभ्य इत्युक्त्वा देवेभ्यः क्षण इत्यपि ॥ २७२ ॥
क्रियतामिति चामन्त्र्य तथेति प्रणवान्वितम् ।
प्रत्युक्तेऽन्यं तथामन्त्र्य पित्रर्थानां निमन्त्रणम् ॥ २७३ ॥
श्राद्धे पितृभ्य इत्येवं कृत्वा तानाचमय्य च ।
आसनेषूपक्लृप्तेषु बर्हिष्मत्सु[४] पृथक् पृथक् ॥ २७४ ॥
प्राङ्मुखानुपवेश्यैनान् 'प्राप्नोत्वि'त्यादि मन्त्रतः ।
उपविष्टान्दैवपूर्वमर्चयित्वा जलादिभिः ॥ २७५ ॥
तिष्ठन्न'ग्नौ करिष्यामी'त्येवं पृष्ट्वा 'कुरुष्व' तैः ।
अनुज्ञातोऽग्निमाधाय लौकिकं तत्परिस्तृतिम्[५] ॥ २७६ ॥
कृत्वा संसाद्य बल्यर्थं गन्धपुष्पाद्युदीरितम् ।
उदुम्बरभवाः[६] काश्चित्[६] समिधः संस्कृतांभसा ॥ २७७ ॥
संप्रोक्ष्याग्निमलंकृत्य मन्त्रवत्परिषिच्य च ।
स्वाहेत्याधाय समिध आज्यलिप्ता यथाविधि ॥ २७८ ॥
परिषिच्योत्तरत्राग्ने[७]'रग्नये कल्पयाम्य'पि ।
'सोमाये'त्यादिभिर्दर्भानास्तीर्याप्तर्पणं ततः ॥ २७९ ॥
अग्निं सोमं तर्पयामि प्रजापतिमतः परम् ।
विश्वान्देवानृषींश्चैव भूतानि च पितृंस्तथा ॥ २८० ॥
सर्वाश्च देवतास्तद्वद्[८] यामीत्येवं करोत्यतः ।
'अग्नये नमः' इत्याद्यैर्गन्धपुष्पफलानि च ॥ २८१ ॥
दत्त्वा व्रीह्यादिपठितं दत्त्वा च[९] तर्पणं ततः ।
कृत्वाऽथ[१०]भोजयेद्विप्रांस्तस्मिन्काले जपेत्स्वयम् ॥ २८२ ॥

१.M oms. २.M द्विजाः. ३.T °मुखपदा°. ४.M बहिवपन्सु. ५.M परिस्मृतिः. ६-६.T भवां कांश्चित्. ७.M सोयेत्या°, T सो येत्यां. ८.M °वतास्तद्वयामी°. ९.M चात्तर्प°. १०.M oms अथ.

'कृणुष्वेन्द्रं व' इत्युपांशु[1] 'ममाग्ने वर्च'[2] इत्यपि ।
पवमानादिकं चापि दर्भपाणिर्जपेदथ ॥ २८३ ॥
तृप्तेषु 'मधु वाता' इत्येकं[3] तृचमुदीर्य च ।
पृष्ट्वा स्वादितमित्येवं दद्यादाचमनं ततः ॥ २८४ ॥
पित्रर्थब्राह्मणोच्छिष्टसन्निधौ तत्र चादितः ।
जलं कृत्वा विकीर्यान्निशेषं[4] दर्भेष्वथोदकम् ॥ २८५ ॥
दत्त्वाऽऽचमय्य सन्त्यज्य तदुच्छिष्टमथांभसा ।
कुंभं संपूर्य विहितं गन्धपुष्पादिसंयुतम् ॥ २८६ ॥
आदाय देवपित्रर्थं[5] ब्राह्मणानां च मध्यतः ।
जानुभ्यामवनिं गत्वा तृणपाणिषु तेष्वपि ॥ २८७ ॥
'प्राङ्मुखे मन' इत्यादि द्वितयं वाचयेत्ततः ।
'नान्दीमुखाश्च पितर' इत्यादि प्रणवानुगम् ॥ २८८ ॥
वाचयित्वा द्विरेतस्मात् कुंभादंभः प्रसिच्य तौ ।
'यथा दिव्येति'[6] मन्त्रेण दत्त्वा तेभ्योऽथ दक्षिणाम् ॥ २८९ ॥
उत्थाप्य पितृपूर्वं तान्प्रदक्षिणसमन्वितः ।
नमस्कृत्य द्विजानेतान् ब्रूयाद् 'दातार' इत्यथ ॥ २९० ॥
आशिषं[7] वाचयित्वाग्निमुखं कृत्वाऽपरास्ततः ।
'ये केशिनो' 'नर्त' इति हुत्वा स्विष्टकृदादिकम् ॥ २९१ ॥
कृत्वाग्नेः पुरतः पर्णेषूदुम्बरभवेष्वपः ।
सकृद्दत्त्वा पक्वशेषान् 'नम'इत्यादिना ततः ॥ २९२ ॥
शतरुद्रीयमन्त्रेण बलिं दद्यान्नमोऽन्वितम्[8] ।
प्रागाननं शिशुं स्वाग्र उपवेश्योप एव च ॥ २९३ ॥
आनीय शीताः उष्णासु गोदाने दक्षिणे शिशोः ।
अद्भिः संक्लेद्य मन्त्रेण समूलानि तृणान्यथ ॥ २९४ ॥
प्रागग्राणि निधायात्र स्वधितिञ्च समन्त्रकम्[9] ।

१.MT °त्याशु. २.T °ग्नेर्मन्व. ३.M इत्येद्यृचमु°, T इत्येकर्त्तृचमु°. ४.MT विदीर्या°. ५.MT °त्रर्थ. ६.MT दिप्यति [T प्या]. ७.M आशिषां. ८.T °न्वितः. ९.T स्वमन्त्रतः, M स्वम°.

प्रोक्ष्यमाणांश्च[१] तान्केशान् 'येनावप'दितीक्षते[२] ॥ २९५ ॥
तिस्रः शिखास्त्र्यार्षेयाणां[३] कुलजानामिहोदिताः[४] ।
पञ्च[५] पञ्चार्षेयाणां यथा[६][र्षमि]त्यादिनोदिता ॥ २९६ ॥
यत्संख्यं वा कुले पूर्वं शिखाकरणमिष्यते ।
तावतीर्वा[७] शिखाः कार्याः स्वमन्त्रेण पृथक् पृथक् ॥ २९७ ॥
दर्भस्तंबे[८] च्छिन्नकेशान्निदध्यान्मन्त्रतस्ततः ।
नापितेन कृते शिष्टवचने हुतशेषतः ॥ २९८ ॥
आज्येनाभ्यज्य चैवैनं मन्त्रेण स्नपयेत्ततः ।
आच्छाद्यैनमलंकृत्य भोजयेद् ब्राह्मणैः सह ॥ २९९ ॥

[विद्यारम्भः]

संप्राप्ते पञ्चमे वर्षे अप्रसुप्ते जनार्दने ।
षष्ठीं प्रतिपदं चैव वर्जयित्वा तथाष्टमीम् ॥ ३०० ॥
रिक्तां पञ्चदशीं चैव सौरभौमदिने तथा ।
एवं सुनिश्चिते[९] काले विद्यारम्भं तु कारयेत् ॥ ३०१ ॥
पूजयित्वा हरिं लक्ष्मीं देवीं चैव सरस्वतीम् ।
स्वविद्यां सूत्रकारांश्च स्वां विद्यां च विशेषतः ॥ ३०२ ॥
एतेषामेव देवानां नामभिर्जुहुयाद् घृतम् ।
दक्षिणाभिर्द्विजेन्द्राणां कर्तव्यञ्चात्र पूजनम् ॥ ३०३ ॥
प्राङ्मुखो गुरुरासीनो वारुणाभिमुखं शिशुम् ।
अध्यापयेत्तु प्रथमं[१०] द्विजान्[११]गीर्भिः[११] स पूजितः ॥ ३०४ ॥
ततः प्रभृत्यनध्यायान् वर्जनीयान्विवर्जयेत् ॥ ३०४क ॥

[स्त्रीसंस्कारः]

उत्थानादिसमुद्दिष्टं चौलान्तं पुरुषस्य यत् ।

१.MT प्रोच्य°. २.M °नावदिन्तिक्षते. ३.MT °शिखास्त्र्या (T °खान्स्त्र्या) र्षेयकुल°. ४.M °नादिहोदिता. ५.M om. ६.MT broken. ७.M तावतिर्वा. ८.M °स्तंभे, T corrected as स्तंबे. ९.M सुनिक्षिते. १०.M प्रथमः. ११-११.T द्विजाशीर्भिः.

स्त्रीणामप्येवमेवैतत् कार्यमित्यतिदिश्यते ॥ ३०५ ॥
उपदेशातिदेशाभ्यां वैलक्षण्यप्रतीतितः ।
पुंल्लिङ्गवर्जनस्यार्थादेव प्राप्तौ च तद्वचः[१] ॥ ३०६ ॥
कुमारदर्शनार्थानां मन्त्राणामूहसिद्धये ।
अतश्च नाम्नि वक्तव्यं स्वस्तिवाचनकर्मणि ॥ ३०७ ॥
अमुष्या इति चौले तु विशेषोऽतः परं भवेत् ।
'पोषेणेमां[२] त्रायस्वैनां'[३] 'मैनां[४] हिंसी'स्तथैव च ॥ ३०८ ॥
'अस्या ऊर्जां' तथैवेमां पौंस्येनेमामिति त्रिषु ।
एक[५] इत्येतत्पक्षत्वं पूर्वोक्तस्याभिधाय तु ॥ ३०९ ॥
[६]मतान्तरमथेत्यादि सूत्रेणानेन वर्ण्यते ।
आवापहोमस्थानीयाः सावित्र्याहुतयो मताः ॥ ३१० ॥
दशभ्य ऊर्ध्वं होमेऽपि न दोष इति गम्यते ।
[७]अपरग्रहणादत्र सावित्री तत्पदादिका[८] ॥ ३११ ॥
[९]पक्वहोमादिसिध्यर्थं प्रसिद्धमिति वर्ण्यते ।
अहोमकर्मणो [१०]मन्त्रप्राप्तस्तूष्णीमितीरितम् ॥ ३१२ ॥
इतिपक्षद्वयं स्त्रीणामाचार्येण समीरितम् ।
तथापि लौकिकाः शिष्टाः स्त्रीणामेतदमन्त्रकम् ॥ ३१३ ॥
अहोमं सर्वमिच्छन्ति शास्त्रान्तरसमाश्रयात् ।
अमन्त्रिका तु कार्येयं [११]स्त्रीणामत्र विशेषतः[११] ॥ ३१४ ॥
संस्कारार्थं शरीरस्य यथाकालं यथाक्रमम् ।
उपदेशातिदेशाभ्यां वैलक्षण्यमिहोदितम् ॥ ३१५ ॥
अहोमकर्मणो मन्त्रवर्जनं च समीरितम् ।
अतः शास्त्रान्तरबलादनुष्ठानं विवक्षितम्[१२] ॥ ३१६ ॥

१.M °यम्ः. २.M पोषणे. ३.M °स्वैना. ४.MT मेनां. ५.T एत. ६.M मातान्त°. ७.T अवर°. ८.M °दिकम्. ९.M पक्वाद्धोमा°, T पश्चाद्धोमा°. १०.T °प्राप्तो तू°. ११-११.M °णामाव्रदशेतः, T broken after स्त्रीणा. १२.MT °क्षिता.

पुण्याहवाचनं स्त्रीणां पुंवदिच्छन्ति पण्डिताः ।
पुण्याहवाचनं कृत्वा भूयः[1] पुण्याहवाचने ॥ ३१७ ॥
गुह्यनाम यथापूर्वं स्त्र्यभिधानं विधाय तु ।
'आयुर्दायै भवन्तो'ऽथ 'स्वस्ती'त्यादि निगद्यते ॥ ३१८ ॥
स्त्रीणां सुखोद्यमक्रूरं[2] विस्पष्टार्थं मनोहरम् ।
मङ्गल्यं दीर्घवर्णान्तमाशीर्वादसमन्वितम्[3] ॥ ३१९ ॥
चौलकर्मणि चाज्याभिलेपनं तु निवर्तते ।
पुंवत्कर्मान्यदुद्दिष्टं मन्त्रहोमविवर्जितम् ॥ ३२० ॥

[स्त्रीपुंसोः साधारणो धर्मः]

अथ साधारणो धर्मः पुंसां स्त्रीणां च वर्ण्यते ।
ज्योतिःशास्त्रोदिते काले वाचयित्वाऽऽशिषो द्विजैः ॥ ३२१ ॥
कण्टकेनापि वा सूच्या कर्णवेधनमाचरेत् ।
उपनीतेः पुरा बालः कामचारी न दुष्यति ॥ ३२२ ॥
अमेध्यदेशगमनेऽस्पृश्यानां स्पर्शनादिषु ।
नाशुचित्वं भवेदन्त्यस्पर्शने स्नानमिष्यते ॥ ३२३ ॥
शूद्रादि[4]भाषणे कामभक्षणेऽपि न दुष्यति ।
[5]महापातकसंबद्धमेतदस्यापि नेष्यते ॥ ३२४ ॥
स्यात्कामचारभक्षोक्तिर्महतः पातकादृते ।
वर्जयेद्ब्राह्मणो[6] नित्यं मद्यमित्याद्यपि स्मृतम् ॥ ३२५ ॥
ब्राह्मण्यमुपनीतस्येत्येतद्वक्तुं न शक्यते ।
ब्राह्मणस्योपनयनं स्मृतौ यस्यां[7] विधीयते ॥ ३२६ ॥
क्रियामयं हि ब्राह्मण्यं नाक्रियो ब्राह्मणो यतः ।
इत्यादिवचनं यत्तत् संस्कृतिस्तुतिसिद्धये ॥ ३२७ ॥
श्रुतौ सृष्ट्यादिवचने ब्रह्मणा[8] जातिसर्जनम् ।

१.M पूयः, T om. २.M द्यमः क्रूरं. ३.M °र्वादानवत्..., T broken after °र्वादा. ४.MT शुक्त्वादि°. ५.M °पातकं बद्धमे°. ६.MT ब्राह्मणे. ७.T यस्या. ८.M ब्राह्मणा, T corrected as ब्रह्मणा.

ब्रह्मणो[१] मुखतोऽप्युक्तं[२] लोकेऽप्यश्वगवादिवत्[३] ॥ ३२८ ॥
ब्राह्मण्यां ब्राह्मणोत्पत्तौ ब्राह्मण्यं प्रथितं तथा ।
उपनीतेः पुरा शूद्रसमस्तं यत्स्मृतौ स्मृतम् ॥ ३२९ ॥
कर्माधिकारविरह[४]ज्ञप्त्यर्थं तत्तथा स्मृतौ ।
[५]वृत्त्या शूद्रसमो ह्येष यावद्वेदे न जायते ॥ ३३० ॥
इति वृत्त्यैव शूद्रेण साम्यं जात्या न तत्ततः ।
ततो द्विजत्ववद्युक्तं ब्राह्मण्यं कर्महेतुकम् ॥ ३३१ ॥
पूर्वं संस्कारविरहेऽप्युपनीतिः स्मृतौ स्मृता ।
तथापि चोपनयनकालादर्वाङ् न कर्मसु ॥ ३३२ ॥
परोद्देशेन विहितेष्वधिकारोऽस्य विद्यते ।
स्यात्कामचारभक्षोक्तिरित्यादिस्मृतिशासनात् ॥ ३३३ ॥
अशक्त्या बाध्यमानत्वात् जन्मनोऽनन्तरं कृते ।
शक्तैश्च[६] नियमाभावात् पुंसा विहितरक्षणे ॥ ३३४ ॥
अधिकारो यदा सिध्येद्विहिताश्रमकर्मसु ।
वर्णधर्माधिकारोऽपि सदैव[७] स्यात्समत्वतः ॥ ३३५ ॥
अतश्चानुपनीतस्य ब्राह्मणस्य पुराऽष्टमात् ।
वर्षात्कर्माधिकारो नेत्येतत्स्मृतिवचोऽर्थवत् ॥ ३३६ ॥
अहुताद्ब्रह्मचारीति हुतशिष्टस्य भक्षणम् ।
वनितागमनं चापि निषिद्धं बालकस्य च ॥ ३३७ ॥
अतो न सर्वभक्षत्वं कामभक्षत्ववादतः ।
भुक्तोच्छिष्टापनयनममेध्यक्षालनं तथा ॥ ३३८ ॥
अशुद्धस्पर्शने कार्यं प्रोक्षणं चेत्यपि स्मृतम् ।
नाभिव्याहारयेद्ब्राह्मेत्येतस्मात् स्मृतिवाक्यतः ॥ ३३९ ॥
अङ्गपाठोऽभ्यनुज्ञात उपनीतेः पुराऽपि तु ।
वर्षाच्च पञ्चमादूर्ध्वमस्पृश्यस्पर्शनादिषु ॥ ३४० ॥

१.M ब्राह्मणा. २.M मुखतोर्युक्तं. ३.MT °श्वनवादि°. ४.M °विरहं. ५.M adds इति before वृत्या. ६.M शक्तेश्च. ७.M सद्दैव.

स पित्रादिः कारयेत्स्नानशौचादीत्यपि च स्मृतः ।
[१]सकृच्च भक्षणं कार्यं सकृच्च परिमार्जनम् ॥ ३४१ ॥
पित्रादिमरणे तस्य संस्काराद्यधिकारिणः ।
तदङ्गमन्त्रवचनं यथाशक्तीति चोदितः ॥ ३४२ ॥
एवमादि विमृश्यास्य कर्तव्यमवधार्यताम् ।
आ विवाहाद् भवेत्स्त्रीणां यथोक्ता कामचारिता ॥ ३४३ ॥
वैदिकत्वं यतस्तस्य विवाहस्य तथा स्मृतेः ।
वैवाहिको विधिः स्त्रीणां संस्कारो वैदिकः स्मृतः ॥ ३४४ ॥

इति सङ्गमग्रामवासिमिश्रविरचिते नारायणीये
वाधूलगृह्यागमवृत्तिरहस्ये
द्वितीयोऽध्यायः

१.M सकृद्भक्ष°, T सकृदभ°

अथ तृतीयोऽध्यायः

[उपनीतेरध्यापनाङ्गत्वम्]

गर्भाष्टमेऽष्टमे वाऽब्दे वसन्ते ब्राह्मणस्य तु ।
उपनीतिं विधायैनं वेदमध्यापयेद् गुरुः ॥ १ ॥
आचार्यस्य समीपे यन्नयनं वेदलिप्सया[१] ।
तत्तूपनयनं ज्ञेयमङ्गमध्यापनस्य तत् ॥ २ ॥
अध्यापनविधिः श्रौतो विद्यामध्यापयेदिति ।
प्रयुङ्क्तेऽध्ययनं स्वार्थनिवृत्त्यनुपपत्तितः ॥ ३ ॥
आचार्यत्वस्य[२] साध्यत्वान्न च तस्या प्रयोक्तृता ।
सोपनीतिप्रवचनकर्ता ह्याचार्य[३] उच्यते ॥ ४ ॥
विहितानेकनियमपूर्वका[४]ध्यापनोद्गतः ।
आचार्यो लौकिको नासौ लौकिकः पाचकादिवत् ॥ ५ ॥
एकोपाधिगृहीतत्वाद्व्यापारनिचयस्य[५] च ।
क्रियाकलापकर्तृत्वमात्रमत्र नियुज्यते ॥ ६ ॥
[६]शिष्यस्याध्ययनापूर्वहेतुव्यापारयोगतः ।
अवैषम्यादुपाध्यायाद् [७]गौरवाद् दृष्टकल्पनात् ॥ ७ ॥
प्रतीतेऽपि[८] च कर्तृत्व आचार्यवर[९]चोदनात् ।
आचार्याय वरो देय इति दानविधौ श्रुतेः ॥ ८ ॥
सम्प्रदानगतं तत्त्वं मुख्यवृत्त्यैव युज्यते ।
तद्रूपं लौकिकं तत्र तदा न ह्युपलभ्यते ॥ ९ ॥
[१०]धूपाग्न्यादिवदेवातो लौकिकं तत् समञ्जसम् ।
अतो लाक्षणिकोऽन्यत्र प्रयोग इति कल्प्यते ॥१० ॥
नालौकिक उपाध्यायनियमस्यानवेक्षणात्[११] ।

१.T लब्धये. २.M आचार्यस्य. ३.M ह्युच्चार्य. ४.T °पूर्वताध्या°. ५.T °निलयस्य. ६.M शिष्य स्वाध्यनापूर्व°, T ध्ययनात्पू° ७.T गौरवाद्दृढक°. ८.M °ते वि. ९.M °पर°. १०.M यूपा°. ११.MT नियमस्य उपनीत्येऽनवेक्षणात्.

अवेदाध्यापके चापि प्रयोगस्तस्य दृश्यते ॥ ११ ॥
परलज्जादिहेतुत्वात् तस्य साध्यत्वसंभवात् ।
प्रसिद्धत्वादुपायस्य विध्यपेक्षा तदुद्भवे ॥ १२ ॥
तदुत्पत्तिविधिश्चायं विद्यामध्यापयेदिति ॥ १२क ॥
आचार्यकरणे साक्षान्नयतेरात्मनेपदम्[१] ।
स्मर्यते व्याकृतौ तस्मादुपनीतिस्तदर्थिका ॥ १३ ॥
तस्याश्चाध्यापनार्थत्वात्तस्यैवाचार्यतार्थता ।
न च [२]सामर्थ्याल्लब्धत्वादुपनीत्यविधेयता ॥ १४ ॥
श्रुतावुपनयीताङ्गं[३] वसन्त इति दृश्यते ।
संस्कारविषयस्तस्मात्तद्विधिस्तस्य युज्यते ॥ १५ ॥
श्रुत्यन्तरे च विस्पष्टमाचार्यकरणार्थिनीम्[४] ।
उपनीतिं समीर्योपनीताध्यापनचोदनात् ॥ १६ ॥
उपनीत्यङ्गकाध्यापनोत्पाद्या सेति गम्यते ।
न च याजनविधिवत्स्वाध्यायविधिरेव सः ॥ १७ ॥
तस्यैव[५] साधिकारत्वादगत्या यानचोदनात् ।
याजनस्यानुवादत्वं युज्यते च धनार्थिनः ॥ १८ ॥
यद्यप्यध्यापनस्यापि धनलोभनिमित्तता ।
तथाप्याचार्यता साध्या वरदानोपयोगिनी ॥ १९ ॥
धनार्थिनस्तु तल्लब्धिरतस्तेन नियम्यते ॥ १९क ॥
परस्मैपदमप्यत्र[६] विशेषेण बुधादिना ।
विधीयते कर्तृगामि[७]फलमेवं च युज्यते ॥ २० ॥
श्रुतिस्मृत्यनुसारेण यद्यपूर्वस्य भाव्यता[८] ।
आचार्यतापि भाव्यैवं दृष्टादृष्टफला हि सा ॥ २१ ॥
उपनीतेस्तदङ्गत्वमतो युक्तं पुरोदितम् ॥ २१क ॥

१.M °नयन्तारात्मने पदम्. २.T सामर्थ्यलब्ध° ३.M श्रुताउपनतीताङ्ग्यं. ४.T करणार्थनीम् ५. M तदस्यैव. ६.M परम°, T corrected as पदम°. ७.M °गामीफल°. ८.T भावृता.

ननु चाचार्यकरणे [१]नयतेरात्मनेपदम् ।
स्मर्यते कर्तृगामित्वं तत्फलस्येह युज्यते ॥ २२ ॥
यद्धि 'स्वरितञित्'[२] सूत्रे क्रियाफलमुदीरितम् ।
तदेतत्कारका[३]वस्थाजातमीप्सितमुच्यते ॥ २३ ॥
क्रियाफलोपनयनसंस्कृतिः कर्मगामिनी ।
इति तत्र न तत्प्राप्तिरिति तत्र विधीयते ॥ २४ ॥
संस्कृतेरग्निगामित्वेऽप्याधाने तच्च युज्यते ।
[४]आत्मसाधारणत्वेन [५]प्रयोगा नापवर्गिताः[५] ॥ २५ ॥
संस्कारान्तरमध्ये स्यात्[६] पाठः श्रुतिषु दृश्यते[६] ॥ २५क ॥
प्रसङ्गादपि वान्यार्थसंस्कृतोऽन्यार्थता[७] व्रजेत् ।
[८]दैक्षार्थसंस्कृतो यूपः सौत्याद्यर्थत्वमेति हि ॥ २६ ॥
क्रत्वर्थवरणस्येह[९] याजनापूर्वशेषता ।
भिन्नत्वेऽप्यधिकारस्य नाङ्गताऽस्य[१०] विहन्यते ॥ २७ ॥
धनस्य यशसः शिष्योपास्तेर्धर्मस्य कारणम् ।
अर्थ्यते[११] केन विदुषा नाचार्यत्वं सुखास्पदम् ॥ २८ ॥
अतश्च [१२]साधिकारत्वात्तस्य युक्ता प्रयोक्तृता ।
विहिताध्ययनस्यैव प्रयोक्तृत्वं समञ्जसम् ॥ २९ ॥
विध्यासन्नवटोः[१३] कर्म स्वाध्यायाध्ययनं यतः ।
अध्यापनस्वरूपं न सिध्येदध्ययनं विना ॥ ३० ॥
विहिताध्ययनस्यैव ग्रहणाद्वारलाभतः ।
विहिताङ्गान्विताधीतेः प्रयुक्तिः प्रथमं ततः ॥ ३१ ॥
तदर्थोपनयस्यापि प्रयुक्तिरत एव च ।
साङ्गप्रयुक्तिदोषश्च न स्यादध्ययनस्य तु ॥ ३२ ॥

१.M नयने°. २.M स्वमितन्त्रीन्सूत्रे. ३.M °त्तारका. ४.M आत्मा°. ५-५.T न प्रयोगापवर्गिताः, M प्रयोगा चापवगिता. ६-६.M स्यादपाठःश्रुति दृ°, T स्याःपाठः. ७.M °तोऽन्यर्थता, T °तोऽन्यार्थतां. ८.T भैक्षार्थ°. ९.T °स्येव. १०.M नागता°. ११.M आथ्यते. १२.M नाधि°. १३.M वभोत्कर्म

आधानवत्प्रयोज्यत्वमतादर्थ्येऽपि युज्यते ।
स्वाध्यायचोदना चेयमन्यथा न विधायिका ॥ ३३ ॥
समर्थाध्यापनविधिमुपजीव्य कृतार्थिनी ।
यतो निरधिकारोऽयं विधिराम्नायते श्रुतौ ॥ ३४ ॥
विद्वद्विषयता [१]वाऽस्याविद्वद्विषयतापि[१] वा ।
न च विद्वद्विषयता[२]ऽदृष्टार्थत्वप्रसङ्गतः ॥ ३५ ॥
अर्थवादानुसारेण न चादृष्टार्थचोदिता ।
फलवत्क्रतुबोधादिदृष्टार्थत्वस्य संभवात् ॥ ३६ ॥
आनर्थक्यं क्रतूनां च दृष्टार्थत्वे प्रसज्यते ।
विध्यभावाद्यथाकामं श्रुतिरप्यधिगम्यते ॥ ३७ ॥
अपि चाध्ययनं न स्याद्विहितानीति लङ्घनात्[३] ।
अविद्वद्विषयत्वेन दृष्टार्थत्वेन बोधकृत्[४] ॥ ३८ ॥
स्वार्थसाधनतां पूर्वां[५] क्रतूनामवगम्य[६] च ।
पश्चाद्बोधकत्वेन पदाधीति[७]नियोजने ॥ ३९ ॥
अन्योऽन्याश्रयतैव स्याद्विधीनां व्यर्थतापि च ॥ ३९क ॥
अधीत्य[८] साधयेदर्थज्ञानमित्यपि न श्रुतम् ।
तस्मादध्ययनापूर्वसाध्यत्वेन विधीयते ॥ ४० ॥
फलवत्क्रतुबोधादि[९] दृष्टार्थमपि तद् भवेत् ।
तस्मादविदुषस्तस्य कर्तव्यत्वाविनिश्चयात्[१०] ॥ ४१ ॥
विध्यन्तरप्रयुक्त्यैव[११] कृतार्थाधीतिचोदना ।
अतश्चाध्यापनाङ्गत्वमुपनीतेरिति स्थितम् ॥ ४२ ॥
न चैवं श्रौतता तस्या[१२] उपनीतेः प्रसज्यते ।
स्मार्तं स्मृत्युपदिष्टत्वात्कर्मैतदवगम्यते ॥ ४३ ॥

१-१.M वास्यादवि च द्विष°, T वास्याः विद्वद्विष°. २.M °यता दृष्टा°. ३.M °द्विनितानति°, T °द्विहितानीविलङ्गनात्. ४.M बन्धकृत्. ५.M पूर्वं. ६.M °वनम्य. ७.T पदाद्धीति. ८.T अधीत्या. ९.M °कृतबो°. १०.M °त्वापि°. ११.M प्रयुक्तैव. १२.M तस्य.

प्रत्यक्षविधिमूलत्वं स्मृतेरपि न युज्यते ।
श्रुतिस्मृत्यभिधेयस्य भिन्नत्वस्यायतो यतः ॥ ४४ ॥
मन्त्रार्थवाद[1]नाम्नाञ्च न स्वातन्त्र्येण[2] मूलता ।
चतुर्विधस्य[3] वेदस्य मूलत्वे सति हि स्मृतेः ॥ ४५ ॥
प्रामाण्यं सर्वथा न स्यादुपपत्त्या निरूपणे ॥ ४५क ॥
अग्निहोत्रादिवत्तस्य वेदविद्भिरनुष्ठिते ।
कल्पितश्रुतिमूलत्वं वायं[4] तदभिधीयते ॥ ४६ ॥
स्वाध्यायाध्यापनविधी स्वशाखाविषयौ श्रुतौ ।
तयोरध्यापनविधेः प्रयोक्तृत्वञ्च युज्यते ॥ ४७ ॥
अन्यस्यापि[5] प्रयोज्यत्वं यथोक्तविधयाऽथवा ।
अपूर्वस्यैव भाव्यत्वमिह स्याद्यजनादिवत् ॥ ४८ ॥
आचाराचयनाद्योगादाचार्यत्वं[6] च युज्यते ।
आचारानाचिनोत्यर्थान्[7] बुद्धिं वेति हि निर्वचः ॥ ४९ ॥
स्वोपकारानुसारेण गुरुमान्यत्वसिद्धये ।
गुर्वादिलक्षणं स्मार्तं व्यवहारार्थमर्थवत् ॥ ५० ॥
उपाध्यायर्त्विगादीनां[8] लक्षणं व्यर्थमन्यथा ।
स गुरुर्यः क्रियां कृत्वा वेदमस्मै प्रयच्छति ॥ ५१ ॥
उपनीय ददद्वेदमाचार्य इति हि स्मृतौ ।
वर्तमानाभिधानं च युज्यते धर्मवित्कृतम् ॥ ५२ ॥
अध्यापनाधिकारश्च बहुधैव भवेच्छ्रुतेः ।
वरचोदनसामर्थ्यादाचार्योपास्यता[9] विधेः ॥ ५३ ॥
विद्यादार्ढ्य[10]निमित्तत्वाच्छ्रेयो हेतुत्ववादतः ।
अप्रमादविधानाच्चार्थ्यनुक्तौ दोषवर्णनात् ॥ ५४ ॥
सर्वार्थसाधनत्वेन प्रयोक्तृत्वं विधेर्भवेत् ।

१.M °पादना°. २.M स्यातन्त्रेण. ३.M °विधन्य. ४.M वाचस्त°. ५.M अन्यस्वज प्र°, T अन्यस्य प्र°. ६.M °गाद्याचा°, T आचार, T...द्योगादा°. ७.T °चिगोत्य°. ८.M °ध्यायर्थिगा°. ९.M वा स्यता°. १०.M °दावद्य°.

तत्प्रयुक्तो विधिश्चान्य उपासीनोपतिष्ठते[१] ॥ ५५ ॥
[२]स्वतन्त्रकर्तृविरहेऽध्यापनानुपपत्तितः[३] ।
[४]विधित्वान्निर्वाहः स्यादनुपपत्तौ विधिद्वयम् ॥ ५६ ॥
विध्यन्तरस्य[५] लिङ्गं स्याद्विहितस्यार्थसिद्धये[६] ।
उपनीतिं विनाऽध्येतुः शक्तोऽध्यापयितुं न सः ॥ ५७ ॥
अतश्चोपनयीतेति[७] विधिरेव प्रकल्प्यते ।
[८]वेदाध्यापनशेषत्वादुपनीतिश्च तादृशी ॥ ५८ ॥
असंस्कृतस्य[९] विदुषः श्रौतकर्म न चोचितम् ।
जातिमात्रमुपादाय विधयश्चेत्प्रयुञ्जते ॥ ५९ ॥
जन्मप्रभृति चैव स्यात्सति सामर्थ्य[वा]न्[१०] हि चेत् ।
स्वाध्यायविधिसंसिद्धकृत्स्नवेदार्थवेदनम् ॥ ६० ॥
सर्वकर्माधिकारी स्यात् स्वाध्यायविधिरादितः ॥ ६०क ॥
प्रयोक्तुमसमर्थत्वाद्विध्यन्तरसहायवान् ।
तदपेक्षोपनयनमुभयानुग्रहाश्रयम् ॥ ६१ ॥
तदनुष्ठानयोग्यत्वापादकं परिकल्पयेत् ॥ ६१क ॥
न ह्यसंस्कृतदेहस्य युज्यते कर्म वैदिकम् ।
सर्वाधिकारहेतुत्वादुपनीत्याख्यसंस्कृतिः ॥ ६२ ॥
सकृत्कृतैव सर्वार्था मरणादनुवर्तते ।
अत एवाष्टवर्षादेरुपनीतश्रुतौ श्रुतम्[११] ॥ ६३ ॥
[१२]कल्पितस्यानुवादेन कालः श्रुतिषु चोदितः ।
अध्यापनविधानार्थं वाऽनुवादो[१३] न सन्निधौ ॥ ६४ ॥
इतिकर्तव्यता सिद्धेरन्यथानुपपत्तितः ।

१.T °नोऽवीत°. २.M स तन्त्र°. ३.M °पवर्तितः. ४.T broken between विधि and निर्वाहा°. ५.M विध्यतर°. ६.M विहितस्वार्थ°. ७.M °नयीचेति. ८.M वैधाध्या°. ९.M °कृत विदु°. १०.M सामर्थ्य हि, T सामर्थ्य...चेत्; here one syllable is required for metrical accomplishment. ११.M श्रिता. १२.M कर्षितस्या°. १३.M °नार्थां नुवा°.

स्वस्वशाखाश्रया चेयं स्वाध्यायाधीति[१]चोदना ॥ ६५ ॥
उपनीतिश्च सर्वासु न शाखासु विधीयते ।
सर्वेषां नित्यता चास्याः[२] श्रौतत्वेन हि युज्यते ॥ ६६ ॥
वैकल्पिकमनुष्ठानं परशाखोदितस्य हि ।
कल्पितश्रुतिमूलत्वे सर्वार्थत्वं समञ्जसम् ॥ ६७ ॥
लिङ्गानि सर्वशाखासु दृश्यन्ते प्रायशोऽपि च ।
अधीतिचोदना चैषा त्रयाणामेव युज्यते ॥ ६८ ॥

[उपनीतेरधिकारिणः]

कर्मानुष्ठानसिध्यर्था वेदाध्ययनचोदना ।
कर्म च ब्राह्मणादीनामग्निमत्त्वे भवेद्धितम् ॥ ६९ ॥
आधानं ब्राह्मणादीनां त्रयाणां श्रुतिचोदितम् ।
आधानचोदनाभावाच्छूद्रादेर्नाधिकारिता ॥ ७० ॥
कामश्रुतिगृहीतत्वादग्निमत्त्वस्य संभवात् ।
ब्राह्मणादेर्वसन्तादिकालार्थत्वाच्च तद्विधेः ॥ ७१ ॥
'विद्वान् [३]य एवमाधत्त' इति सामान्यचोदनात् ।
'चक्षुर्निमील' इत्यादेर्देशस्याप्यस्य संभवात् ॥ ७२ ॥
ब्रह्मसाम्नो विशेषेण ह्यभीवर्तविधानतः ।
व्रतस्याप्यस्य[४] सद्भावादृतुसंबन्धदर्शनात् ॥ ७३ ॥
आधानं कर्म चाप्यस्य साङ्गं सफलमेव हि ।
अतश्चाध्ययनं तस्येत्येतद्वक्तुं न शक्यते ॥ ७४ ॥
'विद्वान् य एवमाधत्त' इत्येषा स्तुतिरेव हि ।
आनुमानिकमेवातो विधानमिदमत्र[५] हि ॥ ७५ ॥
ब्राह्मणादेर्वसन्तादौ श्रुत्याधानं विधीयते ।

१.M °यातीति, T °दिति°. २.MT चास्या. ३.MT विद्वान्न. ४.M संभवात्स्मर्तु°. ५.T broken between विधान and हि.

शूद्रस्याधानमग्नीनां विध्यभावान्न[१] विद्यते ॥ ७६ ॥
अन्यार्थदर्शनञ्चैषां त्रयाणामेव युज्यते ।
तस्माच्छूद्रसमीपे नाध्येतव्यमिति श्रुतेः ॥ ७७ ॥
अवक्लृप्तो न यज्ञोऽसौ शूद्र इत्यादिदर्शनात्[२] ।
यज्ञाधिकारः शूद्रस्य नास्तीत्येवं प्रतीयते ॥ ७८ ॥
ब्राह्मणादेर्वसन्तादावुपनीतिः[३] श्रुतौ श्रुता ।
शूद्रादेर्न श्रुता तस्मादनध्ययनमस्य हि ॥ ७९ ॥
अतश्च रथकारस्याप्युपनीतिर्न विद्यते ।
उपनीतेरश्रुतत्वाद्वचनात्कर्म तस्य तु ॥ ८० ॥
त्रयाणामेव वर्णानां तस्मादध्ययने विधिः ।
तेषामेवोपनयनं तदर्थत्वादतो भवेत् ॥ ८१ ॥
अतश्चोपनयीताधिकारिणो ब्राह्मणादिकान् ।
एवंरूपो विधिः कल्प्यः स स्मृतेर्मूलतां व्रजेत् ॥ ८२ ॥
विधेर्न न्यायसिद्धत्वेऽप्याकाङ्क्षाद्यनुसारिणः ।
मीमांसान्यायसिद्धत्वं पदार्थोत्पादकं[४] त्विति ॥ ८३ ॥
उत्पन्नानां पदार्थानामैदमर्थ्यं स्वशक्तितः ।
तत्रोच्यते तदुत्पत्तिविधिरन्यावृताविति ॥ ८४ ॥
वैषम्यमनयोर्युक्तमतो विद्यान्तरं[५] त्वियम् ।
सावित्र्यध्यापनादेवाध्यापनापूर्वसिद्धितः ॥ ८५ ॥
भेदः स्मृता[६] उपाध्यायगुर्वादेरुपपद्यते ।
अत एवोपनयनकर्ताऽऽचार्य इति स्मृतम् ॥ ८६ ॥
सर्वथाध्यापनाङ्गत्वमुपनीतेर्यथोदितम् ।
अध्यापनाङ्गतां वक्तुमुपनीतेश्च कल्पकृत् ॥ ८७ ॥
ब्रह्मचारिणमित्यादि वाक्यं प्राह महामतिः[७] ।
उपनेता यतश्चास्मिन्नधिकारीति गम्यते ॥ ८८ ॥

१.M °भावन्न. २.M दर्शनाम्. ३.M °नीति. ४.M °पादक त्विति. ५.M °न्तरस्त्वियम्. ६.T °स्मृतार्थ. ७.M oms. महा.

गायत्र्यध्ययनादूर्ध्वं विशेषवचनादिह ।
उपनीतेस्तदङ्गत्वं स्पष्टयत्येव कल्पकृत् ॥ ८९ ॥
'तं[1] हाचार्यं समित्पाणिरुपचक्राम' इत्यतः ।
विशिष्टविद्यासिध्यर्थमुपनीतिश्च गम्यते ॥ ९० ॥
प्रक्रान्ताध्ययनस्याकृतार्थस्याचार्यनाशकम् ।
आचार्यान्तरलाभे सा कार्येत्येतत्समीरितम्[2] ॥ ९१ ॥
अतश्चाध्ययनाङ्गत्वमुपनीतेर्दृढीकृतम् ।
संस्कृतिश्च शिशोरेषा द्विजत्वं यत्कृतं स्मृतम् ॥ ९२ ॥
संस्कारमध्यपाठाच्च [3]शिशुसंस्कारकर्म तु ।
योग्यतापादनद्वारा[4] तत्स्यात्तस्मात्तदङ्गता ॥ ९३ ॥
दीक्षाव्रतादिवद्यस्मात्तदङ्गत्वमिहोचितम् ।
ब्रह्मचारिणमित्यत्र योग्य एव विवक्षितम् ॥ ९४ ॥
अननूक्ता[5] च सावित्री यदेत्याद्यभिधानतः ।
यस्मादनुपनीतस्याप्येष एव विधिर्भवेत् ॥ ९५ ॥
तच्चोपनयनं कार्यं गृहस्थेनैव यत्नतः ।
आचार्यपत्नीं भिक्षेतेत्येतस्माल्लिङ्गदर्शनात्[6] ॥ ९६ ॥
अनुशिष्टं च तं पुत्रं लौक्यमाहुरिति श्रुतेः ।
उपनीतौ पिता मुख्य आचार्यस्तदलाभतः ॥ ९७ ॥

[उपनीतेःकालविचारः]

ब्रह्मवर्चसकामस्य पञ्चमेऽब्देऽग्रजन्मनः ।
आयुष्कामस्य नवमे कार्यं मौञ्जीनिबन्धनम् ॥ ९८ ॥
ब्रह्मवर्चसकामस्य सप्तमेऽष्टम आयुषे ।
तेजस्कामस्य नवमे दशमेऽन्नाद्यकामिनः[7] ॥ ९९ ॥

१.M तमाचार्यं. २.M कार्येत्येत्समी°. ३.MT शिशुं संस्का°. ४.M °पदन°. ५.M अनूक्ता. ६. M °तदकामतः. ७.T °कामिनम्.

एकादशे चेन्द्रियार्थे[1] द्वादशे पशुकामिन:[2] ।
षोडशे सर्वकामस्येत्येते काला: फलार्थिनाम् ॥ १०० ॥

षोडशाब्दमतिक्रम्य नोपनीतिर्विधीयते ।
सावित्रीपतित्वेन तु कर्मस्वनधिकारिण: ॥ १०१ ॥

आषोडशाद् ब्राह्मणस्य सावित्री नातिवर्तते ।
आ द्वाविंशात्क्षत्रबन्धोराचतुर्विंशतेर्विश: ॥ १०२ ॥

अत ऊर्ध्वं पतन्त्येते सर्वधर्मबहिष्कृता: ।
सावित्रीपतिता व्रात्या[3] [4]व्रात्यस्तोमादृते क्रतो: ॥ १०३ ॥

नैतैरपूतैर्विधिवदापद्यपि कदाचन ।
[5]ब्राह्मान् यौनांश्च संबन्धानाचरेद् ब्राह्मण:[6] सह ॥ १०४ ॥

प्रायश्चित्ते कृते तेषामुपनीतिर्विधीयते ।
अतीत्य जातकं[7] कालं व्रात्यस्तोमेन[8] शुध्यति ॥ १०५ ॥

उद्दालकव्रतं पूर्वं कृच्छ्राद्यपि च शोभनम्[9] ।
अष्टमस्यैव वर्षस्य नित्यत्वं श्रुतिचोदितम् ॥ १०६ ॥

गायत्रो[10] ब्राह्मणो यस्मात् गायत्र्यष्टाक्षरा यत: ।
ब्राह्मणं त्वष्टवर्षं तं तस्मादुपनयेदिति ॥ १०७ ॥

नित्यकालमतिक्रम्य सामर्थ्ये दोष एव हि ।
मृगादिमिथुनान्तेषु मासेष्विच्छन्ति केचन ॥ १०८ ॥

वसन्त एव मुख्य: स्यात् काल:[11] श्रुतिविधानत: ।
ब्राह्मणस्य तथा चास्यां श्रुतौ लिङ्गमिदं भवेत् ॥ १०९ ॥

आधाने ब्राह्मणस्यर्तुर्वसन्त इति चोदिते ।
हेतुरुक्तो वसन्तो वै ब्राह्मणस्यर्तुरित्यत:[12] ॥ ११० ॥

प्रसिद्धिश्चोपनीत्यङ्गं कालत्वादस्य गम्यते ।
न हि लोकेऽस्य संबन्ध: प्रसिद्धो ब्राह्मणेन तु ॥ १११ ॥

१.M °न्द्रियात्वे. २.T °कामिनम्. ३.M प्रात्या. ४.M प्रात्य°. ५.T ब्राह्मण्यौनांश्च. ६.M ब्रह्मण°. ७.T जानतं. ८.MT प्रात्यस्तो°. ९.MT शोभनाम्. १०.M गयत्रो. ११.M काल. १२.MT °स्यर्तुमि° [M र्तु].

श्रुत्यन्तरे वसन्तोऽथ[१] ब्राह्मणस्य विधीयते ।
तदपेक्ष्य [२]प्रसिध्यत्वमिहोक्तस्यावगम्यते ॥ ११२ ॥
ब्राह्मणस्योपनयनं वसन्त इति भाषितम् ।
आग्निवेश्येन[३] मुनिना तस्मात्तत्रैव युज्यते ॥ ११३ ॥
चैत्रवैशाखमासौ द्वौ वसन्त इति कीर्त्यते ।
वासन्तिकावृतू[४] यस्मान्मधुमाधव[४] एव च ॥ ११४ ॥
फाल्गुनस्यापि चैत्रस्य वसन्तत्वं प्रतीयते ।
दीक्षाविधौ तयोरब्दमुखत्वं श्रुतिदर्शितम् ॥ ११५ ॥
वसन्तो वत्सरादिः[५] स्यादित्यपि श्रुतिदर्शितम् ।
फाल्गुनस्य वसन्तत्वं कल्पकारोऽपि मन्यते ॥ ११६ ॥
अतो मासास्त्रयो ग्राह्या उपनीतौ श्रुतीरिताः ॥ ११६क ॥
शुक्लपक्षे नृनक्षत्रे[६] कार्या पुण्यदिने तथा ।
सुमुहूर्त इदं कार्यं श्रेष्ठं जन्म यतस्त्विदम् ॥ ११७ ॥

[उपनीतेमर्हत्त्वम्]

शरीरमेव पितरौ [७]यस्माज्जनयतस्ततः ।
श्रेष्ठं जन्म [८]भवेदेतदित्यापस्तंब[९]भाषितम् ॥ ११८ ॥
कामान्माता पिता चैनं यमुत्पादयतां[१०] मिथः ।
संभूतिं[११] तस्य तां विद्याद् यद्योनौ[१२] भुवि जायते ॥ ११९ ॥
आचार्यस्त्वस्य यां जातिं विधिवद्वेदपारगः ।
उत्पादयति[१३] सावित्र्या सा सत्या [१४]साऽजराऽमरा ॥ १२० ॥
तत्र यद्[१५] ब्रह्मजन्मास्य मौञ्जीबन्धनचिह्नितम् ।
तत्रास्य माता सावित्री पिता त्वाचार्य उच्यते ॥ १२१ ॥
वेदप्रदानादाचार्यं पितरं परिचक्षते ॥ १२१क ॥

१.M वसन्तेऽथ, T वसन्ते सा. २.M प्रसिध्यत्वं. ३.M आनिवे°. ४-४.M °वृता यस्मा मधुर्माधव. ५.M °रादि. ६.M oms नृ. ७.M यन्मार्जनयतस्ततः. ८.M broken between जन्म and देत°. ९.M °त्यास्तंभभा°. १०.M °यतामिथः. ११.M संभूतिस्त°. १२.M °द्योनाभ विजा°. १३.M उत्वादयाति. १४.M सां जरा मरा. १५. यं, T यो.

[१]मातुरग्रेऽभि जायन्ते[१] द्वितीयं मौञ्जिबन्धने ।
ब्राह्मणक्षत्रियविशस्तस्मादेते द्विजातयः[२] ॥ १२२ ॥

[स्मार्तयज्ञोपवीतविधानम्]

उच्यतेऽथाग्रजादीनां[३] स्मार्तानां लक्षणं पृथक् ।
यज्ञोपवीतमित्यत्र वर्णितं सूत्रलक्षणम् ॥ १२३ ॥
मौञ्जी त्रिवृत्समा श्लक्ष्णा कार्या विप्रस्य मेखला ।
[४]क्षत्रियस्य तु मौर्वी ज्या वैश्यस्य शणतान्तवी[४] ॥ १२४ ॥
मुञ्जाभावे तु [५]कर्तव्या कुशाश्मन्तकबल्बजैः ।
त्रिवृता[६] ग्रन्थिनैकेन[७] त्रिभिः पञ्चभिरेव वा ॥ १२५ ॥
कृष्णाजिनस्य त्वायाम उपवीतवदिष्यते ।
विस्तारस्त्र्यङ्गुलं तस्य चर्म त्रितयसंहतम् ॥ १२६ ॥
च्छिद्रैश्चतुर्भिः[८] सुदृढं संहतं च तदिष्यते ।
उत्तरीयमिदं तस्य नान्यद्धार्यं तथा स्मृतेः ॥ १२७ ॥
अपीडितो यूपवक्रः सशल्को दण्ड इष्यते ।
पालाश एव स ज्ञेयः[९] केशान्तो ब्राह्मणस्य सः ॥ १२८ ॥
ऋजवस्ते तु सर्वे स्युरव्रणाः सौम्यदर्शनाः[१०] ।
अनुद्वेगकरा नृणां सत्वचोऽनग्निदूषिताः ॥ १२९ ॥
बैल्वो वा याज्ञियो वा स्याद्दण्ड इत्यपि च स्मृतः ।
शाणं कार्पासमप्यस्याविकृतं वास इष्यते ॥ १३० ॥
ईषद्धौतं नवं वस्त्रं साशयं नवघाटितम् ।
अहतस्तद्विजानीयात् सर्वकर्मसु पावनम् ॥ १३१ ॥
नान्दीमुखञ्च पुण्याहं भोजनं वपनं शिशोः ।
सस्नानं समलङ्कारमहतांबरधारणम् ॥ १३२ ॥

१-१.M माधुरग्रे जायन्ते, T मातुरग्रेति जायन्ते. २.M द्विजायतम्. ३.MT °थाजनादिना°. ४-४.MT om; cf Manu II.42. ५.M कुशामन्तक°. ६.M त्रिविना. ७.M °नैतेन. ८.M चकृद्भिः. ९.M ज्ञेयं. १०.M °नाम्.

कारयेदुपवीती सन्नाचान्तोऽग्निगृहंततः ।
स्थितः स्पृष्ट्वा स्वहृदयं प्रागाशावदनः स्वयम् ॥ १३३ ॥
विधाय स्वात्म[१]संस्कारं सकृदाचम्य मन्त्रतः ।
तिरःपवित्रं पीत्वाऽपः शेषमाचम्य पूर्ववत् ॥ १३४ ॥
लौकिकं वह्निमाधाय परिस्तीर्य यथाविधि ।
व्रतावापसमिद्भिस्तु पक्वहोमार्थमेक्षणम् ॥ १३५ ॥
सादयेत्सूत्रं[२] मौञ्जीं[३] च [४]वस्त्रदण्डाजिनान्यपि[४] ।
[५]संसाद्याग्निमुखं कृत्वा परिधानात्पुरोदितम् ॥ १३६ ॥
अपरेणाग्निमाचान्तं प्राङ्मुखं स्वाग्रतः शिशुम् ।
कृत्वोपवीतं[६] तद्धस्तद्वये विन्यस्य दक्षिणे ॥ १३७ ॥
ऊर्ध्वगे तत्करे मन्त्रं 'यज्ञस्ये'त्युच्चरन् स्वयम् ।
प्रतिमुच्य शिशोः स्कन्धे [७]उपवीय्याचमय्य तम्[७] ॥ १३८ ॥
'या अकृन्ता'दिभिर्मन्त्रैः परिधाप्याहतं पटम्[८] ।
आदाय त्रिगुणां मौञ्जीं सपाशाग्राञ्च मेखलाम् ॥ १३९ ॥
दक्षिणे तत्करे पाशं तस्य दत्त्वाग्रमन्यतः ।
वाचय'न्नियमि'त्यादिमन्त्रं नाभ्यां शिशोः स्वयम् ॥ १४० ॥
परिवीय त्रिरेवाथ ग्रन्थिं 'प्राणादि'मन्त्रकम् ।
वाचयंस्त्रिवृतं कुर्यात् पञ्च त्रीन्वा तथा स्मृतेः ॥ १४१ ॥
अजिनं दक्षिणावृत्तलोम 'मित्रा'दि वाचयन् ।
प्रतिमुच्य स्वयं दण्डं दद्या'दग्नि'रिति[९] ब्रुवन् ॥ १४२ ॥
सोऽप्याचम्य समित्पाणिर्भूत्वा चाग्निं प्रदक्षिणम् ।
गत्वा दक्षिणतो[१०] वह्नेर्वटुं प्रत्यङ्मुखोऽग्रतः ॥ १४३ ॥
[११]आचार्यस्योपविश्याथ ब्रह्मचर्यादिकं वदेत् ।
'को नामासी'ति तं पृच्छेद् गुरुर्नाम स्वयं शिशुः[१२] ॥ १४४ ॥

१.M oms. २.MT सूत्र. ३.MT मौञ्जी. ४-४.M दण्डावस्त्राजिनादीन्यपि. ५.M adds तिहैवतुः before संसा°. ६.M °वीतस्तद्धस्थ°. ७-७.M °वीताचमयुतम्. ८.M पटुम्. ९.M °दनिरि°. १०.M तो broken. ११.M आध्वर्युस्यो°. १२.M शिशुम्.

देवदत्तशर्मनामास्मि निर्दिशेत् स्वकं[१] गुरुः ।
शिशोः शिरसि विन्यस्य जपित्वा प्रसवं ततः ॥ १४५ ॥
तृणद्वययुते हस्तपुटे तस्याञ्जलावपः ।
आनीय[२] तृणमुद्धृत्य ताभिरद्भिः शिशुं ततः ॥ १४६ ॥
'अद्भ्य' इत्यादिभिर्मन्त्रैः पृथक् प्रोक्ष्यास्य दक्षिणम् ।
करं साङ्गुष्ठमेवाथ गृहीत्वा मन्त्रतः पृथक् ॥ १४७ ॥
प्रति मन्त्रं गृहीत्वासौ स्थाने नाम वदेच्छिशोः ।
संबुध्यन्तं कृष्णशर्मन्[३] प्राणस्य[४] ब्रह्मचार्यसि ॥ १४८ ॥
ऊर्ध्वं[५] नाभ्यां स्वहस्ताभ्यां देवेभ्यो रक्षणाय तम् ।
[६]परिदद्यात् पृथङ्मन्त्रैस्तदुक्तिर्दानमन्त्रतः[७] ॥ १४९ ॥
परिगृह्य परिष्वज्य 'बोधश्चैति' जपेत्ततः ।
कर्णयोः स्कन्दनधिया 'भूँरित्यादि वदेत्पृथक् ॥ १५० ॥
शिशुं प्राङ्मुखमेवाथ कृत्वोच्छ्वस्यास्य[८] मूर्धनि ।
आत्माग्न्योरन्तरा चैनमुत्तरत्र नयेत्ततः ॥ १५१ ॥
परिधानप्रभृत्यग्निमुखं व्याहृति[९]पश्चिमम् ।
कृत्वा गृहीत्वा[१०] समिधं शिशुमाधाप्य मन्त्रतः ॥ १५२ ॥
जयादि पश्चाद्धोमाख्यं कर्म कृत्वा शिशुं ततः ।
कृत्वा दक्षिणतः पूर्वपथा नीत्वा वदेच्च तम् ॥ १५३ ॥
'ब्रह्मचार्यसि' तस्यार्थो विज्ञाप्य बालमादरात् ॥ १५३क ॥
ब्रह्मचारी यतोऽसि त्वमुपनीतिः कृता हि ते ।
अतश्च कामचारित्वं पूर्ववत्तव नोचितम् ॥ १५४ ॥
उपनीत्युत्तरं स्मार्तं कर्म वैदिकमिष्यते ।
उपनयननियमाः[११] कर्तव्या इति च स्मृतिः॥ १५५ ॥
आसमावर्तनाद् ब्रह्मचारिणो ये स्मृताः स्मृतौ ।

१.M स्वकरं. २.M आहीय. ३.M कृष्णदत्तशर्मन्. ४.M ब्राह्मणस्य. ५.M ऊर्ध्वे. ६.M °दध्यात्. ७.MT °मन्त्र तु. ८.M कृत्वोच्छ°. ९.M व्यावृति°. १०.M गृहीता. ११.T °नयनाद्धि.

मत्तो विज्ञाय तेषां त्वमनुष्ठानं सदा चर ॥ १५६ ॥
अग्नीन्धनं भैक्षचर्यामधःशय्या गुरोर्हितम् ।
आसमावर्तनात्कुर्यात् कृतोपनयनो द्विजः ॥ १५७ ॥
[1]अतस्त्वं मदधीनः स्याः[1] समाहितमना भव ।
विहितस्याननुष्ठाने निन्दितस्य च सेवने[2] ॥ १५८ ॥
परत्रेह च दुःखाप्तिस्तथा च स्मृतिशासनम् ।
विष्वञ्चो विपरीता हि नश्यन्त्याचार्य एव तम् ॥ १५९ ॥
वाचयेदुपदेशेन तस्मान्मद्वचनं त्वया ।
समाहितेन कर्तव्यमुपदेशत एव ते ॥ १६० ॥
धर्माद्यवगतिस्तस्माद् ग्राह्यं मद्वचनं सदा ।
एतमर्थमभिप्रेत्य 'ब्रह्मचार्यस्यु'दीरितम्[3] ॥ १६१ ॥
एवञ्चेत् किं मया[4] कार्यमिति चेत्तच्छृणुष्व मे ।
आधेहि समिधो नित्यं सायं प्रातः समाहितः ॥ १६२ ॥
दूरादाहृत्य समिधः सन्निदध्याद्विहायसि ।
सायंप्रातश्च जुहुयात्ताभिरग्निमतन्द्रितः ॥ १६३ ॥
बहूक्तिः समिधामत्र समावर्तनतः पुरा ।
नियमेन समिद्धोम इत्यस्य प्रतिपत्तये ॥ १६४ ॥
यद्यस्याचार्य एवास्य प्रयोगं नोक्तवानपि ।
'आधेही'त्यत्रनिर्देशादत्र पूर्वं समिद्धुतेः ॥ १६५ ॥
उक्तत्वात् पूर्वमन्त्रेण ज्ञापयत्येष तद्धुतिम् ।
शिष्टाचारानुसारेण तत्प्रयोग इहोच्यते ॥ १६६ ॥

[समिद्धोमप्रयोगः]

शुद्धे देशे निधायाग्निं लौकिकं[5] ज्वलितं ततः ।
समूहनादिकं कृत्वा गन्धपुष्पैरलङ्कृतम् ॥ १६७ ॥

१-१.M अतस्त्वदधीन स्याः°. २.M सेवनम्. ३.T °रितः. ४.M किमुया. ५.M लौकिक.

मन्त्रवत्परिषिच्याग्नावाधाय[१] समिधस्ततः[२] ।
'एषा ते अग्न' इत्यादि मनुना मन्त्रवत्पुनः ॥ १६८ ॥
परिषिच्योत्थितो वह्निं प्राञ्जलि'र्युक्त'[३] आदिभिः ।
'मयि मेधां मयी'त्याद्यैरुपस्थायोपविश्य च ॥ १६९ ॥
'आपो हि ष्ठा' तृचेनाद्भिर्मार्जयित्वानुलेपनम् ।
'केशवाय नमो' मूर्ध्नि कुर्यान्नारायणाय' तु ॥ १७० ॥
ललाटे 'माधवाये'ति कण्ठे तत्पार्श्वयोः पुनः ।
'गोविन्दाय नमो' 'विष्णवे नमो' मधुसूदनः ॥ १७१ ॥
तत्पृष्ठे स्यात्परश्चात्मा हृदये स्यात्त्रिविक्रमः ।
वामनश्चांसमूलस्थौ श्रीधरायोदरे ततः ॥ १७२ ॥
हृषीकेशः पद्मनाभः पार्श्वयोः पृष्ठ एव तु[४] ।
दामोदराय चेत्थं[५] तत्कृत्वा वह्नेरलङ्कृतिम् ॥ १७३ ॥
कुर्यात्पुष्पादिना नित्यमेतत्कार्यमितीरितम् ।
आश्रमोद्देशविहित[६]कर्मणामुपलक्षणम् ॥ १७४ ॥
अपोऽशानाख्यकर्म त्वं साङ्गमाचमनं कुरु ।
सर्वसाधारणं कर्म विहितं यच्छ्रुतौ स्मृतौ ॥ १७५ ॥
आश्रमान्तरसंबद्धविहितं चाविरोधि यत् ।
तत्सर्वमप्रमादेन मदुद्दिष्टं समाचर ॥ १७६ ॥
अतश्च विहितं कर्म कार्यमित्यत्र भाषितम् ॥ १७६क ॥
यद्वा 'समिध आधेही'त्येतं भैक्षादिलक्षणम् ।
तन्निवृत्तौ ब्रह्मचर्यसंपत्तिर्नास्य हीष्यते[७] ॥ १७७ ॥
[८]उपयन् ब्राह्मणो ब्रह्मचर्यं भूतानि गच्छति ।
पादेनाग्निं पदाचार्यं पदा मृत्युं[९] स गच्छति ॥ १७८ ॥
अग्नौ प्रविष्टं यत्तेजः समिदाधानकर्मणा ।

१.M °ग्न्यावाधाय. २.T समिधं ततः. ३.M °लिर्यत्र. ४.T तत्. ५.M चेर्थं. ६.MT °हित. ७.T शिष्यते. ८.M उपनयन्. ९.M मृत्युः.

[1]परकीयान्नभुक्तत्वात् संस्कृत्य प्राप्नुयाद्वटुम् ॥ १७९ ॥
[2]दरिद्रीकृत्य चात्मानं ह्रीर्भूत्वा भिक्षणाद् वटुः[2] ।
आयुर्मृत्युगतं[3] पादं संस्कृत्य प्राप्नुयात्तथा[4] ॥ १८० ॥
आचार्यवचनं कुर्वन् प्रज्ञां प्राप्नोति संस्कृताम् ।
[5]वेदाध्ययनेन स्वात्मसंस्थितं बलमाप्नुयात् ॥ १८१ ॥
एतैर्विहीनः[6] पुरुषो न हि श्रेयः समाप्नुयात् ।
अतश्च नियमेनैते कर्तव्या ब्रह्मचारिणा ॥ १८२ ॥
इत्यस्य प्रतिपत्त्यर्थं[7] समिद्धुतिरिहोदिता ।
साङ्गमाचमनं कार्यमित्यस्य प्रतिपत्तये ॥ १८३ ॥
'अपोऽशानेंति निर्दिष्टमशनं[8] ह्यत्र चोदितम् ।
उपनीतेः पुरा शूद्रसमत्वात् स्पृष्टिमात्रतः ॥ १८४ ॥
शुद्धिप्राप्तावबशनं कार्यमाचमनं त्विति[9] ।
साधारणस्य धर्मस्य लक्षणं ह्येतदिष्यते ॥ १८५ ॥
आश्रमोद्देशविहितं नित्यं नैमित्तिकञ्च यत् ।
कर्म कुर्विति निर्दिष्टं तदेतदिह भण्यते[10] ॥ १८६ ॥

[ब्रह्मचारिणो नित्यनैमित्तिकंकर्म]

रात्रेस्तु पश्चिमो यामो मुहुर्तो ब्राह्म उच्यते ।
तस्मिन्मुहुर्त उत्थाय स्वाचान्तश्चिन्तयेद्धरिम्[11] ॥ १८७ ॥
बोधयित्वा गुरुं चाथ पादसंवाहनादिना ।
[12]गेहान्निष्क्रम्य नैर्ऋत्यामिषुक्षेपाधिकं दिशि ॥ १८८ ॥
कृत्वा यज्ञोपवीतं तु पृष्ठतस्तदलम्बितम्[13] ।
दक्षिणे कर्ण[14] आरोप्य वाग्यतो[15] मेदिनीमपि ॥ १८९ ॥
अयज्ञियैरनार्द्रैश्च काष्ठलोष्टतृणादिभिः ।

१.MT परिक्रियन्न°. २-२.M oms. ३.T आयुर्वृत्तिगतं. ४.M ततः. ५.MT °ध्ययनस्वा°. ६.M °र्विहितं. ७.MT °पत्यर्थं. ८.M °मचनं. ९.M °नस्त्विति. १०.M हन्यते. ११.MT °द्धितम्, cf Vâdh Sm.4. १२.M देहा°. १३.M पृष्ठतं तण्डुलान्वितम्. १४.M कण्ठ. १५.M लाग्यते, T वाग्यते.

आच्छाद्य वामहस्तेन गृहीत्वा मेहनं ततः ॥ १९० ॥
आसित्वोदङ्मुखः कुर्याद्विण्मूत्रोत्सर्जनं दिवा ।
सन्ध्ययोर्निशि चेत्कुर्याद्दक्षिणामुख एव तु ॥ १९१ ॥
प्रत्यङ्मुखस्तु पूर्वाह्णेऽपराह्णे प्राङ्मुखस्तथा ।
उदङ्मुखस्तु मध्याह्ने निशा चेद्दक्षिणामुखः ॥ १९२ ॥
नोर्ध्वं नाधो न तिर्यक् च किञ्चिदीक्षेच्च[१] बुद्धिमान् ।
नभोभूम्यन्तरं पश्येत् कृत्वा मूर्ध्न्युपवीतकम् ॥ १९३ ॥
सदैवोदङ्मुखः प्रातः सायाह्ने दक्षिणामुखः ।
विण्मूत्रमाचरेन्नित्यं संध्यासु परिवर्जयेत् ॥ १९४ ॥
[२]न वेगं धारयेन्नोऽवरुद्धं[२] कुर्यात्क्रियामिति ।
स्मरणात्सन्ध्ययोश्चापि कुर्यान्मूत्रविसर्जनम् ॥ १९५ ॥
अतस्तयोर्निरोधो[३] न सन्ध्ययोरिष्यते[४] बुधैः ।
दिवासन्ध्यासु कर्णस्थ[५]ब्रह्मसूत्र उदङ्मुखः ॥ १९६ ॥
कुर्यादित्यादिवचनमेवमेव समञ्जसम् ।
दिङ्मोहादिनिमित्तेषु नियमो न दिशां स्मृतः ॥ १९७ ॥
छायायामन्धकारे वा रात्रावहनि वा द्विजः ।
यथासुखमुखः कुर्यात्प्राणबाधाभयेषु च ॥ १९८ ॥
वाय्वग्निविप्रमादित्यमपः[६] पश्यंस्तथैव गाः ।
न कदाचन कुर्वीत विण्मूत्रस्य विसर्जनम् ॥ १९९ ॥
न मेहेत नदीच्छायापद्मगोष्ठाम्बुभस्मसु ।
न प्रत्यग्न्यर्कगो[७]सोमसन्ध्यां न स्त्री[८] द्विजन्मनाम्॥ २०० ॥
प्रत्यग्निं प्रति सूर्यं च प्रति सोमोदकद्विजम् ।
प्रति गां प्रति सन्ध्यञ्च प्रज्ञा नश्यति मेहतः॥ २०१ ॥

१.M °दीक्षे च. २-२.M नवेन धारयन्नेहा कुण्डं, T नवेनं धारयेन्नोपक्रुद्धंय; cf infra VI.16.
३.M °र्निरोधेन. ४.MT °योर्नेष्म°. ५.MT कण्ठ°; thus infra VI.16; Vâdh Sm. 8: कर्णस्थ°.
६.M °ग्निप्रभादित्यम...श्यं°. ७.M प्रत्यर्क्रगा°. ८.MT अस्त्री.

दूरादावसथान्मूत्रं [1]दूरात्पादावनेजनम्[2] ।
उच्छिष्टान्ननिषेकं च दूरादेव समाचरेत् ॥ २०२ ॥
मूत्रादिकर्म न बहिर्ग्रामादस्तंगते रवौ ॥ २०२क ॥
न फालकृष्टे मेहेत न चित्यां[3] न च पर्वते ।
न जीर्णदेवायतने न वल्मीके[4] कदाचन ॥ २०३ ॥
न ससत्त्वे न गर्तेषु[5] न गच्छन्नापि च स्थितः[6] ।
न नदीतीरमासाद्य न च पर्वतमस्तके ॥ २०४ ॥
तुषाङ्गारकपालानि देवतायतनानि च ।
राजमार्गश्मशानानि क्षेत्राणि च खलानि च ॥ २०५ ॥
उपक्रुद्धो न सेवेत च्छायादृश्यचतुष्पथम् ।
वर्जयेद् वृक्षमूलानि चैत्यश्वभ्र[7]बिलानि च ॥ २०६ ॥
न चत्वरे गोमये वा न तीर्थे यज्ञभूमिषु ।
नाधस्ताद्याज्ञवृक्षाणां सस्यपूर्णे स्थले तथा ॥ २०७ ॥
नोषरे शाद्वले[8] मूत्रमुद्याने वा समाचरेत् ।
नभोभूम्यन्तरं पश्यन् कृत्वैतद्द्विजने ततः[9] ॥ २०८ ॥
मार्जनं वामहस्तेन [10]वीरणाद्यैरयज्ञियैः ।
कुर्यान्मूत्रपुरीषाणामेवमायुर्न हीयते ॥ २०९ ॥
लोष्टेन परिमृजीत शुष्ककाण्डेन[11] वा गुदम् ।
गृहीतशिश्नश्चोत्थाय जलमुद्धृत्य वान्यतः ॥ २१० ॥
शुद्धां[12] मृदं समुद्धृत्य यावदर्थं विधानतः[13] ।
निधाय मृत्तिकां शुद्धे स्थले त्रेधा विभज्य ताम् ॥ २११ ॥
[14]आसित्वोदङ्मुखः कुर्याद्दिवाशौचमतन्द्रितः[15] ।
दक्षिणाभिमुखो रात्रौ सन्ध्ययोश्च यथा दिवा ॥ २१२ ॥

१.M दूरान्पा°. २. cf Manu IV.151: पादावसचेनम्. ३.MT चित्यं. ४.M adds च after वल्मीके. ५.M नार्तेषु. ६.M स्थितम्. ७.M °श्चभ्र°. ८.M चाध्वले. ९.M ततम. १०.MT वीरणाद्यै°. ११.M कण्टेन. १२.M शुक्ला, T शुक्लां. १३.M विधानतम्. १४.M आसीत्वो°. १५.M शोचम°.

समृद्भिरद्भिः प्रक्षाल्य करावादौ[1] सकृत्ततः ।
[2]आर्द्रामलकमात्राभिः साद्भिः शिश्नस्य शोधनम्[3]॥ २१३ ॥
कृत्वा सव्यकरं[4] षड्भिर्मृद्भिः संक्षाल्य तद्द्वयम्[5]।
तिसृभिः सह संशोध्य गुदे दत्त्वा मृदं सकृत् ॥ २१४ ॥
हस्तौ संशोधयेन्मूत्रशौचमेवं समीरितम् ।
पुरीषोत्सर्जने[6] मूत्रशौचं कृत्वा यथोदितम् ॥ २१५ ॥
गुदं द्वादशभिर्मृद्भिः शोधयित्वा जलान्वितम् ।
एकविंशतिसंख्याभिर्वामहस्तं विशोध्य च ॥ २१६ ॥
उभौ द्वादशसंख्याभिः शोधयित्वा मृदं सकृत् ।
लिङ्गे दत्त्वा पाणिशौचं कृत्वा संशोध्य तत्स्थलम् ॥ २१७ ॥
प्रक्षाल्य पादौ हस्तौ च मुखशौचं विधाय च ।
अपां द्वादशगण्डूषैः समाचम्य यथोदितम् ॥ २१८ ॥
आप्लुत्य दण्डवद् भूयः समाचम्य निजान्तरम् ।
'आपो हि ष्ठा' तृचेनाद्भिर्मार्जयेदाप्लवेत्सकृत् ॥ २१९ ॥
उत्तीर्याच्छाद्य संशोध्य पादावाचम्य तत्परः[7] ।
'दधिक्राविण्ण' इत्याद्यैर्मन्त्रैः संप्रोक्ष्य वारिणा ॥ २२० ॥
गृहीत्वाञ्जलिना चापस्तिष्ठन्प्राङ्मुख आदरात् ।
गायत्र्योर्ध्वं क्षिपेद्धस्तौ प्रक्षाल्याथ प्रदक्षिणम् ॥ २२१ ॥
कृत्वोपविश्य सन्तर्प्य स्वस्वतीर्थैः सुरानृषीन् ।
पितॄंश्च सगणान्मन्त्रैर्निष्पीड्याच्छादनं ततः ॥ २२२ ॥
उपवीती समाचम्य शुद्धे देशे समास्थितः ।
मूर्धास्यहृदयेष्वेवमृष्यादिन्यासपूर्वकम् ॥ २२३ ॥
अभ्यस्य शक्तितस्तारं व्याहृत्यादिसमन्विताम् ।
गायत्रीं त्रिर्जपेद् भूय ऋषिन्यासादिपूर्वकम् ॥ २२४ ॥

१.T करौ पादौ. २.M आद्राम°. ३.M शौध°. ४.M कुप्यकरं. ५.M तद्वयम्. ६.M °सर्जन. ७.M परा.

आ. [१]भूर्भुवः सुवस्तत्सवितुरि'त्याद्यृचं जपेत् ॥ २२४क ॥
उपासीत परं ज्योतिःस्वरूपं ब्रह्म वाग्यतः ।
सज्योतिषसमारभ्य प्रातराभास्करोदयात् ॥ २२५ ॥
जप्त्वासीनो यथाशक्ति जपित्वा संस्थितो रविम् ।
'मित्रस्ये'त्यादिमन्त्राभ्यामुपस्थाय नमस्कृतिम् ॥ २२६ ॥
'मित्राय नम' इत्येवं दक्षिणाभिमुखो यमम् ।
'यमाय नम' इत्येवं 'ब्रह्मणे नम' इत्यपि ॥ २२७ ॥
उदङ्मुखो नमस्कृत्य [२]ब्रह्म तत् त्रिः[२] प्रदक्षिणम् ।
कृत्वा भूमिं समालभ्य 'ध्रुवासि' 'नम' इत्यपि ॥ २२८ ॥
नमस्कृत्य[३] दिशां प्राचीं भूयः 'प्राच्यै दिशे नमः'।
नमस्कृत्य समाचम्य समिद्धोमं यथोदितम् ॥ २२९ ॥

[अभिवादनविधिः]

कृत्वाऽभिवादयेद्[४] वृद्धान् गुर्वाचार्यादिपूर्वकान् ।
उपसंग्रहणं कुर्याद् गुरोरन्वहमादरात् ॥ २३० ॥
तदनुज्ञामवाप्यान्यान्[५] वृद्धानप्यभिवादयेत् ।
'अभिवादय' इत्युक्त्वा 'कृष्णशर्माह'मित्यपि ॥ २३१ ॥
'भो' इत्यन्तं वदेत्कुर्वन्नभिवादनकर्मसु ॥ २३१क ॥
अभिवादात्परं विप्रो ज्यायांसमभिवादयेत् ।
'असौ नामाहमस्मी'ति स्वनाम परिकीर्तयेत् ॥ २३२ ॥
भोः शब्दं कीर्तयेदन्ते स्वस्य नाम्नोऽभिवादने ।
[६]नाम्नां स्वरूपभावो हि भोभाव ऋषिभिः स्मृतः[६] ॥ २३३ ॥
व्यत्यस्तपाणिना कार्यमुपसंग्रहणं गुरोः ।
सव्येन सव्यं स्पृष्टव्यो दक्षिणेन तु दक्षिणम् ॥ २३४ ॥
श्रोत्रे संस्पृश्य मनसः समाधानाय संस्थितः ।

१.M oms. २-२.M ब्रह्मा तत्रिः, T ब्रह्म त त्रिः. ३.M °कृत्वा. ४.M oms °द्. ५.M oms °न्. ६-६.MT om; cf Manu II.124.

स्वर्गाद्यवाप्तिमायुश्च प्रार्थयन्मनसाशिषम् ॥ २३५ ॥
[१]अधस्तादेव जान्वोरा पद्भ्यां हस्तद्वयेन तु ।
व्यत्यस्तेन गुरोः पादौ सुगाढं परिमृज्य तु ॥ २३६ ॥
उपविष्टे गुरुर्मूर्ध्नि स्पृष्ट्वा दद्यादथाशिषम्[१] ।
'आयुष्मान्भव सौम्ये'ति विप्रो [२]वाच्योऽभिवादने ॥ २३७ ॥
अकारश्चास्य नाम्नोऽन्ते वाच्यः पूर्वाक्षरः प्लुतः ॥२३७क॥
अभिवादनकर्मैतदन्यस्मै बहुवेदिने ।
[३]काममभ्युदयार्थी स कुर्याद् गुर्वनुमोदितः ॥ २३८ ॥
ऋत्विङ्मातुलमात्रादीन् संबन्धान्नियमेन तु ।
गत्वाऽभिवादयेत्प्रातरन्यथा दोष एव तु ॥ २३९ ॥
युवतीनां गुरुस्त्रीणां[४] नैतदन्वहमिष्यते[५] ।
दृष्ट्या वन्दनमेवासां जातशुक्लः समाचरेत् ॥ २४० ॥
अजातवीर्यः सर्वासामभिवादनमाचरेत् ।
विप्रोष्यागत्य सर्वेषामभिगम्यैतदाचरेत् ॥ २४१ ॥
निषेकादीनि कर्माणि कृत्वोपनयनान्वितम् ।
वेदमध्यापयेत्साङ्गं सकल्पं यो गुरुः स तु ॥ २४२ ॥
निषेकादीनि कर्माणि यः करोति यथाविधि ।
संभावयति चान्नेन स विप्रो गुरुरुच्यते ॥ २४३ ॥
उपनीय ददद्वेदमाचार्यः स उदाहृतः ॥ २४३क ॥
एकदेशं[६] तु वेदस्य वेदाङ्गस्यापि[७] वा पुनः ।
योऽध्यापयति वृत्त्यर्थमुपाध्यायः स उच्यते ॥ २४४ ॥
ऋत्विक्तु[८] त्रिविधः प्रोक्तः[८] पूर्वैर्जुष्टः स्वयंवृतः ।
यदृच्छया तु यः कुर्यादार्त्विज्यं[९] विधिपूर्वकम् ॥ २४५ ॥
एते मान्या यथापूर्वमेभ्यो माता गरीयसी ॥ २४५क ॥

१-१.M oms. २.MT वाच्यो. ३.M कामेऽभ्यु°. ४.M गुदस्त्री°. ५.M नैतदन्वमिष्यते. ६.M एकदेशस्तु. ७.MT वेदाङ्गस्या [Mस्य] पि. ८-८.M °क्तुक्तविधिं प्रोक्तं. ९.M °दात्वीज्यं.

उपाध्यायान्दशाचार्य[1] आचार्याणां शतं पिता ।
सहस्रं तु पितॄन्माता[2] गौरवेणातिरिच्यते ॥ २४६ ॥
अल्पं वा बहु वा यस्य श्रुतस्योपकरोति यः ।
तमपीह गुरुं विद्याच्छ्रुतोपक्रियया तया ॥ २४७ ॥
श्रेष्ठो[3] गुरुणामाचार्यो मातेत्येक इति स्मृतिः ।
[4]श्रुतिर्गरीयः सर्वेभ्यस्तन्मूलो धर्म इत्यपि ॥ २४८ ॥
गुणवत्या[5]भवेन्मातुराधिक्यमिह चोदितम् ।
निर्गुणत्वे भवेच्छ्रैष्ठ्यमाचार्यादेरिति स्थितिः ॥ २४९ ॥
विद्याकर्मवयोबन्धुवित्तैर्मान्यत्वमीरितम् ।
एतत्सर्वं समालोच्य सन्निपातेऽभिवादयेत् ॥ २५० ॥
मान्यान् यवीयसो दृष्ट्वा[6] प्रत्युत्थायाभिभाषणम् ॥ २५०क ॥
पितुर्भगिन्यां[7] मातुश्च ज्यायस्यां च स्वसर्यपि[8] ।
मातृवद् वृत्तिमातिष्ठेन्माता[9] त्वाभ्यो गरीयसी[10]॥ २५१ ॥
ऊर्ध्वं प्राणा ह्युत्क्रामन्ति[11] यूनः स्थविर आयति ।
प्रत्युत्थानाभिवादाभ्यां पुनस्तान्प्रतिपद्यते[12] ॥ २५२ ॥
अभिवादनशीलस्य नित्यं वृद्धोपसेविनः ।
चत्वारि सम्यग्वर्धन्त[13] आयुः प्रज्ञा[14] यशो बलम्॥ २५३ ॥
नामधेयस्य ये केचिदभिवादं न जानते ।
तान्प्रज्ञोऽहमिति ब्रूयात् स्त्रियः सर्वास्तथैव च ॥ २५४ ॥
[15]यो न वेत्त्यभिवादस्य[15] विप्रः प्रत्यभिवादनम् ।
नाभिवाद्यः स विदुषा यथा शूद्रस्तथैव सः ॥ २५५ ॥
तथा गुरुमुपासीत स्वाध्यायार्थं[16] समाहितः ।

१.MT °ध्यायादृशं. २.MT पितुर्माता. ३.M श्रेष्ठा. ४.T श्रु...र्ग°. ५.M °वत्याद्भवे°. ६.MT दृष्ट्या. ७.T °गिन्या. ८.M स्वसुर्यपि, cf Manu II.133. ९.M मात. १०.M नरीयसी. ११.MT °क्रमन्ति. १२.MT पुरस्तात्, cf Manu II.120. १३. cf Manu II.121: तस्य वर्धन्त. १४. cf Manu II.121: विद्या. १५-१५.M योऽनपे. १६.M साध्यार्थमसमा°.

आहूतश्चाप्यधीयेत[1] लब्धं चास्मै निवेदयेत् ॥ २५६ ॥

[भिक्षाविधानम्]

ततो मध्यन्दिने प्राप्त आचम्य प्रोक्ष्य वारिणा ।
[2]गायत्र्या चाभिमन्त्र्याप ऊर्ध्वं क्षिप्त्वा प्रदक्षिणम्॥ २५७ ॥
कृत्वा प्राङ्मुख आसीनः शक्त्या जप्त्वा समुत्थितः ।
अर्हणार्थमपो दत्त्वा रवये तद्गतात्मवान् ॥ २५८ ॥
'उद्वयं तमसो'दुत्य' 'चित्रं' 'तच्चक्षु'रादिभिः ।
'पुनात्व'न्तैरुपस्थाय रविं भूयः प्रदक्षिणम् ॥ २५९ ॥
कृत्वोपविश्य सन्तर्प्य देवादीन् दण्डमाददत्।
भिक्षार्थं मृन्मयं पात्रं लौहं वादाय संयतः ॥ २६० ॥
वेदयज्ञैरहीनानां प्रशस्तानां स्वकर्मसु ।
ब्रह्मचार्याहरेद् भैक्षं गृहेभ्यः प्रयतोऽन्वहम् ॥ २६१ ॥
सप्ताक्षरो भवेद् भिक्षामन्त्र इत्यनुशासनात् ।
भिक्षेत स्त्रियमित्युक्तेर्भवत्पूर्वत्ववादतः ॥ २६२ ॥
भवतीत्यनुभाष्याथ भिक्षां देहि वदेत्स्त्रियम् ।
याच्ञागतं[3] हि शब्दं स भिक्षाशब्दान्न वर्धयेत् ॥ २ ६ ३ ॥
ब्रह्मचर्ये स्थितो नैकमन्नमद्यादनापदि ।
इति बह्वीभ्य एवैष भिक्षां लिप्सेत वाग्यतः ॥ २६४ ॥
गुरोः कुले न भिक्षेत न ज्ञातिकुलबन्धुषु ।
अलाभे[4] त्वन्यगेहानां पूर्वं पूर्वं विवर्जयेत् ॥ २६५ ॥
आपद्याचार्यपत्नीं स्वां भिक्षेतेत्यपि च स्मृतिः ॥ २६५क ॥

[अशनविधिः]

समाहृत्य तु तद् भैक्षं[5] यावदर्थममायया ।
निवेद्य गुरवेऽश्नीयादाचम्य प्राङ्मुखः शुचिः ॥ २६६ ॥
आयुष्यं प्राङ्मुखो भुङ्क्ते यशस्यं दक्षिणामुखः ।

१.M °धीयीत. २.M गायत्र्याभि°. ३.M याज्ञगतं. ४.M अलोभे. ५. cf Manu II 51: भैक्ष्यं.

श्रियं प्रत्यङ्मुखो भुङ्क्ते ऋतं भुङ्क्ते उदङ्मुखः ॥ २६७ ॥
उपस्पृश्य द्विजो नित्यमन्नमद्यात्समाहितः ।
भुक्त्वा चोपस्पृशेत्सम्यगद्भिः[1] खानि च संस्पृशेत् ॥ २६८ ॥
पूजयेदशनं नित्यमद्याच्चैतदकुत्सयन्[2] ।
दृष्ट्वा हृष्येत्प्रसीदेच्च प्रतिनन्देच्च सर्वतः ॥ २६९ ॥
आहिताग्निरनड्वांश्च[3] ब्रह्मचारी च[4] ते त्रयः ।
अश्नन्त एव सिध्यन्ति नैषां सिद्धिरनश्नताम्[5] ॥ २७० ॥
अनारोग्यमनायुष्यमस्वर्ग्यञ्चातिभोजनम् ।
अपुण्यं[6] लोकविद्विष्टं तस्मात्तत्परिवर्जयेत् ॥ २७१ ॥
चतुरश्रे शुभे पात्रं मण्डले तन्निधाय तु ।
आसीनः परिषिच्यान्नं वारिणा मन्त्रतः सकृत् ॥ २७२ ॥
पीत्वाऽपस्त्वाहुतीः[7] कृत्वा स्वात्माग्ना मन्त्रभिः[8] स्वकैः ।
वाग्यतोऽन्नं यथान्यायं भुक्त्वा पीत्वा पुनर्जलम् ॥ २७३ ॥
मुखशुद्धिं विधायाप आचम्योच्छिष्टपात्रकम् ।
शोधयेत् स्वयमेवैतत् ब्रह्मचारी जलादिभिः ॥ २७४ ॥

[गुरुसेवाकर्म]

गुरुणा चोदितं कर्म यथाकालं समाचरेत् ॥ २७४क ॥
उदकुंभान्सुमनसो गोशकृन्मृत्तिकाकुशान् ।
आहरेद्यावदर्थानि [9]गुरुणाऽचोदितान्यपि[9] ॥ २७५ ॥
अर्धास्तमित आदित्य उपक्रम्य यथाविधि ।
आसीनः[10] पश्चिमां सन्ध्यां प्रत्यङ्मुख उपास्य तु ॥ २७६ ॥
नक्षत्रदर्शनादूर्ध्वमुत्थाये'मं[11] म' इत्यृचा ।
'तत्त्वा यामी'त्युपस्थानमत्र कुर्यात्पुरोदितम् ॥ २७७ ॥

१.M सभ्य...खानि. २.MT °च्चैनवमकुत्स° [Mतून्स°]. ३.M रनध्वांश्च. ४.M पते. ५.M सिद्धिं नग्नताम्. ६.T अपुण्य. ७.M पीत्वा पञ्चाहुतीं. ८.MT मनुभिः. ९-९. cf Manu II-182: भैक्षं चाहरहश्चरेत्. १०.M आसीनं. ११.M °येन्मम.

'अग्नये नम' इत्येवं मित्रस्थाने नमस्कृतौ ।
[१][............] विशेषोऽत्रावदन्मनुः ॥ २७८ ॥
'प्राच्यै दिशे नमः'स्थाने 'प्रतीच्यै च दिशे नमः' ।
प्रत्यङ्मुखत्वमत्रेष्टमुपस्थानादिकर्मणि ॥ २७९ ॥
कृत्वाग्निकार्यं भैक्षञ्च कृत्वा भुक्त्वा यथोदितम् ।
शुश्रूषित्वा गुरुं भूयः पादं संवाहनादिभिः ॥ २८० ॥
गुरौ च शयिते पश्चान्नीचं शयनमाश्रयेत् ।
एतन्नैमित्तिकञ्चान्यत्कर्म कुर्विति भाषितम् ॥ २८१ ॥

[निषिद्धकर्माणि]

तथा च 'मा दिवा स्वाप्सी'र्दिवास्वापो निषिध्यते ।
वर्ज्यवर्जनसिध्यर्थं गौतमेन स्मृतौ यतः ॥ २८२ ॥
'वर्जयेन्मधुमांसे'ति वर्ज्यमध्ये निवेशितः ।
तस्मान्निन्द्यनिवृत्त्यर्थमेतदित्यवगम्यते ॥ २८३ ॥
[२]नेक्षेतोद्यन्तमादित्यं नास्तंयन्तं[३] कदाचन ।
नोपसृष्टं न वारिस्थं न मध्यं नभसो गतम् ॥ २८४ ॥
मधुमांसे गन्धमाल्यदिवास्वप्नाञ्जनस्त्रियम् ।
कामक्रोधौ[४] लोभमोहावुपानच्छत्रधारणम्[५] ॥ २८५ ॥
गन्धानुलेपनाभ्यंगपुष्पस्रग्धारणं भयम् ।
भेर्यादिवादनं नृत्तमास्याभ्यस्य[६] च भाषणम् ॥ २८६ ॥
वाणी[७] च [८]निष्ठुरां गानं [८]हर्षं यानं सुखाप्लवम् ।
दन्तधावनताम्बूलहिंसाद्यूतादिसंग्रहम् ॥ २८७ ॥
हीनसेवां परद्रव्यमदन्तं[९] गुरुदर्शने ।
पादप्रसारणं कण्ठप्रावृतिं चावसक्थिकाम्[१०] ॥ २८८ ॥

१.MT broken. २.M नेक्षेतोऽद्यन्तं. ३.M नास्तयन्तं. ४.M °क्रोधो. ५.M °पानच्छत्रं. ६.M °मस्यभ्यस्य, T °मभ्यस्य. ७.M पाणीञ्च, T पाणी. ८-८.M निष्ठ निष्ठुराङ्गानां, निष्ठ निष्ठरा गानं. ९.T °मद....दर्शने. १०.M °सत्थिकम्.

अपश्रयणं निष्ठिवावस्फोटनविजृम्भणम् ।
हसनं परिवादञ्च सरागं[1] स्त्रीनिरीक्षणम् ॥ २८९ ॥
तत्स्पर्शनञ्च शङ्कायां प्रयत्नेन विवर्जयेत् ।

[गुरुणा गायत्र्युपदेशः]

एवं विज्ञाप्य तं बालं[2] स्पृष्ट्वा'ग्न' इति मन्त्रवत् ॥ २९० ॥
असौ स्थाने च तन्नाम प्रथमान्तमुदीरयन् ।
प्रोच्य चैनं समुत्थाप्य मन्त्रतः स्वयमुत्थितः ॥ २९१ ॥
कारयेदप्युपस्थानं[3] 'तच्चक्षु'रिति मन्त्रतः ।
भिक्षार्थी स वटुः[4] पात्रमादाय तदनुज्ञया ॥ २९२ ॥
मातरं वा स्वसारं वा मातुर्वा भगिनीं निजाम् ।
भिक्षेत भिक्षां प्रथमं या [5]वैनं न विमानयेत्[5] ॥ २९३ ॥
समाहृत्य तु तद्भैक्षं यावदर्थममायया ।
निवेद्य गुरवे[6] तेन वाचाशस्तं निधाय तत्[6] ॥ २९४ ॥
समाचम्योपविष्टेऽस्मिन् गुरुरग्नेरलंकृतिम् ॥ २९४क ॥
मन्त्रवत्परिषेकञ्च विधाय [7]समिधस्तु याः[7] ।
सादिताः[8] संस्कृताः[9] पूर्वञ्चतस्रः संमिताः शुभाः ॥ २९५ ॥
'अग्ने व्रतपते' भूयः सावित्रमिति मन्त्रवत् ।
आधाप्य परिषिच्योर्ध्वमुपसंग्रहणात्परम् ॥ २९६ ॥
उपविष्टे शिशौ प्रत्यङ्मुखे दर्भकुशादिषु ।
प्राङ्मुखस्तृणपाणिः सन्नासीनः सपवित्रकः[10] ॥ २९७ ॥
गृहीत्वा पाणिना सव्यमङ्गुष्ठानन्वितं गुरुम् ।
तथाभूताय शिष्याय निर्दिशेत्प्रणवं[11] तु तम् ॥ २९८ ॥
पच्छोऽनूच्यापि गायत्रीं 'भूरिं'त्याह पदं ततः ।

१.T सराग......निरीक्षणम्. २.M पालं. ३.M कारयेद्द्व्युप°. ४.M वटुं. ५-५. cf manu II.50: या चैनं नावमानयेत्. ६-६. cf Manu II.51: गुरवेऽश्नीयादाचम्य प्राङ्मुखः शुचिः. ७-७.T समिधं तु या. ८.M साधिताः. ९.M संस्कृतां. १०.M सपवित्रकम्. ११.M प्रणयस्तु.

पाठयेच्च यथाशक्ति पुनरर्धर्चशस्तु ताम् ॥ २९९ ॥
उक्त्वा 'भुव' इति प्रोच्य ग्राहयित्वाऽनवानतः[१] ।
'सुव'रित्यन्वितं प्रोच्य निर्दिश्य प्रणवं[२] ततः ॥ ३०० ॥
विसृष्टमिति च ब्रूयादुपसंग्रहणं वटुः[३] ।
कृत्वा गुरोरथान्येषामभिवादनमाचरेत् ॥ ३०१ ॥
उक्तेऽर्थे कल्पवाक्यानां सामर्थ्यमधुनोच्यते ॥ ३०१क ॥

[अग्निग्रहणम्]

संस्कृतिं[४] कर्तुकामो यो विधिना संस्कृतस्य तु ।
भवत्यसौ गृहस्थः सत्कुलीनो वेदपारगः ॥ ३०२ ॥
यज्ञोपवीतं कृत्वाप आचामेद्विधिपूर्वकम् ।
ब्रह्मचारिणमित्युक्तिरोदनं[५] पचतीतिवत् ॥ ३०३ ॥
भाविन्येवोपचारान्न विरुद्धेति पुरोदितम् ।
'यज्ञोपवीत'मित्यादिगतमात्महृदि[६] स्वकम् ॥ ३०४ ॥
अग्निमन्त्रेण गृह्णीयात्[७] संस्पृश्य हृदयं जपेत् ।
स्वस्याग्नेर्ग्रहणं हृत्सु मन्त्रलिङ्गात्प्रतीयते ॥ ३०५ ॥
अथानन्तरमेवाप [८]आचामेद्विधिपूर्वकम् ।
आत्मसंस्कारसिध्यर्थं मन्त्राचमनमिष्यते ॥ ३०६ ॥
उद्धृत्य स्थण्डिलं वह्निं आदध्यात्तदनन्तरम् ।
अपरेणाग्निमित्येवमुत्तरत्राभिधीयते ॥ ३०७ ॥
[९]उचितः संस्कृतो वह्निरग्निशब्दसमीरितः ।
न च दध्येत्तदाधानमश्रुतं परिकल्प्यते ॥ ३०८ ॥
अतस्तत्संस्कार्य एवाग्निः पूर्वमित्यवसीयते ॥ ३०८क ॥
यज्ञोपवीतकरणात्प्रागेवाग्नेर्न[१०] संस्कृतिः ।
आरम्भे विहितं पूर्वमनूद्यात्र विधीयते ॥ ३०९ ॥

१.M °नतम्. २.M श्रवणं. ३.M पटुः. ४.M संस्कृतिः. ५.M °रिणमियुक्ति. ६.M °मात्मन्नृति. ७.M गृह्लीयाः. ८.M आचमे°. ९.M oms. T दध्येतदा°. १०.M °प्रगेवा°.

अग्निग्रहणमात्मार्थं तत आचमनक्रिया ।
समूहनादिभिस्तस्मात् संस्कार्योऽग्निरिहैव तु ॥ ३१० ॥

[सूत्रदण्डमेखलादिधारणम्]

संस्कृतिश्च[1] पदार्थानां ततः कार्या यतो हितैः ।
सूत्रदण्डादिभिर्योग्यैः कर्मयुक्तं प्रसाधितुम् ॥ ३११ ॥
ततश्चाज्यादिसंस्कारः पूर्वमेवात्र युज्यते ।
वाचयित्वा स्वस्त्ययनमाशितस्य शिरोरुहान् ॥ ३१२ ॥
वापयित्वाथ[1क] संस्नाप्य परिधाप्याहतं पटम् ।
[2]इत्याग्निवेश्यगदितमागमादिह गृह्यते ॥ ३१३ ॥
दण्डाजिनोपवीतानि मेखलां चैव धारयेत् ।
इत्यादिवचनान्नित्यमेषां धारणमिष्यते ॥ ३१४ ॥
यद्यप्याचार्य एवैषां ग्रहणं नोक्तवांस्तथा ।
अपि स्मृतौ विधेस्तेषामिहैव ग्रहणं यतः ॥ ३१५ ॥
गर्भाष्टमे[3] तु विप्राणां मौञ्जीधारणमिष्यते ।
मातुरग्रेऽधिजननं द्वितीयं मौञ्जिबन्धने ॥ ३१६ ॥
इत्यादिवचनाच्चैषां पूर्वमेवेह धारणम् ।
आश्रमज्ञापकत्वञ्च तेषामेव स्मृतौ स्मृतम् ॥ ३१७ ॥
मेखलाजिनदण्डैस्तु ब्रह्मचारीति लक्ष्यते ।
यस्येदं लक्षणं नास्ति प्रायश्चित्ती न चाश्रमी ॥ ३१८ ॥
स्वसंस्कृतिं गुरुः[4] कृत्वा साधनानां च संस्कृतिम् ।
विधाय ग्राहयेत्[5] तानि मन्त्रैः शास्त्रान्तरोदितैः ॥ ३१९ ॥
यज्ञोपवीतग्रहणं सर्वादौ विहितं परैः[6] ।
[7]आग्निवेश्योदितो मन्त्रो 'यज्ञस्ये'तीह गृह्यते ॥ ३२० ॥
कौण्डिन्यो मेखलां दत्त्वा वाससो दानमिच्छति ।

१.M °कृतिर्द्विपरदर्थानां. १क.MT °वाचायि. २.T इत्यानिवेश्य°. ३.M °ष्टमेषु. ४.M गुरुं. ५.MT ग्रह्ययेस्तानि. ६.M परे. ७.T अनिवेश्यो°.

परिधाप्याहतं वासो बध्यते मेखलागमात् ॥ ३२१ ॥
'या अकृन्ता'दयो मन्त्रास्तदुक्ता अजिनेऽपि च।
मेखलाग्रन्थिकरणे मन्त्रो बोधायनोदितः ॥ ३२२ ॥
पालाशदण्डदाने तु मन्त्रः कौण्डिन्यसंमतः ।
मेखलाजिनमन्त्राणां लिङ्गाद्वचनमिष्यते ॥ ३२३ ॥
[१]एतैस्तल्लक्षणैर्युक्तो ब्रह्मचार्यभिगम्य[२] तम् ।
ब्रूयाद् गुरुं समित्पाणिर्ब्रह्मचर्याभिमन्त्रकम्[३] ॥ ३२४ ॥
'को नामासी'ति ह्याचार्यप्रश्न एवोपपद्यते ।
हस्तग्रहणवेलायां नामग्रहणसिद्धये ॥ ३२५ ॥
'को नामासी'ति संप्रश्न आचार्यविषयो हि सः ।
यस्योपनीतिमेवासौ कुरुते विधिपूर्वकम् ॥ ३२६ ॥
एनं प्रकृतमेवाथो[४] विद्यार्थिनमथो गुरुम् ।
पृष्टः स निर्दिशेन्नाम[५] ब्रह्मचारी स्वकं गुरोः ॥ ३२७ ॥
जपेत्प्रसवमाचार्यो मन्त्रलिङ्गानुसारतः ।
प्राञ्चमावृत्य चैवैनमभिप्राण्येति[६] वक्ष्यति ॥ ३२८ ॥
उदञ्चमप्यर्जयदित्येतस्माल्लिङ्गदर्शनात् ।
आस्ते दक्षिणतो वह्नेराचार्याभिमुखः शिशुः ॥ ३२९ ॥
प्रत्यङ्मुखो 'ब्रह्मचर्यमागा'मिति[७] वदेत्ततः ।
अथाञ्जलौ शिशोरस्य जलमानीय मन्त्रवत् ॥ ३३० ॥
एताभिरेव नान्याभिर्विनियुक्ताभिरेव तु ।
अद्भिः संप्रोक्ष्य चैवैनं[८] कुमारं प्रतिमन्त्रकम् ॥ ३३१ ॥
वाक्यभेदात्तथा हस्तग्रहणं तदनन्तरम् ।
परिदानं[९] कुमारस्य रक्षणार्थं विधाय च ॥ ३३२ ॥

१.M एतैर्ल्लक्षणै°. २.M °चार्याभि°. ३.M °चर्यादिम°. ४.M प्रकृत.....विद्याथिन°, T प्रकृतमेवा.... विद्यार्थिन°. ५.M निर्दिशे. ६.M प्राणिती; T प्रणिति. ७.M °गामीति. ८.T वैवेनं. ९.M °धानं.

परिगृह्य परिष्वज्य जपित्वा कर्णतृन्दनम् ।
धिया संस्कृत्य[1] तत्कर्णे जपित्वा दक्षिणे तथा ॥ ३३३ ॥
सव्ये जप्त्वाऽथ तत्कर्णं दक्षिणं चाजपत्यधि[2] ।
जपतीत्यर्थ एवास्य सव्ये जप्त्वा यथोदितम् ॥ ३३४ ॥
अभिप्राण्य [3]शिशोर्मूर्ध्नि मन्त्रेणाप्यर्जयत्यथ ।
आसीनमेव चैवैनमुदग्गमयतीति तत् ॥ ३३५ ॥
परिधानप्रभृत्यग्निमुखं कृत्वा समिद्धुतिम् ।
कारयित्वा जयाद्यन्यहोमशेषं विधाय च ॥ ३३६ ॥
अथैनमाह 'ब्रह्मे'ति बोधयित्वार्थमादरात् ।
[4]अग्न्यादिदेवताभ्यस्तं प्रोच्योपस्थापयेत्ततः ॥ ३३७ ॥
प्रतिगृह्येप्सितं दण्डमुपस्थाय च भास्करम् ।
प्रदक्षिणं परीत्याग्निं चरेद् भैक्षं यथाविधि ॥ ३३८ ॥
इति स्मृतेरुपस्थानं कृत्वा भैक्षं चरेद्वटुः[5] ।
एतच्च भैक्षचरणं रात्रिभुक्त्यर्थमिष्यते ॥ ३३९ ॥
दिवाशितस्य चैवास्य संस्कारोऽत्र विधीयते ।
न हि द्विर्भोजनं कार्यं दिवा स्मार्तनिषेधतः ॥ ३४० ॥
सायं प्रातर्द्विजातीनामशनं श्रुतिचोदितम् ।
नान्तराभोजनं कुर्यादग्निहोत्रसमो विधिः ॥ ३४१ ॥
कृतोपनयनस्यास्य व्रतादेशनमिष्यते ।
ब्रह्मणो ग्रहणं चैव क्रमेण विधिपूर्वकम् ॥ ३४२ ॥
अथोपनयनादूर्ध्वं सावित्रमिति चोक्तितः ।
सावित्रं व्रतमादिश्य सावित्र्यध्यापनं[6] ततः ॥ ३४३ ॥
सावित्र्यध्यापिता पूर्वमुपनीय शिशुं यदि ।
[7]त्रियहेऽवनहे तस्मा अदृष्टार्थं ब्रवीति ताम् ॥ ३४४ ॥

१.M संस्कृत्य. २.M °त्यपि. ३.T शिशौ मूर्ध्नि. ४.M अन्यादि°. ५.M वटुम्. ६.M °ध्यापनस्ततः. ७.MT त्र्ययहे.

अनध्यापितसावित्रीकाय तस्मै तदैव तु ।
सन्ध्योपासनसिध्यर्थमेवेत्यत्रावधारणात् ॥ ३४५ ॥
अन्यस्य नियमाभावं ज्ञापयत्येव कल्पकृत् ।
चतुर्थे तां वदेत्तस्मात्तदानीमेव वा ततः ॥ ३४६ ॥
असंस्कृतस्य संस्कारः सर्वत्र प्रतिपाद्यते ।
संस्कृतस्य पुनस्तस्मात्संस्कारो युज्यते कथम् ॥ ३४७ ॥
न च वेदान्तराधीतौ संस्कार इह शंक्यते ।
विद्यार्थस्य नरस्यैव संस्कारः[१] प्रतिपद्यते ॥ ३४८ ॥
सर्ववेदार्थ एवायमादौ संस्कार इष्यते ।
सर्वयज्ञार्थ आधान संस्कारोऽग्नेर्यथा भवेत् ॥ ३४९ ॥
यथोपनयनं पुंसः[२] संस्कारः सार्ववैदिकः[३] ।
अग्न्याधेयं तथाग्नीनां संस्कारः सार्वयाज्ञिकः[४] ॥ ३५० ॥
अस्माच्च वचनात्सर्ववेदार्था संस्कृतिस्त्वियम् ।
संस्कृतस्य शिशोस्तस्मात्संस्कारो न हि युज्यते ॥ ३५१ ॥
कृत्स्नवेदावगमनात्[५] पुराऽऽचार्यो म्रियेत चेत् ।
आचार्यान्तरसंप्राप्तिरर्थात्[६] प्राप्नोति तस्य हि ॥ ३५२ ॥
तदा तेनोपनयनं कृत्वाऽध्याप्य [७]इतीर्यते ।
अनेन संस्कृतं ब्रह्म पुरुषं संस्करोति हि ॥ ३५३ ॥
एवमध्यापनाङ्गत्वं[८] संस्कारस्यास्य युज्यते ।
विशिष्टविद्याग्रहणसमर्थो[९] वा च युज्यते[९] ॥ ३५४ ॥
[१०]तं हाचार्य[१०] समित्पाणिरुपचक्रम[११] इत्यतः ।
नैमित्तिकार्थ एवायं संस्कारो वा समीरितः ॥ ३५५ ॥
लशुनाद्यदने भूयः संस्कारः शास्त्रचोदितः ।

१.MT संस्कारं. २.M पुंस. ३.MT सर्ववेदितः. ४.T °यज्ञिकम्. ५.M °गमनां. ६.M °र्थां. ७.M °ध्याप्याहुतीर्युते. ८.T °पनार्हत्वं. ९-९.M °सिध्यर्थो वाच उच्यते, T °समर्थो वा च पुज्यते. १०-१०.M तमाचार्यं. ११.M °क्रमन.

गत्वा[१] गुर्वन्तरं यस्तु विशिष्टज्ञानसिद्धये ॥ ३५६ ॥
प्रकृष्टं कालमत्रैव वस्तुकामो ब्रवीति हि ।
'प्रब्रवा इद'मित्यादि तदाचार्योऽनुमन्त्रयेत् ॥ ३५७ ॥
शिष्यं प्रयान्तं [२]'याम'ग्निर्वायु'रित्यादिमन्त्रतः ।
संबुध्यन्तमसौ स्थाने शिष्यनाम समुच्चरन् ॥ ३५८ ॥
अन्तः[३]प्राणेषु मन्त्रेषु[४] सकृदेव भवेद्यतः ।
अभ्यासो मङ्गलार्थोऽयं कल्पकृत्समुदीरितः[५] ॥ ३५९ ॥
देशान्तरगतौ चैतत् सर्वत्रेतीतरे जगुः ।
आश्रमान्तरसंप्राप्तावेवेत्यन्ये द्विजोत्तमाः ॥ ३६० ॥
आपूर्विकविधिश्चान्यो विकल्पोक्तो विधीयते ।
श्राद्धादिसकलं कार्यमाहताम्बरधारणात् ॥ ३६१ ॥
यज्ञोपवीतमित्यादि परिधानात्पुरोदितम् ।
ब्रह्म प्रणीतारहितं कृत्वा सूत्रादि दीयते ॥ ३६२ ॥
उदगप्यर्जनान्तेऽग्निमलंकृत्याथ मन्त्रवत् ।
परिषिच्याधाय समिधं चक्षुषी जुहुयात्ततः ॥ ३६३ ॥
आधाप्य समिधं मन्त्र'मेषा त' इति वाचयन् ।
मिन्दाहुती व्याहृतीभिर्हुत्वा मन्त्रवदेव तु ॥ ३६४ ॥
परिषिच्य वदे'द्ब्रह्मचार्यसी'त्यादिपूर्ववत् ।
संस्कारं कुरुते यस्मिन्नग्नौ तस्मिन्[६] समिद्धुतिः[७]॥ ३६५ ॥

[सावित्रव्रतम्]

सावित्रव्रतमोक्षात्प्राग्लौकिकेऽग्नौ[८] ततः परम् ।
अथोपनयनादूर्ध्वं सावित्रव्रतमादिशेत् ॥ ३६६ ॥
आपूर्विकमिदं कर्म शिष्टाः[९] कुर्वन्ति सन्ततम् ।
कृता तु संस्कृतिर्यस्मिन्नग्नौ तस्मिन्[१०] हुताशने ॥ ३६७ ॥

१.T गन्त्वा. २.M यामनि°. ३.T टनु. ४.T मन्त्रे क्तु. ५.M °रितम्. ६.M oms. ७.M °तिम्. ८.M गौ. ९.M शिष्टां. १०.M oms.

परिषेकप्रभृत्याग्नि[१]मुखात्कृत्वा व्रतार्थिने ।
समिधोऽभ्यादधातीति[२] यद्यप्यत्र समीरितम् ॥ ३६८ ॥
तथाप्येवं समाचारो न कुत्राप्युपलभ्यते ।
तस्मिन्नग्नौ परिषेकं कृत्वेत्यन्ये पठन्ति तु ॥ ३६९ ॥
समाचारानुसारेण पाठोऽयमिह[३] युज्यते ।
मध्यायोरपि[४] सावित्रं [५]व्रतमित्यनुषज्यते ॥ ३७० ॥
[६]अभ्याधानात्परं चापि मन्त्रवत्परिषेचनम् ।
प्रसिद्धं व्रतचर्येति व्रतकाले भवेद्धि यत् ॥ ३७१ ॥
कर्तव्यं वर्ज्यमप्यस्य तदेतदिति दिश्यते ।
सावित्र्यध्ययनं[७] तस्मात्तदूर्ध्वमिति गम्यते ॥ ३७२ ॥
पुनः प्रसिद्धमित्युक्तं यदुत्कृष्योत्तरत्र तत् ।
व्रतं विसृजते तस्मिन्निति संबध्यते ततः[८] ॥ ३७३ ॥
'यन्म आत्मन' इत्यादि प्रायश्चित्ताद्यपीष्यते ।
आदेशवदपूर्वत्वं[९] विसर्गस्यापि युज्यते ॥ ३७४ ॥
त्रियहं धारणं वह्नेस्तस्मिन्नग्नावितीरणात् ।
मन्त्राणां प्रतिलोमत्वं विशेषेणेह चोद्यते ॥ ३७५ ॥
चतुर्थे दिवसे प्राप्ते समिद्धोमादनन्तरम् ।
गुरुरग्निं समुच्यैतमादानायुश्च सम्प्रदात्[१०] ॥ ३७६ ॥
पालाशो दृश्यते यत्र यथोक्तायां दिशि स्थितः[११] ।
तस्य[१२] पश्चादधस्ताच्च शुचौ देशेऽग्निमाहृतम् ॥ ३७७ ॥
उद्धृत्योपसमाधाय परिस्तीर्य यथाविधि ।
प्रोक्षणीपात्रदर्व्यौ च समिधः पञ्च संमताः ॥ ३७८ ॥

१.M प्रभृत्या हि. २.T °°भ्यदधा°. ३.M पाठो ह मिह. ४.MT °रवि. ५.M सावित्रमव्रत°. ६.MT अभ्यधा°. ७.M °ध्ययनस्तस्मा°. ८.M ततम्. ९.M आदेशपदपू°. १०.T स..... ११.M °स्थितम्. १२.T तस्या.

आज्यस्थालीं च संसाद्य सूत्रादीनि सहैव तु ।
अन्यानि सादयित्वा संस्कृताद्भिः प्रोक्ष्य तान्यथ ॥ ३७९ ॥
दर्व्याज्यसंस्कृतिं कृत्वा सूपविष्टे शिशौ स्वयम् ।
मन्त्रवत्परिषिच्यैकामाधाय समिधं ततः ॥ ३८० ॥
प्रायश्चित्ताहुतीर्हुत्वाप्याधाप्य समिधः शिशुम् ।
मन्त्रवत्परिषिच्याथ दण्डमादाय तद्धृतम् ॥ ३८१ ॥
पालाशे निहितं गन्धपुष्पधूपादिभिः क्रमात् ।
अर्चयित्वा पायसेन सापूपेन बलिं हरेत् ॥ ३८२ ॥
पर्णोऽसौ[1] सुभ्रवा दण्डस्तस्मात्सुश्रव ते नमः' ।
द्विर्द्विरेतेन संपूज्यो बलिस्वाहान्वितेन तु ॥ ३८३ ॥
अद्भिः सन्तर्प्य चैवैनं मेखलादि शिशोरथ ।
अपनीय पलाशे तन्निधायाचम्य तान्यथ ॥ ३८४ ॥
वाचयित्वा स्वस्वमन्त्रान् ग्राहयित्वा यथाक्रमम् ।
उपस्थाप्य तथा चैनं कृत्वा दण्डप्रदक्षिणम् ॥ ३८५ ॥
जप्त्वा च मन्यते[2] मन्त्रं सशिष्यो ग्राममेत्य च ।
अनेन परिषिच्याथ ब्राह्मणान्[3] स्वस्तिवाचयेत् ॥ ३८६ ॥
यदि दूरे पलाशः [4]स्यादाहृत्योच्छिद्य तत्र तु ।
जपान्तं सकलं कृत्वा [5]स्वानित्यादि वदेद् गुरुः ॥ ३८७ ॥
व्रतं विसृजते तद्वत् गृहीत्वाप्युपतिष्ठते ।
जपेदित्येकवचनं स्वातन्त्र्येणेह वर्णितम् ॥ ३८८ ॥
तथापि कारयेच्छिष्टं समाचारस्थितेर्गुरुः ।
[6]अभ्याधापयतीत्येवं व्रतादेशे समीरणात् ॥ ३८९ ॥
आदेशवद्विसर्गस्य युक्तत्वाद् व्रतकर्मणि ।
प्रसिद्धवचनाच्चात्र विसर्गं कारयेद् गुरुः ॥ ३९० ॥

१.T सो. २.T यन्यते. ३.M ब्राह्मणान्. ४.M स्यामाहृ°. ५.M स्वामीत्या°. ६.M अभ्यध्याप°.

अत आचार्यकर्तृत्वं कर्मणामिह गम्यते ।
मन्त्रलिङ्गादुपस्थानजपा:[१] शिष्यस्य चेष्यते ॥ ३९१ ॥
बलिं दत्त्वाथ विस्रस्येत्येककर्तृत्वं लिङ्गत: ।
नातीव कल्पबाह्योऽयं[२] पक्ष इत्यवगम्यते ॥ ३९२ ॥
अशक्तेर्वा[३] गुरुश्चैनं कारयेदिति युज्यते ।
वासससश्चापि सन्त्यागो धारणं चेह विद्यते ॥ ३९३ ॥
पृथगाचमनं कार्यमुपवीतादिसंग्रह: ॥ ३९३क ॥

[४]इति सङ्गमग्रामवासिमिश्रविरचिते नारायणीये
वाधूलगृह्यागमवृत्तिरहस्ये
तृतीयोऽध्याय:[४]।

१.M °दपस्थानञ्जप:. २.M °वाक्योऽयं. ३.M oms वा. ४-४.T इति संगमग्रामवासिमिश्रिविरचिते वाधूलकगृह्यागमवृत्तिरहस्ये तृतीयोऽध्याय:; M इति संगमग्रामवासिमिश्रिविरचिते वाधूलक गृह्यागमसंग्रहे तृतीयोऽध्याय:.

अथ चतुर्थोऽध्यायः

[ब्रह्मचारिणो यमनियमाः]

उपनीय गुरुः शिष्यं शिक्षयेच्छ्रौत्रमादितः ।
आचारमग्निकार्यञ्च सन्ध्योपासनमेव च ॥ १ ॥
ब्रह्मचारिण एवातो यमाः सन्नियमा अमी ।
लेशतोऽत्र प्रदर्श्यन्ते श्रुतिस्मृतिसमीरिताः ॥ २ ॥
गुर्वधीनो भवेन्नित्यं ब्रह्मचारी समाहितः ।
अन्यत्र पतनीयेभ्यस्तदुक्तं[1] च न लंघयेत् ॥ ३ ॥
हितं प्रियञ्च कुर्वीत विरुद्धं न वदेत् क्वचित् ।
सक्षारलवणं नान्नमद्याच्छ्राद्धं[2] च मासिकम्[2] ॥ ४ ॥
स्वाङ्गप्रक्षालनञ्चासौ सुखार्थं न समाचरेत् ।
अशुचिस्पर्शने तस्य स्वाङ्गक्षालनमिष्यते ॥ ५ ॥
गुरोः सन्दर्शने चैतन्नाङ्गक्षालनमाचरेत् ।
समाजाञ्जनवादांश्च[3] वर्जयेन्नृत्तदर्शनम्[4] ॥ ६ ॥
शान्तो दान्तो मृदु[5]र्धीमान् [6]श्रद्धालुरनसूयकः ।
अक्रोधनो दृढधृती रहःशीलो[7] भवेच्च सः ॥ ७ ॥
उदाचारे गुरौ स्वैरकर्म नासौ समाचरेत् ॥ ७क ॥
विप्रवासे गुरोर्भैक्षं तत्कुलेभ्यो निवेदयेत् ।
तदभावेऽपि चान्येभ्यः श्रोत्रियेभ्यो निवेदयेत् ॥ ८ ॥
नोच्छिष्टं भोजने कुर्यादशक्तौ निखनेद्भुवि ।
अप्सु वा प्रक्षिपेद्यद्वा गुरुदासाय दीयताम् ॥ ९ ॥
उच्छिष्टमगुरोर्नैव भोक्तव्यं ब्रह्मचारिणा ।
आचार्यस्यापि चोच्छिष्टं दोषवत्त्वे न भुज्यते ॥ १० ॥

१.M °दुक्तश्च. २-२.M °च्छ्राद्धमाधिकम्. ३.M °नपादांश्च. ४.M वर्जयेस्रक् तदर्शनम्. ५.M मृदु धी°. ६. T श्लालुर°. ७.M रहलीलो, T रहथीलो.

समिद्धारो न गच्छेत रवावस्तंगते सति ।
होमशिष्टजलेनाथ न कुर्यात्कर्म किञ्चन ॥ ११ ॥
एकहस्तावसिक्तेन पाणिसंक्षुब्धवारिणा ।
नाचामेत्कर्म संयुक्तकर्मभिः पालयेद्गुरोः ॥ १२ ॥
बुद्धिपूर्वं प्रमादाद्वा नियमातिक्रमं गुरोः ।
ज्ञात्वा रहसि चैवैनं बोधयेत्तन्निवृत्तये ॥ १३ ॥
अनिवृत्तौ स्वयं कर्माण्यारभेद्वा निवर्तयेत् ॥ १३क ॥
जघन्यं शयनं[१] तस्य पूर्वोत्थानं चरन्वटुः[२] ।
जागर्त्येव तमुत्थाय पूर्वमेवाभिवादयेत् ॥ १४ ॥
संवेशयेद् गुरुं रात्रौ पादौ प्रक्षाल्य तस्य तु ।
पादप्रसारणं नाभिमुखं[३] तस्य समाचरेत् ॥ १५ ॥
खट्वायां वसतो नाभिप्रसारणमितीतरे ।
तत्सकाशे[४] न संविष्टो भाषेताभाषितं यदि ॥ १६ ॥
आसीनस्तं प्रतिब्रूयादासीनः संस्थितो वदेत् ।
उत्तिष्ठन्तमनुतिष्ठेद् गच्छन्तमनुगच्छते ॥ १७ ॥
उपासीतेश्वरमिव[५] न नग्नां स्त्रियमीक्षेत ।
नोपजिघ्रेन्मुखेनैनां[६] हृदा न प्रार्थयेत् स्त्रियम् ॥ १८ ॥
नाकारणात् स्पृशेदेनामोषधीनां वनस्पतेः ।
आच्छिद्य नोपजिघ्रेत न स्मयेत यदि स्मयेत् ॥ १९ ॥
अपिगृह्य[७] स्मयेदेष रक्तः स्याद्रजस्वलः[८] ।
सत्यवादी प्रयुञ्जीत साधुशब्दान्सुशिक्षितान् ॥ २० ॥
स्नाते गुरौ स्वयं स्नायात् तच्छुश्रूषणकृत्सदा ।
कौपीनं कटिसूत्रं च मेखलादीनि धारयेत् ॥ २१ ॥

१.M °शयनस्त°. २.M वटुम्. ३.M °मुखस्तस्य. ४.M °काशेन, T तत्काल..शेन. ५.M °तेश्चर°. ६.M °जिघ्रं मुखे°. ७.T अविगृ°. ८.M रक्तस्याद्रज°,T रक्तस्य..द्रज°.

यच्च शिष्येण कर्तव्यं कार्यं दासेन वा पुनः ।
कृतमित्येव तत्सर्वं कृत्वा तिष्ठेत्तु पार्श्वतः[१] ॥ २२ ॥
किङ्करः सर्वकारी च सर्वकर्मसु कोविदः ।
नाभुक्तवति[२] चाश्नीयादपीतवति[३] नो पिबेत्[४] ॥ २३ ॥
न तिष्ठति यथासीनः[५] नाप्रसुप्ते[५] स्वपेत्तथा ॥ २३क ॥
नोदाहरेदस्य नाम परोक्षमपि केवलम् ।
न चैवास्यानुकुर्वीत गतिचेष्टितभाषितम् ॥ २४ ॥
गुरोर्यत्र परीवादो निन्दा वापि प्रयुज्यते ।
कर्णौ[६] तत्र पिधातव्यौ गन्तव्यं वा ततोऽन्यतः ॥ २५ ॥
दूरस्थो[७] नार्च्चयेदेनं न क्रुद्धो नान्तिके स्त्रियाः[८] ।
यानासनस्थश्चैवैनमवरुह्याभिवादयेत् ॥ २६ ॥
प्रतिवातेऽनुवाते[९] वा नासीत[९] गुरुणा सह ।
असंश्रये चैव गुरोर्न किंचिदपि कीर्तयेत् ॥ २७ ॥
गोऽश्वोष्ट्रयानप्रासादप्रस्तरेषु कटेषु च ।
आसीत गुरुणा सार्धं शिलाफलकनौषु च ॥ २८ ॥
यथा खनन् खनित्रेण नरो वार्यधि[१०]गच्छति ।
तथा गुरुगतां विद्यां शुश्रूषुरधिगच्छति[११] ॥ २९ ॥
न स्नानेन न[१२]होमेन नैवाग्निपरिचर्यया ।
ब्रह्मचारी दिवं याति स याति गुरुपूजनात् ॥ ३० ॥
अमृतस्य प्रदातारं गुरुं यस्त्ववमन्यते ।
तच्चैनं दहति ब्रह्म तिर्यग्योनौ च जायते ॥ ३१ ॥
ऋचं वा यदि वाऽर्धर्चं पादं वापि तथाक्षरम् ।
सकाशाद्यस्य गृह्णीयान्नियतं तस्य गौरवम्[१३] ॥ ३२ ॥

१.M पार्वतः. २.M °क्तवदपि. ३.M पानीयाद°. ४.T नोत्पिबेत्. ५-५.M सीना प्रसुप्ते T °सीत नाप्रसु°. ६.M कण्ठे न. ७.M दूरे स्था. ८.M स्त्रियाम्. ९-९.M °नुचा..त वनासीत. १०.M वा युधि, T र्यति°. ११.MT °रतिग°. १२.M oms. १३.M नौरवम्.

[1]गुरोर्निर्माल्यशयने च्छायामासनपादुके[2] ।
नाक्रामेज्जितनिद्रः[3] स्याज्जितशिश्नो[4] जितोदरः ॥ ३३ ॥
आचार्यं चैव तत्पुत्रं[5] तद्भार्यां दीक्षितं गुरून् ।
पितरं च पितृंश्चैव मातरं मातुलं तथा ॥ ३४ ॥
हितैषिणं च विद्वांसं श्वसुरं यतिमेव च ।
न ब्रूयान्नामतो विद्वान्मातुश्च भगिनीमथ ॥ ३५ ॥
गुरुभार्यापुत्रयोश्च वृद्धानां धर्मशीलिनाम् ।
शुश्रूषा सर्वदा कार्या प्रणामो भक्तिरेव च ॥ ३६ ॥
उच्छिष्टं न तयोर्भोज्यं स्नापनादीनि वर्जयेत् ।
खट्वासनं च शयनं वर्जयेद्दन्तधावनम् ॥ ३७ ॥
स्वपेदेकः[6] कुशेष्वेव न रेतः स्कन्दयेत् क्वचित् ।
गरूच्छिष्टं भेषजार्थं निषिद्धमपि भक्षयेत् ॥ ३८ ॥
गन्धादिदेवताशिष्टं न निषिद्धमिति स्थितिः ॥ ३८क ॥
नियमातिक्रमे तस्य विद्या कर्म च नश्यति ।
गुरूपदिष्टान्नियमान् प्रयत्नेनाचरेत्ततः ॥ ३९ ॥

[वेदाध्यापनम्]

उपनीय गुरुः शिष्यमुपाकृत्य यथाविधि ।
काण्डव्रतं[7] समादिश्य वेदमध्यापयेत्ततः[8] ॥ ४० ॥
मास्याषाढे श्रावणे वा पूर्वपक्षस्य पर्वणि ।
उपाकृतिः[9] स्यादाषाढे तैष उत्सर्जनक्रिया ॥ ४१ ॥
श्रावणे माघमासे च[10] तथा पूर्णेन्दुपर्वणि ।
अधीयीत तयोर्मध्ये[11] मासानेवार्धपञ्चमान्[12] ॥ ४२ ॥
पूर्वाधिकं शुक्लपक्ष उत्सृज्यापि पठेत्तथा ।
वेदाङ्गानि रहस्यं च कृष्णपक्षे तु संपठेत् ॥ ४३ ॥

१.M गुरोस्तिर्माल्य°. २.M °मासवनादुके. ३.M °निद्र. ४.M °शिश्ने. ५.M twice. ६.M स्ववेदेकं°. ७.MT कन्धव्रतं. ८.M ततम्. ९.M °कृति. १०.MT om. ११.MT मध्यो. १२.T °मात्.

पुनः काल उपाकृत्य पठेत्पूर्वानधीतकम् ।
पारायणसमाप्तौ च कुर्यादुत्सर्जनक्रियाम् ॥ ४४ ॥

[काण्डव्रतानि]

काण्डव्रतानि चत्वारि वेदार्थानि समाख्यया ।
काण्डर्षयश्च चत्वारः प्रजापतिरथापरः[१] ॥ ४५ ॥
सोमोऽग्निश्च विश्वे च देवा इति समीरिताः ।
पौर्णमासार्थमन्त्रा ये ब्राह्मणादिसमन्विताः[२] ॥ ४६ ॥
प्राजापत्याः सोमयागशेषाः[३] सोम्याः समीरिताः ।
अग्न्याधानादिमन्त्रा ये त[४] आग्नेयाः[५] प्रकीर्तिताः ॥ ४७ ॥
इतरे वैश्वदेवाः[६] स्युरेवञ्चैते चतुर्विधाः[७] ।
एकैकस्य[८] बहुत्वेऽपि स्वकाण्डादौ व्रतं धृतम् ॥ ४८ ॥
देशान्तरस्थितानामप्युपकारकमेव तत् ।
प्राजापत्यं समादिश्य यद्वा व्रतमनन्तरम् ॥ ४९ ॥
तं काण्डोक्तं समाहृत्य सर्वमध्यापयेत्तथा ।
सौम्यादीनि समादिश्य काण्डान्यध्यापयेत्पृथक् ॥ ५० ॥
द्वादशाहावमञ्चैषां व्रतानां चरणं मतम् ।
संवत्सरावधि[९] तत्स्याद्गोदानेऽप्येवमेव तु ॥ ५१ ॥
होतॄणां शुक्रियाणां च तथोपनिषदां व्रतम् ।
संवत्सरं चरेत्तानि गोदानसहितानि तु ॥ ५२ ॥
संस्कारार्थानि पुंसा स्युर्वेदव्रतसमाख्यया ।
तेषामध्ययनं तानि निमित्तीकृत्य कुर्वते ॥ ५३ ॥
व्रतानि नृणां[१०] संस्कारं गोदानाख्यं व्रतं स्वतः ।
व्रतेषु नियमाः केचिद्यदि शास्त्रान्तरोदिताः ॥ ५४ ॥

१.M °परम्. २.M °न्वितान्. ३.M यानशेषाः. ४.M ता. ५.M आनीताः, T आग्नेताः. ६.M °देवा. ७.M °र्विधाम्. ८.M कस्य. ९.M °राद्धि, T °रावधिस्तत्. १०.M नृणां.

ग्राह्या आद्यं तयोरेषां वचनं[१] चेष्यतेऽन्तरा[२] ।
कार्यमन्ते नियमादौ वैकल्पिकं [भवेच्][३] च तत् ॥ ५५ ॥
शुक्रियव्यतिरिक्तेषु पालाश्यः समिधो मताः ।
पुण्याहवाचनञ्चेह सर्वेष्विष्टमुपक्रमे ॥ ५६ ॥
गोदानस्य विसर्गेऽपि सश्राद्धकमिदं भवेत् ।
कारीरिकाराव्रतयोर्नैतद्वचनसंयुतम् ॥ ५७ ॥
होमोऽपि नेष्यते तत्र यावदुक्तं समापयेत्[४] ।
उपाकृतौ सपुण्याहं व्याहृत्यन्तं[५] विधाय तु ॥ ५८ ॥
प्रजापतिश्च सोमाग्निर्विश्वे देवा य ईरिताः[६] ।
एतैः काण्डर्षिशब्दान्तैश्चतुर्थ्यन्तैर्जुहोत्यथ[७] ॥ ५९ ॥
'उपहूता'दिभिर्मन्त्रैर्वाग्देव्यन्तैर्दशाहुतीः ।
हुत्वा समाप्य होमं प्राग्वदनो दर्भविष्टरः[८] ॥ ६० ॥
तथाभूतेन शिष्येण सार्धमध्ययनं चरेत् ।
'इषे त्वा'द्यनुवाकांस्त्रीनादितोऽनूच्य कर्मणे ॥ ६१ ॥
'शकेया'न्तं निधायाथ काण्डाद्यध्ययनञ्चरेत् ।
आद्यं काण्ड'मिषे त्वे'ति पूर्वं वाक्यचतुष्टयम् ॥ ६२ ॥
द्वितीय'माप उन्दन्तु वर्चसे'ऽन्तं[९] तृतीयकम् ।
'देवासुराश्च संयत्ता आसन्नि'ति[१०] चतुर्थकम् ॥ ६३ ॥
'उभा वामि'त्यृचं[११] पूर्वमधीत्य प्रणवं ततः ।
सविसृष्टं वदेत्पूर्वं गुरुणोक्तं वदेच्छिशुः ॥ ६४ ॥
उपसंग्रहणं कुर्याद् गुरोराद्यन्तयोः शिशुः ।
वाचयित्वा स्वस्त्ययनं वापयित्वा[१२] शिरोरुहान् ॥ ६५ ॥
व्याहृत्यन्तं विधायाज्यं हुत्वा काण्डर्षये ततः ।

१.M वपनं. २.M न्तमा. ३.MT om; text under bracket conjectured by the editor to meet the metrical requirement. ४.T समाचरेत्. ५.M °हृत्यस्तं. ६.M ईरितम्, T °ताम्. ७.M शब्दास्तैश्चतुर्थ्यास्तैर्जु°. ८.T विष्ठरः. ९.M oms ऽन्तं. १०.M आददेति. ११.M देवामित्यृचं. १२.M वाचयि°.

'सदसस्पति'मन्त्रेणाप्याधाप्य[1] समिधो मिता:[2] ॥ ६६ ॥
चतस्रो व्रतवन्मन्त्रा:[3] प्राजापत्यादिसंयुतैः ।
जयादिहोमं सकलं कृत्वा तत्कालमादिशेत् ॥ ६७ ॥
विसर्गेऽप्येवमेव स्याद्धुत्वा मिन्दाहुती ततः ।
काण्डर्ष्याद्याहुतिं हुत्वा होमान्ते वपनं[4] चरेत् ॥ ६८ ॥
प्राजापत्यं व्रतं सौम्यं व्रतमाग्नेयमेव च ।
वैश्वदेवं च होतारं तथौपनिषदं व्रतम् ॥ ६९ ॥
शुक्रियं चापि गोदानं चरिष्यामि यथाव्रतम् ।
'शकेयं राध्यतां'[5] चैति मन्त्रेषु व्रतसंग्रहे ॥ ७० ॥
विसर्गे'ऽचारिषं' तद्व'दराध्यशक'मेव च ।
होतरि[6] चौपनिषदे व्याहृत्यन्ते हुते ततः ॥ ७१ ॥
हुत्वा पञ्चाहुती'र्याज्ञिकीभ्य' इत्याद्युदीरितैः ।
'सदसस्पतिमि'त्यादि समानं सर्वमाचरेत् ॥ ७२ ॥
तथोपनिषदो होतृशब्दाः सन्त्यज्य तत्र तु ।
'याज्ञिकीभ्यश्चोपनिषद्भ्यः स्वाहे'त्यादिपूर्ववत् ॥ ७३ ॥
'विश्वेभ्यश्चापि देवेभ्यः काण्डर्षिभ्य' इतीह तु ।
पञ्चम्याहुतिरेनां[7] स्यात्प्राजापत्येह नेष्यते ॥ ७४ ॥
विसर्गे[8] याज्ञिकीभ्यः[9] प्राक् प्रायश्चित्ताहुतिर्द्वयोः।

[शुक्रियव्रतप्रयोगः]

उदग्गते रवौ शुक्लपक्षे शुक्रियमादिशेत्[10] ॥ ७५ ॥
[11]यावद्वचनमेवैतत् प्रयोग इह कीर्त्यते ।
पुण्याहवाचनं कृत्वा वापयित्वा शिरोरुहान् ॥ ७६ ॥
भुक्त्वाऽपराह्णे प्राचीं वोदीचीं[12] वा दिशमेत्य तु ।
ग्रहाद्यदर्शने तत्र सूपलिप्ते समुद्धते ॥ ७७ ॥

१.M °णाधाव्य. २.M मिताम्, T मता:. ३.M मन्त्र, T मन्त्र:. ४.M व वनं. ५.T राध्यतं. ६.M होतारेचोप, T होतरे चोप°. ७.T नां broken. ८.M विदग्धे. ९.T याज्ञिकेभ्य:. १०.M मादिशी:. ११.T यावद्वपन°. १२.M वोदीदं.

प्रोक्षितेऽग्निं समाधाय ज्वलयित्वा समूहनम् ।
कृत्वा पर्युक्ष्य दर्भैः संपरिस्तीर्य प्रसिच्य[१] च ॥ ७८ ॥
तृणेषूत्तरत स्थालीं प्रोक्षण्यर्थाहताम्बरे[२] ।
चतस्रः समिधः साग्रा उदुम्बरसमुद्भवाः ॥ ७९ ॥
सपलाशा अशुष्काग्राः सप्ररोहास्तथेतराः[३] ।
[४]वैकङ्कतीः केवलाश्च[४] सादयेत्संस्कृतजलैः ॥ ८० ॥
प्रोक्ष्य स्थालीमधिश्रित्य वह्नौ तत्स्यात्पवित्रवत्[५] ।
आनीय जलमन्यस्मिन्पात्रे तस्मात्प्रसिच्य च ॥ ८१ ॥
सूपविष्टेन शिष्येण[६] गुरुः सार्धं समाहृतैः ।
एतैर्जलैर्दर्भवद्भिर्नमो[७] वाचेऽनुवाकगैः[८] ॥ ८२ ॥
मन्त्रैर्दशभिराम्नातैर्मार्जयित्वा ततो गुरुः[९] ।
गन्धपुष्पैरलंकृत्य मन्त्रवत्परिषिच्य च ॥ ८३ ॥
[१०]वैकङ्कतीर्व्याहृतीभिराधाय समिधः स्वयम् ।
संस्तीर्योत्तरतो वह्नेः प्रागग्राणि तृणान्यथ ॥ ८४ ॥
मदनीरुद्धृतास्तेषु दद्यात्प्रागपवर्गवत् ।
[११]त्रयोविंशतिरेवैते मन्त्रा 'ब्रह्मा'दिका इह ॥ ८५ ॥
ऋष्यादिर्मन्त्रवत्यन्तः[१२] पित्रादिर्धर्ममुपान्तिमः[१३] ।
होत्रन्तो[१४] देवतान्तश्चेत्येते मन्त्रा नमोऽन्विताः॥ ८६ ॥
[१५]'नमोऽग्नय'[१५] इत्यादिप्रयोगो दानकर्मणि ।
रौद्रीं[१६] सपैतृकमुक्त्वा[१७] त्वेकविंशतिरेव ते ॥ ८७ ॥
अतश्च रीतयस्तिस्रः[१८] कार्या एतैस्त्रिसप्तकैः ।
देयं दक्षिणतः पित्र्यं प्राचीनावीतिनान्यथा ॥ ८८ ॥

१.T प्रसिध्य. २.M प्रोक्षस्यर्थाहता°. ३.M रोहस्तथेतराम्, ¯ तथैतराः. ४-४.M °कतीं; T वैकङ्कतीं केवलाश्च broken. ५.M तस्याप°. ६.M धिष्ण्येणन. ७.M °वद्निमो, T °र्दर्भपाणिर्नमो. ८.M वाचानुवादकम्, T °ऽनुवाककैः ९.M गुरुम्. १०.T वै...व्याहृ°. ११.M त्रेधाविं °रेवैतं. १२.T °र्मन्त्रपत्यन्तः. १३.M पित्रादिर्घममुपान्तिकम्, T पित्रादि मुखान्तिमः. १४.M होत्रन्ता. १५-१५.MT नमोऽग्नय. १६.M रौद्र, T रौद्रिं. १७.T सपैतृकं मुक्त्वा. १८.M रीतयन्निस्रः.

रौद्रमुत्तरतो दत्त्वा रीतिशेषं समाचरेत् ।
दत्त्वा[1] पुष्पान्वितैर्मन्त्रैर्मृदन्तिलं[2] यथोदितम् ॥ ८९ ॥
समिधो लौकिकाज्याक्ता[3] उदुम्बरसमुद्भवाः ।
'पृथिवी [4]समिदि'त्याद्यैश्चतुर्भिर्ब्रह्मचारिणः[5] ॥ ९० ॥
आधाप्याग्निमुपस्थाप्य तिष्ठन्तं स्वयमुत्थितः[6] ।
चतुर्भिस्त्रिहवं[7] मन्त्रैः शुक्रियेण समन्वितैः ॥ ९१ ॥
उपविश्या'न्वमंस्था'द्यैः[8] परिषिच्य वटुं ततः ।
श्रावयेच्च दिवाकीर्त्यं मन्त्राख्यं प्रश्नमुत्तरम् ॥ ९२ ॥
'महीनां पय' इत्याद्यं 'देवा वै सत्रमि'त्यपि ।
तद्ब्राह्मणं च संश्राव्य वाससा सशिरोमुखम्[9] ॥ ९३ ॥
शिशोः 'स्वाहे'ति[10] मन्त्रेण वेष्टयित्वा प्रदक्षिणम् ।
'शन्नो[11]वाता'दिभिर्मन्त्रैर्मार्जयित्वा च पूर्ववत् ॥ ९४ ॥
उपास्य सन्ध्यां संप्राप्तां ग्राममेत्य समिद्धुतिम् ।
कृत्वा[12] वाचंयमस्तिष्ठेद्यद्वाऽऽसीनो[13]ऽस्वपन्निशाम् ॥ ९५ ॥
पुरोदयात्तु निष्क्रम्य ग्रामात्सन्ध्यामुपास्य च ।
समिद्धोमे कृते तेन गुरुं पूर्वमुदीरितम्[14] ॥ ९६ ॥
अग्न्याधानादि सकलं कर्म कुर्याच्च कारयेत् ।
व्याहृतीभिः समिद्धोमान् प्राक् तु मिन्दाहुती इह ॥ ९७ ॥
संस्कृताज्येन जुहुयात्समिदभ्यञ्जनं च तत् ।
उपस्थाप्योपविश्याथ परिषिच्याहतं पटम्[15] ॥ ९८ ॥
'[16]वयः सुपर्ण' मन्त्रेण विस्रस्योत्थाप्य तं रविम् ।
'उद्वयं तमसो' [17]'दु त्यं' 'चित्रं' 'तच्चक्षु'रादिभिः ॥ ९९ ॥

१.M पुष्पाणि तै°. २.M °र्मदन्ति च. ३.T °ज्याक्ताः. ४.M समिति द्यौद्यैश्चतु°. ५.M °चारिणम्. ६.M °त्थितम्. ७.M °र्भिस्तन्त्रवन्. ८.M °विश्य समंस्था°. ९.M °मुखः. १०.T स्वाभिमन्त्रेण. ११.T पातादि°. १२.T हुत्वा. १३.M °सीतास्वप°, T °सीत स्वप°. १४.MT पूर्वेद्युदीरि°. १५.M वटुम्. १६.M पयस्यु°, T पयस्सुवङ. १७.M °सोदित्यं.

चतुर्भिर्दिश[1] इत्यन्तैरुपस्थाप्योपविश्य च[2] ।
'शन्नो वाता'नुवाकेन प्रत्यृचं प्रतिमन्त्रतः[3] ॥ १०० ॥
मार्जयेदा[4]मदन्तीभिरादिशेत्कालमन्त्रतः[5] ।
दृष्ट्वाऽमेध्यं[6] जपेन्मन्त्र'मबद्धं मन' इत्यसौ ॥ १०१ ॥
अभिवृष्टो[7] जपेन्मन्त्र'मुन्दतीर्बल'मित्यपि ।
अगुर्व्यासौ स्त्रिया वापि शूद्रेण सह संवदेत् ॥ १०२ ॥
भुक्त्वोज्झितं समुच्छिष्टं स्त्रीशूद्राभ्यां[8] न दीयते ।
न च स्नायान्निमित्तेषु सत्सु स्नानमिष्यते ॥ १०३ ॥
रात्रौ न भोजनं कार्यमुपवासस्तु पर्वसु ।
स्नायात्तत्र विसर्गे तु प्रातर्यं क्रियतेऽखिलम् ॥ १०४ ॥
समिदासादने[9] मन्त्रा 'द्यौ रि'त्याद्यास्त्रयोऽत्र तु ।
'प्राजापत्या म' इत्याद्यश्चतुर्थोऽत्रापि गृह्यते ॥ १०५ ॥
उपस्थापनमन्त्राणां तथेह प्रतिलोमता ।

[गोदानकर्म]

गोदानं चौलवत्कार्यं वर्षे षोडश एव तु ॥ १०६ ॥
पुण्याहवाचनादूर्ध्वं वपनं नेह विद्यते ।
'पक्वं' 'ये केशि' मन्त्राभ्यां हुत्वाथ सदसस्पतिम् ॥ १०७ ॥
हुत्वाधाप्य समिधः[10] स्विष्टहोमादिकं चरेत् ।
भूमावेवास्य शयनं[11] स्नानं च सवनत्रये ॥ १०८ ॥
विसर्गेऽप्येवमेव स्यात् सनखश्मश्रु वापयेत् ।
आचार्यायाथ गां दद्यादन्यस्मै च द्विजातये ॥ १०९ ॥

[स्वशाखाध्ययनमहत्त्वम्]

तपोविशेषैर्विविधैर्व्रतैश्च विधिचोदितैः ।

१.M °भिर्दश°. २.M थ, T तु. ३.M °मन्त्रकम्. ४.MT मुदन्ती°. ५.MT मन्त्र तु. ६.MT मेव्यं. ७.T °पृष्ठो. ८.MT शूद्राद्या. ९.M °साचने. १०.MT समिध. ११.T शयन°.

वेदः[१] कृत्स्नोऽधिगन्तव्यः सरहस्यो द्विजन्मना[२] ॥ ११० ॥
पारम्पर्यागतो येषां वेदः सपरिबृंहणः[३] ।
तच्छाखं[४] कर्म कुर्वीत [५]तच्छाखाध्ययनं तथा ॥ १११ ॥
यः स्वशाखां परित्यज्य [६]पारक्यमधिगच्छति ।
शाखारण्डः[७] स विज्ञेयः सर्वधर्मबहिष्कृतः ॥ ११२ ॥
यच्छाखीयैस्तु संस्कारैः संस्कृतो ब्राह्मणो भवेत् ।
[८]तच्छाखाध्ययनं कुर्यात् त्यक्तेन पतितो भवेत् ॥ ११३ ॥
स्वशाखाश्रयमुत्सृज्य परशाखाश्रयं तु यः ।
कर्तुमिच्छति दुर्मेधा मोघं तत्तस्य[९] चेष्टितम् ॥ ११४ ॥
यन्नाम्नायां स्वशाखायां परोक्तमविरोधि च ।
विद्वद्भिस्तदनुष्ठेयेताग्नि[१०]होत्रादिकर्मवत् ॥ ११५ ॥

[वेदाध्ययनविधिः]

प्राप्ते वेदानुवचने विसर्गे चान्वहं गुरोः ।
उपसंग्रहणं कार्यं विप्रोष्य त्वागतेन च ॥ ११६ ॥
अध्येष्यमाणस्त्वाचान्तो यथाशास्त्रमुदङ्मुखः ।
ततोऽधीयीत[११] वेदं तु वीक्षमाणो[१२] गुरोर्मुखम् ॥ ११७ ॥
हस्तौ तु संयतौ कार्यौ जानुभ्यामुपरि स्थितौ ॥ ११७क ॥
ब्रह्मणः[१३] प्रणवं कुर्यादादावन्ते च सर्वदा ।
स्रवत्यना.कृतं[१४] पूर्वं परस्ताच्च विशीर्यते[१५] ॥ ११८ ॥
पुस्तकप्रत्ययाधीतं नाधीतं गुरुसन्निधौ ।
भ्राजते न[१६] सभामध्ये जारगर्भ[१७] इव स्त्रियाम् ॥ ११९ ॥
ब्रह्म[१८] यस्त्वननुज्ञातमधीयानादवाप्नुयात् ।

१.M वेदं. २.M °जन्मनाम्. ३.M °बृह्मणम्. ३. क MT om. ४.M तच्चाखं. ५.M तच्चाख्याध्य°. ६.M पारत्यम°. ७.M शाखान्दण्ड°,T °दण्ड. ८.M तच्चाख्याध्य°. ९.T तस्य च. १०.M °ष्ठेयस्तान्निहोत्रा°, T °ष्ठेयता°. ११.T ततोपयीत. १२.T प्रेक्षमाणो. १३.T ब्राह्मणा. १४.M °त्येनांकृतं. १५.M विधीयते. cf Manu II.74: विशीर्यति. १६.M भावुके. १७.M जानुगर्भ. १८.M ब्रह्मात्वननु°.

स ब्रह्मस्तेयसंयुक्तो नरकं प्रतिपद्यते ॥ १२० ॥
अनध्यायेष्वधीतं यद्यच्च शूद्रस्य सन्निधौ ।
प्रतिग्रहनिमित्तं[१] च नरकाय तदुच्यते ॥ १२१ ॥
हस्तहीनं तु योऽधीते स्वरवर्णविवर्जितम् ।
ऋग्यजुःसामभिर्दग्धो वियोनिमनुगच्छति ॥ १२२ ॥
हस्तेनाधीयमानस्तु स्वरवर्णान्प्रयोजयेत् ।
ऋग्यजुःसामभिः पूतो ब्रह्मलोकं स गच्छति ॥ १२३ ॥
संस्कारवद्भिः कर्तव्यं वेदस्याध्ययनं द्विजैः ।
शुद्धस्य फलवत्तस्मादन्यथा निष्फलं स्मृतम् ॥ १२४ ॥
योनेरिव गणाद्भीतः सौहित्यान्नरकादिवत् ।
राक्षसीभ्य इव स्त्रीभ्यः स विद्यामधिगच्छति ॥ १२५ ॥
[२]यत्कीटैः पांसुभिः श्लक्ष्णैः वल्मीकः क्रियते महान् ।
न तत्र बलसामर्थ्यमुद्योगं तत्र कारणम् ॥ १२६ ॥
शनैर्विद्यां शनैरर्थान् आरोहेत्पर्वतं शनैः ।
[३][शनैः पन्थाश्च धर्मश्च व्यायामः शनैः शनैः] ॥ १२७ ॥
द्यूतं पुस्तकशुश्रूषा नाटकासक्तिरेव च ।
स्त्रियस्तन्द्री च [मानं च][३क] विद्याविघ्नकराणि षट् ॥ १२८ ॥
ऋक्पादमप्यधीयीत[४] मार्गेणोक्तेन धर्मवित् ।
न त्वेव चतुरो वेदानन्यायेन[५] कदाचन ॥ १२९ ॥
सततं प्रातरुत्थाय दन्तधावनपूर्वकम् ।
स्नात्वा हुत्वाऽथ शिष्येभ्यः कुर्यादध्यापनं नरः[६] ॥ १३० ॥
धर्मार्थौ यत्र न स्यातां [७]शुश्रूषा वाऽपि[७] तद्विधा ।
[८]विद्यया सह मर्त्तव्यं न त्वेनामूषरे वपेत् ॥ १३१ ॥

१.M °निमित्तश्च, T °ग्रहं निरिक्तं च. २.M oms यत्. ३.MT om Second hemistich. ४. M °दमव्यधी°. ५.M वेदानन्यथा यो न. ६.M नरम्. ७-७ M शुश्रूषापि च, T षा...पि; cf Manu II.112. ८. cf Manu II.113 विद्ययैव समं कामं मर्त्तव्यं ब्रह्मवादिना। आपद्यापि हि धोरायां न त्वेनामिरिणे वपेत्॥.

आचार्यपुत्रः शुश्रूषुर्ज्ञानदो धार्मिकः शुचिः ।
कृतज्ञोऽद्रोही मेधावी शुचिः कुल्योऽनसूयकः ॥ १३२ ॥
अध्याप्याः साधुशक्ताप्तस्वार्थदा धर्मतस्त्विमे ।
विनावसेन शिष्यादिशासनं तदशक्तितः ॥ १३३ ॥
भार्या[1] पुत्रश्च दासश्च शिष्यो[2] भ्राता च सोदरः ।
प्राप्तापराधास्ताड्याः स्यू रज्ज्वा वेणुदलेन वा ॥ १३४ ॥
[3]चातुर्वर्ण्यं त्रयो लोकाश्चत्वारश्चाश्रमाः[4] पृथक् ।
भूतं भव्यं भविष्यच्च सर्वं वेदात्प्रसिध्यति ॥ १३५ ॥
वेदमेव सदाभ्यस्येत्तपस्तप्स्यन्[5] द्विजोत्तमः ।
वेदाभ्यासो हि विप्रस्य तपः परमिहोच्यते ॥ १३६ ॥
यं यं क्रतुमधीयीत[6] तस्यतस्याप्नुयात्फलम् ।
त्रिर्वित्तपूर्णपृथिवीदानस्य फलमश्नुते ॥ १३७ ॥
तपसश्च परस्येह नित्यस्वाध्यायवान् द्विजः ॥ १३७क ॥
योऽनधीत्य द्विजो [7]वेदमन्यत्र कुरुते श्रमम् ।
स जीवन्नेव शूद्रत्वमाशु[8] गच्छति सान्वयः ॥ १३८ ॥
न वेदपाठमात्रेण सन्तोषं कारयेद् गुरुः ।
पाठमात्रावसायी तु पङ्के गौरिव सीदति ॥ १३९ ॥
यथा पशुर्भारहारी न तस्य भजते फलम् ।
द्विजस्तथार्थानभिज्ञो न वेदफलमश्नुते ॥ १४० ॥
वेदस्वीकरणं पूर्वं विचारोऽभ्यसनं जपः ।
शिष्येभ्यश्च प्रदानं च वेदाभ्यासो हि पञ्चधा ॥ १४१ ॥
क्रमप्राप्तोपनयनं गृह्यानुक्तमिहोदितम् ।
उपनीतस्य नियमा यमाश्चेह प्रकीर्तिताः ॥ १४२ ॥
उपाकृतिर्व्रतादीनां[9] प्रयोगोऽपि समीरितः[10] ।

१.M भार्यः. २.Cf Manu VIII.299: प्रेष्यो. ३.MT °वर्ण्यस्. ४.MT वेदाश्चत्वारश्चाश्रमात्; thus Manu XII.97. ५.MT तप्यं. ६.M °धीयीते, T °मधीते. ७.M वेदाम°. ८.M wrongly adds न after °माशु. ९.T °कृतिव्रता°. १०.M °रितम्.

इदानीं गृह्यवाक्यानामुच्यतेऽथ समासतः ॥ १४३ ॥

[व्रतसंस्कृतिः]

पूर्वानुवाके चौलान्ता संस्कृतिः समुदीरिता ।
व्रताख्यासंस्कृतिः पूर्वमस्मिन्नध्याय उच्यते ॥ १४४ ॥
एषां व्रतविसर्गे[1] नानेत्यादेरिह दर्शनात् ।
व्रतान्येवेह वक्ष्यन्त इत्येतदवगम्यते ॥ १४५ ॥
इहोपनयनं नोक्तं[2] क्लृप्त्यन्तं[3] समुदीरणात् ।
श्रौतं कर्म द्विजस्येति तस्य तत्र [4]वचो भवेत्[4] ॥ १४६ ॥
उपनीतस्य संस्कारो व्रताख्यस्तेन कीर्त्यते ।
अनन्तरं व्रतान्यत्र वक्ष्यन्ते त्रीणि तानि तु ॥ १४७ ॥
वत्सरं चरितव्यानि पुरुषार्थतया स्मृतौ ।
संस्कारमध्ये चत्वारि [5]व्रतानि चेह[5] गण्यते ॥ १४८ ॥
होत्रादीनां व्रतानीति संबन्ध इह गम्यते ।
होत्रादिशब्दस्तद्वाच्यग्रन्थ एवेह वर्तते ॥ १४९ ॥
तस्य व्रतेन संबन्धो [न][6] तदध्ययनं विना ।
ग्रहणान्तं व्रतं चार्यमिति काण्डं व्रतोदितम् ॥ १५० ॥
होत्राद्यध्यापनार्थत्वमत एषां प्रतीयते ।
तथापि पुरुषार्थत्वमेतेषां न विरुध्यते ॥ १५१ ॥
[7]वेदव्रतसमाख्यानात्तदधीतिमुखेन हि ।
संस्कारार्थत्वमेतेषां स्मृतावपि विवक्ष्यते[8] ॥ १५२ ॥
अन्यान्यपि व्रतान्यत्र विधीयन्ते तथापि तु ।
पुरुषार्थत्वमेतेषामेतेत्यध्यव[9]सीयते ॥ १५३ ॥
मुख्यं संवत्सरं कालो व्रतानामवगम्यते ॥ १५३क ॥

१.M विसर्गेणेत्या°. २.T °नयनोक्तं. ३.M क्लृप्त्यन्ते. ४-४.T वचोक्तवत्. ५-५.M व्रतादिह, T व्रतानि चहि. ६.MT broken. ७.M प्रेतव्रत°, T ...व्रत. ८.T विवक्षिते. ९.T °तेषांमेतेत्य°.

[१]एवंविद्वान् वत्सरं[२] यो[२] व्रतं चरति तस्य तु ।
वत्सरेण व्रतं गुप्तं भवतीति श्रुतौ श्रुतम् ॥ १५४ ॥
ग्रन्थार्थत्वेऽपि होत्रादेः[३] श्रुतकालोऽपि वत्सरम् ।
नियतो[४] ग्रहणान्तोऽन्यव्रतकालो[५]ऽपि कल्पितः[५]॥ १५५ ॥
ततश्चाध्ययनाङ्गत्वमेतेषामवगम्यते ।
पूर्वप्राप्तानि[६] चैतानि प्राजापत्यादिकानि तु ॥ १५६ ॥
त्यक्त्वेह वचनं तेषां संस्कारत्वप्रसिद्धये ।
न चैषां पूर्वचार्यत्वं व्रतानामिह युज्यते ॥ १५७ ॥
स्वाध्यायाध्ययनं प्राप्तमुपनीतस्य तस्य तु ।
उपाकृत्यैव कार्यत्वादादितः स्यादुपाकृतिः ॥ १५८ ॥
स्वाध्यायाध्ययनारंभ उपाकर्मेति कीर्त्यते ।
अध्यायानामुपाकर्म श्रावण्यामिति हि स्मृतिः ॥ १५९ ॥
वेदाध्ययनसामर्थ्यमेतन्मन्त्रा वदन्त्यपि ।
होमान्तेऽध्ययनं चापि विहाय तदनन्तरम् ॥ १६० ॥
अनध्यायान् वर्जयित्वाऽधीयीरन्नितीरितम् ।
उपाकृतेः[७] परं चापि न होत्रादिव्रतं भवेत् ॥ १६१ ॥
होत्राद्यध्ययनं[८] पूर्वं यस्मान्न विधिचोदितम् ।
तैत्तिरीयकशाखेय'मिषे त्वा'द्येह पठ्यते ॥ १६२ ॥
तदाद्यध्ययनं[९] तच्च ज्ञापयत्येव गृह्यकृत् ।
स्वाध्यायाध्ययनारंभ उपाकरणकर्मणि ॥ १६३ ॥
आदितस्त्रीननुवाकाननूच्येत्यादिभाषणात् ।
प्राजापत्यादिकं तस्मात् काण्डार्थं पूवमादिशेत्॥ १६४ ॥
न चाप्युपाकृतेः पूर्वं व्रतमादिश्यते यतः ।
सर्ववेदाध्ययनशेषत्वं स्याद्ध्युपाकृतेः ॥ १६५ ॥

१.M oms एवं. २-२.M वत्सरं वो या. ३.M ह्योत्रादेच्छ्रुत°. ४.T नियतं. ५-५.M °कालो विकल्पितः. ६.M °प्राप्ताग्नि. ७.M °कृतवे. ८.MT होत्राध्ययनं. ९.M तदाध्य°.

[१]तस्मात्काण्डव्रतान्यादावादिश्याधीत्य तान्यथ ।
होत्रादिव्रतमादिश्य होत्राद्यध्ययने कृते ॥ १६६ ॥
[२]अवशिष्टे कृते[२] काले पूर्वाधीतं समभ्यसेत्[३] ।
सौबभ्रुवो[४] ह वाधूल इत्यस्मिन्ननुवाकगे[५] ॥ १६७ ॥
अध्यापनं तु होतृणां दृश्यते प्रथमं तथा ।
इहादौ तद्व्रतं प्रोक्तं तदध्ययनमादितः ॥ १६८ ॥
आहुः[६] केचित्ततोऽप्यत्र[७] विकल्पो न्यायतो मतः ।
ततश्च कार्यपूर्वत्वं[८] व्रतानां न विरुध्यते ॥ १६९ ॥
होमकर्मण एवैतन्नामधेयं व्रतं ततः ।
[९]संवत्सराश्रयो होम इत्येतदवगम्यते ॥ १७० ॥
प्रवृत्तिविषये चापि निवृत्तिविषयेऽपि च ।
परिपाल्यमाने संकल्पे यद्यपि प्रथितं व्रतम् ॥ १७१ ॥
[१०]तथापीहाश्रुतेरन्यशास्त्रसिद्धा भवन्ति चेत्[११] ।
ग्राह्या गोदानसिद्धानां नियमो नेति गम्यते ॥ १७२ ॥
अथ गोदानमित्येवं गोदानेऽपि कृते ततः ।
तस्येति नियमार्थं[१२] स्यादिति तत्रावगम्यते ॥ १७३ ॥
व्रतानां पुरुषार्थत्वं यतः स्मृतिषु चोदितम् ।
संवत्सरस्य कालत्वं व्रतस्यापि श्रुतौ श्रुतम् ॥ १७४ ॥
तस्मात्संवत्सरं [१३]चर्याण्येतानीतीति शब्दनम् ।
तेषां मध्ये[१४] च होतृणां व्रते व्याहृतिपश्चिमम् ॥ १७५ ॥
हुत्वाऽथ[१५] जुहुयाद्धोतृंस्तच्छब्दो देवतापरः ।
सगुणा देवतास्तस्माद्याज्ञिक्याद्या विवक्षिताः[१६] ॥ १७६ ॥
प्रजापतिस्तु काण्डर्षिहोतृशब्दसमीरितः ।

१.T तस्मात् broken. २-२.M °शिष्टकृतेः, T °शिष्ठे°. ३.T समा.... ४.M सौरवभ्रुवो. ५.MT °वाकके. ६.M oms आहुः;T.हुः. ७.M °ततावत्र. ८.MT कायपू°. ९.M oms सं. १०.M °पीह श्रुते°. ११.T च. १२.M नियमा यं. १३.T चार्या°. १४.M मुताध्य. १५.M हुत्वा च. १६.MT °क्षिता.

होत्रादीनां व्रतेष्वेव न च होतॄञ्जुहोति[1] तु ॥ १७७ ॥
न हि [2]चित्तिः स्रुगादीनां होतृत्वमिह युज्यते ।
एष एवोपनिषदां कल्प इत्यतिदिश्यते ॥ १७८ ॥
होतारो यत्र कीर्त्यन्ते तत्रोपनिषदस्त्विह ।
प्रजापतिश्च यत्र स्याद्विश्वे देवास्ततस्त्विति ॥ १७९ ॥
ततश्च होतृशब्देन देवता एव कीर्तिताः ।
'सदसस्पतिमि'त्यत्र प्रतीकग्रहणं त्वृचः ॥ १८० ॥
उत्तमत्वं च सर्वत्र तस्याः प्राप्त्यर्थमुच्यते ।
अपूर्वत्वाच्छुक्रिये सा सावित्रेऽपि न हूयते ॥ १८१ ॥
सदसस्पतिहोमेनाव्यवधानं समिद्धुतेः ।
ज्ञापयत्यथशब्देन [3]व्रतपूर्वसमिद्वचः ॥ १८२ ॥
आख्यया सर्वशेषत्वं समिधां[4] ज्ञापयत्यतः ।
काण्डव्रतेषु चाधाप्याः समिधो[5] व्रतमन्त्रवत् ॥ १८३ ॥
गोदानेऽपि हुते पक्वे हुत्वा च सदसस्पतिम् ।
आधाप्याः समिधो यस्मात् समिन्मात्रमिह[6] श्रुतम्॥ १८४ ॥
साग्रत्वादि गुणास्तस्मात्समिधानेति लक्ष्यते ।
होतृशब्दं विहायान्ये व्रतमन्त्रान् पठन्ति ते ॥ १८५ ॥
होत्रादिरहितञ्चापि कुर्युर्व्रतसमिद्धुतिम् ।
अनुषज्येव होतारं शिष्टा[7] अन्ये पठन्त्यमी ॥ १८६ ॥
अनुषज्येव जुहुयुः समाचारोऽपि तादृशः[8] ।
'वाय्वा'दिमन्त्रयोश्चापि होताराद्यनुषज्यते ॥ १८७ ॥
एतेषामिति होतॄणामिह निर्देश इष्यते ।
एतावदेव नाना स्यादियान्भेदो भवेत्ततः ॥ १८८ ॥
विसर्गेऽपि च होमस्य कार्यत्वमवगम्यते ।

१.T होतृजु°. २.M चित्ति. ३.M पूतपूर्व°. ४.M समिधं. ५.M समिधा. ६.M स्वात्रमिह. ७.T शिष्ठा. ८.M तादृशम्.

एतावदेव नानेति साग्ने[१].....चादिषादिकम्[१] ॥ १८९ ॥
अत्रोक्तं प्रतिलोमत्वं मन्त्राणां नेति गम्यते ।
प्रायश्चित्ताहुती चापि नित्ये व्रतविसर्जने ॥ १९० ॥
याज्ञिकीभ्यः पुरा कार्ये इति बोधायनोदितम् ।
व्रतभ्रेषे च सर्वत्र प्रायश्चित्ताहुती इमे ॥ १९१ ॥
[२]प्रायश्चित्तत्ववचनादाहुतिर्ग्रहणादपि ।
नित्ये व्रतविसर्गे ते[३] इत्येतदवगम्यते ॥ १९२ ॥
'यन्म आत्मन' इत्येतद्यजुरौपानुवाक्यगः[४] ।
तदनन्तरं मन्त्रैव पुनरग्निरऋगीरिताः[५] ॥ १९३ ॥
एष एवोपनिषदां[६] विधिर्होतृव्रतोदितः ।
'याज्ञिक्या'दिषु मन्त्रेषु होतृशब्दानवोद्धरेत्[७] ॥ १९४ ॥
तथा चोपनिषच्छब्दान् प्रक्षिपेत्काण्डदेवताः ।
विश्वे देवा इह ग्राह्याः[८] प्रजापतिपदे तथा ॥ १९५ ॥

[शुक्रियव्रतविधानम्]

शुक्रियाणां व्रतस्येह विधानमधुनोच्यते ।
शुक्रशुक्लमहर्वाचि दिवाकीर्त्यं तु शुक्रियम् ॥ १९६ ॥
शुक्रमादत्त इत्येतद्व्याख्यानसमये गणे ।
आददाना [९]हरेर्वैतच्छुक्रमित्यादिभाषितम् ॥ १९७ ॥
दिवैवाध्ययनं येषां तेषां शुक्रियता ततः ।
प्रवर्ग्यशेषमन्त्रा [१०][.............] मन्त्र तु ॥ १९८ ॥
होतॄणामुपनिषदां पृथग्व्रतमिहोदितम् ।
[११]प्रवर्ग्यशेषता चेह मन्त्रलिङ्गात्प्रतीयते ॥ १९९ ॥
तस्मात्सर्वं दिवाकीर्त्यं शेषत्वं[१२] नास्य[१३] युज्यते ।

१-१.M साग्ने...चादिषा°, T नानेति...षादिकम्. २.M °श्चित्तवच°. ३.T तु. ४.M यजूरौचानु°, T यजुरौचानु°. ५.M °रनिरूगी°. ६.M षदाद्विधि°. ७.MT °नवेद्ध°. ८.M ग्राह्यां, T ग्राह्या. ९.MT हरेवैत°. १०.M broken after शेषमत्र, T शेषमन्त्रा....मन्त्र तु. ११.T प्रपश्यशेष°. १२.M शेष. १३.M adds हि after नास्य.

माघाद्याषाढपर्यन्तः[1] कालस्तस्य[1] नियम्यते ॥ २०० ॥
दक्षिणायनमन्येषां व्रतानां न विरुध्यते ।
अस्मिन्काले क्रियेतैतत्क्रियेतेत्येकवद्वचः[2] ॥ २०१ ॥
अध्याहृतिर्व्रतस्येह विस्पष्टीकरणाय[3] तु ।
यावद्वचनमित्येवं यदप्यत्र समीरितम् ॥ २०२ ॥
पुण्याहं वाचयित्वैव[4] वापयित्वा शिरोरुहान् ।
भुक्त्वापराह्ण इत्यादि सर्वार्थं वचनं यतः ॥ २०३ ॥
[5]वाचेदुपक्रमे तेषामित्याद्यत्रैव वक्ष्यते ।
गृहाद्यदर्शने चैतत् कर्म[6] बोधायनोदितम् ॥ २०४ ॥
अपूर्वत्वेऽपि चैतस्य कृत्वा स्थण्डिलमादितः ।
उद्धृत्य प्रोक्ष्य चैवाग्निमादधीत न हीह तु ॥ २०५ ॥
निषेध एवमग्नीनां[7] संस्काराणामितीरितम् ।
अन्यथा मेध्यदेशेऽग्नेराधानं [8]हि कृतं भवेत् ॥ २०६ ॥
[9]पर्युक्षणादयस्तस्मान्न निषिद्धा इहापि[10] तु ।
व्यस्ताभिश्च समस्ताभिर्व्याहृतीभिः समिद्धुतिम् ॥ २०७ ॥
[11]नमोऽन्वितत्वमन्येषामेवमित्यतिदिश्यते ।
ऋष्यादिषु[12] नमस्कारःसिद्धौ तत्र प्रयुज्यते ॥ २०८ ॥
एकमन्त्रत्वमेतेषामित्यस्य प्रतिपत्तये ।
मदन्ति दानवन्मन्त्रैरेवमित्यतिदिश्यते ॥ २०९ ॥
पुष्पदानं मदन्तीनां दानमूर्ध्वं च पूर्ववत् ।
प्रत्याम्नायोऽत्र समिधां साग्रा औदुम्बरीरिति ॥ २१० ॥
शिष्टां[13] चतुर्थीं समिधमभ्याधापयतीति[14] तु ।
उक्त्वा विसर्ग एवैता विपरीता इति ब्रुवन् ॥ २११ ॥
आदेशवद्विसर्गेऽपि 'प्राजापत्या मं' इत्यृचा ।

१-१.M °पर्यन्तं कालन्तस्य. २.M क्रियतैत्येक°. ३.M विस्विष्टकर°. ४.MT °यित्वेव. ५.MT वचेदुप°. ६.M बौधा°. ७.M °दीनात्, T °मादीनां. ८.M निकृतं. ९.M चर्यु°. १०.M इहीपि. ११.M नमोषित. १२.M पुण्यादिषु°. १३.MT शिष्यं. १४.MT °भ्यापय°.

'द्यौ'रन्तरिक्षं'[१]'पृथिवी'त्यादिमन्त्रैः समिद्धुतिम् ॥ २१२ ॥
प्रातिलोम्येन[२] कृत्वान्ते ज्ञापयत्येव तद्धुतिम् ।
'एता एवे'ति चाप्येवं युज्यतेऽत्रावधारणात्[३] ॥ २१३ ॥
चतुर्थीमिति निर्देशो [४]नार्थवानन्यथा भवेत् ।
उपस्थापनमन्त्राणां प्रतीकग्रहणादिह ॥ २१४ ॥
चतुर्भिर्व्रतवन्मन्त्रैरुपस्थापनमिष्यते ।
एतेषां प्रतिलोमत्वं तद्विसर्गे श्रुतेर्भवेत् ॥ २१५ ॥
प्रावर्गिकं[५] दिवाकीर्त्यं [६]श्रावयेद्वचनादिह ।
कुमारस्योपदेशोऽस्तमिते ग्रामादि यद्वचः ॥ २१६ ॥
पूर्वेद्युरिव तत्सर्वं [७]स्थण्डिलोद्वपनादिकम् ।
परिषेचान्तं सकलं कुर्यादित्यतिदिश्यते ॥ २१७ ॥
'वय' इत्यादिमन्त्रेण शिशोः शिरसि वेष्टितम् ।
अपनीय [८][.................] उपविश्य च ॥ २१८ ॥
उत्तमाः[९] शान्तिमन्त्रोऽपि[१०] कुर्यात्पूर्ववदेव तु ।
'उन्दन्तीर्बलमि'त्यादिमन्त्रः[११] काल्पिक इष्यते ॥ २१९ ॥
भोजनं सकृदेव [१२]स्यात्तन्निश्चित्य पर्वणि[१२] ।
पर्व पञ्चदशी[१३] नान्या पक्षयोरुभयोरिह ॥ २२० ॥
प्रातर्वदिति[१४] निर्देशाद्विसर्गे वरवेष्टनम्[१५] ।
अप्राप्तं 'वय' इत्यादि तदपावृतिवर्जनम्[१६] ॥ २२१ ॥
[१७]अर्थलुप्तमिहैवोक्तं तस्मात्तस्यानुवादता ।
काण्डाख्याप्रक्रियैकत्वे[१८] प्रदेशैकत्व[१९] एव च ॥ २२२ ॥

१.M °रिक्षः. २.M प्रातिलोमयान. ३.°धारणा. ४.M गार्थ°. ५.M प्रावर्ग्यकं. ६.M श्रापमे°. ७.M साण्डिलोद्ध°. ८.MT broken between अपनीय and उपविश्य [T विश्य]. ९.MT उत्तमां. १०.MT मन्त्रापि. ११.M मन्त्रं. १२-१२.T broken after स्या. १३.M °दशिः. १४.T °वदिति...द्विसर्गे, M °द्विसर्गो. १५.M परवेष्टना, T वरवेष्ट°. १६.M °वर्जना. १७.M °लुप्तिमिहैवोक्तस्त°. १८.M °प्रक्रि...येकत्वे. १९.M °कत.

[काण्डव्रतानि]

चतुर्विधत्वं काण्डानां पूर्वमेव समीरितम् ।
विविच्य कथयिष्यामि दिङ्मात्रमिह दर्शितम् ॥ २२३ ॥
'इषे त्वा'द्यनुवाका य उत्तमाध्यायवर्जिता:[१] ।
'सं त्वा[२] सिञ्चादयं' तद्वत् [३]पाकयज्ञादयोऽपि षट्॥ २२४ ॥
'विश्वरूपादय'स्तद्वत् परेऽप्यन्त्यद्वयं[४] विना ।
'तृतीयस्यामि'ति प्रश्नद्वयं 'स त्वा'दिहौत्रकम्[५] ॥ २२५ ॥
दार्शकाण्डमुद्दिष्टं [तत्] सौम्याख्यमथ गीयते ।
'आप उन्दादय:' प्रश्ना उत्तमाध्यायवर्जिता: ॥ २२६ ॥
पाकयज्ञादिके प्रश्ने शिष्टा[६] उत्तमवर्जिता: ।
'प्राचीनवंश'मित्याद्या: षट् प्रश्ना उत्तमान्विता: ॥ २२७ ॥
'ब्रह्म सन्धत्त'मित्यादिरध्याय: [७]प्रथमस्तथा ।
'देवा वै च यथादर्श'मित्याद्या उत्तमं विना ॥ २२८ ॥
'त्रिवृत्स्तोमादय'श्चापि सौम्याध्याया: प्रकीर्तिता: ।
लौकिकं प्रथमे काण्डे पञ्चमोऽन्त्यविवर्जित:॥ २२९ ॥
'युञ्जाने'ति[८] समाम्नाता: प्रश्ना अपि चतुर्दश ।
चत्वारोऽन्त्यविहीनास्तु पञ्चमोऽन्त्यसमन्वित: ॥ २३० ॥
'जीमूता'दींश्च चतुर: परप्रश्नद्वयान्तग:[९] ।
'गायन्त्या'दि द्वयं चापि परप्रश्नद्वयान्तिमम् ॥ २३१ ॥
'इन्द्राय राज्ञ' इत्यादि प्रश्नशेषं तथोपरि ।
'रोहितो धूम्र' इत्यादि 'स्तेगान्दंष्ट्रा'दिकान्[१०] विना॥ २३२ ॥
'कृत्तिकास्वग्नि'मित्याद्या:[११] सोत्तमान् तत्परोऽपि[१२] च ।
अध्यायस्तत्पर:[१३] प्रश्न: प्रथमाध्याय एव च ॥ २३३ ॥
द्वितीये[१४] चाष्टके[१५] प्रश्न:[१६] प्रथमोऽङ्गिरसादिकम्।

१.MT वर्जिताम्. २.M त्वं. ३.MT पादयज्ञा°. ४.T °व्यन्त्य°. ५.M हौन्तकम्. ६.T रिष्टा. ७.M °ध्याय प्रथमन्तथा. ८.MT युञ्जानाति. ९.M °न्तगम्. १०.M स्ते गां °दष्ट्रादितान्, T स्तेनान्दंष्ट्र्यादि°. ११.M °स्वनभि..द्या°. १२.T तत्परापि. १३.M पर. १४.M द्वितीया. १५.M चष्टके. १६.MT प्रश्नं.

[१]संज्ञानाद्यरुणान्ताश्च कृष्यादीष्टिविवर्जिताः[२] ॥ २३४ ॥
आग्नेयास्ते समाख्याता वैश्वदेवास्तथेतरे ।
[३]'चित्तिः स्रुगा'द्यः प्रश्नो यस्तस्य ब्राह्मणमेव च ॥ २३५ ॥
द्वितीये त्वष्टके प्रश्नो द्वितीयः सतृतीयकः[४] ।
प्राजापत्यः सहोत्राख्यस्तस्याधीतिः[५] स्वके व्रते ॥ २३६ ॥
नारायणं चोपनिषत् सवल्युपनिषद्व्रते ।
शुक्रियाणां तु सौम्यत्वमाह बोधायनो मुनिः ॥ २३७ ॥
[६]संक्षेपतोऽत्र निर्दिष्टं[६] विविच्यैवावधार्यताम् ।
अन्यथापि विकल्प्यन्ते[७] काण्डानि बहुधा बुधैः ॥ २३८ ॥
प्राजापत्ये व्रते वीर्ये[८] वैश्वदेव[९] .... ।
.... [१०]मनुवाकार्थं क्रमहानिनिवृत्तये ॥ २३९ ॥
यद्यपीष्टं वृत्तिकृद्भिरन्यथापीह युज्यते ।
यावद्ग्रहणमित्यत्र ग्रहणं तत्त्ववर्णनात्[११] ॥ २४० ॥
[१२]स[प्तम]स्यैव[१२] काण्डानि ह्यधीयीते[१३]ति गम्यते ।
तस्मात्पाठक्रमादेव व्रतचर्याऽवगम्यते ॥ २४१ ॥
'सदसस्पति'मप्योप्याधापयेदिति योजना ।
कारीरयो मारुताद्याश्चत्वारस्त्वनुवाकगाः ॥ २४२ ॥

[काराव्रतम्]

'युञ्जाना'द्याश्च [१४]जातान्ताः काराव्रत[१४]समीरिताः ।
[१५]अक्षारलवणं सर्पिमिश्रं[१६] दध्ना च[१७] संयुतम् ॥ २४३ ॥
परिमृज्योपलिप्तायां भुवि पिण्डीकृतं[१८] च तत् ।
हविष्यं कुशलं[१९] कश्चिन्निदध्याद् भिक्षितं वटुः[२०]॥ २४४ ॥

१.M ज्ञाना...द्यरु°, T संज्ञाना...द्यरू°. २.M कृभ्यादीष्टि°, T °तुभ्यादीष्टिवर्जितम्. ३.M °गाद्यं, T द्वित्तिस्रुगा°. ४.M °तृतीयकम्. ५.M तस्यदिति सवके. ६-६.M संक्षेपतो...दीषं, T सङ्क्षे...निर्दिष्टं. ७.T अन्यथापि च कल्प्यन्ते. ८.T वी..... ९.MT broken after वैश्वदेव. १०.MT broken before मनुवाका°. ११.MT तत्ववर्ण°. १२-१२.M स...स्येव°, T स...काण्डानि. १३.M ह्यभिधीयेत. १४-१४.M जगतां तां कार व्रत. १५.M अक्षरा°. १६.MT सर्पिमित्रं. १७.M प. १८.°कृतश्च. १९.M कुशलाः,T कुशलं. २०.M वटु.

उपविश्य यथान्यायं परिषिच्य पिबेदपः ।
निहितं निहितं पिण्डमादायास्येन वाग्यतः ॥ २४५ ॥
पञ्च पिण्डान् स्वमन्त्रेण 'प्राणा'दिभ्यो जुहोत्यथ ।
यथार्थं भोजनं कुर्यादास्येनादाय पूर्ववत् ॥ २४६ ॥

[कारीरिव्रतम्]

काराव्रतस्य कल्पोऽपि स्यात्कारीरिव्रतोदितः[1] ।
[2]अक्षारलवणं भोज्यञ्चतूरात्र हविः शुचिः ॥ २४७ ॥
तेषामध्ययनं तद्वच्चतूरात्रं समाचरेत् ।
अनयोर्वपनं न स्याद्धोमोऽप्यश्रवणात्कुतः ॥ २४८ ॥
कारीर्याख्यानुवाकानां वैश्वदेवं भवेद् व्रतम् ।
संस्कारत्वाद् व्रतस्यादौ[3] कृतं सर्वोपकारकम् ॥ २४९ ॥
न च काण्डबहुत्वेन प्रतिकाण्डं चरेद् व्रतम् ।
दर्शादियागशेषाणां[4] प्रजापत्यादिसंज्ञया ॥ २५० ॥
निर्देशात्सर्वशेषत्वं व्रतस्यैकस्य युज्यते ।
न च सर्वार्थता सर्वव्रतानामिति शङ्क्यते[5] ॥ २५१ ॥
विशेषवचनादत्र तदानर्थक्यमन्यथा[6] ।
कारीर्यध्ययने[7] तस्मान्नियमान्तरमुच्यते ॥ २५२ ॥
अक्षारलवणं[8] भूमौ गोवदित्यादिभाषितम् ।
कारीर्यादिव्रते[9] तस्माद्यावदुक्तं समाचरेत् ॥ २५३ ॥

[गोदानम्]

गोदानमिति निर्देशात् सामान्यस्मृतिचोदिते ।
वर्षे षोडश एवास्य क्रियेत्याद्यवगम्यते ॥ २५४ ॥
चौलवत्तस्य कल्पः[10]स्याच्छ्राद्धादि सकलं ततः ।
नित्येन ब्रह्मचर्येण सहान्यस्य[11] भवन्त्यमी ॥ २५५ ॥

१.M °कारी विप्रतो°. २.M अक्षराल°. ३.M °व्रंत स्यादौ. ४.M °यानशेषा°. ५.M शक्यंते. ६.M तदनर्थ°, T तदनर्थकम°. ७.M कारीद्ययने. ८.M अक्षरावपनं. ९.M °र्याद्याद्व्रते. १०.M कल्प-स्या°. ११.T सहान्येस्य.

खट्वायां शयनं यस्मान्निषिद्धं ब्रह्मचारिणाम् ।
भूमावेवास्य शयनमनास्तीर्यैव कीर्त्यते ॥ २५६ ॥
उपस्पर्शनं मन्त्रोक्तं स्नानं त्रिषवणं तथा ।
इति शब्दः प्रकारार्थो हेत्वर्थो वा प्रयुज्यते ॥ २५७ ॥
द्वादशाहादयः काला वत्सर[१]प्रतिमा श्रुतेः ।
एते[२]............देशो[२] गोदानाधिकृतेरिह ॥ २५८ ॥
वेदाधीत्यङ्गतामेषां ज्ञापयन्नाह गृह्यकृत् ।
यावद्ग्रहणमित्यस्माद्वचनादिह गम्यते ॥ २५९ ॥
वेदा[धी]ति[३] विनाप्येषाञ्च[४][र्य]मिति तथा स्मृतिः ।
वेदं व्रतानि वाऽऽचारं [५]नीत्वाभ्युपयमेव वा ॥ २६० ॥
संवत्सरमतिक्रम्य न वर्तत इति श्रुतेः ।
वेदार्थत्वेऽपि चैतेषाञ्चर्येवमिह[६] युज्यते ॥ २६१ ॥
यावद्ग्रहणमेतेषामपि वाऽऽचरणं यतः ।
व्रतानां वेदशेषत्वमेतन्मुख्यं तथा स्मृतिः ॥ २६२ ॥
षट्त्रिंशदाब्दिकं चर्यं गुरौ[७] त्रैवेदिकं व्रतम् ।
तदर्धकं[८] वाऽधिकं[९] वा ग्रहणान्तिकमेव वा ॥ २६३ ॥
ग्रहणान्तं व्रतं चार्यं जीवितस्यास्थिरत्वतः ।
श्रुतिश्च 'कृष्णकेशोऽग्नीनादधीते'ति च स्मृतिः ॥ २६४ ॥
समुच्चित्यैव काण्डानां तस्मादध्ययनं भवेत् ।
संवत्सरपरं [१०]चार्यमित्यादिवचनादिह ॥ २६५ ॥
व्रतानां चरणेनापि कृतित्वमवगम्यते ।
गायत्रीमात्रसारैश्च चीर्णवेदव्रतैर्द्विजैः ॥ २६६ ॥
इत्याद्यन्यार्थवाक्यानि [११]तथैवोपलभामहे ॥ २६६क ॥
व्रतस्नातक एष स्याद् वेदस्नातक एव वा ।
वेदव्रतस्नातको वा स्यादित्यादि स्मृतौ स्मृतम् ॥ २६७ ॥

१.M वत्सरः. २-२.M एते....देशो, T broken before देशो. ३.M वेदा...भीं, T वेदा...तिं. ४.M °ञ्च...T निति, T च...णिति. ५.T oms नी. ६.MT चर्येव°. ७.M भूमौ. ८.M तदर्धिकं. ९.T वादिकं. १०.M चायमि°. ११.M मिथैवो°.

[1]सव्रताध्यापनं तस्मादुभयोरग्रहाद्वरम् ।
व्रतानां वेदशेषत्वात्तच्चार्यापदि[2] युज्यते ॥ २६८ ॥
एतेषां वचने सिद्धे तेषामिति समीरणात् ।
होत्रादिसर्वशेषत्वं वचनस्येति गम्यते ॥ २६९ ॥
[3]यथर्षि विभजेच्चूडा[4] इति प्राप्तौ नियम्यते ।
अत्र [5]ह्येकशिखः स्यादित्यनेन[5] व्रतसर्जने ॥ २७० ॥
चरित्वा सनखशमश्रु वपेदिति समीरणात् ।
विसर्ग एव सशमश्रुनखावपनमिष्यते ॥ २७१ ॥

[उपाकर्मसहितस्वाध्यायविधिः]

तपोविशेषैर्विविधैर्व्रतैश्च विधिचोदितैः ।
वेदः कृत्स्नोऽधिगन्तव्य इत्यस्य प्रतिपत्तये ॥ २७२ ॥
वेदव्रतानि तद्धर्मं[6] गोदानं चाभिधाय[7] तु ।
अथानन्तरमारंभः स्वाध्यायस्याधुनोच्यते ॥ २७३ ॥
[8]उपाकर्मापि करणं स्वाध्यायारंभ[9] ईरितः ।
वेदाधीतिमुखेनास्य संस्कारत्वमपि स्मृतम् ॥ २७४ ॥
पौर्णमास्यामिदं कर्म पञ्चदश्यां विवक्षितम् ॥ २७४क ॥
यद्यपि श्रवणेनास्याः संबन्धो वत्सरेषु हि ।
न संभवति सर्वेषु संभवाच्छ्रावणे ततः ॥ २७५ ॥
पौर्णमास्यामिदं कर्म तथाषाढ्यामिदं भवेत् ।
श्रावणादि वार्षिकमित्यादि तथा[10] स्मृतिदर्शनात् ॥ २७६ ॥
अन्वारब्धेषु शिष्येषु जुहुयादिति कीर्तनात् ।
अध्यापनस्य प्राधान्यमस्मिन्कर्मणि गम्यते ॥ २७७ ॥
शिष्यान्वारंभवचनाद्धोमकर्ता गुरुर्भवेत् ।
अध्यापनार्थता[11] चापि कर्मणोऽस्यावगम्यते ॥ २७८ ॥

१.T संप्रता°. २.M °शेषत्वातच्चा°. ३.T यथर्षी. ४.M विभयेजच्पूधा. ५-५.M ह्येकशेषस्या°, T ह्येकशिलस्या°. ६.MT तद्धर्म. ७.M चापिधाय, T चाविधाय. ८.MT °कर्मोपि. ९.M स्याध्याया°. १०.T oms. ११.M °पनर्थता.

तथापि लौकिको वह्निर्होमार्थ इह गम्यते ।
आचार्योपासनेन स्यात् साधारण्यं हि कर्मणाम् ॥ २७९ ॥
साधारणमिदं कर्म बहूनामिति गम्यते ।
शिष्येष्विति बहुत्वोक्तेरेकशिष्योऽपि कर्म तत् ॥ २८० ॥
कुर्यात्सार्धं[1] स्वशिष्येण नाशिष्यस्य विधीयते ।
अतिप्रसङ्गादात्मीयशिष्याः संबन्धिशब्दतः ॥ २८१ ॥
काण्डर्षयस्तु चत्वारः पूर्वमेव समीरिताः ।
कैश्चित्स्वायंभुवं काण्डं पञ्चमं परिकीर्तितम् ॥ २८२ ॥
चत्वार्येवेह निर्दिष्टा [2]ऋषयश्चापि तादृशाः ।
'प्रजापते' 'यदस्येति' वाग्देव्यन्ते समीरितम् ॥ २८३ ॥
'उपहूता'नुवाकेऽतस्तन्निवृत्त्यर्थमीरितम् ।
आवापहोमसमये तन्निवृत्तिर्हि [3]वक्ष्यते ॥ २८४ ॥
तस्मादन्ते [4]तयोर्होमस्तन्त्रेणेतीह गम्यते ।
अधीयीरन्नितीहोक्तेर्नेहाध्यापनमिष्यते[5] ॥ २८५ ॥
असामर्थ्ये निगदति स्वाचार्येऽनुपठेच्छिशुः[6] ।
काण्डादींश्चतुरो भेदादधीयीतेति[7] युज्यते ॥ २८६ ॥

[अनध्यायः]

पर्वण्यपि त्वनध्याये स्वाध्यायाध्ययनं विधेः ।
प्रक्रान्तेऽध्ययने त्वेवमधीतिं वर्जयेत् त्र्यहम्[8] ॥ २८७ ॥
एकाहं वा[9] पर्ववर्जं दिवाऽधीतिर्विधीयते ।
ग्रहणाद्यनुसारेण विकल्प इह युज्यते ॥ २८८ ॥
पक्षयोरुभयोर्मासं[10] प्रदोषं तद्विवर्जयेत् ।
प्रदोषशब्दः पूर्वस्मिन् रात्र्यंशेऽत्र चतुर्थके ॥ २८९ ॥
स्वाध्यायाध्ययनं तत्र वर्जयेन्मासमादरात् ।
अनध्यायवर्जनायैत[11]दुपलक्षणमिष्यते ॥ २९० ॥

१.M स्वार्धं. २.M न्मृषय°. ३.T °वृत्तिर्विपक्ष्यते. ४.M °र्होम. ५.M °ध्यपन°. ६.M °शुम्. ७.M °दधीतेति. ८.M °र्जयत्र्यहम्. ९.T om. १०.M °र्मासः. ११.M °वर्जनादेतदुप°.

अन्येऽपि ये त्वनध्यायाः [१]स्मृतिशास्त्रेषु कीर्तिताः[२] ।
न तेष्वध्ययनं कुर्यात्संक्षेपेण वदामि तान् ॥ २९१ ॥
त्र्यहं प्रेतेष्वनध्यायः शिष्योपाध्यायबन्धुषु[३] ।
उपाकर्मणि चोत्सर्गे स्वशाखे श्रोत्रिये तथा ॥ २९२ ॥
सतानूनप्त्रिषु[४] मृतेष्वृत्विक्ष्वन्येष्वहर्भवेत् ।
आचार्यस्य तथा पित्रोर्द्वादशाहं मृतौ[५] भवेत् ॥ २९३ ॥
आचार्यपुत्रे शिष्ये तद् भार्यायामहरेव तु ।
सब्रह्मचारिणि प्रेते स्वे च भूमिपतावपि ॥ २९४ ॥
सन्ध्यागर्जित[६]निर्घातभूकम्पोल्का[७]निपातने ।
समाप्य [८]वेदाद्यनिशमारण्यकमधीत्य च ॥ २९५ ॥
पञ्चदश्यां चतुर्दश्यामष्टम्यां राहुसूतके ।
[९]ऋतुसन्धिषु भुक्त्वा वा श्राद्धिकं प्रतिगृह्य वा ॥ २९६ ॥
[१०]प्रतिगृह्य द्विजो विद्वानेकोद्दिष्टनिमन्त्रणम् ।
त्र्यहं न कीर्तयेद् ब्रह्म राज्ञो राहोश्च सूतके ॥ २९७ ॥
वर्षविद्युत्स्तनयित्नुसन्निपाते त्र्यहं भवेत् ॥ २९७क ॥
चोरैरुपप्लुते [११]ग्रामे संभ्रमे वाऽग्निकारिते ।
[१२]आकालिकमनध्यायं विद्यात्सर्वाद्भुतेषु च ॥ २९८ ॥
निर्घाते भूमिचलने[१३] ज्योतिषां चोपसर्जने ।
[१४]एतानाकालिकान् विद्यादनृतौ[१५] चाभ्रदर्शने ॥ २९९ ॥
सन्ध्यायां गर्जिते चर्तौ[१६] प्रातश्चेदहरेव तु ।
सायं चेद्रात्रिरेव स्याद्यद्वा प्रातः समुद्भवे ॥ ३०० ॥
अहोरात्रमनध्यायः सायं चेद्रात्रिरेव तु ।
[१७]उल्कापाते भूमिकम्पे शक्रध्वजनिपातने ॥ ३०१ ॥

१.M स्मृतिरात्रेषु. २.M कीर्तिताम्. ३.M बन्धुषः. ४.T सता नूनं त्रिषु. ५.M मृतो. ६.M नर्ज्जित, T नर्जित. ७.M °कम्पोत्कानि°. ८.T वेद...निश°. ९.T केतुस°. १०.M द्विप्रति°. ११.M ग्रासं भ्रमे°. १२.MT आकाविक°. १३.M भूमिवचने, T भूमिपचने. १४.MT एतनाका°. १५.M विद्यादृतो. १६.M वर्तौ. १७.M उल्का°.

अनध्यायस्त्रिरात्रं स्यादिति कैश्चिदुदीरितम् ।
आश्वयुच्छुक्लनवमी कार्तिकद्वादशी तथा ॥ ३०२ ॥
तृतीया चैत्रमासस्य तथा भाद्रपदस्य च ।
एकादशी सिता तैष्य आषाढे दशमी च या ॥ ३०३ ॥
सप्तमी माघमासस्य नवम्येतासु वर्जयेत् ।
प्रदोषे तु त्रयोदश्यां नाध्येयं प्रतिपत्सु च ॥ ३०४ ॥
[१]मेधाकामस्त्रयोदश्यां सप्तम्यां च विशेषतः ।
चतुर्थ्यां च प्रदोषेषु न स्मरेन्नैव[२] कीर्तयेत् ॥ ३०५ ॥
महोत्सवे त्वहोरात्रमुत्सवे भोजनात्परम् ।
सर्पमण्डूकनकुलश्च मार्जारैर्गतेऽन्तरा ॥ ३०६ ॥
अनध्यायस्त्रिरात्रं स्याद्विप्रवासोऽप्यभोजनम् ।
[३]गोमायोर्मूषिकस्यापि गमने चैतदिष्यते ॥ ३०७ ॥
घृतभोजनमन्येषु निमित्तेषु तथा स्मृतम् ।
चण्डालस्य श्वपाकस्य शकस्य गमनेऽन्तरा ॥ ३०८ ॥
षण्मासान्वर्जयेद्धस्तिव्याघ्रयोर्वत्सरं स्मृतम्[४] ।
[५]श्वक्रोष्ट्रगर्दभोलूकवीणाभेर्यादि[६]निस्वने ॥ ३०९ ॥
अमेध्यशवशूद्रान्त्यश्वपाक[७]पतितान्तिके ।
देशे तु चावर्त्मनि[८] च विद्युत्स्तनितसंप्लवे ॥ ३१० ॥
सामध्वनौ चर्ग्यजुषोर्मारुते [९]वाऽतिवायति ।
चतुष्पथे च रथ्यासु[१०] जलान्ते देवसन्निधौ ॥ ३११ ॥
पीठिकानिर्हृते[११] पादे विरिक्ते[१२] चार्तनिस्वने ।
ग्रामान्ते गोव्रजे चापि छर्दीत्वा वर्षसंभवे ॥ ३१२ ॥
वासस्यपि[१३] ह्यनिर्णिक्ते[१३] मैथुनाचरिते सदा ।

१.M मेधाकां. २.M °न्नेव. ३.M °मायोभूषि°. ४.M स्मृतेत्. ५.Cf Manu IV.115: श्वखरोष्ट्र. ६.MT वीणाभिर्या°. ७.M °शूद्रादिन्त्यश्चशानश T शूद्रान्त्यश्व...न. ८.M देशे शुद्धापद्मनि. ९.M पति. १०.M रत्यासु. ११.M °कानि हृते. १२.M विरक्ते. १३-१३.T वासस्य...निर्णिक्ते.

भुक्त्वार्द्रपाणिरंभोऽन्तरर्धरात्रेऽतिमारुते ॥ ३१३ ॥
पांसुवर्षे दिशां दाहे सन्ध्यानीहारभीतिषु ।
धावतः पूतिगन्धे च शिष्टे च गृहमागते ॥ ३१४ ॥
वर्जयेद्वेदवचनमिति दिङ्मात्रमीरितम् ।
द्वावेव वर्जयेन्नित्यमनध्यायौ[1] प्रयत्नतः ॥ ३१५ ॥
स्वाध्यायभूमिञ्चाशुद्धामात्मनाञ्चाशुचिद्विजात् ।
नैत्यके नास्त्यनध्यायो होममन्त्रेषु चैव[2] हि ॥ ३१६ ॥
इत्यादि सर्वमालोच्य यथार्थमवधार्यताम् ।
कृत्स्नवेदानुवचनं[3] रात्रावपि समापनम्[3क] ॥ ३१७ ॥
इष्यते न[4] दिवाकीर्त्यमदिवाकीर्त्यशब्दतः ।

[होतृप्रवर्ग्योपनिषदरुणाम्नायाद्यध्ययनविधिः]

[5]होतृप्रवर्ग्यकाण्डौ च यश्चौपनिषदो[6] विधिः ॥ ३१८ ॥
[7]अरुणाम्नायविधिश्चैव काठके परिकीर्तितम् ।
एतदारण्यकं सर्वं नाव्रती श्रोतुमर्हति ॥ ३१९ ॥
कारीर्योऽप्यथ पित्र्याश्च दिवाकीर्त्यानि यानि च ।
रुद्राः सन्ततिमि[8]त्येतावनुवाकौ च सावित्रौ ॥ ३२० ॥
[9]होतृविध्यनुवाके चेत्यनुवाकचतुष्टयम् ।
सूक्तेषु सूक्तं यत्सौर्यं मेधीयश्चैष[10] चित्रियः[11] ॥ ३२१ ॥
काठकानि च सर्वाणि सर्वाण्यारण्यकान्यथ ।
दिवाकीर्त्यानि शाखायामेतावन्तीति धारणा ॥ ३२२ ॥
दिवैवातो दिवाकीर्त्यं प्रदोषेऽप्यन्यदिष्यते ।
यावदुत्सर्जनं त्वेवमधीयीरन्प्रयत्नतः ॥ ३२३ ॥
उत्सृष्टेऽप्येवमेव स्यादारंभे कुरुते यथा ।

१.T ध्याये. २.M वैव. ३.M °वचना. ३क.MT °समानतम्. ४.M om,T निष्यते. ५.T होतृप्र°. ६.M °निषदे. ७.M अरुणम्नाविधिं, T अ...म्नसाय°. ८.M सन्ततिरित्ये°. ९.M °विध्यानुवाके च त्वनुवाके चतु°. १०.MT मेघो यश्चै°. ११.M चित्रियम्.

ततश्चाध्ययनं[१] तद्वदनध्यायविवर्जनम् ॥ ३२४ ॥
उत्तरत्रापरेणातिदेशार्थं[२] तदनूच्यते ।
न च होमातिदेशोऽत्र[३] यावद्वचनमेव तत् ॥ ३२५ ॥
उत्सृष्टेऽप्येवमेव स्यात्पूर्वाधीतं सिते पठेत्[४] ।

[वेदाङ्गाध्ययनविधिः]

कृष्णेऽङ्गान्यप्यनध्यायान्वर्जयन्निति [५]हैव तु[५] ॥ ३२६ ॥
पाठान्तरमिहाप्यस्ति तथार्थ इह वो भवेत् ।
एतेनैव तु कल्पानामुत्सृष्टे चैवमित्यतः ॥ ३२७ ॥
कल्पाध्ययनमेव स्यात् कृत्वा तूत्सर्जनक्रियाम्[६] ।
एतेनेतीह[७] निर्दिष्टं वेदाध्ययनवद्यथा ॥ ३२८ ॥
अनध्यायनिवृत्त्यादि कल्पस्याध्ययने तथा ।
नित्यस्वाध्याय[८] एवातः कल्पानामपि सिध्यति ॥ ३२९ ॥
कल्पे पितृविधिश्चैव प्रवर्ग्यविधिरेव च ।
काठकानां विधिश्चैव [९]कारीरिविधिरेव च ॥ ३३० ॥
अरुणाम्नायविधिश्च शतरुद्रविधिस्तथा ।
कल्पेषु तु य आम्नाता मन्त्रास्तानप्यतन्द्रितः[१०] ॥ ३३१ ॥
यथाक्रतुमुपाकृत्य त्वधीयीतेति शासनम् ।

[उत्सर्गविधिः]

अथानन्तरमुत्सर्गविधिरत्राभिधास्यते ॥ ३३२ ॥
कस्योत्सर्गः[११] प्रकरणाद्वेदस्येत्यवगम्यते ।
अध्यायानुत्सृजेत्तत्रेत्येवं स्मृतिषु पठ्यते ॥ ३३३ ॥
[१२]कियतोत्सर्जनं तैषे माघे वा सितपर्वणि ।
[१३]येऽत्रान्तेवासिनः शिष्याः समानाचार्यकाश्च ये ॥ ३३४ ॥
समान एक आचार्यो येषामेते तथोदिताः ।

१.M °श्चाध्यायनं. २.MT °त्रापरेणेतिदे°. ३.M °देशात्र. ४.M च वै. ५-५.M हेतवः, T हेव तु. ६.M क्रिया. ७.M एतेनेतिह. ८.M °ध्यायामेवातः. ९.M कारीरी. १०.MT तन्त्रितः. ११.M °त्सर्गं. १२.M क्रियतो°. १३.MT येऽन्यान्ते°.

आचार्येण सहोत्सर्गे प्राप्ते सब्रह्मचारिणा ॥ ३३५ ॥
सहोत्सर्ग इह प्रोक्त इत्येतदवगम्यते ।
नावश्यं गुरुणा सार्धं कुर्यादुत्सर्जनं ततः ॥ ३३६ ॥
समानकल्पसूत्राश्च [१]समानाचार्यका मताः ।
शंखिनी च नदी यस्या[२] शाखास्तत्सदृशा हि वा ॥ ३३७ ॥
शंखिनी सावका यस्यास्त[३]स्मादवकिनी च सा ।
अवतारप्रदेशो हि तीर्थशब्दः प्रयुज्यते ॥ ३३८ ॥
बहूनामवतारार्थं महातीर्थत्वमुच्यते ।
समुद्रगामिनी[४] सा स्यान्न[५] स वर्जनसिद्धये ॥ ३३९ ॥
न समुद्रं विशेद्योऽसौ कथ्यते नद इत्यतः ।
अभिगम्य नदीमेतां शिष्यैः सब्रह्मचारिभिः ॥ ३४० ॥
सार्धं स्नात्वा यथान्यायं कृत्वाऽऽचमनमादितः ।
पवित्रदर्भपाणिः सन्'नापो हि ष्ठा' तृचेन तु ॥ ३४१ ॥
अपां स्तोत्रानुवाकेन पावमानेन चांभसा ।
व्याहृतीभिश्च संप्रोक्ष्य स्वात्मानं शुद्धविग्रहम् ॥ ३४२ ॥
जलमाविश्य तत्रस्थाः[६] प्राणानायम्य ते ततः ।
[७]त्रिर्ब्रह्महृदयं ब्रूयु'र्ऋतं[८] चे'त्यादि तद्भवेत् ॥ ३४३ ॥
विनोच्छ्वासं[९] त्रिरावृत्त्य स्नात्वोत्तीर्य शुभाम्बरम्[१०] ।
सन्तर्प्योत्तीर्यते सर्व[११] आखरान् कल्पयन्त्यथ ॥ ३४४ ॥
स्थण्डिलान्याखराख्यानि प्रत्येकं[१२] तानि पञ्च वै ।
[१३]सर्वमित्येवमर्थं स्यात् त्रीणि प्राक्प्रवणान्यपि॥ ३४५ ॥
सममानानि कृत्वा तदुत्तरापरपार्श्वतः[१४] ।
प्रागायतमुदगग्रावनतं[१५] कल्पयेत् परम् ॥ ३४६ ॥

१.M सामानाचार्य कामतः. २.MT यस्या. ३.M यस्यान्तस्मा°. ४.M °नामिनी. ५.MT स्या न. ६.MT तत्रस्थां. ७.M त्रिवृद्ब्रह्म°. ८.MT ब्रूयुऋतं. ९.M °च्छवासस्त्रि°. १०.M °बराम्. ११.T सवा. १२.M व्रत्येकं. १३.M सर्व इत्ये°. १४.M °परगश्चताः. १५.M °तमुदग्गागापनतं, T तनुदानावनतं.

दक्षिणावनतं चापि दक्षिणापरपार्श्वगम् ।
त्रयाणां मध्यमा यः[१] स्याद्[१] ब्रह्मादीनां स आखरः[२]॥ ३४७ ॥
विश्वामित्राष्टकस्य[३] स्यात् [४][मध्यो]त्तरत आखरः।
तयोर्दक्षिणतो यः[५] स्यादगस्त्यार्थः[५] स इष्यते ॥ ३४८ ॥
कृष्णद्वैपायनादीनामुदक्प्रवण[६] एव च ।
[७]वैशम्पायनकादीनां दक्षिणाखर[८] पार्श्वगः ॥ ३४९ ॥
पाठसिद्धे क्रमोऽप्येष एव स्यादिति कीर्तनम्[९] ।
स्वस्वतीर्थप्रदानार्थं प्राङ्मुखत्वादिसिद्धये ॥ ३५० ॥
उपविष्टेषु सर्वेषु स्वाखरावरभूमिषु ।
प्राङ्मुखेषु ततः स्वान्स्वानाखरान्प्रोक्ष्य वारिणा ॥ ३५१ ॥
दर्भमुष्टीन्समादाय कुर्युर्विनिमयं ततः ।
द्वयोर्द्वयोर्विनिमयः साम्ये स्यादन्यहस्ततः[१०] ॥ ३५२ ॥
विनिमाय हृतं लब्ध्वा प्रदद्यात्स्वीयमन्यथा[११] ।
आसनत्वेन संकल्प्य स्वस्वमुष्टिभ्य उद्धृतम् ॥ ३५३ ॥
एकैकं तृणमेतेभ्यो निदधात्याखरेष्वथ ।
कल्पयामीति सर्वेषु मन्त्रेष्वनुषजेदिति ॥ ३५४ ॥
ज्ञापयन्नेवमित्याह मध्यमाखर[१२] ईरितम्[१३] ।
त्रयोविंशतिरेव स्यू राजशब्दो न केवलः ॥ ३५५ ॥
देवशब्दो विश्वशब्दो विशेषणतयेष्यते ।
इन्द्राय राज्ञ इत्येकस्तथा वैश्रवणान्मतः[१४] ॥ ३५६ ॥
अङ्गिराभ्य इतीत्युक्त्वा विश्वामित्रादिकीर्तनात् ।
तथा दक्षिणतश्चेहागस्त्यायेत्युदीरणात्[१५] ॥ ३५७ ॥
विश्वामित्राष्टकस्य[१६] स्यान्मध्यमोत्तर आखरः[१७] ।

१-१.MT यस्यां. २.M आरवरम्. ३.M °कस्या. ४.MT om. ५-५.M यस्याः अग°. ६.M °मुदत्प्रवण. ७.M adds स before वैशम्पा°. ८.M °णावरपा°, M °णापरपा°. ९.MT कीर्तनम्. १०.M °हस्ततम्. ११.MT त्स्वी...मन्यं. १२.M मारंवार°. १३.M °ईरिता. १४.M °श्रवणादथ. १५.M °गस्त्यायेत्युदीर°. १६.M °कस्या. १७.M आखरम्.

प्रागग्राश्च निधेयाः स्युर्दर्भाः[१] प्राक्प्रवणेषु तु ॥ ३५८ ॥
उदङ्मुखैरुदगग्रा उदक्प्रवण आखरे ।
दक्षिणामुखता तद्वद्दक्षिणाग्रत्वमन्यतः ॥ ३५९ ॥
कृष्णद्वैपायनादीनां निवीतत्वमपीष्यते ।
एकपञ्चाशदेव स्युः कृष्णद्वैपायनादयः ॥ ३६० ॥
षोडश[२] स्युस्तथा मन्त्रा वैशम्पायनकादयः ।
आत्रेयः पदकारान्तः कौण्डिन्यो वृत्तिकारवान् ॥ ३६१ ॥
महान्सौबभ्रुवान्तः स्याद्वाधूलान्तोऽपरो मतः ।
काण्वो बोधायनान्तोऽसावापस्तंबोऽपि[३] सूत्रकृत् ॥ ३६२ ॥
पितृभ्यश्चापि मातृभ्यस्तत् पितृभ्य इतीरिते[४] ।
मन्त्रत्रयभ्रमोऽत्र स्याद्यथा स्वमिति भाषिते ॥ ३६३ ॥
पितृभ्य इति निर्दिष्टाः[५] पिता चापि पितामहः ।
प्रपितामहो [६]मातरश्च माता[६] चापि पितामही ॥ ३६४ ॥
प्रपितामही च मातुर्ये पित्राद्यास्त्रय एव ते ।
पितामह्याश्च पित्राद्या अन्यस्यास्त्रय एव तु ॥ ३६५ ॥
एवं पञ्चदशैवैते मन्त्रा अत्र विवक्षिताः ।
एकत्रिंशदतो मन्त्रा दक्षिणाखरसंश्रिताः[७] ॥ ३६६ ॥

[तर्पणमन्त्रविधानम्]

कल्पयित्वाऽऽसनान्येवमद्भिः सन्तर्पयेदिमान् ।
तर्पणे तु द्वितीयान्ता मन्त्रा एता इतीरिताः[८] ॥ ३६७ ॥
अत्र मन्दहितार्थं ते पठ्यन्तेऽस्माभिरादरात् ।
ब्रह्माणं तर्पयाम्येवं प्रजापतिमतः परम् ॥ ३६८ ॥
बृहस्पतिं तथाग्निञ्च वायुं सूर्यं ततः परम् ।
चन्द्रमसं नक्षत्राणीन्द्रं राजानमेव तु ॥ ३६९ ॥

१.M दर्भा. २.M षोडशस्य. ३.M °स्तंभो°. ४.M °रितेः. ५.T निर्दिष्टां. ६-६.M मातरश्श्वाता. ७.T संश्रुताः. ८.M °रितम्.

यमं च वरुणं सोमं तथा वैश्रवणं क्रमात् ।
वसून् रुद्रानादित्यांश्च [१]विश्वान्देवांस्तदुत्तरम् ॥ ३७० ॥
साध्यानृभून्[२] भृगूंश्चैव मरुतोऽथर्वणस्तथा[३] ।
अङ्गिरसो विश्वामित्रं जमदग्निमतः परम् ॥ ३७१ ॥
भरद्वाजं गौतमं चाप्यत्रिं काश्यपमेव च ।
वसिष्ठं च ततोऽरुन्धतीमगस्त्यं च दक्षिणे ॥ ३७२ ॥
कृष्णद्वैपायनमथ जातूकर्णमनन्तरम् ।
बृहदुक्षं तरुक्षञ्च तृणविन्दुं तदुत्तरम् ॥ ३७३ ॥
सोमशुष्मिणमेवातः सोमश्रवसमित्यपि ।
वाजशुष्मिणमपि च वाजश्रवसमेव हि ॥ ३७४ ॥
वाजरत्नं वामदेवं वर्मणं च वरूथिनम् ।
सनद्वाजं[४] हर्यजिनं दमयं च ततः परम् ॥ ३७५ ॥
उदमयं चैव ततो [५]हूणञ्जयमनन्तरम् ।
तृणंजयं[६] चैव कृतंजयं[७] चापि धनंजयम् ॥ ३७६ ॥
बभ्रूं च त्र्यरुणं[८] चैव त्रिवृषं[९] च क्रमेण हि ।
त्रिधातुञ्चैव शिश्नं च तत ऊर्ध्वं पराशरम् ॥ ३७७ ॥
वसिष्ठमिन्द्रं[१०] मृत्युं च तथा कर्तारमित्यपि ।
अथ धर्तारं त्वष्टारं धातारं समनन्तरम् ॥ ३७८ ॥
विधातारं सवितारमथ सुश्रवसं क्रमात् ।
स्तुतश्रवसमपि वसन्तश्रवसमेव[११] तु ॥ ३७९ ॥
सावित्रीं च्छन्दांस्यृग्वेदं[१२] यजुर्वेदमतः परम् ।
सामवेदं चैवाथर्ववेदं च तदनन्तरम् ॥ ३८० ॥
इतिहासपुराणानि[१३] त्वथर्वाङ्गिरसोऽन्यथा ।

१.T विश्वेदेवां°. २.M °नृभृन्. ३.M °णन्तथा. ४.MT °द्वानं. ५.M ह्यूणं चैवमन°, T ह्यूणञ्जयमन°. ६.M तृणं चयं. ७.M कृतं चयं. ८.T त्र्यरू...चैव. ९.T त्रिवृषं. १०.M °मिन्द्र. ११.M वसत्रशवस°. १२.M च्छन्दांस्यृजुर्वे°. १३.M °णानी.

[१]सर्वदेवजनांश्चातः सर्वभूतान्यतः परम् ॥ ३८१ ॥
तथा सर्वगणांश्चापि त्वन्या उत्सर्गदेवताः ।
वैशम्पायनमित्येवं [२]ह विष्णुं तित्तिरिं[२] तथा ॥ ३८२ ॥
उखं[३] चैव तथात्रेयं पदकारमनन्तरम् ।
कौण्डिन्यं वृत्तिकारं महान्तं सौबभ्रुवं[४] ततः ॥ ३८३ ॥
महान्तं यक्षं वाधूलं काण्वं[५] बोधायनं तथा ।
आपस्तम्बं[६] सूत्रकारमाग्निवेश्यं तथैव च ॥ ३८४ ॥
आचार्यान्वानप्रस्थांश्च वंशस्थानूर्ध्वरेतसः ।
[७]एकपत्नींस्तर्पयामि पितरं च पितामहम् ॥ ३८५ ॥
प्रपितामहमपि च मातरं च पितामहीम् ।
प्रपितामहीं च[८] मातुः पितरं तर्पयामि[९] च ॥ ३८६ ॥
मातुः पितामहं मातुः प्रपितामहमेव च ।
पितामह्याः पितरं च पितामह्याः पितामहम् ॥ ३८७ ॥
तत ऊर्ध्वं पितामह्याः[१०] प्रपितामहमित्यपि ।
अथातः प्रपितामह्याः पितरं तर्पयाम्यपि ॥ ३८८ ॥
तथैव प्रपितामह्याः पितामहमनन्तरम् ।
तथैव प्रपितामह्याः प्रपितामहमित्यपि ॥ ३८९ ॥
'ब्रह्मणे नम' इत्याद्यैर्गन्धपुष्पफलानि तु ।
दत्त्वा पर्यायशोऽपूपधानासक्त्वन्वितं[११] हविः[१२] ॥ ३९० ॥
दद्यात् [१३]स्वाहान्वितैरेतैः पूर्ववत्तर्पयेज्जलैः ।
आवृत्तिश्चेह मन्त्राणां सप्तकृत्वः[१४] ततो भवेत् ॥ ३९१ ॥
वेदिशब्दोऽत्र गौणः स्यादाखरापरभूमिषु ।
उपविष्टा अधीयीरन्नुपाकर्मवदेव तु ॥ ३९२ ॥

१.M सर्ववेद°. २-२.M हविं शुतित्ति°, T हविंशु ३.MT उत्वं. ४.MT सौबभ्रतं. ५.M कंबं. ६.T °स्तंभं. ७.T °पत्नीस्त°. ८.MT तथा; metrical flaw in accepting this reading. ९.M °याम्यथ. १०.M °मह्यां. ११.M सक्तन्वितं. १२.M हविम्. १३.M स्वाहापितै°, T सहान्वितै°. १४.M °कृत्वा.

[कृत्स्नवेदसमाप्तौ स्नानादिकर्म]

गत्वोदकान्तं ते सर्वे [१]'काण्डा'दित्यादिमन्त्रतः ।
रोहयन्ति ततो दूर्वा ऊर्मिमन्तमथोदधिम् ॥ ३९३ ॥
कुर्युः समुद्रो नेह स्यादुदधिर्गौण एव सः ।
उदकं धीयते यस्यामेषा नद्युदधिर्मता[२] ॥ ३९४ ॥
तत उत्तीर्य ते सर्वे आजिं धावन्ति तं पुनः ।
परस्परस्पर्धया ते धावन्त्याश्रमसंभवात् ॥ ३९५ ॥
अथाचार्यगृहानेत्य भोजयन्ति द्विजांस्तथा ।
शिष्टैः सक्त्वोदनाद्यैस्तामेतामुत्सर्जनक्रियाम् ॥ ३९६ ॥
कृत्स्नवेदसमाप्तौ च कुर्यादिति समीरितम् ।
द्रव्यादिबहुकर्तृत्वे सर्वसाधारणं भवेत् ॥ ३९७ ॥
अन्यद्रव्येण यागादि[३] न कर्तुं युज्यते सतः ।
ब्रह्मचर्ये स्थितोऽप्यस्माद्यावदर्थं लभेद्धनम् ॥ ३९८ ॥

[सर्वसाधारणतर्पणकर्मविधानम्]

साधारणमिदं कर्म विधाय तदनन्तरम् ।
सर्वसाधारणमिदं कर्म तर्पणाख्यं विधीयते ॥ ३९९ ॥
देवानृषीन् पितॄंश्चैव तर्पयेदद्भिरन्वहम् ।
नित्यं स्नात्वा शुचिं[४] कुर्याद् देवर्षिपितृतर्पणम् ॥ ४०० ॥
इत्यादि वचनात्[५] स्नानादूर्ध्वमेतत्समाचरेत् ।
स्वाध्यायाङ्गतया चापि विहितं तर्पणं क्वचित् ॥ ४०१ ॥

इति सङ्गमग्रामवासिमिश्रविरचिते नारायणीये
[६]वाधूलगृह्यागमवृत्तिरहस्ये
चतुर्थोऽध्यायः

१.M काण्डादिमन्त्रतम्. २.M नस्युर्दधीमता, T न स्युदधिर्मता. ३.M ययागादि. ४.M शुचिं. ५.M वचनास्नान्नादू°. ६.M वाधूलके, T वाधूलकं.

अथ पञ्चमोऽध्यायः

[समावर्तनस्नानमीमांसा]

यावदध्ययनं त्वेवं पालयेत् स्वाश्रमं वटुः ।
अथाश्रमान्तरं गच्छेत् स्वेच्छया विजितेन्द्रियः ॥ १ ॥
सन्त्यज्य[1] ब्रह्मचर्यं वा गृहस्थोऽसौ भवेत्ततः ।
वने[2] भूत्वा संन्यसेद्वा[3] ब्रह्मचारी गृही भवेत् ॥ २ ॥
संन्यसेद्वा[3] गृहस्थः सन्नित्यादि श्रुतिचोदितम् ।
चीर्णवेदव्रतो वेदान् वेदौ वेदमथापि वा ॥ ३ ॥
अधीत्याथावगम्यार्थं स्नात्वा गुरुसमीपतः ।
समावृत्याश्रमं गच्छेद् गृहस्थादित्रयाश्रमम् ॥ ४ ॥
एतमर्थमभिप्रेत्य कल्पकारो ब्रवीति हि ।
स्नास्यन् वेदमनूच्योपकल्पयेदेरकामिति[4] ॥ ५ ॥
वेदमित्येकवचनं शाखान्तरनिवृत्तये ।
यतोऽध्येया[5]स्त्रयो वेदा ब्रह्मत्वे तद्विधानतः ॥ ६ ॥
यद्वा विवक्षितं [6]तत्स्याज्जात्यपेक्षमथापि वा ।
गुरूक्तं स्वयमुक्त्वा तमधीत्य तदनन्तरम् ॥ ७ ॥
यदि स्नायात्ततः स्नानसंभारानुपकल्पयेत् ।
[7]न प्रसिद्धमिह स्नानं स्नानवाच्येह संस्कृतिः ॥ ८ ॥
इतिकर्तव्यता तस्य यस्मादिह विधीयते ।
स्मृतिष्वपि च संस्कारमध्ये स्नानं प्रकीर्तितम् ॥ ९ ॥
अनूच्य [8]वेदमाचार्यसन्निधावावृत्तेर्यदि[9] ।
वसेन्न तस्य स्नानाख्या संस्कृतिश्चोदिता यतः॥ १० ॥
समावर्तन एवेदं स्नानमित्यवगम्यते ।

१.M स...व्य, T broken. २.M वनं. ३-३.MT सन्य°. ४.M च्योपयेदे°. ५.M अतोऽध्याया°, T यतोऽध्याया°. ६.M त स्यात्. ७.M oms. ८.M वेदानाचार्य°. ९.M °वामतेरिति; यदि given at the beginning of the second hemistitch.

कृत्वा स्नानमुपस्थाय प्रविशेदाश्रमान्तरम् ॥ ११ ॥
इति कल्पे समाम्नातं स्नास्यन्निति च यच्छ्रुतम् ।
तदनर्थकमेव स्यात् सर्वार्थत्वे विशेषतः ॥ १२ ॥
समावर्तनमप्यस्य नेष्यते ब्रह्मचारिणः ॥ १२क ॥
नैष्ठिको ब्रह्मचारी तु वसेदाचार्यसन्निधौ ।
तदभावेऽस्य तनये पत्न्या[1] वैश्वानरेऽपि वा ॥ १३ ॥
[2][...] ।
उत्तराश्रमशेषत्वं युज्यते स्नानसंस्कृतेः ॥ १४ ॥
गृहस्थाश्रमशेषत्वं स्नानस्येत्यपि चोदितम्[3] ।
यत्र कामयते स्नातस्तदेतीत्यत्र वक्ष्यते ॥ १५ ॥
गुरुणाऽनुमतः[4] स्नात्वा समावृत्तो यथाविधि ।
उद्वहेत द्विजो भार्यामिति यद्यपि मानवम् ॥ १६ ॥
यथाविधीति यच्चैतत् स्वरागाद्यनुसारतः ॥ १६क ॥
उद्वहेदन्यथा गच्छेद् वनस्थाद्या नमन्त्विति[5] ।
'विद्यान्ते गुरुरर्थेन निमन्त्र्य' इति गौतमः ॥ १७ ॥
[6]आचार्याय वरं दत्त्वा तदनुज्ञात एव वा[7] ।
स्नायीतेति[8] वदन्तस्य[9] सर्वार्थत्वमिहोक्तवान् ॥ १८ ॥
विधिपूर्वं च स स्नात्वा भार्यां लब्धेति[10] तद्वचः ।
आश्रमान्तरसंप्राप्तौ न निषेधाय तद् भवेत् ॥ १९ ॥
अतश्च स्नानसंस्कार [11]आश्रमान्तरसंश्रयः ।
अधीत्य वेदमध्याप्य शिष्यान्वा स्नानमाचरेत् ॥ २० ॥
एकदेशमधीत्यापि स्नानमत्र विधीयते ।
अधीतवेदवेदाङ्गस्योत्तरत्र विधास्यते ॥ २१ ॥

१.M पत्न्यां. २.M sign of lacuna equal to one line shown. ३.T ...दितंम्. ४.M °मत. ५.M °मस्त्विति. ६.MT उक्त्वाचार्या°. ७.M वः. ८.M स्नायिते°. ९.T वदन्तस्य. १०.M लब्धेति. ११.MT आश्रम...य संश्रयः.

आचार्यासनदानादिविद्वद्योग्यं[१] हि तत्र तु ।
पाठमात्रावसायित्वमि[२]दमित्यत्र नोदितः[३] ॥ २२ ॥
पाठमात्रावसायित्वे[४] प्रमाणं नेह किञ्चन ।
वेदोऽध्येयो ब्राह्मणेन सषडङ्गो हि धर्मतः ॥ २३ ॥
कृत्स्नवेदानधिगमे भवेत्स्नानमिदं कथम् ।
अनधीतश्रुतेरेतत्[५] क्रियते [६]कथमुच्यते ॥ २४ ॥
जात्याश्रयाणां संस्कारकर्मणां नियमो यतः ।
इज्यादेरपि[७] संस्कारकर्म नित्यं विधीयते ॥ २५ ॥
अतोऽध्यापनपर्यन्तमनूच्येतीह चोदितम् ।
दृढीकृतो हि वेदार्थ एवमेव कृते सति ॥ २६ ॥
गुरवेऽपि वरं दत्त्वा तदनुज्ञामवाप्य च ।
स्नानाख्यं कर्म कुर्वीत तदनुज्ञात एव वा ॥ २७ ॥
ऋत्विग्वापनिषेधार्थं नापितं चेति वर्णितम् ।
क्षुरग्रहणमप्यत्र पात्रवत् सादनाय तु ॥ २८ ॥

[समावर्तनसंभरणानि]

दारुग्रहणमिध्मार्थमुपस्तरणमत्र[८] तु ।
होमार्थानि तृणान्येव वकला:[९] शकला मताः ॥ २९ ॥
जिह्वादिर्लेहनार्थस्ते दन्तकाष्ठसहोदिताः ।
वैणवाद्याश्च ते ग्राह्या धर्मशास्त्रानुसारतः ॥ ३० ॥
गन्धद्रव्यैः सुरभिभिः पिष्टं यदनुलेपनम् ।
तदेतत्सर्वं[१०] सुरभिरनुलेपविशेषणम् ॥ ३१ ॥
बहुवाची सर्वशब्द इह पाटलिपुत्रवत् ।
चन्दनं चाञ्जनं चात्र पिष्टमित्यनुवर्तते ॥ ३२ ॥
अहतं च नवं वासः प्रावारमपि सान्तरम् ।

१.M विद्वद्भ्योऽन्यं. २.M °मात्रमवसायित्वा इदमि°, T °मात्रवसायित्वा° इदामि°. ३.T नोदिता. ४.T °मात्रवसा°. ५.M °रेतं. ६.M ऽथेदमु°. ७.M इत्यादे°. ८.M मुपस्तरमत्र. ९.T वक..श्शकला १०.MT सर्व.

प्रावारमुत्तरीयं[१] तत्परिधानीयसंयुतम् ॥ ३३ ॥
एते च वाससी[२] ऊर्ध्वं परिधत्तेऽन्तरं पटम् ।
इत्युक्तेरधिकाराच्च मुक्तादिविश्रुतो[३] मणिः ॥ ३४ ॥
उपधान्यौ तु सौवर्णौ मणयः सुषिरा इमे ।
बादरश्च[४] मणिस्तद्वत् बदरीफलनिर्मितः ॥ ३५ ॥
प्रवर्तौ[५] कुण्डले रौक्मे[६] दण्डो यष्टिर्हि वैणवी ॥ ३५क ॥
वैणवीं धारयेद्यष्टिं सोदकं च कमण्डलुम् ।
यज्ञोपवीतं वेदं च शुभे रौक्मे च कुण्डले ॥ ३६ ॥
वनस्पतित्वं वेणोश्च श्रुतावभ्यर्थमीरितम् ।
अविरुद्धं ततो मन्त्रलिङ्गदण्डपरिग्रहे ॥ ३७ ॥
इति शब्दः [७]प्रकारार्थश्छत्रभोज्यादिसंग्रहः ।

[स्नानकालाः]

स्नानकाला इमे ग्राह्याः स्वेच्छयाऽत्र विकल्पिताः॥ ३८ ॥
विकल्पना च मीमांसा प्राजापत्ये कृते भवेत् ।
प्रजोत्पादनसामर्थ्यं प्राजापत्यं तु वा पदम् ॥ ३९ ॥
अहो[८] अपि च यः[९] सर्वां वृद्धिं प्राप्तुमिहेच्छति ।
अस्मिन् स्नायात्तथा तिष्ये[१०] महर्क्षः[११] पतितो[१२] भवेत् ॥ ४० ॥
ऐश्वर्यस्य समग्रस्य वीर्यस्य यशसः श्रियः ।
ज्ञानवैराग्ययोश्चैव षण्णां भग इतीरणात् ॥ ४१ ॥
एतैर्धनेन संयुक्तो नीरोगश्च भगी मतः ॥ ४१क ॥
सावित्रे [१३]प्रसवयोग्ये नक्षत्रे स्नानमाचरेत् ।
ऐन्द्र ऐश्वर्यसम्पन्नो [१४]विचित्रोऽसौ भवत्यपि[१४] ॥ ४२ ॥

१.M मुत्तीरयन्. २.M वासती. ३.M मुक्ताद्रिश्रुतो. ४.T बादरं...मणि°. ५.T प्रवत्तौ. ६.M रौग्मे. ७.M प्रकारर्थच्छत्र°. ८.T अलो. ९.M om. १०.MT मित्रष्ये. ११.T महतः. १२.M पतिता. १३.M °योग्यो, T [स] वयोग्यो. १४-१४.M प्रजया धनसम्पदा; T प्रजया धनसम्पदा corrected as विचित्रोऽसौ भवत्यपि; M gives अन्नो विचित्रोऽसौ भवत्यपि after प्रजया धनसम्पदा.

ऐन्द्राग्नेहेति[१] योग्यो वा प्रजया धनसम्पदा[१] ।
विस्तीर्णशाखो भवति तेषामन्यतमेऽहनि ॥ ४३ ॥
पूर्वपक्षे शुभदिने स्नायात् स्नायादिति श्रुतेः ।
स्नास्यन्नित्यधिकाराच्च स्वयं कर्तेति गम्यते ॥ ४४ ॥
यस्मिन्नहनि स स्नायादहः[२] कृत्स्नो रविस्तुतः ।
तत्तेजसा च यशसा तपत्येवं यशोऽस्य तु ॥ ४५ ॥
विनश्यत्यभितापेऽतो[३] व्रजं गोष्ठं च च्छादितम् ।
अन्तर्लोम्ना लोहितेन चर्मणाऽनुडुहेन तु ॥ ४६ ॥

[समावर्तनविधिः]

रवेः प्रागुदयात्प्राप्य कृत्वा नान्दीमुखं ततः ।
पुण्याहवाचनं कृत्वा पूर्वार्धाभिवदेत्ततः[४] ॥ ४७ ॥
अग्निं तूपसमाधातुमाहेत्यस्यार्थ ईरितः ।
ततश्चोपसमाधेहीत्येवं कश्चित्प्रचोदितः ॥ ४ ८ ॥
आचम्याग्निमुखं कर्म परिधानादि[५] चोदितम्[५] ।
कुर्यात्सादनवेलायां द्वन्द्वं होमार्थसादनम् ॥ ४९ ॥
आहरन्तीति तत्कर्तृनियमाभावसिद्धये ।
तथाहरणमप्यत्र सादनं ब्रह्मणो[६] गृहात्[७] ॥ ५० ॥
दक्षिणेना[८]ग्र्यमास्तीर्य तृणान्येषूदपात्रकः[९] ।
समिधं च निधायाग्निमपरेणैरकामपि[१०] ॥ ५१ ॥
उदीचीनदिशां स्तीर्त्वा [११]स्वास्तीर्णामुपबर्हणम् ।
निधायोत्तरतो गच्छेन्नापितोऽप्युत्तरत्र तु ॥ ५२ ॥
आस्ते स्नास्यन्[१२] समाचम्य परिधानप्रभृत्यथ ।
व्याहृत्याहुतिपर्यन्तं कृत्वा स गुरवे वरम् ॥ ५३ ॥

१-१.M ऐन्द्राग्नेरिह तिर्योग्यो वा प्रजया धनसम्पदा after अन्नो विचित्रऽसौ भवत्यपि. After धनसम्पदा a long lacuna. २.T स्ना...दहः. ३.M °भिताः पेतो. ४.M पूर्वार्धदि°. ५-५.MT °धाना...रो°. ६.MT ब्रह्मण. ७.M ग्रहात्. ८.M त्रिमा°. ९.M पात्रकम्. १०.T °णैरत्तामपि. ११.M स्वात्तीर्णा°. १२.MT °स्यत्.

दत्त्वासौ तदनुज्ञातः पालाशीं[1] समिधं ततः ।
[2]आज्याक्तामादधातीमं स्तोममित्यादिमन्त्रवत् ॥ ५४ ॥
ब्रह्मचर्याख्यसत्रस्य प्रायणीयः समित्पुरा ।
आहितस्तूपनयन एषा तूदयनार्थिता ॥ ५५ ॥
अह्नो मध्यत्रिभागे स्याद्धोमो मध्यन्दिने समित् ।
आधेया तत्र दद्यात्स्वाद्वन्नं मध्यन्दिनावधि ॥ ५६ ॥
गां पचेत्तत्र चेदिच्छा त्वाधाय समिधं ततः ।
उदक्शिरा एरकायां शेतेऽ'गस्त्या'दिमन्त्रतः ॥ ५७ ॥
'शिवा म' इति मन्त्रेण विद्यमानं स्वकं शिरः[3] ।
अभिमन्त्र्य क्षुरं चापि 'क्षुर' इत्यभिमन्त्रयेत् ॥ ५८ ॥
दत्त्वा तन्नापितायाऽथ श्मश्रवादिप्रोक्ष्य[4] माणवम्[5] ।
अभिमन्त्र्य यत्क्षुरेण श्मश्रूण्यस्योपपक्षकौ[6] ॥ ५९ ॥
शिरोरुहान् वापयित्वाऽन्यान्यङ्गानि कामतः ।
वापयिष्यमाणो भवति लोमानि वपते ततः ॥ ६० ॥
लोमवापस्तु[7] जनतासमूहे[8] क्रियते पुरा ।
[9]अन्नादनसमर्थश्च लोमवापनतो भवेत् ॥ ६१ ॥
[10]भवन्त्यादिबहूक्तिस्तु समूहार्थबहुत्वतः ।
गुणदोषपरिज्ञाने[11] फलमेतदिहोच्यते ॥ ६२ ॥
अविद्वान् [12]रोमवपनात्फलमेतत्समश्नुते ।
गुणदोषपरिज्ञाता यथाकामं समाचरेत् ॥ ६३ ॥
श्मश्रवादीनि समाचम्य दद्यात्तु ब्रह्मचारिणे ।
[13]दर्भस्तम्ब उदपात्रे पातानि हि दधात्यसौ[13] ॥ ६४ ॥

१.M पालाग्निं. २.M °क्तामदधां. ३.M शिरम्. ४.MT प्रोच्य. ५.M माणकम्, T corrected as माणवम्. ६.M °पक्षतौ. ७.MT °वापात्तु. ८.MT समूहो. ९.M अन्नादौ. १०.M भवस्त्यादिरबहू°. ११.MT गुणदोषापरि°. १२.T °वचनात्. १३–१३.M oms.

[१]अमुष्येत्यत्र नामास्य स्नानकर्तुर्वदेत्तथा ।
आमुष्यायन इत्यत्र गोत्रमीशानशर्मणः ॥ ६५ ॥
भार्गवस्यापत्यमिति ततो मन्त्रेण[१] मेखलाम्[२] ।
अपरेणाग्निमासीनो [३]विस्रस्योत्तरमादिना ॥ ६६ ॥
ब्रह्मचारिण एवेमां [४]दद्यान्न्यग्रोध एव वा[४] ।
औदुम्बरे ता निदधात्य'सौ' मन्त्रेण पूर्ववत् ॥ ६७ ॥
जिह्वां विशोध्य शकलैस्तूष्णीमाचम्य मन्त्रतः ।
प्राङ्मुखो दन्तकाष्ठेन दन्तधावनमाचरेत् ॥ ६८ ॥
यथाविधि समाचम्य शीता उष्णास्वपस्ततः[५] ।
[६]निक्षिप्याञ्जलिना ताभिरात्मानमभिषिञ्चति ॥ ६९ ॥
[७]दैवे कर्मणि शीतानां प्रणीताभ्यः स्रुवेण तु ।
आहृतासु निषिञ्चन्ति मदन्तीरत्र मानुषे ॥ ७० ॥
उष्णासु शीताः सिञ्चन्ति तद्व्यावृत्तिरतो भवेत् ।
अभिषेचनमप्यत्र षड्भिर्मन्त्रैः पृथक् पृथक् ॥ ७१ ॥
षोढा विहित इत्येवं षट् कृत्वः[८] स्वाभिषेचने ।
आत्मा हस्तौ च पादौ च शिरस्तैर्विहितः पुमान् ॥ ७२ ॥
स्नात्वा सन्तर्प्य विधिवत् समाचारानुसारतः ।
समुदायं[९] मिश्रयित्वा[१०] गन्धात् किञ्चित्समाददत् ॥ ७३ ॥
उद्दिश्य देवता मन्त्रेणाकाशे त्रिर्निरस्य[११] तत् ।
हस्ताभ्यां गन्धमाहृत्य 'यो गन्ध' इति मन्त्रवत् ॥ ७४ ॥
अनुलिम्पेत आसीनो वह्नेः पश्चाद् द्विजाशिषा ।
अत्रैवं चन्दनस्येति चन्दनालेपनात्पुरा ॥ ७५ ॥

१-१.M oms T भार्गवस्याव..भिति. २.M wrongly reads मेरवलाम् at the beginning of next hemistich. ३.T विस्रप्स्यो°. ४-४.M दद्यान्नोध एव माम्. ५.M उष्णाऽस्व च तम्. ६.M निक्षिच्च्या°, T निषिप्या°. ७.M दैव°. ८.M कत्वा. ९.M °दार्य. १०.M °यित्वाङ्गन्धात्. ११.M त्रीन्निरस्य, T त्रिर्न्निरस्य.

त्रिः प्रसिञ्चेच्चन्दनादित्ययमर्थो[१]ऽतिदिश्यते ।
गन्धस्नानं तथैवोर्ध्वमेतत्पूर्वं समाचरेत् ॥ ७६ ॥
गन्धानुलेपनं कृत्वा 'नमः शाका'दि मन्त्रवत् ।
चन्दनात्त्रिः[२] प्रसिच्याथ 'यो गन्ध' इति मन्त्रतः ॥ ७७ ॥
अनुलिम्पेच्चन्दनेन तदेवमिति गीयते[३] ।
ऊर्ध्वमप्येवमेव स्यात् गन्धचन्दनलेपने ॥ ७८ ॥
[४]अञ्जनेनाक्षिणी आज्य सव्यं मन्त्रेण दक्षिणम् ।
तूष्णीं न्यस्त्वा परिहितं परिधत्तेऽहताम्बरम् ॥ ७९ ॥
[५]समागत्योपविश्याथ सौवर्णमपि[६] मध्यगम् ।
दृढं सूत्रे मणिं प्रोतं[७] सूत्राद्यग्रेऽपि[८] बादरम्[८] ॥ ८० ॥
दर्व्यामाधाय[९] सूत्रेण दण्डे पर्यस्य[१०] बादरम् ।
'इयमि'त्यादिना साज्यं हुत्वा विस्रस्य सूत्रकम् ॥ ८१ ॥
उदपात्रे परिप्लाव्य मन्त्रेणादाय दक्षिणे ।
मणिबन्धसमाख्याते हस्तादग्रे[११]ऽक्ष्णयैव तु ॥ ८२ ॥
बध्नाति तूष्णीमत्यग्रे[१२] बादरप्रोतनोक्षितः ।
एनमित्येकवचनाद्धारयेद्दक्षिणे करे[१३] ॥ ८३ ॥
इति [१४]वात्स्यायनोक्तत्वादयमर्थोऽवगम्यते ।
प्रोत्य सूत्रे कुण्डलेऽथ दर्व्यामाधाय पूर्ववत् ॥ ८४ ॥
[१५]'आयुष्यं' 'शुन'[१५]'मुच्चैर्वा' 'विराजं'[१६] 'यश' इत्यपि ।
हुत्वोदपात्रे प्रक्षाल्य 'विश्वा' इत्यादिमन्त्रवत् ॥ ८५ ॥
दक्षिणे कर्ण आबध्य मन्त्रैः षड्भिश्च कुण्डलम्[१७] ।
'ऋतुभिस्त्वे'ति मन्त्रेण सार्गलं[१८] कुरुते ततः ॥ ८६ ॥

१.T चन्दनादीत्ययमर्थो. २.T चन्दनाद्भिः. ३.M नीयते. ४.M अञ्जनेनाक्षिणीयादी, T °क्षिणी आ... सव्यं. ५.M समाशम्यो°. ६.T सौवर्णमणि. ७.T प्रोतं. ८-८.M सूत्रात्यग्रे वि पादरम्. ९.T °मादाय. १०.T पयस्य. ११.T हस्तभागे. १२.M °मित्यग्रे. १३.M दक्षिणेतरे. १४.T वास्या°. १५-१५.T आयुष्यं...मुच्चै°, M °मुर्च्चर्खं. १६.T विराजा. १७.M °लः. १८.M °णार्गलंकुरु°,T समलंकुरु°.

सव्येऽप्याबद्धमन्त्रैस्तत्कृत्वा मन्त्रेण सार्गलम् ।
मालामादाय मन्त्रेण[1] वाऽधस्ताद्दक्षिणश्रुतेः ॥ ८७ ॥
सव्यश्रुत्युपरिष्टादप्यक्ष्णया[2]बध्य तां स्रजम् ।
स्रजा[3] परिहितं वासः परिधायान्तरं ततः ॥ ८८ ॥
आचम्यासज्य[4] मन्त्रेण चोत्तरीयाम्बरं पुनः[5] ।
आदाय मन्त्रतो यष्टिमुपमुच्याप्युपानहौ ॥ ८९ ॥
छत्रमादाय दृष्टार्थं गत्वा च्छत्रमुपानहौ ।
विमुच्य दण्डमाचम्य जयाद्यं [6]होममाचरेत् ॥ ९० ॥
[7]आनक्षत्रोदयात्तस्मिन्व्रज आस्ते स वाग्यतः ।
सन्ध्यामुपास्य तत्रस्थो दृष्टेष्वृक्षेषु निर्गतः ॥ ९१ ॥
उपस्थाय दिशो 'देवीः षडूर्वी'रिति मन्त्रतः ।
'मा हास्महीं'ति[8] नक्षत्रं 'मा राधामें'ति शीतगुम् ॥ ९२ ॥
यस्मिन्नाश्रम एवैष वस्तुमिच्छेत्तदैव तु ।
तमाश्रमं वसेत्तस्य दोषः[9] स्यादन्यथा यतः ॥ ९३ ॥
अनाश्रमी न तिष्ठेत दिनमेकमपि द्विजः ।
आश्रमेण विना तिष्ठन् प्रायश्चित्तीयते नरः ॥ ९४ ॥
उपस्थाय तदेतीति यत्न[10] एवमतः कृतः[11] ।
संवत्सरं मैथुनं न चरेदित्यादिभाषणम् ॥ ९५ ॥
अवाप्यापि स्वयञ्जायां ब्रह्मचर्यमिहेष्यते ।
परदाराभिगमनमप्राप्तं न निवर्त्यते ॥ ९६ ॥
विवाहानन्तरं यत्तु गमनं कल्प ईरितम् ।
विकल्प्यते तदूर्ध्वं हि निषेधः क्रियतेऽत्र हि ॥ ९७ ॥
इतरस्नानमुद्दिष्ट[12]मथेतरदिहोच्यते ।

१.M मन्त्रेण...धत्ता°. २.T °प्यक्षया°. ३.M स्रज. ४.M °म्यसाज्य. ५.M ततः. ६.M नोसमा°. ७.M आनक्षेत्रो°. ८.M माहास्मनीति, T corrected as °हीति. ९.M दोष. १०.T यत्नमेव°. ११.T कृतम्. १२.M oms.

अमन्त्रकमिदं सर्वं मन्त्रवत् पूर्वमीरितम् ॥ ९८ ॥
मणिकुण्डलसंस्कारहोमवर्जममन्त्रकम् ।
इन्दूपस्थानपर्यन्तं वचनादि यदीरितम् ॥ ९९ ॥
कुर्यादितीह निर्दिष्टं[1] तूष्णीमेवेत्यनेन तु ।
तीर्थे स्नात्वेति चाप्यत्र तीर्थे स्नानं विधीयते ॥ १०० ॥
गन्धस्नानादिसकलमथवा स्नानशब्दितम् ।
अनूद्यत आसनादिदानकालविधित्सया ॥ १०१ ॥

[स्नातकस्य मधुपर्कविधानम्]

[2]अध्यापिते स्नातकस्य मधुपर्कं विधीयते ।
तं प्रतीतं स्वधर्मेण ब्रह्मदायहरं पितुः ॥ १०२ ॥
स्रग्विणं[3] तल्प आसीनमर्हये[4]त्प्रथमं गवा ।
अत आचार्य एवास्मै स्वासनं दापयेत्स तु ॥ १०३ ॥
वचनात्तन्नियोगाच्च तत्रोपविशति स्वतः ।
न ह्यस्य तत्र संस्थानं युक्तं स्मृतिनिषेधतः ॥ १०४ ॥
विद्वद्योग्यं तथा वान्यदासनं तस्य दीयते ।
उपविष्टस्य तूत्थाने तदनन्तरमेव चेत् ॥ १०५ ॥
अदृष्टं तत्र कल्प्यं स्यादन्ते दृष्टार्थमेव तत् ।
अन्तैकार्थं[5] तदुत्थानं प्रसङ्गादभिधीयते ॥ १०६ ॥
प्राङ् सेतुञ्जलमसौ[6] सिञ्चेदाचार्य एव तत् ।
उर्वाकार्थं[7] स्मृतं शिष्यपादप्रक्षालनं ततः ॥ १०७ ॥
अन्येन कारयेदेतदन्यत्कुर्याद्गुरुः स्वयम् ।
मन्त्रावृत्तिश्रुतेरत्र श्रुतिः प्राश्नाति गम्यते ॥ १०८ ॥
आचार्य एव गां प्राह त्वमुष्येत्यस्य[8] नाम यत् ।

१.M oms. २.T आध्या°. ३.T स्रविणं. ४.T °मर्च्चयेत्. ५.T अन्तेका°. ६.T जल...सो. ७.T ...कार्थं. ८.M °ष्येत्वस्य.

वदेत् षष्ठ्यन्तमेवैतद्यं प्राहेत्यविशेषतः ॥ १०९ ॥
अन्यो वा कारयेदेतन्मधुपर्काद्युदीरितम् ।
तस्येत्यन्येन[1] संबन्धो यं[2] प्राहेत्यस्य युज्यते ॥ ११० ॥
कुरुतेति बहूक्तिर्या गुर्वादौ युज्यते हि सा ।
यद्युत्सृजेदुत्सृजत कुरुतेति[3] पदे[4] सति ॥ १११ ॥
पचतेति च तस्यार्थो नैतत्कार्यं कलौ युगे ।
साहाय्ये योजयेत्पुत्रमन्तेवासिन[5] एव वा ॥ ११२ ॥
उपस्थाने कृते तस्य यं वा स्नातः स्वयं लभेत् ।
एकाकी न[6] व्रजेत्स्नात्वेत्येवमस्मात् प्रतीयते ॥ ११३ ॥
[7]रात्रि[र्यावज्]जीवनार्थं गुर्वाद्यर्थं ददाति यः ।
समयो[8] वा कृतो येन कृत्वा स्नानं गृहे मम ॥ ११४ ॥
आगन्तव्यं त्वया पूर्वमाभिमुख्येन तं व्रजेत् ।
तत्र गत्वा लभेदेतद् गृह्णीयान्न्यायतो धनम् ॥ ११५ ॥
रथलाभे विशेषोऽत्र स यदित्यादि कीर्त्यते ।
मध्यं चात्र रथोपस्थं नियमानभिमन्त्रणम् ॥ ११६ ॥
'अयं वामि'ति मन्त्रेण किञ्चिन्नास्मै ददाति चेत् ।
आचम्य 'मयि' मन्त्रेण भूमिस्पर्शनमाचरेत् ॥ ११७ ॥

[वैकल्पिकःसमावर्तनकर्मप्रयोगः]

वैकल्पिकमिदं स्नानं समावर्तनमीरितम् ।
निबध्यते प्रयोगोऽस्य समावर्तनकर्मणः ॥ ११८ ॥
नान्दीमुखान् पितॄनिष्ट्वा पुण्याहं वाचयेत्स्वयम् ।
गुरुरग्निं समाधाय परिस्तीर्य यथाविधि ॥ ११९ ॥

१.M °त्यन्नेन. २.M यः. ३.M कुतेति. ४.T च धे. ५.T °वासिनमेव. ६.M एकाकीनं. ७.M रात्रिर्जीव°, T रात्रि...ज्जीव°. ८.M समयोपाकृतो.

तृणेषूत्तरतः पञ्च पात्राणि समिधं[१] क्षुरम् ।
.... गन्धचन्दनवासांसि ॥ १२० ॥
सुरभ्यञ्जनवासांसि मणिकुण्डलदण्डकान्[१] ।
वल्कलाद्यपि संसाद्य संप्रोक्ष्य प्रोक्षणीजलैः ॥ १२१ ॥
तिरःपवित्रं पात्रेषु[२] [३]जलं दधि तथा मधु[३] ।
उदकान्वितसक्तूनप्योदनं च क्रमेण तु ॥ १२२ ॥
आनीयानुप्रहृत्याग्नौ विस्रस्य च पवित्रके ।
एरकामपरेणाग्निं स्तृणाति स्नानकृत्ततः ॥ १२३ ॥
गन्धपुष्पैरलंकृत्य मन्त्रवत्परिषिच्य च ।
स्वाहेत्याधाय समिधमाज्याक्तां[४] परिषिच्य च ॥ १२४ ॥
एरकायां[५] निपद्याथ शिरसि क्लेदिते परैः ।
क्षुरमादाय दत्त्वाथ कृते[६] वापे नखादिकम्[६] ॥ १२५ ॥
दत्त्वा तेन[७] च निक्षिप्ते दर्भस्तंबे[८]ऽथ मेखलाम् ।
विस्रस्य दत्त्वा तेनास्यां क्षिप्तायां दन्तशोधनम् ॥ १२६ ॥
कृत्वाभिषिच्य षट् कृत्वः शीतोष्णेन च वारिणा ।

१-१. Here text is very much mutilated. In T second Pāda after समि[ध] up to the fourth Pāda before चन्दन वाधा is broken. The first Pāda of the next Verse in T is सुरभ्यञ्जनवासांसि while in M it reads गन्धचन्दन वासांसि and thereafter the text सुरभ्यञ्जन is given but the latter has been cut down and मणिकुण्डलदण्डकान् has been given as the second Pāda. T gives the whole text as:-
तृणेषूत्तरतः पञ्च पात्राणि समि....।
..........................चन्दन वाधा..।।
सुरभ्यञ्जनवासांसि मणिकुण्डलदण्डकान्।
M gives the text as-
तृणेषूत्तरतः पञ्च पात्राणि समिधंक्षुरम्। गन्धचन्दनवासांसि मणिकुण्डलदण्डकाम्।
वासांसि मणिकुण्डल दण्डकान्।
२.M वा मन्त्रेषु. ३-३.M the text was given as प्रसङ्गक्षमिधीयते, but it has been cut down and corrected as जलं दधि तथा मधु. ४ T समिधंमाज्या°. ५.M °कायाग्निवद्याथ. ६-६.M वापेन खादि°. ७.T केन. ८.M °स्तंभे.

तीर्थे स्नात्वा यथान्यायं कृत्वा गन्धानुलेपनम् ॥ १२७ ॥
चन्दनालेपनं[१] लोचनाञ्जनञ्चाहताम्बरम् ।
परिधाय मणिञ्चापि करे बध्वाक्ष्णया तथा ॥ १२८ ॥
कर्णयोः कुण्डले बध्वा[२] प्रतिमुच्य स्रजं शुभाम् ।
वासश्च परिधायान्यदासज्याप्युत्तरीयकम् ॥ १२९ ॥
दण्डं गृहीत्वोपानहावुपमुच्यातपत्रकम् ।
गृह्णीयाद् गुरुरप्यस्मै स्वासनं वाऽन्यदेव वा ॥ १३० ॥
अत्रा'स्वे'ति निधायामुं [३]ब्रूयात्स्नातं प्रतीक्ष्य तत् ।
तत्रोपवेशनं कृत्वा स्वाचार्येणाहृतं[४] जलम् ॥ १३१ ॥
'आ मा गादि'ति वीक्ष्याथ ब्रूयात् 'प्राङ् सेक्तवा'[५] इति ।
तेन सिक्ते जलेऽथान्यवारिणा पादशोधनम् ॥ १३२ ॥
कारयित्वा[६] गुरुस्तस्मै मध्वाहरति तत् स तु ।
वीक्ष्य 'यन्मधुनो'[७] मन्त्रेणाश्नाति ब्रह्ममन्त्रवत् ॥ १३३ ॥
आहृतं दधि मन्थं चाप्योदनं त्रिस्त्रिरेव तु ।
आचान्तेऽस्मिन् गुरुर्ब्रूयाद् 'गामियं[८] गौस्तवे'त्यसौ॥ १३४ ॥
मम चेत्यभिमन्त्र्यैनां[९] ब्रूयादुत्सृजतेत्यतः[१०] ।
उत्सृष्टायां समुत्तिष्ठेदासनादनुमानिना[११] ॥ १३५ ॥
आनक्षत्रोदयात्तस्मिन्नासित्वा वाग्यतस्ततः ।
दिङ्नक्षत्रशशीनामप्युपस्थानं[१२] समाचरेत् ॥ १३६ ॥
अत्र तूदयनीयार्थसमिद्धोमौ श्रुतं ततः ।
विना होमेन चाप्येतत् कर्म कुर्यादितीरितम्[१३] ॥ १३७ ॥
शुचौ देशे ततः सर्वं संसाद्य प्रोक्ष्य संस्कृतैः ।

१.T चन्दनानुले°. २.M प्रबध्व. ३.M °धायामुद्र्या°, T °स्नातं. ४.MT स्वावार्येणा°. ५.M °त्तपा, T त्तवा. ६.M मारयि°. ७.M °मधुषौ, T मधुषो but corrected as मधुनो. ८.M गामीयं. ९.M °मन्त्र्येनां. १०.M °जतेऽत्यतः. ११.T °मादिना. १२.M °क्षत्रमुपस्थानामप्युस्थान°. १३.M °तीतरम्.

पवित्रवज्जलादीनि पात्रेष्वानीयते क्वचित् ॥ १३८ ॥
विसृज्य सन्त्यजेत्[१] स्नास्यन्नथ [२]वापनमारभेत् ।
यदूर्ध्वं तत्समानं स्याद् यावदुक्तमपीष्यते ॥ १३९ ॥
तूष्णीं स्नात्वेति तत्पक्षे स्नानस्यैव विशेषणम् ।
स्नाताय याचते पूर्वं प्रत्याख्यानं करोति चेत् ॥ १४० ॥
आरंभो व्यर्थ[३] एवेह स्नातकस्येति गम्यते ।
भूमिस्पर्शनलिङ्गेन प्रत्याख्यानभयात्ततः ॥ १४१ ॥
धनसिध्यर्थमप्यत्र वशीकरणसाधनम् ।
उच्यते निर्धनस्येह विवाहादेरसंभवात् ॥ १४२ ॥
यमसौ सनिमेष्यन्[४] स्याद् द्रव्यमर्थयितुं व्रजेत् ।
तं दृष्ट्वा मन्त्रयेऽदन्न'मित्याद्यभिमुखो वदेत् ॥ १४३ ॥
संबुध्यन्तमसौ स्थाने निर्दिशेन्नाम तस्य तु ।
अभिमन्त्र्यावबोध्यार्थं प्रयोजनमथो वदेत् ॥ १४४ ॥

[क्रोधादिशमनार्थकर्म]

क्रोधादिशमनायान्यत् प्रसङ्गादिह कथ्यते ।
'यत्त' इत्यादिनाऽऽमन्त्र्याप्यधिक्रोधोऽस्य[५] शाम्यति॥ १४५ ॥
शूद्रा दासी तथा भार्या कुपिताऽन्यत्र गच्छति ।
आकर्षफलकश्चेह द्यूतादिफलकं[६] मतम् ॥ १४६ ॥
चतुरङ्गार्थफलकः सस्यकर्षक एव वा ।
संस्कार्यो लौकिको वह्निस्तत्र होम इहोदितः ॥ १४७ ॥
पर्यग्निमात्रं कर्तव्यं हस्तेन जुहुयात्ततः[७] ।
एकादशापरो होमः संख्याया अश्रुतेरिह ॥ १४८ ॥
आगमिष्यति भार्या वा दासी वेति प्रतीयताम् ।
न्याये[८]ऽध्वास्तृणपिण्डाः स्युर्वृक्षत्वक् पिण्डकाश्च[९] वा॥ १४९ ॥

१.M °त्यजत्. २.M अथवा पानमा°. ३.M भोप्यर्थ. ४.M निमेषंस्या. ५.M मन्त्र्य प्यैधिकोधा°, T °नामन्त्र्य प्यैधि°. ६.M °फलतो. ७.M तथा. ८.T न्याये...स्तृण°. ९.M °कास्य.

रज्जुपिण्डाश्च वाऽऽधेयास्त्रयो बहुवचो यतः ।
जीवत्यागो पतेच्छन्नं[१] स्वयमेव तदाहरेत् ॥ १५० ॥
मदाश्रया न चान्यत्र गच्छेयुरिति कामयेत् ।
ग्राम्या ओषधयस्तद्वदारण्याश्च चतुर्दश ॥ १५१ ॥
तिलमाषा व्रीहियवा अणवश्च[२] प्रियङ्गवः ।
गोधूमाश्चेत्यमी सप्त ग्राम्या ओषधयः स्मृताः ॥ १५२ ॥
श्यामाकाश्चापि नीवारा जर्तिलाश्च गवीधुकाः[३] ।
[३क]गार्मुताश्चापि वास्तानि त्वन्ये वेणुयवान्विताः ॥ १५३ ॥
समीपस्थेषु तेष्वग्नौ जुहुयात्तेभ्य इत्यपि ।
तादर्थ्येऽत्र चतुर्थी स्यात्तेषां भोजनसिद्धये ॥ १५४ ॥
[४]स्थाल्यादावन्नमुद्धृत्य दत्त्वाऽमुत्रेण तान्परि ।
स्रावर्ये'च्छश्वं'दित्येवं तेभ्य आरभ्य मन्त्रवत् ॥ १५५ ॥
आत्मानं प्रतिलेखां च लिखेन्नैतेऽन्यसंश्रयाः ।
असौ स्थाने [५]'नाम चास्य'[५] संबुध्यन्तं विनिर्दिशेत् ॥ १५६ ॥
वशीकरणसिध्यर्थमुपायाः केचनेरिताः ।
आरंभः सर्व एवेह निष्फलोऽप्यन्यथा भवेत् ॥ १५७ ॥
स्मृतावपि तथैवोक्तं भार्यादाससुतादिभिः[६] ।
विवादं वर्जयित्वा तु सर्वान्लोकाञ्जयेद् गृही ॥ १५८ ॥

[विवाहसंस्कारः]

अधीत्य वेदान् साङ्गान्स्तदर्थानप्यवगम्य[७] च ।
गृहाश्रमे[८] वसेत् स्नात्वा भार्यां लब्ध्वेत्यतः परम् ॥ १५९ ॥
हस्तग्रहणमित्यादिविवाहोऽत्राभिधीयते ।
प्रत्यक्षाः श्रुतयश्चैवं कृतकृत्या भवन्ति हि ॥ १६० ॥
स्नानानन्तरमेवातो हस्तग्रहणमुच्यते ।

१.M वते च्छृङ्गं २.MT अणचश्च. ३.MT °धुका. ३क.MT °गाम्मुता. ४.T स्थालादाव°. ५-५.M नमावास्य. ६.T °सनादि.... ७.T °र्थानवग°. ८.M यथाश्रमे.

यत्र[1] कामयते स्नातः कन्यां लब्धुं तदेत्यसौ ॥ १६१ ॥
यत्रेत्यादिवचोऽर्थोऽन्यत् स्नानमुक्त्वाप्यनन्तरम् ।
कन्यादातारमेवासावभिप्रैतीति कीर्तितम् ॥ १६२ ॥
मैथुनं वर्जयेत्संवत्सरमित्याद्युदीरितम् ।
आश्रमान्तरसंप्राप्तिरर्थश्चेन्न समञ्जसम् ॥ १६३ ॥
गृहस्थाश्रमशेषत्वं स्नानस्य स्मृतिदर्शितम् ॥ १६३क ॥
गुरुणानुमतः स्नात्वा समावृत्तो यथाविधि ।
उद्वहेत द्विजो भार्यां सवर्णां लक्षणान्विताम् ॥ १६४ ॥
ऐकाश्रम्यं तथा चार्या[2] प्रत्यक्षश्रुतिदर्शनात् ॥ १६४क ॥
ब्रुवते गार्हपत्यस्य[3] तल्लोपो तेन युज्यते ।
सुगमो मुक्त्युपायोऽसौ [4]सत्त्वशुद्ध्यनुसारतः ॥ १६५ ॥
सर्वाभीष्टास्तथा भोगा लभ्यन्तेऽस्मिन् गृहाश्रमे ।
नित्यं नैमित्तिकं कुर्वन् भजन् भोगान् गृहाश्रमी ॥ १६६ ॥
विरक्तो वनमाश्रित्य[5] तपस्तप्त्वा सुदुश्चरम् ।
संन्यस्त आत्मज्ञानेन मुच्यते कर्मबन्धनात् ॥ १६७ ॥
एकाधिकारिणा वेदः[6] कृत्स्नोऽध्येयस्तथा सति ।
ऋणानि त्रीण्यपाकृत्य[7] मनो मोक्षे निवेशयेत् ॥ १६८ ॥
अनपाकृत्य मोक्षं तु सेवमानो व्रजत्यधः ।
अतोऽयमर्थ आचार्यवचसामिति गम्यते ॥ १६९ ॥
अर्थान्तरोक्तिः[8] पूर्वत्र श्रुतिस्मृत्यनुसारतः ।
हस्तग्रहणशब्देन विवाह इह लक्ष्यते ॥ १७० ॥
अस्मिन् कर्मणि कन्याया[9] हस्तग्रहणमुच्यते ।
[10]स्नानानन्तरमुक्तत्वाल्लिङ्गात्संवेशनोक्तितः ॥ १७१ ॥
ज्ञात्वानुष्ठाने प्रवृत्तस्य[11] स्त्र्यपेक्षा[12] स्यादनुष्ठिते ।

१.T पुत्रं. २.M चायां. ३.M नार्हस्थस्य, T गार्हस्थ°. ४.MT सत्वशुध्य°. ५.T °माविश्य. ६.MT वेदं. ७.M °ण्यवाकृत्य. ८.M °रोक्तिं. ९.M कन्यायां १०.T स्नानान्तरमु°. ११.M प्रवर्तस्य. १२.M स्त्यपे°.

[1]उत्पत्तिविधिसामर्थ्याद्यज्ञविध्यनुसारतः ॥ १७२ ॥

[वरकन्ययोर्गुणदोषविचारः]

अनन्यभुक्ता मेध्या[2] सा स्वीकार्या प्रथमं ततः ।
गुणवत्येव सा ग्राह्या पुत्रोत्पत्तिर्हि कामतः ॥ १७३ ॥
दृष्टार्था अप्यदृष्टार्था द्विविधाश्च गुणाः स्मृताः ॥ १७३क ॥
अव्यङ्गाङ्गी[3] सौम्यनाम्नी हंसवारणगामिनी ।
तनुलोमकेशदशना मृद्वङ्गी मेघवर्णिनी ॥ १७४ ॥
हंसस्वना तना हृद्या दत्ता वाचापि याऽऽदितः ॥ १७४क ॥
असपिण्डाऽसगोत्रा च मातृतः पितृतस्तथा ।
अरोगिणी भ्रातृमती स्वात्मनोऽपि यवीयसी ॥ १७५ ॥
दशपुरुषविख्यातश्रोत्रियाणां कुलोद्भवा ।
स्त्रीगुणैरन्विता सा च ग्राह्या धर्मार्थकामदा ॥ १७६ ॥
समानपुरुषोत्पन्न[4]पुरुषापत्यसंभवाः ।
पुरुषा ये स्त्रियश्चापि पितृबन्धव[5] एव ते ॥ १७७ ॥
समानपुरुषोत्पन्न[6]स्त्र्युद्भवाः पुरुषो स्त्रियः ।
मातृबन्धव एतेषां सापिण्ड्यं च परस्परम् ॥ १७८ ॥
[7]सप्तकात् पितृबन्धुभ्यः पञ्चमान्मातृबन्धुतः ।
ऊर्ध्वं कन्या परिग्राह्या पञ्चमी सप्तमी च वा ॥ १७९ ॥
[8]जमदग्निभरद्वाजभृग्वाद्युत्पन्नसन्ततिः ।
गोत्रमित्युच्यते तत्र भेदाश्च बहुधा स्मृताः ॥ १८० ॥
[9]पञ्चार्षेयास्तु तत्रैके द्व्यार्षेयादयोऽपरे ।
भृगूनङ्गिरसो मुक्त्वा विवाहः स्वेषु नेष्यते ॥ १८१ ॥
पञ्चानां त्रिषु सामान्यादविवाहस्त्रिषु द्वयोः ।
भृग्वङ्गिरो गणेष्वेवं[10] शेषेऽप्येकोऽपि[11] वारयेत्॥ १८२ ॥

१.M उत्वत्ति. २.M °भुक्त्वामे°. ३.MT °ङ्गानी. ४.M °षोत्वन्न. ५.M °बान्धव. ६.MT °षोत्वन्न. ७.M सप्ततात्. ८.M °दग्निर्भर°. ९.MT °र्षयास्तत्र. १०.T °रोहणेष्वेवं. ११.M °को विवार°.

भर्तृगोत्रसपिण्डत्वे स्त्रीणां दाने[1] कृते सति ।
तथापि पूर्वसद्भावात् सापिण्ड्यं[2] स्मृतिचोदितम् ॥ १८३ ॥
स्त्रीसन्ततौ सुप्रसिद्धं मातृगोत्रं च लोकतः ॥ १८३क ॥
महान्त्यपि समृद्धानि गोऽजाविधनधान्यतः ।
स्त्रीसंबन्धे दशेमानि कुलानि परिवर्जयेत् ॥ १८४ ॥
हीनक्रियं निष्पुरुषं निश्छन्दो रोमशार्शसम् ।
[3]क्षय्यामयाव्यपस्मारिश्वित्रिकुष्ठिकुलानि च ॥ १८५ ॥
कपिलामधिकाङ्गीमप्यसमाधेयरोगिणीम्[4] ।
अलोमिकां चातिलोमां [5]वाचाटां पिङ्गलामपि[5] ॥ १८६ ॥
काकस्वरां कामवाक्यां श्मश्रुव्यञ्जनयोगिनीम् ।
अनिबद्धेक्षणां वृत्तनयनां पुरुषाकृतिम् ॥ १८७ ॥
अतिरुक्षच्छविं पाण्डुकरजामरुणेक्षणाम् ।
आपीनहस्तपादां च घर्घरस्वरसंयुताम् ॥ १८८ ॥
वामनामतिदीर्घां च करालवदनां तथा ।
ऋक्षवृक्षनदीनाम्नीमन्त्यपर्वतनामिकाम् ॥ १८९ ॥
क्रूरनाम्नीमतिच्छिद्रदशनां संहतभ्रुवाम्[6] ।
पक्ष्यहिप्रेष्यनाम्नीञ्च[7] कृशां स्थूलां पुनर्भुवम् ॥ १९० ॥
यस्याश्च रोमशे जंघे गुल्फे यस्यास्तथोन्नतौ ।
गण्डयोः कूपकौ यस्या हसन्त्यस्तां च नोद्वहेत् ॥ १९१ ॥
दोषाल्पत्वे गुणाधिक्ये ग्राह्या विधिनिषेधतः ॥ १९१क ॥
एतैरेव गुणैर्युक्तः सवर्णः श्रोत्रियो वरः ।
यत्नात्परीक्षितः पुंस्त्वे युवा धीमान् जनप्रियः[8] ॥ १९२ ॥

[स्त्रीणां संस्कारमीमांसा]

संस्कृता कर्मयोग्याऽतः संस्कार्या[9] पुंवदेव सा ।

१.M माने. २.M सपिण्डयं. ३.M °मय्याव्यवस्थानिरिश्चित्रि°. ४.M °धिकां नीमव्यसमाधायरोहिणीम्. ५–५.M वाचा भाविङ्गलामपि; cf Manu III.8. ६.M साहतभ्रु°. ७.M °नाम्निञ्च. ८.M °प्रियम्. ९.M संस्कर्ता.

विवक्षितत्वाल्लिङ्गस्य नोपवीत्यधिकारिणी[१] ॥ १९३ ॥
पत्नीवतो हि कर्माणि विहितानि श्रुतौ स्मृतौ ।
संस्कृतायां च पत्नीत्वं पत्न्यर्थो लभ्यतेऽप्यतः[२] ॥ १९४ ॥
'पत्युर्नो यज्ञसंयोग' इति व्याकरणे[३] स्मृतम् ।
स्त्रीणां[४] वैदिकसंस्कारो विवाहः स्मृतिचोदितः[५] ॥ १९५ ॥
वैवाहिको विधिः स्त्रीणां संस्कारो वैदिकः स्मृतः ।
विवाहसंस्कृता पत्नी तस्माद्यज्ञाधिकारिणी ॥ १९६ ॥
प्रजार्थ एव संस्कारः स्त्रीद्वाराऽ[६]त्राभिधीयते ।
'मृत्युपाशात्प्रजामस्यै मुञ्चत्वि'त्यादिलिङ्गतः ॥ १९७ ॥
अत एवर्तुगमनं गर्भस्थैर्यादिसाधनम् ।
जातकर्मापि चेहोक्तमन्यथा तदनर्थकम् ॥ १९८ ॥
प्रजोत्पत्तिविधिश्चापि प्रयुङ्क्ते[७] संस्कृतिं स्त्रियाः ।
धर्मापाये प्रजापाये दारस्वीकरणं स्मृतेः ॥ १९९ ॥
प्रजामात्रार्थता तस्मात्संस्कृतेरवगम्यते ।
यत्प्रयुक्त्या गृहीता या तदर्था सेति युज्यते ॥ २०० ॥
न रागतः प्रवृत्तस्य पुमर्थे दुःखवर्जिते ।
सक्तस्य वैदिकोपायः[८] साध्ये चेतः प्रवर्तते ॥ २०१ ॥
संसेव्य विहितं कर्म प्रतिषिद्धं निवर्त्य च ।
तत्प्राप्तिरत एवादौ जायमानादिवादतः ॥ २०२ ॥
ऋणद्वयविमोकार्थं स्त्रियं संस्कर्तुमीप्सति ।
तस्या अपि पुमर्थेषु वैदिकेष्वेव तुल्यता ॥ २०३ ॥
अधिकारस्य तुल्यत्वादैककर्म्यं[९] यतस्तयोः ।
तस्या अपि फलं तुल्यं श्रूयते सर्वकर्मसु ॥ २०४ ॥
संस्कारेऽस्याः कृते द्रव्यसंबन्धस्तुल्य एव तु ।

१.M नोपनीत्यधि°. २.M °प्यसौ. ३.T °करणं. ४.M स्त्रियं. ५.M चोदितम्. ६.M °द्वारत्रा. ७.M संयुक्ते. ८.T °पायसाध्ये. ९.MT ऐककर्मं.

श्रुतेः स्मृतेर्मध्यकं [१]स्वं नैकस्त्यक्तुं च सक्षमः ॥ २०५ ॥
स्त्रिया एवैष संस्कारः सर्वार्थ इति गम्यते ।
मन्त्रलिङ्गानुसारेण स्त्रीफलत्वं प्रतीयते ॥ २०६ ॥
पुत्रयज्ञादिसिध्यर्थं विवाह इति दर्शयन् ।
उक्त्वा स्नानं विवाहं[२] च जातकर्मान्त ईरिते ॥ २०७ ॥
अष्टकाश्राद्धमत्राह नित्यं यद् गृहमेधिनः ।
विवाहाग्नौ च गृह्येऽस्मिन् कर्म कार्यमितीरितम् ॥ २०८ ॥
स्वीकृतिश्च स्त्रिया रागः[३] प्रयुक्तेति हि युज्यते ।
अन्यथा ब्रह्मचारी सन् संस्कुर्वीत स्त्रियं विधेः ॥ २०९ ॥
धर्माद्यपाये ग्रहणं तदर्थमिति न प्रमा ।
विवाहसंस्कृता पत्नी तस्मात्सर्वाधिकारिणी ॥ २१० ॥
एवं च नियमस्तत्र विवाहे क्रियते यया ।
कया च कार्ये धर्मेऽस्मिन्ननयैव[४] सह स्त्रिया ॥ २११ ॥
कुर्यात्कर्मेति तच्चैतत् प्राजापत्येह गम्यते ।
सहधर्मश्चर्यतामित्युक्त्वा दीयतेऽर्थिने ॥ २१२ ॥
दात्रा दाने स्वकन्याया वरो ह्यत्र[५] नियम्यते ।
अतश्च तामतिक्रम्य नोद्वहेत्कामकारतः[६] ॥ २१३ ॥
धर्माद्यलब्ध[७]वचनाद्वनितान्तरसंग्रहम् ।
अधिवेदने च सर्वत्र पूर्वानुमतिरिष्यते ॥ २१४ ॥
पूर्वाग्नेरुत्तराग्नेश्च नाशान्न्यायानुसारतः ।
सर्वार्थं पुनराधानं कार्यं पूर्वसमीरितम् ॥ २१५ ॥
पत्न्यन्तरस्य मरणे पूर्वोपात्तेन वह्निना[८] ।
दाहयित्वा मृतां शुद्धौ पुनराधानमाचरेत् ॥ २१६ ॥

१.MT श्रुतेस्मृते°. २.MT स्नाने. ३.T राग. ४.M °न्नतयेव. ५.T वरोऽप्यत्र. ६.M कारकामतः. ७.M °लब्ध्वा. ८.M वर्णिना.

[विवाहसंस्कृतिमीमांसा]

प्रसङ्गादिदमत्रोक्तमथ प्रकृतमुच्यते ।
हस्तग्रहणमत्रोक्तं प्राधान्येन स्मृतीरितम् ॥ २१७ ॥
कन्यकायाः करस्तस्मान्मन्त्रतो ग्रहणात्पुरा ।
न स्पृष्टव्यो वरेणात्र[1] हस्तग्रहणलक्षणः[2] ॥ २१८ ॥
विवाहस्तत्र सामर्थ्यात् वरदत्तां वधूं स्वयम् ।
स्वीकृत्य संस्कृतिं तस्याः[3] कुर्यात्तद्दातृवेश्मनि ॥ २१९ ॥
एनां गृहानानयतीत्युत्तरत्राभिधास्यते ।
बाह्यतः श्रोत्रियागारादग्निमाहृत्य लौकिकम् ॥ २२० ॥
आधाय संपरिस्तीर्येत्यादितन्त्रोपलक्षणम् ।
शम्याकारांस्तु परिधीन् विधत्तेऽत्र विशेषतः ॥ २२१ ॥
परिधायाहतं वासः सोत्तरीयो वधूमपि ।
परिधाप्य तथा वास उपवेश्यासने शुभे ॥ २२२ ॥
आवापदेशे जुहुया'द्या तिरश्च्या'दिमन्त्रतः[4] ।
द्वितीयामिति निर्देशाद् द्वितीया च 'समि'त्यृचा ॥ २२३ ॥
अन्वारभ्यैव होतव्या जयादौ नैष चोद्यते ।
विधानादुत्तरत्रान्वारब्धाया जुहुयादिति ॥ २२४ ॥
विवाहे नित्यतां[5] वक्तुमनूद्यन्ते जयादयः ।
यावदुक्तविधावेषां निवृत्तिर्ह्यन्यथा भवेत् ॥ २२५ ॥
तत्रापि चैते होतव्याः कल्पकृद्वचनं तथा ।
येनेच्छेत्[6] कर्मणा तत्र ते[7] होतव्या इति श्रुतौ ॥ २२६ ॥
अनारभ्यैव विहिता युष्माकं दर्विहोमकः[8] ।
इत्यादि [9]गुणवादाच्च दर्विहोमेषु चोदिताः ॥ २२७ ॥
तां पुष्टिं मिथुने पश्यन्नित्यादिश्रुतिलिङ्गतः ।

१.M °णात्रो. २.M °लक्षणम्. ३.M तस्मात्. ४.M जुहुयात्यतिरिच्यातिमन्त्रतः. ५.M विवाहेत्येतां. ६.M येनैतत् सकर्म°. ७.M oms. ८.M °होमकम्. ९.M गणवादा°.

ऋध्यर्थे दारसंयोगे नियता इति युज्यते ॥ २२८ ॥
एवं चाधारवत्पक्षे जयादेरर्थवादता[१] ।
अथशब्दप्रयोगादप्यन्वारंभ[२]विधानत: ॥ २२९ ॥
उत्तरासामाहुतीनां वैलक्षण्यं प्रतीयते ।
इत: प्रभृत्याहुतीनां संस्रावानयनं तत: ॥ २३० ॥
अवाचीनकरेणास्या[३] उत्तानं दक्षिणं करम् ।
गृह्णीयादिति शास्त्रान्तरोदितं ग्राह्यमेव तु ॥ २३१ ॥
असाविति स्त्रिया नाम प्रथमान्तं समुच्चरेत् ।
अस्यासावहमित्यत्र स्वीयं नाम तथोच्चरेत् ॥ २३२ ॥
एतच्च पाणिग्रहणं मन्त्रेण क्रियतेऽत्र[४] यत् ।
पत्नीत्वं च पतित्वं च तयोरेतेन कर्मणा ॥ २३३ ॥
स्त्रीपुंसयोश्च संबन्धाद्वरणं प्राग्विधीयते ।
वरणाद् ग्रहणं पाणे: संस्कारोऽथ विलक्षणम् ॥ २३४ ॥
तयोरनियमं[५] प्रोक्तं वरणं दोषदर्शनात् ।
पाणिग्रहणमन्त्राभ्यां नियतं दारलक्षणम् ॥ २३५ ॥
नोदकेन न वाचा न कन्याया:[६] पतिरुच्यते ।
पाणिग्रहणसंस्कारात्पतित्वं सप्तमे पदे ॥ २३६ ॥
ततश्च सप्तमे क्रान्ते पदेनान्यस्य सा भवेत् ॥ २३६क ॥
ततश्च सप्तमपदात् प्रागन्यस्मै मृते सति ।
पतिते वापि नष्टे वा क्लीबत्वे वा विनिश्चिते ॥ २३७ ॥
सगोत्रत्वेऽपि संन्यस्ते जातिहीनत्ववेदने ।
पित्रादिभिश्च सा कन्या[७] देयेत्येवं प्रतीयते ॥ २३८ ॥
अद्भिर्वाचा च दत्तायां म्रियेतादौ वरो यदि ।
गतमन्त्रोपनीता स्यात् कुमारी पितुरेव सा[७] ॥ २३९ ॥

१.M °रनुवादता. २.M °दावन्वा°. ३.M °करेणाया. ४.M क्रियते यत्. ५.T तयोरनिय...प्रोक्तं. ६.M कन्यायां. ७–७.M oms.

[१]पाणिग्राहे मृते कन्या[१] केवलं मन्त्रसंस्कृता ।
[२]सा चेदक्षतयोनिः स्यात् पुनः संस्कारमर्हति ॥ २४० ॥
विधिवत्प्रतिगृह्यापि त्यजेत्कन्यां विगर्हिताम् ।
व्याधितां[३] विप्रदुष्टां वा च्छद्मना चोपपादिताम्[४] ॥ २४१ ॥
वरश्चेत्कुलशीलाभ्यां न युज्येत कथंचन ।
न मन्त्राकरणं[५] तत्र न च कन्यानृतं भवेत् ॥ २४२ ॥
समाकृष्य तु तां कन्यां बलादक्षतयोनिकाम् ।
पुनर्गुणवते दद्यादिति शातातपोऽब्रवीत् ॥ २४३ ॥
ऊर्ध्वं तु सप्तमपदाद्विधुरा सा मृते पतौ ।
ततश्च संस्कृतिस्तस्या नान्येन क्रियते क्वचित् ॥ २४४ ॥
न विवाहविधावुक्तं विधवावेदनं क्वचित् ।
न द्वितीयश्च साध्वीनां क्वचिद् भर्तोपदिश्यते ॥ २४५ ॥
परिणीयापि वा साग्निं विधवेति निगद्यते ।
मनसा यापि[६] वा यस्मै दत्ता तस्यैव सा[७]शुभा ॥ २४६ ॥
सप्त पौनर्भवाः[८] कन्या[९] वर्जनीयाः[१०] कुलाधमाः[११] ।
वाचा दत्ता मनोदत्ता कृतकौतुकमङ्गला ॥ २४७ ॥
उदकस्पर्शिता या च या च पाणिगृहीतिका ।
अग्निं परिगता या च पुनर्भूप्रसवा च या ॥ २४८ ॥
इत्येताः काश्यपेनोक्ता दहन्ति कुलमग्निवत् ॥ २४८क ॥
मङ्गलार्थं स्वस्त्ययनं यज्ञश्चासां प्रजापतेः ।
प्रयुज्यते विवाहेषु प्रदानं स्वामिकारणम् ॥ २४९ ॥
न दत्त्वा कस्यचित्कन्यां [१२]पुनर्दद्याद्विचक्षणः ।
दत्त्वा पुनः प्रयच्छन् हि प्राप्नोति पुरुषोऽनृतम् ॥ २५० ॥
एवमादिविमृश्यापद्यासां[१३] संस्कारमाचरेत् ॥ २५०क ॥

१-१.M oms. २.M या. ३.M oms. ४.T चोपपपादि°. ५.M मन्त्रां करणं. ६.M वापि, T या वि. ७.M याशुभा; T सा शुभा. ८.MT °र्भवां. ९.MT कन्यां. १०.T नीयां. ११.T °धमाम्. १२.M पुनर्भूद्या°. १३.M °श्या च यासां.

[विवाहप्रकारः]

ब्राह्मेण विधिना दत्ता मुख्या विप्रस्य कन्यका ।
नाना स्मृतिसमुद्दिष्टं तत्प्रकारोऽधुनोच्यते ॥ २५१ ॥
वरमाहूय सदृशमर्थिनं ब्रह्मचारिणम् ।
श्रुतशीलान्वितं विप्रं नीरोगं चरणान्वितम् ॥ २५२ ॥
सुभगं मधुपर्केण त्वर्हयित्वा स्वलङ्कृतम् ।
अलंकृत्य स्वयं कन्यामम्बराभरणादिभिः[१] ॥ २५३ ॥
तस्मै दद्यात्पिता तूष्णीं[२] मन्त्रोऽपि क्वचिदीरितम्[२] ॥ २५३क ॥
प्राजापत्ये विवाहे यो मन्त्रः स्मृतिषु पठ्यते ।
वैकल्पिकत्वं[३] ब्राह्मेऽस्य प्राजापत्ये तु नित्यता ॥ २५४ ॥
पुनन्ति साधवः पुत्रा[४] दशपूर्वान्दशावरान् ।
आत्मानं[५] च पुनात्येष ब्राह्मोढावहितोद्भवः[६] ॥ २५५ ॥
यज्ञे तु वितते सम्यगृत्विजे[७] कर्म कुर्वते ।
अलंकृत्य सुतादानं दैवं धर्मं प्रचक्षते ॥ २५६ ॥
एकं [८]गोमिथुनं द्वे वा वरादादाय धर्मतः[९] ।
कन्याप्रदानं विधिवदार्षो धर्मः स उच्यते ॥ २५७ ॥
[९क]सहोभौ धर्मश्चर्यतामिति वाचाऽनुभाष्य तु ।
कन्याप्रदानमभ्यर्च्य[१०] प्राजापत्यो[११] विधिः स्मृतः ॥ २५८ ॥
दैवोढायाः[१२] सुतश्चैव सप्त सप्त परावरान्[१३] ।
आर्षोढायाः[१४] सुतस्त्रीन्स्त्रीन्[१५] षट्षट् कायोदजः[१६] सुतः॥ २५९ ॥
पिता दद्यात्स्वकन्यां[१७] च[१८] भ्रातर्यनुमते पितुः ।
मातामहो मातुलश्च सकुल्यो बान्धवस्तथा[१९] ॥ २६० ॥

१.M °भरणादिदम्. २-२.M तूष्णीमन्त्रोक्त...रीरितम्. ३.T °कत्वाद्. ४.MT पुत्रान्. ५.M आत्मनश्च. ६. ब्राह्मोढाविहि°. ७.MT °त्विजं. ८.M द्वे मिथुनं. ९.MT कर्मतः; thus Manu III.29. ९क. MT सहधर्मश्च°. १०.T मन्यच्च. ११.MT °पत्ये. १२.Cf Manu III.38; दैवोढाजः. १३.M वरा°. १४. Cf Manu III.38. आर्षोढाजः. १५.M स्वत्स्त्रीं°. १६.T कार्याहृता, M कायाहृ°. १७.MT सुकन्यां. १८.MT om. १९.M बान्धवन्त°.

माता[१] त्वभावे सर्वेषां प्रकृतौ यदि वर्तते ।
तस्यामप्रकृतिस्थायां दद्युः कन्यां स्वजातयः ॥ २६१ ॥
यदा तु नैव कश्चित् स्यात् कन्या राजानमाव्रजेत् ।
अप्रयच्छन् समाप्नोति भ्रूणहत्यामृतावृतौ ॥ २६२ ॥
त्रीणि वर्षाण्यृतुमती कांक्षेत पितृशासनम् ।
ततश्चतुर्थे वर्षे तु चिन्तेत सदृशं पतिम् ॥ २६३ ॥
अलभ्यमाने सदृशं गुणहीनं समाश्रयेत् ॥ २६३क ॥
अन्येऽप्यासुरगान्धर्वा राक्षसाः सपिशाचकाः ।
विवाहाः कीर्तितास्तेषां प्रकाराः स्मृतिदर्शिताः ॥ २६४ ॥
ज्ञातिभ्यो द्रविणं दत्त्वा कन्यायै चैव शक्तितः ।
कन्याप्रदानं स्वाच्छन्द्यादासुरो धर्म उच्यते ॥ २६५ ॥
इच्छयाऽन्योऽन्यसंयोगः कन्यायाश्च[२] वरस्य च ।
गान्धर्वः स विधिर्ज्ञेयो मैथुन्यः[३] कामसंभवः[४] ॥ २६६ ॥
हत्वा[५] च्छित्त्वा च भित्त्वा च क्रोशन्तीं[६] रुदतीं गृहात्।
प्रसह्य कन्याहरणं[७] राक्षसो विधिरुच्ये ॥ २६७ ॥
सुप्तां मत्तां प्रमत्तां वा रहो यत्रोपगच्छति ।
स पापिष्ठो[८] विवाहानां पैशाचः प्रथितोऽष्टमः[९] ॥ २६८ ॥
श्रेयान् गृहाश्रमस्तस्मात् सुगमः स्मृतिचोदितात्[१०] ।
अहोमकर्मणोऽपीदं स्नानमत्र विधानतः ॥ २६९ ॥
निहितं चोत्तरेणाग्निमश्मानं दृषदादिकम् ।
गृहीतहस्तामास्थाप्य[११] चोत्तरेण च तं व्रजेत्[१२] ॥ २७० ॥
[१३]अन्नत्वादिह लाजानां तत्संस्काराः पुरोदिताः ।

१.MT मता. २.M °यास्य. ३.T मैथुन्यं. ४.T °संभवम्. ५.MT हित्वा. ६.MT रोदन्तीं, thus Manu III.33. ७.M oms क. ८.M चाविष्टो, T वासिष्ठो. ९. Cf Manu III.34: पैशाचश्चाष्टमोऽधमः. After this two Verses (263.263क) त्रीणि वर्षाण्यृतुमती=गुणहीनं समाश्रयेत् have been repeated in both M and T. १०.M °चोदिताः. ११.MT °मस्थाप्य. १२.M wrongly puts व्रजेत् at the beginning of next Verse. १३.M कार्यस्त°,T कार्यं.

कार्यस्तद्धोमकरणाञ्जलिसंस्कृतिरत्र तु ॥ २७१ ॥
[१]प्रक्षालितेऽञ्जलौ तस्या उपस्तीर्य परार्धतः[२] ।
ओप्य मन्त्रेण पूर्वार्धा[३]त्तूष्णीमोप्याभिघार्य च ॥ २७२ ॥
परिहोमान्वितं तेन जुहुयाद् देवतीर्थतः ।
एवमेवोक्तमार्गेण त्रिरुक्तेन सहैव तु ॥ २७३ ॥
लाजानामचरुत्वेन[४] निवृत्तिः[५] स्विष्टकृद्धुतेः[६] ।
सर्वस्माद्धविषः शेषात् कार्यान्त्येति पुरोक्तितः[७] ॥ २७४ ॥
जुहोति सौविष्टकृतीं 'यदस्ये'तीह वादतः ।
कौण्डिन्यवचनाच्चाज्यं सलाजं जुहुयादिह ॥ २७५ ॥
मार्जनान्ते प्रणीतानामुत्थाप्यैनां [८]पदानि च ।
अनुनिष्क्रम्य चाप्येनामुपस्थाप्य 'ध्रुवा'दिना ॥ २७६ ॥
ध्रुवं 'सप्तर्षय'श्चारुन्धतीमप्युपतिष्ठते ।
वैवाहिकाग्निना सार्धं पुरस्कृत्य वधूं गृहात् ॥ २७७ ॥
प्राप्योपवेशनगृहं द्वारेयीं दक्षिणा स्पृशेत् ।
हस्तभागमभिप्रेत्य दक्षिणामुत्तरामिति ॥ २७८ ॥

[विवाहप्रयोगः]

श्रतिस्मृतिसमाचारगृह्यकल्पानुसारतः ।
प्रयोगमधुना वक्ष्ये विवाहस्य समासतः ॥ २७९ ॥
कन्याया आशिषो दाता वाचयित्वा वराय तु ।
कृत्वार्घ्यं भोजयित्वैनामलंकृत्य यथाविधि ॥ २८० ॥
दद्यादर्घ्यं[९] सदानादिदातृधर्मोऽभिधीयते ।
विधानेनानुपदिकेनार्घ्यं[१०] कुर्यात्तदुच्यते ॥ २८१ ॥
यज्ञर्त्विग्वरणादौ यद्विधानं परिकीर्तितम् ।

१.M adds न before प्रक्षा°. २.M °पराद्धतम्. ३.M पूर्वार्धा तूष्णी°. ४.M °नामाचरु°. ५.M निर्वृत्ति. ६.M °कृद्धुतेः. ७.M पुरोर्तितः. ८.MT °प्येनां. ९.M °दर्घ्यत्यदा°, T दद्याद...त्यदा°. १०.MT °नानुवदि°.

अन्वहं क्रियमाणेषु पाकयज्ञेषु यत्स्मृतम् ॥ २८२ ॥
आचार्यशिष्यराजार्थं प्रतिसंवत्सरं तथा ।
विवाहे वत्सरादर्वाग्यज्ञेऽप्यर्घ्यं तथाचरेत् ॥ २८३ ॥
शोभयित्वा स्ववेश्मानि मार्जनालेपनादिभिः ।
प्रागग्राणि तृणान्यत्र शुचौ देशे विधाय तु ॥ २८४ ॥
[1]प्रोक्षण्याज्यपिधानार्थपात्रे कंसं[1] घृतं मधु ।
दधिसक्तून् कुण्डिकां च स्रजं च्छत्रमुपानहौ ॥ २८५ ॥
भूषणं कुण्डले तोयमेरकां[2] वसनद्वयम् ।
एरकास्तरणं कूर्चमोदनं सोपदंशकम् ॥ २८६ ॥
सह संसाद्य संप्रोक्ष्य तानि संस्कृतवारिणा ।
उदीचीनदशां वेश्ममध्य आस्तीर्य चैरकाम् ॥ २८७ ॥
वासस्तदुपरि न्यस्य कूर्चं तस्योपरि न्यसेत् ।
त्रिवृदासनमेवेदं ब्रूयादासनमित्यथ ॥ २८८ ॥
अर्घ्ये तत्रोपविष्टे तु कुण्डिकायां पवित्रवत् ।
उदकुंभात् समानीय पद्यमित्याहरज्जलम् ॥ २८९ ॥
पादप्रक्षालनाय[3] यज्जलं[3] पाद्यमिहोच्यते[4] ।
हस्तयोर्वदनस्यापि क्षालनायार्घ्यमुच्यते ॥ २९० ॥
वैकल्पिकं पाद्यदानं पूर्वमत्र विधीयते ।
व्यवस्थासिद्धये[5]ऽथार्घ्यमित्यर्घ्यमिति भण्यते ॥ २९१ ॥
[6]तदाहृतं जलं सिञ्चेद्[7] भार्या[8] प्रक्षालयेत् स्वयम् ।
प्रक्षालको[9] ब्राह्मणश्चेद् दक्षिणं पूर्वमस्य तु ॥ २९२ ॥
दद्यात्पादं क्षत्रियस्य सव्यं वैश्यस्य चादितः ।
यः पादौ क्षालयेत्तस्य पाणी प्रक्षालयेन्मृदा ॥ २९३ ॥
'दोहोऽसी'ति[10] स्वहृदयमुपस्पृश्यालभेन्'मयि' ।

१-१.M °ण्यर्थविधानार्थ कंसं, T कं सघृ°. २.M तोयीमे°. ३-३.T °नायाऽलं जलं. ४.T पद्यमि°. ५.M सिद्धयेदार्घ्य°. ६.M अतदा°. ७.M सञ्चात्. ८.M भार्यो. ९.M प्रक्षल°. १०.M दोहसीति.

पूर्ववज्जलमाहृत्य ब्रुवन्नर्घ्यमितीतरः[१] ॥ २९४ ॥
सिञ्चेत्तदञ्जलौ[२] तेन क्षालयेत्स्वमुखं वरः[३] ।
तथैव जलमाहृत्य तूष्णीमाचामयेत्ततः[४] ॥ २९५ ॥
अविभक्तधना येऽस्य पुत्रदारादिबान्धवाः ।
उपासीरंश्च ते सर्वे परिवार्यार्घ्यमादरात् ॥ २९६ ॥
आचम्यागत्य तद् द्रव्यं दूरात्पश्येति[५] दर्शयेत् ।
तिरःपवित्रं कंसेऽथ दधिमध्वाज्यसक्तवः[६] ॥ २९७ ॥
क्रमेणानीय विस्रस्य पवित्रे च निरस्य तु ।
वर्षीयसा तैजसेन विधायार्घ्यं करे शुचौ ॥ २९८ ॥
न्यस्य[७] कूर्चं तदुपरि न्यस्यार्घ्यं च विधानवत् ।
उपरिष्टाच्च कूर्चेन विधाय मुखसंमितम् ॥ २९९ ॥
आहृत्य तदपावृत्य[८] ब्रूयात्[९] पर्क[९] इतीतरम् ।
आनीयमानमामन्त्र्य 'यशोऽसी'त्यप्यपावृतम्[१०] ॥ ३०० ॥
'देवस्ये'ति मन्त्रेण प्रतिगृह्यावनौ च तत् ।
पृथिव्या इव संसाद्य सव्य आधाय तत्पुनः ॥ ३०१ ॥
आवर्जिते जले तेन पीत्वा त'दमृता'दिना ।
सर्वाङ्गुलीभिरावेष्ट्य प्रसलै'स्तेज'[११]आदिभिः ॥ ३०२ ॥
[१२]त्रिरशित्वाङ्गुलीभिस्तदपः पीत्वा'ऽमृत'ादिना ।
यं कामयेत मच्छ्रेयान् स्यादित्यस्मै ददाति सः[१३] ॥ ३०३ ॥
ततोऽपि संस्कृतान्पर्कान् [१४]दद्यान्नान्यस्य कस्यचित् ।
पृथगाहार्य दध्यादीन् येभ्यो दीक्षां प्रयच्छति ॥ ३०४ ॥
अर्घ्याय शुचयेऽपीयमर्हणीयेति[१५] गां वदेत् ।
तस्या उत्सर्जनं शास्ति वरो 'गौ'रितिमन्त्रतः ॥ ३०५ ॥

१.M °मितीतरम्; °मिती करम्. २.M सिञ्चेत्तञ्जलौ. ३.M परम्, T परः. ४.M °माचम्य यत्ततः. ५.MT पूजात्प°. ६.T °सक्तवम्. ७.M अस्य. ८.M तदावृत्य. ९-९.M ब्रूयाच्चक्र, T °पर्ण. १०.M °त्यपावृ°. ११.T प्रसलैतेज. १२.T त्रिशिरत्वाङ्गु°. १३.T oms. १४.T पर्णान्. १५.M °पीहमर्ह°.

अर्घ्याय दद्यात्कंसं तत् पिधानमहताम्बरम्[1] ।
कुण्डले चन्दनं मालां भूषणं च्छत्रमेव च ॥ ३०६ ॥
उपानहौ पर्कदुहं[2] गामन्यामपि गां क्रमात् ।
[3]उपानहान्तान्येतानि देयानि नियमेन तु ॥ ३०७ ॥
अन्यान्यपि यथाश्रद्धं[4] देयानीत्यादि भाषितम्॥ ३०७क ॥
एतेषामपि देयत्वे नियमेनेत्यपीरितम् ।
प्रसार्येत्यादि यज्ञार्थमृत्विजां[5] वरणेषु[6] तत् ॥ ३०८ ॥
अथौदनं समाहृत्य ब्रूयादन्नं ततो 'भूतम्' ।
[7]ततः 'सुभूत'मितीतरः[7] [8]प्रत्याह तदनन्तरम्[8] ॥ ३०९ ॥
एवं संभोज्य विधिवद्वरं तमभिवादयेत् ।
यथावारं मङ्गलानि शुचौ देशे निधाय तु ॥ ३१० ॥
नवतन्तुकृते कण्ठसूत्रे प्रोत्यापि[9] भूषणम् ।
सुवर्णनिर्मितं तत्र निधायाथाहतांबरः[10] ॥ ३११ ॥
परिधाप्य वधूं[11] तत्र स्रगादिभिरलंकृताम् ।
उपवेश्य यथान्यायं पूजयित्वा विनायकम् ॥ ३१२ ॥
कामदेवं महादेवं पार्वतीं श्रियमच्युतम् ।
पूजयित्वा भूषणस्थामिन्द्राणीमपि पूजयेत् ॥ ३१३ ॥
दत्त्वा दानानि विप्रेभ्यो गृहीत्वा भूषणं ततः ॥ ३१३क ॥
दशहोत्रादिकन्यासं[12] श्रुतिसिद्धं विधाय तु ।
भूषयित्वा समुत्थाप्य तया सार्धं वरान्तिकम्[13] ॥ ३१४ ॥
गत्वा प्रत्यङ्मुखस्तिष्ठन् प्राङ्मुखाय वराय ताम् ।
संस्थितताननुसंस्थाना नद्याद्युदकपूर्वकम्[14] ॥ ३१५ ॥

१.M °विधानमहता खरे, T विधानमहताम्बरे. २.M चर्कदुहं. T वर्क°. ३.M उपानधन्ता°. ४.MT °श्रद्धं. ५.M °मृर्त्विजां. ६.MT om षु of वरणेषु . ७-७.T तत् सुभ्रमतीतरत्, M तत्सुभ्रमतितीतरः; cf Baudh GS I.2.55-56. ८-८.MT om; the text under bracket conjectured by the Editor. ९.M प्रोत्याविभू°. १०.M °हतां वरः. ११.M वधूस्तत्र. १२.M सः श्रुति°. १३.M साधमपरान्ति°. १४.M नद्यादुक°, T नद्यादुदक°.

स्वकराहिततोयं[1] यं कन्याहस्तनिपातितम् ।
संस्रावयेत्तस्य हस्ते दानं त्रिरिह मन्त्रवत् ॥ ३१६ ॥
समाचारानुसारेण प्रयोगो दान ईरितः ।
परिणेता यथामन्त्रं शुद्धदेहो जपादिभिः ॥ ३१७ ॥
ज्योतिःशास्त्रोदिते काले कृत्वा श्राद्धं पुरोदितम् ।
भोजयित्वा द्विजान् भुक्त्वा ज्ञातिबन्धुसमन्वितः॥ ३१८ ॥
अभिवाद्य गुरून् वृद्धान् यथान्यायमलंकृतान्[2] ।
नानासुगन्धकुसुमविचित्ररचितस्रजान्[3] ॥ ३१९ ॥
चूर्णैर्गन्धादिभिः स्त्रीभिः शाकुनं सूक्तमादरात् ।
जपद्भिर्ब्राह्मणैर्ज्ञातिबन्धुभिश्च समन्वितः ॥ ३२० ॥
[4]देशजात्यात्मसदृशं ततो यानमधिष्ठितः ।
कन्यादातृगृहं[5] गत्वा स्नात्वा पुण्याहवाचनम् ॥ ३२१ ॥
कृत्वा तद्गृहमाविश्य पूजितः समलंकृतः ।
परिधायाहतं वासः 'स्वा मे'त्यप्युत्तरीयवत् ॥ ३२२ ॥
प्रतिगृह्य ततः कन्यामुपवेश्यासने शुभे ।
अग्निमाधाय विधिवल्लाजैः पात्राणि सादयेत् ॥ ३२३ ॥
उत्तरेणाग्निमश्मानं निधाय प्रोक्ष्य संस्कृतैः ।
आहुतिद्वयमावापदेशे[6] हुत्वा जयादिकान् ॥ ३२४ ॥
हुत्वा तन्मूर्ध्नि संस्रावं मन्त्रेणासिच्य संस्थितम् ।
प्राङ्मुख्याः [7]प्राङ्मुखस्तस्यास्तिष्ठन्त्या दक्षिणं करम्॥ ३२५ ॥
[8]'आयुर्दा त्वमसी'त्येवं गृहीत्वा दृषदादिकम् ।
आस्थाप्य परिणीयैनां[9] हुत्वा [10]लाजान्यथोदितम्॥ ३२६ ॥
ततो वास्तोष्पतीयादिहोमशेषं समापयेत् ।

१.M स्वकरारहितः कार्यं. २.M °कृता. ३.M स्रजा. ४.M दशजा°. ५.M कन्यादातृगृहं. ६.M °मावाचदेशे. ७.M प्रङ्मुखन्तस्या°. ८.MT आर्यादा°. ९.M °णीतैनां. १०.M oms ला.

तस्या दक्षिणपादस्य पदान्येषोऽश्मनि[१] क्रमेत् ॥ ३२७ ॥
'भूरि'ति प्रथमं क्रामेद् द्वितीयं 'भुव' इत्यपि ।
तृतीयं[२] 'सुव'रित्येव तूष्णीं चत्वारि निष्क्रमेत् ॥ ३२८ ॥
उपस्थाय समारूढवह्निना ज्वलितेन वा ।
सार्धं गच्छेद् गृहानङ्के पितुर्भ्रात्रादिकस्य वा ॥ ३२९ ॥
आसीनां स्ववधूं हस्ते गृहीत्वोत्थाप्य मन्त्रवत् ।
यानमारोप्य विधिवदानीय स्वगृहानथ ॥ ३३० ॥
उद्धृत्याग्निं समाधाय द्वारेयीस्पर्शनं ततः ।
कृत्वाऽलंकृतभवनमध्य[३] आस्तीर्य रोहितम् ॥ ३३१ ॥
[४]चर्म तत्रोपविशतो दम्पती मन्त्रवत्ततः ।
आदित्येऽस्तमिते होमं कुर्यात्स्वस्त्ययनान्वितम् ॥ ३३२ ॥
विधिवत्संपरिस्तीर्य कस्मिंश्चिद् भाजने शुचौ ।
उपस्तीर्य शुचीन्[५] व्रीहीनानीयाप्यभिघार्य तान् ॥ ३३३ ॥
पर्यग्निकृत्यौषधिभिरलंकृत्य हुताशनम् ।
मन्त्रवत्परिषिच्याग्नावाज्याक्तां[६] समिधं शुभाम् ॥ ३३४ ॥
'स्वाहे'त्याधाय तस्याश्च द्व्यङ्गुले देवतीर्थतः ।
जुहुयादग्नये व्रीहीन् ज्यायसीमुत्तरां[७] ततः ॥ ३३५ ॥
हुत्वाहुतिं तु तत्पार्श्वे प्राजापत्यामथेन्धनैः ।
ततश्चोपसमिध्याग्निं मन्त्रवत्परिषिच्य च ॥ ३३६ ॥
भस्मानुलेपनं कृत्वा कुर्यादग्नेरलंकृतिम्[८] ।
सन्निधौ वर्तते सायं प्रातः शब्दोऽत्र सन्ध्ययोः ॥ ३३७ ॥
उपास्य सन्ध्यां कुर्वीत होमं तस्मादनन्तरम् ।
वेदव्रतान्यपि चरेत्त्रियहं[९] नानृतं वदेत् ॥ ३३८ ॥

१.M °दान्येषो...नि, T °न्येषोशनि. २.T तृतीयस्सुव°. ३.M स्वभवन°, T स्वभवमध्य. ४.MT add त before चर्म. ५.T शुची,T शुचि. ६.M °च्याग्नौ-आज्या°, T च्याग्नौ वाज्या°. ७.M मुत्तरं. ८.M °कृतिः. ९.M °त्र्यहं.

मांसाशनं स्त्रीगमनं वासःपल्पूलनं[१] तथा ।
आञ्जनाभ्यञ्जने कोशीधान्यं खट्वासनादिकम्[२]॥ ३३९ ॥
शूद्रोच्छिष्टं तथा श्राद्धं मृन्मयेन[३] जलाशनम् ।
अन्यच्च[४] गर्हितं शास्त्रे वर्जयेद् भोजनं हविः ॥ ३४० ॥

[पञ्चमहायज्ञाः]

हुत्वोदिते [५]रवौ गत्वा प्रागुदीचीं दिशं गृहात् ।
गृहाद्यदर्शने[६]ऽरण्ये समीपे वाथ सांशुचौ॥ ३४१ ॥
प्राणायामैर्दग्धदोषः[७] शुक्लाम्बरधरः शुचिः ।
आचम्य ब्रह्मयज्ञेन यज्ञ इत्यध्यवस्य तु ॥ ३४२ ॥
उपस्पृश्य जलं विद्युदब्लिङ्गाभिः[८] पिबेदथ ।
दशप्रणवगायत्र्या रुद्रसंख्याविभक्तया ॥ ३४३ ॥
परिमार्जनादिश्रुत्युक्तं हृदयालंभनान्तिकम्[९] ।
कृत्वा प्रसव्यमावृत्य नमस्कृत्योपविश्य च ॥ ३४४ ॥
बहुषु स्तीर्णदर्भेषु चोपस्थं दक्षिणोत्तरम् ।
संहतौ दर्भसंयुक्तौ [१०]पाणी कृत्वा पवित्रवत्[११] ॥ ३४५ ॥
नभोभूम्यन्तरं पश्यन् प्राङ्मुखो यतमानसः ।
ओङ्कारं व्याहृतीस्तिस्रः[१२] सावित्रीं च 'तदि'त्यृचम् ॥ ३४६ ॥
पच्छोऽर्धर्चशो[१३]ऽनवानं[१४] वेदादीनप्यनूच्य[१५] च ।
अनुवाकाञ्चमं[१६] वेदं स्वमधीत्य यथाविधि ॥ ३४७ ॥
'नमो ब्रह्मण' इत्येतं त्रिरनूच्य 'ध्रुवं' जपेत् ।
'वृष्टिं'रित्युदकं स्पृष्ट्वा काण्डर्षींस्तर्पयेत्ततः ॥ ३४८ ॥
ब्रह्मयज्ञोऽयमुद्दिष्टः प्रत्यक्षश्रुतिचोदितः ।
श्रुतिस्मृत्यनुसारेण नियमाः स्मृतिदर्शिताः ॥ ३४९ ॥

१.MT पल्लूलनं. २.M खल्वा°. ३.M मृन्मशेन, T मृमशेन. ४.M अनच्च. ५.M रवो. ६.MT °दशने°. ७.M °यामैर्दुग्ध°. ८.T विद्युद...गाभिः. ९.MT °यालभना°. १०.M पाणिकृत पवित्रवित्. ११.M °मानसम्. १२.M °हृतीन्तिस्रः. १३.MT °र्धच्चशो. १४.T °शोन्वाकं. १५.T °नूद्य. १६.M °वाकाचमं, T °कावमं.

मन्द्रमेव[१] पठेत्प्रातरुच्चैर्मध्यन्दिने स्थिते ।
उच्चैरेवापराह्णे तु सन्ध्याकाल[२] उपांशुमत्[३] ॥ ३५० ॥
अनध्यायादिविषयमृगाद्यध्ययनं स्मृतम् ।
ब्रह्मयज्ञविधाने हि च्छन्दांसीति निगद्यते ॥ ३५१ ॥
अनुवाकादिकः[४] पूर्वन्दिने[५] योऽस्मिन्समापितः ।
तदुत्तरानुवाकादिरारंभः प्रतिपन्मतः[६] ॥ ३५२ ॥
ग्रामादौ मनसा कुर्यात्स्वाध्यायं शक्तिसंभवे[७] ।
सर्वथाऽध्ययनं कार्यं शुचौ शुचिरिति स्मृतिः[८] ॥ ३५३ ॥
अतो नित्यो ब्रह्मयज्ञो द्विजातेः स्मृति[९]चोदनात् ।
आचार्यो[१०] नोक्तवानस्य विधिं श्रुतिविधानतः ॥ ३५४ ॥
इतिकर्तव्यतासिद्धेर्देवयज्ञाद्युदीरितम् ।
शाखान्तरानुसाराद्या तथा[११] सति समुच्चयः ॥ ३५५ ॥
अत एव नृयज्ञोऽपि नोक्तो न ह्यनवेक्षणात् ।
देवयज्ञसमाख्यानाद्देवेभ्योऽग्नौ जुहोति यत् ॥ ३५६ ॥
आधाय समिधं तेन देवयज्ञः समाप्यते ।
स्वधा करोति स्वान्नेन जलं दत्त्वाऽथ पित्रियम्[१२]॥ ३५७ ॥
नित्यत्वख्यापनार्थो वा विशब्दोऽत्र प्रयुज्यते ।
यद्यप्यन्ते समाम्नातो ब्रह्मयज्ञस्तथापि तु ॥ ३५८ ॥
पाठादर्थक्रमो न्याय्य[१३] उदिते विहितत्वतः ।
कार्यः[१४] पूर्वं ब्रह्मयज्ञ इति वाधूलकागमः ॥ ३५९ ॥
कालान्तरेऽपि कार्योऽसौ श्रुतिस्मृत्यनुसारतः ।
स चार्वाक् सर्पणात्कार्यः[१५] पश्चाद्वा प्रातराहुतेः॥ ३६० ॥

१.MT मन्द°. २.M °काला. ३.M उपामर्शेत्. ४.M °वातादिकः. ५.T पूर्वदिने. ६.M °पद्मभूः. ७.T शक्त्यसं°. ८.M श्रुतिः. ९.M श्रुति°. १०.MT आचार्या. ११.M द्या थो. १२.T पित्रियः. १३.M न्याय. १४.MT कार्यं. १५.MT कार्यं.

वैश्वदेवावसाने वाथान्यदर्थे[१] निमित्ततः ।
यदि स्यात्तर्पणादर्वाग् ब्रह्मयज्ञः कृतो न हि ॥ ३६१ ॥
कृत्वा मनुष्ययज्ञं वै ततः स्वाध्यायमारभेत् ।
आपद्यपि हि कर्तव्या नित्यमेते महामखाः ॥ ३६२ ॥
पञ्च सूना गृहस्थस्य चुल्ली पेषण्युपस्करः[२] ।
खण्डनी[३] चोदधानी च [४]वध्यन्ते यांस्तु[४] वाहयन् ॥ ३६३ ॥
तासां[५] क्रमेण सर्वासां निष्कृत्यर्थं महर्षिभिः ।
पञ्च क्लृप्ता महायज्ञाः प्रत्यहं गृहमेधिनाम्[६] ॥ ३६४ ॥
पञ्चैतान् यो महायज्ञान्न हापयति शक्तितः ।
स गृहेऽपि वसन्नित्यं सूनादोषैर्न लिप्यते ॥ ३६५ ॥
प्रवासं गच्छतो यस्य गृहे कर्ता न विद्यते ।
पञ्चानां महतामेष स यज्ञैः सह गच्छति ॥ ३६६ ॥
प्रवासं कुरुते चैनान् यदन्नमुपपद्यते[७] ।
न चेदुपपद्यते[८]ऽन्नमद्भिरेव समाचरेत् ॥ ३६७ ॥
अद्भिरेव व्रतं कुर्याद्यथालाभमनुव्रतम् ।
देवानां देवयज्ञेन द्विजो गच्छति[९] सात्म्यताम्[१०] ॥ ३६८ ॥
पितॄणां पितृयज्ञेन भूतयज्ञेन भूतिनाम्[११] ।
[१२]मनोर्मनुष्ययज्ञेन ब्रह्मयज्ञेन ब्रह्मणः[१३] ॥ ३६९ ॥
एतासां सात्म्यतां गत्वा देवतानां शतं समाः ।
[१४]आनन्त्यं ब्रह्मणो याति ध्रुवं शाश्वतमव्ययम्[१५] ॥ ३७० ॥
यत्फलं सोमयागेन प्राप्नोति धनवान्द्विजः ।
सम्यक् पञ्चमहायज्ञैर्दरिद्रस्तदवाप्नुयात् ॥ ३७१ ॥

१.M वादान्यर्थे, T वा दान्यदर्थे. २.M वुषैषन्यवस्करः, T वुपैष ह्यवस्करम्. ३.M; Cf Manu III.68: कुण्डनी. ४-४. Cf Manu III.68: बध्यते यास्नु. ५.M सा तां. ६.M °धिनम्,T मेधिनः, thus Manu III.69. ७.T यदन्यमुप°. ८.MT चेदुत्पद्दते. ९.M द्विगृहाच्छति. १०.MT साम्यताम्. ११.M भूतिनम्, T भूतिनः. १२.M oms मनोः. १३.M ब्रह्मणम्. १४.MT आन्त्य. १५.M शाश्चतंव्ययम्.

पञ्चयज्ञांस्तु यो मोहान्न करोति गृहाश्रमी[१] ।
तस्य नायं न च परो लोको भवति धर्मतः ॥ ३७२ ॥
सूना निर्णिक्तदोषा ये सर्वे ते वृषलाः स्मृताः ।
न तेषामधिकारोऽस्ति क्वचिद्धर्मे दुरात्मनाम् ॥ ३७३ ॥
देवादिनिःश्वासहतं[२] शरीरं यस्य वेश्मनि ।
[३]न तेन संकरं कुर्याद् गृहासनपरिच्छदैः ॥ ३७४ ॥
अकृत्वा वैश्वदेवं तु भुञ्जते[४] ये[५] द्विजाधमाः ।
वृथा तेनान्नपाकेन काकयोनिं व्रजन्ति ते ॥ ३७५ ॥

[औपासनहोमबल्योर्विधानम्]

ब्रह्मयज्ञं विधायैवं कृत्वा पुण्याहवाचनम् ।
पूर्ववत्संपरिस्तीर्य वह्निमौपासनं ततः ॥ ३७६ ॥
हविष्यमोदनं लोकवह्निपक्वं घृताप्लुतम् ।
व्यञ्जनक्षाररहितं पात्रे[६] कस्मिंश्चिदाहृतम् ॥ ३७७ ॥
पर्यग्नि कृत्वौषधीभिरलंकृत्य हुताशनम् ।
समन्तात्परिषिच्याथ[७] तूष्णीमाज्यावसेचिताम्[८] ॥ ३७८ ॥
'स्वाहे'त्याधाय समिधं देवेभ्यो देवतीर्थतः ।
हुत्वा हविष आदाय समन्तात्[९] परिषिच्य च ॥ ३७९ ॥
[१०]अग्नेर्दक्षिणतः[११]सव्यं जान्वाच्य[११]पितृतीर्थतः ।
प्राचीनावीतवद्दत्त्वा जलगन्धतिलानपि[१२] ॥ ३८० ॥
पितृभ्योऽपि स्वधेत्यन्नं हविषो जलसंयुतम् ।
दत्त्वा जलान्तिकं भूय उपवीत्यथ दक्षिणम् ॥ ३८१ ॥
जान्वाच्योत्तरतो वह्नेर्भूतेभ्यो नम' इत्यपि ।
जलादीनि प्रदायान्नं दत्त्वा स्वाहान्वितं जलम् ॥ ३८२ ॥

१.M ग्रहा°. २.M °श्वासगतं. ३.M oms न. ४.M भञ्जतो. ५.M यो. ६.M पात्रं. ७.M समन्तं परि°. ८.M °सेविताम्. ९.M समन्तः. १०.M °र्दैक्षिण°. ११-११.M सर्वव्यञ्जान्वाच्य. १२.M °गन्धात्तवान्यपम्; T °गन्धात्तवान्यपः.

दत्त्वा मन्त्रवदेवाथ परिषिच्य जुहोति तु ।
सूर्यादिभ्योऽग्नये सायं सूर्यस्तत्र निवर्तते ॥ ३८३ ॥
अष्टौ मन्त्रा इमे ज्ञेयाः [1]सगणास्तु त्रयोऽन्तिमाः[1] ।
हुत्वाऽग्नये स्विष्टकृते [2]समन्तात्परिषिच्य च ॥ ३८४ ॥
अग्नेरुत्तरतः शुद्धे देशे दद्याद् बलिं ततः ।
मध्ये तु[3] ब्रह्मणः स्थानं दिशि प्राच्यां शतक्रतोः॥ ३८५ ॥
अग्निकोणे भवेदग्नेर्दक्षिणायां यमस्य तु ।
स्वस्यां दिशि निर्ऋत्यास्तु[4] प्रतीच्यां वरुणस्य तु ॥ ३८६ ॥
स्वस्यां[5] दिशि तथा वायोर्दिश्युदीच्यां तु शीतगोः ।
ईशानस्यापि चैशान्यां पुरुषाः स्वामिपूर्वगाः ॥ ३८७ ॥
[6]वायव्यानलयोर्मध्य आरभ्येशानशक्रयोः ।
मध्यान्तं गृहदेवानां क्रमेण स्थानमिष्यते ॥ ३८८ ॥
अथ दक्षिणतः स्थाने पितृभ्योऽन्नं प्रदीयते ॥ ३८८क ॥
स्वाहान्वितं हविर्देयं [7]जलादिनमसायुतम् ।
स्वधा पितृभ्य इत्यस्य न विकारं[8] क्वचिन्मतम् ॥ ३८९ ॥
समन्तात्[9] परिषिच्यान्नं व्याहृतीभिर्जुहोत्यथ ॥ ३८९क ॥
मन्त्रवत्परिषिच्याग्निमलंकृत्योत्तरत्र तु ।
'सर्वेभ्यश्चापि भूतेभ्यः स्वाहे'त्यन्नं क्षिपेत्पुनः ॥ ३९० ॥

[गृह्यवैश्वदेवकर्मविधिः]

समाचारानुसारेण देवयज्ञाद्युदीरितम्[10] ।
धर्मशास्त्रानुसारेण गृह्यार्थो वर्ण्यतेऽधुना ॥ ३९१ ॥
तर्पणानन्तरं कार्यं वैश्वदेवमितीह तु ।
अनन्तरं वैश्वदेवविधिरत्राभिधास्यते ॥ ३९२ ॥
यस्मिन्कर्मणि विश्वेभ्यो देवेभ्यो हूयते हविः ।

१-१.M सगुणास्तु त्रयोन्तिमाम्, T °योन्तिमाम्. २.M समन्तं. ३.M तद्. ४.MT निर्ऋत्यान्तु. ५.M स्वान्दिशि. ६.M पार्वत्य°, T वाष्पत्यनिल°. ७.MT जलादी°. ८.M नवीकारं. ९.M समन्तं. १०.M °यज्ञाप्युदी°.

ब्रह्मादिभ्यो बलिर्यस्मिन् पितृभ्यश्च विधीयते ॥ ३९३ ॥
तद्वैश्वदेवमित्युक्तमधिकारी गृहाश्रमी ।
वैवाहिकेऽग्नौ कुर्वीत गृह्यकर्म यथाविधि ॥ ३९४ ॥
पञ्चयज्ञविधानं च पङ्क्तिञ्चान्वाहितिं[१] गृही ।
साग्निकं[२] पितृयज्ञान्तं बलिकर्म[३] समाचरेत् ॥ ३९५ ॥
अनग्निहुतशेषेण बलिं काकबलिं हरेत् ।
पुरुषयज्ञादृते नास्ति निरग्नेस्तु महामखः ॥ ३९६ ॥
अन्नं व्याहृतिभिर्हुत्वा[४] हुत्वा मन्त्रैश्च शाकलैः ।
प्रजापतेर्हविर्हुत्वा[५] शिष्टं काकबलिं हरेत् ॥ ३९७ ॥
गृहस्थस्याधिकारोऽतो वैश्वदेव इहोदितः[६] ।
अन्नस्येत्यदनीयस्य[७] हविषः स्मृतिदर्शनात् ॥ ३९८ ॥
यदन्नं पुरुषो भुङ्क्ते तदन्नास्तस्य देवताः ।
इति भोज्यं हविः [८]सर्वशेषमन्नमिहोच्यते ॥ ३९९ ॥
लवणव्यञ्जनक्षारपरान्नादि[९]समन्वितम् ।
निषिध्यन्ते स्मृतौ होमे विहितं च तदापदि ॥ ४०० ॥
तथापि[१०] माषवरककोद्रवादि न गृह्यते ।
[११]निवपेच्छेषमित्युक्तेरिह षष्ट्याश्च दर्शनात् ॥ ४०१ ॥
होमादिसिद्धये पात्र उद्धार्यं सर्वशेषतः ।
उद्धृत्य हविषासिच्य हविष्येण घृतादिना ॥ ४०२ ॥
स्वशाखाविधिना[१२] हुत्वा तच्छेषेण बलिं हरेत् ।
जुहुयात्सर्पिषाऽभ्यक्तं[१३] तैलक्षारविवर्जितम् ॥ ४०३ ॥
दध्यक्तं पयसाक्तं वा तदलाभ.ऽभसापि[१४] वा ।
अलाभे येन केनापि[१५] फलशाकोदकादिभिः ॥ ४०४ ॥

१.M न्वाहि किं. २.M सानिकं. ३.M बली°. ४.M °भिर्हत्वा, T °भिर्भत्त्वा. ५.M °र्हत्वा. ६.M दिते. ७.M अन्नस्येत्वद°. ८.M सर्व शेषमग्र°. ९.M °वरणादि°. १०.M तदापदि. ११.M दिवविच्छेषमि°. १२.M °शाखविधि°. १३.M °षाभिक्तं. १४.M भेसापि. १५.M तेनापि.

पयो दधिघृतौ कुर्याद्वैश्वदेवं स्रुवेण तु ।
हस्तेनान्नादिभिः कुर्यादद्भिरञ्जलिना जले ॥ ४०५ ॥
उत्तानेन तु हस्तेन अङ्गुष्ठाग्रेण पीडितम् ।
संहताङ्गुलिपाणिस्तु वाग्यतो जुहुयाद्धवम् ॥ ४०६ ॥
यदप्यौपासने होमे मनुना विहितः स्वयम् ।
तथापि लौकिके वह्नौ पचनार्थे[१] विकल्प्यते ॥ ४०७ ॥
गृह्येऽग्नौ वेति निर्देशाद्धोमाग्नौ पच्यते च तत् ।
यस्मिन्नग्नौ[२] पचेदन्नं तस्मिन्[३] होमो विधीयते ॥ ४०८ ॥
[४]लौकिके वैदिके चापि हुतोत्सृष्टे जले क्षितौ ।
वैश्वदेवस्तु कर्तव्यः पञ्च सूनापनुत्तये[५] ॥ ४०९ ॥
अग्नाविति[६] समिद्धेऽग्नौ [७]होमः स्यादिति[७] भण्यते[८] ।
बहुशुष्केन्धने वह्नौ सुसमिद्धे विशेषतः ॥ ४१० ॥
विधूमे लेलिहाने च होतव्यं कर्मसिद्धये ।
[९]अनर्चिषु जुहोत्यग्नौ व्यङ्गारे चैव मानवः[९] ॥ ४११ ॥
प्रतीयतेऽत आरंभः प्रातरेवास्य कर्मणः ।
सांयप्रातरिति ह्येतदहोरात्रोपलक्षणम् ॥ ४१२ ॥
[१०]मन्दाग्निरामयावी* च दरिद्रश्चोपजायते ।
अग्नये सायमित्यादि तत्कालान्वयसिद्धये[१०] ॥ ४१३ ॥
मध्याह्ने त्वथ संप्राप्ते[११] बलिं कृत्वात्मनो गृहे ।
पितृदेवमनुष्याणां शिष्टं भुञ्जीत वाग्यतः[१२] ॥ ४१४ ॥
ब्रह्मादिगृहदेवान्तबलिदानं यदुच्यते ।
भूतयज्ञसमाख्याऽस्येत्यथेत्याद्या[१३]विधीयते ॥ ४१५ ॥

१.MT वचनार्थे. २.M तस्मि°. ३.M broken between त and होमो. ४.M adds द्वौ before लौकिके. ५.M च नु ये. ६.M अनाविति. ७-७.M होमस्या°. ८.T oms ण्यते. ९-९.M oms. १०-१०.T gives this Verse between बिधूमे=मानवः (411) and प्रतीयत=लक्षणम् (412). ✱.M मन्दाग्नीराम°; T broken between °रामया and [°न्द्र]श्चोप°. ११.T सम्प्राप्ते...हे. १२.M वान्यतः. १३.M °त्याद्य.

यत्पितृभ्यो [..............................][१] ।
पितृभ्यः स्वधा[२] इत्यत्र स्वधाकारः श्रुतो यतः ॥ ४१६ ॥
बलिं हरेच्छेषमन्नं[३] निर्वपेदिति[४] भेदतः ।
कीर्तयन् गृह्यकारोऽपि तयोर्भेदमिहोक्तवान् ॥ ४१७ ॥
अथवा भोजयेद्विप्रान्[५] [६]पित्रर्थं स्मृतिदर्शनात्[६] ।
[७]दद्यादहरहः श्राद्धमन्नाद्येनोदकेन वा ॥ ४१८ ॥
पयोमूलहवैर्वापि[८] पितृभ्यः प्रीतिमावहन्[९] ।
एकमप्याशयेद्विप्रं पित्रर्थं पाञ्चयाज्ञिके ॥ ४१९ ॥
न चैवात्राशयेत्[१०] कञ्चिद्वैश्वदेवं[११] प्रति द्विजम् ॥ ४१९क ॥
नामन्त्रणं न होमं च नाह्वानं न विसर्जनम् ।
न पिण्डदानं न सुरान् नित्यं कुर्याद् द्विजोत्तमः ॥ ४२० ॥
उपवेश्यासनं दत्त्वा संपूज्य कुसुमादिभिः ।
निर्दिश्य भोजयित्वा तु किंचिद् दत्त्वा विसर्जयेत् ॥ ४२१ ॥
उद्धृत्य वा यथाशक्ति[१२] किंचिदन्नं समाहितः[१३] ।
वेदतत्त्वार्थविदुषे ब्राह्मणायोपपादयेत् ॥ ४२२ ॥

[बलिवैश्वदेवकर्म]

ब्रह्मादिभ्यो बलिं दद्याद्यथादिशमितीरणात् ।
वेश्मपर्यन्तसंस्थानां[१४] गृहरक्षणकर्मणाम् ॥ ४२३ ॥
अष्टदिङ्मध्यरचित[१५]कुसुमादिषु शिलासु[१५] वा ।
निहितासु बलिं दद्यात्परिक्रम्य यथाविधि ॥ ४२४ ॥
अन्नेन सुमनोभिश्च गन्धधूपैः प्रदीपकैः ।
गृहस्थः[१६] पूजयेन्नित्यं स्वगृहे गृहदेवताः ॥ ४२५ ॥

१.M broken after पितृभ्यो up to the end of the 2nd Pāda. २.M oms; T broken from the beginning of the 3rd Pāda up to its end. ३.M °मन्न. ४.MT निवपेदिति. ५.T विप्रं. ६-६.M broken. ७.M broken before दहशरहः and T before °द्येनो[Mथो]दकेन. ८.MT °हवै°. ९.M °माहरहन्. १०.M चैवात्रेश°. ११.M किञ्चिद्वैश्व°. १२.T यथा.. किञ्चि°. १३.M °हितम्. १४.M संस्थानं. १५-१५.T °रचित...सु वा. १६.M गृहस्थं.

इन्द्रादिपुरुषेभ्यश्च स्वामिस्थाने पृथग्बलिम्[१] ।
एवं विधाय भवनं प्रविश्य गृहदेवताः ॥ ४२६ ॥
पूजयेद् बलिदानेनेत्येतदर्थमिहोच्यते ।
गृहदेवताभ्य इत्यादिसमाख्यानाच्च[२] गम्यते ॥ ४२७ ॥
उलूखलाद्यधिष्ठात्री देवता विद्यते ततः ।
शुचौ देशे विधेयास्ते न[३] पदाद्येन तांस्पृशेत् ॥ ४२८ ॥
उलूखलादिकं यत्र गृहे नित्यं निधीयते ।
गत्वा [४]तत्रोपरि तयोः[४] सकृन्मन्त्रेण दीयते ॥ ४२९ ॥
[५]एकवत् स्थलनिर्देशाद् द्विवन्मन्त्रोपदेशतः[५] ।
उदधानि जलाधारः[६] कलशोऽस्य समीपतः ॥ ४३० ॥
देयः [७]समीपसिध्यर्थमुदधान्यामुदीरितम्[८] ।
द्वार इत्येकवचनान्मुख्यद्वारे[९] बलिक्रिया ॥ ४३१ ॥
द्वारेष्विति वदन्त्यन्ये[१०] सर्वेष्वेव ततो बलिः ।
सामर्थ्यात्स्थलभेदे तु मन्त्रो व्यावर्तते बलौ ॥ ४३२ ॥
'दिवाचारिभ्य' इत्येवं द्वार ऊर्ध्वं क्षिपेद् बलिम्[११] ।
अधिकारादन्यदेशाः श्रवणादेवमीरितम् ॥ ४३३ ॥
अवशिष्टं कृत्स्नमन्नं पितृभ्यो निवपेत्ततः ।
यज्ञशिष्टाशनोक्त्याऽन्नं शेषयेदिति केचन ॥ ४३४ ॥
एवं गृहबलिं कृत्वा गृहे गृहपतिः शुचिः ।
ततोऽन्यदन्नमादाय हितकारी समाहितः ॥ ४३५ ॥

देवा मनुष्याः पशवो वयांसि[१२]
सिद्धाः सयक्षोरगदैत्यसङ्घाः।
प्रेताः पिशाचास्तरवः समस्ता

१.M बलिः. २.M °नाश्च. ३.M विधायास्ते, T विधे°. ४-४.M तत्रोपचरितयो. ५-५.M एकवस्थलेः निदेशाद्विपमन्त्रो°. ६.M °धारं. ७.M समिध्यर्थ°. ८.M °मुरीरितम्. ९.M °वचना मुख्य°. १०.M परन्त्य°. ११.M क्षिपेब्दलिः. १२.M पयांसि.

ये चान्नमिच्छन्ति मयात्र दत्तम् ॥ ४३६ ॥
पिपीलिकाः कीटपतङ्गकाद्या
बुभुक्षिताः कर्मनिबन्धबद्धाः[१]।
प्रयान्तु ते तृप्तिमिदं मयाऽन्नं
तेभ्यो निसृष्टं सुखिनो[२] भवन्तु ॥ ४३७ ॥
येषां न माता न पिता न बन्धु-
[३]र्नैवान्नसिद्धिर्न तथाऽन्यदस्ति[३]।
[४]तत्तृप्तयेऽन्नं भुवि दत्तमेतत्
ते यान्तु[५] तृप्तिं मुदिता भवन्तु ॥ ४३८ ॥
भूतानि सर्वाणि तथान्नमेत-
दहं च विष्णुर्नियतो यदस्ति[६]।
तस्मादहं भूतनिकायभूत-
मन्नं प्रयच्छामि भवाय तेषाम् ॥ ४३९ ॥
चतुर्विधो भूतगणो य एषः
तत्र स्थिता येऽखिलभूतसङ्घाः
तृप्त्यर्थमन्नं हि मया निसृष्टं
तेषामिदं ते मुदिता भवन्तु ॥ ४४० ॥
इत्युच्चार्यावनौ दद्याद् गृही सर्वाश्रयोऽन्वितः[७] ॥ ४४०क ॥
शुनां च पतितानां च श्वपचानां[८] च रोगिणाम् ।
वायसानां[९] कृमीणां च शनकैर्निवपेद् भुवि[१०] ॥ ४४१ ॥
श्वानौ द्वौ श्यामशबलौ वैवस्वतकृतोद्भवौ ।
ताभ्यां पिण्डं प्रदास्यामि रक्षतां पथि मां सदा ॥ ४४२ ॥
ऐन्द्रवारुणवायव्या याम्या[११] वै नैर्ऋतास्तथा[१२] ।

१.M बध्याः. २.M सुखिना. ३-३.M नैंवसिद्धि न तथान्यदन्तिक. ४.M oms तत्. ५.MT यान्ति. ६.M ऽन्यास्ति. ७.M ऽन्वतः. ८.M °वचनां. ९.M वयसा°. १०.Cf Manu III.93: निर्वपद्भुवि. ११.M यार्ष्या, T यार्षा. १२.M नैरुता°, T नैऋता°.

वायसाः[1] प्रतिगृह्णन्तु भूमौ पिण्डं मयार्पितम् ॥ ४४३ ॥
पतितानां तु यद्दानं तन्न कार्यमितीतरे ।
दत्त्वाऽनेन[2] विधानेन [3]बलिं पश्चादुपस्पृशेत् ॥ ४४४ ॥

[भिक्षादानमीमांसा]

एवं बलिं विधायाग्रं दत्त्वा वेदविदे ततः ।
भिक्षुकेभ्यो यथाशक्ति[3] भिक्षां दद्यात्समाहितः ॥ ४४५ ॥
ब्रह्मचारी यतिश्चैव विद्यार्थी गुरुपोषकः ।
अध्वगः[4] क्षीणवृत्तिश्च व्याधितश्च[5] गृहाच्च्युतः॥ ४४६ ॥
एते भिक्षार्थिनस्तेभ्यः स्वस्तिवाचनपूर्वकम् ।
हस्ते दत्त्वा जलं भैक्षं सर्वव्यञ्जनसंयुतम् ॥ ४४७ ॥
दत्त्वा भूयोऽपि यतये जलं दद्यात्तथोदितम्[6] ॥ ४४७क ॥
ग्रासमात्री भेवद् भिक्षा[7] अग्रं[8] ग्रासचतुष्टयम् ।
अग्रं चतुर्गुणीकृत्य हस्तकारो[9]ऽभिधीयते ॥ ४४८ ॥
दद्याच्च भिक्षात्रितयं परिव्राड्[10]ब्रह्मचारिणाम् ।
इच्छया च ततो दद्याद्विभवे सत्यवादितः ॥ ४४९ ॥
हस्तदत्ता तु या भिक्षा [11]लवणव्यञ्जनानि च ।
भुक्त्वा त्वशुचितां याति[12] दाता स्वर्गं न गच्छति[13] ॥ ४५० ॥
भैक्षदानेऽधिकारोऽपि स्त्रीणामेव निरूपितः ॥ ४५०क ॥
सत्कृत्य भिक्षां भिक्षुभ्यो यः प्रयच्छति मानवः।
गोप्रदानसमं पुण्यं तस्याह भगवान्यमः ॥ ४५१ ॥
यतिश्च ब्रह्मचारी च पक्वान्नस्वामिनावुभौ[14] ।
तयोरन्नमदत्त्वा तु भुक्त्वा चान्द्रायणं चरेत् ॥ ४५२ ॥
अव्रता ह्यनधीयाना[15] यत्र भैक्षचरा द्विजाः ।
तं ग्रामं दण्डयेद्राजा चोरभक्तप्रदो हि सः ॥ ४५३ ॥

१.M वयसाः. २.M दत्वा नो. ३-३.M oms. ४.M अध्वगं. ५.M व्यधित°. ६.M दद्यात्स्तथो°. ७.M °भिक्षां. ८.T अग्र°. ९.M हन्त°. १०.M परिव्राक्. ११.T लक्षण°. १२.M यान्ति. १३.M गच्छन्ति. १४.M पक्वान्नस्स्वामि°. १५.M अव्रतान्यनधियाना.

अकृते वैश्वदेवे तु भिक्षुके गृहमागते ।
वैश्वदेवार्थमुद्धृत्य[1] भिक्षां दत्त्वा विसर्जयेत् ॥ ४५४ ॥
गोदोहनात्परं[2] कालमतिथ्यर्थं गृहाङ्गणे[3] ।
तिष्ठेदतिथिमायान्तमदृष्टाश्रुतपूर्वकम् ॥ ४५५ ॥
अज्ञाप्यमान[4]गोत्रादिं पण्डितं मूर्खमेव वा ।
श्रान्तं[5] दृष्ट्वा प्रसन्नात्मा स्वागतं प्रोच्य संयतः ॥ ४५६ ॥
प्रियपूर्वाभिभाष्यार्घ्यं पाद्यमाचमनीयकम् ।
आसनं च प्रदायास्मा अन्नं दद्याद् घृताप्लुतम् ॥ ४५७ ॥
ज्योतिष्कृत्वा गुणैरन्यैः संयुतं हृदयंगमम् ।
हिरण्यगर्भं बुध्वैनं[6] प्रीणयित्वा समाहितः ॥ ४५८ ॥
गच्छन्तं श्रोत्रियं तृप्तमासीमान्तादनुव्रजेत् ।
अश्रोत्रियं नानुगच्छेदुत्थानं चागते सति ॥ ४५९ ॥
उदकादि यथान्यायं श्रोत्रियत्वधियाऽर्पयेत् ।
श्रोत्रियत्वादपि [7]ज्ञानं लोकतो न स पृच्छ्यते ॥ ४६० ॥
यद्याहिताग्निरतिथिः स्वयमभ्युपगम्य तु ।
व्रात्य क्वावात्सिरित्येवं संभाष्योदकमस्य तु ॥ ४६१ ॥
व्रात्योदकमिति[8] प्रोच्य दद्यादर्घ्यादि पूर्ववत्[8] ।
अन्नं व्रात्य[9] तर्पयस्वेत्यस्मै दद्यात्सुपूजितम् ॥ ४६२ ॥
उपसेचनं पयः सर्पिर्मधु वोदकमेव वा ।
आपस्तम्बमुनिप्रोक्त[10] आहिताग्नौ समीरितः ॥ ४६३ ॥

[आतिथ्यविधिः]

बोधायनोदितश्चापि विधिरातिथ्य उच्यते ॥ ४६३क ॥
वर्तमानोऽध्वनि ब्रह्मचारी गुर्वर्थसिद्धये ।
आगच्छेदसमुत्थाय संप्रोच्य स्वागतं ततः ॥ ४६४ ॥

१.T °देवात्तमु°. २.T गोदोहना...रं. ३.T गृहाङ्कणे. ४.M अज्ञाप्यमन°. ५.M शानतं. ६.M °बुध्यैनं. ७.T °दर्वि. ८-८.M प्रोच्याद्यादर्घ्यादि°, T प्रोच्यात्यादर्घ्यादि°. ९.T प्रात्य. १०.M °मुनिः प्रोक्त, T °स्तंभ°.

कुशलं चापि भाष्यैनमुपासित्वाऽस्य पात्रिकाम् ।
[१]दद्यान्नियममेवानुतिष्ठस्वेत्यभिधाय तु ॥ ४६५ ॥
भिक्षां दद्याद् गृहस्थादौ पूर्वोदितविधानतः ।
यतये स्वागतं प्रोच्याभ्युत्थायासनमादरात् ॥ ४६६ ॥
पादशौचं तथाऽभ्यङ्गं दत्त्वाभ्यर्च्य यथाविधि ।
भिक्षुकायागतायास्मै भिक्षां दद्यात्सुपूजिताम् ॥ ४६७ ॥
अष्टाक्षरेण मन्त्रेण विष्णुरेव यतो यतिः ।
पादुकासनशय्यादीन् यतीन्दृष्ट्वा[२] त्यजेत्सदा ॥ ४६८ ॥
रथी वा यद्यनड्वी[३] वाऽऽगच्छेत्पूज्यतमे[४] श्रुते[४] ।
बहवश्चेत्तु तं प्राप्ताः[५] पूज्यास्ते सर्व आदरात् ॥ ४६९ ॥
आसनावसथौ शय्यामनुव्रज्यामुपासनाम्[६] ।
उत्तमेषूत्तमं कुर्याद्धीने हीनं समे समम् ॥ ४७० ॥
विद्यातपोऽधिकानां तु प्रथमासनमुच्यते ।
पङ्क्तौ सहस्थितानां[७] तु भोजनादि समं स्मृतम् ॥ ४७१ ॥

यद्येकपङ्क्तौ विषमं ददाति
स्नेहाद् भयाद्वा यदि वाऽर्थहेतोः[८] ।
वेदेषु दृष्टामृषिभिश्च भीतां[९]
तां ब्रह्महत्यां मुनयो वदन्ति ॥ ४७२ ॥

यदि त्वतिथिधर्मेण क्षत्रियो गृहमाव्रजेत् ।
भुक्तवत्सु ब्राह्मणेषु कामं तमभिभोजयेत् ॥ ४७३ ॥
वैश्यशूद्रावपि प्राप्तौ कुटुम्बेऽतिथिधर्मणा[१०] ।
भोजयेत् सहभृत्यैस्तावानृशंस्यं प्रयोजयेत् ॥ ४७४ ॥
शूद्रमभ्यागतं कर्म कारयित्वैव भोजयेत् ।
स्त्रियश्चैषां प्रपूज्याः स्युर्यदि शक्तिर्न विद्यते ॥ ४७५ ॥

१.M °न्नियमेवा°. २.M यदीनृष्ट्वा. ३.M °नस्वी. ४-४.T °तमश्रुते. ५.M प्राप्तां. ६.M °पूज्या°. ७.M संस्थिता°. ८.M पार्थ°. ९.M गीतां. १०.Cf Manu III.III: °धर्मिणौ.

दद्यादन्नं गुणवते पूर्वं वा य उपागतः ॥ ४७५क ॥
नैकग्रामीणमतिथिं विप्रं साङ्गतिकं तथा ।
उपस्थितं गृहे विद्याद् भार्या यत्राग्नयोऽपि[1] वा ॥ ४७६ ॥
मांसमन्नं तथा शाकं गृहे यच्चोपपादितम् ।
न वै[2] स्वतस्तदश्नीयादतिथिं[2] येन नार्चयेत्[3] ॥ ४७७ ॥
तृणानि[4] भूमिरुदकं वाक् चतुर्थी च सूनृता ।
एतान्यपि सतां गेहे नोच्छिद्यन्ते[5] कदाचन ॥ ४७८ ॥
देवतानामृषीणां च संवादेषु पुनः पुनः ।
श्रुतपूर्वो मया धर्मो महानतिथिभोजने ॥ ४७९ ॥
सुदूरादाशयात्प्राप्तं क्षुत्तृष्णाश्रमकर्षितम् ।
यः पूज्यतेऽतिथिः सम्यगयूपक्रतुरेव सः ॥ ४८० ॥
अतिथिर्यस्य भग्नाशो गृहात्प्रति निवर्तते ।
स तस्य दुष्कृतिं दत्त्वा पुण्यमादाय गच्छति ॥ ४८१ ॥
दिनातिथौ तु विमुखे गते यत्पातकं[6] स्मृतम् ।
[7]तदेवाष्टगुणं पुंसां सूर्योढे विमुखे गते ॥ ४८२ ॥
एते पञ्च महायज्ञा गृहस्थस्य समीरिताः ।
प्रवासेऽपि च ते नित्या गृहे कर्ता न चेद् भवेत् ॥ ४८३ ॥

[विवाहशेषकर्म]

विवाहशेषगमनं वक्ष्यामोऽतः परं वयम् ।
स्वकर्म वैश्वदेवान्तं रात्रौ कृत्वा यथोदितम् ॥ ४८४ ॥
पुण्याहवाचनं कृत्वा होमं व्याहृतिपश्चिमम् ।
कृत्वा'ग्ने प्राय' इत्याद्यैश्चतुर्भिर्जुहुयाद् घृतम् ॥ ४८५ ॥
ततो जयादिकं होमं सान्त्यपक्वं समाचरेत्[8] ।
अथ संवेशनगृहं श्लक्ष्णरूढ्यादिशोभितम्[9] ॥ ४८६ ॥

१.MT यत्रान्नयो°. २-२.M वैवस्वतन्तदग्नीया°. ३.T नार्थयेत्. ४.T तृणादि. ५.MT विद्यन्ते; T shows a sign of omission after विद्यन्ते. ६.M पतातं. ७.M oms त. ८.T समापयेत्. ९.T °रूड्यादि°, M °सेवितम्.

दृढानिम्नोन्नतभुवं दर्पणोदरसन्निभम् ।
सुसन्मृष्टं[१] सूपलिप्तमनार्द्रं गन्धसंयुतम्[२] ॥ ४८७ ॥
विधानाढ्यं पुष्पमाल्यैर्गन्धवद्भिर्विराजितम् ।
[३]लाजादध्यक्षतफलपूगपल्लवशोभितम् ॥ ४८८ ॥
सारांगारविनिक्षिप्तगुग्गुल्वगरुधूपितम्[४] ।
प्रतिवेशं[५] तु विन्यस्ततल्पास्तीर्णैरर्कोज्ज्वलम्[६] ॥ ४८९ ॥
पयःफेननिभास्तीर्णशय्यान्यस्तोपबर्हणम्[७] ।
[८]तल्पाग्रन्यस्तरुचिरदर्पणोदधगादिकम्[९] ॥ ४९० ॥
[१०]विचित्राम्बरनिष्पन्नपरिश्रयणराजितम् ।
[११]तल्पपर्यन्तदिङ्न्यस्तवृतसूत्रोत्थतेजसम्[१२] ॥ ४९१ ॥
सुविन्यस्तलसद्दीप[१३]निकरोद्भूषणोचितम्[१४] ।
हृद्यं प्रविश्य मनुजं[१५]सर्वभूषणभूषितम् ॥ ४९२ ॥
तथाविधां वधूं तस्मिंच्छयने शाययेत्ततः ।
अधिरुह्य स्वयं तल्पमुपस्थस्यापि दर्शनम् ॥ ४९३ ॥
स्वदक्षिणकरेणास्याः[१६] कृत्वर्तुगमनोदितम् ।
अभिप्राणनपर्यन्तं कुर्यात्संवेशनं ततः ॥ ४९४ ॥
स्नात्वा भृत्यादिसहितो रात्रिभोजनमाचरेत् ।
इतः प्रभृति साऽश्नीयात्पत्युच्छिष्टं दिने दिने ॥ ४९५ ॥

इति सङ्गमग्रामवासिमिश्रविरचिते नारायणीये
वाधूलगृह्यागमवृत्तिरहस्ये[१७]
पञ्चमोऽध्यायः

१.M सुसद्वृष्टं, T ससन्मृष्टं. २.T लिप्तम...गन्ध°. ३ M लाजदध्य°. ४.M सारां गां वि° गुग्गुल्य°. ५.MT °वंश. ६.M °रतोज्ज्व°,T °रकोज्ज्व°. ७.M रय्याग्रन्यन्तोप°. ८.M कल्पाग्र°. ९.M °दर्पणोदकंगादि°, M दर्पणोदधगा°. १०.M विचित्रां खरनि°. ११.M कल्प°. १२.M घृतसूत्रोत्थ तेचसम्, T वृतसूत्रोत्थतेचसम्. १३.M °दीप. १४.M °रोमितः, T °रोचितम्. १५.M मनुज. १६.M °णास्यां. १७.MT वाधूलकगृ°.

अथ षष्ठोऽध्यायः

[नित्यशौचकर्म]

रात्र्यः[१] षोढाविभक्ताया अन्त्ये[२] ब्राह्ममुहूर्तके ।
उदिते [३]वा क्षणे[३] बोध्यो[४] मृदुसंभाषणैः शनैः ॥ १ ॥
पत्न्या[५] शिष्येण वाचान्तः[६]प्रसन्नकरणः शुचिः ।
चिन्तयेत्परमात्मानं हृदब्जेऽव्यतिरेकिणम्[७] ॥ २ ॥
सुसूक्ष्मं सच्चिदानन्दविग्रहं भवनारणिम् ।
ब्रह्माणं शंकरं विष्णुमिष्टां[८]वाऽन्यां स्वदेवताम् ॥ ३ ॥
धर्मार्थकामाश्चेहैव[९] संचिन्त्यास्तद्दिनोचिताः ॥ ३क ॥
परित्यजेदर्थकामौ यौ स्यातां धर्मबाधकौ[१०] ।
धर्ममप्यसुखोदर्कं लोकविद्विष्टमेव च ॥ ४ ॥
इति स्मृत्यनुसारेण कायक्लेशांश्च[११] सोद्भवाः ॥ ४क ॥
एतत्सर्वं[१२] विनिश्चित्य गुरुगोविप्रदेवताः[१३] ।
मनसा वा नमस्कृत्य शौचार्थं मृदमाहरेत् ॥ ५ ॥
कूलात्ससिकताच्छुद्धदेशाद्वा[१४] जन्तुवर्जितात् ॥ ५क ॥
यस्मिन्देशे तु यत्तोयं या च यत्रैव[१५] मृत्तिका ।
सैव तत्र प्रशस्ता स्यात्तथा शौचं विधीयते ॥ ६ ॥
अङ्गारतुषकूटास्थिशर्कराकेशसंयुताम् ।
वल्मीकोषरतोयान्तः कुड्यापूतश्मशानजाम् ॥ ७ ॥
[१६]आहृतामन्यशौचार्थमाखुकृष्टां च पांसुलाम् ।
मार्गकर्दमकृष्टस्थां गेहस्थां[१७] लेपसंभवाम् ॥ ८ ॥
तरुगेहसमुत्पन्नां[१८] नान्नादितनमृत्तिकाम् ।
वापीकूपतटाकेषु बाह्यतो [१९]नाहरेन्मृदम् ॥ ९ ॥

१.M रात्राः. २.M अन्त्य°. ३-३.M वांकणे. ४.M बोध्या. ५.T पत्ना. ६.M प्रसन्नः. ७.M °रेकणम्. ८.M °ष्टवोऽन्यां. ९.M °श्चैवेह. १०.MT °बोधकौ. ११.M °केशाश्च. १२.M सर्वमपि नि°. १३.M गुरुकोविप्र°. १४.M °कता च्छद्धदे°, T °सिकता...द्धदे°. १५.M येऽत्रैव. १६.M °हृतामान्य°. १७.T गृहस्थां. १८.M समत्वन्ना°. १९.T वा हरे°.

आहरेज्जलमध्यात्तु[१] परतो मणिबन्धनात्[२] ।
सजलं भाजनं[३] स्थाप्य मृत्तिकां च परीक्षिताम् ॥ १० ॥
घ्राणास्ये वाससा वेष्ट्य वस्त्रप्रावृतमस्तकः[४] ।
निवीती[५] देहमाच्छाद्य विण्मूत्रं तु विसर्जयेत् ॥ ११ ॥
एकवासा ब्रह्मसूत्रं कण्ठ आरोप्य मेहते।
मूत्रादिसर्जने जातु[६] न करेण[७] स्पृशेच्छिरः ॥ १२ ॥
प्रत्यङ्मुखस्तु पूर्वाह्णेऽपराह्णे प्राङ्मुखस्तथा ।
उदङ्मुखस्तु मध्याह्ने निशायां दक्षिणामुखः ॥ १३ ॥
सदैवोदङ्मुखः प्रातः सायाह्ने दक्षिणामुखः ।
विण्मूत्रमाचरेन्नित्यं सन्ध्यासु परिवर्जयेत् ॥ १४ ॥
नोऽवरुद्धः[८] क्रियां कुर्यान्न वेगं धारयेदिति ।
स्मरणात्सन्ध्ययोश्चापि कुर्यान्मूत्रविसर्जनम् ॥ १५ ॥
[९]अतस्तयोर्निरोधो न सन्ध्ययोरिष्यते बुधैः[९] ।
दिवासन्ध्यासु कर्णस्थब्रह्मसूत्र उदङ्मुखः ॥ १६ ॥
कुर्यादित्यादिवचनमेवमेव समञ्जसम् ।
दिङ्मोहादिनिमित्तेषु नियमो न दिशां स्मृतः ॥ १७ ॥
छायायामन्धकारे वा रात्रावहनि वा द्विजः ।
यथासुखमुखः कुर्यात् प्राणबाधाभयेषु च ॥ १८ ॥
न मेहेत[१०] नदीच्छाया[११]पद्यगोष्ठाम्बुभस्मसु ।
[१२]न प्रत्यङ्ङर्कगोसोमसन्ध्याम्बुस्त्रीद्विजन्मनाम् ॥ १९ ॥
[१३]वाय्वग्निविप्रमादित्यमपः पश्यंस्तथैव गाम् ।
[१४]न कदाचन कुर्वीत विण्मूत्रस्य विसर्जनम्[१४] ॥ २० ॥
दूरादावसथान्मूत्रं दूरात्पादावसेचनम् ।

१.M °मस्या तु. २.M °बन्धगात्. ३.M भाजनस्थाप्य. ४.M °मस्तकम्. ५.M निवीति. ६.M मातु. ७.M करणे. ८.MT नोवरुद्धं. ९-९.MT om, See Supra III.196. १०.T न...हेत. ११.M वद्य°. १२.MT प्रत्यन्नर्क°. १३.M वार्याग्नि. १४-१४.MT om. Cf Manu IV.48 .

[१]उच्छिष्टान्ननिषेकं च दूरादेव समाचरेत् ॥ २१ ॥
न फालकृष्टे मेहेत न [२]चित्यां न[२] च पर्वते ।
न जीर्णदेवायतने न वल्मीके कदाचन ॥ २२ ॥
[३]न ससत्त्वेषु गर्तेषु[३] न गच्छन्नापि च स्थितः ।
न नदीतीरमासाद्य न च पर्वतमस्तके ॥ २३ ॥
तुषाङ्गारकपालानि देवतायतनानि च ।
राजमार्गश्मशानानि क्षेत्राणि च खलानि च[४] ॥ २४ ॥
वर्जयेद् वृक्षमूलानि चैत्यश्वभ्रबिलानि च[५] ॥ २४क ॥
[६][न च]त्वरे गोमये वा न तीर्थे यज्ञभूमिषु ।
नाधस्ताद्याज्ञवृक्षाणां[७] सस्यपूर्णे स्थले तथा ॥ २५ ॥
नोषरे शाद्वले[८] मूत्रमुद्याने वा समाचरेत् ।
मूत्रादिं न बहिः कुर्यात् [९]ग्रामादस्ततंगते रवौ ॥ २६ ॥
सोपानहो[१०] न मेहेत न पश्येदात्मनः शकृत् ।
अथावकृष्य विण्मूत्रं[११] लोष्टकाष्ठतृणादिना ॥ २७ ॥
उदस्तवासा[१२] उत्तिष्ठेद्[१३] दृढं विधृतमेहनः ।
आशौचान्नोत्सृजेच्छिश्नं प्रस्रावोच्चारयोः[१४] स्वयम् ॥ २८ ॥
मूत्रोच्चारे कृते शौचं न स्यादन्तर्जलाशये ।
अन्यत्रोद्धृत्य तत्कुर्यात् सर्वदैव समाहितः ॥ २९ ॥
अरत्निमात्रं जलं त्यक्त्वा कुर्याच्छौचं जलाशये ।
यस्मिन् स्थाने कृतं शौचं वारिणा तत्तु शोधयेत् ॥ ३० ॥
न शुद्धिस्तु भवेत्तस्य मृत्तिकां[१५] यो न शोधयेत् ।
वामहस्तेन कुर्वीत शौचं नाभेरधस्तु यत् ॥ ३१ ॥

१.M उद्दिष्टान्न°. २-२.T चित्यासु. ३-३.M सत्वेन न गर्तेषु, T न सत्वे नगगर्तेषु. ४.MT om. ५.M चैत्यश्चभ्र°, T चैत्यश्वभ्र°. ६.MT broken. ७.T °द्याज्ञवृ°. ८.M शाद्वल. ९.M broken between कुर्यात् and Tमाद°. १०.M सोवानामको. ११.MT °मूत्र. १२.M उदन्त°. १३.M उत्तिष्ठो. १४.T प्र...राच्चारयोः, M °च्चारेयाः. १५.M वृत्तिकां.

दक्षिणेन करेणोर्ध्वं नाभेः सर्वत्र सर्वदा ।
एतच्छौचं गृहस्थानां तथा गुरुनिवासिनाम् ॥ ३२ ॥
इति शौचं गृहस्थस्य समानं ब्रह्मचारिणा ।
नानाविधाः शौचकल्पाः स्मृता[१] आश्रमभेदतः ॥ ३३ ॥

[विट्शौचप्रयोगः]

गृहस्थविहितो वा स्याद्वर्ग्यो[२] स्वाश्रमचोदितः ।
मूत्रशौचं विधायादौ विट्च्छौचं च समाचरेत् ॥ ३४ ॥
यद्वादावुदकेनैव गुदं प्रक्षाल्य तत्र तु ।
मृदं प्रसृतिसम्पूर्णां दत्त्वा तत्क्षयकृज्जलैः[३] ॥ ३५ ॥
प्रक्षाल्यार्धप्रसृतिमान् दत्त्वा[४] प्रक्षाल्य पूर्ववत् ।
तृतीयां च चतुर्थीं च त्रिभागकरपूरणीम् ॥ ३६ ॥
पञ्चमीं च तथा दत्त्वा वामहस्ततलं[५] ततः ।
अङ्गुष्ठपर्वमितया मृदालिप्योदकेन तु ॥ ३७ ॥
[६]शोधयेद्दशकृत्वोऽथ मृद्भिः[७] करतलं त्वयम् ।
सप्तभिः शोधयेत्सव्यहस्तपृष्ठे मृदश्च षट्[८] ॥ ३८ ॥
एवं दत्त्वा नखेष्वेवं षड् दत्त्वा जलसंयुतम् ।
ततो गुदे मृदं दत्त्वा त्रिभागकरपूरणीम् ॥ ३९ ॥
हस्तयोः पञ्चभिर्मृद्भिः कुर्याच्छौचं च पूर्ववत् ।
विट्च्छौचस्य प्रयोगोऽयं मूत्रशौचस्य तूच्यते ॥ ४० ॥

[मूत्रशौचप्रयोगः]

जलेन लिङ्गं प्रक्षाल्य त्रिभागकरपूरणीम् ।
दत्त्वाऽद्भिः क्षालयेदेवं [९]द्विः सकृद्वा[९] विधाय तु ॥ ४१ ॥
वामहस्तं त्रिभिर्मृद्भिः शोधयित्वाऽथ मृद्द्वयम् ।
उभयोः करयोर्दत्त्वा जलेन क्षालयेद्यदा ॥ ४२ ॥

१.M विकल्पाः. २.T स्या...स्वाश्रम°. ३.M तत्क्षय तु जलैः. ४.M °सृतिमा दत्वा.
५.T °तलस्ततः. ६.M शोधय°. ७.T मद्भिः. ८.M तत्. ९-९.M द्विधा कृत्वा.

एवं कृतेऽपि गन्धो[1] वा लेपो वा नापगच्छते[2] ।
उक्तसंख्यातिरेकेण[3] तन्निवृत्त्यन्तमाचरेत् ॥ ४३ ॥
यावत्तु[4] शुद्धिं मन्येत तावच्छौचं विधीयते ।
प्रमाणं शौचसंख्याया न शिष्टैरुपदिश्यते[5] ॥ ४४ ॥
अर्वाग्गन्धक्षये संख्या पूरणीया विधानतः ।
न्यूनाधिकं न कर्तव्यमित्यादिस्मरणादपि ॥ ४५ ॥
[6]अह्निशौचं तु यत्प्रोक्तं निश्यर्धं तत इष्यते ।
परिवादं तु विज्ञेयमार्त्तः कुर्याद्यथाबलम् ॥ ४६ ॥
देशं कालं तथात्मानं द्रव्यं द्रव्यप्रयोजनम् ।
उपपत्तिमवस्थां च ज्ञात्वा शौचं प्रकल्पयेत् ॥ ४७ ॥
उपविष्टस्तु विण्मूत्रं कर्तुं यस्तन्न विन्दति ।
स कुर्यादर्धशौचं तु स्वस्य शौचस्य सर्वदा ॥ ४८ ॥
न यावदुपनीयन्ते[7] द्विजाः शूद्रास्तथाङ्गनाः ।
गन्धलेपक्षयकरं[8] शौचं तेषां विधीयते ॥ ४९ ॥

[द्विजानां शौचविधानम्]

भुञ्जानस्य तु विप्रस्य कदाचित्स्रवते गुदम् ।
उच्छिष्टमशुचित्वं च ततः शौचं कथं भवेत् ॥ ५० ॥
पूर्वं कृत्वा तु शौचं वै ततः पश्चादुपस्पृशेत् ।
ततः कृत्वोपवासं च पञ्चगव्येन शुध्यति ॥ ५१ ॥
शौचे यत्नः सदा कार्यः शौचमूलो द्विजः स्मृतः[9] ।
शौचाचारविहीनस्य समस्ता[10] निष्फलाः क्रियाः ॥ ५२ ॥
यस्य शौचेऽपि शैथिल्यं वृत्तं तस्य परिक्षतम्[11] ।
मुहूर्तमप्यप्रयतो न स्याच्छक्ताविति स्मृतम् ॥ ५३ ॥
वसा[12]शुक्रमसृङ्मज्जामूत्रविट्कर्णविट्नखाः ।

१.M नद्धो. २.M नावग°. ३.M °तिकोण. ४.T यावत्तु...म्मन्ये°. ५.M °दृश्यते. ६.T अग्नि°. ७.M यादवुचनी°. ८.M °क्षयक्षयकरं. ९.M द्विजन्मतः. १०.M समस्तान्नि°. ११.M परीक्षतः. १२.MT शुक्ल°.

[१]श्लेष्माश्रुपूयिकाः स्वेदो[२] द्वादशैते [३]नृणां मलाः[३]॥ ५४ ॥
[४]विण्मूत्रोत्सर्गशुध्यर्थं [५]मृद्वार्यादेयमर्थवत् ।
दैहिकानां मलानां च शुद्धिषु[६] द्वादशस्वपि ॥ ५५ ॥
आददीत मृदं षट्सु[७] पूर्वेषु तु विशुद्धये ।
उत्तरेषु तु षट्स्वद्भिः[८] केवलाभिर्विशुध्यति ॥ ५६ ॥
विकल्पः संभवापेक्षः [९]कर्मापेक्षोऽपि वेह[१०] तु ।
[११]आत्मीयमूत्रसंस्पर्शे पाण्योस्तिस्रो मृदः स्मृताः ॥ ५७ ॥
पादयोश्च तथाऽमेध्ये मृदः[१२] पञ्चदश स्मृताः ।
मानुषास्थिवसां विष्ठामार्त्तविण्मूत्ररेतसी[१३] ॥ ५८ ॥
मज्जानं शोणितं वापि परस्य[१४] यदि संस्पृशेत् ।
स्नात्वापमृज्य लेपादीनाचम्य स शुचिर्भवेत् ॥ ५९ ॥
नाभेरधः[१५] प्रवाहौ च सुराभिः कायिकैर्मलैः ।
मद्यैर्वोपहतो[१६] मृद्भिस्तदङ्गं जलसंयुतम् ॥ ६० ॥
तिसृभिः क्षालयित्वाऽथ समाचान्तो विशुध्यति ।
परस्य शोणितस्पर्शे रेतो विण्मूत्रजे तथा ॥ ६१ ॥
चतुर्णामपि वर्णानां द्वात्रिंशन्मृत्तिका स्मृताः ।
तिसृभिश्च ततः पादावाजानुभ्यां पृथक् पृथक् ॥ ६२ ॥
आकूर्पाद्वापि[१७] संक्षाल्य हस्तावामणिबन्धनात् ।
तथैव मृद्भिः प्रक्षाल्य शौचस्थानं विशोध्य च ॥ ६३ ॥

[आचमनविधिस्तत्कालाश्च]

उपविष्टः शुचौ देशे स्पृशन्वामेन तज्जलम् ।
आयतं पूर्वतः कृत्वा गोकर्णाकृतिवत्करम् ॥ ६४ ॥
संहताङ्गुलिना[१८] तोयं गृहीत्वा पाणिना द्विजः ।

१.M श्लेषाश्रु, T शेषाभ्रु. २.M स्वेदा. ३-३.M तृणा मुलाः. ४.M विस्फूत्रो°. ५.T मृद्वार्ये°. ६.M शु...षु. ७.M सु twice. ८.M oms षट्°. ९.M कर्मप्रेक्षो°. १०.M चेह. ११.T आत्मीयं. १२.M मृदं. १३.M °मार्तविस्फूर्तरे°. १४.M वरस्य. १५.M नाभेनुधं. १६.M °र्वोवहतो. १७.T आ. ..द्वापि. १८.M साहता°.

मुक्ताङ्गुष्ठकनिष्ठे तु शेषेणाचमनं चरेत् ॥ ६५ ॥
शृङ्खिणिकायाश्चालंभे केशानां रुधिरस्य च ।
अग्नेर्गवां ब्राह्मणानाममेध्या प्रयतस्य च ॥ ६६ ॥
स्त्रीशूद्रोच्छिष्टसंभाषेऽश्रुपाते रोदनेऽपि च ।
उपक्रमे विशिष्टस्य गुरोरप्युपसंग्रहे ॥ ६७ ॥
नित्यकर्मसमारंभे ताम्बूलस्य च चर्वणे ।
मार्जारमूषिकास्पर्शे क्रोधानृतसमुद्भवे[1] ॥ ६८ ॥
अवतीर्य समुत्तीर्य जलं दैवतदर्शने ।
विना यज्ञोपवीतेन शिखाकक्ष्यविमोचने ॥ ६९ ॥
[2]क्रूरदृश्येऽक्षणेऽशुचिश्व[3]चण्डालादिदर्शने ।
प्रयतोऽपि समाचामेत्तथा तीर्थादिसेवने ॥ ७० ॥
दक्षिणप्रवणं[4] भूमिं गोमयं वा तथौषधिम् ।
अशक्तौ संस्पृशेद्यद्वा भास्करं संविलोकयेत् ॥ ७१ ॥
स्नात्वा पीत्वा क्षुते सुप्ते भुक्त्वा रथ्या प्रसर्पणे ।
भोजने वहने दाने [5]रेतोविण्मूत्रसर्जने ॥ ७२ ॥
चण्डालम्लेच्छसंभाषे[6] हविषामपि भक्षणे ।
स्नाने[7] होमे सन्ध्ययोश्च [8]जपदेवार्चनेषु च ॥ ७३ ॥
ओष्ठौ विलोमतौ स्पृष्ट्वा वासो विपरिधाय[9] च ।
निष्ठीवने [10]शुक्तभाषे [11]कासश्वासविनिर्गमे ॥ ७४ ॥
चत्वरं वा श्मशानं वा गत्वा वापि महापथम् ।
वेदाध्ययनयज्ञेषु द्विर्द्विराचमनं स्मृतम् ॥ ७५ ॥
आनन्त्यात्तन्निमित्तानां दिङ्मात्रमिह दर्शितम् ।
नानाप्रयोजनमिदं स्मृतिभाष्यकृतोदितम् ॥ ७६ ॥
मूत्राद्युत्सर्जने शौचं यज्ञादौ कर्मसाधनम् ।

१.M क्रोधोऽनृत°. २.M क्रूरादृश्येक्षुणे. ३.M °शुचिश्च. ४.M दक्षिणां श्रवणं. ५.M रेकेता. ६.M समाभाषे. ७.M दाने. ८.M जलदेवा°. ९.MT विपदिधाय. १०.T शुत्क°. ११.M कासा°.

क्षुते नैमित्तिकं [१]शुक्तभाषणे चापनाशनम् ॥ ७७ ॥
जाह्नव्यादौ च धर्माय प्रस्थानादौ च सिद्धये ।
क्रूरदृश्येक्षणे क्षुण्णलक्षणाद्यपनुत्तये ॥ ७८ ॥
स्मृत्यन्तरात् समाचारादाम्नायाच्चैवमादिभिः ।
प्रकारैस्तद्विचेतव्यं[२] सदा [३]तत्त्वबुभुत्सुभिः ॥ ७९ ॥
य एवं ब्राह्मणो नित्यमुपस्पर्शनमाचरेत्[४] ।
ब्रह्मादिस्तम्बपर्यन्तं जगत्स परितर्पयेत् ॥ ८० ॥
त्रिः प्राश्नीयाद् यदंभस्तु प्रीतास्तेनाद्यदेवताः ।
ब्रह्मा विष्णुश्च रुद्रश्च [५]भवन्तीत्यनुशुश्रुमः ॥ ८१ ॥
गङ्गा च यमुना चैव प्रीयेते[६] परिमार्जनात् ।
स्पृष्टे लोचनयुग्मे तु प्रीयेते[६] शशिभास्करौ ॥ ८२ ॥
नासत्या[७] दस्रौ प्रीयेते स्पृष्टे नासाबिलद्वये[८] ।
कर्णे युग्मे तथा स्पृष्टे प्रीयेते त्वनिलानलौ[९] ॥ ८३ ॥
संस्पृष्टे हृदये चास्य प्रीयन्ते[१०] सर्वदेवताः[११] ।
मूर्धसंस्पर्शनादस्य प्रीतस्तु पुरुषो भवेत् ॥ ८४ ॥
क्रियां यः कुरुते मोहादनाचम्येह नास्तिकः ।
भवन्ति हि वृथास्तस्य क्रियाः सर्वा न संशयः ॥ ८५ ॥
सोपानात्को जलस्थो वा मुक्तकेशोऽपि वा पुनः ।
उष्णीषी वापि नाचामेद् वस्त्रेणावेष्ट्य वा शिरः ॥ ८६ ॥
न गच्छन्न शयानश्च न चलन्न परं[१२] स्पृशन् ।
[१३]न हसन्नैव[१३] सञ्जल्पन्नात्मानं चैव वीक्षयन् ॥ ८७ ॥
केशान्नीवीमधःकायं न स्पृशन् धरणीमपि ।
यदि स्पृशति चैतानि भूयः प्रक्षालयेत् करम् ॥ ८८ ॥

१.T शुक्ल°. २.M °द्वि...त्तव्यं. ३.M कत्व°. ४.M स्पृर्शन°. ५.T भवतीत्य°. ६-६.MT प्रीयते. ७.T नासत्य. ८.MT नासावृगद्वये. ९.M °निलोनलौ. १०.MT °यते. ११.T °दैवतम् °ता. १२.M चरं. १३-१३.M स सन्नैव.

नान्तर्वासा न निर्वासा न क्रुध्यन्न च यानगः ।
विना यज्ञोपवीतेन तथाधौतेन[1] वाससा ॥ ८९ ॥
मुक्त्वा[2] शिखां वाऽप्याचान्ते कृतस्यैव पुनः क्रियाः।
आसनारूढपादो वा जान्वोर्वा जङ्घयोस्तथा ॥ ९० ॥
कर्णं शिरो वा प्रावृत्य रथ्यापणगतोऽपि वा ।
अकृत्वा पादयोः शौचमाचान्तोऽप्यशुचिर्भवेत् ॥ ९१ ॥
भुक्त्वासनस्थोऽप्याचामेन्नान्यकाले[3] कदाचन ।
जान्वोरूर्ध्वं जले तिष्ठन्नाचान्तः शुचितामियात् ॥ ९२ ॥
अधस्ताच्छतकृत्वोऽपि समाचान्तो न शुध्यति ।
जलस्थो वा स्थलस्थो वा द्वयोर्वा समुपस्थितः ॥ ९३ ॥
जलस्थो जलकृत्येषु स्थलस्थः स्थलकर्मसु ।
उभयोस्तूभयस्थस्तु[4] कर्मस्वधिकृतो भवेत् ॥ ९४ ॥
स्नात्वाऽऽचामेद् यदा विप्रः पादौ कृत्वा जले स्थले।
उभयोरप्यसौ शुद्धस्ततः कार्यक्षमो भवेत् ॥ ९५ ॥
आर्द्रवासा जले कुर्यात्तर्पणाचमनञ्जपम् ।
शुष्कवासाः स्थले कुर्यादिति धर्मो व्यवस्थितः ॥ ९६ ॥
न वामहस्तेनोद्धृत्य पिबेद्वस्त्रेण वा जलम् ।
शूद्राशुच्येकहस्तैश्च दत्ताभिर्न कदाचन ॥ ९७ ॥
[5]अलाबुताम्रपात्रस्थैः करकस्थं च दृत्यपः ।
गृहीत्वा स्वयमाचामेन्न तेनाप्रयतो भवेत् ॥ ९८ ॥
शुचिगोतृप्तिकृत्तोयं[6] प्रकृतिस्थं महीगतम् ।
अव्याप्तमप्यमेध्येन[7] गन्धपर्ण[8]रसान्वितम् ॥ ९९ ॥
सबुद्बुदाः सफेनाश्च[9] गन्धपर्णादि[10]दूषिताः ।
वह्नितप्ताश्च कलुषा एकरात्रोषिता अपि ॥ १०० ॥

१.MT °धो तेन. २.T मुक्त्वा. ३.T °न्नानुकूले. ४.M स्थन्तु. ५.M अमाम्बु. ६.M °कृत्तोऽयं. ७.M °मप्यमध्येन. ८.T गन्धवर्ण°. ९.M सथेना°. १०.MT °वर्णादि°.

क्षारा विवर्णाः सुभृताः प्रदरादपि निर्गताः ।
गोस्तर्पणासमर्थास्तास्त्याज्या[1] आपोऽशुभागमाः[2] ॥ १०१ ॥
येषु देशेषु ये देवा येषु देशेषु ये[3] द्विजाः ।
येषु देशेषु यत्तोयं या च यत्रैव मृत्तिका ॥ १०२ ॥
येषु स्थानेषु यच्छौचं धर्माचाराश्च यादृशः ।
तत्र तान्नावमन्येत धर्मस्तत्रैव तादृशः ॥ १०३ ॥

[दन्तधावनविधिः]

मुखे पर्युषिते नित्यं भवत्यप्रयतो द्विजः ।
तस्मात्सर्वप्रयत्नेन भक्षयेद्दन्तधावनम् ॥ १०४ ॥
विधानतः समाचम्य प्राङ्मुखो वाग्यतः शुचिः[4] ।
उपविष्टस्त्वराहीन उद्धृतं दक्षिणं करम् ॥ १०५ ॥
कृत्वा जान्वन्तरे तिक्तकषायकटुकार्दितम्[5] ।
सुगन्धं कण्टकिक्षीरवृक्षोत्थं[6] द्वादशाङ्गुलम् ॥ १०६ ॥
कनिष्ठिकाग्रवत्स्थूलं कीटवह्न्याद्यदूषितम् ।
सत्वचं क्षालितमृजुं मन्त्रेण परिजप्य तु ॥ १०७ ॥
धावयेद्दन्तकाष्ठेन दन्तांस्तेन समाहितः ॥ १०७क ॥
आयुर्बलं यशो वर्चः प्रजापशुवसूनि च ।
ब्रह्म प्रज्ञां च मेधां च त्वं नो देहि वनस्पते ॥ १०८ ॥
सुसूक्ष्मं हीनदन्तस्य मध्यदन्तस्य मध्यमम् ।
स्थूलं विषमदन्तस्य त्रिविधं[7] दन्तधावनम् ॥ १०९ ॥
सज्जे धैर्यं वटे दीप्तिं करञ्जे विजयी रणे ।
प्लक्षे चैवार्थसंपत्तिर्बदर्यां मधुरस्वरः ॥ ११० ॥
[8]खदिरे चैव सौगन्ध्यं बिल्वे[9] तु विपुलं[10] धनम् ।
औदुम्बरे वाक्यसिद्धिर्बन्धूके च दृढा श्रुतिः ॥ १११ ॥

१.M °र्थास्ताज्या. २.M आपोश्शुभा°. ३.M या. ४.T शुचौ. ५.M °कादितम्. ६.M वृक्षार्थं. ७.M न्त्रिविधं. ८.M यदिरे. ९.MT बिले. १०.M षिपुलं.

सैध्र्ये[1] च [2]कीर्तिः सौभाग्यं[2] पलाशे सिद्धिरुत्तमा ।
कदम्बे[3] सकला लक्ष्मीराम्रे चारोग्यमेव च ॥ ११२ ॥
अपामार्गे धृतिर्मेधा प्रज्ञा शक्तिर्वपुः[4] श्रुतिः ।
आयुः शीलं यशो लक्ष्मीः सौभाग्यञ्चोपजायते ॥ ११३ ॥
अर्केण हन्ति रोगांस्तु बीजपूरेण तु व्यथाम् ।
कुरुम्बेन[5] तथाऽऽयुष्मान्[6] भवेत्पलितवर्जितः ॥ ११४ ॥
दाडिमे[7] सिन्धुवारे च कुब्जके[8] कूटजे[9] तथा ।
जाती च करमर्दा च दुःष्वप्नं चैव नाशयेत् ॥ ११५ ॥
शाल्मलाश्वत्थभव्यानां[10] सवकिंशुकयोरपि[11] ।
कोविदारशमीपीलुश्लेष्मातकविभीतकान् ॥ ११६ ॥
गुल्गुलुं क्रमुकं चापि बिल्वं श्लेष्मातकं[12] तथा ।
कोविदारं पलाशं च शिरीषं शुष्कमेव च ॥ ११७ ॥
करवीरं च बदरीं कुशं काशं च वर्जयेत् ।
प्रतिषेधाद् विधानाच्च पलाशादौ विकल्पना ॥ ११८ ॥
इष्टका लोष्टपाषाणैरितराङ्गुलिभिस्तथा ।
मुक्त्वा चानामिकाङ्गुष्ठौ वर्जयेद्दन्तधावनम् ॥ ११९ ॥
प्राङ्मुखस्तु धृतिं विद्यां शरीरारोग्यमेव च ।
दक्षिणेन तथा क्रौर्यं पश्चिमेन पराजयम् ॥ १२० ॥
उत्तरेण गवां नाशः स्त्रीणां परिजनस्य च ।
पूर्वोत्तरे तु दिग्भागे सर्वान्कामानवाप्नुयात् ॥ १२१ ॥
चतुर्दश्यष्टमी दर्शपूर्णिमा संक्रमे रवेः[13] ।
श्राद्धे जन्मत्रये चैव विवाहे जीर्णदूषितः ॥ १२२ ॥
व्रते चैवोपवासे च षष्ठ्यां च प्रतिपद्यपि ।
नवम्यां भानुवारे च दन्तकाष्ठं विवर्जयेत् ॥ १२३ ॥

१.M सैध्रे, T सैन्ध्र्ये. २-२.T कीर्त्तिर्नौभाग्यं. ३.T कदाये. ४.M वपु. ५.MT कुरुमेन. ६.M युष्टान्. ७.M डाडीमे. ८.MT कुब्जजे. ९.कूगजे. १०.T °व्याना°. ११.T सवकिं°. १२.M श्लेष्ट्रतकं. १३.M रवौ.

अलाभे दन्तकाष्ठानां प्रतिषिद्धदिने तथा ।
अपां[१] द्वादशगण्डूषैः पत्रैर्वा दन्तधावनम् ॥ १२४ ॥
मध्यमाङ्गुलिवत्स्थूलं पर्वाग्रक्रतुकूर्चकम्[२] ।
जिह्वोल्लेखनिका वापि दन्तकाष्ठेन कीर्तिताः ॥ १२५ ॥
तया विशोधयेज्जिह्वां प्रतिषिद्धदिनेऽपि च ।
प्रक्षाल्य भुङ्क्त्वा[३] तज्जह्याद्[४] दन्तकाष्ठं शुचिस्थले॥ १२६ ॥
पतितेऽभिमुखे सम्यग् भोज्यमाप्नोत्यभीप्सितम् ॥ १२६क ॥

[स्नानफलम्]

[५]अगम्यागमनात् स्तेयात्[५] पापेभ्यश्च प्रतिग्रहात् ।
रहस्याचरितात्पापान्मुच्यते स्नानमाचरन् ॥ १२७ ॥
मनःप्रसादजननं रूपसौभाग्यवर्धनम् ।
शोकदुःष्वप्नहं स्नानं [६]मोक्षदं याजनं[६] तथा ॥ १२८ ॥
स्नानमूलाः क्रियाः सर्वाः श्रुतिस्मृत्युदिता नृणाम् ।
तस्मात्स्नानं निषेवेत श्रीपुष्ट्यारोग्यवर्धनम्[७] ॥ १२९ ॥
अस्नात्वा नाचरेत्कर्म जपहोमादि किंचन ।
लालास्वेदसमाकीर्णः शयनादुत्थितः पुमान् ॥ १३० ॥
अत्यन्तमलिन[८]कायो नवच्छिद्रसमन्वितः[९] ।
स्रवत्येष दिवा रात्रौ[१०] प्रातःस्नानं विशोधनम् ॥ १३१ ॥
प्रातःस्नानं प्रशंसन्ति दृष्टादृष्टकरं हि तत् ।
सर्वमर्हति शुद्धात्मा प्रातःस्नायी जपादिकम् ॥ १३२ ॥
नित्यं नैमित्तिकं काम्यमिति स्नानं त्रिधा स्मृतम्[११] ।
नित्यं सततनिर्वर्त्यं काम्यं कामाय यद्धितम्[१२] ॥ १३३ ॥
निमित्तादुपजातं तु स्नानं नैमित्तिकं स्मृतम् ।
तच्च पञ्चविधं प्रोक्तं दिव्यमाग्नेयवारुणे[१३] ॥ १३४ ॥

१.T broken. २.M कूर्चकः. ३.M ...त्वा. ४.T तर्जन्या. ५-५.M गमनान्ते या. ६-६.M मोक्ष... दाह्वान°. ७.M °पुण्यारोग्य°. ८.M मलिनं, T मलिनः. ९.M समन्वितम्. १०.M दिमामात्रौ. ११.T त्रिधा स्मृतम्. १२.M तत्. १३.M °वारुणेः.

ब्राह्मं वायव्यमप्येषां लक्षणं स्मृतिषूदितम् ।
यत्तु सातपवर्षेण दिव्यं स्नानं प्रकीर्तितम् ॥ १३५ ॥
आग्नेयं भस्मना प्रोक्तमवगाह्य तु वारुणम् ।
'आपो हि ष्ठा' तृचेनाद्भिर्मार्जनं ब्राह्ममुच्यते ॥ १३६ ॥
वायव्यं गोरजः स्नानं मुख्यं वारुणमापदि ।
कालदोषादसामर्थ्यादाग्नेयादि समाचरेत् ॥ १३७ ॥
यद्वा शिरस्कं स्नायीत मार्जयेद्वार्द्रवाससा ॥ १३७क ॥
नदीषु देवखातेषु[१] तटाकेषु सरःसु च ।
स्नानं समाचरेन्नित्यं गिरिप्रस्रवणेषु च ॥ १३८ ॥
कूपेषूद्धृततोयेन स्नानं कुर्वीत वै भुवि ।
स्नायीतोद्धृततोयेन ह्यथवा भूमिसंभवैः ॥ १३९ ॥
भूमिष्ठमुद्धृतात्पुण्यं ततः प्रस्रवणोदकम्[२] ।
ततोऽपि धारासलिलं[३] तस्मान्नादेयमुच्यते ॥ १४० ॥
तीर्थतोयं ततः पुण्यं गाङ्गं पुण्यं तु सर्वतः ।
त्रिभिः सारस्वतं तोयं पञ्चाहेन तु यामुनम् ॥ १४१ ॥
सद्यः पुनाति गाङ्गेयं दर्शनादेव नर्मदा ।
त्रिरात्रफलदा नद्यो[४] याः काश्चिदसमुद्रगाः ॥ १४२ ॥
समुद्रगास्तु[५] पक्षस्य मासस्य सरितांपतिः ।
नद्यामस्तमये स्नानं वर्जयेत्तु सदा बुधः ॥ १४३ ॥
स्रवन्नदीषु च स्नायात्प्रविश्यान्तःस्थितो द्विजः ।
तटाकादिषु सर्वेषु प्रत्यक्षं स्नानमाचरेत् ॥ १४४ ॥
नद्या यच्च परिभ्रष्टं नद्या यच्च[६] विविर्जितम् ।
गतप्रत्यागतं यच्च तत्तोयं परिवर्जयेत् ॥ १४५ ॥
अगाह्यास्त्वग्रिमा आपो [७]नद्यः प्रथमवेगिताः[८] ।

१.M देवमातेषु, T देवपातेषु. २.M °दिकम्; T °दितम्. ३.MT धार संपुण्य. ४.M नाद्यो. ५.M समुद्रगा तु. ६.T यच्च...वर्जितम्. ७.M नद्या. ८.M वेदिताः.

प्रक्षोभिताश्च केनापि याश्च तीर्थास्त्वनिन्दिताः ॥ १४६ ॥
अजा गावो महिष्यश्च[१] ब्राह्मणी च प्रसूतिका ।
दशरात्रेण शुध्यति भूमिष्ठं च नवोदकम् ॥ १४७ ॥
प्रभूते विद्यमाने तु सोदके[२] सुमनोहरे ।
नवोदके[३] द्विजः स्नायान्नदीं चोत्सृज्य कृत्तिमे ॥ १४८ ॥
मासद्वयं श्रावणादि सर्वा नद्यो रजस्वलाः ।
तासु स्नानं न कुर्वीत वर्जयित्वा समुद्रगाः ॥ १४९ ॥
प्रावृट्काले महानद्यः सन्ति नित्यं रजस्वलाः ।
तासु स्नानं न कुर्वीत वर्जयित्वा तु जाह्नवीम् ॥ १५० ॥
गोदावरी भीमरथी कृष्णवर्णा सरस्वती ।
तुङ्गभद्रा सुप्रयोगा साह्या[४] कावेरिकैव च ॥ १५१ ॥
दुग्धोदा नलिनी रेवा वारिशीता कलस्वना ।
महा अपि महानद्यः सह्यमूलाद्विनिसृताः ॥ १५२ ॥
अलाभे देवखातानां[५] सरसां[६] सरितां तथा ।
[७]उद्धृत्य चतुरः पिण्डान् वारक्ये स्नानमाचरेत् ॥ १५३ ॥
नित्यं नैमित्तिकं काम्यं क्रियाङ्गं मलकर्षणम् ।
तीर्थाभावे तु कर्तव्यमुष्णोदकवरोदकैः ॥ १५४ ॥
मृते जन्मनि संक्रान्तौ श्राद्धे जन्मदिने तथा[७] ।
अस्पृश्यस्पर्शने भानुवारे राहोश्च दर्शने ॥ १५५ ॥
पर्वद्वये च सप्तम्यां न स्नायादुष्णवारिणा ।
शीतास्वप्सु निषिच्योष्णा मन्त्रसंभारसंभृताः ॥ १५६ ॥
गृहेऽपि शस्यते स्नानं तद्धीनमफलं बहिः ।
सपवित्रः क्रियां[८] कुर्यात् स्नानहोमजपादिकम् ॥ १५७ ॥
पवित्रं दर्भनिष्पन्नं कौशं वा हैमराजतम् ।

१.M महिष्या°. २.MT उदके. ३.M ...दके. ४.T सांह्या. ५.M देवतानां. ६.M सरतां. ७-७.M oms. ८.M यः.

धारयेद् ग्रन्थिसंयुक्तं दक्षिणोपकनिष्ठया ॥ १५८ ॥
ग्रन्थिर्यस्य पवित्रस्य न तेनाचमनं चरेत् ।
नोच्छिष्टं तत्पवित्रं तु भुक्तोच्छिष्टं तु वर्जयेत् ॥ १५९ ॥

[प्रातःस्नानविधिः]

अरुणोदयकाले वाप्युषस्युदयसंनिधौ ।
शक्तः स्नानं प्रकुर्वीत तद्विधिः प्रतिपाद्यते ॥ १६० ॥
अल्पत्वाद्धोत्रकालस्य[१] बहुत्वात् स्नानकर्मणः ।
प्रातः संक्षेपतः स्नानं होमलोपो विगर्हितः ॥ १६१ ॥
दन्तान् विशोध्य स्वाचान्तः[२] स्नानशाटीं[३] वसन्मृदा ।
तीरदेशे समासीनः शिरोमलमपोह्य तु ॥ १६२ ॥
प्रक्षाल्य मृद्भ्यां नाभ्यन्तमधस्तात्तिसृभिस्तथा[४] ।
पादौ विशोध्यान्यतमं[५] प्रयतं परिधाय च ॥ १६३ ॥
स्वाचान्तो[६] जलमाविश्य निमज्ज्योन्मज्ज्य पाथसि ।
नाभिमात्रे स्थितो नित्यमाचान्तश्चिन्तयन्पितॄन् ॥ १६४ ॥
प्राचीनावीतवत्प्रातरा[७]शाथावदनोऽम्बरे ।
त्रींस्त्रीञ्जलाञ्जली[८]र्दद्यादुच्चै[९]रुच्चतरं बुधः ॥ १६५ ॥
'आगच्छन्त्वा'दिभिर्मन्त्रैः पितृतीर्थेन सादरम् ।
अथोपवीतवत्तीर्त्वा[१०] पादौ कृत्वा जले स्थले ॥ १६६ ॥
आचम्याब्दैवतैर्मन्त्रैर्ऋष्यादिस्मरणान्वितम् ।
मार्जयेत्तदविज्ञाने[११] दोषः स्मृतिषु भण्यते ॥ १६७ ॥
[१२][अविदित्वा ऋषिं छन्दो दैवतं योगमेव च ।
योऽध्यापयेज्जपेद्वापि पापीयाञ्जायते तु सः] ॥ १६८ ॥

१.M अतत्वाद्धोत°. २.M स्वापन्ते. ३.M °शामीं. ४.M °स्ततम्. ५.MT न्यत्प्रयतं. ६.M स्वापान्तो. ७.M प्रातनाशा°. ८.M ञ्जलि°, T ञ्जलीं. ९.M दद्यारुच्चै°. १०.M °पवीत्युत्तीर्युः, T °वी...त्युत्तीर्य. ११.M °त्तदपि ज्ञाने. १२.T shows sign of broken text equal to one Verse. M, however, does not show any sign of broken text. The text given in the bracket possibly be conjectured as has been lost.

सिन्धुद्वीप ऋषिश्छन्दो गायत्र्यापश्च देवताः ।
मार्जने विनियोगोऽस्येत्येवं व्यासेन कीर्तितम् ॥ १६९ ॥
एवं संमार्जनं [1]कृत्वा छन्द आर्षं च दैवतम्[2] ।
अघमर्षणसूक्तस्य संस्मरेत् प्रह्वतः[3] सदा ॥ १७० ॥
निमज्ज्यान्तस्ततः[4] पश्चात् त्रिः पठेदघमर्षणम् ॥ १७०क॥
पुण्यतीर्थानि[5] संस्पृश्य स्नात्वा सम्प्राप्य च स्थलम् ।
जलमञ्जलिना मूर्ध्नि सिञ्चेत् 'प्राणा'दिमन्त्रवत् ॥ १७१ ॥
कञ्चित्कालं स्थितो वस्त्रजलं भूमौ निपातयेत् ।
शुचिना वाससावेष्ट्य शिरोजलमपि त्यजेत् ॥ १७२ ॥
अपमृज्यान्न च स्नातो गात्राण्यम्बरपाणिभिः ।
न च निर्धुनुयात्केशान् वासश्चैव न निर्धुनेत् ॥ १७३ ॥
पिबन्ति शिरसो देवाः पिबन्ति पितरो मुखात् ।
मध्यतः सर्वगन्धर्वा अधस्तात् सर्वजन्तवः ॥ १७४ ॥
तस्मात् स्नातो नापमृज्यात् स्नानशाट्या न पाणिना ॥१७४क॥
तिस्रः कोट्यर्धकोटी च यावन्त्यङ्गरुहाणि वै ।
स्रवन्ति सर्वतीर्थानि तस्मान्न परिमार्जयेत् ॥ १७५ ॥
स्नानशाट्यादिवचनात्तन्निषेधोऽत्र गम्यते ।
स्नातोऽङ्गानि निमृज्य[ती][6]त्येवं स्मृतिषु दृश्यते ॥ १७६ ॥

[वस्त्रधारणविधिः]

अथ वासस्तु निर्णिक्तमुपवातमनुल्बणम् ।
अजीर्णं धवलं प्रोक्ष्य परिधाय तथाविधम् ॥ १७७ ॥
विदध्यादुत्तरीयं तत् प्रसङ्गादिदमुच्यते ॥ १७७क ॥

१.T कुर्यात्. २.M देवताम्. ३.M प्रण्वतः. ४.M निमज्ज्यान्ततः. ५.M broken after पुण्यतीर्थानि, covering verses 171 to 207 before °केशं तु कण्ठके p. 216. M indicates the loss of text with the marginal remark चिह्नितस्थल अत्र ग्रन्थपातः. T, however, gives the full text. ६.T broken.

स्वयं धौतेन कर्तव्या क्रिया धर्म्या विपश्चिता ।
न च नेजकधौतेन नाहतेन च कर्हिचित् ॥ १७८ ॥
अहतं यन्त्रनिर्मुक्तमुक्तं वासः स्वयंभुवा ।
शस्तं तन्माङ्गलिक्येषु तावत्कालं न सर्वदा ॥ १७९ ॥
शयने लोकयात्रायां रथ्यास्वीश्वरदर्शने ।
देवार्चनादिकार्येषु वासो भेदोऽभिधीयते ॥ १८० ॥
स्नानं दानं जलं होमं स्वाध्यायं पितृतर्पणम् ।
नैकवस्त्रो द्विजः कुर्याच्छ्राद्धभोजनसत्क्रियाः ॥ १८१ ॥
सव्यादीषत्परिभ्रष्टकटिदेशधृताम्बरः ।
एकवस्त्रं तु तं विद्याद् दैवे पित्र्ये च वर्जयेत् ॥ १८२ ॥
विकक्ष्योऽनुत्तरीयश्च नग्नश्चावस्त्र एव च ।
श्रौतस्मार्तं न कुर्वीत न नग्नश्चिन्तयेदपि ॥ १८३ ॥
नग्नो मलिनवस्त्रः स्यान्नग्नश्चान्धवदस्मृतः ।
नग्नो द्विगुणवस्त्रः स्यान्नग्नो रक्तपटः स्मृतः ॥ १८४ ॥
नग्नस्तु स्निन्धवस्त्रः स्यान्नग्नः स्यूतपटः स्मृतः ॥ १८४क ॥
न रक्तमुल्बणं वासो दशाहीनं मलान्वितम् ।
काषायमुपवस्त्रं च केशकीटादि[1]दूषितम् ॥ १८५ ॥
नीलश्च परिधातव्यः सामर्थ्ये मलिनं त्यजेत् ।
अभावे धौतवस्त्रस्य शोणक्षौमाविकानि च ॥ १८६ ॥
कुतपं योगपट्टं वा द्विवासापि न वै भवेत् ।
यज्ञोपवीते द्वे धार्ये श्रौते स्मार्ते च कर्मणि ॥ १८७ ॥
तृतीयमुत्तरीयं च वस्त्राभावे तदिष्यते ।
द्व्यङ्गुलं त्र्यङ्गुलं वापि द्व्यङ्गुलद्वितयाङ्गुलम् ॥ १८८ ॥
सूत्रैर्वस्त्राकृतिं करोत्युत्तरीयमिति स्मृतम् ।
अथाचम्य स्वतीर्थेन कुर्याद् देवादितर्पणम् ॥ १८९ ॥

१.T कीठादि°.

द्वौ हस्तौ युग्मतः[१] कृत्वा पूरयित्वोदकाञ्जलिम् ।
गोशृङ्गमात्रमुद्धृत्य जलमध्ये जलं क्षिपेत् ॥ १९० ॥
साक्षतैस्तर्पयेद्देवानृषीनपि च तद् गणान् ।
तिलचन्दनदर्भाग्रयुतैः सन्तर्पयेत् पितॄन् ॥ १९१ ॥
तिलानामप्यभावे तु सुवर्णरजतान्वितम् ।
तदलाभे निषिञ्चेत्तु दर्भैर्मन्त्रेण वा पुनः ॥ १९२ ॥
निष्पीडयेत्ततो वस्त्रं प्राचीनावीतवत्[२] स्थले ॥ १९२क ॥
स्नानार्थमभि[३] गच्छन्तं देवाः पितृगणैः सह ।
वायुभूतास्तु गच्छन्ति तृषार्ताः[४] सलिलार्थिनः ॥ १९३ ॥
निराशास्ते निवर्तन्ते वस्त्रनिष्पीडने कृते[५] ।
तस्मान्न पीडयेद् वस्त्रमकृत्वा[६] पितृतर्पणम् ॥ १९४ ॥
वस्त्रनिष्पीडनं तोयं श्राद्धेषूच्छिष्टभागिनाम् ।
भागधेयं श्रुतिः प्राह तस्मान्निष्पीडयेत् स्थले ॥ १९५ ॥
अपुत्रा ये मृताः केचिदस्मद् गोत्रेषु गोत्रिणाम् ।
ते पिबन्तु मया दत्तं वस्त्रनिष्पीडनोदकम् ॥ १९६ ॥
त्रिगुणीकृत्य यो वस्त्रमज्ञानात्पीडयेन्नरः ।
तस्य त्रिरात्रमाशौचमिति वेदविदो विदुः ॥ १९७ ॥
एवं सम्पीड्य तद् वस्त्रं पुनराचमनं चरेत् ।
ऊर्ध्वपुण्ड्रं ततः कुर्यान्मृदा तद्विधिरुच्यते ॥ १९८ ॥

[मृदोर्ध्वपुण्ड्रधारणविधिः]

पर्वताग्रे नदीतीरे विष्णुक्षेत्रे विशेषतः ।
सिन्धुतीरेऽथ[७] वल्मीके तुलसीमूलमाश्रिते[८] ॥ १९९ ॥
मृद एतास्तु संग्राह्या वर्जयेत्त्वन्यमृत्तिकाः ॥ १९९क ॥

१.T यागतः; thus Vādh Sm.56. २.T प्राचीनावत्. ३.T °स्नानार्थमिह. ४.T तृष्णार्ता; thus Vādh.Sm 59. ५.T तु ते; thus Vādh Sm.60. ६.T वस्त्रं कृत्वापि; thus Vādh Sm.60. ७.T च. ८.T माश्रिता; thus Vādh Sm 110.

श्यामा शान्तिकरी प्रोक्ता रक्ता वश्यकरी भवेत् ।
पीता मृच्छ्रीकरी ज्ञेया श्वेता मृद्वैष्णवी स्मृताः ॥ २०० ॥
अङ्गुष्ठः पुष्टिदः प्रोक्तो मध्यमायुष्करी भवेत् ।
अनामिकाऽन्नदा नित्यं मुक्तिदा च प्रदेशिनी ॥ २०१ ॥
एतैरङ्गुलिभेदैस्तु कुर्वीत न नखैः स्पृशेत् ॥२०१क॥
वर्त्तिदीपाकृतिं वापि वेणुपत्राकृतिं तथा ।
पद्मस्य मुकुलाकारं तथैव कुमुदस्य च ॥ २०२ ॥
मत्स्यकूर्माकृतिं वापि शङ्खाकारमतः परम् ॥२०२क॥
दशाङ्गुलप्रमाणं तु उत्तमोत्तममुच्यते ।
नवाङ्गुलं मध्यमं स्यादष्टाङ्गुलमतः परम् ॥ २०३ ॥
सप्तषट्पञ्चभिः पुण्ड्रं मध्यमं त्रिविधं स्मृतम् ।
चतुस्त्रिद्व्यङ्गुलैः पुण्ड्रं कनिष्ठं त्रिविधं भवेत् ॥ २०४ ॥
ललाटे केशवं विद्यान्नारायणमथोदरे ।
माधवं हृदि विन्यस्य गोविन्दं कर्णकूपके ॥ २०५ ॥
उदरे दक्षिणे पार्श्वे विष्णुरित्यभिधीयते ।
तत्पार्श्वबाहुमध्ये तु मधुसूदन उच्यते ॥ २०६ ॥
त्रिविक्रमं कण्ठदेशे वामे कुक्षौ तु वामनम् ।
श्रीधरं बाहुके वामे हृषीकेशं[१] तु कण्ठके ॥ २०७ ॥
पृष्ठे तु पद्मनाभं तु ककुद्दामोदरं स्मरेत् ।
द्वादशैतानि नामानि वासुदेवं च मूर्धनि ॥ २०८ ॥
पूजाकाले च होमे च सायंप्रातः समाहितः ।
नामान्युच्चार्य विधिना धारयेदूर्ध्वपुण्ड्रकम् ॥ २०९ ॥
अशुचिर्वाप्यनाचारो मनसा पापमाचरन् ।
शुचिरेव भवेन्नित्यमूर्ध्वपुण्ड्राङ्कितो द्विजः ॥ २१० ॥

१.M restarts with केशं तु after loss of the text from verse 171 to verse 207.

ऊर्ध्वपुण्ड्रधरो[१] मर्त्यो म्रियते यत्र कुत्रचित् ।
श्वपाकोऽपि विमानस्थः[२] पूज्य एव न संशयः ॥ २११ ॥
जाह्नवीतीरसंभूतां मृदं मूर्ध्ना बिभर्ति यः ।
बिभर्ति रूपं सोऽर्कस्य तमोनाशाय केवलम् ॥ २१२ ॥

[सन्ध्योपासननिर्णयः]

अत ऊर्ध्वं प्रवक्ष्यामि सन्ध्योपासननिर्णयम् ।
अहोरात्रकृतैः पापैर्यामुपास्य प्रमुच्यते[३] ॥ २१३ ॥
सर्वावस्थोऽपि यो[४] विप्रः सन्ध्योपासनतत्परः ।
ब्रह्मण्याच्च न हीयेत जन्मान्तरगतोऽपि सः ॥ २१४ ॥
यावन्तोऽस्यां[५] पृथिव्यां तु विकर्मस्था[६] द्विजातयः ।
तेषां हि पावनार्थाय सन्ध्या सृष्टा स्वयंभुवा ॥ २१५ ॥
त्रिंशत्कोट्यस्तु विख्याता [७]मन्देहा नाम राक्षसाः ।
प्राद्रवन्ति सहस्रांशुमुदयं तद्[८] दिनेदिने ॥ २१६ ॥
अहन्यहनि ते सर्वे सूर्यमिच्छन्ति खादितुम् ॥ २१६क ॥
ततो देवगणाः सर्वे ऋषयश्च तपोधनाः ।
सन्धौ तु समुपासीना यत्क्षिपन्ति महज्जलम् ॥ २१७ ॥
ब्रह्मव्याहृतिसंयुक्तं गायत्र्या चाभिमन्त्रितम् ।
तेन दह्यन्ति ते दैत्या वज्रीभूतेन वारिणा[९] ॥ २१८ ॥
एतद्विदित्वा यः सन्ध्यामुपास्ते संशितव्रतः ।
दीर्घमायुः स विन्देत सर्वपापैः प्रमुच्यते ॥ २१९ ॥
यस्तु तां केवलां सन्ध्यामुपासीत स पुण्यभाक् ।
तां परित्यज्य कर्माणि कुर्वन्प्राप्नोति किल्बिषम् ॥ २२० ॥
सन्ध्याहीनोऽशुचिर्नित्यमनर्हः सर्वकर्मसु ।
यदन्यत्कुरुते कर्म न तस्य फलभाग्भवेत् ॥ २२१ ॥

१.M °पुण्ड्रतरो. २.M °स्थाः. ३.M स्रमु°. ४.MT add देवा after यो. ५.MT यावतो स्यात्. ६.M °कर्मस्थो. ७.M मन्देना. ८.M तं. ९. Cf Tait Âr.2.2.1-2

सन्ध्या येन न विज्ञाता सन्ध्या नैव ह्युपासिता ।
जीवमानो भवेच्छूद्रो मृतः श्वा[1] चाभिजायते ॥ २२२ ॥
योऽन्यत्र कुरुते यत्नं धर्मकार्ये द्विजोत्तमः ।
विहाय सन्ध्याप्रणतिं स याति नरकायुतम्[2] ॥ २२३ ॥
तस्मान्नोल्लङ्घनं कार्यं सन्ध्योपासनकर्मणः ॥ २२३क ॥
अनातुरश्चोत्सृजेद्यः स विप्रः शूद्रसंमितः ।
प्रायश्चित्तिर्भवेच्चैव लोके भवति निन्दितः ॥ २२४ ॥
अहोरात्रस्य यः सन्धिः सूर्यनक्षत्रवर्जितः ।
सा तु सन्ध्या समाख्याता मुनिभिस्तत्त्वदर्शिभिः ॥ २२५ ॥
[....][3] ।
तत्र यत्क्रियते तच्च सन्ध्यापदसमीरितः ॥ २२६ ॥

[सूर्योपासना]

योऽसौ सूर्यो जगत्स्वामी सर्वलोकप्रकाशकः ।
चिद्रूपः सर्वभूतात्मा निर्विशेषो निरञ्जनः ॥ २२७ ॥
साक्षी सर्वस्य लोकस्य मण्डलान्तर्गतः पुमान् ।
ऋङ्मण्डलो रश्मिसामा यजुरात्मा हिरण्मयः ॥ २२८ ॥
ब्रह्मविष्णुशिवाद्याख्यस्तेजोमूर्तिर्विराट् स्वराट् ।
[4]सदानन्दोऽद्वयो नित्यः स्वतन्त्रो भगवान् विभुः[5] ॥ २२९ ॥
स्वात्मन्यतिरेकेण[6] हृन्मध्ये तस्य दीपवत् ।
उपलभ्यस्य यद् ध्यानमभिन्नस्य स्फुलिङ्गवत् ॥ २३० ॥
तदेतद्विहितं तत्र श्रूयते हि तथा श्रुतौ ।
उद्यन्तमस्तमित्यादि तस्यार्थो वर्ण्यतेऽधुना ॥ २३१ ॥
'उद्यन्तमि'ति निर्देशात् सन्धौ ध्येयो रविस्ततः ।
कालयोगाद्रविः सन्ध्याशब्दलक्ष्योऽवगम्यते[7] ॥ २३२ ॥

---

१. मृतश्चा. २.M °यतम्. ३.T shows the sign of broken text in the first hemistich; M, however does not show it. ४.M स्वादनन्दो. ५.T प्रभुः. ६.M °न्यवितिरे°. ७.M °लक्ष्योऽपग°.

सत्यं ज्ञानमनन्तं यद् ब्रह्मत्रय्यं[१] तु दर्शितम् ।
आदित्योऽसौ दृश्यमानस्तदेवेत्यागमोक्तिभिः ॥ २३३ ॥
विदित्वा स्वात्मनोऽप्यस्मादभेदं विष्फुलिङ्गवत् ।
अयःपिण्डादग्नितप्तादथ स्वीयहृदम्बुजे ॥ २३४ ॥
आत्मभूतं रविं तेजोराशिं ब्रह्मद्वयात्मकम् ।
पुनःपुनरनिर्वेदाद्[२] ध्यायन् विहितमाचरन् ॥ २३५ ॥
ब्राह्मणः सकलं भद्रमश्नुते मुच्यते च सः ।
ब्रह्मोपासनमेवातः सूर्योपासनमुच्यते ॥ २३६ ॥
सन्ध्यामुपासितुं [३]छिन्धीत्यारभ्य ब्राह्मणान्तरे ।
य एषोर्गन्तरोऽव्यक्त[४] आत्मैतं सन्धिमेव वै ॥ २३७ ॥
सन्ध्यां ब्रह्मविदो नित्यमुपासत इतीरितम् ।
व्यासेनाप्येतदेवेह प्रधानमिति दर्शितम् ॥ २३८ ॥
युधिष्ठिरादिवृत्तान्तं ब्रुवता रणमूर्धनि ।
तथैव ते महाराज दर्शिता[५] रणमूर्धनि ॥ २३९ ॥
सन्ध्यागतं सहस्रांशुमादित्यमुपतस्थिरे ।
सर्वस्मृतिषु चैषोऽर्थः प्राधान्येन विधीयते ॥ २४० ॥
न भिन्नं प्रतिपद्येत गायत्रीं ब्रह्मणा सह ।
[६]'सोऽहमस्मी'त्युपासीत विधिना येन केनचित् ॥ २४१ ॥
मन्त्रवाच्यश्च सविताऽसावित्यत्र[७] निगद्यते ।
'उद्यन्तमस्त'मित्यादि श्रुत्यर्थो बाध्यतेऽन्यथा ॥ २४२ ॥
तथा च वचनान्यत्र गदितानि महर्षिभिः ॥ २४२क ॥

[गायत्र्युपासनारहस्यम्]

प्रातःकाले तु गायत्री सांयकाले सरस्वती ।
मध्यन्दिने च सावित्री उपास्या नामभेदतः ॥ २४३ ॥

१.M त्रैय्यं, T corrected as त्रय्यं. २.M °रहिवेदा. ३.T श्चिन्धी°. ४.M एषोन्तरो, T एषोगन्तरो.
५.MT दंसिता. ६.T साहम°. ७.M सावित्रीत, T ऽसाविति.

प्रतिग्रहादन्नदोषात्पातकादुपपातकात् ।
गायत्री प्रोच्यते तस्माद् गायन्तं त्रायते यतः[१] ॥ २४४ ॥
सवितृद्योतनाच्चैव सावित्री परिकीर्तिता ।
जगतः प्रसवित्री सा[२] वाग्रूपत्वात्[३] सरस्वती ॥ २४५ ॥
गायत्रीह भवेद्रक्ता सावित्री शुक्लवर्णिका[४] ।
सरस्वती तथा कृष्णा उपास्या वर्णभेदतः ॥ २४६ ॥
गायत्री ब्रह्मरूपा तु सावित्री रुद्ररूपिणी ।
सरस्वती विष्णुरूपा उपास्या रूपभेदतः ॥ २४७ ॥
उपास्ते[५] सन्धिवेलायां निशाया[६] दिवसस्य च ।
[७][त्रिविधरूपां] तामेव प्रवदन्ति मनीषिणः[७] ॥ २४८ ॥
या सन्ध्या सा[८] जगत्सूतिर्मायातीता हि निष्कला ।
ईश्वरी केवला शक्तिस्तत्त्वत्रयसमुद्भवा ॥ २४९ ॥
ध्यात्वार्कमण्डलगतां सावित्रीं वै[९] जपेद् बुधः ॥ २४९क ॥
ततश्च विहिता [१०]येऽत्र मरुदाय मनादयः[१०] ।
स्वात्मशुद्धिविधानेन तदङ्गत्वं प्रयान्ति ते ॥ २५० ॥
विदुषो ध्यानमन्यस्य जप एवेति चेन्न हि ।
रविं ध्यायंस्तथा कुर्वन् न [११]तूर्ध्वक्षेपणादिकम् ॥ २५१ ॥
प्राप्नोति मुक्तिपर्यन्तं कल्याणमिति हि श्रुतम् ।
न चैवमधिकारोऽत्र [१२]मुमुक्षोर्वा फलार्थिनः[१३] ॥ २५२ ॥
निष्कामेन कृतस्यैतत् फलं यस्मादिहोच्यते ।
अकृतौ दोष एव स्याद् यत्र प्रीत्युपलब्धितः ॥ २५३ ॥
प्रवृत्तिस्तत्र शास्त्रं न तथा तदनुवर्तने ।

१.M ततः. २.MT om. ३.M वाभूपत्वा°. ४.M °वर्णिता. ५.M उपान्ते. ६.M निशायां. ७-७.T broken before तामेव; M neither shows any sign of broken text nor gives the entire second hemistich. ८.MT या. ९.M यो. १०-१०.MT यत्र [T येऽम] मरुदाय मनादयः? text not clear. ११.M broken between कुर्वन् and र्ध्व°. १२.M मुमुक्षु°. १३.M ऽथवार्थिनः.

नरकं गच्छतीत्येवं [1]स्मृतसन्ध्यादिकर्मसु ॥ २५४ ॥
'मा कर्मफलहेतुर्भू'रित्यादि भगवद्वचः ।
सन्ध्याहीनोऽशुचिर्नित्यमित्यादि बहुशः स्मृतम् ॥ २५५ ॥
अतः सर्वाणि कर्माणि निष्कामेन कृतानि हि ।
ज्ञानवन्ति सृतिध्वंसं कुर्वन्तीत्यवगम्यते ॥ २५६ ॥
[2]न च ज्ञानवता[2] नित्यं कर्मणा संसृतेर्हतिः[3] ॥ २५६क ॥
श्रवणादिभिरेवास्य स्वरूपं वेद यो द्विजः ।
[4]रविर्ब्रह्माहमस्मीति मुच्यते सोऽपि संसृतेः ॥ २५७ ॥
ब्रह्मैव सन्नित्यस्यार्थो ब्राह्मणः सन्निहैव तु ।
मुच्यते स सृतेर्यद्वा ब्रह्माभिन्नस्फुलिङ्गवत् ॥ २५८ ॥
उपाधिभेदाद् भिन्नः सन्नुपाधिविरहे सति ।
सम्पद्यतेऽद्वयं ब्रह्म घटध्वस्तौ यथा वियत् ॥ २५९ ॥
अतो ज्ञानान्वितं कर्म नित्यं ज्ञानं[5] च केवलम् ।
संसारमुक्तये पुंसामनर्थं तद्विसर्जने ॥ २६० ॥

[प्रणवोपासनाया रहस्यम्]

तस्य प्रणव[6]साध्यत्वं ध्यानस्य श्रूयते द्विधा ।
वाचकालम्बनत्वेन वाचकत्वेन भण्यते ॥ २६१ ॥
ओमित्यनेन पुरुषं परं[7] ध्यायेत्तथोमिति[8] ।
एवं ध्यायत[9] आत्मानं ओमित्येतद्[10] ब्रवीमि ते ॥ २६२ ॥
'एतद्ध्येवाक्षरं ब्रह्मे'त्येवमादि श्रुतौ श्रुतम् ।
तथैवालम्बनत्वेन तद्यथा शङ्कुनेत्युप ॥ २६३ ॥
क्रम्याहो'ङ्कार एवेदं सर्वं ब्रह्मापि चोमि'ति ।
'एतदालम्बनं श्रेष्ठमेतदालम्बनं परम्' ॥ २६४ ॥
इति श्रुत्यनुसारेण व्यवस्थाऽत्रापि विद्यते ।

१.M स्मृतशा°. २-२.M लज्जानवता. ३.T हतिम्. ४.MT स सृते°. ५.M ज्ञानश्च. ६.MT प्रवण°. ७.M चरुं. ८.M ध्येयेन्त°. ९. MT ध्यायथ. १०.M आ. इत्ये°.

[१]आगमाच्चार्थनिर्णीतब्रह्मभूतात्मनो यतेः ॥ २६५ ॥
अतिक्रान्तोपसर्गस्य निवृत्तस्यापि कर्मणः ।
वाचकत्वेन तद्ध्यानमन्यस्यालम्बनेन तु ॥ २६६ ॥
अभिधानविशेषोऽयं स्वाभिधेयोपसंहृतः ।
सत्स्वभिधेयसामान्य[२]व्यतिरिक्तो मृदा यथा ॥ २६७ ॥
घटादिस्तदनुरक्तः [३]समबाध्यतयापि च ।
अभिन्नस्तद्वदोङ्कारस्त्रयी सारतया श्रुतेः ॥ २६८ ॥
अभिधानाभिधेयस्वरूपे प्रत्यङ्गविष्णुवत् ।
विधीयते ब्रह्मदृष्टिरालम्बनमिदं श्रुतम् ॥ २६९ ॥
ओङ्कारालम्बनो[४] विद्वान् क्रमान्मुच्येत संसृतेः ।
जपन्नासीत सावित्रीमित्यादिवचनेन तु ॥ २७० ॥
तज्जपोऽपि तदर्थानुध्यानयुक्तो विधीयते ।
मानसस्य जपस्यापि विशिष्टत्वं प्रतीयते ॥ २७१ ॥
न चेह जपमात्रस्य प्राधान्यं प्रतिपद्यते ।
जपेदासीन इत्येवं स्मर्यतैवं न चासनम् ॥ २७२ ॥
प्रधानश्रुतिबाधेन मन्त्रार्थध्यानतोऽपि च ।
क्रियमाणानुवादित्वं[५] मन्त्रस्यापि समीरितम् ॥ २७३ ॥
[६]विद्यया यत्करोत्येनद्वीर्यवत्तरमीरितम् ।
मन्त्रार्थचिन्तनं चापि स्मर्यते तत्त्वदर्शिभिः ॥ २७४ ॥
यथाशक्ति ततः कार्यं ध्यातं[७] मन्त्रप्रकाशितम् ।
प्रधानजप्यमन्त्रार्थस्तस्मादत्राभिधीयते ॥ २७५ ॥
एतमक्षरमेतां च जपन्[८] व्याहृतिपूर्विकाम् ।
सन्ध्यामोमिति[९] निर्देषान्मन्त्रो[१०] जप्यस्तथाविधः ॥ २७६ ॥

१.MT °गमार्च्चार्य°. २.M °सामान्या. ३.M समपित बाध्य°. ४.M ओङ्कारल°. ५.M °णानुवात्वेवं. ६.M विद्यायावत्करोम्येतद्, T विद्याया यत्क°. ७.M ध्यानमन्त्र°. ८.M जप्य. ९.MT सन्ध्यायोमि°. १०.M निर्दिशोमन्त्रो.

एकाक्षरोऽयं[१] प्रणवस्त्र्यक्षरः स्मृतिदर्शितः[२] ।
अकारः[३] प्रथमस्तत्र तदर्थोऽयममी श्रुताः ॥ २७७ ॥
ऋक् पृथिव्यग्निभूर्ब्रह्मजाग्रद्[४]गेहेशवह्नयः ।
प्राणश्च प्रातःसवनमुकारस्तु द्वितीयकः ॥ २७८ ॥
अन्तरिक्षयजुर्वेदवायुदक्षिणवह्नयः ।
भुवोऽपान[५]स्वप्नवृत्तिर्विष्णुर्मध्यन्दिनस्त्वमी ॥ २७९ ॥
उकारमात्रया ध्येया मकारस्तु तृतीयकः ।
द्यौरादित्यः सामवेदः पूर्वाग्नि[६]व्यानशङ्कराः ॥ २८० ॥
तृतीयसवनं स्वश्च सुषुप्तिश्चेति तद्गताः[७] ।
एतैरेव जगत्सर्वं भिद्यते प्रणवोद्भवैः ॥ २८१ ॥
[८]अत आ.कार[८] एवेदं जगद् ब्रह्मणि युज्यते ।
आ. तद्ब्रह्मेति[९] निर्देशात्सोऽहमित्योमितीरितम्[१०] ॥ २८२ ॥
एवं च निष्कलं शुद्धं नित्यमुक्तं[११] निरञ्जनम्[१२] ।
अद्वयं सच्चिदानन्दं [१३]ब्रह्मास्म्यहमितीरितम् ॥ २८३ ॥
त्रिमात्रो[१४]ऽसौ प्रयोक्तव्यः स्वाध्यायादिषु कर्मसु ।
अर्धम् गातिरिक्तः[१५] स मध्याह्ने[१६] विनियुज्यते ॥ २८४ ॥
तैलधा गाच्छिन्नं[१७] दीर्घमर्णो निनादवत्[१८] ।
अवाप्तं प्रणवस्याग्रं यस्तं वेद स वेदवित् ॥ २८५ ॥

[व्याहृतिरहस्यम्]

यदेतदद्वयं ब्रह्म प्रणवप्रतिपादितम्[१९] ।
भूरित्यनेन [२०]तस्यैव विद्यमानत्वमुच्यते[२०] ॥ २८६ ॥

१.M एकाक्षरयोयं. २.MT दर्शितम्. ३.M अकारं. ४.M °मूर्ब्रह्म जाग्रत. ५.MT °भुवो वा न. ६.M पूर्वाणि. ७.M ते गताः. ८-८.M सततं धार. ९.M तन्तद्ब्रह्मे°. १०.M सोह मित्यामि°. ११.T नित्यमुक्तनि°. १२.M निरञ्चनम्. १३.MT नन्दब्रह्मा°. १४.M रात्रिमात्रे°. १५.M मात्रादिरिक्तेस्स,T °मिरिक्ते. १६.M मध्याने. १७.T °धारा...च्छिन्न, M °च्छिन्न. १८.M दीर्घं घण्टनि°,T दीर्घंम°. १९.T प्रणवप्रतिपदितम्. २०-२०.M सस्यै रविद्यमानत्व°.

भूरादेः[1] प्रणवात्मत्वात् तासां ब्रह्मार्थता यतः ।
सत्तायां भूरिति प्राहुरसत्वं न ततोऽस्य हि ॥ २८७ ॥
विनाशिकार्यसंघस्य[2] कारणं नित्यमिष्यते ।
घटादेर्मृत्तिका यद्वद् भुव इत्यत उच्यते ॥ २८८ ॥
तस्मात्सर्वाणि भूतानि भवन्तीति भुवः पदम् ।
जगत्कारणतां तस्य ब्रवीति ब्रह्मणः सतः[3] ॥ २८९ ॥
'तस्मादात्मन आकाशः संभूत' इति हि श्रुतिः ।
अनादिमध्यनिधनाविद्यासंरूषितात्मनः ॥ २९० ॥
ब्रह्मणो जायते व्योम तिमिरादिव चन्द्रिका ।
मायापि जगदुत्पाद्य माययैवेश्वेरच्छया[4] ॥ २९१ ॥
सर्पादीन् कल्पितान् स्रग्वत्[5] प्रविष्टस्तद्वतः सुवः ।
'तत्सृष्ट्वा प्राविशत्सृष्ट'मित्याद्या श्रूयते श्रुतिः ॥ २९२ ॥
सुखदुःखान्यवाप्नोतीत्यात्मैव सुवरुच्यते[6] ।
चिद्रूपः सर्वभूतेषु वेत्ता लब्धा च[7] शासिता ॥ २९३ ॥
कर्ता भोक्ता विभुर्नित्यो[8] निश्चलो यः प्रकाशते ।
आनन्दं वाहयत्येष[9] ज्ञात[10]स्वात्मतयेश्वरः ॥ २९४ ॥
[11]द्युमणिर्वास्तवस्तस्मांद् दीप्तिमत्वादिलक्षितः ।
अतो ब्रह्मात्मता[12] सर्वजगतो व्याहृतीरिता ॥ २९५ ॥
'ब्रह्माहमस्मी'त्येषोऽर्थो व्याहृतीनां भवेदतः ।
पूर्वोक्तो विस्तरेणार्थो गायत्र्याः प्रतिपाद्यते ॥ २९६ ॥

[गायत्रीमन्त्रार्थः]

यद् भर्गो भजनीयं तद्धीमहीतीह योजना ।
कस्य स्वभूतं देवस्य द्योतमानस्य कस्य तत् ॥ २९७ ॥

१.M भूमादेः. २.M बिना त्रिकाय संघ°. ३.M स्वतः. ४.T °वेश्वरेश्वरः. ५.M स्रग्वन्. ६.MT सुवमुच्यते. ७.M वशा°. ८.M स्थित्यो. ९.M वा वहत्येषु. १०.M ज्ञातः. ११.M द्युमणीर्वा°. १२.M ब्रह्मता.

सवितुः स्वेन भासाऽसौ बिभर्ति द्योतयञ्जगत् ।
वरेण्यं वरणीयं[१] तत् प्रार्थनीयं मुमुक्षुभिः ॥ २९८ ॥
ईदृशः सविता यस्मात् तस्मादात्मतया[२] यतः ।
स्थितोऽपरोक्षो नोऽस्माकं कार्यसंघस्य यद्धियः ॥ २९९ ॥
धर्मार्थकाममोक्षार्थश्रुतिस्मृत्युक्तकर्मसु ।
प्रचोदयान्नित्यमेव चोदयत्येष ईश्वरः ॥ ३०० ॥
अध्याहारं विनाप्यर्थो[३] युज्यते यत्तदीरितः[४] ।
दृष्टयोर्व्यत्ययेनापि विभक्तेः कथमुच्यते ॥ ३०१ ॥
योऽन्तर्यामीश्वरो[५] नित्य आत्मत्वेनात्मनि स्थितः ।
अपरोक्षोऽर्करूपेण भासयन्[६] दिविविष्ठितः[६] ॥ ३०२ ॥
अनादिमध्यनिधना[७]विद्यासंरूषितात्मनाम् ।
अस्माकं कार्यकरणसंघानां प्रतिनाशिनाम् ॥ ३०३ ॥
धियो नियुङ्क्ते धर्मादिगोचरा अनिशं विभुः ।
अस्य[८] स्वभूतिं[९] सवितुः कार्यसंघप्रसूतिनः ॥ ३०४ ॥
संसारोच्छेदकं[१०] भर्गो मण्डलान्तर्गतं परम्[११] ।
हीनताररहितज्योतिः सर्वकल्याणकृत्तमम् ॥ ३०५ ॥
सुसूक्ष्मं सच्चिदानन्दं पुरुषं पूर्णमद्वयम् ।
देवस्य द्योतमानस्य राजमानं स्वतस्ततः ॥ ३०६ ॥
वरेण्यं चिन्तयामोऽस्मद्धृदि स्वात्मतयाऽनिशम् ॥ ३०६क ॥

[दशप्रणवसंयुक्तगायत्र्यर्थः]

दशप्रणवसंयुक्ता या गायत्री शिरोऽन्विता[१२] ।
शङ्करोदितमार्गेण तस्या [१३]अर्थोऽधुनोच्यते ॥ ३०७ ॥
भूपदाद्या व्याहृतयो भूशब्दस्तदिह[१४] वर्तते ।

१.M वरीरणीयं, T यरीरणीयं. २.M कस्मा°. ३.M °व्यर्थो. ४.M °रिह. ५.T °मीयतो. ६-६.M भासयन्ति दिविष्ठितः. ७.M °मन्ध्यदिनादि. ८.T सस्य. ९.M स्वभूतं. १०.M °च्छेदिकं. ११.M चरम. १२.MT ऽन्विताः. १३.M तस्यार्थो°. १४ M °शब्दस्तदिह°, T शब्दस्त...वतंतै.

तत्पदं सदिति[१] प्रोक्तं तन्मात्रत्वं[२] तु भूरतः[३] ॥ ३०८ ॥
भूतत्वात् कारणत्वाच्च भुवः शब्दस्य संगतिः ।
सर्वस्वीकरणात् स्वात्मतया सुवरितीरितम्[४] ॥ ३०९ ॥
महत्त्वाच्च महस्त्वाच्च महः शब्दः समीरितः ।
तदेव सर्वजनता तस्मात्तु व्याहृतिर्जनः[५] ॥ ३१० ॥
तपो ज्ञानतया चैव तथा तापतया[६] स्मृतम् ।
सत्यं परत्वादात्मत्वादनन्तज्ञानतः स्मृतम् ॥ ३११ ॥

[प्रणवस्य व्याहृतीनामात्मसंबन्धः]

प्रणवस्य व्याहृतीनामात्मसंबन्ध[७] उच्यते ।
अकारो भूरुकारस्तु भुवो मार्णः स्वरीरितः ॥ ३१२ ॥
बिन्दुर्महस्तथात्मादौ[८] जनः शक्तिस्तपस्तथा ।
शान्तिः सत्यमिति प्रोक्तं यत्तत्[९] परिकरं[९] पदम् ॥ ३१३ ॥

[व्याहृतीनां प्रणवस्य च गायत्र्यैक्यसंबन्धः]

प्रणवस्य[१०] व्याहृतीनां गायत्र्यैक्यमथोच्यते ।
अत्रापि तत्पदं पूर्वं प्रोक्तं तदनुवर्ण्यते ॥ ३१४ ॥
[११]तद्विहितैकवचनमनेनाखिलवस्तुनः ॥ ३१४क ॥
सृष्ट्यादिकारणं तेजोरूपमादित्यमण्डले[१२] ।
अभिध्येयं सदानन्दं परं ब्रह्माभिधीयते ॥ ३१५ ॥
[१३]यत्तत्सवितुरित्युक्तं [१४]षष्ठ्येकवचनात्मकम् ।
धातोरिह विनिष्पन्नं प्राणिप्रसववाचकात् ॥ ३१६ ॥
[१५]सर्वासां प्राणिजातीनामेव[१५] प्रसवितुः सदा ।
वरेण्यं वरणीयत्वात्सेवनीयतया तथा ॥ ३१७ ॥
[१६]भजनीयतया सर्वैः प्रार्थनीयतया स्मृतम् ।

१.M सभिस्ति. २.T तन्मात्रं. ३.M भूरयः. ४.M सुवरीरितम्, T सुपरिकीर्तितम्. ५.T जनम्. ६.M तावत्तया, T तापकतया. ७.T °तीनां...मस्सम्बन्ध. ८.T तथास्मादौ. ९-९.M यच्च तच्चरतरं. १०.M प्राणस्य. ११.M तद्वितैव, T तद्वि...वचन°. १२.M रूपादित्य°. १३.M यन्तत्स°. १४.M षष्ठ्यैक°. १५-१५.M सर्वासामेव प्राणीनामेव. १६.M oms.

पूर्वस्याष्टाक्षरस्यैवं व्याहृतिर्भूरिति स्मृताः ॥ ३१८ ॥
पापस्य भर्जनाद् भर्गो भक्तस्निग्धतया तथा[१] ॥ ३१८क ॥
देवस्य वृष्टिदानादिगुणयुक्तस्य नित्यशः ।
प्रभूतेन प्रकाशेन दीप्यमानस्य या तथा ॥ ३१९ ॥
'ध्यै चिन्तायाम्'मतो[२] धातो[३]र्निष्पन्नं धीमहीत्यतः ।
निगमाद्येन नित्येन[४] विद्यारूपेण चक्षुषा ॥ ३२० ॥
दृश्यो हिरण्ययो देव आदित्ये नित्यसंस्थितः ।
हीनतारहितं[५] तेजो यस्य स्यात्स हिरण्मयः ॥ ३२१ ॥
यः[६] सूक्ष्मः सोऽहमित्येवं[६] चिन्तयामः सदैव तु ।
द्वितीयाष्टाक्षरस्यैवं व्याहृतिर्भुव ईरिता[७] ॥ ३२२ ॥
धियो बुद्धिर्मनोरस्य[८] च्छान्दसत्वात्स ईरितः ।
कृतश्च लिङ्गव्यत्यासः सूत्रात्सुप्तिषु च ग्रहात् ॥ ३२३ ॥
यत्तु तेजो निरुपमं सर्ववेदमयात्मकम् ।
भजतां पापनाशस्य हेतुभूतमिहोच्यते ॥ ३२४ ॥
[९]न इति प्रोक्त आदेशः षष्ठ्यसौ युष्मदस्मदोः ।
[१०]तस्मादस्माकमित्यर्थः प्रार्थनायां[११] प्रचोदयात् ॥ ३२५ ॥
तृतीयाष्टाक्षरस्यापि व्याहृतिः स्वरितीरिता[१२] ।
एवं [१३]दशपदान्यस्यास्त्रयश्चाष्टाक्षराः स्मृताः ॥ ३२६ ॥
षडक्षराश्च चत्वारः स्युश्चतुर्विंशदक्षराः ।
इत्थंभूतं यदेतस्य देवस्य सवितुर्विभोः ॥ ३२७ ॥
वरेण्यं भजतां पापविनाशनकरं परम् ।
भर्गोऽस्माकमभिध्यातं धियस्तन्नः प्रचोदयात् ॥ ३२८ ॥

[गायत्रीशिरसोऽर्थः]

उक्तैवमत्र गायत्री पुनस्तच्छिर उच्यते ।

१.M oms. २.M चिन्ताया अतो, T चिन्तायां मतो. ३.M धीतो. ४.M निर्व्येन, T निर्व्त्येन. ५.T रहितस्तेजो. ६-६.M सूक्ष्म सोममित्येवं. ७.M ईरितः. ८.M °रस्या. ९.M oms. १०.M तस्मादस्मादहमित्यर्थः. ११.M प्रार्थनाय. १२.MT °रिताः. १३.M °पदान्त्यस्या°.

'आपो ज्योती रस' इति सोमाग्न्योस्तेज उच्यते ॥ ३२९ ॥
तदात्मकं जगत्सर्वं रसस्तेजोद्वयं युतम् ।
अमृतं तदनाशित्वाद् बृहत्वाद् ब्रह्म गद्यते ॥ ३३० ॥
यदानन्दात्मकं ब्रह्म [1]सत्यं ज्ञानमनादि तत्[1] ।
भूर्भुवः [2]सुवरित्युक्तं सोऽहमित्योमुदाहृतम् ॥ ३३१ ॥
एतत्तु वेदसारस्य शिरस्त्वाच्छिर[3] उच्यते ।
लक्षणैरिति निर्दिष्टे वेदसारे सुनिष्ठितः ॥ ३३२ ॥

[गायत्रीजपफलम्]

फलार्थी तदवाप्नोति मुमुक्षुर्मोक्षमिच्छति ।
बहुधाऽस्या वदन्त्यर्थं मुनयस्तत्त्वदर्शिनः ॥ ३३३ ॥
सर्वथा पुरुषो नित्यः 'सोऽहमस्मी'ति भावयेत् ।
'हिरण्मयेन पात्रेणे'[4]त्याद्या बह्वयो[5] यतः[6] श्रुताः ॥ ३३४ ॥
निष्कलोपासनाशक्तौ ध्यायेदर्कस्थमीश्वरम्[7] ।
ब्रह्माणं शंकरं विष्णुं क्रमात्सन्ध्यासु[8] संयमी ॥ ३३५ ॥
विष्णुरेवाथवा ध्येयः सर्वसन्ध्यासु शक्तितः ॥ ३३५क ॥
ध्येयः सदा सवितृमण्डलमध्यवर्ती
नारायणः सरसिजासनसन्निविष्टः ।
केयूरवान्मकरकुण्डलवान् किरीटी
[9]हारिहिरण्मयवपुर्धृतशंखचक्रः ॥ ३३६ ॥
केचिज्जपस्य प्राधान्यं मन्यते [10]धृतितः स्मृतौ[10] ।
[11]न च[11] स्वाध्याय इत्यादि [12]बहुधा श्रूयते[12] श्रुता॥ ३३७ ॥
योऽधीतेऽहन्यहन्येतां[13] त्रीणि वर्षाण्यतन्द्रितः ।
स ब्रह्म परमभ्येति[14] पर्यभूतः[15] खमूर्तिमान् ॥ ३३८ ॥

१-१.MT सत्यज्ञानदि. २.MT स्वरि°. ३.M शिवस्त्वा°. ४.M वात्रेण. ५.M बाह्यो. ६.M यत. ७.M स्थायेदर्कसमीश्वरम्, T स्थायेदर्क. ८.M सन्ध्या तु. ९.T हारी. १०-१०.M श्रुति च स्मृतौ; T स्मृतो. ११-११.M तच्च. १२-१२.T बहु यच्छ्रूयते. १३.M oms एतां. १४.M °भ्यैति. १५.M °भूतं,T वर्य°.

[1]जप्येनैव हि[1] संसिध्येद् ब्राह्मणो नात्र संशयः ।
कुर्यादन्यं न वा कुर्यान्मन्त्रो ब्राह्मण उच्यते ॥ ३३९ ॥
पूर्वां सन्ध्यां जपेत्तिष्ठन्नासीनः पश्चिमां तथा ।
[2]रात्र्यन्तयामनाडी द्वे सन्ध्यादिकाल उच्यते ॥ ३४० ॥

[सन्ध्याप्रयोगः]

दर्शनाद्रविरेखायास्तदन्तो मुनिभिः स्मृतः ।
प्रयोगमधुना वक्ष्ये स्नात्वाचान्तो यथोदितम् ॥ ३४१ ॥
'प्रातः सन्ध्यामुपासिष्य' इति संकल्प्य वाग्यतः ।
'सूर्यश्चे'ति सकृत्पीत्वा मन्त्रहीनमथेतरत् ॥ ३४२ ॥
साङ्गमाचमनं कृत्वा त्रिर्जपेद् द्विपदामृचम् ।
प्राणानायम्य विधिवद् 'दधिक्राविण्ण' इत्यृचा ॥ ३४३ ॥
पवित्रदर्भपाणिः सन्नब्लिङ्गाभिश्च[3] मार्जयेत्[4] ।
धाराच्युतेन तोयेन सन्ध्योपास्तिर्विगर्हिता ॥ ३४४ ॥
मन्त्रपूतं जलं यस्मा'दापोहिष्ठा'भिमन्त्रितम् ।
पतत्यशुचिदेशे तु तस्मात्तत्परिवर्जयेत् ॥ ३४५ ॥
नद्यां[5] तीर्थे ह्रदे वापि सौवर्णे[6] दारुसंभवे ।
ताम्रे वा राजते पात्रे जलमानीय तेन तु ॥ ३४६ ॥
मार्जनादि समाम्नातं कुर्यान्नित्यमिति स्मृतम् ॥ ३४६क ॥
ऋगन्ते मार्जनं कुर्यात्पादान्ते वा समाहितः ।
तृचस्यान्तेऽथवा कुर्याच्छिष्टानां मतमीदृशम् ॥ ३४७ ॥
'आपोहिष्ठे'ति तिसृभिर्ऋग्भिः[7] संप्रयतः शुचिः ।
[8]नवप्रणवयुक्ताभिर्जलं[8] शिरसि [9]निक्षिपेत् ॥ ३४८ ॥
विप्रुषोऽष्टौ क्षिपेदूर्ध्वमधो 'यस्य क्षया'दिना ।
[10]संवत्सरकृतं पापं मार्जनान्ते विनश्यति ॥ ३४९ ॥

१-१.T °नैवति. २.M रात्र्यन्धयामनाडि°. ३.M °सन्नाभिं गाभिश्च. ४.M मर्ज्जयेत्. ५.M नद्यास्तीर्थे. ६.M सोवर्णे. ७.M °रद्भि स्सं°. ८-८.MT न च प्रणव°. ९.M निर्दहेतिति. १०.MT om.

रजस्तमो[१]मोहजाताञ्जाग्रत्स्वप्नसुषुप्तिजान् ।
वाङ्मनःकर्मजानेतान्नवभिर्निर्दहेदिति ॥ ३५० ॥
अभ्युक्ष्य शुद्धदेहः सन् गृहीत्वाञ्जलिना जलम् ।
आदित्याभिमुखस्तिष्ठन् तद्गतात्मोर्ध्वलोचनः ॥ ३५१ ॥
वेदसारं परं ज्योतिर्मूलभूतं परात्परम् ।
हृत्स्थं सर्वस्य लोकस्य मण्डलान्तर्व्यवस्थितम् ॥ ३५२ ॥
चिन्तयन् परमात्मानं सुगन्धिकुसुमान्वितः ।
प्रणवव्याहृतियुतगायत्र्या मन्त्रिता अपः ॥ ३५३ ॥
सकृदेव क्षिपेदूर्ध्वमविशेषेण हि श्रुतिः ।
एनस्ताः प्रति निघ्नन्ति जगदाप्याययन्ति च ॥ ३५४ ॥
'यव यवे'तिमन्त्रं[२] च जपित्वा क्षालयेत्करौ ।
'भर्गोऽसी'ति हिरण्यादिविधेमान्तमनु[३] जपन् ॥ ३५५ ॥
प्रदक्षिणं परिक्रम्या'प्या. ब्रह्मे'त्यादि मन्त्रवत् ।
उपविश्'या. तमि'त्यादि मन्त्राभ्यां च करौ क्रमात् ॥ ३५६ ॥
प्रक्षाल्य दद्यादर्घ्यं 'हिरण्यगर्भा'दिमन्त्रतः ।
'आयातु वरदा देवी'त्यमुना चाथ तर्पयेत् ॥ ३५७ ॥
'सवितारं तर्पयामि ब्रह्मरूपिणमेव च ।
भूः पूर्वपुरुषं तद्वदृङ्मयं मण्डलाधिपम्' ॥ ३५८ ॥
'आत्मान'मित्यथाचम्य स्थलशुध्यर्थमंभसा ॥ ३५८क ॥
'उत्क्रमन्तु पिशाचा ये भूता ये भूमिहारकाः ।
सर्वविघ्नकराः पुंसां ब्रह्मकर्म समारभे' ॥ ३५९ ॥
विशुद्धभूमिं प्रोक्ष्यात्र प्राक्कूलेषु तृणेषु च ।
आस्थितः प्राङ्मुखो मौनी नियतेन्द्रियमानसः ॥ ३६० ॥
[४]मार्जनात्तु बहिः शुद्धिराभ्यन्तरविशुद्धये ।
त्र्य[गर्थ][५]ज्ञानसहितं प्राणायामत्रयं चरेत् ॥ ३६१ ॥

१.M मोहजाताजा°. २. MT आयवायव्यमन्त्रं. ३.T °मान्तं मनुं. ४.MT °नाप्त बहिः. ५.MT broken.

गायत्रीं शिरसा सार्धं जपेद् व्याहृतिपूर्विकाम् ।
प्रतिप्रणवसंयुक्तां[1] त्रिरयं[2] प्राणसंयमः ॥ ३६२ ॥
प्रणवस्य मुनिर्ज्ञेयः परमेष्ठी प्रजापतिः ।
च्छन्दस्तु देवी गायत्री परमात्मा च देवता ॥ ३६३ ॥
जमदग्निभरद्वाजभृगुगौतमकाश्यपाः[3] ।
विश्वामित्रवसिष्ठाख्यावृषयो व्याहृतीरिताः ॥ ३६४ ॥
गायत्र्युष्णिगनुष्टुप् च बृहती पङ्क्तिरेव च ।
त्रिष्टुब्जगत्यौ च्छन्दांसि कथ्यन्ते देवता अपि ॥ ३६५ ॥
सप्तार्चिरनिलः सूर्यो वाक्पतिर्वरुणो वृषा ।
विश्वेदेवा इति प्रोक्ताः सप्तव्याहृतिदेवताः ॥ ३६६ ॥
विश्वामित्रस्तु गायत्र्या ऋषिश्छन्दः स्वयं स्मृतम् ।
सविताऽस्या[4] देवता च ब्रह्मा शिर ऋषिः स्मृतः ॥ ३६७ ॥
च्छन्दश्च दैवी गायत्री परमात्मा च देवता ।
यथोदितेन मार्गेण शक्त्या प्रणवमभ्यसन् ॥ ३६८ ॥
ध्यायेद् ब्रह्माथ[5] गायत्रीं मन्त्रार्थगतमानसः ।
सप्तव्याहृतिसंयुक्तां शिरसा च समन्विताम् ॥ ३६९ ॥
त्रिर्जपित्वाथ योऽस्माकं धिय इत्यादिकाञ्जपेत्[6] ।
यो देवः सविताऽस्माकं धियो धर्मादिगोचराः ॥ ३७० ॥
प्रेरयेदस्य यद् भर्गस्तद्वरेण्यमुपास्महे ।
तुरीयपादसंयुक्तां व्याहृतिप्रणवान्विताम् ॥ ३७१ ॥
जपेत्तुरीयपादं[7] तु 'परो[8] रजसि सावदोम्' ।
महावाक्यानि संजप्य[9] चर्ष्यादिन्यासपूर्वकम्[10] ॥ ३७२ ॥
सहस्रकृत्वो गायत्रीं शतकृत्वो दशापराम् ।
अमितं वा समभ्यस्येत्तृणपाणिर्यथोदितम् ॥ ३७३ ॥

१.M °प्रणमसं°,T प्रतिप्रतिमसं°.२.M मत्रिरयं. ३.MT काश्यपः. ४.MT स्याद्देव°. ५.M °येद्ब्राथ. ६.M इत्यधिताञ्ज°. ७.M °पादस्तु. ८.M वरो. ९.M संज्ञप्य. १०.M ष्यादीन्यास°, T °जप्यर्ष्यादि°.

दृष्टेऽर्के तमुपस्थाय परिक्रम्य प्रणम्य च ।
गत्वा गृहं स्वपत्न्यादि मार्जनालेपनादिकम्[१] ॥ ३७४ ॥
विहृताग्निः परिस्तीर्य हुत्वा व्रीहीन्यथोदितम् ।
उपासीत स्वयं होमे मुख्यः पुत्रो[२]ऽपि शिष्यकः ॥ ३७५ ॥
गुरुर्भ्राता भागिनेय ऋत्विजो विट्पतिस्तथा ।
सावित्रान् रौद्रमन्त्रांश्च हुत्वाऽग्निं शक्तितो जपेत् ॥ ३७६ ॥
गायत्रीं त्रिष्टुभं शक्त्या 'हंसः शुचिषदि'त्यृचम् ।
त्र्यम्बकं 'पौरुषं सूक्तं' विरजामृत्युमाङ्गलम्[३] ॥ ३७७ ॥
कूष्माण्डीः पावमानीश्च शिवसंकल्पमेव च ।
'अग्ने नया'दिकं[४] मन्त्रं द्रुपदामघमर्षणम्[५] ॥ ३७८ ॥
पावनानि तथान्यानि जपेद् विग्रहशुद्धये ।
विद्याकराँ श्रीकराँश्च धर्मदान्मोक्षदानपि ॥ ३७९ ॥
ऋग्यजुःसामसंभूताञ्जपेदायुष्करानपि ।
दशवारं[६] वाष्टशतमग्निहोत्रे जपेत्ततः ॥ ३८० ॥
हुत्वाग्निहोत्रं विधिवदुपास्याग्नीन्समाहितः ।
सावित्रीं शक्तितो दत्त्वा दीर्घसन्ध्यत्वसिद्धये ॥ ३८१ ॥
ततः सूर्यमुपस्थाय जपेज्जप्यान् यथोदितान् ।
मङ्गलार्थानि[७] कर्माणि ततः कुर्याद्यथाविधि ॥ ३८२ ॥
रोचनां चन्दनं होमं मृदङ्गं[८] दर्पणं[९] मणिम् ।
गुरूनग्निं च विप्रांश्च सर्पीरादित्यमप्यपः ॥ ३८३ ॥
पश्येत्प्रदक्षिणं कुर्यादश्वत्थं च तथा स्पृशेत् ।
उपगम्य गुरून् सर्वान् विप्रांश्चाप्यभिवादयेत् ॥ ३८४ ॥
गोभ्यश्च यवसं दद्याद् गोमतीश्च[१०] तथा जपेत् ।
दूर्वाः[११] समालभेत् 'काण्डात्काण्डादि'त्यादिमन्त्रतः ॥ ३८५॥

१.T लेपनेऽधिकम्. २.M मुख्य...त्रो, T पुत्रो विशि°. ३.M लाङ्गलम्. ४.M अग्नेऽग्नया° ५.M °मर्षणीम्. ६.M दशाकरा. ७.M मङ्गलत्वानि. ८.M मृदङ्गां. ९.M दर्पणिं. १०.M गोमतीं च. ११.M दूर्वात्.

तिसृभिस्तिसृभिस्ताभिः 'क्षुत्पिपासा'दिना मुखम् ।
संमृज्य त्रिरुपस्पृश्य 'गन्धद्वारे'ति मूर्धनि ॥ ३८६ ॥
'सहस्रपरमा दूर्वे' इत्येतैर्विन्यसेत्पृथक् ।
'काण्डादि'त्यादिनाघ्राय चाञ्ज्यादपि च लोचने ॥ ३८७ ॥
'दूर्वे अमृतसंभूते शतपत्रे शताङ्कुरे ।
शतं हन्सि[1] च पापानि शतमायुश्च वर्धय' ॥ ३८८ ॥

[वेदशास्त्राध्ययनम्]

वेदाभ्यासं[2] ततः कुर्यात् प्रयत्नच्छन्दितो द्विजः ।
वेदार्थानधिगच्छेत शास्त्राणि विविधानि च ॥ ३८९ ॥

[दिनस्य तृतीयभागे पोष्यवर्गार्थसाधनम्]

तृतीये च ततो भागे [3]पोष्यवर्गार्थसाधनम् ।
माता पिता गुरुर्भार्या प्रजा दीनः[4] समाहितः ॥ ३९० ॥
अभ्यागतोऽतिथिश्चाग्निः[5] पोष्यवर्ग उदाहृतः ॥ ३९०क ॥
भरणं पोष्यवर्गस्य प्रशस्तं स्वर्गसाधनम् ।
नरकं[6] पीडने तस्य तस्माद्यत्नेन तं भरेत् ॥ ३९१ ॥
यात्रामात्रप्रसिध्यर्थं स्वैः कर्मभिरगर्हितैः ।
अक्लेशेन शरीरस्य कुर्वीत धनसंचयम् ॥ ३९२ ॥
सप्त वित्तागमा धर्म्या दायो लाभः[7] क्रयो जयः ।
प्रयोगः कर्मयोगश्च सत्प्रतिग्रह[8] एव च ॥ ३९३ ॥
ऋतामृताभ्यां[9] जीवेत मृतेन प्रमृतेन वा ।
सत्यानृताभ्यामपि[10]वा न श्ववृत्त्या[11] कथञ्चन ॥ ३९४ ॥
ऋतमुञ्छशिलं[12] ज्ञेयममृतं[13] स्यादयाचितम् ।
मृतं तु याचितं भैक्षं प्रमृतं कर्षणं स्मृतम् ॥ ३९५ ॥

१.MT हन्ति. २.M °भ्यासा. ३.MT चोष्य°. ४.T प्रजाधीनः. ५.M °गतोति...श्चाग्निः. ६.M नरकः. ७.MT लोभः. ८.MT संप्रति°. ९.M ऋतांमृता°. १०.M °भ्यां वि, T सत्यार्ज्यं तेन चै वापि and thereafter text broken up to जीव्यते (Verse 398). ११.M श्चवृ°. १२.M तमुञ्छसिलं. १३.M ज्ञेयं मृतं.

सत्यानृतं तु वाणिज्यं तेन चैवापि जीव्यते[१] ।
सेवा श्ववृत्तिर्व्याख्याता[२] तस्मात्तां[३] परिवर्जयेत् ॥ ३९६ ॥
कुसूलकुंभीधान्यो वा त्र्यैहिकोऽश्व[४]स्तनोऽपि वा ।
जीवेद्वापि शिलोञ्छेन[५] श्रेयानेषां परं परम् ॥ ३९७ ॥
राजानं चाधिगच्छेत योगक्षेमार्थसिद्धये ।

[दिनस्य तुरीयभागे विहितकर्माणि]

चतुर्थे तु ततो भागे[६] स्नानं कुर्यात्तदुच्यते ॥ ३९८ ॥
यथाविध्यप आचम्य मृत्तिकामाहरेच्छुभाम् ।
'अश्वक्रान्ता'दिभिर्मन्त्रै'र्गन्धिद्वारां' जपंस्ततः ॥ ३९९ ॥
तया पूर्ववदङ्गानि विलिप्योत्सृज्य चाम्बरम् ।
[७]परिधायान्यदाचम्य प्रपद्येत जलं ततः ॥ ४०० ॥
'हिरण्यश्रृङ्गं'[८] मन्त्रेण गृहीत्वाञ्जलिना जलम् ।
'सुमित्रा'[९] इति 'दुर्मित्रा'[१०] नैर्ऋत्यां दिशि तज्जलम् ॥ ४०१ ॥
तीरे सन्त्यज्योपस्पृश्य 'यदपां क्रूरमि'त्यपः ।
प्रदक्षिणं त्रिरावृत्य निमज्ज्योन्मृज्य[११] तत्र सन् ॥ ४०२ ॥
'नमोऽग्नय' इति प्रोच्य प्राञ्जलिः पूर्ववत्पितॄन् ।
तर्पयित्वा समाचम्य पुन'राप: पुनन्त्वि'ति ॥ ४०३ ॥
आचम्य दर्भपाणिः 'सुरभिमत्या' तृचेन च ।
[१२]'आपोहिष्ठामया'दिभिर्ऋग्भिश्चतसृभिस्ततः ॥ ४०४ ॥
'हिरण्यवर्णा' 'यासांरा' 'यासां देवा:' शिवेन मा' ।
पवमानानुवाकेन व्याहृतीभिश्च मज्जयेत्[१३] ॥ ४०५ ॥
निमग्नार्धशरीरः स'न्नृतं चे'ति [१४]जपंस्त्रिशः ।
प्राणायामान्धारयित्वा निमज्ज्योन्मज्ज्य[१५] पाथसा ॥ ४०६ ॥

१.M जीर्यते. २.M सर्वाश्चवृत्तिर्व्याख्याता; T °व्याख्याता. ३.MT तत्. ४.M °श्च°. ५.MT सिलो°. ६.M भोगे. ७.M परिधाप्यथाचम्य. ८.M हिरण्यगर्भश्रृभृङ्गं ९.MT add न after सुमित्रा. १०.T इति...त्रां. ११.MT निमज्योन्मज्य. १२.M अपोदिमन्त्राद्यभि°, T अपोदिमन्तदाद्याभिः. १३.M वर्जयेत्. १४.M oms. १५.MT निमज्योन्मज्य.

'प्राणापाना'दिभिर्मन्त्रैर्व्यष्टिभिः[१] पौरुषैरपि ।
'सहस्रशीर्षं देवमि'ति नारायणोदितैः ॥ ४०७ ॥
'विष्णोर्नुका'दिभिः षड्भिः[२] श्रीसूक्तेनापि शक्तितः ।
अभिषिच्य सुसंमृष्टदेहः पूर्ववदेव तु ॥ ४०८ ॥
परिधाय[३] शुभं वासः प्रतिमुच्योत्तरीयकम् ।
आचम्यापः [४]'पुनन्त्वा'द्येनाचम्य सन्नियम्य च ॥ ४०९ ॥
द्रुपदां[५] पूर्ववज्जप्त्वा मार्जयित्वा यथोदितम् ।
अर्घ्यं दत्त्वा 'यवयवे'[६]त्यादि जप्त्वा ततः करौ[७] ॥ ४१० ॥
'उद्वर्गोसी'ति संक्षाल्य 'हंसः शुचिषदि'त्यृचा ।
प्रदक्षिणं प्रक्रिम्य विष्णुसावित्रीमन्त्रतः ॥ ४११ ॥
उपविश्य पाणी संक्षाल्य मन्त्रवत्तर्पयेदिह ।
ब्रह्मशब्दमपोद्धृत्य विष्णुशब्दः प्रयुज्यते ॥ ४१२ ॥
ऋक्पदे भूः पदे चैव[८] यजुर्भुव इति क्षिपेत् ।
आत्मस्थानेऽन्तरात्मेति प्राङ्मुखो वाप्युदङ्मुखः ॥ ४१३ ॥
तृणेष्वासीन आदित्यं ध्यायन्पूर्ववदेव तु ।
[९]सहस्रकृत्वो गायत्रीं शतकृत्वो दशापराम् ॥ ४१४ ॥
अमितं वा समभ्यस्य दत्त्वार्घ्यं पूर्ववद्रविम् ।
उपस्थाय च सौरीभि[१०]रुपविश्याथ तर्पयेत् ॥ ४१५ ॥
अग्निः प्रजापतिः सोम इति बोधायनोदितैः[११] ।
स्नानोदितैर्वा [१२]निष्पीड्य वस्त्रमाचम्य[१२] पूर्ववत्॥ ४१६ ॥
यथोदितं ब्रह्मयज्ञं विधाय तदनन्तरम् ।
'इदं चापि' जपन्नम्बु दद्यादात्मेच्छयादरात् ॥ ४१७ ॥
उपकाराय भूतानां[१३] गृही सर्वाश्रयो यतः ।
देवासुरास्तथा यक्षा नागगन्धर्वराक्षसाः ॥ ४१८ ॥

१.M व्यंष्टिभिः. २.M अकारादिभिः. ३.M परिधायाशुभं. ४.M पुनस्ताद्येना°. ५.T ...पदां. ६.M यव्ये°, T.° त्वाय वायव्ये. ७.M करे. ८.M चैथ, T चेह. ९.M सह कृत्वो. १०.M चमसे... भि°. ११.M बौधा°. १२-१२.M निष्पीड्यप आचम्य. १३.M भूतानं.

पिशाचा गुह्यकाः सिद्धाः कूष्माण्डास्तनुवः खगाः ।
जलेचरा भूनिलया वाय्वाहाराश्च जन्तवः ॥ ४१९ ॥
तृप्तिमेतेन यान्त्वाशु[1] मद्दत्तेनाम्बुनाखिलाः ॥ ४१९क ॥
नरकेषु समस्तेषु यातनासु च ये स्थिताः ।
तेषामाप्यायनायैतद्दीयते सलिलं मया ॥ ४२० ॥
[2]बान्धवा अबान्धवा[2] ये [3]येऽन्यजन्मनि बान्धवाः[3] ।
ते तृप्तिमखिला यान्तु यश्च मत्तोऽभिवाञ्छति ॥ ४२१ ॥
आचम्य च ततो दद्यात् सूर्याय सलिलाञ्जलिम् ॥ ४२१क ॥
'नमो विवस्वते ब्रह्म भास्वते विष्णुतेजसे ।
जगत्पवित्रे शुचये पवित्रे कामदायिने' ॥ ४२२ ॥
ततः पुष्पाञ्जलिं दद्याद् भानवे तद्गतात्मवान् ॥ ४२२क ॥
अत्रोपतिष्ठेदादित्यं 'हंसः शुचिष'दित्यृचा ।
'हिरण्मयेन पात्रेणे'त्यादिमन्त्रेण मन्त्रवत् ॥ ४२३ ॥
'घृणि ब्रह्म प्रपद्ये' चाप्य'हं वृक्षस्य रेरिवा'[4] ।

[नैमित्तिकस्नानम्]

नित्यस्नानं समुद्दिष्टं नैमित्तिकमथोच्यते ॥ ४२४ ॥
दिवाकीर्त्यमुदक्याञ्च पतितं[5] सूतिकां तथा ।
शवं तत्स्पृष्टिनञ्चैव स्पृष्ट्वा स्नानेन शुध्यति ॥ ४२५ ॥
अबुद्धिपूर्वसंस्पर्शे तेषां स्नानं विधीयते ॥ ४२५क ॥
त्रयाणां बुद्धिपूर्वे तु तत्स्पृष्टिन्याय[6]कल्पना ।
उपस्पृशेच्चतुर्थस्तु तदूर्ध्वं प्रोक्षणं स्मृतम् ॥ ४२६ ॥
[7]चण्डालपतितौ दृष्ट्वा नरः पश्येत भास्करम् ।
स्नातस्त्वेतौ समालोक्य सचेलस्नानमाचरेत् ॥ ४२७ ॥

१.M यात्वा°. २-२.MT बान्धवाबान्धवा. ३-३.M ये जन्मनि च बान्धवाः, T wrongly corrected as ये अन्य°. ४.T वृक्षस्य...रिव. ५.M पतितो. ६.M तत्सृष्टिन्यां°, T स्पृष्टिन्या°. ७.M wrongly adds स्मृतं also before चण्डाल°.

यस्तु च्छायां श्वपाकस्य ब्राह्मणो ह्यधिरोहति ।
तत्र स्नानं प्रकुर्वीत घृतं प्राश्य विशुध्यति ॥ ४२८ ॥
एकच्छायां समारूढश्चण्डालादिर्यदा[१] भवेत् ।
ब्राह्मणस्तत्र निवसन्त्स्नानेन[२] शुचितामियात् ॥ ४२९ ॥
[३]तीर्णे संस्तर एकस्मिन्नस्पृश्यैः[४] सह[५] तिष्ठति ।
अस्पृष्टैस्तैरदुष्टोऽस्मीत्येवं[६] मूढस्तु मन्यते[७] ॥ ४३० ॥
चितिं च चितिकाष्ठं च यूपं चण्डालमेव च ।
स्पृष्ट्वा देवलकं चैव सचेलो जलमाविशेत् ॥ ४३१ ॥
देवार्चनपरो विप्रो वित्तार्थी वत्सरत्रयम् ।
स वै देवलको नाम ब्रह्मवादिषु गर्हितः ॥ ४३२ ॥
श्ववराहे[८] [९]खरानुष्ट्रान्वृकगोमायुवानरान् ।
काककुक्कुटगृध्रांश्च पक्षिणश्चाप्यमेध्यता ॥ ४३३ ॥
बौद्धान्पाशुपतान् जैनान् लोकायतिकनास्तिकान् ।
विकर्मस्थान् कापिलांश्च शूद्रांस्पृष्ट्वाविशेज्जलम्॥ ४३४ ॥
रजकव्याधशैलूषवेणुचर्मोपजीविनः ।
निर्णेजकं सौतिकं[१०] च नटं चापि मुखे भगम् ॥ ४३५ ॥
सोमविक्रयिणं [११]वध्यघातिनं ध्वजिनं तथा ।
श्वपाकं [१२]पतितं व्यङ्गमुन्मत्तं शवहारकम् ॥ ४३६ ॥
चूतिकां साविकां नारीं रजसा च परिप्लुताम् ।
अशुद्धान्स्वयमप्येतानशुद्धस्तु यदि स्पृशेत् ॥ ४३७ ॥
[१३]विशुध्यत्युपवासेन तथा कृच्छ्रेण [१४]वा पुनः[१४]॥ ४३७क ॥
नीलीं[१५]नीलीविकारांश्च मानुष्यास्थ्यपि वा पुनः ।
चण्डालपतितच्छायां स्पृष्ट्वा स्नानं समाचरेत् ॥ ४३८ ॥

१.T रूढःश्वच°. २.MT निवासं. ३.T तार्णे. ४.M एतस्मि°. ५.MT सहि. ६.M °त्येव. ७.M मन्यन्ते. ८.T श्ववरोहे. ९.M खलमानुष्ठान्वृकान्, T °वृकगो°. १०.T सौनिकं. ११.M वन्ध्य°. १२.M चतितव्य°. १३.M शुध्य°. १४-१४.M वा पुनः. १५.M नीली.

अजीर्णेऽभ्युदिते वान्तेऽश्रुकर्मणि मैथुने ।
दुःस्वप्ने दुर्जनस्पर्शे स्नानमात्रं विधीयते ॥ ४३९ ॥
स्पृष्ट्वा रुद्रस्य निर्माल्यं सवासा आप्लुतः शुचिः॥ ४३९क ॥
अष्टम्यां च चतुर्दश्यां दिवापर्वणि मैथुनम् ।
कृत्वा सचेलं स्नात्वा तु वारुणीभिश्च मार्जयेत् ॥ ४४० ॥
न स्नानमाचरेद् भुक्त्वा नातुरो न महानिशि ।
न वासोभिः सहाजस्रं नाविज्ञाते जलाशये ॥ ४४१ ॥
राहुदर्शनसंक्रान्तिविवाहात्ययवृद्धिषु ।
स्नानदानादिकं कुर्यान्निशि काम्यव्रतेषु च ॥ ४४२ ॥
विप्रः स्पृष्टो[१] निशायां[२] तूदक्यया पतितेन वा ॥ ४४२क ॥
दिवाहृतं तु यत्तोयं कृत्वा स्वर्णयुतं तु तत् ।
रात्रिस्नाने तु संप्राप्ते [३]स्नायादनलसन्निधौ ॥ ४४३ ॥
दिवाहृतं तु यत्तोयं गृहे यदि न विद्यते ।
प्रज्वाल्याग्निं ततः स्नायान्नदीषु पुष्करणीषु च ॥ ४४४ ॥
स्नानार्थं[४] यो निमित्तेन कृत्वा तोयावगाहनम् ।
आचम्य प्रयतः पश्चात् स्नानं[५] विधिवदाचरेत् ॥ ४४५ ॥
चण्डालादेस्तु संस्पर्शे वारुणं स्नानमाचरेत् ।
इतराणि तु चत्वारि यथा योग्यं स्मृतानि वै ॥ ४४६ ॥
आतुरस्नान उत्पन्ने दशकृत्वो ह्यनातुरः ।
स्नात्वा स्नात्वा स्पृशेदेनं ततः शुध्येत्स आतुरः[६] ॥ ४४७ ॥
स्मृत्याचारं[७] देशकालाद्यनुसारेण नित्यशः ।
स्नानं नैमित्तिकं कुर्यान्निमित्तानन्तता[८] यतः ॥ ४४८ ॥
दृष्टादृष्टफलं काम्यं स्नानं तीर्थादिसेवनम् ।

१.M पुंस्ना, T स्पृंस्ना. २.MT निशाशान्तू°. ३.M स्नामादानल°, T corrected as स्नानादानल. ४.M स्नानार्थे, T स्नानार्हे. ५.M आत्मानं. ६.M शुध्येत्समाचरेत्. ७.M wrongly adds आतुरः before स्मृत्साचारं. ८.M निमित्तानन्ददायतः.

[1]मलापकर्षणाद्यर्थमस्मिनकाले समाचरेत् ॥ ४४९ ॥

[नैमित्तिकतर्पणम्]

देवादितर्पणं सर्वस्नानेषूक्तं समाचरेत् ।
नैमित्तिकमथो वक्ष्ये तर्पणं शास्त्रचोदितम् ॥ ४५० ॥
कृष्णपक्षे चतुर्दश्यामङ्गारकदिनं यदा ।
तदा[2] स्नात्वा शुभे तोये दक्षिणाभिमुखस्तिलैः ॥ ४५१ ॥
पवित्रदर्भपाणिः सन् तर्पयेद्यमनामभिः ।
यमाय धर्मराजाय मृत्यवे चान्तकाय च ॥ ४५२ ॥
वैवस्वताय कालाय सर्वभूतक्षयाय च ।
औदुम्बराय दध्नाय नीलाय परमेष्ठिने ॥ ४५३ ॥
वृकोदराय चित्राय चित्रगुप्ताय वै नमः ।
यमाय नम इत्येवं मन्त्रयोग[3] इहेष्यते ॥ ४५४ ॥
इह जन्मकृतं पापं जन्मान्तरकृतं च यत् ।
अङ्गारकचतुर्दश्यां तर्पयन्स्तद् व्यपोहति[4] ॥ ४५५ ॥

[अब्-अग्नि-हृत्-सूर्य-स्थण्डिल-प्रतिमासु देवतार्चनम्]

कुर्वीत देवतापूजां जपयज्ञादनन्तरम्[5] ।
अप्स्वग्नौ हृदये सूर्ये[6] स्थण्डिले प्रतिमासु वा ॥ ४५६ ॥
अग्नौ क्रियावतां देवो दिवि देवो मनीषिणाम् ।
प्रतिमास्वल्पबुद्धीनां योगिनां हृदये मतः ॥ ४५७ ॥
आपो ह्यायतनं तस्य तस्मात्तासु सदा स्थितः ।
तस्य [7]सर्वगतत्वाच्च स्थण्डिले भावितात्मनाम् ॥ ४५८ ॥
न विष्ण्वाराधनात्पुण्यं विद्यते कर्म वैदिकम् ।
तस्मादनादिमध्यान्तं नित्यमाराधयेद्धरिम् ॥ ४५९ ॥
'तद्विष्णों'रिति मन्त्रेण सूक्तेन पुरुषेण वा ।

१.M मलसदिकर्षणाव्यर्थ°, T °कर्षणार्द्यर्थ...काले. २.M तथा. ३.M मन्त्रहोम. ४.M तर्पयेत्तद्दिने-ष्विति. ५.M जपन्...ज्ञादन°. ६.M आर्ये. ७.M सर्वग्रत°.

नैताभ्यां सदृशो मन्त्रो वेदेषूक्तश्चतुर्ष्वपि[1] ॥ ४६० ॥
अथवा देवमीशानं भगवन्तं सनातनम् ।
आराधयेन्महादेवं भावभूतो महेश्वरम् ॥ ४६१ ॥
मन्त्रेण रुद्रगायत्र्या प्रणवेनाथवा पुनः ।
ईशानेनाथवा रुद्रैस्त्र्यम्बकेण समाहितः ॥ ४६२ ॥
तथा 'नमः शिवाये'ति मन्त्रेणानेन वा यजेत् ॥ ४६२क ॥
[2]येऽर्चयन्ति सदा विष्णुं शंखचक्रगदाधरम् ।
सर्वपापविनिर्मुक्ता ब्रह्माणं[3] प्रविशन्ति ते ॥ ४६३ ॥
यः प्रदद्याद् गवां लक्षं दोग्ध्रीनां वेदपारगे ।
एकाहमर्चयेल्लिङ्गं तस्य पुण्यं ततोऽधिकम् ॥ ४६४ ॥
यो मोहादथवाऽऽलस्यादकृत्वा देवतार्चनम् ।
भुङ्क्ते स याति नरकान् सूकरेष्विह जायते ॥ ४६५ ॥

[देवताराधनविधिः]

अस्मदीयाः पठन्त्येकमाराधनविधिं शुभम् ।
पुंसस्तदनुसारेण [4]परिचर्या प्रदर्श्यते[4] ॥ ४६६ ॥
शोभितांस्तु गृहान्प्राप्य स्वाचान्तः सपवित्रकम् ।
शुचिः शुचौ समे देशे गोमयेनोपलिप्य तु ॥ ४६७ ॥
अलङ्कृतेऽक्षतैः पुष्पैस्तत्रस्थे मङ्गलासने ।
स्वास्तीर्णे मणिलोहादिसंभवं पुरुषोत्तमम् ॥ ४६८ ॥
प्रतिष्ठाप्यानिषिद्धैः[5] सुगन्धिभिः कुसुमाक्षतैः ।
तूष्णीं समर्च्य पुरुषं सौवर्णे राजतेऽपि वा ॥ ४६९ ॥
शंखशुक्त्यादिके पात्रे शुद्धास्तदहरुद्धृताः ।
अपो गन्धवतीः[6] क्षिप्त्वा विकीर्य[7] कुसुमानि च ॥ ४७० ॥
आदायाञ्जलिनोत्क्षिप्य तत्पात्रं सजलं नरम् ।

१.M चतृस्वपि, T चतसृष्वपि. २.M oms ये. ३.M ब्रह्मणं. ४-४.M परिचर्याच्च दृश्यते. ५.M प्रतिष्ठाप्य...षिद्धै°. ६.M °वतीं. ७.M विकीर्ण.

'ओमायात्वि'ति[१]मन्त्रेण सम्यगावाह्य तज्जलम् ॥ ४७१ ॥
देवस्य [२]पुरतस्तूष्णीं निनीयास्यासनोचितान् ।
दर्भान् दत्त्वाऽथ तत्पात्रं गायत्र्याभिमृशेत्ततः ॥ ४७२ ॥
पात्रे प्रक्षालिते तस्मिन्पवित्रे विन्यसेदपः ।
क्षिप्त्वाऽभिमन्त्र्य गायत्र्या सपवित्रं[३] तु तज्जलम्॥ ४७३ ॥
'ओमि'त्यातमितो:[४] सूर्यं दर्शयित्वा जलात्ततः ।
उद्धृत्य पाद्यं त्रीणीति दत्त्वार्घ्याचमनीयके[५] ॥ ४७४ ॥
दत्त्वा व्यपोह्य[६] निर्माल्यं व्याहृतीभिरमुं ततः ।
अब्लिङ्गाभिस्तु[७] तिसृभि'र्ब्रह्मजज्ञानं'मित्यृचा ॥ ४७५ ॥
'कया न'[८] इत्यृचा चा'पो अस्मा'नित्या[९]दिनाम्भसा ।
स्नापयित्वापि चाचामं दत्त्वा देवं प्रदक्षिणम् ॥ ४७६ ॥
परिषिच्योदकुंभेन चान्तरीयोत्तरीयके ।
यज्ञोपवीतं पाद्यं च दत्त्वा साचमनीयकम् ॥ ४७७ ॥
गन्धं दद्या'दिदं विष्णु'रित्यृचाऽथ किरीटके ।
[१०]केयूरकुण्डलहारादिभूषणैर्भूषयेत्ततः ॥ ४७८ ॥
'तद्विष्णो'रिति पुष्पाणि दत्त्वा धूपं च दीपकम् ।
गायत्र्योद्दीप्य मन्त्रेण दत्त्वा साचमनीयकम् ॥ ४७९ ॥
दत्त्वा [११]षष्टिकशाल्यन्नं गव्ये पयसि साधितम् ।
अनिषिद्धदधिमधुमूलमोदकसंयुतम् ॥ ४८० ॥
शोभनव्यञ्जनोपेतमाज्यक्षीरसमन्वितम् ।
शुद्धान्नमाज्यसिक्तं वा सौवर्णे राजतेऽपि वा ॥ ४८१ ॥
कांस्यादौ[१२] भाजने शुद्धे आहृत्य साग्रतः[१३] शुचौ ।
निधा'यामृत'मन्त्रेण दत्त्वा [१४]पानीयमादरात् ॥ ४८२ ॥

१.MT ओमायत्वि°. २.M पुरुषस्तू°. ३.MT सपवित्रस्तु. ४.T ओमित्याकृतितो. ५.M °नीयते. ६.M °प्यपोह्य. ७.M अप्सिंगाभिस्तु. ८.M कायान. ९.M स्मानीत्या°. १०.T oms के. ११. MT षाष्टि° १२.M पाकांस्यादौ. १३.T स्याग्र°. १४.M चानीय°.

'प्राणा'दिभिस्ततो मन्त्रैः पञ्चभिस्तन्निवेदयेत् ।
बोधायनोक्तमन्त्रेण 'देवस्ये'त्यादिनाऽपि वा ॥ ४८३ ॥
कंचित्कालं ततो देवं ध्यात्वा सामृतमन्त्रवत् ।
अपिधानं प्रदायाथ व्यपोह्यैतन्निवेदितम् ॥ ४८४ ॥
क्षालनाचमनं दत्त्वा ताम्बूलाद्यपि शक्तितः ।
दत्त्वा द्वादशभिर्मन्त्रैर्दद्यात्पुष्पाणि नामभिः ॥ ४८५ ॥
नारायणो माधवश्च गोविन्दः केशवस्तथा ।
उरुपूर्वो[१] विक्रमोऽन्यः श्रीधरश्चक्रहस्तकः ॥ ४८६ ॥
लोककर्ता लोकधरो ब्रह्मेत्यन्यो[२] महापुरु[३] ।
[४]षायों भूर्भुवः सुवरों पुरुषाय[५] नमोऽन्तिकाः[६] ॥ ४८७ ॥
चतुर्थ्यन्ता इमे मन्त्राः प्रयोक्तव्या इहार्चने ।
पूर्वोक्तैः केशवाद्यैर्वा दद्यात्पुष्पाणि नामभिः ॥ ४८८ ॥
अथ 'त्रीणि पदे'त्याद्यैः पादैः षोडशभिः क्रमात् ।
'सुमृडीको[७] भवत्व'न्तैर्दद्यात्पुष्पाणि सादरम् ॥ ४८९ ॥
वैष्णवीभिस्तथान्याभिर्ऋग्भिः स्तुत्वा प्रदक्षिणम् ।
परिक्रम्यावनिं प्राप्य जानुभ्यां शिरसा हरिम् ॥ ४९० ॥
नमस्कृत्य[८] 'प्रयात्वा'दि[९] मन्त्रेणोद्वासयेदमुम् ॥ ४९०क ॥

[बोधायनोक्तपूजाविधिः]

अथ बोधायनेनोक्तो [१०]विधिरत्र प्रदर्श्यते ।
पूर्वोक्तमनुसृत्येह विशेषः प्रतिपद्यते ॥ ४९१ ॥
'ओं भूः पुरुष'मित्यादिमन्त्रेणावाहयेदिह ।
अथैनं स्वागतेनाभिनन्दन्ति स्वागतादिना ॥ ४९२ ॥
आसनार्थं ततः कूर्चं दद्याद् 'भगवदा'दिना ।

१.M गुरुपूर्वो. २.M °त्यग्न्यो. ३.M महापुरुषाय. ४.M begins the Pāda with ओं भुर्भुवः°. ५.M पुरुष...श्च, T पुरुषे च. ६.M नमोन्तिताः. ७.T सुमृद्धीका. ८.M नमस्तुत्य. ९.M प्रयात्वाति. १०. See Baudh GS, II.14.1-15.

यश्'चों भू'रादिनावाह्य तूष्णीं दत्त्वा कुशासनम् ॥ ४९३ ॥
पात्राभिमन्त्रणादीनि कृत्वा 'त्रीणि पदे'त्यृचा ।
पाद्यमर्घ्यमि'दं विष्णु'रित्यृचा प्रणवेन वा ॥ ४९४ ॥
'दिवो वा [१]विष्ण'वाचामं दत्त्वा व्याहृतिभिस्ततः ।
व्यपोह्य देवनिर्माल्यं कुशपाणिरमुं ततः ॥ ४९५ ॥
[२]अब्लिङ्गाभि'र्हिरण्या'द्यैः 'पवमानः सुवा'दिभिः ।
मार्जयेद् 'ब्रह्म जज्ञानं'[३] 'कया[४]नश्चित्र' इत्यृचा ॥ ४९६ ॥
यजुषा चापि संस्नाप्य प्रदायाचमनीयकम् ।
अग्रतस्तर्पयेदद्भिः 'केशवा'द्यैः समीरितैः ॥ ४९७ ॥
'भूर्भुवः सुवरि'त्येनं[५] परिषिच्योदकेन तु ।
अन्तरीयोत्तरीये च वाससी प्रणवेन तु ॥ ४९८ ॥
यज्ञोपवीतं सावित्र्या पाद्यमाचमनान्वितम् ।
दत्त्वा गन्धमि'दं विष्णु'रिति दत्त्वाऽथ भूषिते ॥ ४९९ ॥
इरावत्याक्षतं[६] दत्त्वा पुष्पं[७] धूपं[८] च दीपकम्[८] ।
दत्त्वा निवेदयेदन्नं 'देवस्ये'ति यथोदितम् ॥ ५०० ॥
प्रसिद्धैर्नामभिर्दत्त्वा कुसुमानि पृथक् पृथक् ।
'त्रीण्या'दिभिश्च तं स्तुत्वा नमस्कृत्यापि पूर्ववत् ॥ ५०१ ॥
उद्वासये'दों भूरा'द्यै[९]रेतत् सर्वार्थदं स्मृतम् ।
अप्स्वग्नौ च निषिध्येते आवाहनविसर्जने ॥ ५०२ ॥

[पुरुषसूक्तेन पूजाविधिः]

पौरुषेणापि सूक्तेन पूजाविधिरथोच्यते ।
पौरुषं चापि तत्सूक्तं षोडशर्चञ्च बह्वृचम् ॥ ५०३ ॥
आनुष्टुभस्य[१०] सूक्तस्य त्रिष्टुबन्तस्य[११] देवता ।
पुरुषो यो जगद्योनिर्ऋषिर्नारायणः स्मृतः ॥ ५०४ ॥

१.MT विष्णु°. २.M अब्जिगाभि°. ३.T ब्रह्मजित्ज्ञानं. ४.M काया. ५.M °त्यिवं. ६.M इतराक्तत्यक्षतं. ७.M पुष्प. ८-८.M दीपं च धूप्कम्. ९.M भूरेद्यै°. १०.M अनुष्टुतस्य. ११.M त्रिष्टुबस्तस्य.

प्रथमां[1] विन्यसेद्वामे द्वितीयां दक्षिणे करे ।
तृतीयां वामपादे तु चतुर्थीं दक्षिणे तथा ॥ ५०५ ॥
पञ्चमीं वामजंघायां दक्षिणस्यां तथोत्तराम् ।
सप्तमीं वामकट्यां[2] तु दक्षिणायां तथाष्टमीम् ॥ ५०६ ॥
नवमीं नाभिमध्ये तु दशमीं हृदि विन्यसेत् ।
एकादशीं कण्ठदेशे द्वादशीं वामबाहुके ॥ ५०७ ॥
त्रयोदशीं दक्षिणेऽपि चास्यदेशे चतुर्दशीम् ।
अक्ष्णोः पञ्चदशीं न्यस्य षोडशीं मूर्ध्नि विन्यसेत् ॥ ५०८ ॥
यथात्मनि तथा देवे न्यासकर्म समाचरेत् ।
एवं न्यासस्तु कृत्वादौ पश्चाद्देवस्य पूजनम् ॥ ५०९ ॥
गन्धमाल्यैः सुरभिभिरात्मानमर्चयेद् [3]बुधः ।
ततः पीठं समाराध्य गन्धपुष्पाक्षतैः शुभैः ॥ ५१० ॥
आद्ययावाहयेद्देवमृचा तु पुरुषोत्तमम् ।
द्वितीययासनं दद्यात्पाद्यं चैव तृतीयया ॥ ५११ ॥
चतुर्थ्यार्घ्यं प्रदातव्यं पञ्चम्याचमनीयकम् ।
षष्ठ्या स्नानं प्रकुर्वीत सप्तम्या वस्त्रमेव च ॥ ५१२ ॥
यज्ञोपवीतमष्टम्या नवम्या गन्धमेव च ।
दशम्या पुष्पदानं स्यादेकादश्या तु धूपकम् ॥ ५१३ ॥
द्वादश्या तु तथा दीपं त्रयोदश्या चरुं तथा ।
चतुर्दश्या नमः कुर्यात्पञ्चदश्या प्रदक्षिणम् ॥ ५१४ ॥
षोडश्योद्वासनं कुर्याच्छेषमष्टाक्षरेण तु ।
[4]पुष्पाण्यन्वहमेताभिर्ऋग्भिर्दद्यात्समाहितः ॥ ५१५ ॥
अष्टाक्षेरण वा पूजा कार्या विष्णोस्तथा श्रुतिः ॥ ५१५क ॥
पत्रं पुष्पं फलं तोयं यो मे भक्त्या प्रयच्छति ।
तदहं भक्त्युपहृतमश्नामि प्रयतात्मनः ॥ ५१६ ॥

१.M प्रथमं. २.M °कल्यां. ३.M चाप्यर्चयद्. ४.M पुष्पाण्यबहुमेता°.

इत्येतद् भगवानाह भक्तिनम्रोऽर्चयेदतः ॥ ५१६क ॥
यादृशं फलमाप्नोति विष्णुमभ्यर्च्य मानवः ।
महादेवं समभ्यर्च्य तादृशं फलमश्नुते ॥ ५१७ ॥
यथाकामी[1] भवेत्तस्माद् देवयोरनयोर्नरः[2] ॥ ५१७क ॥
शुभमर्चन[3]साध्यं स्यात् फलमेकार्चनेन तु ।
इति बोधायनेनोक्तो[4] विकल्पोऽतोऽर्चने तयोः ॥ ५१८ ॥

[महादेवार्चनविशेषविधिः]

महादेवार्चनं चात्र पुरुषार्चनवन्मुनिः ।
आह बोधायनस्तस्य विशेषः प्रतिपाद्यते[5] ॥ ५१९ ॥
महापुरुष इत्यत्र महादेव इतीरयेत् ॥ ५१९क ॥
'भूर्महारुद्र' इत्यत्र देवमावाह्य पूर्ववत् ।
'सर्वो वै रुद्र' इत्यादि 'नमोऽस्त्व'न्तेन पाद्यकम्[6] ॥ ५२० ॥
दातव्यं प्रणवेनार्घ्यं पाद्यमित्यादिभिस्तु वा ।
स्नाने यथोदिता मन्त्रा 'ब्रह्म जज्ञा'न्तिकास्तथा[7] ॥ ५२१ ॥
'कद्रुद्राये'ति मन्त्रोऽनुवाकः सर्वादिरीरितः[8] ।
'कयानश्चित्र' 'आपो वा इदं सर्वमि'तीरिताः ॥ ५२२ ॥
'भवं देवं' तथा 'शर्वं देव'मित्यष्टभिस्तथा ।
सन्तर्प्य परिषिच्याद्भिश्चान्तरीयोत्तरीयके ॥ ५२३ ॥
उपवीतं च पाद्यादि दत्त्वा [9]व्याहृतिभिस्ततः ।
'सर्वो वै रुद्र' इत्यादिना दत्त्वा गन्धमुत्तमम् ॥ ५२४ ॥
हाराद्यैर्भूषयित्वाऽथ पुष्पं [10]धूपं च दीपकम्[10] ।
तेनैव दद्यादथवा 'नमस्ते रुद्र' इत्यृचा ॥ ५२५ ॥
गन्धं दत्त्वा भूषयित्वा 'सहस्राणी'ति पुष्पकम् ।
'ईशानं त्वा'क्षतं धूपं दीपं पुरुषयागवत् ॥ ५२६ ॥

१.T याथाकामी. २.M °रनयो...रः. ३.MT शुभयार्थ°. ४.M °नोक्तः. ५.M °पद्यते. ६.M पाद्यकक्. ७.M ब्रह्मज्ञन्तिका°,T °जिज्ञान्तिका°. ८. M °रितम्. ९.M oms व्या. १०-१०.M दीपं च धूपकम्.

दत्त्वा [१]निवेद्य पूर्ववत्[२] प्रोक्ष्य[३] त्रियम्बकेण तत् ।
परिषिच्यामृतजलं दत्त्वा मन्त्रेण पूर्ववत् ॥ ५२७ ॥
'देवस्यें'ति निवेद्यास्मै स्वकाले कुसुमाञ्जलिम् ।
'भवाये'त्यादिभिर्मन्त्रैरष्टाभिर्नमसान्वितैः ॥ ५२८ ॥
दत्त्वा रौद्रीभिर्ऋग्भिस्तं[४] स्तुत्वा कृत्वा प्रदक्षिणम् ।
उद्वासये'दमुं' मन्त्रैर्नमस्कृत्य यथापुरम् ॥ ५२९ ॥
पुष्पं तु स्याद् द्रोण[५]खदिरशमीबिल्वसमुद्भवम् ।
तथा बकुलनन्द्यादिवर्ताख्यं[६] करवीरकम् ॥ ५३० ॥
पलाशं चम्पकाशोकमल्लिकाजातिसंभवम् ।
तुलसीकुसुमं[७] मुख्यं मल्लिका[८]कुसुमं तथा ॥ ५३१ ॥
न शुष्कैः पूजयेद्देवं [९]कुसुमैर्न महीगतैः ।
न विशीर्णदलैः[१०] शुष्कैर्नाशुक्लैर्नाविकासिभिः[११] ॥ ५३२॥
पूतिगन्धोऽग्रगन्धानि केशकीट[illegible]तानि च ।
वर्जयेदूर्णनाभेन[१२] वासितं य[illegible] शोभनम् ॥ ५३३ ॥
हविः शाल्योदनं दिव्यमाज्ययुक्तं सशर्करम् ।
नैवेद्यं देवदेवस्य यावकं पायसं तथा ॥ ५३४ ॥
[१३]नैवेद्यवस्त्वलाभे तु फलान्यपि निवेदयेत् ।
फलानामप्यभावे तु तिलगुल्मौषधीरपि ॥ ५३५ ॥
ओषधीनामभावे तु तोयान्यपि निवेदयेत् ।
तदलाभे[१४] तु सर्वत्र मानसं प्रवरं स्मृतम् ॥ ५३६ ॥
नमस्कारेण चैकेन साष्टाङ्गेन हरिं व्रजेत् ॥ ५३६क ॥
उरसा शिरसा दृष्ट्या मनसा च धियापि च ।
पद्भ्यां कराभ्यां वाचा च प्रणामोऽष्टाङ्ग उच्यते ॥ ५३७ ॥

१.MT निवेद्यं. २.MT पूर्वोक्त. ३.T प्रोक्षि...त्र्यम्ब°. ४.M भिरुग्भि°, T भिऋग्भि°. ५.M स्याद्रोणखरिर, T °रवरिर. ६.M वर्तारवः, T वर्ताख्यं. ७.M कुसुम°. ८.T मल्लयका°. ९.M कुसुमैस्त. १०.M नवशीर्ण°. ११.M °शुकैस्थाविका°. १२.M दूर्णुना°. १३.M नैवेद्यं वस्त्व°. १४.T तदभावे.

एवं संपूज्य देवेशं क्षणं ध्यात्वा निरञ्जनम् ।
ततोऽवलोकयेत्सूर्यं 'हंसः शुचिष'दित्यृचा ॥ ५३८ ॥

[वैश्वदेवकर्मविधिः]

यथोक्तविधिना कुर्याद् वैश्वदेवमतः परम् ॥ ५३८क ॥
पिबेत्पादोदकं विष्णोर्'तदस्य प्रिय'मित्यृचा ।
वैष्णवीभिस्तथान्याभिर्ऋग्भि[१]श्चरणमन्त्रतः ॥ ५३९ ॥
अकालमृत्युशमनं[२] सर्वव्याधिविनाशनम् ।
विष्णोः पादोदकं तीर्थं तत्पिबामि जनार्दन[३] ॥ ५४० ॥
बालः स्ववासिनीवृद्धगर्भिण्यातुरकन्यकाः ।
सखीन्भृत्यान् बान्धवांश्च संस्कृतान्नेन भोजयेत् ॥ ५४१ ॥
मधुपर्केण संपूज्याः श्रोत्रियाचार्यशिष्यकाः[४] ।
ऋत्विक्प्रियविवाह्याश्च[५] राजा च प्रतिवत्सरम् ॥ ५४२ ॥
भुक्तवत्सु तु सर्वेषु भुञ्जीयातां तु दम्पती ।
नात्मार्थं पाचयेदन्नं[६] विधाता शीर्यते[७] गृही ॥ ५४३ ॥
[८]पाचयेत्पुनरप्यन्नं देवब्राह्मणपूजने ।
[९]सुगन्धिचन्दनालिप्तगात्रः शुक्लाम्बरः शुचिः ॥ ५४४ ॥
उपवीती शिखी स्रग्वी स्वाचान्तः सपवित्रकः ।
सुसंवृते शुचौ देशेऽलंकृते सुमनोरमे ॥ ५४५ ॥
जाज्वल्यमानदीपोत्थप्रभया सुविराजिते ।
सूपलिप्ते[१०] मण्डलं च चतुरश्रं जलेन वा ॥ ५४६ ॥
भस्मना वा विधायात्र कांस्यं श्लक्ष्णं सुशोधितम् ।
सौवर्णं राजतं ताम्रमब्जं वाऽश्मविनिर्मितम् ॥ ५४७ ॥

१.M °रुग्भि°. २.M °गमनं. ३.T जनादर्दन. ४.M °बान्धवाः, T बान्धवाः corrected as शिष्यकाः; M adds शिष्यकाः at the beginning of next hemistich. ५.MT विवाहाश्च. ६.M वाचये°, T वा° corrected as पा°. ७.MT विघ्नाताशी यतो. ८.M वाच°. ९.M adds पूजने also before सुगन्धि° at the beginning of the next hemistich. १०.M oms सूप.

विन्यस्य पात्रं पत्रं वा सूपविष्टः शुभासने ।
क्रोधलोभविनिर्मुक्तः प्राङ्मुखः सुप्रसन्नधीः ॥ ५४८ ॥
[1]दक्षिणाभिमुखः प्रत्यङ्मुखः सौम्याननोऽपि वा ।
प्रशस्तरत्ननिकराबद्ध[2]होमाङ्गुलीयकः ॥ ५४९ ॥
पाणिना दक्षिणेनैतद् भाजनं[3] परिमृज्य तु ।
अन्नं सुसंस्कृतं हृद्यमाहृतं शुचिभिः शुभैः ॥ ५५० ॥
तत्कालागतभिक्षुभ्यः शक्त्या दत्त्वाऽथ रोचते[4] ।
इति दृष्ट्वाभिपूज्यान्नं 'भूर्भुवः सुवरो'मिति ॥ ५५१ ॥
उपस्थायाहृतपात्रे पाणिना दक्षिणेन तु ।
उद्धृतेन नमस्कृत्य[5] मधुरव्यञ्जनान्वितम्[5] ॥ ५५२ ॥
अभ्यज्य सर्पिषा तस्माद्धर्मराजाय वै बलिम् ।
दत्त्वाऽथ चित्रगुप्ताय प्रेतेभ्यश्च बलिं हरेत् ॥ ५५३ ॥
यत्र क्वचन संस्थानां क्षुत्तृष्णोपहतात्मनाम् ।
प्रेतानां तृप्तयेऽक्षय्यमिदमस्तु यथासुखम् ॥ ५५४ ॥

[भोजनविधिः]

अथोपस्पृश्य पात्रस्थमन्नं दक्षिणपाणिना ।
अभिमृज्य जपेन्मन्त्रा'नहमस्म्या'दिसूक्तगान्[6] ॥ ५५५ ॥
'अन्तश्चरसि' मन्त्रं च 'मधुवाता'दिकं तृचम्[7] ।
मन्त्रवत्परिषिच्यान्नं ध्यायन्प्राणाम्बरं जलम् ॥ ५५६ ॥
पीत्वा'ऽमृता'[8]द्यमन्त्रेण स्पृष्ट्वा 'विद्युदसी'त्यपः ।
सग्रहं दशहोतारं[9] सञ्जप्य मनसा ततः ॥ ५५७ ॥
साङ्गुष्ठसर्वाङ्गुल्यग्रैरवदानसमं[10] हविः ।
अवदाय मुखे प्राणे 'निविष्टाये'ति पञ्चभिः ॥ ५५८ ॥
दन्तानतीत्य जुहुयात्प्राणाद्याप्यायनाय तत् ।

१.M क्षीणाभि°. २.M °बन्ध होमा°. ३.M भार्जनं. ४.M रोचके. ५-५.M कृत्यं सुख्यञ्जनादिकम्. ६.M सूक्तनात्. ७.MT तृचाम्. ८.M पीतामृताद्य°. ९.M °होन्तारं. १०.M °ग्रैरपदानसं.

अश्नीयाच्छ्रद्धया भूयस्तूष्णीं ध्यायन्प्रजापतिम् ॥ ५५९ ॥
मधुरं पूर्वमश्नीयाल्लवणाम्लौ[१] तु मध्यतः ।
कटुतिक्तादिकं चान्ते सूपक्षीरादिसंयुतम् ॥ ५६० ॥
[२]प्राग्द्रवं मध्यकठिनं द्रवान्तं[३] चापि तत्स्मृतम्[४] ।
बलारोग्यविवृद्ध्यर्थं क्लेशा स्युर्मृत्युरन्यथा ॥ ५६१ ॥
पञ्चार्द्रो भोजनं कुर्याद्धस्तयोः पादयोर्मुखे ।
पञ्चार्द्रस्तेषु[५] चार्द्रेषु वाग्यतः स्याच्च सर्वदा ॥ ५६२ ॥
दर्व्या देयं घृतान्नं तु समस्तव्यञ्जनानि च ।
उदकं यच्च पक्वान्नं न दर्व्या दीयते क्वचित् ॥ ५६३ ॥
आहृतेऽन्ने तु तत्पात्रं स्पृशन्सव्येन पाणिना ।
भुञ्जीत नोत्सृजेन्मध्ये भोज्यं स्यात्तद्विसर्जने[६] ॥ ५६४ ॥
अष्टौ ग्रासा मुनेर्भक्तं षोडशारण्यवासिनः ।
द्वात्रिंशस्तु गृहस्थस्यामितं ब्रह्मचारिणः ॥ ५६५ ॥
गृहस्थो ब्रह्मचारी वा योऽनश्नंस्तु तपश्चरेत् ।
प्राणाग्निहोत्रलोपेन ह्यवकीर्णी[७] भवेत्ततः ॥ ५६६ ॥
प्राणाग्निहोत्रमन्त्रांस्तान्निरुद्धो[८] भोजने जपेत् ।
सायं प्रातर्द्विजातीनामशनं श्रुतिचोदितम् ॥ ५६७ ॥
नान्तरा[९] भोजनं कुर्यादग्निहोत्रसमो विधिः ।
नैकवासाः समश्नीयात्[१०] कपाटमपिधाय च ॥ ५६८ ॥
ताम्ररौप्याब्जसौवर्णवर्जं भिन्नेऽपि भाजने ।
लवणं व्यञ्जनञ्चैव घृतं तैलं तथैव च ॥ ५६९ ॥
लेह्यं पेयञ्च[११] विविधं हस्तदत्तं न भक्षयेत् ।
कार्ष्णायसे[१२] मृन्मये वा न भुञ्जीत कदाचन ॥ ५७० ॥
[१३]वटार्काश्वत्थपत्रेषु कुंभीतिन्दुकजेषु वा ।

१.T °लवणाम्रौ. २.M प्राग्रूप. ३.M द्ररवास्तं. ४.M °तस्मृतम्. ५.M पञ्चार्द्रतेषु, T पञ्चार्द्रतैषु. ६.M oms सर्जने. ७.M ह्यवतीर्णी. ८.M °मन्त्रान्त निरूद्धो. ९.M नान्तरं. १०.M सपत्नीयात्. ११.M चेयञ्च. १२.M तक्ष्णायसे. १३.M वटर्का°.

कोविदारे पर्णपृष्ठे कार्पासे तान्तवेऽपि[१] वा ॥ ५७१ ॥
करञ्जपत्रे विकर[२] आसनेऽशुभभाजने[३] ॥ ५७१क ॥
भिन्नं शकृन्मयं लोहबद्धं पालाशमेव च ।
वर्जयेदासनं क्लिन्नं शीर्णं दग्धं तथाऽशुचि ॥ ५७२ ॥
शाकमूलफलापूपमोदकेक्ष्वादिकानि च[४] ।
दन्तैः सञ्छिद्य नाश्नीयान्नासन्दीसंस्थितस्तथा[५] ॥ ५७३ ॥
नोच्छिष्टं[६] भक्षयेत्किञ्चिन् न गच्छन्नापि च स्थितः।
नास्नातो[७] न च संविष्टो नासीनः शयने भुवि ॥ ५७४ ॥
प्रौढपादो नार्द्रवासा न यन्त्रारूढपादुकः ।
बहूनां[८] पश्यतामेक[९] एकस्य बहवोऽपि च ॥ ५७५ ॥
पादप्रसारणं[१०] कृत्वा न च वेष्टितमस्तकः ।
नोच्छिष्टं[११] ग्राहयेदाज्यं जग्धशेषं न संत्यजेत् ॥ ५७६ ॥
शूद्रभुक्तावशिष्टं तु नाद्याद् भाण्डस्थितं[१२] त्वपि ।
न पिबेन्न च भुञ्जीत द्विजः सव्येन पाणिना ॥ ५७७ ॥
[१३]नैकहस्तेन च जलं शूद्रेणावर्जितं पिबेत् ।
पिबतो यत्पतेत्तोयं भोजने मुखनिःसृतम् ॥ ५७८ ॥
अभोज्यं तद् भवदन्नं [१४]न पिबेत्पीतशेषकम् ॥ ५७८क ॥
न स्पृशेद् वामहस्तेन भुञ्जानोऽन्नं कदाचन ।
न पादौ न शिरो वस्तिं[१५] न पदा भाजनं स्पृशेत् ॥ ५७९ ॥
उत्सर्गस्थं न भुञ्जीत सशब्दं पाणिना धृते ।
न सन्ध्ययोर्न मध्याह्ने नार्धरात्रे कदाचन ॥ ५८० ॥
शून्यालये न चाश्नीयान्न च[१६] देवादिवेश्मनि[१७] ॥ ५८०क ॥
एकपंक्त्युपविष्टानां विप्राणां सहभोजने[१८] ।

१.M तातवेपि. २.M °ऽपिकर. ३.T शुद्ध°. ४.M तु. ५.M संस्थितन्तथा, T °तदा. ६.M °च्छिष्टो. ७.M न स्नातो. ८.M बाहूनां. ९.M °मेकः. १०.M °प्रसरणं. ११.MT नोच्छिष्टो. १२.M नाद्यात्मण्ड°, T नाद्यान्भाण्ड°. १३.M oms न. १४.M oms न. १५.M विस्तिं. १६.M oms. १७.M देवानिवे°. १८.M °णामह्निभो°.

यद्येकोऽपि त्यजेत्पात्रं नाश्नीयुरितरेऽप्यनु ॥ ५८१ ॥
अग्निना भस्मना वापि स्तंबेन[1] सलिलेन वा ।
द्वारेण वापि मार्गेण पङ्क्तिभेदो बुधैः स्मृतः ॥ ५८२ ॥
न कुत्सिताहृतं भोज्यं जुगुप्सावदसंस्कृतम् ॥ ५८२क ॥
आयसेन तु पात्रेण यदन्नमुपदीयते ।
भोक्ता विष्ठासमं भुङ्क्ते दाता च नरकं व्रजेत् ॥ ५८३ ॥
भुक्त्वा पीतामृताद्येन तच्छेषं निनयेद् भुवि ॥ ५८३क ॥
'रौरवे नरके घोरे पद्मार्बुदनिवासिनाम् ।
अर्थिनां सर्वभूतानामिदमस्तु 'स्वधा नमः' ॥ ५८४ ॥
अपसृत्य मनाक् शुद्धिं विधायास्य कराश्रयाम्[2] ।
दन्तलग्नानि सन्त्यज्य दन्तकाष्ठेन यत्नतः ॥ ५८५ ॥
आचान्तः पुनराचम्य स्पृष्ट्वा 'विद्युदसी'त्यपः ।
'प्राणानां ग्रन्थि'रित्यादिनात्मानमभिमृश्य च ॥ ५८६ ॥
देशान्तरस्थः[3] पादौ च पाणी प्रक्षाल्य पूर्ववत् ।
आचम्य दक्षिणेऽङ्गुष्ठे पादोऽर्थे स्रावयेत्करौ ॥ ५८७ ॥
'अङ्गुष्ठमात्रः पुरुष' इत्युभे जानुनी स्वके ।
तूष्णीमुभाभ्यां हस्ताभ्यामभिमृश्योर्ध्वबाहुकम् ॥ ५८८ ॥
प्राणे निविश्'यामृता'द्यैरनुमन्त्र्य हुतस्ततः ।
प्रणवेन स्वमात्मानं चिन्तयेद् ब्रह्म निष्कलम्[4] ॥ ५८९ ॥
[5]स्वस्थः प्रशान्तचित्तस्तु[6] कृतासनपरिग्रहः ।
अभीष्टदेवतानां तु कुर्वीत स्मरणं ततः ॥ ५९० ॥
'अग्निराप्याययन् धातुं पार्थिवं[7] पवनेरितः ।
दत्तावकाशं नभसो जरयेदस्तु मे सुखम्' ॥ ५९१ ॥
अन्नं[8] बलाय मे भूमेरपामग्न्यनिलस्य च ।

१.T स्तवेन. २.M °श्रयम्. ३.M देशान्तमस्थः. ४.M निष्ककात्. ५.MT स्वस्थ°. ६.M °वित्तस्तु. ७.M पार्थिवं. ८.T अग्नं.

भवत्वेतत् परिणतो ममास्त्वविहतं[1] सुखम् ॥ ५९२ ॥
प्राणापानसमानानामुदानव्यानयोस्तथा ।
अन्नं पुष्टिकरं मेऽस्तु ममास्त्वव्याहतं सुखम् ॥ ५९३ ॥
[2]आनस्तिरग्निर्वडवानलश्च
भुक्तं मयान्नं जरयेदशेषम् ।
सुखं च मे तत्परिणामसंभवं
[3]यच्छत्वरोगं मम चास्तु[3] देहम् ॥ ५९४ ॥
विष्णुः समस्तेन्द्रियदेहदेही
प्रधानभूतो भगवान् यथैकः ।
सत्येन तेनान्नमशेषमत्त-
मारोग्यदं मे परिणाममेतु ॥ ५९५ ॥
विष्णुरत्ता[4] तथैवान्नं परिणामश्च वै तथा ।
सत्येन तेन तद् भक्तं जीर्यत्वन्नमिदं तथा ॥ ५९६ ॥
इत्युक्त्वाऽथ स्वहस्तेन परिमार्जेत्तथोदरम् ।
ताम्बूलभक्षणं कृत्वा समाचान्तो यथाविधि ॥ ५९७ ॥

[दिनस्य षष्ठसप्तमयोर्भागे इतिहासपुराणश्रवणम्]

इतिहासपुराणानि शृणुयाच्च समाहितः ।
षष्ठं च सप्तमं भागं शिष्टैरिष्टैश्च बन्धुभिः ॥ ५९८ ॥
समासीत ततः काले विहृत्याग्नीन् समाहितः ।
अर्धास्तगे[5] रवौ गत्वा बहिराचम्य पूर्ववत् ॥ ५९९ ॥
'अग्निश्चे'त्यादिनाऽऽचम्य प्रदायार्घ्यं प्रदक्षिणम् ।
'आ सत्येने'ति चावर्त्य तर्पयेत्पूर्ववत्ततः ॥ ६०० ॥
रुद्रं सरस्वतीमत्र प्रयुञ्जीत यथोदितम् ।
'परमात्मा' 'सुवः'[6] 'सा मे'त्यत्रोपपदमिष्यते ॥ ६०१ ॥

१.M °विहितः. २.M आनस्तिम°. ३-३.M यच्चत्वरोगममुचारस्तु. ४.M विष्णुमत्त, T तुथै°. ५.T अर्धास्तगौ. ६.MT सुपः.

आसीनः पूर्ववत्सन्ध्यां वारुण्याशामुखस्ततः ।
उपासित्वाऽथ हुत्वाग्निमग्नीन्वा[१] तनुमास्य च[१] ॥ ६०२ ॥
वारुणीभ्यामुपस्थाय कृत्वा यामन्यथापुरम्[२] ।
सायं सिद्धेन शुद्धेन नाम्नामपि सहस्रकम् ॥ ६०३ ॥
जपेत् स्तोत्राणि चान्यानि[३] स्वाध्यायं चापि शक्तितः ।
भृत्यैः परिवृतो भुक्त्वा यथापूर्वं समाहितः ॥ ६०४ ॥

[शयनविधिः]

दैविकीं[४] मानुषीं रक्षां गेहादीनां विधाय च ।
आचम्य देवतामिष्टां संस्मृत्य स्वावृते गृहे ॥ ६०५ ॥
सुगुप्तेऽलङ्कृते[५] रम्ये स्वास्तीर्णे[६] मंगलान्विते ।
शयने प्राक्शिरा [७]स्वप्यान्माधवार्पितमानसः ॥ ६०६ ॥
स्फुटितां च विशालां च भग्नाङ्गां मलिनीमपि ।
न च दन्तुमयीं[८] शय्यामधितिष्ठेदनास्तृताम्[९] ॥ ६०७ ॥
प्राच्यां दिशि शिरः शस्तं याम्यायामपि वा दिशि ।
सदैव स्वपतः[१०] पुंसो विपरीतं तु रोगदम् ॥ ६०८ ॥
नास्नातां[११] तु स्त्रियं गच्छेन्नातुरां[१२] न रजस्वलाम् ।
नानिष्टां न प्रकुपितां[१३] नाप्रशस्तां न गर्भिणीम् ॥ ६०९ ॥
नादक्षिणां नान्यकामां [१४]नाकामां नान्ययोषितम्[१४] ।
क्षुत्क्षामामतिभुक्तां वा स्वयं चैतैगुणैर्युतः ॥ ६१० ॥
नाति[१५]स्रग्गन्धधृक् प्रीतो नाध्मातः[१६] क्षुधितोऽपि वा ।
सकामः सानुरागश्च व्यवायं[१७] पुरुषो व्रजेत् ॥ ६११ ॥

[संस्कृतायाः स्त्रिया धर्माः]

आन्वाहिका[१८] गृहस्थस्य धर्माः प्रायेण दर्शिताः ।

१-१.T वा...च. २.MT यान्यथापुरम्. ३.M वान्यानि. ४.M देवकीं. ५.M °कृते...म्ये. ६.M °स्तीर्णं. ७.M स्व प...न्माधवा द्वीत°. ८.M दस्तु मर्यां. ९.M °दनावृताम्. १०.M स्वतः ११.MT नास्नाता. १२.M नातुरा. १३.M प्रकुर्वीतां. T corrected as प्रकुपितां. १४-१४.M नाकामामन्ययोषितम्, T मान्ययोषितम्. १५.MT नातः [M त]. १६.M नात्मातः, T नाध्मातः. १७.T व्यवायं. १८.M आन्वाति हा, T आन्वातिना.

संस्कृतायाः स्त्रिया धर्मान् नित्यान् वक्ष्यामि साम्प्रतम्॥ ६१२ ॥
अस्वातन्त्र्यं भवेत्स्त्रीणां सर्वकर्मसु सर्वदा ॥ ६१२क ॥
भर्त्रैकदेवता नार्यस्तच्छुश्रूषापराः सदा ।
अनन्यमानसाः शास्ता[1] गच्छन्ति परमं पदम् ॥ ६१३ ॥
उत्थाय पूर्वं स्वपतिमवबोध्य मनोरमैः ।
मृदुभिर्वचनैः सार्धं पादसंवाहनादिना ॥ ६१४ ॥
मूत्राद्युत्सर्जनं कृत्वा सुगुप्ते समृदम्भसा ।
गन्धलेपक्षयकरं शौचं कृत्वा समाहिताः[2] ॥ ६१५ ॥
प्रक्षाल्य पाणिपादौ[3] च मुखशुद्धिं यथोदिताम् ।
विधाय पचनार्थानि[4] पात्राणि क्षालयेज्जलैः ॥ ६१६ ॥
वेश्मसंमार्जनं कृत्वा संप्रोक्ष्य सकृज्जलैः[5] ।
आलिप्य गुप्ते पात्राणि यथास्थानं निधाय च ॥ ६१७ ॥
अप्सु स्नात्वा शुभं वास उपवासमनुल्बणम् ।
गुल्फकौ पर्यधोनाभिः परिधायोपविश्य च ॥ ६१८ ॥
प्रक्षाल्य चरणौ पाणी जिह्वासंस्पर्शनोचिता ।
अपः पीत्वा सकृत्तद्वत् परिमृज्यान्मुखं ततः ॥ ६१९ ॥
एतदाचमनं स्त्रीणां सर्वकर्मसु चोदितम् ।
कृतानुलेपना[6] पुष्पधारिण्यपि वृतस्तनी[7] ॥ ६२० ॥
[8]पुरान्यगमनात् प्राप्य देवतायतनं रहः ।
तामाराध्य नमस्कृत्य परिक्रम्य प्रदक्षिणम् ॥ ६२१ ॥
प्राप्याग्निगृहमाचम्य विहृत्याग्निं समाहिता ।
सुसंमृज्योपलिप्यात्र होमयोग्यवसूनि च ॥ ६२२ ॥
समित्पुष्पतृणव्रीहि[9]घृतवारीणि चन्दनम् ।

१.T शान्ता. २.MT °हितः. ३.M पाणि°. ४.M वचना°, T वपना°. ५.T सजतुं जलैः. ६.M °लेपनं. ७.M पृतस्तनी. ८.T पुरान्याग. ९.M व्राहि.

यथास्थानं यथापेक्षं निधाय स्वामिना हुते ॥ ६२३ ॥
होमेऽनुलेपनं कृत्वा वह्न्युत्थसितभस्मना ।
दुग्ध्वा गाः क्षीरपचनं कृत्वा निर्मथ्य वै दधि ॥ ६२४ ॥
गणेशानं हरिं भक्त्या पूजयित्वा यथाविधि ।
वैनायकान् वैष्णवांश्च जपेन्मन्त्रान् समाहिता[1] ॥ ६२५ ॥
कलशानुदधानीं च पूरयित्वाऽच्छवारिणा ।
धूपोदनव्यञ्जनानि संपच्य विधिवत्ततः ॥ ६२६ ॥
अपिधाय शुचौ देशे निधायैकत्र संवृते ।
सपर्या वैश्वदेवादिसाधनं परिकल्प्य च ॥ ६२७ ॥
विज्ञाप्य स्वामिनं[2] तेन वैश्वदेवकृते सति ।
आगतेभ्योऽथो[3]भिक्षुभ्यो भिक्षां दत्त्वा यथाविधि ॥ ६२८ ॥
भुक्तवत्सु तु सर्वेषु संमृष्टे [च][4] स्ववेश्मनि ।
विधाय मण्डलं तत्र पात्राण्यास्तीर्य भोजनम् ॥ ६२९ ॥
शोधितं कांस्यरौप्यादि न्यस्त्वा शुक्लशुभाम्बरा ।
अलंकृतानुलिप्ताङ्गी संयता सुमनोहरा ॥ ६३० ॥
तत्कालागतभिक्षुभ्यो दत्त्वाऽन्नं व्यञ्जनान्वितम् ।
अस्कन्दयन्ती[5] भर्त्रेऽन्नं मेक्षणेनावदाय च ॥ ६३१ ॥
क्षिप्त्वा यथार्थं तत्पात्रे व्यञ्जनं सघृतं ततः ।
दत्त्वा दर्व्यापि च जलं भुङ्क्ते[6] पात्रावशेषितम् ॥ ६३२ ॥
अपिधाय जलं दत्त्वा संस्पृश्यास्मिन्बहिर्गते ।
कृतशौचे[7] स्वयं भुङ्क्त्वा[8] कृतास्यकरशोधना[9] ॥ ६३३ ॥
उच्छिष्टपात्राण्युद्धृत्य शोधनैः संविशोध्य च ।
उच्छिष्टभूमिमालिप्य वेश्मान्ते सर्वपात्रिकाः ॥ ६३४ ॥
निधाय चासनादीनि कृत्वा ताम्बूलभक्षणम् ।

१.M °हितः. २.M स्वामिनस्तेन. ३.M oms ऽथ. ४.MT om. ५.MT °यन्ति. ६.T भुक्ते. ७.M कृतं शौचे. ८.T भुक्त्वा. ९.M शोधनम्, T °शोधनाः.

सुवृत्ताभिः सुवृद्धाभिर्वधूभिः सह संयुता[१] ॥ ६३५ ॥
उपविश्य कथाः श्रुत्वा पुराणादिसमीरिताः ।
प्रक्षाल्य सर्वपात्राणि ततः संमृश्य वेश्म च ॥ ६३६ ॥
स्थालीविधानदर्व्यादिपाचनार्थानि[२] गुप्तिमत् ।
कृत्वा दुग्ध्वा पयः काले विधायाग्निं गृहाङ्गणे[३] ॥ ६३७ ॥
दीपान् निरूप्य संस्थाप्य यथास्थानं यथाविधि ।
संपृच्छ्यान्नं हुते होमे वैश्वदेवे कृते सति ॥ ६३८ ॥
भुक्ते स्वामिनि भुक्त्वाऽथ[४] स्थाल्यादिक्षालने कृते ।
बहिरुत्तरपूर्वस्मिन्वास्तुभागे प्रविश्य च ॥ ६३९ ॥
गुप्ते निधाय पात्राणि द्रव्याण्यन्यानि भागशः ।
सर्वरक्षां विधायाथ कृतपादावसेचना[५] ॥ ६४० ॥
शुश्रूषयित्वा[६] भर्तारं पादसंवाहनादिना ।
प्रीणयित्वा हितैर्वाक्यैः प्रियैस्तद्गतमानसा ॥ ६४१ ॥
सुप्तेऽस्मिन्च्छयने[७] नीचे स्वप्स्यात्तत्सन्निधौ ततः[८] ।
पतिप्रियहिते युक्त्वा स्वाचारा संयतेन्द्रिया ॥ ६४२ ॥
सेह कीर्तिमवाप्नोति प्रेत्य[९] चानुत्तमं सुखम् ॥ ६४२क ॥
स्त्रियः श्रियश्च गेहेषु न विशेषोऽस्ति कश्चन[१०] ।
पूज्या[११] भूषयितव्याश्च बहुकल्याणमीप्सुभिः[१२] ॥ ६४३ ॥
गृहस्थः परमो [१३]लोको गृहस्थः सुखमेधते ।
गृहस्थश्च जगत्सर्वं बिभर्ति सचराचरम् ॥ ६४४ ॥

इति सङ्गमग्रामवासिमिश्रविरचिते नारायणीये
वाधूलगृह्यागमवृत्तिरहस्ये
षष्ठोऽध्यायः

१.T संयता. २.M वचनार्थानि, T वाचना°. ३.M गृहाङ्कणे. ४.MT भुक्त्वा°. ५.M °सेचने. ६.M शुश्रूषित्वाऽथ. ७.M °याने. ८.M puts ततः at the beginning of next hemistich before पति°. ९.M प्रेत्या. १०.M केचन. ११.MT भुज्या. १२.M बहुभ्योऽर्णमी°. १३.MT लोके.

अथ सप्तमोऽध्यायः

[पितृश्राद्धमीमांसा]

चन्द्रक्षयेऽग्निमान्कुर्यात् पितृभ्यः श्राद्धमास्तिकः ।
यस्मिन्कृतेऽस्य पितरः प्रेतास्तृप्तिं[1] प्रयान्ति हि ॥ १ ॥
पित्रादिभ्यः[2] प्रमीतेभ्यः श्राद्धकर्म विधीयते ।
न जीवन्तमतिक्रम्य किंचिद्दद्यादिति श्रुतेः ॥ २ ॥
पित्रादिभोजनं श्राद्धे पाक्षिकं मनुना स्मृतम् ।
कामं वा[3] तदनुज्ञात इत्यनेन निराकृतम् ॥ ३ ॥
पिण्डान्दद्यात्तत्पितृभ्यो ददातीत्यादिदर्शनात् ।
तृप्तिः[4] पितृणां तेन स्यादित्येतदवगम्यते ॥ ४ ॥
उद्दिश्य न पितॄनत्र त्यागमात्रं विधीयते ।
[5]कर्त्रभीष्टार्थसिध्यर्थं स्वर्गकामादियागवत् ॥ ५ ॥
दद्यात्पितृभ्य इत्येवमुत्पत्तौ दानचोदनात् ।
[6]तद्गतस्वत्वसंबन्धस्तत एवावगम्यते ॥ ६ ॥
[7]यत्तु तन्निदधातीति निधानं दानमेव तत् ।
तिस्रो दर्वीर्ददातीति दानशब्दसमीरणात् ॥ ७ ॥
न चोपपत्तिरन्वेष्या[8] शास्त्रसिद्धेऽत्र वस्तुनि ॥ ७क ॥
यथैव स्वकृतं कर्म फलदं पुरुषस्य हि ।
तद्वत्परकृतं चापि फलदं शास्त्रचोदनात् ॥ ८ ॥
अत एव हि पुत्रत्वं नरकोद्धरणात्स्मृतम् ॥ ८क ॥
अपुण्यकारिणां चातः सर्वदेहानुयायिनाम् ।
श्राद्धेनाप्यायमानानां[9] विद्वद्भिः स्वसुतादिभिः ॥ ९ ॥
क्रमेण पुण्यनिचयान्निवृत्तिः[10] संसृतेर्भवेत् ।

१.M प्रेतातृप्तिं. २.M चित्रादिभ्यः. ३.M oms. ४.M तृप्तिं. ५.M कर्तृभीष्टा°. ६.M oms वद्. ७.M यत्तुनिद°. ८.°न्वेष्यो. ९.M °नाप्यार्यमा°. १०.M °चयां त्रिवृत्तिः.

कर्तुश्च फलदातृत्वं[१] तेषामेवोचितं ततः ॥ १० ॥
यद्वा [२]वस्वादयो देवाः पितरः श्राद्धतर्पिताः ।
प्रीणयन्ति मनुष्याणां पितॄंस्तिर्यग्गतानपि ॥ ११ ॥
अचिन्त्यशक्तयो नित्याः सर्वभूतानुयायिनः ।
तत्तज्जन्मानुरोध्यन्नपान[३]भक्षादिदानतः ॥ १२ ॥
प्रीणयन्ति [४]मनुष्याणां पितॄंस्तिर्यग्गतानपि[४] ॥ १२क ॥
यद्वा संसारिरूपत्वमसंसारिस्वरूपता ।
तेषामेव पितॄणां स्यादत एव मृते सति ॥ १३ ॥
देहान्तरगते कर्मवशगे तस्य साक्षिणः ।
नित्यस्याप्यतिरिक्तस्य[५] सर्वभूतानुयायिनः ॥ १४ ॥
दाहोदकक्रियाद्येन संस्कारेण यथाविधि ।
विशिष्टदेहमुत्पाद्य प्रीणाति श्राद्धकर्मणा ॥ १५ ॥
[६]प्रेतोऽपि भुक्त्वा[६] प्रीणाति स्वाभिन्नं भोक्तृरूपिणम् ।
सर्वभूतात्मनस्तस्य प्रीतिः श्राद्धादिना स्मृताः ॥ १६ ॥
ये यजन्ति पितॄन्देवान् ब्राह्मणांश्च हुताशनान्[७] ।
सर्वभूतान्तरात्मानं विष्णुमेव यजन्ति ते ॥ १७ ॥
आयुः पुत्रान् यशः स्वर्गं कीर्तिं पुष्टिं बलं श्रियम् ।
पशून् सुखं धनं धान्यं प्राप्नुयात्पितृपूजनात् ॥ १८ ॥
त्रैविध्यमत एतेषां युज्यते स्मृतिदर्शितम् ।
देवतिर्यक्पितृस्थत्वं होमपिण्डद्विजाशनैः ॥ १९ ॥
बहुधावस्थितस्यास्य तृप्तिः स्याच्छास्त्रचोदिता ।
एवञ्च विदुषः श्राद्धेऽधिकार इति गम्यते ॥ २० ॥
देवतिर्यक्पितृस्थत्वाद् यद्वा ते त्रिविधास्ततः[८] ॥ २०क ॥

१.M फलदेवत्वं. २.M च स्वादयो. ३.M °त्वन्न च. ४-४.M मनुष्याणामपि निस्तीर्य श्रुतानपि. ५.T °स्याव्यति°. ६-६.M प्रीतोपि भुक्त्वा, T प्रीतो विभुत्वात्. ७.M °शनात्. ८.M °ऽत्रविधा°.

होमः स्याद् देवतास्थानां[१] तिर्यक्स्थाः पिण्डभोजिनः[२]।
विप्राशनं पितृस्थानां होमदानाशनात्मकम् ॥ २१ ॥
श्राद्धं तदङ्गमन्यत्स्यात् ब्राह्मणामन्त्रणादिकम् ।
ग्रन्थव्याख्यान एवेदं स्पष्टमेवाभिधास्यते ॥ २२ ॥
सर्वथा तृप्तिरेतेषामस्ति दानविधिः श्रुतेः ।
उपपत्तिस्तथा कल्प्या मन्त्रपादानुसारिणी ॥ २३ ॥
तच्छ्राद्धं त्रिविधं नित्यकाम्यनैमित्तिकत्वतः ।
कालमात्रनिमित्तं [३]सच्छ्राद्धं नित्यमिहोच्यते ॥ २४ ॥
[४]जननादिनिमित्तं[४]यन्नैमित्तिकमिहोच्यते ।
पितृयज्ञाष्टकामासश्राद्धान्वा एकनित्यता ॥ २५ ॥
अनाहिताग्नेर्नित्यत्वं[५] पितृयज्ञस्य शेषतः ।
स्मृतितश्च[६] न जीवन्तमति[७] दद्यादिति श्रुतेः ॥ २६ ॥
स्वपित्रादिविहीनस्य न जीवपितृकस्य च ।
विशेषः काल्पिका यः स आहिताग्नेः क्रतौ भवेत्॥ २७ ॥
कस्मिंश्चिज्जीवति ततो न श्राद्धं पिण्डभोक्तरि ।
मृतेषु सर्वथा श्राद्धं पितृयज्ञादिकं भवेत् ॥ २८ ॥
निषेधः पतितादीनां सपिण्डीकरणान्तिकः ।
निषिद्धोदककल्पानां पतितानां[८] द्विजन्मनाम् ॥ २९ ॥
ऊर्ध्वं संवत्सरात्कुर्यात् सर्वमेवौर्ध्वदेहिकम् ।
सर्वाधिकारमेव स्याच्छ्राद्धमान्वाहिकं स्मृतम् ॥ ३० ॥
विवाहपुत्रजन्मादिनिमित्तं स्मर्यते च यत् ।
अनग्निकस्य चापि स्याच्छ्राद्धं मरणहेतुकम् ॥ ३१ ॥
सप्तसंबन्धिनः श्राद्धे दातृभोक्तृस्वरूपतः ।
पित्राद्याः पिण्डभोक्तारस्त्रयो लेपभुजोऽपरे ॥ ३२ ॥

१.M स्थान, T देव...स्थानां. २.M °भाजिनः. ३.M स्याच्छ्राद्धं. ४-४.M यजनादिषु निमित्तं यत्तन्नैमि°, T यत्तन्नैमि°. ५.M ग्ने...त्यत्वं. ६.M स्मृतिश्च. ७.M जीवन्तं तम°. ८.T पतितादि°.

त्रयो दाता च सप्तैवं सपिण्डा इति ते स्मृताः ।
धर्मादानाच्च पुत्रत्वं सापिण्ड्यं चापि जन्मवत् ॥ ३३ ॥
जन्मसंबन्ध एव स्यात्तत्र[1] मुख्यो यथा पितुः ।
दुःखत्राणनिमित्तत्वात् पुत्रः श्राद्धेऽधिकारवान् ॥ ३४ ॥
[2]मातृश्राद्धेऽधिकारोऽपि तथैव स्यात्समत्वतः ।
मातृमातामहाद्येषु मृतेषु स्याच्च तत्ततः ॥ ३५ ॥
केचिन्मातामहादीनां श्राद्धमानं प्रचक्षते ।
कैश्चिदेवोपदिष्टत्वादनिष्टत्वं तथापरे ॥ ३६ ॥
तुल्यत्वान्नित्यता युक्ता पित्रोर्यद्यपि तद्विधिः ।
नोपलभ्यत आचार्येणोपदिष्टस्तथा पितुः ॥ ३७ ॥
ब्राह्मणान्भोजयेच्छक्त्या स्मृतिन्यायानुसारतः ।
पर्वणि क्रियमाणं सच्छ्राद्धं पार्वणमुच्यते ॥ ३८ ॥
जन्मकर्मश्रुतेत्यादि तद्विधिः परिपठ्यते ।
[3]तामेव प्रकृतिं प्राहुरष्टकारहितं बुधाः ॥ ३९ ॥
अष्टकासु यतो धर्मा विशेषेण समीरिताः ।
पार्वणेऽपि समाम्नाताः परस्परविलक्षणाः ॥ ४० ॥
आकाङ्क्षितास्तु सर्वत्र सर्वे ग्राह्या इतीरितम् ।
अष्टकाया[4] विवाहान्ते कल्प एव समीरणात् ॥ ४१ ॥
सैव प्रकृतिरित्यन्ये तत्प्रयोगकृते सति ।
मासश्राद्धं पर्वणि[5] स्यात्प्रयुक्तप्रकृते[6]स्तथा ॥ ४२ ॥
पिण्डानामावृतेत्यादि पिण्डाप्रदतिदेशनात् ।
नित्यत्वात् पितृयज्ञस्य प्राथम्यं सर्वथा भवेत् ॥ ४३ ॥

[श्राद्धकालविचारः]

कालोऽधिवृक्षःसूर्योऽस्य कल्प एव समीरितः ।

१.M स्यास्तत्र. २.T °श्राद्धेऽधिकारो०ऽपि. ३.M wrongly adds ते before तामेव. ४.M अष्टका या. ५.M पार्वणि. ६.M प्रयुक्तः प्रकृते°.

विधिश्च शेषवचनान्मानवे यद्यपीरितम् ॥ ४४ ॥
पितृयज्ञं तु निर्वर्त्य विप्रश्चन्द्रक्षयेऽग्निमान् ।
पिण्डान्वाहार्यकं[१] श्राद्धं कुर्यान्मासानुमासिकम्[२] ॥ ४५ ॥
तथापि पार्वणात्पूर्वं विशेषवचनादिह ।
भूमिं विधाय सूर्यांशुरधिरूढो[३] यथा द्रुमान् ॥ ४६ ॥
कालोऽधिवृक्षसूर्याच्छ्रुतिकल्पानुसार्यसौ ।
इन्दुक्षये च विहितः[४] श्राद्धमिन्दुक्षयेऽपि च ॥ ४७ ॥
अष्टमेऽपि चतुर्दश्यां[५] जन्मपर्वाष्टमांशके ।
प्रातः सन्ध्यागमः सोमः सूर्यो यस्यां तु दृश्यते ॥ ४८ ॥
तस्यां श्राद्धतिथौ कार्यं काले पर्व भवेद्यदि[६] ।
अपराह्णश्च कालोऽस्य सोऽपि [७]मध्यन्दिनात्परम् ॥ ४९ ॥
आन्त्यात् त्रिमूतत्रितयाद्[८] आरंभः क्षुतवे सृतः ।
कुतपश्च मुहूर्तोऽह्नो योऽष्टमः स निगद्यते[९] ॥ ५० ॥
नाति सन्ध्या समीपे तत् कार्यं रात्रौ च सन्ध्ययोः ।
[१०]विनोपरागमित्यन्ये पञ्चधाहर्विभज्य[११] च ॥ ५१ ॥
अपराह्णश्चतुर्थोंऽशः श्रुतिदृष्टिस्त्रिधापि[१२] च ।
विभज्य तत्तृतीयांशः स्मार्तो भागद्वयोत्तरः ॥ ५२ ॥
उत्तरेद्युश्च तत्कार्यं यदि पर्वापराह्णिकम् ।
कालान्तरेषु चाप्येष कालः[१३]स्यात्पितृकर्मणि ॥ ५३ ॥
एकोद्दिष्टं तु मध्याह्ने प्रातर्दैविकमिष्यते[१४] ।
निमित्तानन्तरं कार्यं तथा नैमित्तिकं स्मृतम् ॥ ५४ ॥
नित्या एवाष्टकावृद्धिः कृष्णपक्षायनद्वयम्[१५] ।
द्रव्यब्राह्मणसंपत्तिर्विषुवः[१६] सूर्यसंक्रमः ॥ ५५ ॥

१.MT पिण्डबाहार्यकं. २.M °सितम्. ३.M सूर्यात् गुरधि रूढो. ४.MT विहिता. ५.T चतुर्दश्या. ६.MT भवेद्यपि. ७.M मन्ध्यन्दि°. ८.M आन्तयान्त्रिभूत्रत्रितयान,T आम्त्यान्. ९.M सन्निग°. १०.M विहोप. ११.T पञ्चधाह वि°. १२.T श्रुतिदृस्टस्त्रि°. १३.M काल. १४.M देविक°. १५.M पक्षोऽयनं द्वयम्. १६.M विष्टपः.

व्यतीपातो गजच्छाया ग्रहणं चन्द्रसूर्ययोः ।
श्राद्धं [१]पितृरुचिश्चैव श्राद्धकालाः प्रकीर्तिताः ॥ ५६ ॥
कृष्णपक्षे दशम्याद्या वर्जयित्वा चतुर्दशीम् ।
श्राद्धे प्रशस्तास्तिथयः पञ्चम्याद्यास्तु मध्यमाः ॥ ५७ ॥
श्रवणाश्विधनिष्ठार्द्रा[२] नागदैवतमस्तके ।
यद्यमा रविवारेण व्यतीपातः स उच्यते ॥ ५८ ॥
यदि स्याच्चन्द्रमाः पित्र्ये हस्ते चैव दिवाकरः ।
वर्षासु च त्रयोदश्यां सा च्छाया कुञ्जरस्य तु ॥ ५९ ॥
शक्तितः कालनियम इति स्मृतिनिदर्शनात् ।
सति सामर्थ्य एतेषु श्राद्धमावश्यकं भवेत् ॥ ६० ॥
नभस्यापरपक्षस्थत्रयोदश्यां विधुक्षये ।
यथाकथंचिदपि तत्कार्यं माघाष्टकासु च ॥ ६१ ॥
नभस्यकृष्णपक्षस्थ[३]त्रयोदश्यां तथा दिवि ।
अष्टकास्वप्यसामर्थ्ये तत्तृप्तिस्तर्पणात् स्मृता[४] ॥ ६२ ॥

[श्राद्धस्य महत्त्वम्]

अनयैव दिशा श्राद्धमालोच्य श्राद्धमाचरेत् ।
कन्यां कन्यावेदिनश्च पशून्मुख्यान्सुतानपि ॥ ६३ ॥
वृषं[५] कृषिवाणिज्यं च [६]विशं चैकशफं[६] तथा ।
ब्रह्मवर्चस्विनः पुत्रान्[७] स्वर्णरूप्येक[८]रूप्यके ॥ ६४ ॥
ज्ञातिश्रैष्ठ्यं[९] सर्वकामानाप्नोति श्राद्धदः समा ।
प्रतिपत्प्रभृति ह्येता वर्जयित्वा चतुर्दशीम् ॥ ६५ ॥
क्षेत्रं बलं तथा पुत्रं[१०] ज्यैष्ठ्यं [११]सौभाग्यमुख्यताम् ।
[१२]सुतान्प्रवृत्तचक्रतां ज्ञातिभ्यः प्रभुतां तथा ॥ ६६ ॥

१.T पित्ररू°. २.M °ष्ठाद्रा. ३.MT °पक्षस्थ. ४.M °स्मृतात्. ५.M द्युषं, T द्वषं. ६-६.M मितमेक°. ७.M पुत्रात्. ८.T रूप्ये...कुप्यते. ९.M °श्रेष्ठं, T श्रैष्ठं. १०.M पुत्र. ११.MT ससौभाग्य°. १२.T puts सुतान् at the end of preceding hemistich and along with M पुत्रान् between चक्रतां and ज्ञातिभ्यः.

अरोगित्वं यशो वीतशोकतां परमां गतिम् ।
धनं विद्यां[१] भिषक्सिद्धिं कुप्यङ्गावो[२]ह्यजाविकम् ॥ ६७ ॥
[३]अश्वानायुश्च विधिवद् यः श्राद्धं परिवेषयेत् ।
कृत्तिकादिभरण्यन्तं स कामानाप्नुयादिमान् ॥ ६८ ॥

[पङ्क्तिपावनब्राह्मणाः]

अग्र्यः सर्वेषु देवेषु श्रोत्रियो वेदविद् युवा ।
[४]वेदार्थविज्ज्येष्ठसामा [५]त्रिषुवस्त्रिसुपर्णकः ॥ ६९ ॥
स्वस्रीयः ऋत्विग्जा[६]मातृयाज्यश्वशुरमातुलाः ।
[७]त्रिनाचिकेतदौहित्रशिष्यसंबन्धिबान्धवाः ॥ ७० ॥
कर्मनिष्ठतपोनिष्ठपञ्चाग्निब्रह्मचारिणः[८] ।
पितृमातृवराश्चैव ब्राह्मणाः पङ्क्तिपावनाः ॥ ७१ ॥

[श्राद्धेऽभोज्याः]

रोगी हीनातिरिक्ताङ्गः काणः[९] पौनर्भवस्तथा ।
अवकीर्णी कुण्डगोलौ कुनखि श्यावदन्तकः ॥ ७२ ॥
[१०]भृतकाध्यापकः क्रूरः कन्यादूष्याभिशस्तकः[११] ।
मित्रध्रुक् पिशुनः सोमविक्रयी परिविन्दकः[१२] ॥ ७३ ॥
मातृपितृसुतत्यागी कुण्डाशी वृषलात्मकः ।
विधुरो नष्टवह्निश्च श्राद्धकर्ता च तद्दिने ॥ ७४ ॥
पूर्वेद्युः श्राद्धभोक्ता च शाखारण्डो[१३] निराकृतिः ।
अतिवृद्धो देवलकोऽतिबालो वृषलीपतिः ॥ ७५ ॥
उपपातकिनः सर्वेऽप्यभोज्यान्नाश्च निन्दिताः ॥ ७५क ॥

[श्राद्धे भोज्याभोज्यद्रव्याणि]

द्रव्याणि तु हविष्यान्नं[१४] पायसं कृसरं मधु ।

१.M विद्यां...सिद्धिं. २.M गापो. ३.M अश्वागायु°. ४.M cms वेदार्थ. ५.M त्रिसु...स्त्रिसुपर्ण°, T त्रिमसुस्त्रिसुप°. ६.M ऋत्विजां मातृ याज्व°. ७.M °नापिके°. ८.M °चाग्निर्ब्रह्म°. ९.M काणं न...भव°. १०.M हृतका°. ११.T °दूष्यभि°. १२.M °विन्दकम्. १३.M शालारण्डो. १४.M मुन्यन्न.

कालशाकं च मुन्यन्नं श्यामाकाद्यपि शोभनम् ॥ ७६ ॥
तिलाः शाकं पयो गव्यं दधि मस्तु[1] तथा घृतम् ।
माषा अप्याढकीमुद्गा राजमाषादिवर्जिताः ॥ ७७ ॥
अजानानस्तु[2] यः श्राद्धं द्विदलैः परिवेषयेत् ।
रक्षांसि तद्विलुम्पन्ति श्रुतिरेषा पुरातनी ॥ ७८ ॥
राजतानि तु पात्राणि सौवर्णान्यपि वाऽऽपदि[3] ।
आयसव्यतिरिक्तानि शुद्धानि धवलानि तु ॥ ७९ ॥
न्यायार्जितानि[4] द्रव्याणि शोधितानि यथाविधि ।
मृन्मयानि विशुद्धानि दहनक्षालनादिभिः ॥ ८० ॥
विशोधितानि मृद्भस्मगोशकृद्भिर्यथाविधि ।
तैजसानि विशोध्यानि पूर्वेद्युः श्राद्धवेश्म तु ॥ ८१ ॥
संमार्जनोपलेपाभ्यां विशोध्याम्बुजवालुकाः ।
नादेयाः सतिलास्तत्र वितरेत्तद्दिनेऽपि च ॥ ८२ ॥
अखण्डितानि शुक्लानि निर्मलानि च तद्दिने ।
[5]प्रक्षालितोपवातानि वसनान्यासनानि च ॥ ८३ ॥

[श्राद्धभोजिब्राह्मणनिमन्त्रणविधिः]

भोक्तारश्चापि शुचय आत्मवन्तो जितेन्द्रियाः ।
आस्तिकः श्रद्दधानश्च व्यपेतमदमत्सरः ॥ ८४ ॥
आत्मवान् शुचिरेव स्याच्छ्राद्धकर्ता च संयमी।
निमन्त्रयीत पूर्वेद्युः ब्राह्मणानुक्तलक्षणान् ॥ ८५ ॥
अभिगम्योपविश्यैनानुपविष्टान् सुसंस्तरे ।
'श्राद्धं करिष्ये श्वस्तस्माद्युष्माभिस्तत्र भुज्यताम्' ॥ ८६ ॥
तद्दिने वा निमन्त्र्याः स्युर्यदि संबन्धिनस्तु ते ॥ ८६क ॥
निमन्त्रिता[6]हि पितर उपतिष्ठन्ति तान्द्विजान् ।

१.T ..स्तु. २.M अजानानास्तु. ३.M वापदि, T वाऽपदि. ४.M न्यार्जि°. ५.M °लितो वा. ६.M निमन्त्रितानि.

वायुभूतास्तु गच्छन्ति तथासीनानुपासते ॥ ८७ ॥
अतो निमन्त्रितैर्भाव्यं मनोवाक्कायसंयतैः[1] ।
जन्मकर्मादिवाक्येन तदेतदभिधीयते ॥ ८८ ॥
निमन्त्रयीत पूर्वेद्युः स्नातकानिति योजना ।
किंलक्षणान्कथं चेति तदेतदभिधीयते ॥ ८९ ॥
मातृतः पितृतः शुद्धा विख्याताश्च स्वकर्मभिः ।
वेदार्थज्ञानिनः काममदक्रोधादिवर्जिताः ॥ ९० ॥
शिष्टाचारपरा विप्रा जन्मकर्मादिशब्दिताः ॥ ९०क ॥
श्रुतशब्देन वा स्वात्मविषये[2] ज्ञानमुच्यते ।
कर्मशब्देन तद्विद्यासिद्धिस्तदधिकारतः ॥ ९१ ॥
ज्ञाननिष्ठाय देयानि [3]कव्यानीत्यपि हि स्मृतिः ।
शीलवन्तोऽपि वा नित्यं[4]मङ्गला इह कीर्तिताः ॥ ९२ ॥
स्नातका गृहिणो यद्वा स्नातकव्रतसंयुताः ।
ब्राह्मणा एव ते ज्ञेया ब्राह्मणाश्चेति वक्ष्यते ॥ ९३ ॥
तृप्त्यर्थं पितृदेवानां विप्रसृष्टिः स्मृतेरपि ।
आश्रमान्तरसंबन्धविधिर्दैविक[5]भोजने ॥ ९४ ॥
विश्वान्देवान् समुद्दिश्य पैतृके यत्प्रदीयते ।
स्वंस्वमावसथं तेषामधिगम्य पृथक् पृथक् ॥ ९५ ॥
निमन्त्रयीत पित्रर्थान्[6] दैवपूर्वान्यथोदितम् ।
दैवे[7] युग्मःस्मृताः पित्र्ये[8] त्वयुग्माः शक्तितो[9] द्विजाः ॥ ९६ ॥
द्वौ वा दैवे त्रयः पित्र्य एकैक उभयत्र वा ।
[10]मातामहानामप्येवं[11] तन्त्रं वा वैश्वदेविकम् ॥ ९७ ॥
सत्क्रियां देशकालौ च शौचं ब्राह्मणसम्पदः ।
पञ्चैतान्विस्तरो हन्ति तस्मान्नेहेत विस्तरम् ॥ ९८ ॥

१.T °वाचा च संयतैः. २.M °विषय°. ३.M काव्या°. ४.T नित्य°. ५.M देविक°. ६.M पित्रार्थान्. ७.M देवैर्युग्म. ८.MT पित्रे. ९.M शक्तिते. १०.M puts वा at the beginning of next hemistich before माता°. ११.M °प्यवस्तन्त्रं.

कृष्णपक्षान्तशब्देनामावास्यात्राभिधीयते ।
नित्यमत्र भवेच्छ्राद्धं कालमात्रनिमित्ततः ॥ ९९ ॥

[प्रयतत्वमीमांसा]

शौचातिशयसिध्यर्थं प्रयतत्वमनूच्यते ।
शक्तौ मुहूर्तमपि नाप्रयतः[1] स्यादिति स्मृतेः ॥ १०० ॥
तदङ्गस्नानसिध्यर्थं कृतशौचत्वमुच्यते ।
यद्वा[2] प्रयतता स्वात्मशुद्धिरत्र विवक्षिता ॥ १०१ ॥
मृतिजन्मनिमित्तायामन्तःशुद्धौ[3] न तद् भवेत् ।
शुद्धान्तःकरणत्वं वा प्रयतत्वमिहोच्यते ॥ १०२ ॥
श्राद्धकर्माधिकारो हि तस्यैव स्मर्यते यतः ।
कृतशौचत्वमप्यत्रातिशयार्थं समीर्यते ॥ १०३ ॥
मनागपि ततोऽशुद्धिः पितृकार्ये निरस्यते ।
परिश्रित्य श्रुतौ देशे शुचिभिः साधनैस्ततः ॥ १०४ ॥

[श्राद्धे द्रव्यसंस्काराः]

तत्कार्यं पूर्वमेवान्नभक्ष्यपेयादिसंस्कृतिम् ।
विधिवत्कारयेत्स्त्रीभिः पिष्टैर्मांसक्रिया कलौ ॥ १०५ ॥
तिलादयो यथा भोज्यो संस्कार्या विधिवत्तथा ।
क्षीरतण्डुलसर्पीभिः सतिलैः कृसरक्रिया ॥ १०६ ॥
[4]भृष्टतण्डुलचूर्णानि सिताद्यैरन्वितानि तु ।
अन्यानि श्राद्धयोग्यानि विहितानि श्रुतौ स्मृतौ ॥ १०७ ॥
संस्कार्याण्यपि देयानि मध्वाज्यं घृतमेव वा ।
विष्टराश्च त्रयः कार्या दर्भैर्विरचिताः[5]शुभाः ॥ १०८ ॥
होमार्थौदुम्बरी दर्वी [6]सोग्रमज्जबिलान्विता ।
सकृदाच्छिन्न एव स्याद्[7] बर्हिर्मुष्टिर्मृदः[8] शुभाः ॥ १०९ ॥

१.M °प्रयत. २.M यद्वः. ३.M °मतो शुद्धो. ४.M ...ष्ट°. ५.M दर्भेऽपि रचिताः. ६.M स्वोग्र°. ७.M स्याः. ८.M मृदुः.

यत्र पिण्डाः प्रदीयन्ते पितृभ्यः श्रुतिदर्शनात् ।
औदुम्बर्यश्च समिधो श्रिता[1] मेक्षणमेव च ॥ ११० ॥
अर्घ्यार्थं राजतं पात्रं तद्युक्तं कांस्यमेव वा ।
अर्घ्यादिसंस्कृतिः कार्या पूर्वमेवागमादिह ॥ १११ ॥
दक्षिणाग्रैस्तृणैरत्र परिस्तरणमिष्यते ।
च्छिन्नैस्तृणाग्रैर्बहुभिर्दक्षिणोत्तरपार्श्वयोः ॥ ११२ ॥
स्वकर्तृत्वमपूर्वत्वं पैतृकेषु पुरोदितम् ।
हविषो लौकिके वह्नौ पाकं कुर्वन्ति पैतृके ॥ ११३ ॥
सकृत्प्रक्षालनं कार्यं तण्डुलानां च पैतृके ।
पात्राणां सादनं चापि वह्नेर्दक्षिणतः स्मृतम् ॥ ११४ ॥
[2]आज्यस्थाली प्रोक्षण्यर्थपात्रं दर्वी च मेक्षणम् ।
विष्टरावुदपात्राणि तृणमुष्टिस्तथा हविः ॥ ११५ ॥
औदुम्बर्यश्च समिधः सकृदाच्छिन्नमेव च ।
वह्नेर्दक्षिणतश्चार्घ्यक्लृप्तिः[3] स्यात् सैकते स्थले ॥ ११६ ॥
तस्माद्दक्षिणतः पश्चाद्वि[4]प्रभोजनमिष्यते ॥ ११६क ॥
पादशौचार्थमवटं[5] वर्तुलं द्वादशाङ्गुलम् ।
शुद्धे स्थले प्रकर्तव्यं[6] तस्य दक्षिणतः शुभम् ॥ ११७ ॥
निधाय चासनं गर्तमुपलिप्य सकृज्जलैः ।
तृणानि दक्षिणाग्राणि वोदगग्राणि वा क्षिपेत् ॥ ११८ ॥
निदध्याच्च मृदं गर्तपूर्वपश्चिमपार्श्वयोः ।
पश्चाद्दक्षिणतो [7]भुक्तेर्निदध्यादासनानि च ॥ ११९ ॥
प्रागग्रे द्वे तृणे [8]पश्चान्निहितेषु विनिक्षिपेत् ।
दक्षिणाग्रं[9] तथैकैकं निदध्याद्दक्षिणासने ॥ १२० ॥
राजतेषु तु शुद्धेषु पात्रेषु द्विजभोजनम् ।

१.M मिता. २.M अज्य°. ३.M °श्चार्घ्यः. ४.M °द्विप्रे°. ५.M °मभवं. ६.M प्रकर्तव्यस्तस्य.
७.M भुंक्ते नि. ८.M तृणे...निहि°. ९.M °णाग्रस्तथै°.

तदन्वितेषु पात्रेषु[१] विशिष्टेष्वपि तद्भवेत् ॥ १२१ ॥
चतुरश्रस्थण्डिले तन्निधानमपि च स्मृतम् ॥ १२१क ॥
जलेन भस्मना वापि पङ्क्तिदोषनिवृत्तये ।
मर्यादा परितः कार्या पृथक्पृथगिति स्मृतम् ॥ १२२ ॥
अर्घ्यदानविधानार्थे[२] पत्रे[३] सव्यपुटे समे ।
स्यातां[४] पवित्रकरणं दर्भेणैकेन पैतृके ॥ १२३ ॥
प्रोक्षण्याज्यादिसंस्कारधर्मा अपि सकृत्सकृत् ॥ १२३क ॥
प्राचीनावीतिना पित्र्यं कर्म कार्यमितीरितम् ।
वैश्वदेविकमत्रापि कार्यं यज्ञोपवीतिना ॥ १२४ ॥
अलङ्कृतिस्तथा वह्नेरभिवादो जपोऽपि च ।
पैतृकं चापसव्यं[५] स्याद्वैश्वदेवं प्रदक्षिणम् ॥ १२५ ॥
निषिद्धानुपनीतानां सन्निधिः पितृकर्मणि ।
स्नात्वा विशुद्धवसनः साचान्तः[६] सपवित्रकः ॥ १२६ ॥
कृतवह्न्यादिसंस्कार आसनस्थस्तृणासनः[७] ।
प्राङ्मुखो दर्भपाणिः सन् ब्रूयात्स्वागतमागतान् ॥ १२७ ॥
अथाभिवाद्य तान्विप्रान् निमन्त्र्य च यथाविधि ।
प्रक्षाल्य चैव तत्पादौ क्लृप्तकेशनखादिकान्[८] ॥ १२८ ॥
तैलेनाऽभ्यज्य[९] संस्नाप्य सुगन्धामलकादिभिः ।
आचमय्य च तान्विप्रान् अर्घ्यपाद्यादिसंयुतम् ॥ १२९ ॥
अथ सव्यं स्वयं वासो[१०] वसित्वाऽथोपवेशयेत् ।
सहपिण्डक्रियामासश्राद्धप्रकृतिरिष्यते ॥ १३० ॥
आहूय ब्राह्मणान्पादौ प्रक्षाल्येत्यादि तत्र च ।
एवमेव समाम्नातं ततः पाद्यमितीह च ॥ १३१ ॥
ततः शब्दप्रयोगोऽयमन्यथा[११] स्यान्निरर्थकम् ।

१.T पत्रेषु. २.M पिधानार्थे. ३.T पत्रे. ४.M स्यातामप°. ५.T चाऽसव्यं. ६.T स्वाचान्तः. ७.M आसनस्थ. ८.M °दिगान्. ९.T तैलैर्वाभ्य°. १०.T वासोऽव°. ११.M प्रयोगो यः अन्य°.

[१]स्नानानन्तरमेवेह यद्वा पाद्यादिचोदना ॥ १३२ ॥
न [२]तूपवेशनादूर्ध्वं स्नानमत्र विवक्षितः ।
भोजनार्थं यतश्चात्र प्राङ्मुखाद्युपवेशनम् ॥ १३३ ॥
अन्यथा तददृष्टार्थं स्मृतिशास्त्रविरोध्यपि[३] ।
स्मृतिन्यायानुसारेण यत्रौपयिकं स्मृतम्[४] ॥ १३४ ॥
आनूद्यतेऽर्घ्यदानार्थं ततः स्नानादिना ततः ।
उपवेश्य ततो दद्यादर्घ्यमित्यत्र योजना ॥ १३५ ॥
तिलावकिरणं चोक्तं सर्वपैतृककर्मसु ।
जलपात्रान्नभूम्यादौ[५] तत्प्रक्षेपविधित्सया ॥ १३६ ॥
[६]अर्घ्यपाद्यादि पित्रर्थं ब्राह्मणेभ्यस्तिलान्वयात्[६] ।
कस्मिंश्चिद्भाजने दर्भं निधायैव क्षिपेज्जलम् ॥ १३७ ॥
तिलांश्च पाद्यमित्युक्त्वा तत्पादाववनेजयेत्[७] ।
पादप्रक्षालनविधिर्मधुपर्के समीरितः ॥ १३८ ॥
अन्यत्राचमनं[८] कार्यं संस्कृतैः पूर्ववज्जलैः ।
यज्ञोपवीतमित्यत्र ब्रह्मसूत्रं विवक्षितम् ॥ १३९ ॥
तस्यापसव्यता चेह सर्वपित्रर्थमिष्यते ।
अत एवोपवीती सन् प्राङ्मुखान्वैश्वदेविकान् ॥ १४० ॥
उपवेश्य द्विजान्पित्र्यानुदीचमुपवेशयेत् ।
समुच्चयार्थ एवेह वाशब्दोऽस्तीति[९]दर्शनात् ॥ १४१ ॥
युग्मान् प्राच उदीचश्चायुगांच्छक्त्यनुसारतः ॥ १४१क ॥
द्वौ दैवे पितृकार्ये त्रीनेकैकमुभयत्र वा ।

१.M स्नाननन्त°. २.M तु च वेश°. ३.M विरूध्यपि. ४.M °पयिकमुतम्. ५.T °पात्रान्न...दौ. ६-६.T reads the text in two lines as :

अर्घ्यपादादिदानं................................ ।।
..................पित्रर्थब्राह्मणेभ्यस्तिलान्मयात्।

M, however reads the whole text as forming the first hemistich; here दानं seems to be superfluous. ७.M °वपनेज°. ८.T अन्यत्रासंस्कृतैः. ९.M शब्दस्ति, T शब्द...स्ति.

भोजयेत्सुसमृद्धोऽपि न प्रसज्येत विस्तरे ॥ १४२ ॥
सत्क्रियां देशकालौ च शौचं ब्राह्मणसम्पदः ।
पञ्चैतान् विस्तरो[1] हन्ति तस्मान्नेहेत विस्तरम् ॥ १४३ ॥
अन्वारभ्यांसं पूर्वव[2]त्तद्दक्षिणकरं ततः ।
गृहीत्वा दक्षिणेनामूनुपवेश्य यथाविधि ॥ १४४ ॥
प्राप्नोत्वित्युपवेश्याथ[3] .... ।
तिलोदकसमाख्यानां पित्रर्थानां द्विजन्मनाम् ॥ १४५ ॥
दक्षिणेषु करेष्वर्घ्यं पवित्रान्तर्हितेषु च ।
दद्यादर्घ्यमिहैकं स्यात् सर्वेषामेकवच्छ्रुतेः ॥ १४६ ॥
एकदर्भविनिष्पन्नपवित्रवति भाजने ।
जलमासिच्य सुरभिमत्तिलानोप्य तज्जलम् ॥ १४७ ॥
सिकतोपरि संस्तीर्णदक्षिणाग्रतृणस्थिते ।
पात्रे पवित्रवत्सिक्त्वा जलगन्धार्कवोदकैः ॥ १४८ ॥
अभ्यर्घ्यावाह्य[4] च [5]पितॄनब्गन्धकुसुमैरपि ।
सधूपदीपमाल्यैश्च समभ्यर्घ्य तृणादिभिः ॥ १४९ ॥
आच्छादयेदर्घ्यक्लृप्तिर्व्यष्टके पितृकर्मणि ।
तत्र पात्रान्तरं[6] सर्वं सुरभ्यपि च नेष्यते ॥ १५० ॥
पाणिप्रक्षालनं दत्त्वा स्वासनेषूपवेश्य च ।
उपविश्य स्वयं सव्यं जान्वाच्य[7] द्विजहस्तके ॥ १५१ ॥
अर्घ्यस्थितं दक्षिणाग्रं विन्यस्य च पवित्रकम् ।
जलं दत्त्वार्घ्यमादाय पात्राभ्यां मन्त्रवत्क्षिपेत् ॥ १५२ ॥
आद्यन्तयोर्जलं दद्यादर्घ्यदानमिदं[8] मतम् ।
पैतृकं पितृतीर्थेन कर्म कार्यमिति स्मृतम् ॥ १५३ ॥
बद्धप्रतिसरत्वं स्यादूर्णासूत्रेण बन्धनात् ॥ १५३क ॥

१.M पञ्चैतद्विस्त मोहन्ति. २.M सं पूर्वं तद्दक्षि°. ३.MT broken after वेश्याथ [M वेश्य च].
४.M अभ्यर्ध्यमावा°. ५.M वितृन्गान्ध°. ६.T पात्राकरं. ७.M °न्वाप्य. ८.M दत्वाद्यादर्ध्यदानं.

उपवीती दर्भपाणिरुत्थायावाहयेत्ततः ।
प्राङ्मुखः सन् सुरौ द्वौ द्वौ श्राद्धकर्मसु चोदितौ ॥ १५४ ॥
नान्दीमुखे क्रतु[१]सत्यावष्टेत्यां कालकाम्यकौ ।
क्रतुदक्षौ सपिण्ड्यां तु काम्येषु च धुरीरुचः ॥ १५५ ॥
पुरूरवाद्रवौ[२] चैव पार्वणे विनियोजयेत् ।
गन्धपुष्पतृणाम्भोभिस्तूष्णीमावाहयेत्सुरान् ॥ १५६ ॥
तत्सन्निधित्संस्मरणं[३] द्विजेष्वावाहनं 'पितॄन् ।
आवाहयिष्य' इत्युक्त 'ओमद्यावाहये'ति[४] च[५] ॥ १५७ ॥
पित्रर्थैरभ्यनुज्ञातः पितॄनावाहयेदृचा ।
दत्त्वा तिलान्वितजलं पूर्ववत् पूजयेद्[६] द्विजान् ॥ १५८ ॥
जलवासोगन्धपुष्पधूपदीपस्रगादिभिः ।
भूषणैः संस्कृतं घृतसंयुतं संस्कृतं हविः ॥ १५९ ॥
आदाय पृष्ट्वानुज्ञातः सर्वैर्वह्नावलंकृतैः[७] ।
मन्त्रवत्परिषिच्याज्यं 'याः [८]प्राची'र्जुहुयादिह ॥ १६० ॥

[आहिताग्नेः श्राद्धकर्म]

अनूद्यते पूर्वमेव कर्तव्या वह्निसंस्कृतिः ।
वह्न्यादिनियमार्थतो[९] लौकिकस्य न संग्रहः ॥ १६१ ॥
[१०]औपासनाग्निरामात्यश्रौतार्थो वा द्विजाहृतः ।
अपराह्णे [११]तमुद्धरेत्यस्मदादीयेनोक्तितः ॥ १६२ ॥
कृत्स्नस्य चैकदेशस्य पितृदानार्थतोदिता ।
उच्यतेऽत्र व्यवस्थाऽतो लौकिकाग्निनिवृत्तये ॥ १६३ ॥
आहिताग्नेः श्राद्धकर्मप्राप्त एवैतदीर्यते ।
पैतृयाज्ञिकहोमस्य लौकिकाग्नौ निषेधतः ॥ १६४ ॥

१.T तु. २.M पुरूरवार्द्रवौ. ३.T तत्सन्निधानस्म°. ४.T °द्यावहयेदिति. ५.T oms. ६.M oms द्. ७.M °कृते. ८.M प्राचीं. ९.T °मार्था तो. १०.M °सनानि समारभ्य श्रोतार्थो. ११.M तममुद्धृत्येत्यस्मादीयेन; T तमुद्धृत्येत्यस्मदादीपनो°.

स्मार्ताग्निसंभवे स्मार्तं तत्रैवेति नियम्यते ।
आमात्याद्यभिधानेन श्राद्धं तस्माद् द्वयोरपि ॥ १६५ ॥
श्राद्धाभावोऽनाहिताग्नेरत एव न शङ्क्यते[१] ।
सर्वस्मृतिषु तस्यैव श्राद्धकर्म विधीयते ॥ १६६ ॥
आचार्योऽप्यष्टकां नित्यां विवाहानन्तरं वदन् ।
गृहस्थमात्रसाध्यार्थं श्राद्धस्य ज्ञापयत्यसौ ॥ १६७ ॥
दर्भाः परिधयो ज्ञेया नापरे वृक्षसंभवाः ।
दक्षिणाग्रत्वमत्रोक्तमेषामेवं समञ्जसम् ॥ १६८ ॥
परितोऽग्नेर्निधीयन्ते दक्षिणाग्रा यतो हि ते ।
[२]छिन्नैस्तृणाग्रैः परितो दक्षिणोत्तरपार्श्वयोः ॥ १६९ ॥
परिस्तरणसिद्ध्यर्थं परिधिरिति[३] भण्यते ।
पूर्वपश्चिमपार्श्वस्था दक्षिणाग्राः स्युरन्यथा ॥ १७० ॥

[आमात्येऽग्निकार्यम्]

ततोऽस्मिन्दक्षिणे वह्नौ कृत्स्नाग्निविनियोजने ।
आमात्ये त्वन्यथा कुर्यादग्निकार्यं तदुच्यते ॥ १७१ ॥
'याः प्राची'रिति हुत्वेति मन्त्राः पञ्चदशोदिताः ।
उदुम्बरोत्थया दर्व्या हुत्वाज्यं मेक्षणेन तु ॥ १७२ ॥
संस्कृतेन चरोर्हुत्वा[४] तदग्नौ प्रास्य मेक्षणम् ।
मन्त्रवत्परिषिच्यान्नं हुतशेषं तु साज्यकम् ॥ १७३ ॥

[पित्रर्थब्राह्मणभोजनविधिः]

[५]पित्रर्थद्विजभुक्त्यर्थपात्रेषु विनियोजयेत् ।
ददत्तन्मनसा[६] ध्यायन्पितॄननुदिशोदिति ॥ १७४ ॥
लिङ्गादन्यस्य कृत्स्नस्य विनियोगो न चोदितः ।
प्रकृता[७] न विकारं हि कुर्युरित्यभिधास्यते ॥ १७५ ॥

१.M शक्यते. २.M हिंस्रैस्तृ°, T च्छिन्नेस्तृ°. ३.MT परिधीरि°. ४.T चरोहु°. ५.M पित्रर्थं. ६.M मनसा साध्यायत्पितृ°. ७. T प्रकृता...वि°.

वैश्वदेविकभुक्त्यर्थमतः पाकान्तरक्रिया ।
दैवपूर्वमुपस्तीर्य दत्त्वान्नं व्यञ्जनान्वितम् ॥ १७६ ॥
श्राद्धाभिमन्त्रणेनान्नं पितृदत्तं तृणान्वितम् ।
अभिमृज्य द्विजाङ्गुष्ठांस्तदन्येषु[१] नियोजयेत् ॥ १७७ ॥
अङ्गुष्ठमात्रो भगवान् विष्णुः पर्यटते महीम् ।
राक्षसानां वधार्थाय तेन रक्षो न बाधते ॥ १७८ ॥
दत्त्वोपस्तरणीयं च जलं तेभ्यः समाहितः ।
'इदमन्नमि'ति प्रोच्य दक्षिणाभिमुखः पितॄन् ॥ १७९ ॥
तेषां प्राणाहुतीः 'प्राणे निविश्ये'त्यभिमन्त्र्य च ।
उपवीय स्वहृदयं 'ब्रह्मणी'त्यभिमृश्य च ॥ १८० ॥
यथारुचि यथान्यायमुक्तान्नं[२] परिवेषयेत् ।
जपेद्वा स्वयमन्नं तत् [३]पथ्येव परिवेषयेत् ॥ १८१ ॥
अनसूयं[४] द्विजा ब्रूयुर्नान्नदोषगुणानपि ।
तदर्था 'ब्राह्मणाश्चे'ति[५] च शब्दोक्तिस्तथा[६] स्मृतेः॥ १८२ ॥
अनुष्णस्य प्रशंसाया[७] निषेधस्तुतिदर्शनात् ।
च शब्दो वाग्यमाद्यर्थः संस्थितः प्रागुदङ्मुखः ॥ १८३ ॥
जप्त्वादौ मधुवातीयं तृचं राक्षोघ्नसंज्ञितम् ।
'सोमासो' 'शं त' इत्येतौ गायत्रीं [८]तद्वदादिताः ॥ १८४ ॥
'आशुः शिशान' इत्येत'मिन्द्रो वृत्रा'दि पैतृकम् ।
अनुवाकं पित्र्ययज्ञवचनौ पावमानकीः ॥ १८५ ॥
तथा चेदमनूच्येति नाचिकेतमयादिकम्[९] ।
विनान्त्य[१०]त्रिसुपर्णं च पौरुषं पावनी[११] स्मृतिः ॥ १८६ ॥
दर्भपाणिर्जपेत्त्वेषु[१२] सुतृप्तेषु द्विजातिषु ।

१.M °स्तदन्नेषु. २.M न्यायं मुक्ता°. ३.M °तत्...वत्परि°, T पत्स्येव. ४.M adds वा after अनुसूयं. ५.M ब्राह्मणांश्चेति. ६.M शब्दोक्षिस्त°. ७.M प्रशंसायां. ८.M गायंत्रीन्तत्पदादिताम्. ९.M गाचितेतमयाचितम्. १०.M विनान्त्यं. ११.M चापनी. १२ M °र्जपत्वैषु, T र्जपेत्वेषु.

दक्षिणाभिमुखो जप्त्वा मधुवातादिकं[1] तृचम् ॥ १८७ ॥
पृष्ट्वा 'स्वदितमि'त्येतत् ज्ञात्वा दत्त्वा पिधानकम्।
शिष्टमन्नमनुज्ञाप्य विप्रैरिष्टनियोजनैः[2] ॥ १८८ ॥
कृत्स्नादन्नात्समुद्धृत्य पैतृकोच्छिष्टसन्निधौ ।
दर्भानास्तीर्य निक्षिप्य तेषूच्छिष्टाशयेषु च ॥ १८९ ॥
जलान्वितं ततः पात्रीं यस्यामन्नं समुद्धृतम् ।
संक्षाल्य तज्जलं सिक्त्वा[3] दक्षिणां दिशमेत्य तु ॥ १९० ॥
तस्मादुद्धृत्य निक्षिप्य मेलनादन्नविक्रिया ।
बहूक्तेः कर्तृनियमस्तत्र नास्तीति गम्यते ॥ १९१ ॥
[4]जलगन्धात्तिलजलदानपूर्वं पितॄंस्तथा ।
आवाह्य विष्टरेष्वेतानभ्यर्च्य[5] जलपूर्वकम् ॥ १९२ ॥
धूपगन्धार्तवस्रग्भिरादर्शेन यथाक्रमम् ।
[6]प्रदीयाञ्जनतैलाद्यैः सूत्रैरेभिर्यथा[7] पृथक् ॥ १९३ ॥
[8]दर्भान् प्रक्षालितान् याज्यतूलांस्तत्सन्निधौ[9] ततः ।
आस्तीर्य मूलमध्याग्रेष्वम्भसा परिषिच्य च ॥ १९४ ॥
पिण्डान् कृत्वा दक्षिणेन पाणिनैकैकमाददत्[10] ।
उपसंगृह्य सव्येन पाणिं पित्रादिनाम तु ॥ १९५ ॥
संबुध्यन्तं 'देवदत्तशर्मणेतत्त' इत्यपि ॥ १९५क ॥
उक्त्वा तृणेषु संन्यस्य मूलादितः[11] करौ ततः ।
निमृज्यान्तेषु दर्भेषु लेपभाक्पितृतृप्तये ॥ १९६ ॥
सर्वत्र पिण्डदानार्था मन्त्रा अन्य इवाहिते ।
इत्यत्रैव [12]स्व आम्नाने ह्यतैर्मन्त्रैरिहेष्यते ॥ १९७ ॥
सव्यावृतो नियम्यासूंस्त्रिः परावृत्य[13] वारिभिः ।

१.M °वाकाद°. २.M °योजने. ३.M सित्वा. ४.M °गन्धात्तजलदा°. ५.T °रेषूक्तानभ्य°. ६.M प्रदीपाञ्ज°. ७.M सूत्रैरुग्भिर्य°. ८.M wrongly adds पृथक् at the beginning of next Verse before दर्भान्. ९.M प्रक्षान्य कान्या ताम्बूलांस्त°. १०.M °ददत्सतु. ११.T मूलादी... करौ. १२.M स्वनाम्ने°. १३.M adds च between परावृत्य and वारिभिः.

उदपात्रस्थितैः पिण्डान्परिप्लाव्यापसव्यकम् ॥ १९८ ॥
[१]न्युब्ज्य पात्राणि विप्रेभ्यः प्रदाय च तिलोदकम् ।
जलादिभिः[२] समभ्यर्च्य पितृनुद्वास्य तैर्जलैः ॥ १९९ ॥
मार्जयित्वा 'यथा दिव्या' इत्यनेन स्वशक्तितः ।
विप्रेभ्यो दक्षिणां दत्त्वा सुवर्णाद्याञ्जलान्वितम् ॥ २०० ॥
स्वनामगोत्रे संश्राव्य द्विजांस्तानभिवाद्य च ।
दक्षिणाभिमुखो [३]याचेद् 'दातार' इति तैर्द्विजैः ॥ २०१ ॥
'एवमस्ति'वति निर्दिष्ट उपविश्य पितृंस्ततः ।
अभ्यर्च्योद्वास्य तान्पिण्डान् प्रक्षिपेदनलेऽप्सु वा ॥ २०२ ॥
[४]वा शब्दद्वयसामर्थ्याद् वयोभिः खादयेद् द्विजान् ।
आशयेदप्यजां [५]गां वा पितृपूर्वं[५] द्विजांस्ततः ॥ २०३ ॥
उत्थाप्य तान् नमस्कृत्य प्रदक्षिणसमन्वितम् ।
प्रार्थयेद्याम्यवदनस्तृप्तानेतान्द्विजोत्तमान् ॥ २०४ ॥
'दातारो नोऽभिवर्धन्तां[६] वेदसन्ततिरेव च ।
श्रद्धा च नो मा व्यगमद् बहुदेयञ्च नोऽस्त्विति' ॥ २०५ ॥
अनुज्ञातस्ततो विप्रैर्वैश्वदेवसमन्वितम् ।
सगणोऽन्नं तदश्नीयान्नियमार्थमिदं वचः ॥ २०६ ॥
तच्छिष्टस्यैव भुक्तिः स्यात् सकृन्नोपत्रसेदतः ।
परिहारो निषिद्धानां कर्तुर्भोक्तुश्च वर्जनम् ॥ २०७ ॥
पुनर्भोजनमध्वानं भाराध्ययनमैथुने ।
दानं प्रतिग्रहं यज्ञं श्राद्धभुक् परिवर्जयेत् ॥ २०८ ॥
दन्तधावनताम्बूलक्षौराभ्यङ्गमभोजनम् ।
[७]रत्योषणपरान्नं च श्राद्धकर्ता विवर्जयेत् ॥ २०९ ॥
उच्छिष्टं न प्रमृज्यात्तु यावन्नास्तमितो रविः ।

१.M न्युब्ज°. २.M जालादि°. ३.M याचैद्दर्ता°. ४.M oms. ५-५.M च पितृपूर्व°. ६.M नो विवर्धन्तां. ७.M रव्योषधप°, T रत्योषडपरान्नं.

उत्थितेष्वेषु विप्रेषु यद्वोच्छिष्टं प्रमार्जयेत् ॥ २१० ॥
पितृतुष्टिनिमित्तत्वात् पुत्रोत्पत्तेरनन्तरम्[1] ।
निन्द्यपुत्रनिवृत्त्यर्थं सत्पुत्रोत्पत्तयेऽपि च ॥ २११ ॥
आरभ्यते परं वाक्यं न दिवामैथुनादिकम् ।
मघास्वित्यत्र[2] वर्षर्तौ त्रयोदश्यां मघास्विति ॥ २१२ ॥
मघासु[3] माघमासे वा पञ्चदश्यां तथा स्मृतेः ।
मध्वादिभिर्नियोगेन श्राद्धं कार्यं स्तुतेरतः ॥ २१३ ॥
यथाविधि सुतोत्पत्तौ प्रवृत्या श्राद्धकर्मणि ।
पैतृकर्मविमुक्तिः स्यात् इत्यस्मादपि गम्यते ॥ २१४ ॥

[श्राद्धानुष्ठानक्रमः]

अनुष्ठानक्रमं वक्ष्ये विदुषामुपकारकम् ।
प्राचीनावीतवद्बर्हिं परिस्तीर्य यथोदितम् ॥ २१५ ॥
संसाद्यैकैकशः सर्वं प्रोक्ष्य संस्कृतवारिणा ।
सकृद्दर्वीं मेक्षणं च संमृज्याज्यं[4] निरुप्य च ॥ २१६ ॥
वह्नेर्दक्षिणतोऽङ्गारेष्वधिश्रित्यान्नसंयुतम् ।
पर्यग्न्यपसलैः[5] कृत्वा घृतमुत्पूय तद्धविः ॥ २१७ ॥
प्रतिष्ठाप्य पवित्रं च कृत्वा पाद्यं तिलोदकम् ।
विधिवत्स्वागतं प्रोच्य ब्राह्मणानभिवाद्य च ॥ २१८ ॥
मासश्राद्ध इति प्रोच्य वैश्वदेवं निमन्त्र्य च ।
प्राचीनावीतवत्पित्र्यमेकं मातामहं द्विजम् ॥ २१९ ॥
तथा मातामहश्राद्धं क्षणमित्या.[6] तथेति तैः ।
हस्तं[7] प्रक्षाल्य तत्पादावाचमय्याम्बरं स्वयम् ॥ २२० ॥
अपसव्यं वसित्वा समाचान्त उपवेश्य तान् ।
दत्त्वा तिलोदकं देवांस्तूष्णीमावाह्य मन्त्रतः ॥ २२१ ॥
पितॄन् मातामहांस्तूष्णीमर्घ्यं दत्त्वा समर्च्य तान् ।

१.M पित्रोत्वत्तेरन°. २.M मघास्थित्य°. ३.MT मघ. ४.M adds च between °ज्यं and निरुप्य. ५.T °पसद्यैः. ६.T °मित्यां. ७.M हक्तं, T उक्तं.

दत्त्वा तिलोदकं स्पृष्ट्वा साज्यमादाय तद्धविः ॥ २२२ ॥
सर्वैः[1] .... ।
.... ॥ २२३ ॥
[2]नैयोगिकी पुमुत्पत्तिरुत्पन्नस्य सुतस्य च ।
विहितोत्पत्तिः संस्कार[3]करणादिति ॥ २२४ ॥

[अष्टकाश्राद्धनिरूपणम्]

जातकर्मात्र निर्दिष्टमष्टकाकर्मणो वचः ।
नित्यत्वख्यापनार्थं तत् संस्कारे गृहिणः कृते ॥ २२५ ॥
न चार्थवादजनितफलक्लृप्तिरिहोचिता ।
अपूपेनापि कार्यत्वादन्नादिविरहे सति ॥ २२६ ॥
न त्वेवानष्टकः[4] स्यादित्येवं कैश्चिच्च पठ्यते ।
[5]सर्वस्मृतिभिरप्यस्यानित्यत्वं प्रतिपाद्यते ॥ २२७ ॥
[6]अष्टम्यर्थोऽष्टकाशब्दस्तस्यां यत्क्रियते तिथौ ।
तदष्टकेति निर्दिष्टं कालद्वारेण कर्मणः ॥ २२८ ॥
[7]स्वरूपावगतिर्मन्त्रलिङ्गलभ्या[8] तदाख्यया ।
एकस्यामपि शाखायां न ह्येता पठ्यतेऽष्टका ॥ २२९ ॥
अधीयन्तेऽष्टका मन्त्राः स्वाध्यायविधिचोदिताः ।
तदाख्यान्वितमन्त्राणां तदाख्याते हि कर्मणि ॥ २३० ॥
विनियोगे कृतार्थत्वं जपयज्ञान्वयेन हि ।
समाख्यानोपपत्तिः स्यादग्निष्टोमादिवत्ततः ॥ २३१ ॥
मन्त्रलिङ्गानुसारेण [9]तत्कर्म परिकल्प्यते ।
पितृतृप्तिसुधापूपाद्यन्वितान् मन्त्रवाक्यतः ॥ २३२ ॥

१.MT indicates the loss of one Folio after this text: अत्र चिह्नित कोष्ठ पत्रिकायाभावः (M); इत उपरि पत्रमेकं मातृकायां लुप्तं दृश्यते (T). २.M नैर्यो°. ३.MT broken, T indicates the sign of broken tet by dots after संस्कार. M, however, does not show it. ४.M त्वेवाष्टक. ५.MT °स्मर्तृभि°. ६.T अष्टम्यथोऽ°. ७.T °गतिं मन्त्र°. ८.MT लभ्यां. ९.M oms.

द्रव्यदैवतसंयोगः साधिकारोऽवगम्यते ।
ततस्तदनुसारेण[1] प्राप्नोत्येवोपकारकम् ॥ २३३ ॥
मन्त्रार्थवादैरेवार्थैः श्रुतिभिः परिकल्प्यते ।
अष्टकामिति निर्दिश्य माघस्यैकामिति ब्रुवन् ॥ २३४ ॥
[2]माघ्यष्टकाया नित्यत्वं ज्ञापयत्येष कल्पकृत् ।
स्तुतिरप्यर्थवत्येव [3]मन्त्रराधादियोगिनी ॥ २३५ ॥
'संवत्सरस्य या पत्नी सा न' इत्यपि युज्यते ।
[4]अन्वर्थत्वादष्टकायाः सर्वत्र करणं यदि ॥ २३६ ॥
[5]प्रत्यक्षत्वात्कृष्णपक्षाष्टमीष्वेतत्क्रियादिति ।
तिस्रस्तैषस्य मासस्य कृष्णपक्षाष्टमीष्विति ॥ २३७ ॥
अध्याहृत्याष्टमीं योज्य अथवाध्यष्टकामिति ।
सप्तमाद्या नवम्यान्ताः[6] पक्षेऽस्मिन्नष्टका मता ॥ २३८ ॥
अष्टकामिति निर्देशात् तृतीये दानचोदनात् ।
एकत्वमष्टकाख्यातकर्मणोऽस्यावगम्यते ॥ २३९ ॥
[7]भोक्तॄणां विप्रवर्याणां यदर्थं यन्निमन्त्रणम् ।
तदर्थतैव तस्य स्यादात्मनेपदयोगतः ॥ २४० ॥
स्वयं कर्तृत्वमेव स्यादुपकल्पनवर्णनात् ।
प्रयोगः प्राशुभावाच्च पूर्वं तद् द्रव्यसंगतः ॥ २४१ ॥
स्वगर्भघातिनियोगौ[8] यावेहेत्यभिधीयते[9] ।
अन्नग्रहणमप्यत्रापूपादेरुपलक्षणम् ॥ २४२ ॥
मधुग्रहणमप्यत्र यागद्रव्योपलक्षणम् ।
अतः स्मृत्युदितं श्राद्धयोग्यमापाद्यमेव[10] तु ॥ २४३ ॥
इहाष्टकायाः प्राधान्यं तस्य कर्मण उच्यते ।

१.M oms. २.M माध्याष्ट°. ३.M मन्त्राराधा°. ४.M अष्टकार्थत्वाद°. ५.M पित्रर्थत्वाम्कृष्ण-पक्षाष्टमीष्वेतत्; M gives क्रियादिति at the beginning of the second hemistich. ६.M नवम्यास्ताः...क्षस्मिन्न°. ७.M °णामपिप्रवर्या°. ८.M स्वर्ग...तिनिर्यागौ; T °निर्योगौ. ९.M यावेहदित्य°. १०.M °मापद्यवे तु ह.

होमभोजनदानानां प्राधान्यमिह वर्ण्यते ॥ २४४ ॥
होमस्य लिङ्गसामर्थ्यात्प्राधान्यं प्रतिपादितम् ।
ददातीतीह निर्देशात्पितृभ्यो दानचोदनात् ॥ २४५ ॥
प्राधान्यमेव पिण्डानां होमस्य न तदर्थता ।
ओदनस्यैव[1] देयत्ववचनात्पिण्डदानवत् ॥ २४६ ॥
अपूपमांसमात्रस्य मध्वादिविरहेऽपि च ।
देयत्वनियमोक्त्या च प्राधान्यं[2] द्विजभोजनम् ॥ २४७ ॥
[3]मध्वादिवद्गुणत्वेऽपि नैतद्वच इहोऽर्थवत्[4] ।
अतो न प्रतिपाद्यार्थं[5] शिष्टापूपस्य युज्यते ॥ २४८ ॥
अतस्त्रयाणां [6][नित्यत्व]मित्यत्राप्यवसीयते[7] ॥ २४८क ॥
देवतिर्यङ्मनुष्यस्थान् होमदानद्विजाशनैः ।
प्रीणाति श्राद्धकृदिति स्मृतिरेवं च युज्यते ॥ २४९ ॥
स्मृतिप्राप्तस्य शौचस्य प्रसिद्धत्वमिहोच्यते ।
स्मार्तानामेतदन्येषां धर्माणामुपलक्षणम् ॥ २५० ॥
सप्तमी माघमासस्य कृष्णपक्षस्य या तिथिः ।
अनूराधान्वयस्तस्याः प्रायेण भवतीति सः ॥ २५१ ॥
अनूराधोपलक्ष्यार्थ[8]स्तद्युक्तायां तिथाविति ।
कृष्णपक्षस्य नित्यत्वमष्टकास्विति दर्शितम् ॥ २५२ ॥
सर्वेषु कृष्णपक्षेषु न ह्यनूराधसंभवः ।
माघ्यामेवैककरणमित्यप्यत्र[9] प्रदर्शितम् ॥ २५३ ॥
अनूराधादि शब्दोऽतः सप्तम्याद्युपलक्षणः[10] ॥ २५३क ॥
अग्नेरुपसमाधानं स्मार्तस्याविष्कृतिर्यतः ।
पैतृयज्ञिकहोमस्य निषेधोऽलौकिकेऽनले ॥ २५४ ॥

१.M °स्येव. २.T प्रधानं. ३.M adds कृत्वा before मध्वा° at the beginning of the Verse. ४.M इहोर्थवत्. ५.M अज्ञानप्रतिपाद्यार्थं. ६.MT broken. ७.M °त्रापसीयते, T नित्यत्राव्यवसीयते. ८.M °लक्ष्यासु तद्युक्ताया. ९.M °करण इत्य°. १०.T °द्युक्तलक्षणः.

अतो गृहिण एवास्मिन् श्राद्धकर्मण्यधिकृताः[१] ।
शोभयित्वा परिस्तीर्येत्येतत्तस्योपलक्षणम्[२] ॥ २५५ ॥
आपूर्विकत्वमस्येष्टमन्नस्विष्टकृदुक्तितः[३] ।
अतः पात्राणि संसाद्य प्रोक्ष्य संस्कृतवारिणा ॥ २५६ ॥
अष्ट प्रस्थमितान् व्रीहीन् पवित्रवति शूर्पके ।
[४]सकृन्निरुप्य शूर्पस्थान् प्रोक्ष्य शिष्टेन वारिणा ॥ २५७ ॥
अवहत्य फलीकृत्य प्रक्षाल्य च कपालकम् ।
उपधायाश्रुतेरेकमुपवेषेण केनचित् ॥ २५८ ॥
पिष्ट्वा पिष्टानि संस्कृत्येत्याद्यथ प्रतिपाद्यते ।
पुरोडाशवदित्यत्रापूपश्रपणवर्णनात्[५] ॥ २५९ ॥
व्रीहिनिर्वापवचनादेतत्सर्वं यथोदितम् ।
प्राप्तं कर्तव्यमेव स्यादनुक्तमिति गम्यते ॥ २६० ॥
निर्वापादेर्मन्त्रवत्त्वदर्शनाच्छ्रपणादिषु[६] ।
तत्तन्मन्त्रनिवृत्त्यर्थं तूष्णीमित्यभिधीयते ॥ २६१ ॥
निर्वापप्रोक्षणे कृत्वा[७] पिष्टसंस्कारवर्णनात् ।
लिङ्गाद्विरोधान्निर्वापे पिष्टग्रहणमिष्यते ॥ २६२ ॥
[८]पाकार्थत्वात्तण्डुलानां स्थालीपाके यथा ग्रहः ।
अपूर्वार्थतया पिष्टग्रहणं च तथोदितम्[९] ॥ २६३ ॥
तथैव च समाचारः शिष्टानामुपलभ्यते ।
अतोऽत्र पिष्टग्रहणं निर्वापेऽपि विकल्प्यते[१०] ॥ २६४ ॥
[११]प्रागपि [१२]श्रपणादाज्यनिर्वापाद्युदितं[१३] क्रतौ ।
शृतेऽस्मिन्नाज्यमित्यादि श्राद्धेऽस्मादभिधीयते ॥ २६५ ॥
पर्यग्निकरणं तस्मादपूपस्य तृणैः पुरा ।
पवित्रमेकमेव स्यादपूपाज्यादिसंस्कृतौ ॥ २६६ ॥

१.MT °क्रिया. २.M परिप्री...र्येत्येतत्तोपलक्षणः. ३.M °मन्नस्तिष्ट°, T °ष्टकुत्थितः. ४.MT शकृ°. ५.MT श्रवणवर्ण°. ६.MT °वत्वदर्शनाच्छ्रवणा°. ७.T उक्त्वा. ८.M पाकार्तत्वा°. ९.T तथोचितम्. १०.M विकथ्यते. ११.M प्राग्वपि. १२.MT श्रवणदाज्य° [Mज्यं]. १३.M निर्वाप्युदितं.

साधारणत्वादाज्येऽत्र संस्कृते प्रतिपाद्यते ।
[१]पुरोडाशवदेवास्यापूपस्योद्वासनं भवेत् ॥ २६७ ॥
तिलोदकं [२]विधायोपवेश्याभ्यर्च्य द्विजोत्तमान्[२] ।
अनुज्ञातो द्विजैर्दर्व्या जुहुयात्परिषिच्य तु ॥ २६८ ॥
औदुम्बर्येतिवचनं पितृपात्रोपलक्षणम् ।
पिण्डार्थाः समिधश्चात उदुम्बरसमुद्भवाः ॥ २६९ ॥
इहोपस्तरणाद्वित्तेरिष्टा[३] दर्व्यपरा तु सा ।
पूर्वोपात्ता विशेषेण तद्योग्या पर्णनिर्मिता[४] ॥ २७० ॥
उत्तरानधरान्देशान्त्समारभ्याग्निकोणतः[५] ।
होमावदानवचनादन्यत्रापि तथेष्यते ॥ २७१ ॥
उपांशुत्वमिहापीष्टं प्राजापत्याहुतेः सकृत् ।
अभिघारणमेव स्यात् स्विष्टकृत्यपि पैतृके ॥ २७२ ॥
पिण्डावृत् पितृयज्ञोक्ता तन्मात्रवचनादिह[६] ।
तच्च होम[७] उपस्थानमपि नास्तीति गम्यते ॥ २७३ ॥
उद्धृत्य त्वभितप्याद्भिः प्रोक्ष्यास्तीर्य कुशान् पितॄन्।
अभ्यर्च्य मार्जयित्वा त्रिः पिण्डान् दर्व्या प्रदाय च॥ २७४ ॥
उपस्थाय नियम्यासून् परावृत्योदपात्रतः ।
मार्जयित्वा दशान्दद्यादथापूपाभिमर्शनम्[८] ॥ २७५ ॥
[९]श्रद्धाभिमर्शनेनेति समाख्यावचनं त्विह ।
एतैरेवाभिमर्शनं मासश्राद्धे भवेदिति ॥ २७६ ॥
विद्याग्रहणमप्यत्र शीलादेरुपलक्षणम् ।
अविद्वत्प्रतिषेधोऽपि सर्ववर्ज्यनिषेधकृत्[१०] ॥ २७७ ॥
स्मृत्युक्तसंख्याप्राप्त्यर्था बहूक्तिर्ब्राह्मणानिति ।

१.MT °मेकमास्याद°. २-२.M विद्यायेवोपवेश्याभ्यर्च तं द्विजान्. ३.M इहोहस्तरणाद्विरेतरिष्टा, T °रणाद्वित्तेरिष्टा. ४.M वर्णनि°. ५.M °देशात्स°, T उत्तरापरदेशात्समारभ्यैवाग्नि°. ६.M °मात्रमवनादिह. ७.M तद्वद्धोम. ८.M °पातिम°. ९.T भ्रद्धाभि°. १०.M °वर्ज°.

[१]परिवेषणोपदेशाच्च ब्राह्मणामन्त्रणादयः ॥ २७८ ॥
शास्त्रान्तरानुसारेण कार्या आकङ्क्षिता इह ।
उदकाञ्जलिदानं च द्विजोत्थापनतः[२] परम् ॥ २७९ ॥
कूपादिगतमम्भः संप्राप्य याम्याननः पितॄन्[३] ।
[४]स्वतीर्थेन तिलाम्भोभिस्तर्पयेद्दर्भसंयुतैः ॥ २८० ॥
ज्येष्ठान्वितायामष्टम्यां संपरिस्तीर्य पूर्ववत् ।
संस्कृत्याज्यं मन्त्रवच्च परिषिच्य समिद्वति ॥ २८१ ॥
अग्नावुपाकृतीर्हुत्वा दर्व्याज्यं[५] बर्हिषा पशुम् ।
उपाकरोति मन्त्रस्य विकारो नेह विद्यते ॥ २८२ ॥
[६]समानविधितो गोत्वाल्लिङ्गस्याप्यनिरोधतः[७] ।
अभिषिच्याभिषिच्याद्भिस्तूष्णीमाप्याययेदसून् ॥ २८३ ॥
श्रपयित्वावदानानि[८] शूलैः सन्तृद्य[९] पूर्ववत् ।
द्विजान्समर्च्य जुहुयाद्वपां[१०] दर्व्या यथाविधि ॥ २८४ ॥
त्रिधाविच्छेदवचनाद् होमत्रित्वं प्रतीयते ।
आवृत्तिरस्य मन्त्रस्य तथान्यानभिधानतः ॥ २८५ ॥
लौकिकानलसंसिद्धमन्नं संस्कारसंस्कृतम् ।
मांसेन जुहुयात्सार्धमुपस्तीर्याभिघार्य च ॥ २८६ ॥
शिष्टं पूर्ववदेव स्याद् गुणवत्त्वेऽर्थिनां[११] सति ।
दद्यान्निमन्त्रितैः सार्धं गौर्निषिद्धा कलौ ततः ॥ २८७ ॥
चरुः प्रतिनिधेयः स्यात्तृतीयेऽह्नि नियोगतः ।
बहुव्यञ्जनसंयुक्तं[१२] [१३]सार्वजन्यं व्रतं चरेत्[१३] ॥ २८८ ॥
[१४]श्राद्धभुग्द्विजमुख्येभ्यः शक्त्या [१५]दद्याद् धनं बहु[१५] ।
[१६]मासश्राद्धोक्तमार्गेण निमन्त्र्य गुणवद् द्विजान्॥ २८९ ॥

१.M परिवे...णोप°. २.M द्विजोर्थावनतः. ३.M puts पितॄन् before स्व at the beginning of next hemistich. ४.M पितॄन् स्व...र्थेन. ५.MT हुत्वाज्यं, T oms दर्व्या. ६.T समानि. ७.M गत्वा लिङ्ग°, T °प्यनिरोधतः. ८.M °यित्वापदा°. ९.M सन्तृद्यः, T स...द्य. १०.M वचा. ११.M स्यात् गुणत्वेऽर्थिनां, T स्या...गुणत्वेऽ°. १२.M °संयुक्तान्नं. १३-१३.M सर्वजन्यं प्रकर्षयेत्. १४.M °भुक्तिज°. १५-१५.M द ...नम्, T दा...बहु. १६.M adds बहु before मास° at the beginning of the next hemistich.

यथास्मृत्यन्नमापाद्य[१] स्नात्वा काले यथोदिते ।
प्राचीनावीतमासज्य दर्भैः प्राग्दक्षिणाग्रकैः[२] ॥ २९० ॥
दैववत् संपरिस्तीर्य दक्षिणेन हुताशनम्[३] ।
[४]....दक्षिण .... कपालकम्[४] ॥ २९१ ॥
तिस्रो दर्वीश्च समिध उपवेषं सवेदकम् ।
उदकुंभं[५] दशामघ्यर्यसाधनं द्विजभूषणम् ॥ २९२ ॥
आज्यस्थालीं मदन्त्यर्थां[६] प्रोक्षण्यर्थां[७] च पात्रिकाम् ।
पिण्डं [८]पचनोद्वासन ...... दानपात्रिकाम्[८] ॥ २९३ ॥
न्युब्ज्य[९] संसाद्य चैकैकं पित्र्यवत् संस्कृतांभसा ।
सकृत्प्रोक्ष्यावशिष्टांभो निधाय सपवित्रके ॥ २९४ ॥
यथोक्तदेशे[१०] निहिते [११]भाजने मन्त्रतः सकृत् ।
निरुप्य[१२] प्रोक्ष्य कृत्स्नेन[१३] सकृन्निहितवारिणा ॥ २९५ ॥
[१४]अङ्गारद्वयमावर्त्य तयोरेकं निरस्य च ।
उपस्पृश्यान्यमावर्त्य कपालमुपधाय तु ॥ २९६ ॥
[१५]साङ्गारं तत्र निक्षिप्य त्यक्त्वा तैरभिवास्य च ।
प्रतप्तपात्रे[१६] पिष्टानि पवित्रवति निक्षिपेत् ॥ २९७ ॥
मदन्तीरप आनीय केनचिन्मेक्षणेन तु ।
संयूय[१७]तानि प्रम्णाय पिण्डीकृत्याभिमृश्य च ॥ २९८ ॥
वेदेनापोह्य चाङ्गारानधिश्रित्य सकृत्त्वचम्[१८] ।
ग्राहयित्वाथ पर्यग्नितृणैः कृत्वाभिमृश्य च ॥ २९९ ॥
अवज्वाल्य तृणैर्भस्मनाभिवास्याप्यपूपकम् ।
स्पृष्ट्वा वेदेन[१९] सुशृते[२०] दर्वीसंमार्जनं सकृत् ॥ ३०० ॥

१.M °मापद्य. २.T प्रागग्रैर्दक्षिणाग्रकैः. ३.T broken. ४-४.M ...दक्षिण...कपालकम्, T ... कपालकम्. ५.M °कुंभ. ६.M °त्यर्थाः, T मृद°. ७.M प्रोक्तान्यर्थां. ८-८.M वचनोद्वास... दानपात्रिकाम्, T पवनोद्वा...दनपात्रिणा. ९.MT न्युज्य. १०.M यथोदकदेशे. ११.M भाजनेन्मन्त्र°. १२.T नी... १३.M कृत्स्नौ. १४.T °द्वयामा°. १५.M अङ्गारं. १६.T पदात्त°. १७.M संयुतानि, T सम्पूय°. १८.M सकृत्त्वचः. १९.MT वेद. २०.T सुश्रिते...दर्वी.

कृत्वाज्यमपि संस्कृत्य वेदेनापूपभस्म तु ।
त्यक्त्वा पात्र उपस्तीर्यापूपे[1]ऽप्युद्वास्य भाजने ॥ ३०१ ॥
अभिघार्य समज्याधस्तादुपानज्य सर्वतः ।
क्लेदयित्वा कपालं च प्रत्यज्योद्धृत्य भाजने ॥ ३०२ ॥
पिण्डार्थमोदनं तत्र श्रपयित्वाप्यधस्ततः[2] ।
अपरेणाग्निमासाद्य तृणेष्वेतत्त्रयं ततः ॥ ३०३ ॥
कृत्वा पवित्रमापाद्य[3] तिलांभो विधिवत्ततः ।
पितृमातामहसुतशेषभूतान् द्विजोत्तमान् ॥ ३०४ ॥
अष्टकाश्राद्ध इत्येवं निमन्त्र्य तु यथाविधि ।
प्रक्षाल्यापि च तत्पादौ विना पाद्यादिकल्पना[4] ॥ ३०५ ॥
समाचम्योपवेश्यैतान्[5] 'प्राप्नोत्वि'त्यादिना ततः ।
अर्घ्यं दत्त्वा स्वमन्त्रेण समभ्यर्च्य तिलोदकम् ॥ ३०६ ॥
प्रदाया'ग्नौ[6] करिष्यामी'त्युत्थायोक्त्वा[7] 'कुरुष्व' तैः ।
अनुज्ञातश्चोपवीय वह्नौ पुष्पैरलंकृते ॥ ३०७ ॥
प्राचीनावीतमासज्य मन्त्रवत्परिषिच्य च ।
'स्वाहे'त्याधाय समिध उपस्तीर्यावदाय च ॥ ३०८ ॥
पाण्याभिघार्य[8] प्रत्यज्य पुरस्ताद्धोमपूर्वकम् ।
यथोक्तं पञ्चभिर्हुत्वो[9]परिष्टाद्धोमसंयुतम् ॥ ३०९ ॥
औदुम्बर्यैव दर्व्याऽऽज्यं[10] हुत्वा स्विष्टकृतं तथा ।
हुत्वा प्रक्षाल्य दर्वीञ्च मन्त्रवत्परिषिच्य च ॥ ३१० ॥
दत्त्वा पिण्डानुपस्तीर्य दैवपूर्वमपूपकम्[11] ।
मध्वादिव्यञ्जनयुतं परिविष्य च पैतृकम् ॥ ३११ ॥

१.T °स्तीयापूपे°. २.M °प्यधर्मकः. ३.M wrongly indicates the sign of broken Text between पवित्र and मापद्य. ४.M कत्वना. ५.M indicates the sign of broken text between समाचम्ये and पवेश्यैतान्. ६.M प्रदायान्नेन. ७.M °त्युक्त्वायोक्त्वा. ८.M पङ्क्त्याभि°. ९.M हुत्वोवरिष्टा°. १०.M °म्बर्यैः पदव्याजं. ११.M °मपूपकः.

अभिमृश्य त्रिभिर्मन्त्रैस्तूष्णीं मातामहादिकान्[१] ।
दत्त्वोपस्तरणाम्भोऽथ[२] राक्षोघ्नादि यथोदितम् ॥ ३१२ ॥
गायत्रीमप्रतिरथं विना जप्त्वा मधुत्रयम् ।
जप्त्वा पिधानकजलं दत्त्वा निक्षिप्य पूर्ववत् ॥ ३१३ ॥
अन्नशेषं ततः पिण्डं दत्त्वाऽऽचम्य तिलोदकम् ।
दत्त्वोद्वास्याभिवाद्याथ पितृनुद्वास्य पिण्डकान् ॥ ३१४ ॥
पितृपिण्डं[३] समुत्थाप्य द्विजानेतान् प्रदक्षिणम् ।
कृत्वा नमस्कृतः प्रार्थ्य 'दातार' इति चाशिषः[४] ॥ ३१५ ॥
उदकाञ्जलिदानञ्च कृत्वा कुर्यात्तु भोजनम् ।
श्वोभूते संपरिस्तीर्य प्रोक्ष्य शिष्टं निधाय च ॥ ३१६ ॥
दर्वीसंमार्जनं कृत्वा संस्कृत्याज्यं च मन्त्रवत् ।
परिषिच्य समिद्धोमपूर्वं दर्व्या जुहोत्यथ ॥ ३१७ ॥
बर्हिषा तण्डुलाञ्छुद्धानुपाकृत्य समन्त्रतः ।
[५]संप्रोक्ष्य संस्कृतमंभोभिरधिश्रित्याथ पात्रिकाम् ॥ ३१८ ॥
पवित्रवदपस्तस्यां क्षिप्त्वा क्षालिततण्डुलान् ।
[६]ओप्यास्मिन्पचमानेऽस्मान् कस्मिंश्चिद् भाजने शुचौ ॥ ३१९ ॥
[७]वपाश्रपण्यौदुम्बर्या समुद्धृत्य पचौदनम्[८] ।
पर्यग्नि प्रसलैः[९] कृत्वा तृणैस्तस्मिंच्छ्रितं सति ॥ ३२० ॥
[१०]पूर्वञ्चरुमुपस्तीर्याभिघार्यासादयेत् क्रमात् ।
[११]आज्यसंस्करणादूर्ध्वमन्नसादनमिष्यते ॥ ३२१ ॥
पिण्डार्थोदनपाकादि[१२] कुरुष्वान्तं विधाय तु ।
तूष्णीं समन्तात् प्रसलैः परिषिच्य समिद्धति ॥ ३२२ ॥

१.M °महाहितम्. २.M °भोग. ३.M पितृवाद्य, T पितृपा...समु°. ४.M वाशिषः. ५.M oms सं. ६.M आ.प्यास्मि वचनेऽस्मान. ७.M °श्रवण्यौ°. ८.M त्रचौद°. ९.T पर्याग्नि- वसलैः. १०.M वचारुपस्तिर्या°, T ...वचारुप°. ११.M wrongly adds पूर्व before आज्य°. १२.M पिण्डार्थादौ च पाका°.

अग्नौ दर्व्यामुपस्तीर्य वपां समवदाय च ।
अभिघार्य पुरस्ताच्च हुत्वा [१]वेह वपादिना[१] ॥ ३२३ ॥
हुत्वोपरिष्टाद्धुत्वाऽथ प्रास्य तच्छ्रपणीमपि[२] ।
संस्रावेणाभिघार्याथ हृदयादि विधाय च ॥ ३२४ ॥
चरोरुपस्तीर्यावदायावदाय[३] सकृत् सकृत् ।
प्रत्यज्य चोभयत्रेयमाद्यैः पञ्चभिराहुतीः[४] ॥ ३२५ ॥
हुत्वाज्येन[५] ततो[६] हुत्वा प्राजापत्याहुतिं ततः ।
अन्नात् स्विष्टकृतं [७]हुत्वा दर्वीप्रक्षालनादिकम्[७] ॥ ३२६ ॥
पूर्वेद्युरिह कर्तव्यं साज्यं पश्ववशिष्टकम्[८] ।
[९]पित्रर्थद्विजभुक्त्यर्थपात्रेष्वेवेह निक्षिपेत् ॥ ३२७ ॥
वैश्वदेवान्नपाकस्तु पृथगिष्ट इहापि तु ।
एवमेव तृतीयेऽह्नि विशेषस्तत्र वर्ण्यते ॥ ३२८ ॥
अन्नासादनपर्यन्तं कृत्वा संपच्य चौदनम् ।
आसाद्यार्घ्यौदकं कृत्वा द्विजानभ्यर्थ्य [१०]पूर्ववत् ॥ ३२९ ॥
तिलांभोर्मार्जनं कृत्वा गत्वा दत्त्वोदकाञ्जलिम् ।
आचम्यागत्य विप्रेभ्यः शक्त्या मन्त्रेण दक्षिणाम् ॥ ३३० ॥
दत्त्वाभिवादनं तूष्णीं कृत्वोद्वास्य पितॄंस्ततः ।
आशीः प्रार्थनापर्यन्तं कृत्वा भुञ्जीत बान्धवैः ॥ ३३१ ॥

इति सङ्गमग्रामवासिमिश्रविरचिते नारायणीये
वाधूलगृह्यागमवृत्तिरहस्ये
सप्तमोऽध्यायः[११]।

१-१.M वप वहादिना. २.T °च्छ्रवणी°. ३.M °वदायान्नवदाय. ४.M °हुतीम्. ५.M °त्वाभ्येन. ६.M तथो. ७-७.M oms. ८.M पश्वावितीष्टकम्. ९.M पित्रर्थं. १०.T °भ्यर्घ्य. ११.M oms.

अथाष्टमोऽध्यायः

[स्त्रीपुरुषधर्माः]

आन्वाहिकप्रसङ्गेन श्राद्धकर्म समीरितम् ।
धर्मानिदानीं वक्ष्यामः पुरुषस्य स्त्रिया अपि ॥ १ ॥
रक्षेत् स्त्रियं प्रयत्नेन पुरुषो दुर्बलोऽपि सन् ।
स्वां प्रसूतिं चरित्रं च कुल -मात्मानमे- [1]व च ॥ २ ॥
स्वं च धर्मं प्रयत्नेन जायां रक्षन् हि रक्षति ॥ २क ॥
अस्वतन्त्राः स्त्रियः कार्याः पुरुषैः स्वैर्दिवानिशम् ।
स्वातन्त्र्याद्धि प्रदुष्यन्ति कुलजा अपि योषितः ॥ ३ ॥
न कश्चिद्योषितः शक्तः प्रसह्य परिरक्षितुम् ।
मानस्यव्यभिचारस्य दुर्निवारतया तथा ॥ ४ ॥
उपायैरत एवैता रक्षणीयाः प्रसङ्गतः ।
शौचे धर्मेऽन्नपक्त्यां[२] च वारणेऽप्यन्यरक्षणे[२] ॥ ५ ॥
आयव्यये धनादीनां गृहे तस्कररक्षणे ।
अग्निशुश्रूषणादौ च नियोक्तव्याः स्त्रियः सदा ॥ ६ ॥
अर्घनीया च सा तेन भूषणाच्छादनाशनैः ॥ ६क ॥
भर्तृभ्रातृपितृव्यैश्च[३] श्वश्रूश्वसुरदेवरैः ।
बन्धुभिश्च स्त्रियः पूज्या उत्सवेषु विशेषतः ॥ ७ ॥
बालया वा युवत्या वा वृद्धया वाऽपि योषिता ।
न स्वातन्त्र्येण कर्तव्यं किञ्चित्कार्यं गृहेष्वपि[४] ॥ ८ ॥
बाल्ये पितृवशे[५] तिष्ठेत्पाणिग्राहस्य यौवने ।
पुत्राणां भर्तरि प्रेते न भजेत[६] स्वतन्त्रताम् ॥ ९ ॥
मृते भर्तर्यपुत्रायाः पतिपक्षः[७] प्रभुः स्त्रियाः[८] ।

१.T कुल...वच, cf Manu 9.7. २.Cf Manu पाक्त्या [Tपत्थां] च पारिणाह्यस्य चेक्षणे. ३.T °पितृव्याश्च. ४.T गृहेण्वपि. ५.Cf Manu V.148 पेतुर्वशे. ६.Cf Manu V.148: भजेत्स्त्री. ७.T broken. ८.MT स्त्रियः..

[विनियोगात्मरक्षासु भरणे च स ईश्वरः][1] ॥ १० ॥
परिक्षीणे पतिकुले निर्मनुष्ये निराश्रये ।
तत्सपिण्डेषु चासत्सु पितृपक्षः प्रभुः स्त्रियाः ॥ ११ ॥
पक्षद्वयावसाने तु राजा तस्याः प्रभुः स्त्रियाः[2] ॥ ११क ॥
अतस्ताः [3]परतन्त्राः स्युर्योषितस्तु[4] स्तुता[4] अपि ।
यथाधिकारं बिभृयू रक्षणीयाः प्रयत्नतः ॥ १२ ॥
जामयोग्यानि देहानि[5] शपन्त्यप्रतिपूजिताः ।
तानि कृत्याहतानीव विनश्यन्ति समन्ततः ॥ १३ ॥
जायापत्योर्न धर्मस्य विभागो विद्यते क्वचित् ।
भर्तृद्रव्ये पुण्यफले धर्मे साम्यमतः स्त्रियाः[6] ॥ १४ ॥
सत्यामापद्यतो भार्या अभीप्सेदुत्तमां गतिम् ॥ १४क ॥
परान्नं तु कदाचित् स्त्री [7][न गृह्णीयादनापदि] ।
[.......][7] स्वभर्तारमतिक्रम्यापरं लभेत् ॥ १५ ॥
विशीलः कामवृत्तो वा गुणैर्वा परिवर्जितः ।
उपचर्यः स्त्रिया साध्व्या सततं देववत्पतिः[8] ॥ १६ ॥
मृतेऽपि [9]तस्मिन्वचसाऽपि [9]नेच्छत्यपरं पतिम् ।
इह कीर्तिमवाप्नोति प्रेत्य चानुत्तमां गतिम् ॥ १७ ॥
सुरापी व्याधिता धूर्ता[10] वन्ध्यार्थघ्न्यप्रियंवदा ।
स्त्रीप्रसूर्गर्भभर्तृघ्नी[11] प्रतिकूला च सर्वदा ॥ १८ ॥
[12]वैनासिक्यनवेक्षव्या पुरुषद्वेषिणी[13] अपि ।
आसु[14] दुष्टाः परित्याज्या[15] अदुष्टा अक्षराः[16] स्त्रियः॥ १९ ॥
भर्तृप्रियहिते युक्ता अनुज्ञाप्यापरां लभेत् ॥ १९क ॥
कृतदारोऽपरान्[17] दारान् भिक्षित्वा योऽधि[18]गच्छति ।

१.MT om; cf Nârada Smṛti IV.13.28. २.MT स्त्रियः. ३.MT °स्तत्पर°. ४-४.T °स्ते तु ता. ५.M गेहानि. ६.T स्त्रियः. ७-७.T broken. ८.T दैव°. ९-९.MT तस्मिन्न च सा अनिच्छन्त्य°. १०.M धूर्त, T oms धूर्ता. ११.MT भर्त्रघ्नी. १२.MT वैनासिक्यनवेक्तव्या [T°त्तव्या]. १३.T पुरुष...।. १४.T ...सु, M आ सु. १५.MT °ज्याः. १६.T अक्षमाः. १७.M कुदारोपरान्. १८.M योथ, T योऽथ; Cf Manu XI.5: योऽधि°.

रतिमात्रं फलं तस्य द्रव्यदातुस्तु सन्ततिः ॥ २० ॥
एकामुत्क्रम्य कामार्थमन्यां लब्धुं[१] यदीच्छति ।
अर्थैः सन्तोष्य[२] पूर्वोढामनुज्ञाप्यापरां लभेत् ॥ २१ ॥
यथा वश्याऽनुरक्ता च भवेद् भार्या गुणैः स्वकैः ।
तस्यां तथा वर्तितव्यं भर्तर्यपि [३]तया तथा[३] ॥ २२ ॥
यत्रानुकूल्यं दम्पत्योस्त्रिवर्गस्तत्र वर्धते ।
स्वर्गेऽपि दुर्लभं ह्येतदनुरागं परस्परम् ॥ २३ ॥
धर्मे सर्वा[४] नियुञ्जीत क्रमेण ज्येष्ठया विना ।
कनिष्ठा न नियोक्तव्या स्नानादिस्वार्थकर्मसु ॥ २४ ॥
स्वाधिकारानुसारेण[५] प्रवृत्तिर्न विहन्यते ।
इज्याऽध्ययनदानादि कुर्यात्काले यथाविधि ॥ २५ ॥
धनैर्न्यायार्जितैस्तानि विप्रस्याध्यापनादिभिः[६] ।
प्रतिग्रहैर्याजनैश्च सद्भ्यो[७] लब्धानि धर्मतः[८] ॥ २६ ॥
कुसूदकृषिवाणिज्यः पशुरक्षोऽर्थितान्यपि[९] ।
चौर्यादन्येन[१०] मार्गेण लब्धं धर्म्यं [११]तथाऽऽपदि ॥ २७ ॥
स्वल्पैरपि गुणैर्नित्यं[१२] कुर्यान्नैमित्तिकं तथा ।
वयोबुद्ध्यर्थवान्वेष[१३]श्रुताभिजनकर्मणाम् ॥ २८ ॥
सदृशं कर्म कर्तव्यं काम्यं वृत्तिश्च तादृशी ।
इज्या श्रुत्युदिता धर्मा यागहोमस्वरूपिणः ॥ २९ ॥
ब्रह्मयज्ञादिरूपोक्ताः[१४] धीतिर्दानमिहोच्यते ॥ २९क ॥

[दानमीमांसा]

दातव्यं प्रत्यहं पात्रे निमित्तेषु विशेषतः ।
याचितेनापि दातव्यं श्रद्धापूतं तु शक्तितः ॥ ३० ॥

१.T लक्ष्मीं. २.M सन्त्येष. ३-३.T तथा तया. ४.M सर्वान्. ५.M °कारानुरागेण. ६.T °नादि...॥. ७.M सद्ध्या, T सन्ध्या. ८. T सर्वतः. M सर्वतः but corrected as धर्मतः. ९.T ऽत्थितान्य°. १०.M यायादन्येन. ११.M यथा°. १२.M गुणैश्चिन्त्यं. १३.T सुताभि°. १४.M °पोक्ता ऽधीति°.

पात्रता च द्विजाग्र्याणां विदुषां वेदतत्परा:[१] ।
कर्मनिष्ठा ब्रह्मनिष्ठा श्रेष्ठा एते यथाक्रमम् ॥ ३१ ॥
न विद्यया केवलया विप्रजात्या[२] च पात्रता[२] ।
यत्र वृत्तमिमे चोभे तद्धि पात्रं प्रकीर्तितम् ॥ ३२ ॥
नापात्रे विदुषा किञ्चिद् देयं [३]श्रेयोऽर्थिना सदा[३] ॥ ३२क ॥
विद्यातपोभ्यां हीनेन न तु ग्राह्य: प्रतिग्रह: ।
गृह्णन् प्रदातारमधो नयत्यात्मानमेव[४] च ॥ ३३ ॥
सुसंमृष्टे शुचौ[५] देशे[६] गन्धमाल्याद्यलङ्कृते ।
आहूय वेदवेदाङ्गपारगं[७] संशितव्रतम् ॥ ३४ ॥
तपस्विनं जितक्रोधं ब्राह्मणं[८] ब्रह्मवादिनम्[८] ।
सानुष्ठानं परं शान्तं दरिद्रं गुरुदैवतम् ॥ ३५ ॥
नववासोभि:[९]संवीतं चन्दनार्तवभूषणै: ।
अभ्यर्च्य दक्षिणकरे तस्य प्राग्वदन:[१०] शुचि: ॥ ३६ ॥
[११][...................................... ।
.....] जलं दत्त्वा गन्धपुष्पोदकान्वितम् ॥ ३७ ॥
[१२]गोभूमितिलहेमानि शक्त्या मूलफलाद्यपि ।
'अ तत्सं'दिति निर्दिश्य दत्त्वा भुक्तवते तत: ॥ ३८ ॥
दद्याज्जलमसौ विप्र: समावाह्य[१३] यथाश्रुति ।
मन्त्रेण प्रतिगृह्णीयादाशीर्भिर्वर्धयेच्च तम् ॥ ३९ ॥
वाचयित्वाऽऽशिषो दद्यादित्यपि स्मर्यते बुधै: ।
अन्नस्य क्षुधित: पात्रं हिरण्यादेरिहोदितम् ॥ ४० ॥
पुत्रजन्मविवाहादौ ग्रहणेन्दुक्षयादिषु ।
हिरण्यादेर्विशिष्टस्य दानं नैमित्तिकं स्मृतम् ॥ ४१ ॥

१.M वेद...पमा:, T वेदतत्परा:. २-२.M जात्यात्पा°. ३-३.M श्रेयार्थितात्मन:. ४.M नयन्यात्मा°. ५.M शुचे. ६.M देश. ७.M °पारग:. ८-८.M ब्राह्मण...वादिनम्. ९.M °वासोऽभि. १०.M प्रावावद°. ११.MT text under bracket broken but shown as broken in the beginning of second bemistich only . १२.M नाभूमि°. १३.M समावान्य.

देशकालद्रव्यपात्रविशेषापेक्षयापि च ।
नानाविधानि दानानि स्मृतानि फलवन्ति हि ॥ ४२ ॥
देशतस्तानि वर्ण्यन्ते दातृवित्तानुसारतः ॥ ४२क ॥
भूमिपश्वन्नवस्त्राम्भ[१]स्तिलसर्पिः प्रतिश्रयम् ।
नैवेशिकं[२] स्वर्णधुर्यं दत्त्वा स्वर्गे महीयते ॥ ४३ ॥
स्वर्णशृङ्गी शफै[३] रौप्यैः सुशीला वस्त्रसंयुता ।
सकांस्यदोहा दातव्या क्षीरिणी गौः सदक्षिणा ॥ ४४ ॥
दाताऽस्याः स्वर्गमाप्नोति वत्सरान् रोमसम्मितान्[४] ।
कपिला चेत्तारयति[५] भूयश्चासप्तमं कुलम् ॥ ४५ ॥
वत्सरान्[६] रोमतुल्यानि युगान्युभयतोमुखीम् ।
दाता स्वर्गमवाप्नोति पूर्वेण विधिना ददत् ॥ ४६ ॥
गृहधान्योभयोपानत्[७]छत्रमाल्यानुलेपनम् ।
यानं वृक्षजलं शय्यां दत्त्वाऽत्यन्तं सुखी भवेत् ॥ ४७ ॥
शान्तसंवाहनं रोगीपरिचर्या सुरार्चनम् ।
पादशौचं द्विजोच्छिष्टमार्जनं गोप्रदानवत् ॥ ४८ ॥
सान्तानिकं यक्ष्यमाणमध्वगं सार्ववेदसम् ।
[८]गुर्वम्बपितृभृत्यार्थं[९] स्वाध्यायार्थ्युपतापिनौ[१०] ॥ ४९ ॥
दशैतान् स्नातकान्विद्याद् ब्राह्मणान्धर्मभिक्षुकान् ।
निःस्वेभ्यो देयमेतेभ्यो दानं[११] विद्या विशेषतः ॥ ५० ॥
एतेभ्यो[१२] हि द्विजाग्र्येभ्यो देयमन्नं सदक्षिणम् ॥ ५०क ॥
सर्वधर्ममयं ब्रह्म प्रदानेभ्योऽधिकं ततः ।
प्रददत्तत्समाप्नोति ब्रह्मलोकमविच्युतम्[१३] ॥ ५१ ॥
प्रतिग्रहे[१४] समर्थोऽपि नादत्ते यः प्रतिग्रहम् ।

१.M °न्नपात्रांभः°. २.T °वेशिकः. ३.T शफे रोप्यै. ४.M संयुतान्. ५.M चोत्तार°. ६.T वत्सा. ७.M °धान्यादयोपान°. ८.M गुर्वं च. ९.M cf Manu XI.1. १०.M °ध्यायाप्युपता°. ११.T दातं. १२.M एतेभ्योऽपि. १३.M °मपिच्युतः, T °मविद्युतम्. १४.M °ग्रह.

ये[1] लोका दानशीलाना [मेता]नाप्नोति[2] पुष्कलान् ॥ ५२ ॥
कर्माण्येतानि विप्रस्य धर्मवृद्धिकराणि[3] षट् ।
पूर्वोत्थानं गुरुष्वर्चा भोजनानि[4] .... ॥ ५३ ॥

[पत्नीधर्माः]

जघन्यासनशायित्वं भर्तृप्रियहिते रतिः ।
सहधर्मचर्या [5]पूज्यपूजाद्वेषश्च तद्द्विषाम् ॥ ५४ ॥
तदानुकूल्यं तत्कार्यपरताऽदुष्टभावना ।
समानव्रतचारित्वं श्वश्रूश्वशुरयोर्गुरोः ॥ ५५ ॥
पूजातिथीनां देवानां शुचिता प्रियभाषिता[6] ।
पातिव्रत्यं सुगुप्तत्वममुक्तकरताऽपि च ॥ ५६ ॥
सुगुप्तभाण्डता दानप्रियता मृष्टवेश्मता ।
लाजदध्यक्षतैर्दूर्वा[7]प्रवालकुसुमादिभिः ॥ ५७ ॥
बलिर्वास्त्वर्चनं भर्तृशुश्रूषा तद्वचःकृतिः ।
तदीश्वरत्वं तत्पूजा मङ्गलाचारता स्त्रियाः ॥ ५८ ॥
परदाररतिं[8] जायाविप्रियं कलहं स्वकैः[9] ।
नास्तिक्यं दुष्टसंसर्गं वर्जयेत्सर्वदा पुमान् ॥ ५९ ॥
पानं दुर्जनसंसर्गः स्वभर्तृविरहाटनम् ।
द्वारावलोकनं हास्यं गवाक्षावेक्षणाक्रिये ॥ ६० ॥
अनुत्सवे गन्धपुष्पविकृताम्बरधारणम् ।
वणिग्वृद्धयतिभ्योऽन्यभाषणं नाभिदर्शनम् ॥ ६१ ॥
गणिकाधूर्तमायावि[10]कुहकादिसहासनम् ।
परशय्यासनोद्यानयानवासो गृहानपि ॥ ६२ ॥
अनु[11] ..... तान् देवभृत्यपत्यग्रभोजनम् ।
प्रकीर्णोपस्करद्रव्यभाण्डभाजनतामपि ॥ ६३ ॥

१.M एते. २.M °शीला...नाप्नोति, T °शीलानां...ना°. ३.M °वृत्तिकराणि, T °वृत्ति° corrected as °वृद्धि°. ४.MT broken after भोजनानि, [T भो...]. ५.MT तत्पुज्य°. ६.M °भूषिता. ७.T °दूर्वा. ८.T °रतिर्जा°. ९.M सकैः. १०.M यावीकु°. ११.M अनु...तान्देव°, T अनु...देव°.

असंस्कृतोच्छिष्टपात्रभुक्तिं भर्तुः पितुः सुतान् ।
अन्योच्छिष्टं भर्तृनामाशुद्धौ देवगृहे गतिम् ॥ ६४ ॥
अमाङ्गल्यानि[1] कर्माणि मूलकर्म च वर्जयेत् ॥ ६४क ॥
विधाय प्रोषिते [2]वृत्तिर्जीवेन्नियममास्थिता ।
प्रोषिते त्वविधायैव जीवेच्छिल्पैरगर्हितैः[3] ॥ ६५ ॥
क्रीडाशरीरसंस्कारसमाजोत्सवदर्शनम् ।
हासं परगृहं यानं त्यजेत्प्रोषितभर्तृका ॥ ६६ ॥
पितृमातृसुतभ्रातृश्वश्रूश्वशुरमातुलैः ।
हीना न स्याद्विना भर्त्रा गर्हणीयाऽन्यथा भवेत् ॥ ६७ ॥
पतिशुश्रूषयैव स्त्री सर्वान् कामान् समश्नुते ।
स्वर्गं पुनः समायाता [4]सुखानामम्बुधिर्भवेत् ॥ ६८ ॥
पूर्वोत्थानपरा दक्षा जघन्यासनशायिनी ।
अवाग्दुष्टानुकूला च भवेद्वैपुण्यकर्मणः ॥ ६९ ॥
अहिंसा सत्यमस्तेयं शौचमिन्द्रियनिग्रहः ।
दमः क्षमार्जवमिति धर्मः साधारणः स्मृतः ॥ ७० ॥

[दृष्टे रजसि स्त्रियाः नैमित्तिकधर्माः]

दृष्टे रजसि वक्ष्यामि धर्मान्नैमित्तिकांस्त्रियाः ।
तद्रागरोगद्रव्योत्थं रक्षाख्यं कालजं रजः ॥ ७१ ॥
गर्भिण्या गर्भविश्लेषे शोणितं यद्विनिःस्रवेत् ।
तद्रोगजं[5] गर्भशोषनिमित्ता तद्विनिःसृतिः ॥ ७२ ॥
भर्त्रादिदोषवैषम्यादसकृत् स्यात्तु रोगजम् ।
द्रव्यजं धातुवैषम्यहेतुद्रव्योपयोगजम् ॥ ७३ ॥
आरभ्याद्यार्तवदिनादेकविंशतिवासरे ।
मासाञ्चोर्ध्वं[6] रजो यत्स्यात्तत्कालजमुदाहृतम्[7] ॥ ७४ ॥
रागद्रव्योत्थिते तस्मिञ्छौचमादौ समीर्यते ।

१.M अ...गल्यानि. २.M वृत्तिर्जी°, T वृत्तीर्जी°; cf Manu IX.75: वृत्तिं जी°. ३.T जीवेद् बिन्वैर°. ४.MT सुखनांशेविनिर्भ°; cf Kât.Smṛti 19.12. ५.T तद्राजजं. ६.T मायो चोर्ध्वं. ७.M कालजमु...हृतम्.

आद्वादशाहान्नारीणां त्रिरात्रेऽपगते[1] सति ॥ ७५ ॥
मूत्रवच्छौचमिष्टं स्यात् स्नानमूर्ध्वं तु षड्स्वतः ।
एवं सप्तदशाहानि त्रिरात्रैः सह विंशतिः ॥ ७६ ॥
त्रिरात्रं विंशतेरूर्ध्वमाशौचं कालजोद्भवम् ।
आरभ्याद्यार्तवदिनात् सततं तत्प्रवर्तने ॥ ७७ ॥
रोगजे मूत्रवच्छौचं क्षालनाद्यपि वाससाम् ।
रोगजे वर्तमानेऽपि काले निर्याति कालजम् ॥ ७८ ॥
तस्मात्कालेऽप्रमत्ता[2] स्यादन्यथा सङ्करो भवेत् ।
अकाले यद् भवेत्स्त्रीणां रक्तमाहुर्मनीषिणः ॥ ७९ ॥
अशुद्धं तु भवेत्स्त्रीणां मासि मासि तु यद् भवेत् ।
इति मासस्य मुख्यत्वात्तत्प्रवृत्तौ तु रोगतः ॥ ८० ॥
प्रतिमासं[3] त्रिरात्रं स्यादाशौचमिति गम्यते ।
रागद्रव्योत्थिते[4]ऽप्यस्मिन् स्यात्तत्सप्तदशात्परम् ॥ ८१ ॥
आद्वादशाहान्नारीणां[5] मूत्रवच्छौचमिष्यते ।
अष्टादशाहात् स्नानं स्यात्त्रिरात्रं परतोऽशुचिः ॥ ८२ ॥
आद्वादशाहादित्यादि प्रारभ्य स्नानवासरम् ।
द्वादशाहप्रभृत्येव स्नानं षट्सु दिनेष्वतः ॥ ८३ ॥
इति कालजधर्मत्वं विंशते[6]रूर्ध्वमिष्यते ॥ ८३क ॥
उत्पन्नगर्भस्रावादौ स्यात्त्रिरात्रं न सर्वदा ।
मासत्रये[7] त्रिरात्रं स्याच्चतुर्थादित्रये तु तत् ॥ ८४ ॥
[8]माससंख्यासमदिनं [9]सप्तमासचतुष्टये ।
दशाहं मातुरेव स्यादचेतनसमुद्भवे[10] ॥ ८५ ॥
साध्वाचारा[11] न तावत् स्याद्रजो यावत्प्रवर्तते ।
निवृत्तौ रजसः कुर्याद् गृहकर्माणि नित्यशः ॥ ८६ ॥

१.M °रात्रेऽवगते, T °रात्र्यवगते, corrected as रात्र्यपगते. २.MT प्रमात्ता. ३.M °मासस्त्रिरात्रं. ४.M रोगद्रव्योऽर्थिते. ५.T °दशाहं ना°. ६.T विंशते...मिष्यते. ७.M °त्रयेऽतिरात्रं. ८.T यथामास; T (यथा) मास°. ९.T सप्तमासप्तचतु°. १०.M °भवेत्. ११.T स्वाध्यायादानतावत्.

नास्पृश्या रोगजे[१] तस्मिन्निति केचित्प्रचक्षते ।
प्रसूतिकासु रजसा स्नानतो विंशतेः परम् ॥ ८७ ॥
रजस्वलेति सा प्रोक्ता विना नैमित्तिकं रजः ।
रजस्युपरते तत्र स्नानेनैव विशुद्ध्यति ॥ ८८ ॥
[२]यस्मिन्नहनि वा रात्रौ मलवद्वसनाङ्गना ।
तद्दिनादित्रिरात्रं स्यान्न [३]संख्याताधिकावशात् ॥ ८९ ॥
तृतीयभागे सम्प्राप्ते मलं स्यान्निशि चेत् स्त्रियाः[४] ।
प्रभातादित्रिरात्रेण शुद्धिस्तत्र विनिर्दिशेत् ॥ ९० ॥
[५]अविज्ञाते मले स्रावे मलवद्वसना[६] यदि ।
करोति गेहे तद् दुष्टं ज्ञानाद्वा शुद्धिरिष्यते[७] ॥ ९१ ॥
निःसन्दिग्धं परिज्ञातेत्यार्तवे शुद्धिकारणम् ।
सन्दिग्धरात्रे[८] स्नानं स्यादित्युवाच प्रजापतिः ॥ ९२ ॥
सार्तवा तु यदा नारी नैकवेश्मनि संवसेत्[९] ।
न संसर्गं व्रजेत्सद्भिः स्नात्वा पापात्प्रमुच्यते ॥ ९३ ॥
अधुनाद्यार्तवे कार्यमात्रेयप्रोक्तमुच्यते ।
कन्याया अप्यकन्याया [१०]आर्तवे प्रथमोद्भवे[१०] ॥ ९४ ॥
अक्षतैरासने क्लृप्ते सदीपे[११] वासयेत् स्त्रियम् ।
अपूपं लवणं मुद्गं गुडमिश्रं च शक्तितः ॥ ९५ ॥
दत्त्वा ब्राह्मणपत्नीभ्यः पादुके ह्यधिरोहयेत् ।
त्रिरात्रेऽवगते स्नात्वा पुण्याहमपि वाचयेत् ॥ ९६ ॥
आञ्जनाभ्यञ्जने स्नानं प्रवासं दन्तधावनम् ।
नखानां कृन्तनं[१२] रज्जुताळपत्रादिबन्धनम् ॥ ९७ ॥
गन्धपुष्पं दिवास्वप्नं ताम्बूलं च गृहेक्षणम् ।

१.T °श्याद्रोगजे. २.T तस्मि°. ३.M संख्या नाधिका°. ४.M स्त्रियम्, T स्त्रियः. ५.M अपि ज्ञाते. ६.M °वासना. ७.T शुचिरिष्यते. ८.T सन्दिग्धमात्रे. ९.T संभवेत्. १०-१०.T सूत्रोक्तं प्रथमोऽश्नुते. ११.सदीवे. १२.M कृन्त.

वर्जयेन्मधुमांसादि पर्णे खर्वे च भोजनम् ॥ ९८ ॥
अखर्वपात्रे भुञ्जीत पेयं चाञ्जलिना पिबेत् ।
जह्यात् प्रजादोषकरमन्यच्च श्रुतिदर्शितम् ॥ ९९ ॥
मलैः शरीरजैर्मुक्ता सांगोपांगसमाश्रितैः ।
दन्तानां धावनं कृत्वा संगवे[1] स्नानमाचरेत् ॥ १०० ॥
पञ्चधाह्नो विभक्तांशो[2] द्वितीयः सङ्गवः श्रुतः[3] ।
ऊषैरुत्स्वेदनेनाथ खण्डनक्षालनै[4]स्तथा ॥ १०१ ॥
यथालेपं [5]विधातव्ये [6]मलवद्वस्त्रशोधनम् ।
अवगाहेन शुद्धि [7][......................] ॥ १०२ ॥
अनापदि भवेत्स्नानमवगाहनलक्षणम् ।
असम्भवेऽप्यसामर्थ्ये स्यादापद्यभिषेचनम् ॥ १०३ ॥
स्नात्वा शुद्धं परिधाय[8] गन्धपुष्पैरलङ्कृता ।
आचम्य पुष्पैरादित्यमर्चयित्वा 'ऋता'दितः[9] ॥ १०४ ॥
'ऐन्द्रं पदं प्रभो मह्यमिदानीं दातुमर्हसि' ।
इत्युक्त्वाथेन्द्रभावेन प्रार्थयेत् स्वपतिं वधूः ॥ १०५ ॥
ऋतुस्नाता सती नारी यं स्नेहान्नरमीक्षते ।
तादृशं जनयेत्पुत्रं तस्मात्पश्येन्निजं पतिम् ॥ १०६ ॥
यदि कांस्ये तु भुक्तिः स्यात्त्रिरात्रेऽवगते सति ।
त्रिः सप्तकृत्वः संमृज्य भस्मना चोदकेन च ॥ १०७ ॥
अग्निसंस्पर्शनं कृत्वा व्यवहारक्षमा भवेत् ॥ १०७क ॥
रजस्वला सती नारी यत्र देशे वसेत्सदा ।
शयीत वाथ भुञ्जीत स देशो गोमयैः पुनः ॥ १०८ ॥
उपलिप्तो गवाक्रान्तः शुद्धिमर्हति[10] नान्यथा ॥ १०८क ॥

१.M साङ्गवे. २.T विभक्ता.शो. ३.T साह्नवः श्रुतः, M सङ्गवच्छुतः. ४.T °क्षाळनै°. ५.MT तव्ये. ६.T मूलव°. ७.MT broken. ८.MT परीधाय. ९.M दृतादितः,T दृतादृतः. १०.M शुद्धिम...ति.

क्षालनं स्यात्कटादीनां [1]नीत्वा [2]ज्ञान्तं यशोऽर्थिना[2] ।
[3][................] तृणानां त्याग एव च ॥ १०९ ॥
[4]तक्षणं दारवाणां[5] स्याच्छोध्यमन्यच्च शोधनैः ।
प्रायश्चित्तमुदक्यायाः प्रसंगादधुनोच्यते ॥ ११० ॥

[उदक्यायाः प्रायश्चित्तिः]

आर्तवाभिप्लुता नारी शवं स्पृष्ट्वापि[6] को हिता[6] ।
आस्नानकालान्नाश्नीयादासीना वाग्यता बहिः ॥ १११ ॥
भुञ्जानायां शवस्पर्शे त्रिरात्रेऽवगते सति ।
कृच्छ्रचान्द्रायणे कुर्यात्पञ्चगव्यं तथापदि ॥ ११२ ॥
चण्डालदर्शने भुक्ता वाऽऽस्नानात्स्यादभोजनम्[7] ।
शुद्धौ कुर्याद् बालकृच्छ्रं[8] ब्रह्मकूर्चं पिबेद् द्विजान्॥ ११३ ॥
भोजयेद्यदि चण्डालं पतितं वा स्पृशेत्ततः ।
अतिकृच्छ्रं चरेत्कृच्छ्रमेकं वाऽनशनं त्र्यहम् ॥ ११४ ॥
कृत्वा[9] पिबेत् ब्रह्मकूर्चमुच्छिष्टा यदि संस्पृशेत् ।
कुर्यात्सान्तपनं[10] कृच्छ्रं यद्वा चान्द्रायणव्रतम् ॥ ११५ ॥
स्पृष्ट्वान्त्यान् वायसपशून्सरीसृपविहङ्गकान्[11] ।
अशुद्धानपरां स्नात्वा भुञ्जीत यतमानसः ॥ ११६ ॥
अस्नात्वा यदि भुञ्जीत प्राजापत्यं समाचरेत् ।
उपवासत्रयं कुर्यात्स्पृष्ट्वा च शवसूतिके ॥ ११७ ॥
आशौचिनं च संस्पृश्य श्रुत्वा बन्धुमृतिं तथा ।
आस्नानकालान्नाश्नीयात्पिबेद् ब्राह्मीं सुवर्चकाम्॥ ११८ ॥
उदक्या सूतिका वापि संस्पृशेदन्त्यजं यदि ।
त्रिरात्रेण विशुद्धिः स्यादिति शातातपोऽब्रवीत् ॥ ११९ ॥

१.M कटान्नीत्वा,T कटादी-त्वा. २-२.M oms; T ज्ञान्तं यथोर्थिना. ३.MT broken. ४.M तत्क्षणं. ५.M दारपाणं. ६-६.M विकोहिता. ७.M °स्नानात्तस्याद°. ८.M कृच्छ्रा. ९.T कृत्त्वा. १०.M सान्तवनं. ११.M पतङ्गकान्.

आर्तवाभिप्लुते[१] नार्यौ[२] स्पृष्टे[३] चेदिच्छया मिथः ।
उपवासत्रयं कार्यमभिषेके तु भोजनम् ॥ १२० ॥
स्पृष्ट्वा भुक्त्वा विना स्नानं चरेच्चान्द्रायणव्रतम् ॥ १२०क ॥
स्पृष्टे रजस्वलेऽन्योऽन्यं सगोत्रे चैकभर्तृके ।
कामादकामतो[४] वापि त्रिरात्रेण विशुद्ध्यतः ॥ १२१ ॥
[५]सवर्णे पञ्चगव्येन ब्रह्मकूर्चेन शुद्ध्यतः[५] ।
तस्मिन्नेवाहनि स्नात्वा भुञ्जीतेत्यपि च स्मृतम् ॥ १२२ ॥
शूद्रां रजस्वलां स्पृष्ट्वा ब्राह्मणी कृच्छ्रतः शुचिः ॥ १२२क ॥
रजस्वला तु संस्पृश्य श्वजम्बुकखरान् क्वचित् ।
निराहारा भवेत्तावद्यावत्स्नानमिति स्मृतम् ॥ १२३ ॥
पतितान्त्यश्वपाकैश्च संस्पृष्टा चेद्रजस्वला ।
तान्यहानि व्यतिक्रम्य[६] प्रायश्चित्तं समाचरेत् ॥ १२४ ॥
प्रथमेऽह्नि त्रिरात्रं स्याद् द्वितीये द्व्यहमेव तु ।
अहोरात्रं तृतीयेऽह्नि परतो नक्तमाचरेत् ॥ १२५ ॥
सार्तवां वीक्ष्य भुञ्जाना [७]नाद्यादास्नानकालतः ।
ब्रह्मकूर्चं पिबेदूर्ध्वं संभाषेतां मिथो यदि ॥ १२६ ॥
उपवासं तयोराहुरबुद्धौ शुद्धिकारणम् ॥ १२६क ॥
द्विविधा शौचसम्पाते मध्ये स्नात्वा तु भोजनम् ।
तन्मध्ये रजसि प्राप्ते स्नात्वा भोजनमिष्यते ॥ १२७ ॥
उद्धृतेनाम्बुना स्नानं [८]नावगाहेत्कथंचन ।
कृतेऽवगाहने[९] कुर्यादुपवासं विशुद्धये ॥ १२८ ॥
श्वस्पृष्टमङ्गं प्रक्षाल्य नक्तमग्नौ प्रतापयेत् ।
अधो नाभेस्तु संस्पृष्टं प्रक्षाल्याचम्य शुध्यति ॥ १२९ ॥

१.MT °प्लुता. २.MT नार्यो. ३.MT स्पृष्टेच्चेदि°. ४.M कामदाकाम°. ५-५.M puts this hemistich after तस्मिन्नेवाहनि°. ६.T व्यति...प्राय°. ७.M थाद्यादा°. ८.T नावनाहेत्. ९.M °गाहेन.

शुभा पुष्पवती स्पृष्ट्वा पुष्पवत्या प्रसूतिका ।
शेषाण्यहान्युपवसेत्स्नात्वा शुद्ध्येद् घृताशनात् ॥ १३० ॥
प्रक्रान्ता[1] चेदुदक्या स्यादुपवासतपोव्रते ।
नैतेन दोषं[2] प्रकान्तं[3] नियमो न निवर्तते ॥ १३१ ॥
आतुरा चेदृतुमती यस्याः स्नानमिहोच्यते ।
स्पृष्ट्वा तामपरःस्नाया[4]द् दशकृत्वो ह्यनातुरः ॥ १३२ ॥
वासोभिर्दशभिश्चैव परिधाप्य यथाक्रमम् ।
ब्राह्मणान् भोजयित्वाऽथ पुण्याहेन विशुध्यति ॥ १३३ ॥
आतुराणां तु सर्वेषामेवमेव विधीयते ।
मृतिसूतकसम्पर्के रजो दृष्ट्वा कथं भवेत् ॥ १३४ ॥
ब्राह्मणानां करैर्मुक्तं तोयं शिरसि धारयेत् ।
द्विजेभ्यः शक्तितो दत्त्वा पुण्याहेन विशुध्यति ॥ १३५ ॥
उदक्यायां प्रसूतायां[5] मृतायां[6] वाप्यशौचिनि ।
स्वाशौचे समतिक्रान्ते शवं धर्मेण दाहयेत् ॥ १३६ ॥
तद्रक्षणे यद्यशक्तिस्तदाशौचं समाचरेत् ॥ १३६क ॥
आशौचरहितो विप्रान् परिधाप्याम्बरं पृथक् ।
स्नापयित्वान्तरा स्नातः सप्तकृत्वो विशुद्धये ॥ १३७ ॥
एकविंशतिकृत्वो वा द्वात्रिंशत्कृत्व एव वा ।
दशद्वादशकृत्वो वा यथाशौचं समाहितम् ॥ १३८ ॥
कुशगोमयगोमूत्रमृद्भस्मस्वर्णवारिभिः ।
स्नापयित्वा ततः कृत्वा पुण्याहं बाह्वृचं ततः ॥ १३९ ॥
दाहयेत्तां सदाचारादयं पक्ष इहेष्यते ।
बुद्ध्यबुद्ध्यादिभेदेन स तु दद्यात्सतस्तथा ॥ १४० ॥
व्यवस्था कल्पनीयाऽत्र परस्परविरोधिनाम् ।
देशकालाद्यपेक्ष्यापि शौचक्लृप्तिः पुरोदिता ॥ १४१ ॥

१.T प्रकान्ते. २.M दोषः. ३.M प्रकान्त. ४.M °मपरस्नायाः शकृ°, T स्नाया दश°. ५.T °ताया. ६.T मृताया.

रजःसम्बन्धमेतत्स्त्रीकृत्यं प्रायेण दर्शितम्[१] ।
नाना [२]स्मृतिसमुद्दिष्टमवधार्य समाचरेत् ॥ १४२ ॥

[यमनियमाः]

वक्ष्यामो नियमानन्यान् यमानपि समासतः ।
यानातिष्ठन्नरो नित्यं ब्रह्मलोके महीयते ॥ १४३ ॥
शुक्लाम्बरधरः शुक्लमाल्यगन्धानुलेपनः ।
क्लृप्तकेशनखश्मश्रु नित्यमात्महिते रतः ॥ १४४ ॥
द्राक्षायणी ब्रह्मसूत्री यष्टिमान् स्याद् घृतं मधु ।
[३]मृदं गां[३] दैवतं विप्रं प्रज्ञातांश्च[४] वनस्पतीन् ॥ १४५ ॥
गच्छेत् प्रदक्षिणं नित्यं चतुष्पथसमन्वितम् ।
अश्वत्थं सिन्धुराजं च दृष्ट्वा वन्देत न स्पृशेत् ॥ १४६ ॥
मन्दवारे स्पृशेदाद्यमपरं[५] पर्वणि स्पृशेत् ।
सर्वभूतहितः शान्तः क्षमावाननसूयकः[६] ॥ १४७ ॥
सुगन्धस्नानशीलः स्यात् सत्यवादी जितेन्द्रियः ।
अनायासेन कर्माणि कुर्यान्मङ्गलतत्परः ॥ १४८ ॥
अस्पृहो[७]ऽकृपणो नित्यमात्मशौचपरायणः[८] ।
न जीर्णमलवद्वासा भवेच्च विभवे सति ॥ १४९ ॥
[९]नान्वाध्यायविरोध्यर्थमीहेत[१०] न यतस्ततः ।
नाश्नीयाद् भार्यया सार्धं नैनामीक्षेत चाग्निकीम्[११] ॥ १५० ॥
क्षुवतीं[१२] जृम्भमाणां[१३] वा [१४]न संस्थिता[मनावृताम्][१४] ।
नेक्षेत चाश्नतीमेनामासीनां च यथासुखम् ॥ १५१ ॥
नान्नमद्यादेकवासा[१५] न नग्नः स्नानमाचरेत् ।

१.M दर्शितः. २.MT °धृति°. ३-३.T मृद्वंगं. ४.M प्रज्ञतां°. ५.M °दाद्यं परं. ६.M क्षमा...अन°. ७.T अस्पृहः कृपणः. ८.M परायणा. ९.MT नन्वाध्या...विरो°. १०.M मिहेत्. ११.Cf Manu IV.43: चाश्नतीम्. १२.T क्षवती. १३.MT जृम्भित [T ता] वासा. १४-१४.M वासा..न संस्थितः; T संस्थितः..।. १५.MT क्षुवतीं जृम्मयाणां वा wrongly put here; thus ManuI V.45.

न संशयं प्रपद्येत नाकस्मादप्रियं वदेत् ॥ १५२ ॥
नाहितं नानृतं चैव न स्तेनः[१] स्यान्न वार्धुषी ।
नेक्षेतार्कं [न][२]नग्नां स्त्रीं न च संस्पृष्टमैथुनाम् ॥ १५३ ॥
'अयं मे वज्र' इत्येनं सर्वमन्त्रमुदीरयेत् ।
वर्षत्यप्रावृतो गच्छन्न प्रधावेच्च वर्षति ॥ १५४ ॥
[३]ष्ठीवनासृक्च्छकृन्मूत्रविषाण्यप्सु[४] न संक्षिपेत् ।
पादौ प्रतापयेन्नाग्नौ न चैनमवलङ्घयेत् ॥ १५५ ॥
न धारयेदपश्चाग्नि[५]मपश्चान्नं[६] तथैव च ।
युगपत्स्नातको[७] विप्रस्तद् भार्या च तथैव च ॥ १५६ ॥
जलं पिबेन्नाञ्जलिना न श्रेयांसं प्रबोधयेत् ।
नाक्षैः क्रीडेन्न धर्मघ्नैर्व्याधितैरपि[८] संवसेत् ॥ १५७ ॥
न बाहुभ्यां[९] निशि नदीं नदं वा[१०] सन्तरेद् बुधः ॥ १५७क ॥
बालातपप्रेतधूमौ[११] वर्ज्यौ भिन्नं[१२] तथासनम् ।
न छिन्द्यान्नखरोमाणि दन्तैर्नोत्पाटयेन्नखान्[१३] ॥ १५८ ॥
[१४]न मृल्लोष्ठं[१५] विमृद्नीयान्न[१५] छिन्द्यात्करजैस्तृणम्।
न वृथा[१६] प्रलिखेद्[१७] भूमिं बहिर्माल्यं न धारयेत् ॥१५९ ॥
[१८]केशभस्मतुषाङ्गारकपालेषु च संस्थितिम्[१८] ।
वर्जयेत्परकीयां गां धयतीं न निवेदयेत् ॥ १६० ॥
अद्वारेण च नातीयाद् ग्रामं वा वेश्म[१९] वावृतम् ।
रात्रौ च वृक्षमूलानि दूरतः परिवर्जयेत् ॥ १६१ ॥
[नाधार्मिके वसेद् ग्रामे न व्याधिबहुले भृशम्][२०] ।

१.T स्तोथ. २.MT broken. ३.M ष्ठिवना°,T जीवना°. ४.M विषाण्य...न. ५.M °पश्वाग्नि°. ६.M पश्वान्नं,T °पश्चान्नस्त°. ७.M स्नानतो. ८.M रत्र्यातिभित रवि. ९.T नन्वाहुत्यां. १०.M वासस्तरेद्. ११.M तालातपत्रे धूमौ, ज्यया तु वप्रे तद्धूममौ; Thus Manu IV.70. १२.T भिन्नस्तथा°. १३.MT °पाटयेत्तथा; thus Manu IV.70. १४.M oms. १५-१५.M मृलोष्टमपि मृश्नी°, T विमृश्नीया°. १६.T वृद्ध्या. १७.T प्रक्षिपेद्. १८-१८.T केश भर्तु...ङ्गारातपालेपानि...; M संस्थितीम्. १९.M वेश्मलावृतः. २०.MT om.

प्रपद्येताटवीं[१] नैको न चिरं पर्वते वसेत् ॥ १६२ ॥
न [२]शूद्रराज्ये निवसेन्नाधार्मिकजनावृते[३] ।
न पाषण्डिजनाक्रान्ते नोपसृष्टेऽन्त्यजैर्नृभिः[४] ॥ १६३ ॥
नैकः [५]स्वप्न्याच्छून्यगृहे न व्रजेत्सार्तवां स्त्रियम् ।
समानशयने चैव न शयीत तया सह ॥ १६४ ॥
नाग्निं मुखेनोपधमेन्नात्मनोऽभिहरेत्[६] स्रजम् ।
नाश्नीयात्सन्धिवेलायां न गच्छेन्नापि संविशेत् ॥ १६५ ॥
नोदक्ययाऽभिभाषेत यज्ञं गच्छेन्न चावृतः ।
नमस्कर्तुं व्रजेत्कामं [७]दिदृक्षुर्यज्ञकर्म वा ॥ १६६ ॥
कुलात्कुलं रहस्यार्थी संचरेन्नानिमित्ततः ।
न दिवीन्द्रायुधं[८] दृष्ट्वा कस्यचिद्दर्शयेद् बुधः ॥ १६७ ॥
न चोदकेऽभिवीक्षेत वत्सतन्त्रीं न लङ्घयेत् ।
[९]परशय्यासनोद्यानगृहयानानि वर्जयेत् ॥ १६८ ॥
अदत्तान्यग्निहीनस्य[१०] न चाश्नीयादनापदि ।
कदर्यबद्धचोराणां क्लीबरङ्गावतारिणाम्[११] ॥ १६९ ॥
[१२]षण्डाभिशस्तवार्धुषिगणिकागणदीक्षिणाम् ।
अवीरास्त्रीस्वर्णकारस्त्रीजितग्रामयाजिनाम् ॥ १७० ॥
शस्त्रविक्रयिकर्मारतुन्नवायश्ववृत्तिनाम्[१३] ।
नृशंसराजरजक[१४]कृतघ्नवधजीविनाम्[१४] ॥ १७१ ॥
चैलधावसुराजीवसहोपपतिवेश्मनाम्[१५] ।

१.M प्रपद्येता...नैको. २.T न...दिवसे. ३.M °न्नार्मिकजना°, T नाधारितजना°. ४. T नोत्सृष्टेन्त्यजैस्थितम्. ५.MT स्वप्न्या°. ६. cf Manu IV.55 : °ऽपहरेत्. ७.M adds वा after दिदृक्षुः. ८.M नदिचीन्द्रायधं, T नटि चीन्द्रायुधं; cf Manu IV.59. ९.MT शय्यासहोद्या°. १०.M अदत्तान्यनिही°. ११.MT क्लीबांगावतारिणाम्; see Yâjña Smṛ I.161. १२.MT ...भिगस्त. १३.MT °कर्मातिन वा [T चा] य श्ववृत्ति°. १४-१४.M कृतघ्न...जीवि..., T रजक...; see Yâjña Smṛ I.163. १५.M °सहोपवतिवे°, T °सहो वपति वे° see Yâjña Smṛ I.164.

पिशूनानृतिनोश्चैव[१] तथा चाक्रिकबन्दिनाम्[२] ॥ १७२ ॥
एषामन्नं न भोक्तव्यं सोमविक्रयिणस्तथा ॥ १७२क ॥
अनर्चितं वृथामांसं[३] केशकीटसमन्वितम् ।
[४]शुक्तं पर्युषितोच्छिष्टं श्वस्पृष्टं पतितेक्षितम् ॥ १७३ ॥
उदक्यास्पृष्टं संघुष्टं पर्यायान्नं[५] च वर्जयेत् ।
गोघ्रातं शकुनोच्छिष्टं पादस्पृष्टं च कामतः ॥ १७४ ॥
सन्धिन्यनिर्दशावत्सगोःपयः परिवर्जयेत् ।
औष्ट्रमेकशफं[६] स्त्रैणमारण्यकमथाविकम् ॥ १७५ ॥
देवतार्थं हविः शिग्रुं[७] लोहितान् व्रश्चनानि च ।
अनुपाकृतमांसानि विड्जानि कवकानि च ॥ १७६ ॥
च्छत्राकं विड्वराहं[८] च लशुनं ग्रामकुक्कुटम् ।
पलाण्डुं[९] गृञ्जनं चैव मत्स्याञ्जग्ध्वा[१०] पतेद् द्विजः[१०]॥ १७७ ॥
यत्किञ्चित् स्नेहसंयुक्तं भक्ष्यं भोज्यमगर्हितम्[११] ।
[१२]तत्पर्युषितमप्याद्यं हविःशेषं च सर्वशः ॥ १७८ ॥
दधिभक्ष्यं तु शुक्तेषु[१३] सर्वं च दधिसंभवम् ।
यानि चैवाभिषूयन्ते पुष्पमूलफलैः शुभैः ॥ १७९ ॥
पक्षिजग्धं गवाघ्रातमवधूतमवक्षुतम्[१४] ।
दूषितं केशकीटैश्च मृत्प्रक्षेपेण शुध्यति[१५] ॥ १८० ॥
शूद्रेषु दासगोपालकुलमित्रार्धसीरिणः ।
भोज्यान्ना नापितश्चैव यश्चात्मानं निवेदयेत् ॥ १८१ ॥
आहृताभ्युद्यतां[१६] भिक्षां पुरस्तादप्रचोदिताम्[१७] ।

१.M °नृतिङ्गाश्चैव, T पशूनां पत्रिणश्चैव, cf Manu IV.214. २.M चात्रिकवादिनाम्, T चा...कवादिनाम्. ३.M मांसः. ४.M शुक्र...पर्यु°. ५.MT पर्यायान्तं. ६.M ओष्ट्रमैकं शफं. ७.Cf Manu V.6: शेलुं. ८.M विध्वराहं. ९.M oms. १०-१०.MT मत्याजाध्वा य [T प] ते द्विजः. ११.M भोज्यमह...तम्. १२.M oms तत्. १३.M गुप्तेषु, T शुप्तेषु corrected as गुप्तेषु. १४.M गवाक्रान्त° क्षुतः, T °गवाभुक्त° मक्ष्वक्षुतम्. १५.M विशुध्यति. १६.M आहृत्याभ्यु°, T सूनृताभ्यु°. १७.M पुरस्ता...दितम्, T पु...म्; thus Manu IV.248.

मेने प्रजापतिर्भोज्यामपि[१] दुष्कृतकर्मणाम्[२] ॥ १८२ ॥
चिकित्सकस्य मृगयोः शल्यकर्त्तृविवासनम्[३] ।
षण्ढस्य[४] कुलटायाश्च[५] पतितस्य च वार्धुषेः[६] ॥ १८३ ॥
शत्रूणां च कृतघ्नानां[७] सूद्यतामपि वर्जयेत् ।
कुशाः शाकं पयो मत्स्या[८] गन्धाः पुष्पं दधि क्षितिः ॥ १८४ ॥
मांसं[९] शय्यासनं धान्यं प्रत्याख्येयं[१०] न वारि च ।
सुरातिथ्यर्चनकृते गुरुवृत्त्यर्थमेव च ॥ १८५ ॥
सर्वतः प्रतिगृह्णीयादात्मवृत्त्यर्थमेव च ।
न राज्ञः [११]प्रतिगृह्णीयाल्लुब्धस्यो[१२]च्छास्त्रवर्तिनः ॥ १८६ ॥
प्रतिग्रहे सूनिचक्रिध्वजिवेश्यानराधिपाः ।
दुष्टा दशगुणाः पूर्वपूर्वदिते[१३] यथोत्तरम् ॥ १८७ ॥
देवर्त्विक्स्नातकाचार्य[१४]राज्ञां च्छायां वरस्य[१५] च ।
न क्रामेद्रक्तविण्मूत्रष्ठीवनो[१६]द्वर्त्तनानि च ॥ १८८ ॥
विप्रा हि क्षत्रियात्मानो नाव[ज्ञेयाः कदाचन][१७] ।
[१८]आमृत्योः श्रियमन्विच्छन्न कञ्चिन्मर्मणि स्पृशेत् ॥ १८९ ॥
श्रुतिस्मृत्युदितं सम्यङ् नित्यमाचारमाचरेत् ।
न [१९]निन्दा ताडने[१९] कुर्यात्सुतं शिष्यं च ताडयेत् ॥ १९० ॥
कर्मणा मनसा वाचा यत्नाद्धर्मं समाचरेत्[२०] ॥ १९०क ॥
क्षात्रेण कर्मणा जीवेद्विशां वाऽप्यापदि द्विजः ।
निस्तीर्यार्थं तमुत्सृज्य वाप्यात्मानं[२१] न्यसेत्पथि ॥ १९१ ॥
फलोपलक्षौमसोममनुष्यापूपवीरुधः ।
तिलौदनरसक्षारान्दधिक्षीरं घृतं जलम् ॥ १९२ ॥

१.M °पतिर्भोक्ताज्यामपि. २.M दुष्कृतक्षिणात्. ३.M °कन्तु...वाशनः. ४.M षाण्डश्च, T षडस्य. ५.MT कुलदाया°. ६.MT वार्धुषे. ७.M कृतस्नानां, T कृतस्नानां corrected as कृतघ्नानां. ८.MT मत्स्याः. ९.M oms मां°. १०.T व्रत्या°,M प्रकुर्वत्या°. ११.M पूतिगृ°. १२.MT ल्लबधस्यो°. १३.MT पू...वदिते. १४.M °स्नातकावायु°. १५.M परस्य. १६.M °ष्ठिवनो°. १७.MT broken see Yājña Smṛ I.153. १८.T ...त्यो. १९-१९.M निन्दितादने. २०.M समाचरत्. २१.M चाप्या°.

शस्त्रासवं[१] मधूच्छिष्टं मधुलाक्षाऽथ बर्हिषः ।
मृच्चर्मपुष्पकुतपकेशतक्रविषैरकान् ॥ १९३ ॥
कौशेयनीर[२]लवणमांसैकशफहेतवः ।
[३]शाकार्द्रौषधिपिण्याकतूलगन्धांस्तथैव च ॥ १९४ ॥
वैश्यवृत्त्यापि संजीवन् विक्रीणीत न कर्हिचित् ।
धर्मार्थं विक्रयं नेयाः तिला धान्येन तत्समाः ॥ १९५ ॥
रसा रसैर्निमातव्या न त्वेव[४] लवणं तिलैः[५] ।
कृतान्नं चाकृतान्नेन [६]स्वकृष्योत्पादितांस्तिलान् ॥ १९६ ॥
विक्रीणीयाद्धर्महेतोश्चिरकालमसंस्थितान् ॥ १९६क ॥
भोजनाभ्यञ्जनाद्दानाद्यदन्यत्[७] कुरुते तिलैः ।
कृमिभूतः श्व[८]विष्ठायां पितृभिः सह मज्जति ॥ १९७ ॥
सद्यः पतति मांसेन लाक्षया[९] लवणेन च ।
त्र्यहेण शूद्रो भविता[१०] ब्राह्मणः क्षीरविक्रयी[११] ॥ १९८ ॥
आपद्युत्तमया[१२] वृत्त्या जीवेदुत्कृष्टवर्णजः[१३] ।
न त्वेव ज्यायसीं वृत्तिं नीचः कुर्यात्तु कर्हिचित् ॥ १९९ ॥
श्रेयान् स्वधर्मो विगुणः परधर्मात्स्वनुष्ठितात् ।
परधर्मेण जीवा[न् हि सद्यः पतति जातितः][१४]॥ २०० ॥

॥ इतः परं ग्रन्थपाताः ॥

[इति सङ्गमग्रामवासिमिश्रविरचिते नारायणीये
वाधूलगृह्यागमवृत्तिरहस्ये
अष्टमोऽध्याय][१५]

१.M शस्त्रानुवं. २.M °नीलि°. ३.M शाकादोषधि. ४.M त्वंच. ५.Cf Manu X.94:. रसैः. ६.M °न्नेना वै स्व°. ७.M °भ्यञ्जना...न्यत्र, T °भ्यञ्जना...कुरुते. ८.M कृमी °भूताश्च वि°, T कृमी भूतश्च वि°; cf Manu X.91. ९.M लाक्षाया. १०.M भस्मता. ११.Cf Manu .92: क्षीरविक्रयात्. १२.M °द्युधमया. १३.T जीवेदुष्कृष्ट १४.MT broken after जी; Cf Manu X.97: M indicates the loss of remaining text with the statement 'इतः परं ग्रन्थपाताः'. १५.MT. Not given; remaining folios seem to have been lost; or damaged.

उत्तरप्रदेशस्थ-बलियाजनपदान्तर्गत-जवहींग्रामवास्तव्येन
माध्यन्दिनशुक्लयजुर्वेदशाखिना
विश्वामित्र-कात्य-उत्कील-त्रिप्रवरेण,
कात्यायनगोत्रोत्पन्नेन पं. सीतारामपौत्रेण
अंजोरिया-नारायणयोः कनिष्ठसूनुना
आचार्य व्रजबिहारी चौबे द्वारा सम्पादितं
वाधूलगृह्यागमवृत्तिरहस्यं
समाप्तिमगात्

★ ★ ★

ओम्
नम ऋषिभ्यः पूर्वेभ्यः पथिकृद्भ्यः
नम आचार्येभ्यो धर्मसूत्रकृद्भ्यः

★ ★ ★

INDEX – I

उद्धृतमन्त्रानुक्रमणी

आ

द

ध

ब

भ

श

स

ह

—o—

INDEX – II

श्लोकानुक्रमणी

अ

आ

इ

ई

उ

ऊ

ऋ

ए

ख

ग

ज

त

द

ध

न

प

भ

म

य

र

ल

व

श

स

ह

—o—

INDEX – III

प्रमुखपदानुक्रमणी

अ

इ

ई

उ

ओ

औ

क

क्ष

ख

घ

च

छ

ज

ज्ञ

त

द

न

प

फ

ब

भ

य

ल

व

श

ष

स

ह

—०—